Guide to the Records of the Lord Chancellor's Department

Dr. Patrick Polden

LONDON
HER MAJESTY'S STATIONERY OFFICE

First published 1988
ISBN 0-11-380015-0

ACKNOWLEDGEMENT TO THE
ECONOMIC AND SOCIAL RESEARCH COUNCIL

The report on which this book is based was commissioned by the Economic and Social Research Council, whose support is gratefully acknowledged.

Sponsored for publication by the
Lord Chancellor's Department

Printed in the United Kingdom for Her Majesty's Stationery Office
Dd. 240057 5/88 C8

ACKNOWLEDGEMENTS

I should like to record my grateful thanks to the various people who have assisted with in this undertaking, and in particular to the following.

First, to Mr Duncan Chalmers and the staff of the Public Record Office at Kew, for their courtesy and efficiency in keeping me constantly supplied with unusually large quantities of material.

Second, to the Departmental Records Officer of the Lord Chancellor's Department, Mrs Enid Smith, whose meticulous reading of my drafts enabled several errors to be corrected.

Third, to Cyril Glasser, whose knowledge and understanding of many of the matters covered here far exceeds my own and who managed to remedy some of my more egregious blunders. I am particularly indebted to him for his help with the section on legal aid.

Last, to Mrs Angela Duncan, who coped imperturbably with the eccentricities of man and machines over a period far longer than was originally envisaged and helped to produce something like order out of something not far removed from chaos.

For those errors which remain, the responsibility is of course my own.

TABLE OF CONTENTS

Chapter 2

THE SUPREME COURT OF JUDICATURE

Chapter 4

THE MAGISTRATES' COURTS

Chapter 5

LOCAL, MILITARY AND CORONERS COURTS, AND COURTS OUTSIDE GREAT BRITAIN

Chapter 6

ADMINISTRATIVE TRIBUNALS

Chapter 7

THE LEGAL PROFESSION AND LEGAL AID

Section 3

REFORMS IN THE LAW

Chapter 1

THE PROCESS OF LAW REFORM: THE LAW REVISION COMMITTEE

Chapter 4

DEBTOR AND CREDITOR

Chapter 5

TORTS AND ACCIDENT COMPENSATION

Chapter 6

FAMILY LAW

Chapter 7

LUNACY

Chapter 8

CRIMINAL LAW AND PROCEDURE

Chapter 9

WARTIME EMERGENCY LEGISLATION

Chapter 10

INTERNATIONAL LAW AND NATIONALITY

Section 4

CHURCH AND STATE

Chapter 1

THE CROWN, THE CONSTITUTION AND THE EMPIRE

Chapter 2

PARLIAMENT AND LEGISLATION

Chapter 3

THE CROWN OFFICE

Chapter 4

THE CHURCH

Appendix 1

THE LORD CHANCELLORS AND THEIR STAFF, 1872–1951

Appendix 2

Appendix 3

STATUTES AND BILLS

Appendix 4

BIBLIOGRAPHY

INTRODUCTION

1 The Aims of the "Guide"

The purpose of this guide is to encourage and facilitate the use of those records of the Lord Chancellor's Department[1] which have been deposited in the Public Record Office and opened to public inspection, by providing a more detailed description of the contents of individual files, particularly those in the general series (classes PRO LCO 1 and 2) than is available in the Public Record Office list, and arranging them according to their subject matter rather than serially. As is explained below, the records of the department date back to about 1870, although systematic record keeping was not begun until 1889, and the guide covers the period from the beginning of the records to November, 1951, when Lord Jowitt resigned as Lord Chancellor.

Two reasons suggested that date as the *terminus ad quem*; the first is that by that time, in common with the records of other government departments, the main series was expanding at such a rate that it becomes impracticable to continue to itemise the contents of each file; the second is that as one approaches nearer to the limit of closure under the "thirty year rule" an increasing and significant proportion of the files remain closed because they contain later material which is not yet ready for release. This stopping point, though convenient, is of little significance in the administrative history of the department and inevitably makes for an incomplete coverage of several important subjects; thus the deliberations of the Evershed Committee on the Administration of Justice were not completed until 1953, and the Morton Committee on Intestate Succession gave rise to legislation passed in 1952. In such cases some indication is given of the remaining files in the sequence.

The detailed examination of files upon which this guide is based is only possible because of the relatively small number which have been preserved, but their fewness does not mean that they are of little value to the researcher. On the contrary, they contain an unusually high proportion of interesting and significant matter and have been unduly neglected by historians of legal institutions and law reform, by those interested in the processes of government and legislation and by students of recent social history. Avner Offer and Gavin Drewry, in widely different fields,[2] have each demonstrated the usefulness of the LCO papers when combined with those of other government departments and private individuals, and it is hoped that this guide may suggest other topics which they can be used to explore.

2 The Contents and Organisation of the "Guide"

The guide is based upon an examination of all the files in classes PRO LCO and 1 and 2 which were open in January, 1987 and which had been started before Jowitt left office. They number some six thousand files and the examination was necessarily not a thorough one; given the diversity of their subject matter and the internal complexity of some files (such as those relating to the Supreme and County Court Rule Committees) it is not claimed that the most significant features have always been noticed and recorded. In particular, the earlier files, down to 1915, are for the most part wholly in manuscript and outgoing letters are noted on the file's cover rather than on separate sheets within the file, which makes them especially difficult to examine quickly and accurately. The other classes of LCO files which contain pre-1952 material were not examined in the same detail where they comprised large numbers of files of basically similar structure, such as classes LCO 26 (records of adjustment officers appointed under the Liabilities (War-Time Adjustment) Acts) and LCO 12 (County Courts Department), but all are included in the "Guide" for the sake of completeness.

In deciding between the merits of selectivity and comprehensiveness, the difficulty of predicting the interests of scholars and researchers in the future—to which the destruction of all too many public records wrongly deemed to be of no value bears melancholy witness—prevailed, although the consequence has been to swell the size of the work undesirably. Likewise, no attempt has been made in the lists to indicate which files are likely to be of importance and which (such as most of the Crown Office files) are not, but it is hoped that the descriptions of their contents will enable the user to decide whether they are germane to his enquiry, something that the present PRO list, which takes its descriptions mostly from the file covers, does not do.

A guide of this sort is not intended to be read from cover to cover but to be consulted on specific questions. It is envisaged that some users will be seeking information on a well-defined and very specific matter, such as the history of a particular Act of Parliament or the consequences of a judicial decision, but it is hoped that it will also assist those whose enquiry is of a more wide-ranging or elusive kind, relating for example to the influence of a particular judge or minister, to changes in the machinery of justice or to the evolution of government policy in a particular area. In addition, there may be those who are not engaged on a particular quest but are seeking for topics which they might wish to investigate. The introductory passages which precede most of the sub-sections in the "Guide" are aimed chiefly at the latter classes of user. They do not pretend to original scholarship and are, for the most part, based only upon the most readily accessible printed sources and the LCO records themselves. The lack of reliable accounts of quite important aspects of the administration of justice and the operation of the law is quite marked and it is hoped that this guide will encourage others to make it good.

There is a more substantial introduction to the Lord Chancellor's Office itself, because an understanding of its role, methods and leading personalities is indispensable to the effective use of its records: even this, however, falls well short of a history of the LCO, for neither the records of other government departments nor the papers of private individuals have been consulted.

The internal organisation of the "Guide" is straightforward. The greater part is contained in two sections, on the administration of justice and the reform of the law respectively. The degree of overlap between the two is, of course, substantial, particularly in matters such as divorce, and a degree of duplication was considered preferable to extensive cross-references. The other sections deal with the LCO itself and with a whole variety of subject matter which cannot easily be accommodated in the main sections. It has not been feasible to provide an index sufficiently detailed to be useful without extending the length of the "Guide" even further; instead there are appendices listing some of the legislation, decided cases and committee reports mentioned in the "Guide", which should enable the user to go straight to the files in question if he wishes to avoid searching here for a fuller description of their contents; it should be emphasised however that the appendices are far from comprehensive.

Obviously, there will be many cases in which the researcher will need to look at the records of other government departments, notably those of the Treasury, Home Office, Law Officers Department and the Office of the Parliamentary Counsel,[3] as well as those of the Lord Chancellor's Office but it has not been practicable to indicate in any detail which classes of those records are likely to be of most importance. Similarly, the private papers of Lord Chancellors and others are an essential counterpart to the departmental records on many issues but they were not used in compiling the "Guide".

It was hoped to be able to complete this guide in time to mark the centenary of the Lord Chancellors' Department in its modern form, which is conventionally ascribed to the year 1885, but the temporary closure of the Public Record Office and various other delays have defeated that aim.

3 The Records of the Lord Chancellor's Department

As is explained below, the secretaries who have served the Lord Chancellors in the nineteenth century regarded their correspondence as their personal property and usually removed it when they left. Even the creation of the permanent secretaryship in 1884 did not immediately bring about the adoption of record keeping practices which had become standard in other departments, and it was not until 1889 that the systematic registration and indexing of documents was begun. New matters were then entered in a large ledger and numbered serially according to the stamped numbers on its pages;[4] because sub-numbers were used extensively for related matters some of the entries covered several pages and consequently some page numbers were never used at all. The earliest surviving file in this sequence is number 3/9 (now PRO LCO 2/1), a file begun in March, 1889 and the last surviving file from this first ledger, 386/1 (now PRO LCO 2/54), was opened in December, 1891. Because of the numbering system, and because some files were re-opened and re-numbered when the matter to which they related was subsequently revived, it would be a laborious task to establish the proportion of files which have survived, but from this ledger only LCO 2/1–54 remain under the departmental numbers originally given them and a small sample from the first register shows that numbers 201 to 250 covered 386 separate files, an average of seven and three-quarters files per main number. This would indicate a total of some 3,000 files opened during the period 1889 to 1891 and a survival rate of only 1.8%. To judge from this sample (it is much too small to be reliable) a high proportion (more than 20%) of the total of the files opened in those years related to lunacy.

Experience evidently suggested changes, for the next register, begun in 1892, was divided in advance into alphabetically arranged subject headings and when a page was completed the heading was repeated on a new page at the end of the sequence. The numbering was continued from the end of the previous register but again there are unused numbers, this time because a few of the headings proved redundant. This system remained essentially unchanged until 1919 and index volumes were also compiled to facilitate access to the papers.

When the first register was opened, there was already a large and motley collection of unsorted documents of varying ages in the office, stuffed into cupboards and largely forgotten. Liddell records that in May, 1895.

> I have taken advantage of a lull in the work to clear out, sort and destroy old papers in the office, of which there are several cupboards full, which no-one has had time to touch.[5]

Liddell made an index to these documents, which he arranged in packets according to their subject matter, and presumably Muir McKenzie took the decision about which were to be retained. The eight-eight bundles which were preserved have become PRO class LCO 1 and are still numbered in Liddell's original alphabetical sequence. Not surprisingly, they are difficult to use, for the bundles are often incomplete and in some cases material has been wrongly sorted; much of it goes back to Lord Selborne's time and the last documents are from 1888. The next major examination and weeding out of unwanted material was carried out in December, 1915, probably on the initiative of Sir Claud Schuster, the new Permanent Secretary, and it was then that the greater proportion of registered files were classified as "valueless documents" and destroyed.

From 1919, the form of entries in the registers was changed; the contents of letters began to be briefly summarised and when a file was subsequently destroyed the entry relating to it was stamped accordingly. In 1924 loose leaf ledgers were introduced in place of registers and the indexes became more detailed, which makes it feasible to reconstruct some of the destroyed files, at least in outline, from the summaries of letters and from the records of other departments.

By that time, more important changes had also taken place in the records system. The business of the secretaries of presentations and commissions seems always to have been kept apart from the general business of the office and none of the former has been deposited in the Public Record Office.[6] Otherwise the single general series included all types of business, including even that of the Crown Office. However, in 1921 the "E" series of files was begun for establishment business; in the following year the transfer of the County Courts Department of the Treasury and all of its records demanded a second separate series and from 1924 Crown Office papers were separately recorded in a "CO" series. All remaining business seems to have been left in the general series and there were no further important changes throughout the remainder of the period covered by this guide. The original number sequence had reached about 2,260 by 1930 when it was stopped and a new sequence begun from number 3,000. By the end of 1951 this had barely advanced past 3,500 because the main numbers were now allocated only to major areas of business, such as County Courts and Magistrates; within these subjects new files were opened under sub-numbers, many of which naturally became very numerous. Unfortunately it continued to be the LCO practice to re-open and re-number existing files when new matter arose in the same connection, even if many years had elapsed since the opening of the original file, and some files therefore came to cover extremely long periods.

The Public Record Office has kept together the whole of the general series under class LCO 2 and only a few of the other LCO classes, of which there are currently about 30, contain materials from within this period. Important exceptions, which are included in the "Guide", are LCO 3, which contains records of the Reconstruction Committee on the acquisition and transfer of land; LCO 4, the establishment series; LCO 5, which contains miscellaneous materials on the presentations to crown livings; LCO 6, Crown Office registered files; LCO 8, County Courts "headquarters files", which deal with e.g. registrars' salaries, and "walking possession"; LCO 26, records of the adjustment officers appointed under the Liabilities (Wartime Adjustment) Acts; and LCO 32, papers of the Lawrence Committee on Poor Persons, 1919. Very few of the general series files containing pre-1952 materials have not been transferred to the Public Record Office, and the number of files which are subject to an extended closure is very small.

ABBREVIATIONS

1 The Records

The correct designation for the files referred to in the main body of the "Guide" is PRO 1 LCO 2 (or whatever is the appropriate class number) followed by the piece number. For convenience, and to save space, they are referred to by their numbers alone, because no records of other departments are listed and there seems therefore no likelihood of confusion. The full reference should, of course, be quoted when ordering files or referring to them in any other context.

The great majority of the files listed are in class LCO 2 and to avoid the necessity of constant repetition, the following practice has been adopted: the *first* reference to a file which follows any heading or sub-heading in the lists gives both the class number and the piece number(s) for that file, e.g. 2/1596–7. Subsequent files within the same sub-section are referred to *only* by their piece number(s) e.g., 1604–6, unless they are from a different class to those in the entry immediately preceeding, in which case the class number is also provided and that class number then governs subsequent entries until it is in turn displaced or the [sub-] section ends, thus:

Staffing and Expenses

1/11	Judges' allowances and expenses: correspondence with Treasury and memoranda and resolutions by judges, especially in 1884. Other papers in 1/5 (1883 resolution).
1/12, 13	Negotiations with Treasury on salaries and appointments to various clerkships and subordinate offices, 1876–88. 1/13 deals with clerks in the Associates Department of the QBD.
2/2643	Clerk of assize at Lancaster's delayed accounts: long correspondence on complaints against him (1942–7), especially with the Clerk to the Duchy and the Home Office.
4608	Responses of clerks of assize to Judges' Widows Pensions Scheme 1950.
6652	Appointment of recorders from other circuits (see ***infra***, 323).
1563–6, 2794–5, 3475, 5302	Sheriffs: discussions (1920–41) on expense and shortage of candidates (1563), especially Howarth's memorandum. Wartime economies and minor matters.
4769–73	Circuit Officers Committee. Discussions with Master Bonner, 1934 on control of SC staff. Preliminary meetings of 1944 and Lord Greene MR's complaint re drafting of orders. Correspondence on membership of committee, minutes, evidence, Schuster's papers (including discussions on patronage) interim report. Draft report discussed with Treasury and publication considered.
2/4471–2	SCJ (Circuit Officers) Bill 1946. Caldecote report considered in cabinet. Drafting correspondence with PCO, and correspondence with Law Society on qualifications of circuit officers. Parliamentary papers.

2 Other Abbreviations

For the most part, these are in the familiar form for judicial officers (e.g. LCJ, MR, LJJ) and government departments (e.g. HO, FO). The only important departure from conventional practice is that PCO refers to the Parliamentary Counsel's Office, *not* to the Privy Council Office. The abbreviations SCRC and CCRC refer to the Supreme Court and County Court Rule Committees respectively.

Notes

1 *Since 1970 this has been the correct and official designation of the department. In the period covered by this guide, the staff more commonly referred to it as the Lord Chancellor's Office, and this form has been adopted throughout.*

2 *A. Offer,* **The Origins of the Law of Property Acts, 1910–25***(1977) 40 MLR 505; G. Drewry,* **Lord Haldane's Ministry of Justice: Stillborn or Strangled at Birth?** *(1983) 61 Public Administration, 396.*

3 *The following, however, may be mentioned as likely to be useful:*

T 1 Treasury Board papers, to 1920
10 Out letters, County Courts, 1849–1913
15 General law Out letters, 1807–1913
129 Out letters, Lord Chancellor, 1914–21
162 Establishments Files, 1880–1948
163 General Files, 1888–1948
215 Establishments (General) Division, 1921–54

TS 25 Law Officers' Opinions, 1870–1927
27 Registered Files, 1843–1971
HO 34 Public Offices Entry Book, 1836–98
43 Domestic Entry Books, 1782–1898
45 Registered Papers, 1839–1963
117 Letter Books, 1806–1922
LO 2 Registered Files, 1885–1971
BT 23 Solicitors Department Indexes and Registers, 1879–1902
103 Solicitors Department papers, 1860–1965
FO 83 General Correspondence, G.B. and General, 1745–1967.

The papers of the Parliamentary Counsel's Office are not held by the P.R.O.

4 *These registers and indexes are kept in the offices of the Lord Chancellor's Department at the House of Lords.*

5 **Notes from the Life of an Ordinary Mortal** *(1911), 311.*

6 *Most of the earlier documents relating to the appointment of justices have been destroyed. In 1945 the Secretary of Commissions wrote that "most of our papers prior to 1930 have been pulped" (2/3497, to R. Somerville, 25.10.1945) and in the following year he explained to another correspondent that "the records of this office prior to 1930 were destroyed in the war" (2/2908: to G. F. Clark, 8.11.1946).*

7 *This practice has now been discontinued. There was no Department Records Officer during this period and the smallness of the department and its recruitment of lawyers rather than generalist civil servants encouraged the persistence of old-fashioned practices.*

Section 1

THE LORD CHANCELLOR AND HIS OFFICE

1
THE LORD CHANCELLOR

1 Introduction

If you have seen upon the street
a man who absolutely beat
the ordinary band,
a human orchestra complete
who played the cymbals with his feet
instead of with his hand,
and in some way contrived to blow
a cornet or a piccolo
not with his mouth but with his toe,
and never ceased to strike
a multitude of drums and things
by simply pulling little strings—
you knew it not, but that is what
the Chancellor is like.

Poor gentleman—he has to mix
with barristers and lords
he is in charge of lunatics;
and coroners and wards;
and what with listening to Earls,
and looking after orphan girls,
and imbeciles of every kind and judges of the County Court,
and all that kind of thing;
he gets extremely little sleep;
and then, of course, he has to keep
the Conscience of the King;
and sometimes at the close of day
he gives a Vicarage away;
the reason why is dark to me,
but, anyhow, he has to be
a most religious man,
and often in the "Sunday Chime"
explains the need for overtime
to every artisan.

But round his neck the GREAT BIG SEAL
is permanently tied;
He wears it for the common-weal;

by night, by day, at every meal;
it is a source of pride;
for many a man has sought to steal
that ornament. They died.
But all the same it weighs a deal—
and by a rotten chance
it's not allowed to leave the land,
and so, of course, you understand,
he cannot go to France.

And oft, upon the lonely shore,
men see the sad eyed Chancellor
at Folkestone or at Dover;
astride of some convenient groyne
he looks with longing at Boulogne,
as cattle do at clover;
till, feeling that he must relax,
he takes a stick of sealing-wax,
an envelope and lots of string
and writes a letter to the King,
to ask if it is very wrong to look with longing at Boulogne—
and seals it up all over.
But I should take IT off, I own
and quickly travel to Boulogne.
Or I should simply keep IT on, and quickly travel to Boulogne.

Sir Alan Herbert's whimsy[1] neatly expresses the layman's bewilderment at the peculiar agglomeration of functions acquired by the Lord Chancellor. The first Lord Hailsham, from personal experience, described him as "the most anomalous creature in the constitution because his very existence contradicts what at least used to be generally regarded as the essential characteristic of our English system",[2] namely the separation between the legislative, executive and judicial powers. The Lord Chancellor might, within the duties of his own department, order the preparation of a bill. As a cabinet minister[3] he would introduce and discuss it with his ministerial colleagues. If it reached the House of Lords he would (unless he had appointed a Deputy Speaker) preside over the debates from the Woolsack[4] and would probably vacate the Woolsack to introduce or defend the bill. If it passed into law he might be the minister charged with issuing those orders or instruments necessary to bring it into operation and with making rules under the Act. Disputes arising out of its provisions would almost certainly be adjudicated by persons appointed by him, whether judges, magistrates or members of administrative tribunals, and an appeal against their decision might ultimately fetch up in the House of Lords, where he might be one of the judges ultimately responsible for interpreting his own measure. Truly, he is a remarkable officer of state and it is scarcely surprising that on occasion he found difficulty in reconciling the claims made upon him in these different capacities. The Machinery of Government Committee, whose report sought to divest him of some of them, summarised his duties less felicitously but more accurately than Herbert:[5]

The Lord Chancellor may be described as President of the Supreme Appellate Court of Great Britain and Ireland [and] the House of Lords in its judicial capacity.

The House of Lords sits judicially on four days of the week during a period of the year which corresponds roughly with, but is a little shorter than, the time of the legal sittings of the Supreme Court. During all this time therefore, the Lord Chancellor on four days of the week is sitting from 10.30 to 3.45 or 4 o'clock, with an interval of half an hour for lunch. The work while it lasts is exceedingly laborious, and it is easy to imagine that on those days on which the House sits as a Court of Appeal from 10.30 to 3.45, and when he has to deal with ordinary Parliamentary business from 4.15 to 7.30 or 8, only a man of very exceptional physical vigour can find either leisure or strength to cope with the many other duties of his high office. Yet it is in the hasty intervals between these sittings that the Lord Chancellor must communicate, and discuss Government measures, with his colleagues, must attend to the extensive patronage which is in his gift, and must exercise a general supervision over the many other matters which lie within his province. The mere enumeration of the number of hours consumed in judicial business, however, does not exhaust the matter, for, especially of recent years, the judgments of the House of Lords have been put into written form. He must write his judgment, read the judgments of his colleagues, and must frequently discuss with them the points of law or matters of fact which arise in the course of the case.

The functions of a Judge are necessarily personal to himself, and the Lord Chancellor can obtain little or no help from his officers in these matters, except, and that by no means always, in the purely ministerial work of searching for references or finding books. But the fact that the Lord Chancellor presides over judicial business in the House of Lords gives him, by courtesy at least, a power and influence over the proceedings of the Judicial Office, and special responsibilities in respect of the Standing Orders which govern the judicial proceedings in the House of Lords. The Lord Chancellor exercises no patronage in the Judicial Office, which carries on its work as an integral part of the House of Lords Offices, but the Heads of that Office are in the habit of seeking instructions and advice from the Lord Chancellor in an informal way, while as President of the Court it is in the Lord Chancellor's duty to determine what causes should be placed in the list and to see that an adequate Court is present to hear them.

The actual work of arranging for the attendance of Peers for this purpose is performed, under the close supervision of the Chancellor, by his Permanent Secretary. This might seem a routine matter, but in practice it is important and difficult, and occupies much time and thought.

The Lord Chancellor also sits, whenever he is able, in the Judicial Committee of the Privy Council as President of that Court. When he is not sitting he bears a responsibility for the proceedings of that Court and exercises supervision over it. He is regarded both by himself and others as responsible for seeing that the work is done; as the Peers sit either at the House of Lords or on the Judicial Committee in accordance with his requests, he is, in fact, responsible for the constitution of the Court, and the appointment to be Privy Councillors of those who are not Peers, and who are considered to be suitable members of the Committee, is largely dependent upon his advice.

The Chancellor is by origin a Judge of first instance and by statute a member of the Court of Appeal. In practice these offices do not often impose any work upon him, but in emergencies they do.

The Chancellor is by statute head of the Chancery Division of the High Court of Justice and President of the Supreme Court. The former of these offices implies little more than a titular supremacy, together with the performance of certain not very onerous duties. The Lord Chancellor's consent is required to the temporary transfer of a Judge from the Chancery Division to some other Division of the High Court or vice versa; of causes from one Chancery Judge to another Judge of that Division, or to or from that Division, and the hearing of summonses on these latter matters on the very rare occasions when the transfer is not made by consent. None of these duties imposes any material amount of work upon the office.

But the duties of the President of Supreme Court, with the numerous functions attached thereto, are exceedingly onerous, difficult, and responsible, and all the more so because some of them are undefined and indefinable. It is upon the recommendations of the Lord Chancellor that all the Judges of the Supreme Court — though technically not those of the Court of Appeal — are appointed by the King, a patronage the exercise of which is one of great anxiety, and which requires that the Lord Chancellor should be in constant touch with the Bar.

All the other appointments to Masterships and Clerkships in the Courts (except the Masters on the King's Bench side, the officers of the Probate and Admiralty Registries, the Clerks in the Office of the Masters in Lunacy, and the personal clerks of the Lords Justices and Judges), and all the promotions in the Courts outside the Probate and Admiralty Registries, are made by the Lord Chancellor, and over the whole of the Courts and all the operations of all these officials he exercises a control, the extent of which, in the case of the Judges, is not explicit, and in the case of the other officials depends largely upon the personal characteristics of the Lord Chancellor and his Permanent Secretary.

Mention must also be made of the extensive powers of the Lord Chancellor as a rule-making authority. The procedure in the High Court is regulated by rules of the Supreme Court, made, under the authority conferred by the Judicature Acts, by the Rule Committee of the Supreme Court. The Lord Chancellor of the day is Chairman of this Committee, which comprises also the Lord Chief Justice, the Master of the Rolls, the President of the Probate, Divorce, and Admiralty Division, four other Judges of the Supreme Court, two barristers, being members of the General Council of the Bar, and two Solicitors, one a member of the Council of the Law Society, and the other a member of the Law Society and also of the Provincial Law Society. The members, other than the ex-officio members, are appointed by the Lord Chancellor. The general body of rules was made long ago. They are comprised in 72 Orders, each divided into many rules. These Orders and Rules, and the comments upon them, occupy 1,362 closely-printed pages in the book called "The Annual Practice", which is in common use in the profession. The rules are constantly added to and amended in small particulars.

It must not be supposed that the Rules deal with unimportant matters. In many respects they have a far-reaching effect upon the rights of His Majesty's subjects. The Lord Chancellor is concerned with the Rules both as Chairman of the Committee, and because his Secretary is

Secretary to the Committee, and the staff of his office is the only staff available for the work of the Committee, so that all proposals for revision and all complaints of the working of the Rules come to the Lord Chancellor through his Secretary.

He has also authority, conjointly with the Treasury, and in some cases with the consent of certain Judges of the Supreme Court, for the making of Orders and Rules as to the fees to be taken on proceedings in the High Court. He has, further, the duty of approving rules made under the County Courts Act and the Workmen's Compensation Act by the County Courts Rule Committee, a small body of County Court Judges appointed by the Lord Chancellor, to which his Permanent Secretary acts as Secretary.

The Lord Chancellor is responsible for the County Court system of the country. There are 55 County Court Judges and 600 Courts. All the Judges are appointed by the Lord Chancellor alone, and are removable by him. The Registrars, who are themselves minor Judges, besides being responsible for the finance of their Courts, are appointed by these Judges, subject to the approval of the Lord Chancellor, and are removable by the latter. The Courts vary greatly in size and importance; the method of remuneration of the Registrars varies according to the size of the Court; the clerks are technically the servants of the Registrars and not servants of the State. It will readily be understood that the administrative work connected with the appointment of so many Judges, their conduct when appointed, and the innumerable complaints which arise in the course of administration, constitute a gigantic task.

Comparatively recent statutes have placed under the Lord Chancellor's control the Land Registry. This is not the place to discuss the probable future developments of the system of registration of title to land. It suffices to say that the present Land Registry, whatever the success of the system may be, is conducted quietly and efficiently, and, on its administrative side, imposes but little labour on the Lord Chancellor or his officers. If, as seems inevitable, the interest in this subject should revive after the war, it would fall to the lot of the Lord Chancellor to prepare legislation dealing with the matter, a task which would entirely absorb his activities and those of his officers.

The Public Trustee Act, 1907, placed under the Lord Chancellor's control the then newly-constituted office of the Public Trustee. Here again very considerable problems will arise for consideration after the war. From the point of view of the Lord Chancellor and his officers the question of moment is the enormous labour which the creation of this office imposes upon them on the "Establishment" side.

Notwithstanding the passing of the Mental Deficiency Act, 1913, the Lord Chancellor still retains duties in relation to lunatics. His judicial powers in this matter have in effect passed away since legal proceedings for the administration of the estates of lunatics were instituted. The duty of inquiring into the sanity of alleged lunatics (in the very rare cases in which a formal inquisition into the matter is now taken), and the power of making orders in the case of certain persons who are lunatics, but not so found by inquisition, has become a matter dealt with by regular Judges, that is, the Masters in Lunacy or, on appeal, the Lords Justices. Similarly, the Commissioners in Lunacy, who were the Lord Chancellor's officers, have been absorbed into the Board of Control. The Masters are, however, appointed by the Lord Chancellor, the Visitors are the

Lord Chancellor's Visitors, and a certain proportion of the members of the Board of Control are appointed by him; while he retains, and sometimes exercises, power to give instructions to the Visitors and to the Board of Control to inquire formally or informally into cases specially brought to his knowledge. Further, as every lunatic has a right to write to the Lord Chancellor, and very many lunatics exercise this right— some of them many times a day—the complaints of lunatics are constantly brought before the Lord Chancellor, and the time of his officials is very largely occupied in reading these letters, with a view to satisfying themselves that they do not in isolated instances suggest that the writer may be submitting a justifiable complaint.

There is vested in the Lord Chancellor the sole power of appointing Justices of the Peace throughout England—outside the Duchy of Lancaster—Wales, and Scotland. In 1909 a Royal Commission, presided over by Lord James of Hereford, was appointed to consider whether any, and if so what, steps should be taken to facilitate the selection of the most suitable persons as Justices of the Peace, irrespective of creed and political opinion. Until that time Justices had been appointed usually upon the recommendation of the Lords Lieutenants, and it was notorious that the system was not a satisfactory one. To avoid the evils complained of, the Commission, which reported in 1911, recommended that the Lord Chancellor should nominate within each county one or more small representative Committees to inform and advise the Lord Chancellor and the Lords Lieutenants as to the persons to be selected as members of the Committees, and that the practice and procedure of the Committees should be left to the discretion of the Lord Chancellor. There are in England—outside Lancashire—and Wales 62 Counties or quasi-Counties, and 222 Boroughs having separate Commissions of the Peace, and in Scotland 37 Counties, including Counties of Cities, having separate Commissions of the Peace. The work of setting up Advisory Committees for all these places was taken in hand shortly after the Commission had reported, and has proceeded ever since. It is exceedingly laborious and delicate, and has not yet been fully completed. The work is done by the Secretary of Commissions under the direct supervision of the Lord Chancellor himself, without the intervention of the Permanent Secretary. In practice, however, difficult points, when they arise, are sometimes discussed by the Lord Chancellor with his principal adviser. When a Committee has been established, it recommends to the Lord Chancellor, through the Lord Lieutenant in the case of a county committee, the names of the persons thought suitable for appointment as Justices of the Peace. In dealing with these recommendations, again, great labour and some tact is required, and the Lord Chancellor is often very fully occupied by questions of this nature, which, as in the case of most personal questions, absorb a disproportionate amount of the time of himself and his officials. Stipendiary Justices of the Peace are appointed by the Home Secretary, and complaints against either kind of Justices are apt to be sent indiscriminately either to the Lord Chancellor or to the Secretary of State.

The Lord Chancellor is patron of 12 canonries and 659 benefices, in addition to all those benefices below a certain value at a certain date which lapse to the Crown by reason of the appointment of their holders to certain ecclesiastical offices in the gift of the Crown, the failure of the patron to appoint within a specified time, or the incapacity of the patron. The remainder of the Crown patronage in respect of benefices rests with the Prime Minister, who disposes of all benefices which in a certain year of Henry VIII, were of the value of £20 or more as stated in the King's Book, those below that figure at that date falling to the Lord Chancellor. The work of appointment to these benefices is dealt with by an officer who is usually called the Secretary for Presentations. That office has been abolished by statute, but by the custom of the Lord Chancellor's Department one of the Lord Chancellor's Private Secretaries fulfils the duties of the office without the supervision of the Permanent Secretary. This matter would fully occupy the time of this official if he had not other duties to perform. The presentations are made on an average one a week throughout the year, and almost every presentation involves the interviewing of numerous candidates and much correspondence, while it also makes serious inroads upon the time of the Lord Chancellor himself. As patron, the Lord Chancellor is also concerned with certain matters relating to the property of the benefices. These are not very numerous or important, but they require legal knowledge. They are dealt with as appertaining to the permanent office. Naturally, if any such difficulty arises in connection with any part of the ecclesiastical jurisdiction of the Lord Chancellor, the office at large, as distinct from the Private Secretary already mentioned, is ready to afford such assistance as the Lord Chancellor may require.

In addition, Hailsham said "He is even said to be the keeper of the King's conscience"; I have never yet discovered what responsibilities exactly were entailed in that department of my office";[6] it had, however, provided Lord Loughborough with a justification for disloyalty to his cabinet colleagues over the question of Roman Catholic disabilities in 1801.

During the period covered by this guide the Lord Chancellor's role underwent significant changes. He had already ceased to sit as a judge at first instance in his own court following the reform of Chancery in 1852 and after the Judicature Acts his judicial activities were usually confined to the House of Lords and the Judicial Committee of the Privy Council.[7] The circumstances in which the House of Lords Appellate Committee came into existence in 1948 have been described elsewhere[8], and it tended to attenuate further his judicial role. Against that diminished burden, and largely responsible for bringing it about, must be set the relentless growth in his responsibilities connected with the administration of justice, in particular the proliferation of administrative tribunals. Even before the recommendations of the Franks report it had become common practice to vest the appointment of legally qualified members in the Lord Chancellor, and in many instances he was also responsible for making or confirming the rules under which they operated.[9] The provision of legal aid and advice to poor litigants, especially in civil cases, had long been among the responsibilities of the Lord Chancellor and the passing of the Legal Aid and Advice Act 1949 massively increased its importance.[10] The courts of justice themselves, at almost all levels, underwent an unspectacular but significant expansion in personnel throughout the period, thereby increasing the patronage at the Lord Chancellor's disposal, and the exercise of patronage, whether judicial, magisterial or ecclesiastical, was one function to which he clung tenaciously and wished to exercise personally.[11] The gradual extension of government into spheres of activity hitherto the exclusive preserve of private enterprise also made itself felt, notably with the creation of the Land Registry and the Public Trustee.

Cabinet duties too became more onerous, with more frequent meetings, more and more committees (the Lord Chancellor's experience usually put him in demand to act as chairman[12]) and a deluge of papers, while the mass of legislation to which their deliberations gave rise in turn increased the burden on government ministers in the Upper

House. Not all Lord Chancellors were suited to the role of government spokesman[13] but some, particularly those serving Liberal and Labour governments weak in debating talent, had to undertake a good deal of this work; Jowitt in particular experienced nightmares in trying to get to grips with the details of Labour's welfare and nationalisation measures.[14]

The Lord Chancellor was a political appointee and in contrast with the other great legal officers, the Lord Chief Justice, the Master of the Rolls and the President of the Probate, Divorce and Admiralty Division, he came and went with successive administrations. Hewart was wont to allude scornfully to this contrast,[15] and undoubtedly the more rapid turnover of Chancellors between the wars did hamper the development of a consistent approach to law reform and legal administration: from the appointment of Muir McKenzie as Principal Secretary in 1880 to his retirement in 1915 there were eight changes of Chancellor, but because Halsbury served three terms and Herschell two, Muir McKenzie served only five masters.[16] During Schuster's time as Permanent Secretary (1915–1944) there were thirteen changes of Chancellor and he served ten different masters (Haldane, Cave and Hailsham each served two terms). Between 1944 and 1986 there was greater stability: in over forty years there were only nine changes, and only eight Chancellors; a recent incumbent, the second Lord Hailsham, has served twice and held the office for longer than any post-Restoration Lord Chancellor other than Hardwicke, Thurlow, Eldon and Halsbury. Halsbury's total of seventeen years and four months is remarkable for modern times, since the average for the thirteen who succeeded him down to Jowitt is only five years.

The list of modern Chancellors contains some distinguished names in the wider political field, such as Haldane, Birkenhead and Simon, several distinguished as judges and a few who are little remembered for anything. During the reign of Queen Victoria they have been said to be coming to be "regarded as something of a race apart, ineligible for the offices which gave real power"[17] but any such tendency was checked early this century; indeed the career of Rufus Isaacs shows even the Lord Chief Justice becoming involved in more narrowly political business. Nevertheless it is probably true that after Haldane's second term few Chancellors in the next thirty years carried much weight in cabinet, and at least one (Sankey) was a distinct embarrassment there.[18] Only the first Lord Hailsham went from the Chancellorship to other cabinet office and for those who were not really politicians at all—Cave, Sankey, Maugham and Simonds—such a move was out of the question.

The Chancellors from Halsbury to Caldecote are the subject of the first volume of R. F. V. Heuston's admirable and accurate **Lives of the Lord Chancellors**, and Simon and Jowitt will take their place in the second volume.[19] Heuston draws extensively on the private papers of his subjects and others in these volumes, which form a continuation of **The Victorian Chancellors** by J. B. Atlay, a work of great elegance and judicious balance and which deals, *inter alia*, with Selborne and Cairns. The inspiration for these collective biographies, though almost their opposite in its unreliability and partisan spirit, is Lord Campbell's **Lives of the Lord Chancellors**, which was said to have "added a new terror to death".[20] They may be supplemented in some cases by the autobiographies of the Chancellors themselves: these vary considerably in their usefulness, but Selborne's compendious **Memorials**, and those of Haldane and Birkenhead are valuable; Simon's is characteristically unrevealing, Maugham's even more so.[21] The same applies to the full length biographies which have appeared.[22] They also tend to concentrate on the role of their subject in politics and affairs of state, and on the famous trials in which he was concerned, and few have much to say about his role as head of a government department; a glance at their indexes for references to the Lord Chancellors' Permanent Secretaries is enlightening.

Unfortunately, it is not easy to redress the balance from the departmental papers which survive and are open to public inspection. If the nineteenth century Lord Chancellor can be described as "a minister without a ministry",[23] his department in this period gives the impression of being "a ministry without a minister". Liddell records being impressed with the evidence of how much of the work Selborne had done personally[24] but even in the better documented era of Schuster's secretaryship, it is necessary to look very hard to discern the personal stamp of a Lord Chancellor on the work of his department. To some extent, this is a false impression created by the absence of the papers dealing with the patronage on which the Lord Chancellor expended considerable time and attention, but it remains striking nevertheless. Sometimes where a Chancellor had a particular interest in a subject, such as Jowitt's in statute law revision and Maugham's in the law of evidence, it is reflected in the office files but even that is not always the case, for they contain very little on Loreburn's attempted codification of the criminal law and virtually nothing on Halsbury's reform of criminal evidence. Evidence of initiatives from the Chancellor is scarce and it would be easy to accede to Hewart's allegation that some of the Chancellors were little more than ciphers who reigned while Schuster ruled.[25] Again, appearances may be deceptive. The knowledge that the Lord Chancellor opposed a particular course of action may have led his permanent officials to desist from any initiative in that area: the first Lord Hailsham's opposition to the reform of crown proceedings is one example.

Two things militated against a Lord Chancellor taking a more personal part in the activities of his department. One was the shortage of time he could spare from his other duties: both Haldane and Hailsham have described their daily routine in terms which make it clear how little time they could give to their departmental duties,[26] and Simon's working method is indicative of *his* shortage of time.[27] The other is that hardly any of these Chancellors entered upon his duties with anything resembling a party programme of measures, or even a policy. Most, no doubt, had some pet project of their own which they hoped to forward, but it is indicative of the marginalisation of law reform in the political agenda of this century that if it figured in party manifestos at all, it did so usually only in small print and vague terms; even the Labour party in 1945, encumbered with a mass of ideological baggage, scarcely had any policy towards the law. As a result, the conventional caricature of the relationship between a minister and his civil servants, in which the latter seek to thwart and deflect the former's large proposals for change, is almost reversed in the case of the LCO, where the civil servants had projects which faced the obstacles presented by the conservative and cautious disposition of most Lord Chancellors.

The papers in this collection do show some of the more personal aspects of the Lord Chancellor's situation. For example, there is material on Birkenhead's vain claim to exemption from income tax on his salary, on the replacement of the state coach by a more prosaic motor car, several speeches to the Lord Mayor's annual dinner for the judges, and a good deal on his role as visitor to various academic and charitable institutions.

The most interesting, perhaps, are the entertaining files concerning his official flat, which had been created in Sir Henry Graham's house at the Palace of Westminster. The Treasury attempted to extract £500 p.a. rent from Birkenhead but their proposal was rebuffed both by the Chancellor and the House of Lords. Birkenhead's later money troubles give point to his dismissal of an attempted analogy with the First Lord of Admiralty: "First Lords do not divorce themselves for ever from an income of £25,000 per annum".[28] The House of Commons, however, strongly criticised his extravagant plans for alterations to the flat, leading him to abandon his plans to live there. Only Cave ever did, for Hailsham found it too small for his family and Sankey gave it up to the Yeoman Usher of the Black Rod to aid the economy drive.[29]

The concession quickly threatened to become permanent: the Stanhope Committee on Accommodation in Parliament in 1944 admitted the Lord Chancellor's claim to it, but nevertheless proposed to give it to Black Rod.[30] Simon was furious and got the recommendation reversed, but Black Rod, Esmè Gordon-Lennox, took to his bed and Jowitt had to engage in unpleasant and embarrassing exchanges with his wife before he was able to get them out.[31]

Notes

1 *A copy of this poem is in 2/3632.*

2 *"**The Duties of a Lord Chancellor**", p. 5. This was the Holdsworth Lecture for 1936. To judge from the titles of lectures by subsequent Lord Chancellors, the office has become less enjoyable: Lord Gardiner "**The Trials of a Lord Chancellor**" (1968), Lord Hailsham, "**The Problems of a Lord Chancellor**" (1972). Lord Kilmuir's account is in (1956) 9 **Parliamentary Affairs** 132.*

3 *The Lord Chancellors in this period were all members of the cabinet, but were excluded from the "war cabinets" of Lloyd George and Churchill.*

4 *Since the Woolsack was technically outside the House of Lords a Lord Chancellor could preside over the House while still a commoner, as Sir Douglas Hogg did in 1928. He could not, however, "enter" the House to address it until he had been introduced as a peer.*

5 *PP 1918 (Cd. 9230) XII, 1, abbreviated from pp. 64–70. The standard account of the history of the office is Sir W. S. Holdsworth, **A History of English Law**; N. Underhill, **The Lord Chancellor** (1978) is also useful.*

6 ***Op. cit.**, 17.*

7 *The last Lord Chancellor to sit as a judge at first instance was Lord Birkenhead in 1921, setting an example in helping to clear a backlog of divorce petitions. Lord Gardiner later heard a bail application in the Kray case.*

8 *See **infra, House of Lords**, 45.*

9 *PP 1957 (Cmd 218) VIII, 1. See 2/4319: "Statutory Rules and Orders for which the Lord Chancellor is wholly or partly the Rule-making Power" (1947), 2/4630 "Appointment of Arbitrators, Referees etc. under Statutory Powers" (1948), and "**Administrative Tribunals**", **infra**, 159 ff.*

10 *See **infra**, 187 ff.*

11 *See e.g. 2/3409 on the subject of ecclesiastical patronage.*

12 *Lord Hailsham, **op. cit.**, 12–3.*

13 *Sankey, for example, waited almost a year before making his maiden speech and that was one learned by heart on a subject (the Coal Mines Bill) on which he had first hand knowledge (R. F. V. Heuston, **Lives** . . ., 509–10).*

14 *e.g. 2/4334, Coal Industry Nationalisation (Superannuation) Regulations, 1950.*

15 *A. Mockler,* ***Lions Under the Throne*** *(1983), 271.*

16 *This excludes Buckmaster, who was sworn in on 1st June, 1915.*

17 *N. Underhill,* ***op. cit.****, 183.*

18 *Sankey's production of a school atlas in cabinet to assist his geography was much ridiculed (R. F. V. Heuston,* ***Lives*** *. . ., 527).*

19 *Prefigured in (1986) 102 LQR 90: "Judicial Prosopography".*

20 *E. B. Sugden (Lord St. Leonards) quoted this in the volume that he produced to refute Campbell's criticisms of him.*

21 *Lord Selborne,* ***Memorials*** *(4 vols. 1896–8), Lord Haldane,* ***An Autobiography*** *(1929), Lord Birkenhead,* ***Life, Law and Letters*** *(1927), Lord Maugham,* ***At the End of the Day*** *(1954) and Lord Simon,* ***In Retrospect*** *(1952).*

22 *See bibliography,* ***infra.*** *See also R. F. V. Heuston's discussion in* ***Judges and Biographers*** *(1967).*

23 *N. Underhill,* ***op. cit.****, 188.*

24 *A. G. C. Liddell,* ***Notes from the Life of an Ordinary Mortal*** *(1911), 311.*

25 *R. Jackson,* ***The Chief*** *(1959).*

26 *Lord Haldane,* ***Autobiography*** *(1929), 324–7; Lord Hailsham,* ***op. cit.****, 7–13. Schuster made a point of praising Haldane's willingness to devolve responsibility to his officials (Lord Grey and others,* ***Viscount Haldane of Cloan*** *(1928), 33).*

27 *2/3711: Coldstream to A. B. Ashby, 18.6.1946: "what he looks for is a case put to him on a side, or a side-and-a-half, of paper, supplemented by as much 'oral evidence' as witnesses care to put before him."*

28 *2/5653: to Lord Curzon, 26.2.1919.*

29 *2/5656: summary of events, 1944.*

30 ***Ibid.****.*

31 *2/5656.*

2 Salaries, Appointments, Pensions

2/409,633, 933–4, 936–7, 1518, 1520–4, 3623, 5650	Formal correspondence about appointment and coats of arms (1915–51). 936 includes notes on current business and the office structure in 1928, also Hailsham's letter of 1929.
326, 632	Discussions on allowances and LC's coach, 1912, 1915 (cost of patents) 1918, 1921 (state coach).
1547	Brief for PQs on Roman Catholic disabilities and the LC, 1932.
3624–7	Various minor questions on regalia, rules, titles, procedence, 1945–54.
171, 687	Formal grants of pensions; re-calculation of Lord Buckmaster's pension.
480, 631	Birkenhead's memoranda on suggested reduction of his salary and his claim to exemption from income tax, with correspondence on precedents, especially Law Officers' opinion on *Argyll* v *IRC*.
933	Haldane accepts voluntary cut of £4,000 p.a., 1924.
1518–9	Sankey agrees to economy reductions in salary and expenses.
2608–23	LC's breakfasts, reception of the Lord Mayor and Westminster Abbey service arrangements, 1931–41.

2624, 2665 LC's speeches to Lord Mayor's dinner for the judges (1931, 1933, 1937–8) and correspondence on its future after the war.

3 Accommodation

2/5653–6, 5649 Extensive correspondence with Privy Council Office, Treasury etc. over LC's official flat in Sir H. Graham's house; its acquisition (1918), rent and conversion. Resumes 1944: LC's correspondence with Lord and Lady Esmè Gordon-Lennox, Simon's evidence to the Stanhope Committee on Accommodation and subsequent correspondence on recovering the flat for the LC. Also an offer of Capel House as an official residence, 1951.

4 Incapacity and Absence

2/822, 935 Cave's illness 1927; discussions with officials about the opening of Parliament; arrangements for memorial service.

3244 Correspondence with Nihill CJ, Colonial Office and Prime Minister on Jowitt's trip to open the East African Court of Appeal, 1951.

5677–81 Jowitt's visit to Australia, 1951: correspondence with Prime Minister, Inns of Court and others.

5 Miscellaneous

1/58 Actions by the former Clerk of the Patents, Leonard Edmunds, against Lord Selborne in 1877; Treasury Solicitor's summary of proceedings against Edmunds for misappropriation of funds (1864–6) and his subsequent legal and political campaign, updated to 1878.

2/3628, 3632 Lectures and broadcasts on the office of Lord Chancellor by H. A. Hollond and Lord Simon, 1944, 1949.

3638 Jowitt's role in election of Chichele Professor of International Law, 1947.

4705 Jowitt consulted by the Lord Chamberlain on theatre censorship, 1951.

4706 Correspondence with Lord Nathan on the "History of Parliament", 1940, 1948.

4707 F. L. Caunter's letters to Jowitt on the problems of the Cornish tin industry, 1951.

5663 Sundry requests for information on the work of the Lord Chancellor, 1951–5.

5676 Jowitt declines to debate in the Oxford Union, 1951.

5681 Jowitt's address to the Holdsworth Club, 1951.

5683 Correspondence and meetings with Treasury on insuring pictures from the National and Tate Galleries (LC as trustee) on loan to government departments, 1951. Complications over the Lane bequest.

5833 Eldon Law Scholarship: correspondence with the secretary, various dates 1923–52 with Tomlin's opinion on the interpretation of the regulations, 1928.

5836 A few papers on the Hunterian collection, 1925.

5837 Radcliffe Travelling Scholarship 1923–57: opinion of LC (1926) on eligibility of women and correspondence on war-time suspension and post-war difficulties.

5845 By-laws of Royal College of Surgeons sent for his approval, 1929–57.

6 Lord Chancellor as Visitor

(see also *"Westminster Abbey"*, *infra*, 320)

2/1534–9, 2766–7, 3637, 5835–6, 5842, 5845, 5847

Various institutions, (see list in 3637) mostly Oxford and Cambridge colleges but also the Harpur Trust, sometimes requiring the Visitor's opinion on legal questions (e.g. 2766, Christchurch College, 1930).

2
THE LORD CHANCELLOR'S OFFICE

1 The creation of the office

The Victorian Lord Chancellor might be a Minister without a Ministry, but he was far from being a dignitary without servants, and in most of his diverse capacities they were sufficient at least in numbers.[1] Thus, the Chancellor's own court, the Court of Chancery, had never been regarded as suffering from a shortage of staff (other than judges)[2] even when its business was disgracefully in arrears and the House of Lords was well enough served by the clerks of the Parliaments and sundry other officials.

In his capacity as Keeper of the Great Seal[3] moreover, the Chancellor presided over several offices (the Patent Office, the Petty Bag and the Crown Office in Chancery) which were the veritable home of Circumlocution. They were overmanned and of doubtful public utility: the "candid and intelligent" Clerk of the Petty Bag confessed as much[4] and the office of the Clerk of the Crown was underworked except after a General Election.[5] The Royal Commission on the Legal Offices commented that "some less cumbrous method of passing documents under the Great Seal might be advantageously adopted"[6] and legislation was already in train which would give the Treasury, subject to the concurrence of the Lord Chancellor and the Master of the Rolls, the power to abolish the Patent Office and Petty Bag and transfer their work to the Crown Office.[7] But although the Clerk of the Crown described himself as "an officer of Parliament, and of the Lord Chancellor in his non-judicial capacity"[8] he said of his clerks "they are not [the Lord Chancellor's officers] in any respect. They are not appointed by him, and although he is in frequent communication with them, they act independently in their own department and the Lord Chancellor is not responsible for them: nor are they responsible to him".[9]

As a great officer of state the Chancellor also had a small retinue of attendants, which included his Trainbearer and Pursebearer, a Sergeant at Arms, the Messenger (or Porter) to the Great Seal and a Clerk of the Chamber, the equivalent of the "body clerk" of a common law judge. This retinue also included what might be termed his departmental officers.[10] They comprised three secretaries, two of whom handled the patronage which was so important a part of the Chancellorship. The Secretary of Commissions was responsible for the Chancellor's appointment of justices of the peace and the Secretary of Presentations dealt with ecclesiastical patronage. The Principal Secretary was a general factotum whose duties were summarised thus:[11]

> Letters from departments of state, from members of both Houses of Parliament, and others relating to bills dealing with legal subjects, from legal associations and private individuals suggesting alterations in the law, from applicants for patronage in legal and other civil departments,

and from judges and officers of the courts (as well as from the Treasury) on the subjects of duties, salaries and pensions. To investigate (when necessary) any matter of complaint affecting the administration of justice made to the Lord Chancellor, and to place papers relating to suitors and their claims before the solicitor to the suitor's fund under his lordship's direction. To take the Lord Chancellor's directions upon matters affecting the bankruptcy and county courts administration, and to communicate under those directions with the officer of the Treasury appointed to assist his lordship in such matters. To communicate constantly with the following legal officers: — The Patent Office, the Crown Office, the Registrar's Office, the Record and Writ Office, the Lunacy Office, the Paymaster-General's Office, and to daily transact business with the clerks in the principal secretary's office. To assist the Lord Chancellor, in any way required by him in the preparation and revision of legislative measures under his charge in the House of Lords. To examine the evidences of pedigree for the purpose of issuing the writ to enable a peer to take his seat in the House of Lords, and to report upon the same to the Lord Chancellor . . . To receive all memorials . . . relating to the magistracy of the country . . .

This establishment had not changed very much since the time of Lord Eldon, whose method of business is related in a tradition handed down among the Haldanes:

"In those days the Lord Chancellor lived in Seymour Street; he had no rooms in the Palace of Westminster at all, except his court, which was situate at the top of the steps at the south end of Westminster Hall. Thither he came to business every morning in his coach, accompanied by his Principal Secretary, his Secretary of Commissions, his Secretary of Presentations, his Secretary of Bankrupts, his Groom of the Chamber, his Mace Bearer and his Purse Bearer — a most impressive arrival. He kept no papers of any kind; when he or any Lord Chancellor of that day went out of office such records as had accumulated during his term of office were destroyed lest they should prove either too embarrassing or too informative to his successors.".[12]

The Lord Chancellor now had rooms in the House of Lords, but they did not constitute a ministry in any sense. There was no corpus of departmental records and no permanent, established official "who has all the traditions of the office in his breast"[13] to supply the want of them. It is true that in an office in Quality Court, off Chancery Lane, there lurked two permanent clerks under the supervision of the Principal Secretary, but the senior's time was wholly, and his junior's largely, occupied in scrutinising "attendable petitions" for formal defects; these petitions were part of the process in Chancery suits, most of them necessitated by the fact that the act creating the Vice-Chancellor's court did not provide a means to move him directly in a suit. It was an essentially unnecessary job the clerks performed, but the senior clerk was on the point of retiring and unwilling to travel out of his accustomed path.[14]

It is not surprising that Lord Chancellors sometimes felt the want of more and better assistance,[15] and in particular a measure of continuity. Nevertheless both Cairns and Selborne were positive that none of the existing secretaryships could be made a permanent, non-political post as their work was considered too sensitive;[16] yet E. P. Thesiger, appointed Secretary of Presentations by his father Lord Chelmsford, had been kept on by Lords Hatherley, Selborne and Cairns.[17] The other secretaryship was less burdensome and the Treasury was pressing for it to be combined with the Principal Secretaryship, which Selborne agreed to do on an experimental basis.[18]

During the previous fifty years, as a later Royal Commission noticed,[19] the lines upon which reform of the courts and associated offices was approached had diverged significantly from those applied to the civil service generally. In particular, little attention was paid to the process of appointment and promotion within the former: they were ignored in the Northcote-Trevelyan report and omitted from the Order in Council of 1870 which established open competition. Now there were ominous signs that this immunity from Benthamite trends in public administration was drawing to an end and the "closed corporations"[20] over which the judges held almost uncontrolled sway were threatened not only by the proposal for a single Supreme Court of Judicature but also by attempts to assimilate the entry, promotion, and conditions of service of the non-judicial officers to those in force in other government departments. Yet when the Childers Committee, which reported in 1873, virtually adopted the position of the Treasury officials who gave evidence before it, lawyers reacted strongly and indignantly to the unfamiliar assumption that the legal officers could be evaluated by the same criteria as the civil service generally, even though by the Judicature Act 1873 s.85 all new appointments not personally attached to a judge were "deemed to be civil servants".[21]

The select committee's recommendation for a royal commission to examine the legal departments had to be conceded, if only to make the case for a different set of criteria, but with two Treasury men, William Law and G. O. Trevelyan, on the Commission and the great common law judge and champion of individualism Baron Bramwell out of his element in its Benthamite atmosphere, it is not surprising that the tendency of its reports was towards a closer assimilation with civil service practice. Most threatening to the Lord Chancellor however was its acceptance of the need "to entrust to some Department of the Government directly responsible to Parliament the power to administer and organise these officers in such a manner as to ensure the greatest amount of efficiency, combined with all practicable economy";[22] the argument that such a responsibility was inappropriate for the judges was dressed up in constitutional terms but was essentially a recognition that retrenchment, the catchword of the day, was unlikely to be effected through them.[23] The Commission fell short of adopting the plausible proposal of H. C. E. Childers (formerly Financial Secretary to the Treasury), to locate this "Ministry of Justice" in the Home Office; Selborne contended that this was outside their terms of reference and also opposed it on its merits. It was allowed to expire, partly because no Home Secretary particularly wanted it, but mostly because it would need legislation, involving as it must "a reconstruction of two important departments, and a great interference with several others";[24] any bill vesting substantial judicial patronage in a lay government minister would be highly controversial. Since the Lord Chancellor was more acceptable to the judges, and was to be the President of the new Supreme Court of Judicature, he was the logical person to be made responsible for its officials and to be placed on the same footing vis-à-vis the Treasury as the heads of other government departments.[25] This new role should extend to his having all the "superior appointments" in the SCJ.

These responsibilities generated a great deal of work in the 1870s and 1880s, as the re-organisation of bankruptcy business, the creation of a Central Office and numerous other investigations and inquiries had to be undertaken to create a sound working infrastructure for the SCJ.[26] Moreover the Judges' Council and the Rule Committee both needed secretarial services and the rule making power, in particular, made permanent records and at least a rudimentary filing system necessary. Selborne and Cairns worked extremely hard themselves and had the valuable assistance of Henry Nicol, the veteran head of the Treasury's county courts branch, and Henry Leigh Pemberton, Official Solicitor to the Court of Chancery, who became almost an additional secretary for a time. Even so, it was no longer possible to agree to abolish the Secretary of Commissions, revived as a separate post by Cairns, and by 1882 Cairns, although out of office, had become convinced that the Judicature Acts had thrown such "a network of Departmental Business" onto the Lord Chancellor that he needed an "efficient Permanent Secretary" at the considerable salary of £1,500 p.a.[27] This was an important step, because the creation of a permanent secretary by Selborne would *ipso facto* deprive the succeeding Conservative Chancellor of the right to replace him. It seems possible that Selborne was already thinking along similar lines, and by appointing his nephew Ralph Palmer to be Clerk of the Crown when Romilly retired in September, 1880, after he had been Principal Secretary for only a few months, Selborne was able to make the Crown Office available for any future re-organisation. His new Principal Secretary, a radical young barrister, Kenneth Muir McKenzie, immediately asked to be able to combine it with the Secretaryship of Commissions, but the claims of Carrington Francis were held "irresistible".[28]

Among the Secretary's surviving papers are Muir McKenzie's scribbled permutations among the various offices within the Lord Chancellor's gift. It was useful that changes in Chancery practice had freed the Quality Court clerks for general duties and that the Judges' Council had requested a secretary for their meetings, which could be offered up to the Treasury as a tactical sacrifice.[29] No plans had been finalised when the Secretary of Commissions (Evelyn Murray, Francis's successor) resigned in August, 1883, and a renewed Treasury demand for its abolition had to be fended off,[30] but shortly afterwards Selborne proposed to Cairns that Quality Court be closed and all staff concentrated in the Houses of Parliament, where the "hitherto very insufficient and inconvenient accommodation" had been augmented, that there should be a Permanent Secretary ("in fact a permanent secretary to the Ministry of Justice") and a Private Secretary to handle confidential and political business.[31]

Having secured the approval of Cairns and the Treasury, Selborne was able to put the new arrangement into effect. The first stage was a Treasury Minute of 12 May, 1884 making the Principal Secretary, who should be a barrister of not less than seven years' standing, a permanent officer at a salary of up to £1,500 p.a. On the next vacancy in the office of Clerk of the Crown he was to hold that office also (which was in the Prime Minister's gift) and perform its duties.[32] In fact, Muir McKenzie was to receive only £1,200 a year until Nicol's retirement; he was to have the services of the two clerks formerly in Quality Court, and the Crown Office clerks would continue to do its business. A Private Secretary would be appointed and would also act as Secretary of Commissions, and when Thesiger retired the Secretaryship of Presentations would be left vacant; as a Conservative it was evidently impossible to make him Selborne's Private Secretary, and he had a *de facto* status of permanence. The following March, Palmer was translated to Visitor in Lunacy and Muir McKenzie became Clerk of the Crown.[33] In June Gladstone's government fell and Lord Halsbury became Lord Chancellor in the short-lived Conservative administration, a prologue to his long occupation of the Woolsack. Cairns had died in April and Selborne was never to hold office again: the creation of the Lord Chancellor's Office was the last fruit of their bi-partisan collaboration on judicial reform, a collaboration which the widening gulf between the political parties and the personal antipathy between Halsbury and Herschell made unlikely to recur.

In November, 1886 Muir McKenzie invited an unsuccessful and unhappy barrister Adolphus Liddell, a friend of his Balliol days, to become Chief Clerk in the Crown Office, and later Assistant Secretary. Liddell eagerly embraced the opportunity to quit the uncongenial round of circuit life and having found his niche, occupied it contentedly for more than thirty years.[34] Between 1886 and Muir McKenzie's own retirement in 1915 the structure of the office remained almost unchanged. The Secretary of Commissions was revived as a separate office in 1910 in anticipation of the work of creating advisory committees on the recommendation of the Royal Commission on the Appointment of Justices of the Peace. By 1900 the Permanent Secretary had acquired a private secretary of his own, employing his own relations whenever possible;[35] Lord Loreburn also made use of a relative, his nephew, for a short time as an assistant private secretary and paid his salary out of his own pocket[36] but the office remained tiny in comparison with most government departments.

Notes

1 *All except the officers of the Houses of Parliament are dealt with in reports of the Legal Departments Commission, PP 1874 [C-949] XXIV, 557; 1874 [C-1107] XXIV, 583; 1875 [C-1245] XXX, 163.*

2 *They were "excessive in numbers" according to the Childers Committee: PP 1873 (248) VII, 391 at p. vi.*

3 *H. C. Maxwell-Lyte,* **Historical Notes on the Great Seal** *(1926) is the standard account.*

4 *PP 1867 [547] XXXIX, 425 at p. 13. This is the report of the Goschen Committee on Fees on Appointments.*

5 *PP 1875 (C-1245) XXX, 167 at qq. 2343–2424.*

6 *PP 1874 (C-1101) XXIV, 583, at p. 36.*

7 *Great Seal (Offices) Act 1874. The Master of the Rolls' concurrence was necessary only in the case of the Great Seal Patent Office, to which he appointed.*

8 *PP 1874 [C-1007] XXIV, 583 at p. 39.*

9 *1/59: memorandum of March, 1878.*

10 *The Suitors in Chancery Relief Act 1852 (15 & 16 Vic c. 87) abolished several of the Lord Chancellor's officers and regulated the salaries of the rest; see ss. 23–6.*

11 *PP 1875 [C-1245] XXX, 163, q. 2547 quoted by A. H. Manchester,* **Modern Legal History** *(1980), 105–6.*

12 **The Duties of a Lord Chancellor** *(1936), 6.*

13 *PP 1875 [C-1245] XXX, 163 at q. 2899.*

14 **Ibid.**, *qq. 2825–2920.*

15 *See e.g. Lord Westbury's complaint quoted in N. Underhill,* **op. cit.**, *188–9.*

16 *PP 1874 [C-1107] XXIV, 583 at p. 34; 2/262: Selborne to Cairns, 16.8.1883.*

17 *PP 1875 [C-1245] XXX, 163 at qq. 2470–2540.*

18 *1/59: Selborne's memorandum to Treasury, 1873.*

19 *PP 1914–16 (Cd 7832) XII, 1 at p. 4.*

20 *PP 1874 (C-1107) XXIV, 583, at p. 103.*

21 *"A strong* **prima facie** *case has been made out by the officers of the Treasury, to the*

effect that both with respect to cost, and to administrative regulation, these establishments should undergo a searching investigation. Almost without exception, they are considered by the Treasury to be unduly expensive; and is clear to your Committee that the absence of any uniform principle in their regulation must produce mischievous results." 2nd report, PP 1873 (248) VII, 391 at p. ix.

22 *PP 1874 [C-1107] XXIV, 583 at p. 104.*

23 *PP 1874 (C-1107) XXIV, 583 at pp. 103–7.*

24 *PP 1875 (C-1245) XXX, 163 at q. 1245 (Childers).*

25 *PP 1874 (C-1107) XXIV, 583 at p. 107.*

26 *PP 1914–16 (Cmd 7832) XII, 1 summarises the main measures at pp. 7–9.*

27 *2/262: Cairns to Selborne, 29.2.1882.*

28 *The precise sequence of events between 1880 and 1885 has been incorrectly stated by a number of writers, including Heuston. There were no fewer than four principal secretaries in 1880: H. J. L. Graham, whose appointment to be a Master in Lunacy was criticised in Parliament ((1879–80) 68 LT 295) was succeeded by W. L. Selfe, the future county court judge. When the Conservatives resigned Selborne appointed first Palmer, then Muir McKenzie. For Francis's claims see 2/262: Selborne to Muir McKenzie, 24.9.1880. Francis had been Selborne's Principal Secretary from 1872 to 1874, but had not proved wholly satisfactory: 1/59; Selborne to Treasury, 1873.*

29 *1/60, especially H. Leigh Pemberton to Muir McKenzie, 24.4.1883; 1/61: Muir McKenzie to Selborne, 14.8.1883.*

30 *1/60: Treasury to Lord Chancellor, 28.7.1883, 14.8.1883.*

31 *2/262: Selborne to Cairns (draft), 16.8.1883.*

32 *2/262: Treasury to Lord Chancellor, 3.5.1884; PRO 30/51/9: Selborne to Cairns, 12.5.1884.*

33 *During Palmer's time, the Clerk of the Crown had also reluctantly acquired the duties of the Clerk of the Patents (abolished 1882, see 1/74) and the Clerk of the Petty Bag.*

34 *A. G. C. Liddell,* **Notes from the Life of an Ordinary Mortal** *(1911), 243–7, 251. Liddell's father, also named Adolphus, was Permanent Under Secretary at the Home Office 1867–85 (see J. Pellew,* **The Home Office, 1848–1914** *(1982)).*

35 *His son W. Muir McKenzie (1899–1901) and nephew Ronald Muir McKenzie (1908–15). Kenneth's younger brother Montague was a well-known expert on commerical law and was frequently called upon for advice in that field; he was also an Official Referee.*

36 *PP 1914–16 (Cd 7832) XII, 1, q. 50,663.*

2 The Office under Muir McKenzie, 1884–1915

Throughout this time it can be said without exaggeration that Muir McKenzie *was* the Lord Chancellor's Office, yet for such an influential figure in such a pivotal position he remains curiously elusive and it is difficult to take his measure. He makes only fleeting appearances in contemporary memoirs and diaries,[1] published nothing of the kind himself and left no papers which are known to historians. Unfortunately these deficiencies cannot easily be supplied from official records, for he ran the office in an idiosyncratic style which was almost the antithesis of the bureaucratic model. His successor explained its features with a mixture of admiration and disapproval.[2]

First "he was a man naturally secretive" and practised an occult mode of business which extended so far that "he wrote his letters himself and kept no copies, and he directed the envelopes and stuck them up",[3] for "it was always at once the pride and the reproach of

Lord Muir McKenzie's methods of business that he carefully prevented anyone but himself from knowing what was really being done in the office."[4]
Secondly, he would delegate nothing of the slightest importance. Liddell proved to be an ideal choice to be Assistant Secretary to such a man for while "the most charming of men"[5] he was unambitious, complaisant and entirely untrained in office methods. The Private Secretaries seldom stayed long in the office and left no impact and the clerks' duties gave them no scope for initiative.

Thirdly, records were kept to a bare minimum. "His memory was so far reaching and so infallible and his prestige so great that the committing of decisions to paper was either unnecessary or indiscreet . . . he kept no records of the understandings or pledges to which he became a party."[6] At most he would scribble a précis of his letters on the cover of a file, but he seldom made minutes either for the Chancellor or for his subordinates. It was not only matters of policy that were kept locked up in that mighty memory but others, where precedent and practice were of greater importance: "thus the Treasury constantly complained, and with reason, that the staff records of the very large staff controlled from this office were not properly kept . . . There is no record of the very great number of offices to which the Lord Chancellor appoints, nor the origin of any particular office, nor how the patronage falls to the Lord Chancellor".[7] Not surprisingly, the Permanent Secretary's disdain for record keeping set the tone for the whole office, with the direct consequence that when the advisory committees on magistrates' appointments were set up, no record was kept even of their composition and the political allegiance of the members.[8]

Fourthly, "although an advanced Radical in politics, he was in many matters exceedingly conservative. He, for example, detested the use either of shorthand or of typewriting".[9] When he retired there was only one typewriter in the LCO, used solely for the preparation of commissions, and only the Clerk of the Chamber, by now "a kind of odd-job man" was capable of using it or of taking shorthand.[10] This conservatism mirrored that which permeated the Royal Courts of Justice, where male law writers still copied out documents in longhand.[11]

As a final peculiarity of some importance, Muir McKenzie "abstained almost ostentatiously from taking any part either in the work relating to magistrates or in that relating to the ecclesiastical patronage",[12] this in marked contrast to the influence which the legal profession ascribed to him over judicial patronage.[13] The magistracy was in some ways the most troublesome of all the Lord Chancellor's duties because of the importance which politicians attached to the party complexion of the bench. It drove Herschell near to distraction and led Loreburn and Haldane to follow him in asserting that in its existing form the Lord Chancellorship was beyond the capacity of any individual to perform properly.[14] It is significant that they were all Liberals, for it was their party's demands for the Conservative domination of the bench to be ended that made such inroads into the Lord Chancellor's time, and once the advisory committees got working properly, no later Chancellor repeated the claim.

It follows that much of Muir McKenzie's activity will have to be teased out from the records of other departments, particularly the Treasury, and perhaps from the private papers of Lord Chancellors and others. For that part of the work of the LCO which was concerned with the administration of the higher courts, the report of the MacDonnell

Commission on the Civil Service, which sat near the end of his term, provides a useful contemporary appraisal.[15] His work was praised and the limitations imposed by the legislation governing the SCJ, for example that the Lord Chancellor's "legal power to exercise . . . control [over the Central Office] is open to some doubt" and that the PD & A division was left "semi-independent", were recognised.[16] Nevertheless when tested by the yardstick of contemporary good practice, the courts were found seriously wanting. Clerical appointments made by patronage not open competition; promotion by seniority rather than merit; octogenarians (and even a nonagenerian) clinging to their posts; departments run as independent units by masters and registrars, between which transfers were almost unknown; lack of uniformity in office practice and discipline and the lack of any inbuilt provision for regular reviews of performance, all these offended against the canons of public administration and in condemning them the Commission implicitly condemned the President of the SCJ and his department. The declaration that "we believe that it will be possible to effect large economies in the Chancery Offices" echoes ironically Muir McKenzie's note to Selborne's **Memorials**: "when he left office in 1885 he was engaged on a scheme for consolidating the Chancery Offices, which he believed would have greatly conduced to reducing the delays and expenses which are still characteristic of that branch of the High Court, while diminishing by nearly one-half the cost of the department."[17]

Between the 1880s, when strong Treasury pressure was being exerted to modernise the court offices and the LCO was itself engaged in the same process, and the MacDonnell Commission set up in 1912, the impetus for such reforms had slackened. The impression created by the LCO papers, but which requires to be tested by a closer examination, is that the failure of the SCJ (Officers) Bill in the mid-1890s marked the end of steady and persistent Treasury efforts to effect economies and introduce administrative reforms, while Halsbury's decision to refer to the Council of Judges calls for a royal commission on the operation of the Judicature Acts signalled his unwillingness to countenance major changes.[18] The climate gradually changed: under Selborne and Cairns the judges and inferior court officers had been on the defensive; their private fiefs were made part of a single organisation over which the Lord Chancellor and the Treasury had large, if sometimes ill-defined powers; the country was "almost pathologically afraid of jobbery"[19] and their patronage was threatened; the Judicature Acts did not seem to be the necessary limit of reorganisation since there was powerful agitation for permanent provincial outposts of the High Court. By the time Muir McKenzie retired they had re-grouped and entrenched themselves behind the formidable bulk of the White Book. Not only were provincial sittings off the agenda, the very assizes had been preserved almost intact and the atavistic tendencies of the divisions of the High Court had been allowed to flourish to such good effect that they were almost independent courts. To a surprising extent, the judges (or at least the heads of divisions) had regained control of their courts, and their independence was protected by the solid phalanx of barristers in the House of Commons which by and large shared the judges' views and interests.

Schuster (admittedly not an unprejudiced nor disinterested observer) wrote that "during the long reign of Lord Halsbury [Muir McKenzie] gradually lost heart in the reforms which he had either planned himself or the idea of which he had inherited from Lord Selborne"[20] and there is no reason to question his verdict. In those years reforms were undertaken, but they were piecemeal and tentative and do not seem to be part of any wider scheme. One major obstacle was patronage, which frustrated Muir McKenzie's attempts to amalgamate the district probate registries with the district registries;[21] another was the sensitivity of the heads of division to any threat to their effectively independent position, a good example being Coleridge's ludicrous assertion that:

> . . . if I could have foreseen, as perhaps I ought, how the Judicature Acts would be worked, I would have resigned sooner than be a party to it. The steady lowering of the Judges of first instance, and the enthroning of the Chancellor upon the necks of all of us, have altered the Profession, so far as the Common Law is concerned, and made success in it, except so far as money making is concerned, not an object of ambition to a high-minded man. It frets me more than I can tell you to feel that the great place I hold is being let down year by year, and I don't know how to prevent it . . . I find the great traditional influence of the Chief Justice and the deference to him lessened materially, in every way, year by year . . .[22]

Halsbury was too indolent and too much in sympathy with the judges to encounter such hostility for the sake of reforms in which he had little interest. Muir McKenzie resigned himself to the postponement of his schemes the more readily because he found Halsbury "the most loveable man I ever knew in public life"[23] and when at last the Liberals returned in 1906 first Loreburn and then Haldane were so preoccupied with other business that there was little time for legal reforms. By then, in any case, although his subsequent career, culminating in his appointment as an octogenarian junior minister in the first Labour government, shows that he retained much of his vigour and "his great knowledge and subtlety"[24] were little impaired, Muir McKenzie seems to have been content to coast towards retirement and "hardly realised how very large a proportion of the work [of the office] was either done in a slovenly way or not done at all".[25]

In the wider field of law reform the record of the LCO was by no means unimpressive. For example, Halsbury imposed compulsory registration of title on London and piloted the Criminal Evidence Act into law; Loreburn created the Public Trustee and set on foot codifying bills in the criminal law and Haldane introduced measures radically reforming the law of property in 1914. That more was not achieved was largely due to factors beyond the control of Lord Chancellors. Muir McKenzie attributed the "slaughter of County Court bills" to the lack of a departmental minister in the House of Commons,[26] but the reasons are probably more complicated than that. Increasingly, governments were committed to controversial legislation on other subjects, which congested the Parliamentary timetable and the Whips would not give a place to legal reforms which were of secondary concern compared with, say, Ireland, education, taxation and labour law. That meant that they had to be bi-partisan if they were to become law, since only thus could they pass through Parliament in the time grudgingly conceded to them, yet vested interests such as the Bar, the solicitors and bankers were all strongly organised in defence of their privileges. That sort of co-operation, between the diehard Halsbury and the radicals Loreburn and Haldane, was scarcely likely in the increasingly polarised world of Edwardian politics.

Notes

1 *According to his obituarist "a difficult man to know and a dangerous man to thwart or underestimate; his tact and astuteness were acknowledged, but what was not so generally appreciated was that under his apparently cynical manner were concealed great human sympathy and kindness" (***'The Times'***, 23.5.1930).*

2 *2/3630: Schuster's memorandum of 1943. See also 4/221: memorandum of 1919 to Lord Birkenhead explaining his plans to remodel the office.*

3 *2/3630 p. 5.*

4 *4/221 p. 6.* **Cf. 'The Times'**, *23.5.1930: "his position 'behind the throne' always seemed to be agreeable to him".*

5 *2/2629 p. 5. His autobiography includes selections from his diary.*

6 *4/221, pp. 5–6.*

7 **Ibid.**, *p. 2.*

8 **Ibid.**, *pp. 3–4.*

9 *2/3630, p. 5.*

10 **Ibid.**, *p. 6.*

11 *PP 1914–16 (Cd. 7832) XII, 1 at p. 26.*

12 *2/3630, p. 6.*

13 *See his obituary and Schuster's appreciation in* **'The Times'**, *23, 24.5.1930.*

14 *R. F. V. Heuston,* **Lives** *. . ., 114–17; PP 1918 (Cd. 9230) XII, 1, at p. 64.*

15 *PP 1914–16 (Cd. 7832) XII, 1. This report, their sixth, was prepared under the chairmanship of Sir H. B. Smith.*

16 **Ibid.**, *pp. 9–11.*

17 **Ibid.**, *p. 37; Selborne,* **Memorials**, *(1885) 2, p. 156.*

18 *On the SCJ (Officers) Bill, see 2/91. Lord Esher had pleaded for a royal commission in 1890 (2/47).*

19 *W. L. Burn,* **The Age of Equipoise** *(1964), 114.*

20 *2/3630, p. 5.*

21 *PP 1914–16 (Cd. 8130) XII, 91 at q. 44,147.*

22 *E. Coleridge,* **Life and Correspondence of Lord Coleridge** *(1904) vol. 2, p. 359: to Lindley LJ, 17.9.1889.*

23 *Quoted in A. W. Fox,* **Lord Halsbury** *(1929), 125.*

24 *4/221, p. 2.*

25 **Ibid.**

26 *PP 1914–16 (Cd. 8130) XII, 91 at q. 44,334. The fate of successive Public Trustee Bills, the last of which succeeded in passing in dramatic and fortuitous circumstances is another instance (S. H. Jeyes and F. D. How,* **Life of Sir Howard Vincent** *(1912) 291–2).*

3 The "Ministry of Justice" project and the Re-organisation of the Office

Halsbury, Herschell and Loreburn would not have found the organisation and methods of the LCO particularly striking; they had served only as Law Officers, whose department was even more exiguous and atypical than the Lord Chancellor's. Haldane, however, was quite different. He came fresh from the War Office, where his jocular threat to create a "Hegelian" army veiled a crusading belief in Britain's need to raise her public administration to Teutonic levels of efficiency. Schuster's comment that it was "not unnatural . . . that he should have been struck not only with the lack of method for discharge of the ordinary business of the Department, but with the complete absence of any organisation for a continuous examination of the functions which the Department supervised, and for laying plans for the future"[1] is probably rather restrained: Haldane was incredulous that a prominent cabinet minister and judge in the highest courts in the land should be submerged in a detailed consideration of the merits of parsons and magistrates. It is therefore strange at first sight that Haldane's three years as Lord Chancellor did not produce any obvious alterations in the Office. In part this no doubt stemmed from the realisation that it would be tactful to await Muir McKenzie's retirement and bring in a new broom, and in part from the fact that Haldane was tremendously busy with the judicial work of the House of Lords and his beloved Privy Council, with the reform of the land law and as a cabinet minister at a time of chronic domestic and international crisis. Primarily, however, it can be attributed to his desire to promote a much more thoroughgoing reorganisation than could be accomplished merely on the Lord Chancellor's own initiative within his department.[2] Haldane's project involved nothing less than the creation of a Ministry of Justice which would assume most of the Lord Chancellor's executive functions. Schuster summarised the plan thus:

> (a) The office of the Lord Chancellor should remain in being. He should be in the Cabinet as "a legal and constutional adviser of the highest standing". He should be President of the Imperial Court of Appeal; but he should be "freed from the duty of daily or even frequent judicial sitting". He would cease to be Speaker of the Second Chamber—a result which Lord Haldane in any event expected would follow from the reconstitution of the Second Chamber. He would be the Minister responsible for the appointment of all judicial officers, that is to say not only the Judges of the High Court, the County Court Judges, such Masters of the Supreme Court as were then appointed by him, and the ordinary unpaid Justices of the Peace, but also the members of the Imperial Court of Appeal, the Lords Justices of the Court of Appeal (at present appointed by the Prime Minister), the Recorders and the Stipendiary Magistrates (at present appointed by the Home Secretary) and those Masters of the Supreme Court whose appointment then rested and still rests with other judicial personages. But in making these appointments he would be under a duty to consult a Committee which would include the Prime Minister, the Minister of Justice, any ex Lord Chancellors, and the Lord Chief Justice, but though bound to consult this Committee he should be free to act on his own opinion. He would have a duty to watch and master all questions relating to legislation, and would take the place of the Treasury as the channel of communication between departments desirous of initiating legislation and the Parliamentary Counsel Office.
>
> (b) All the other functions of the Lord Chancellor, including apparently those relating to the administration of the staff of the Supreme Court and of the County Court would pass to the Minister of Justice who would in fact be the Home Secretary relieved of certain functions specified in the Report as being more congruous with the work of other departments.[3]

The history of this ill-fated project has been meticulously traced by Gavin Drewry in an article which is a model of good administrative history and it need not be recounted here.[4] By the time Haldane returned to office in 1923 it was effectively dead and buried, although to preserve his *amour propre* it was still treated as a live possibility. It is ironical that no-one did more to ensure its defeat than the man Haldane had chosen to be his Permanent Secretary with a view to carrying through the scheme, Claud Schuster, who for thirty years was widely considered to be the real ruler of the LCO.

It is a further irony, in view of the way Haldane's philo-Germanism got him hounded from office, that his last appointment was himself the grandson of German immigrants, sporting a decidedly German-sounding name. Haldane had had a free hand since Muir

McKenzie had made no effort to find or train a successor,[5] and he chose one who had gained a good deal of varied experience of public administration and the business world: Schuster was Secretary successively to the Local Government Act Commission (1899–1902) and to the Great Northern Railway Company, then went to the Board of Education as a legal assistant, rising to Assistant and finally Principal Assistant Secretary in its legal department (1903–11), became Chief Registrar of Friendly Societies (1911–2) and joined the new National Health Insurance Commission as Secretary and legal adviser, becoming the legal member of the Commission in 1913. He was still only forty-five years old, as physically fit as was to be expected from a devoted Alpine climber, and possessed "one of the acutest minds in the public service".[6] He excelled as a writer of fluent and persuasive minutes which adroitly shepherded the recipient down the path mapped out for him to a conclusion carefully prepared in advance and he quickly acquired a reputation for getting his own way.[7] The legal profession, among whom there had been a good deal of speculation about Muir McKenzie's successor, was surprised at Haldane's choice but quickly came to recognise that he was a man to be reckoned with; no less formidable than Muir McKenzie but more direct and outspoken. Schuster evidently relished his new position and had no intention of presiding over the dismantling of the LCO, so he set about the task of defeating the Ministry of Justice proposal not only by encouraging the Chancellor, Lord Birkenhead (who needed little persuasion) to oppose it but by confuting the arguments deployed by its supporters. These were principally that the Lord Chancellor was so overworked and his departmental resources so meagre that he could neither give enough attention to ensuring that the administration of justice became efficient and economical and was regularly modified to accommodate the changing needs of litigants, nor could he provide the impetus for an ongoing programme of reforms in the substance of the law.[8]

In order to demonstrate the falseness of this view Schuster did require a modest increase in resources for the office. Apart from the ritual sparring inseparable from such applications, the Treasury made few difficulties[9]—it was, at all events, likely to be a cheaper expedient than a Ministry of Justice. The only real obstacle was raised to Schuster's desire to instal as Liddell's successor Albert Napier, who had come in as Buckmaster's unestablished Private Secretary in 1915 and had been pronounced unfit for war service. Schuster stuck to his guns and won: Napier made his whole career in the office, succeeded Schuster in 1944 and retired ten years' later.[10] The remodelling of the department at the end of the Great War produced this structure shown in Figure 1.

The County Courts Department was moved wholesale from the Treasury in the early 1920s and was itself a sizeable organisation, but occupied separate premises and enjoyed a largely independent existence under the supervision of the Assistant Secretary. The patronage secretaries also remained largely separate: the qualifications needed by these officials were essentially personal rather than professional and some were far from the orthodox model of a civil servant.[11] The Secretary of Ecclesiastical Patronage tended to have a military background and Schuster's sketch of Dallas Waters gives a good idea of the qualities requisite for a successful Secretary of Commissions.[12]

Few of the other inferior officers in the department exercised very much personal responsibility, though the role of Establishment Officer—one of the recommendations made by the MacDonnell Commission for civil service departments—was potentially important as his duties extended to the offices of the SCJ. Several, however, gave long

Figure 1

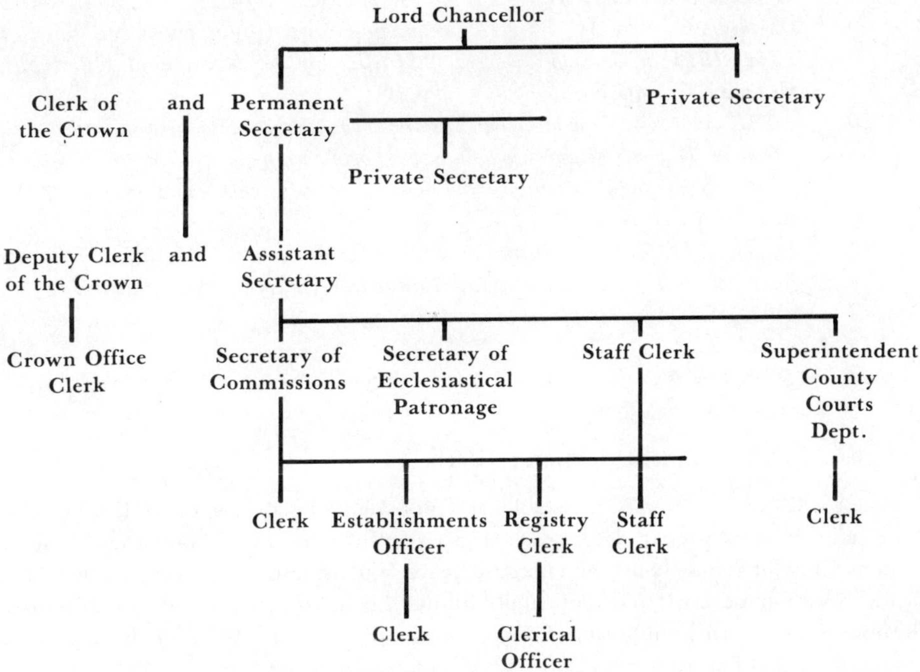

service to the LCO; thus Sir Robert Overbury, later Clerk of the Parliaments, was transferred from the RCJ as a class III clerk in 1919 and served successively as staff clerk in the Crown Office then Secretary of Commissions and Chief Clerk before his promotion to be Reading Clerk in the House of Lords in 1934; J. W. Macaree, who succeeded him as Chief Clerk and retired in 1948, had joined as registry clerk in 1919; E. C. Martin, a Principal Officer at the Treasury, came over with the County Courts Department and retired as Superintendent only in 1949; Major L. P. Haviland was Secretary of Ecclesiastical Patronage from 1928 to 1950 and Percy Lee, formerly of the Land Registry, was successively Establishment Officer and Chief Clerk between 1919 and 1930.[13] Even the post of private secretary to the Lord Chancellor turned into a permanent one held by R. W. Bankes (1919–29), J. D. Waters, A. J. N. Paterson and Vernon Harington (1934–49), so that Hailsham demanded to employ in addition his old judge's clerk as a personal secretary.[14]

Notes

1 *2/3630, p. 8.*
2 *Lord Haldane,* ***Autobiography*** *(1929) 249–53.*
3 *2/3630, pp. 1–3.*
4 *(1983) 61* ***Public Administration****, 396–414.*
5 *PP 1914–16 (Cd 8130) XII, 91 at q. 55, 417.*

6 *'**The Times**', 29.7.1956.*

7 *Hailsham referred to one such memorandum, on the Ministry of Justice project, in his defence of Schuster against Hewart:* ***Parl. Debs.*** *(H of L) 1934–5, vol. 95 cols. 382–3.*

8 *PP 1918 (Cd. 9230) XII, 1, at pp. 64–78.*

9 *On this process see M. Wright,* ***Treasury Control over the Civil Service, 1854–1914*** *in G. Sutherland (ed.),* ***Studies in the Growth of Nineteenth Century Government*** *(1972), 195.*

10 *4/221. As a son of one of Queen Victoria's most celebrated soldiers, Lord Napier of Magdala, Napier's delicate health must have been a source of some chagrin to him. He perpetuated his family's military traditions indirectly by marrying a daughter of Field Marshal Sir G. S. White.*

11 *See e.g. E. W. Swanton's description of Major G. H. Cartwright, Ecclesiastical Secretary from 1911 to 1925 in A. Ross,* ***The Penguin Cricketer's Companion*** *(1978).*

12 *4/222: Schuster's minute, August 1940.*

13 *4/221–2.*

14 *4/221.*

4 The Reign of Schuster, 1915–44

Schuster's LCO was small and stable and not generally overworked. Unlike Muir McKenzie he was prepared to delegate, so that, for instance, Napier took on the responsibility for county courts and because he worked fast himself and because the nature of the Lord Chancellor's routine usually limited his attendance on him to an hour in the mornings he had ample time for his own work. It would be difficult to find any contemporaries of his rank who could airily confess that "I am anything but busy" even if they were frank enough to do so.[1] He was not idle, however. His moderate workload enabled him to become an inveterate member of committees and inquiries on any number of subjects, in the course of which he acquired a knowledge of men and business which made him formidable indeed, as well as a reputation for incisive and sometimes impatient interventions.[2] In Whitehall he became a legendary figure, who stands out in high relief compared with his predecessor,[3] and it is not inappropriate that he earned the rare notoriety of being made the victim of a personal attack by the Lord Chief Justice. It is hardly surprising that he made enemies; Napier's obituary records that "his method of obtaining his ends did not, however, always escape criticism and with the years an increasing dislike of opposition tended to strain his relations with certain members of the judiciary and heads of department with whom he was brought into contact";[4] this impatience and over-confidence sometimes led him astray, most notably in his unsuccessful attempt to dismember the PD & A division. His dictatorial tone and assumptions of power lent plausibility to Hewart's charge that the Lord Chancellor was a puppet in the hands of an over-mighty civil servant. Nor is it entirely without substance: as we have seen, the turnover of Chancellors between the wars was faster than before and few had time to acquire a real mastery of the job, which inevitably increased their dependence on the Permanent Secretary. Nevertheless some of these Chancellors were men of strong character like Haldane, Birkenhead and Hailsham, hardly likely to settle for subordination, and others, such as Maugham and Simon, were notoriously wilful and difficult to work for. If Schuster seemed at his most overbearing under Sankey, it was probably because they shared reforming intentions and were anxious to make hay while the sun shone — certainly Schuster had no cause to welcome the return of the conservatively inclined Hailsham.

Nearing his retirement in 1943, and in the shadow of another Machinery of Government Committee, Schuster penned a lengthy memorial in which he defended the Department's record over twenty-five years, addressing himself to the two functions identified by the Haldane Committee as crucial to a "Ministry of Justice", viz. the promotion of law reform and the supervision of the machinery of justice. The document[5] is a convenient starting point for the researcher who wishes to appraise the record of the LCO in this period and to examine the soundness of Schuster's claim that its performance demonstrated that the Haldane proposals were either unnecessary or undesirable. There is no space to attempt that here, but a brief outline of the issues may be useful.

It was common ground that in this century proposals for law reform in the narrow sense, affecting the structure and organisation of the courts and matters of evidence and procedure, and those substantive areas of law which formed a residual category for which no other government department took responsibility (such as the law of real property and succession, and the general parts of the law of torts and contract) had become more difficult to translate into legislation. Some interested observers, including Muir McKenzie, attributed this largely to the absence of a minister sitting in the Commons and possessing departmental responsibility for such bills,[6] while Haldane and Schuster regarded the cabinet as the critical forum,[7] but the problem was essentially the same—to persuade the government of the day to give Parliamentary time to law reform. The relentless expansion of government business pressing on an inelastic Parliamentary timetable obliged the Whips to deal ruthlessly with bills which were regarded as being secondary importance and increasingly law reform came to be seen as marginal in the politics of the day. Social welfare and the management of the economy were coming to dominate the political scene: votes were in housing and health, not bankruptcy and negligence. The stuff of most law reform was seen as of interest only to a limited range of persons, not to the great masses who now made up the electorate.[8] Moreover, as the tentacles of state intervention reached further into the life of the country and grasped more tightly, existing departments expanded their activities and new ministries were created whose responsibilities took in matters with a strongly "legal" content, such as workmen's compensation (Home Office), lunacy (Ministry of Health) and landlord and tenant (Ministry of Health and later the Ministry of Housing). By the middle of this century, the only areas which were likely to be neglected unless the LCO or a Ministry of Justice fought for them were those already mentioned and the law of divorce, which no government dared to touch.

Within this context the LCO operated and its record must be judged accordingly. In the long term, the creation of the Law Revision Committee in 1934 may be seen as the outstanding feature. This went some way towards playing the part which seems to have been intended for the Judges' Council, and its value lay not so much in its actual achievements, though they were considerable, as in demonstrating the value of a standing body to which subjects might be referred for expert consideration. Despite the narrow limits imposed upon it, which excluded anything politically controversial,[9] it made its mark and it was precisely the ground of Jowitt's objection to reviving it—that it would embarrass the government to be faced with a mounting pile of reports awaiting implementation—that was one of its main attractions to reformers, for its continuing activity made it harder to sideline law reform.[10] The attraction remains, and despite the disappointingly high casualty rate among proposals from its successor bodies, the Law Reform Committee and the Law Commission, few would argue for a reversion to a position where *ad hoc* committees are the primary method of initiating changes.

The greatest triumph of the office in substantive law reform was unquestionably the vast legislation on real property which was finally completed in 1926. The concessions which were made to vested interests in the course of its passage have been criticised but the achievement remains a notable one. The various reforms brought about in the common law, mainly as a result of Law Revision Committee reports, are also on the credit side, but against that must be set the unconscionable delay in reforming crown proceedings and the department's reluctance to support, let alone initiate, improvements in private international law.[11]

In the administration of justice, the record is perhaps less impressive. In the longer view, it is possible to regard the whole period, almost a century, between the Judicature Acts and the Beeching Report, as essentially static: with the single—and notable—exception of the Legal Aid Act 1949, the changes in the structure, organisation and practice of the courts over that period can be fairly described as minor adaptations. This can be seen as a predictable consequence of placing responsibility for justice with the Lord Chancellor and a department staffed by lawyers rather than generalist civil servants; for with the legal profession in charge of its own destinies, radical developments, such as the substitution of tribunals for courts and the wider use of arbitration, were hardly likely to be given much encouragement. Nevertheless it would be wrong to dismiss the changes that were made as insignificant or call the period sterile.

The inter-war years fall into three reasonably distinct phases. In the first, which ended with the SCJ (Consolidation) Act 1925, many of the recommendations of the Royal Commission on the Civil Service were implemented, together with other improvements that the LCO had long wished to bring about, and the authority of the Lord Chancellor over the courts was increased. The relocation of the Treasury's county courts department in the LCO, and the legislation which gave the Lord Chancellor the appointment of registrars and placed the terms of employment of the staff of the county courts on a more satisfactory footing, were a major advance for the LCO and although it had little success in widening the jurisdiction of county courts, the report of the Austin Jones Committee in 1947 gave a generally favourable verdict on their organisation.[12]

In the SCJ vested interests were far stronger and the Lord Chancellor's authority much weaker, but the diligent labours of the Tomlin Committee enabled a considerable rationalisation to be effected among the administrative departments, whose staffs were also brought more closely into line with the civil service on promotions, pay, pensions etc. Legislation also put paid to the ''peculiarly vicious form of organisation''[13] which complicated the courts' financial and accounting arrangements. At the same time the operation of patronage in appointments which the Commission had criticised was modified:

> The Royal Commission on the Legal Departments of the Civil Service had recommended that all rights of appointment in the Offices of the Courts, including the Probate, Divorce and Admiralty Division, should be taken from the various Judges in whose gift they lay and given to the Lord Chancellor. In order to proceed upon the line of least resistance this recommendation was not pursued to its extremity, but those Judges who had rights of appointment of clerks agreed to exercise them only upon the recommendations of a Committee presided over by the Lord

> Chancellor's officers. The few cases where the Lord Chief Justice and the Master of the Rolls had rights of appointment to Masterships were left undisturbed, as it was thought that the change was not worth the friction which would result from an attempt to make it. In the Probate, Divorce and Admiralty Division, where the arrangements were peculiarly chaotic, the President, while retaining the nominal power to appoint, agreed to exercise it only in favour of those who had passed the ordinary Civil Service examination.[14]

Here Schuster's bland account is less convincing: it conceals the fact that even the "line of least resistance" was only achieved after a hard struggle and at the price of alienating the newly appointed Lord Chief Justice, who declared in positively Eldonian terms:

> "When the time comes for me to relinquish the office to my successor, whoever he may be, I desire to relinquish it entirely unimpaired and undiminished in any of the duties, rights or privileges, however apparently unimportant or uninteresting some of them may be thought to be".[15]

With Lloyd George as Prime Minister, the times were hardly propitious to transfer patronage from the judiciary to the executive, and it is not surprising that the Machinery of Government Committee's proposal that the Prime Minister should yield up his judicial patronage in exchange for participation in a committee which would advise the Lord Chancellor was not pursued; indeed, it was all that Birkenhead could do to defend the ground conceded by Asquith and keep puisne judgeships from again becoming a legitimate reward for party political services.[16]

Whatever its initial cause, the mutual antagonism between Hewart and Schuster quickly became an important stumbling block to any plans which the latter might devise for the courts, although it did not become public knowledge until Hewart's famous outburst in the Lords in 1934. Hewart's accusation that Schuster was engaged in Machiavellian plot to substitute for the Lord Chancellor a layman as Minister of Justice who would necessarily be in the hands of his Permanent Secretary, particularly in making judicial appointments and promotions, is quite without substance.[17] But his hostility to the importance that the LCO had assumed in such matters was more than merely personal, nor was he the first LCJ to voice a grievance about the subordination of his own office.[18]

The central plank in the argument deployed first by Selborne and later by Birkenhead and Schuster to repulse the demand for a Minister of Justice who would be accountable to Parliament for the public service which the courts of law were intended to provide, was that the Lord Chancellor *was* already such a minister, at least in relation to the superior and county courts; indeed it was to enable him to fulfil that function that he was allowed a permanent staff and on that basis he had explicitly equated his relationship with the Treasury with that of the heads of other government departments.[19] Moreover in the argument as developed by Schuster, the hybrid qualities of the Lord Chancellor—which his officers, by virtue of their legal qualifications, partook—ceased to be an anomaly and became a positive virtue:

> Lord Haldane in reaching the conclusion that the Lord Chancellor should continue to exist both as a Minister and as a Judge rejected the theories on the Lord Chancellor's position which had been prevalent among many

> of those who took an interest in this subject, particularly during the second half of the nineteenth century. Acting under the influence of Montesquieu, who supposed that the excellence of the British Constitution lay in the complete separation of the legislative, executive and judicial functions, these persons found it impossible to justify union in the person of the Lord Chancellor of a legislator in the House of Lords, a Minister and a Judge. Even when conceding that Montesquieu was wrong, and that there is not and never has been in England any such separation of functions, it is in theory difficult to reconcile such a union in one man or to understand how one man can, to take an instance be technically responsible as a legislator for the legislation which produced Regulation 18B, share with the Home Secretary the responsibility for action taken under it, and pronounce in his place as a Judge judgment on the question whether that action was rightly taken. The answer to this criticism is first that the system works, and second that it may be greatly doubted whether any other system would work. The advantages which accrue to the Cabinet from the presence of a colleague who is not only of high judicial reputation but who can represent to them the view of the judiciary; to the legislature from the presence in it of one who is both a Judge and Minister; and to the judiciary from the fact that its President is in close touch with current political affairs, are enormous. In a Democracy, whose legislation may be advancing, or at least moving, rapidly, and whose judiciary remains static, there is always present a serious risk of a collision between the two elements. Where the Constitution is written and the static condition of the judiciary is absolute, as in the United States, the danger of such a collision is very great. Even in England, with an unwritten Constitution and an unwritten common law, unless there is some link or buffer (whichever term may be preferred) between the two elements, the situation would be perilous. We may, therefore, accept with confidence Lord Haldane's conclusion on this side of the matter.[20]

This view of the LCO as a "ministry of justice" necessarily implied that it possessed the authority over the courts which was the counterpart to responsibility for them. Yet in the SCJ the scope of the Lord Chancellor's office and its interaction with the heads of divisions was unclear, a 'divisum imperium' perpetuated and aggravated when the common law divisions were merged in a Queen's Bench Division that dwarfed its fellows.[21] The question of patronage was important intrinsically and also because it symbolised power relations, but it could be compromised in a way that the wider issues of authority could not. Any attempt by the Lord Chancellor to interfere in the management of a division or to re-organise the allocation of business among them, still less to alter the divisional or appellate structure, was likely to be resented and resisted by its chief, yet unless he was able to do so, the Lord Chancellor would be obliged to take responsibility for their shortcomings without having the power to correct them.

Hewart, and those judges who thought like him, clearly rejected the constitutional and administrative role which the LCO was seeking to carve out for itself. In their view, the courts were not really part of "the machinery of government" at all and where Schuster's model carefully blurred the demarcation line between executive and judiciary, they drew it clean and sharp not around the judge's courtroom but around the RCJ itself. The independence of the judiciary meant freedom for the judge to arrange the business of his court, for the master to control the business of his office, and for the head of a division to organise the flow of work within it. Co-ordination among the divisions could be achieved by informal contacts, by the Rule Committee and, if necessary, by the Judges' Council.

No "link" or "buffer" was necessary, and in view of their embittering experience in connection with the enforced salary reduction in 1931, they might reasonably be sceptical as to its value. In this picture, the staff of the LCO were civil servants *simpliciter* and for the LCJ to receive communications through the Lord Chancellor's Permanent Secretary was a grave discourtesy.

Given the reluctance within the legal establishment to air their differences in public and the conservative views of Cave and Hailsham, it is not surprising that there was a period of relative inactivity between 1925 and 1930. However, Sankey demonstrated his interest in promoting reforms and the publication of the London Chamber of Commerce's attack on the cost of litigation in April, 1930, generated enough public concern to put legal reforms back onto the political agenda. There is little doubt that Schuster had been waiting for some such opportunity, and he produced a "review of the present system" which dealt summarily with the question of costs which was at the heart of the public agitation and concentrated mainly on delays, for which he had more plausible remedies.[23] His proposals were certainly drastic, involving the abolition of the Court of Appeal and the dismemberment of the PD & A and Kings Bench, which would be reconstituted in three divisions (Chancery remaining unchanged as a fourth), furnishing judges in rotation to handle appeals. Since each division would have a President, the LCJ would, perhaps not entirely coincidentally, become merely the head of one much smaller division.

The tone of this paper, with its calculations of 'judge hours', Lord Atkin found more distasteful than the proposals themselves.[24] It was however the start of a campaign which led to the setting up of the Hanworth Committee, who were enjoined

> "To consider the state of business in the Supreme Court, and to report whether greater expedition in the dispatch of business, or greater economy in the administration of justice in the Court is practicable and would be effected by any, and, if so, what, rearrangements in the constitution of the Supreme Court and of the Divisions comprised in the High Court of Justice. . . ."[25].

Other initiatives were Sankey's earnest attempts to cajole the judges of the KBD into streamlining their practice,[26] and the appointment of the Peel Commission, whose terms of reference were a clear aspersion on Hewart's management of the KBD.[27] The snub administered, at best negligently, to the LCJ in announcing publicly the appointment of the Commission without giving him prior notice, was probably as influential as the slight to Slesser in the Administration of Justice (Appeals) Bill in bringing on the dramatic scene in the House of Lords.

The results of all this endeavour may look modest enough, and certainly came nowhere near carrying out Schuster's original ideas, but they created a momentum which might have been sustained and increased but for the war, and the deliberations of the Hanworth Committee and the Peel Commission contain some interesting material.

The war put an end to work of this kind but in his memorandum Schuster outlined some of the tasks that the office ought to tackle when it ended. New legislation on poor persons' litigation, the extension of title registration, "a fresh impulse" to the Statute Law Committee and a wider remit for the Law Revision Committee were among them, but

but he gave the highest priority to the administration of criminal justice. He envisaged a rule committee "to whom should be referred the general duty of continual supervision and revision of the practice and procedure in criminal matters in the High Court, at Quarter Sessions, and particularly in Petty Sessional Courts"[28] and a major overhaul of magistrates' courts to enable them to cope properly with the work which was being steadily devolved upon them. The illogical division of responsibility between the Lord Chancellor and the Home Secretary had hitherto prevented the effective supervision of the criminal courts and to end this "it is suggested that the time has come when there should be committed to the Lord Chancellor the duty of supervising the whole of the machinery of the Petty Sessional Court whether sitting as a court of examination or as a court of trial".[29] This represented a bold bid to capture the magistrates' courts from the Home Office but Schuster never had the opportunity to pursue it further: he retired in August 1944, and was ennobled like his predecessor.[30]

Notes

1 *2/696: to T. W. Chitty, 18.2.1926.*

2 *For Professor Robson's unfavourable view of Schuster's performance on the Donoughmore Committee see* **Justice and Administrative Law** (2nd ed., 1947) 340–1. *The papers of the "Committee on Diplomatic Women" (2/1150) show him in action as chairman under trying circumstances.*

3 *See e.g. Sir H. S. Kent,* **In On The Act** *(1979), 35–7, 108–10. Symbolically, Schuster appropriated the grandest room in the office for himself.*

4 '**The Times**', *29.7.1956.*

5 *2/3630, memorandum of 31.1.1943. Its context is explained by G. Drewry,* **op. cit**.

6 *PP 1914–16 (Cd. 8130) XII, 91 at qq 44,332–5.*

7 *Lord Birkenhead,* **Points of View** *(1922) vol. 2, 108.*

8 *This was not, however, without compensating advantages: for example, the presentation of the Law of Property Bill as a "technical" reform was designed to reduce the attention given to it by lay MPs; A. Offer (1977) 40 MLR 505.*

9 *This even extended to tortious liability for the acts of animals; 2/5611: Napier's note, 5.6.1951.*

10 *Cf. A. L. Goodhart,* **Law Reform** *(Holdsworth Club Lecture, 1952).*

11 *On these topics, see Section 3,* **infra**.

12 *2/3630: Schuster's memorandum, pp. 10–13. See also* **infra**, *132–3.*

13 **Ibid.**, *p. 10.*

14 **Ibid.**, *p. 9.*

15 *4/300: to the Lord Chancellor, 1.4.1925. The peculiar circumstances surrounding Hewart's appointment may have made him unusually sensitive to any slights to the office.*

16 *2/3630: Schuster's memorandum, pp. 2, 16–19. The "sharp conflict of opinion between the Prime Minister and the Lord Chancellor as regards the appointment to another high judicial office and the single occasion on which a Lord of Appeal in Ordinary was created without consultation with the Lord Chancellor" referred to on p. 17 both probably relate to Birkenhead's Chancellorship.*

17 *See* **infra**.

18 *See* **supra**, *21 for Coleridge's complaint. For a more recent example of the disparagement of the "unsuccessful barristers" who make up the LCO, see A. Mockler,* **Lions Under the Throne** *(1983), 329.*

19 *2/3630: Schuster's memorandum, p. 13: "The effect of the changes was that the relations between the Treasury and the Lord Chancellor's Department became . . . similar to those between the Treasury and any other department of the Government."*

20 ***Ibid.**, pp. 3–4.*

21 *The phrase is Liddell's:* **Notes from the Life of an Ordinary Mortal** *(1911), 191.*

22 *Hewart made this complaint in his House of Lords speech. In the debate a former Lord Chief Justice, Lord Reading, called the LCJ "the permanent head of the judiciary".* **Parl. Debs.** *(H of L) 1933–4, vol. 95 col. 367.*

23 *2/1702. The "Review" is in 2/1596.*

24 *2/1596. The paper was sent to Atkin in error. Lord Tomlin was more favourable.*

25 *Schuster, of course, was on the Committee, and cajoled Hanworth into sitting with him on the Peel Commission.*

26 *2/1703: notes of meeting, 3.3.1932.*

27 *In a cabinet paper (CP 226(34)) the Lord Chancellor set down the KBD arrears principally to utter mismanagement: 2/1610.*

28 *2/3630, pp. 23–4.*

29 ***Ibid.**, pp. 24–5.*

30 *Like Muir McKenzie, Schuster was not put out to grass for long. At the end of the war he was appointed to head the legal section of the British Control Commission in Austria.*

5 The Lord Chancellor's Office, 1944–51

This time there was a potential successor within the department, for Albert Napier had been Assistant Secretary for nearly thirty years, complementing Schuster as the emollient to his abrasive, and it is not surprising that Simon was content to promote him, rather than seeking to bring in an outsider who must learn the job in exceptionally difficult conditions. Moreover, Napier had been taking an increasing share of the Permanent Secretary's regular work because Schuster had been obliged to give much of his time to the work of committees, particularly the cabinet's war legislation committee and the civil liabilities sub-committee.[1]

So it was Napier who had to guide the office through the difficult years of staff and equipment shortages, when every typist had to be fought for—an unfamiliar situation for the LCO, which Schuster had deliberately kept as small as possible and which had consequently been on easy terms with the Treasury.[2] The workload was significantly increased by the incessant outpouring of rules and regulations on every conceivable subject, which required at least to be carefully scrutinised and often engaged the office in complicated discussions on drafting with the Parliamentary counsel. Although the rule committees were in suspension, a constant liaison had to be maintained with the senior officers at the RCJ and with a favoured coterie of county court judges and registrars. The emergency legislation included much that was complicated and novel, affecting large numbers of people and powerful vested interests, and it necessarily required careful supervision and frequent amendment. Tribunals of all descriptions sprang up in wartime and some, especially the Pensions Appeal Tribunals, imposed heavy burdens and operated in areas where public and political sensitivity was acute.[3]

Fortunately government departments did not undergo the same tribulations as had been felt during the Great War, when they were denuded of their experienced men who volunteered for war service; but the usual pace of changes in personnel was inevitably much accelerated and the specialised nature of much of the LCO's work made it difficult to secure suitable replacements, and still more difficult to ensure that they received the sort of thorough training that was needed.[4] It was fortunate indeed that just before the war began, G. P. Coldstream had been recruited from the Parliamentary Counsel's Office, for his drafting expertise was invaluable, and also that when Dallas Waters was given up to the Privy Council in 1940 Leo Page, who had already established a reputation as an authority on the magistracy, was available to take over the Commissions work.[5] When Page's health gave way Sir Rupert Howarth then brought to the job the formidable experience he had gained in the cabinet secretariat.[6] Even so, the manpower struggle grew desperate in the last years of the war and some who were recruited through informal contacts stayed on and made a career in the office. Thus, R. T. Thesiger came to Schuster's attention in Austria and proved to be a major asset, imperturbably assuming the considerable responsibility of putting together the legal aid machinery; he engaged in delicate negotiations with the often touchy representatives of the two professional bodies, carrying them through with only minimal supervision. W. T. C. Skyrme (later Sir Thomas) was another who came expecting to do a brief stint of office work and stayed to become a long serving Secretary of Commissions;[7] Denis Dobson entered by a more conventional route in 1947 and became Permanent Secretary after Sir George Coldstream in 1968.

When peace returned, Napier found himself with a department which was bigger than the one he had entered in 1915 but (discounting the county courts department which had been exiled to Thame during the war and remained geographically detached even when it returned to London) not by very much. Nomenclature was changed to accord with civil service practice during a re-organisation in 1947 but all the senior posts were still filled by lawyers and although the structure was now closer to that of other small government departments, it was still quite distinctive.

The department was able to remain small partly because reforms in the administration of justice were given a low priority in the programme of the Labour government which came into office in 1945. Its huge and far-reaching programme of economic and social reform so congested the Parliamentary timetable that it was not even considered worthwhile to revive the Law Revision Committee, lest further reports gather dust and become an embarrassment.[9] Nor does the Labour Party seem to have given much attention to the subject: at all events there was no party programme of law reform, whereas a Conservative party sub-committee had issued a report earlier in 1945, following a renewed correspondence in *The Times* on the cost of litigation.[10]

The Haldane Society, it is true, did hurry out a proposal for a Ministry of Justice, which attracted little support, and when it produced a lengthy and radical manifesto for law reforms at the end of 1948, Jowitt condemned it as a "farrago of foolishness" and denounced it in unmeasured terms to Morrison.[11] The Attorney-General (Sir Hartley Shawcross) was more temperate, but certainly not enthusiastic, and Chuter Ede, the Home Secretary, backed Jowitt on those matters which affected his own department. The report came far too late in the life of the government to have any chance of making a real impact and its rejection testifies to their essential conservatism in legal matters.

In 1945 the cabinet established a committee under Jowitt to "consider whether there are grounds for an enquiry into the system of administering civil justice in Great Britain, with a view to reducing the cost of litigation''[12] but the LCO persuaded it to concentrate first on measures to deal with the ''avalanche of divorce suits'' and on implementing the Rushcliffe Report on legal aid; it was offered a choice on the wider issues between ''a full-scale enquiry into the administration of justice in all its aspects'' (including fusion of the legal professions, state-subsidised litigation etc.) and ''some more detailed enquiry, for example into the question whether procedure can be still further simplified with a view to expediting and cheapening litigation within the general framework of the existing system.''[13] The decision to opt for the latter effectively ended the possibility of any overall review of the legal system for years to come and the Chancellor of the Exchequer vetoed any alteration in the terms of the committee to permit it to consider wider questions, although Jowitt was prepared to trust the chairman, Sir Raymond Evershed MR, ''not to pursue hopeless hares'' and to control the more adventurous spirits like Gerald Gardiner.[14]

The reform of divorce procedure turned out to be less noteworthy than had been expected—Jowitt had initially assumed that the county courts would be given jurisdiction—and the legal aid scheme finally implemented in 1950 was maimed by the Treasury's stringent economies, so the end product of the Attlee government's reforms in legal administration was not spectacular. However, Jowitt can claim considerable credit for the Crown Proceedings Act and, especially, for the programme of statute law reform which was his particular interest.[15] The Evershed Committee became, in effect, a successor to the Hanworth Committee and quickly got bogged down in copious evidence. Its papers are, however, of real value to the historian of legal institutions and reforms and the resistance of the Chancery division to its experiment with fixed dates for trials showed how little change had been wrought in attitudes by the war.

The conservatism and independence which prevailed within the RCJ had effectively prevented the LCO's Establishment Officer from making the authority which it claimed over the RCJ staff real. A Treasury O & M report, noting that ''in the past, laymen establishment officers have often found the professionally trained heads of offices intractable on establishment matters''[16] suggested that it needed someone of ''high status possessing legal qualifications'' to assist the Permanent Secretary in ''the difficult task of reconciling the individual independence of different parts of the Judiciary with his general responsibility of ensuring that the most effective and economical use is made of the staff supplied to assist the business of the courts''.[17]

Altogether, the LCO papers do not give the impression that the department was on top of its work and pursuing clear goals in the immediate post-war years. The Evershed Committee does not seem to have been used as an instrument of LCO policy in the way Schuster would have attempted; there seems not to have been any systematic attempt to come to grips with the increasing number and importance of tribunals and to integrate them into the legal system (perhaps a reflection of the narrow perspectives engendered by the traditional legal training and background of the LCO staff); and despite the changes in the magistrates' courts after the Du Parcq Commission report, Schuster's bolder plans for criminal justice were not pursued with much vigour. This may be attributable in part to the fact that Napier was now in charge. He was an altogether less flamboyant character than Schuster, and though undoubtedly a most capable administrator and a well liked man, he was sixty-three when he became Permanent Secretary and perhaps

Figure
2

LORD CHANCELLOR'S DEPARTMENT-HEADQUARTERS OFFICE

Present organisation 6th November 1947

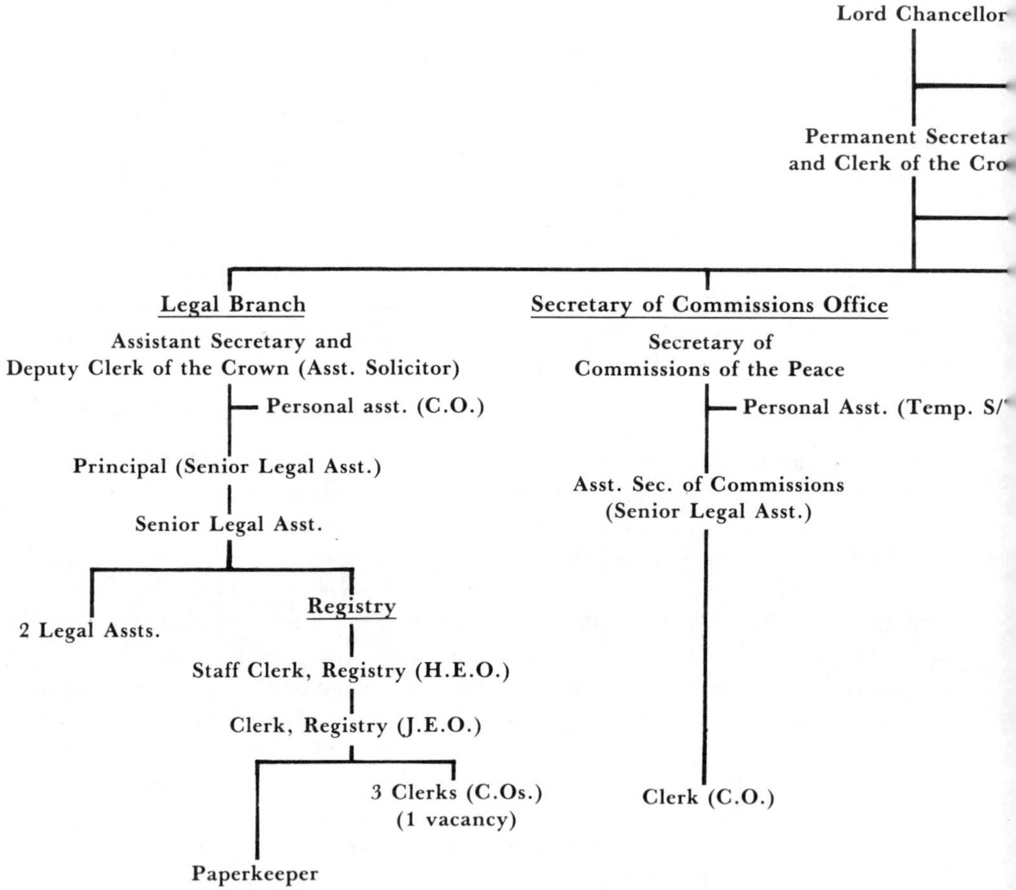

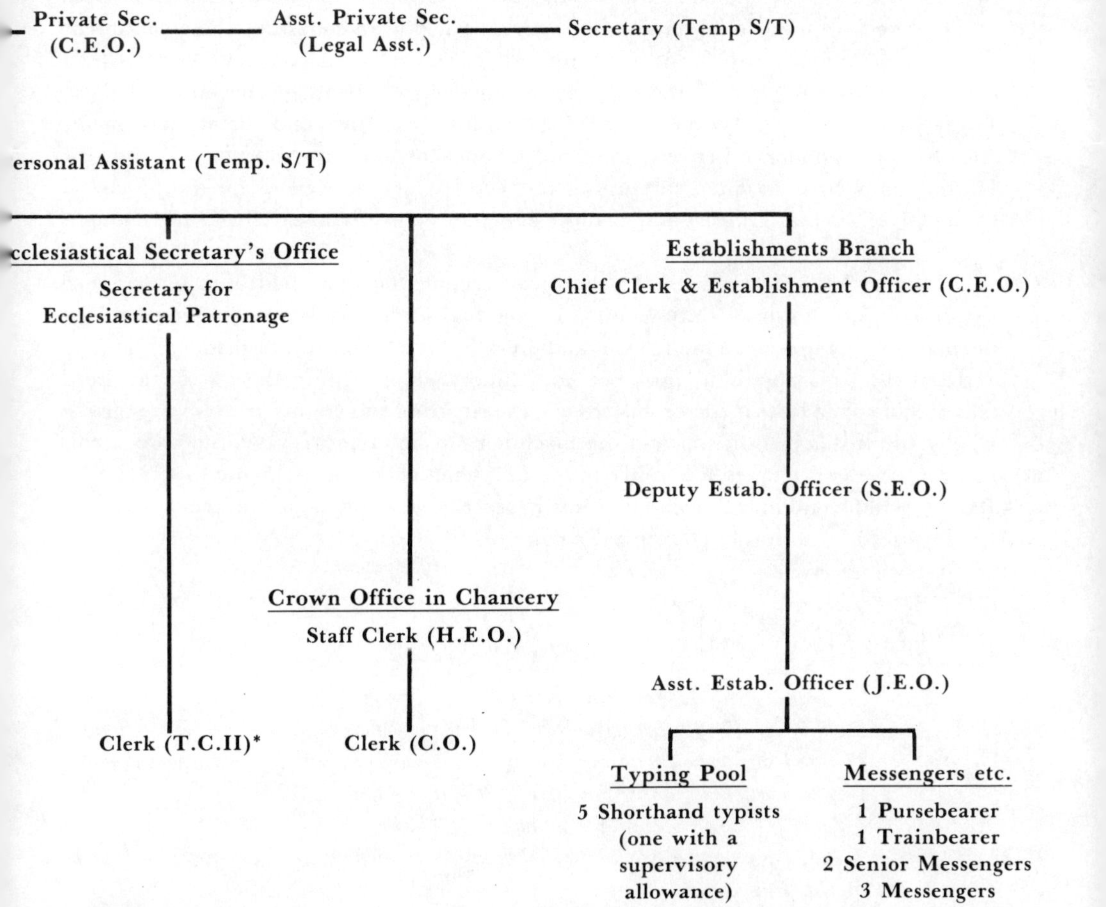

**Assists with Establishment work*

by then lacked both the physical vigour and the mental agility which his predecessors had brought to the job; nor, of course, did he possess Schuster's range of experience. The papers which have been examined yield few clues as to his personal pet projects or his aims for the office, but show a self-effacing man much closer to the conventional model of a civil servant than Schuster. He had, in any case, quite enough to do without seeking to expand his responsibilities. The LCO acquired responsibility for the appointment of stipendiary magistrates and for the staff of the Judge-Advocate General and Judge-Advocate of the Fleet, as well as responsibilities in connection with tribunals and the burden of the legal aid scheme which, because of the decision to opt for "syndicalism rather than nationalisation",[18] required the LCO to foster that close working relationship with the Law Society which Schuster had fathered.

The Lord Chancellor's own role in government is particularly interesting at this time, for although Bevan's threat to deal with attempted "judicial sabotage"[19] proved empty rhetoric in view of the appeal courts' continued unwillingness to countenance challenges to the exercise of ministerial powers, the very drastic powers sought by the government e.g. on Exchange Controls, and the multitude of controls, old and new, under which the population chafed were bound to be viewed unfavourably by many lawyers and judges. Jowitt and other Labour lawyers were acutely sensitive to changes of despotic government, and the correspondence between the Lord Chancellor and the Attorney-General, Sir Hartley Shawcross, is often interesting on these points, as well as on the perennial complaint of the Law Officers at the failure of departments to consult them early enough.

When Jowitt left office with the Labour government, the LCO had been in existence in a recognisable form for sixty-seven years and had succeeded in installing itself almost unchallengeably in a position of power and prestige. The "Ministry of Justice" was dead and buried, legal appointments were now almost wholly within the gift of the Lord Chancellor, or at least made on his advice, the superior and county courts were almost wholly within his jurisdiction and the machinery of law reform was largely under his control. Hewart's feigned ignorance of the LCO had been unconvincing in 1934;[20] by 1951 it would be unthinkable and it is only in recent times that the role of the department has begun to be seriously challenged again.

Notes

1 *See H. S. Kent,* ***In On The Act*** *(1979) 108–10.*

2 *2/3630, pp. 29–30. Before the Royal Commission on the Civil Service in 1930, Schuster expressed satisfaction with the existing measure and methods of Treasury control.*

3 *On the wartime legislation see* ***infra****, 265 ff.*

4 *4/221; 2/4081: Coldstream's minute, 31.7.1947.*

5 *4/221. Page was the author of several books on criminal justice, including* ***The Justice of the Peace*** *(1936).*

6 *4/221.*

7 *Skyrme described the circumstances of his recruitment in* ***The Changing Image of the Magistracy*** *(1979) ix.*

8 *4/22.*

9 *2/3565: meeting of 3.10.1946.*

10 *2/3927: draft memorandum, November, 1945, p. 15.*

11 *2/4115, 22.12.1948. The report was eventually published in 1951 as* ***The Reform of the Law****, edited by Glanville Williams.*

12 *2/3927: draft memorandum to the cabinet committee, November 1945, p. 1. The memorandum was drafted by Coldstream.*

13 ***Ibid.****, p. 11.*

14 *2/3929.*

15 ***Infra****, 296–8.*

16 *4/22 (March, 1949), p. 11.*

17 ***Ibid.****, p. 2. Napier had proposed this to the Treasury in 1946: 4/22.*

18 *B. Abel-Smith and R. Stevens,* ***Lawyers and the Courts*** *(1967), 327.*

19 ***Ibid.****, 285.*

20 ***Parl. Debs.*** *(H of L) 1934–5, vol. 95 col. 236.*

1/37 Papers on the Crown Office in Chancery, 1880–1, including notes by R. C. Palmer, correspondence with Treasury and arrangements for C. Romilly's retirement.

1/59 Papers on the Lord Chancellor's officers, including memoranda by Lord Selborne and on duties of principal secretary; correspondence with Treasury on appointments, salaries etc. 1870–80.

1/74 Correspondence with Treasury, Clerk of the Crown and Clerk of the Patents (C. Cardew) on abolition of this office, and memoranda on functions, 1881–3.

1/60 Lord Chancellor's officers, 1883: drafts of proposals for reorganisation and correspondence with Treasury; statement of duties in the office of Secretary of Presentations by R. White.

1/61 Lord Chancellor's officers, 1884–8; memoranda by H. Nicol, E. P. Thesiger and E. Preston on their offices, correspondence with Treasury and Lord Cairns re appointments and accommodation; draft proposals for a Secretary to the Law Officers.

2/262 Proposals by Muir McKenzie (1880); correspondence between Selborne and Cairns on the future of the office; negotiations with the Treasury (1884); memorandum on work of Principal Secretary and Official Solicitor.

1/79 Correspondence with Home Office and Treasury on appointment of revising barristers under Redistribution of Seats Act, 1885, and draft list, 1885.

2/15 1888–90, four files on non-clerical staff.

35 Discussions with Treasury on preparation of estimates, 1889.

263, 329 Re-arrangements of duties, 1909 and negotiations with Treasury on salaries; K. Muir McKenzie's salary and pension discussed, 1912 and 1915.

410 Memorandum on the functions of the office for the Reconstruction Committee by C. Schuster, 1917.

673 Formation of the Civil Service Legal Society, 1919, minutes and report, 1922 and correspondence with Treasury.

677, 1070 Permanent Secretary appointed Accounting Officer under Supreme Court Vote, 1921; memorandum by M. F. Headlam on his position as a National Debt Commissioner, 1928.

3630 "Ministry of Justice": responses of Law Society and Bar Council to Machinery of Government Committee report, 1918–9 and Schuster's correspondence with them. PQ, 1932. Memorandum by Schuster, 1943; PQ and correspondence with Attorney-General on revived proposals 1946.

682, 4701 Correspondence re pictures of ex-Lord Chancellors to hang in the LCO, 1921–37. Also on pictures in the Palace of Westminster, 1950.

938 Memorandum by Schuster on the constitution of the office and state of business, 1924.

964 Role of LCO in the House of Lords: memorandum for the new administration, 1924.

939 Memorandum for Donoughmore Committee, on Lord Chancellor's power to make regulations under statutes, 1929.

1225 Cabinet papers and Law Officers' opinion on recovery of cabinet papers, 1934. Correspondence with successive LCs on return of papers. Correspondence with Foreign Office, 1938, on LCO practice with secret papers.

4751, 5667, 2291 Correspondence with Lord Esme Gordon-Lennox on access to the Bar of the House of Lords for LCO staff, 1934, 1947, 1956, and papers on the right of the Permanent Secretary to sit on the steps of the throne, 1952–4. Attendance of Clerk of the Crown at the Speaker's levees, 1923.

3634 List of accounts and papers presented to Parliament annually by the LCO, 1950.

3635 Discussions with Scottish Home Department on improving liaison, 1948.

4/22 Staff complement 1945–9, including correspondence with Treasury on appointments, salaries and office organisation; report by Treasury O & M team 1949.

4/121 Evidence to Royal Commission on the Civil Service, 1929–30.

4/122–3 LCO evidence and response to Barlow Committee on Legal Administrative Staff, 1945 and Treasury circulars.

4/124 Working parties on civil service organisation, 1946: reports and LCO minutes on application, to 1950.

4/126 Establishment lists and seniority, correspondence 1922–55.

4/131 Appointments without a civil service certificate.

4/149 Correspondence on part-time etc. officers, 1931–2, 1934, 1954.

4/212 LCO reply to Prime Minister's memorandum on reduction of government expenditure, 1949, with office minutes.

4/221–2 LCO staff complement, 1919–44, including appointments and promotions, office organisation, correspondence with Treasury on LCO and other Supreme Court offices.

6 Relations with the Law Officers

The Machinery of Government Committee recommended that the Lord Chancellor "should have arrangements and an establishment which should bring him more nearly than at present into close relation with the Attorney and Solicitor-General in giving advice on legal questions".[1]

Relations with the Law Officers had not always been good in the past and inevitably much depended on the personalities of those holding the posts; thus Sir J. D. Coleridge can be found complaining that the office of Attorney-General was being disparaged by the Lord Chancellor in much the same terms that he later used as Lord Chief Justice.[2] On the whole, however, friction appears to have been the exception rather than the rule. The incumbents faced similar problems in that their workload tended to increase beyond the resources at their disposal. The conviction expressed by Liberal Chancellors on the first quarter of the twentieth century that the burden was too great for any man echoes the laments of the Law Officers in the last quarter of the nineteenth century[3] and they both suffered from the absence of a regular, permanent staff: indeed Sir William Harcourt's evidence to the Jessel Committee on the Legal Business of the Government discloses a state of affairs strikingly similar to that which the Lord Chancellor's officers had recently revealed to the Lisgar Commission.[4] Perhaps because the Law Officers had no equivalent to those offices, like that of the Clerk of the Crown, where compensating savings might be made or clerks converted to more useful duties and perhaps because their establishment did not facilitate government supervision over the courts as the Lord Chancellor's might, they had to wait a little longer for assistance; the Law Officers' Department, even smaller than the Lord Chancellor's, was created in 1893 and given rooms in the RCJ.[5]

In one respect, however, the Law Officers were conspicuously luckier than the Lord Chancellor — they continued to receive fees for parts of their work in addition to their salary. Down to 1894 they were still allowed to undertake private practice, but even when they were restricted to government business their fees continued to exceed their salaries: F. E. Smith could afford the politic gesture of taking a cut in salary in 1916, whereas when he became Lord Chancellor he made great play with his pecuniary sacrifices. One of the periodic assaults on this anomaly was made by a select committee in 1920, when the very high fees which wartime work had brought in, coupled with the overwork and delays that were its natural counterpart, gave rise to dissatisfaction in cabinet and Parliament, and the Lord Chancellor was involved in ineffectual discussions on various suggested expedients.[6]

The Law Officers were particularly important to the LCO because they usually had the duty of introducing its bills into the Commons and dealing with questions relating to its functions. Schuster said "in this respect the relationship between the Lord Chancellor and the Attorney-General is very like that which prevails in other departments where one Minister is in the House of Lords and one in the House of Commons"[7] and he explained that the answers to Parliamentary questions were usually settled by the Permanent Secretary with the Attorney-General and that the Law Officers allowed the LCO to approach their own officers without any formality. There is no reason to suppose that this idealises the situation significantly, although there were occasions on which the LCO found an Attorney-General unco-operative; thus the Law Officers became so burdened by the mass of questions arising out of the operation of war disability pension tribunals that they refused to continue answering them and the government's Chief Whip had to undertake the job, *faute de mieux*.[8]

The Attorney-General's position as head of the bar also brought him into a close working relationship with the Lord Chancellor. He had to be the channel through whom the Bar Council was consulted and when a barrister was sought for an appointment to a tribunal or committee his opinion was asked.[9] Obviously, some Law Officers were on better terms with the Lord Chancellor and his Permanent Secretary than others, and so were more likely to involve themselves in the processes of law reform. The poorer documentation of the earlier part of this period distorts the picture, but certainly Sir Donald Somervell stands out from these papers as one whose participation was more sustained and extended over a wider area than most of his predecessors.[10] He even adopted a less defensive view in relation to the reform of proceedings against the crown, where the Law Officers had a departmental interest in limiting the encroachments which the reforming elements wished to make; Sir Douglas Hogg had been particularly pugnacious in his defence of the *status quo* and did not modify his attitude when he became Lord Chancellor.[11]

Like other departments, the LCO had sometimes to seek a formal "opinion" on a legal question from the Law Officers, though its own in-house legal expertise was such that it rarely needed to.[12] The papers, however, contain a substantial number of opinions (well over sixty), some of which are of considerable interest. The position of the Law Officers if their opinion was disregarded by a department, either upon the contrary views of its own legal advisers or (very occasionally) on the views of the Lord Chancellor, was distinctly awkward, since they had to defend actions which they had already pronounced unlawful. There are several examples from the Attlee government, which may simply reflect the preponderance of later material in these files: thus in 1947 the Colonial Secretary defended his refusal to intervene on behalf of six men under sentence of death for sacrificial murder in the Gold Coast by a reference to "the highest legal advice" that he could not do so; the advice was Jowitt's and the Attorney-General, who had advised in the contrary sense, was furious.[13] He was still more upset when the Central Land Board was being encouraged by the Ministry of Town and Country Planning to act against the Law Officers' narrow construction of Town and Country Planning Act 1947 s. 43, which threatened to thwart their object of reducing the price of all land purchased by the Board to its "existing use value". On this occasion Jowitt, although he and the Act's draftsman differed from the Law Officers' opinion, would not countenance a departure from it.[14] Shawcross became disgruntled both at not being consulted timeously and at the fact that the Lord Chancellor was sometimes consulted instead (no doubt his presence in the cabinet made this convenient), telling Attlee that "I now have quite a list of matters here about which we were clearly involved but in regard to which we were not consulted before action had been taken" and seeking an understanding that the Lord Chancellor would send him copies of all opinions he gave to the cabinet.[15] It was probably a perennial complaint, aggravated by the accelerating speed of government business in the age of the telephone; it was certainly not confined to Attlee's administration, for the Conservatives had been in office only a few months when their Law Officers were protesting vigorously about the cabinet's preference for Simonds' opinion on a delicate and complicated question on the status and control of imported labourers in Egypt.[16]

The other legal department with which the LCO necessarily enjoyed a close working relationship was the Treasury Solicitor, whose role in modern times has not attracted much scholarly attention. Occasional conflicts were inevitable between an office charged with protecting the interests of the crown and the LCO, with its broader concern with the workings of the judicial system, and they can be seen here in connection with wartime tribunals, land charges, limitations and, especially, with the discovery of documents.[17]

Notes

1 *PP 1918 (Cd. 9230) XII, 1 at p. 74.*

2 *J.Ll.J. Edwards,* ***The Law Officers of the Crown****, (1964), 148–9. Coleridge's pretensions to forward the codification of English law may have given rise to some of his discontents.*

3 ***Ibid.***, *65.*

4 ***Ibid.***, *143.*

5 ***Ibid.***, *142.*

6 ***Ibid.***, *90–118, especially 108–9. 2/622.*

7 *2/3630, p. 15.*

8 *2/2787, especially Schuster to Col. Wilson, 5.5.1921.*

9 *Good examples are in 2/3619, 3659–60. See also 2/4625: Jowitt to Shawcross, 6.10.1948, apologising for meeting representatives of the Bar without the presence of anyone from the L.O.D.*

10 *Somervell, however, was Attorney-General from 1936 to 1945, a much longer tenure than average; within this period only Sir Richard Webster's (Lord Alverstone) exceeds his, and he did not hold the post continuously (1886–92, 1895–1900).*

11 ***Infra***, *201.*

12 *J.Ll.J. Edwards* (**supra**), *151–2, points out a gradual decline in the number of formal opinions after the end of the Great War. Sir Hartley Shawcross, the Attorney-General in the cases referred to below, described this part of his job in* **The Office of the Attorney-General** *(1953), p. 6. For an instance where the Law Officers categorically refused to give an opinion see 2/1148.*

13 *2/3231.*

14 *2/4292.*

15 *2/3633: to Attlee, 19.4.1950. A previous instance in which both the LCO and the LOD were kept in the dark, perhaps because it was feared they would be obstructive, occurred in connection with the proposed Geneva Conventions (2/4309).*

16 *2/6351.*

17 *Examples are 2/4273, 4519, 4591, 4661–3, 5251.*

1/61 Proposal for a secretary to the Law Officers, 1884.

2/622 Treasury suggestions for alterations discussed with the Lord Chancellor. Cabinet paper, note on remuneration (1922).

3018 LOD circular 1945 on departmental re-organisation and Lord Chancellor's letter to Chancellor of Exchequer on salaries.

3367 Proposal by Attorney-General that all government litigation should go through the Treasury Solicitor discussed, 1947.

3231 Dispute over colonial criminal appeals, 1946–7. Correspondence with Law Officers.

4292 Dispute over s. 43 Town and Country Planning Act 1947: meeting to discuss Law Officers' opinion, views of draftsman and Lord Chancellor and subsequent correspondence with Ministry of Town and Country Planning, 1947–8.

3633 Correspondence of Prime Minister, Attorney-General and Lord Chancellor on procedure in important legal matters, 1950.

4309 Geneva Convention: cabinet committee to discuss proposals, 1949.

6351 Dispute over position of imported labourers in Egypt: see Coldstream's minute of 6.12.1951.

5149 Cabinet discussions on the independence of the Law Officers in deciding whether to prosecute for the theft of the Stone of Scone, 1951.

Section 2

THE ADMINISTRATION OF JUSTICE

INTRODUCTION

Among the multiplicity of functions performed by the Lord Chancellor and his department, those bearing on the administration of justice have become in modern times the most demanding and burdensome. It is, of course, well known, if not notorious, that the Lord Chancellor's Department does not have exclusive jurisdiction over the courts and that the Home Office and the Treasury, in particular, retain important powers and duties in the same field; nevertheless it remains the case today, as it was throughout the period under review, that primary responsibility for the smooth running of the machinery of justice and for its adjustment to changing social and political needs, falls upon the Lord Chancellor.

The LCO records begin during the throes of a long overdue attempt to re-model the superior courts of justice on more rational and efficient lines and show Selborne and Cairns engaged in the lengthy and sensitive task of giving effect to the Judicature Acts and reorganising the personnel and administration of the new Supreme Court of Judicature. When Jowitt left office in 1951 that structure, now three quarters of a century old, remained substantially intact despite recurrent bouts of public agitation for substantial changes. Likewise the jurisdiction and workings of the county courts, the lower tier of courts for most civil litigation, were not fundamentally altered from the 1870s and the wide ranging civil and (especially) criminal jurisdiction of lay magistrates, primary responsibility for which still lay with the Home Office, was intact despite considerable public criticism. Even some of those local courts of record which had survived earlier purges clung tenaciously to their anomalous existence. The most important changes in the landscape of litigation during this period took place altogether outside the hierarchy of courts, in the growth of administrative tribunals. With regard to the courts themselves, Selborne would probably have been surprised, and perhaps disappointed, at the familiarity of the scene which would have confronted him in 1951.[1]

Notes

1 *The best overview is B. Abel Smith and R. Stevens,* ***Lawyers and the Courts*** *(1967). A. H. Manchester,* ***Modern Legal History*** *(1980) is a more recent account. Successive editions of R. M. Jackson's classic work,* ***The Machinery of Justice in England*** *(1st ed., 1940) show the changes since 1939. On the business of the courts the annual Judicial Statistics are an invaluable source of detailed information, especially before 1922, when the LCO assumed responsibility for their production and a more economical and less exhaustive form was adopted.*

Chapter 1

THE HOUSE OF LORDS AND THE JUDICIAL COMMITTEE OF THE PRIVY COUNCIL

1
THE HOUSE OF LORDS

1 Introduction

The judicial functions of the House of Lords have been extensively and thoroughly investigated by scholars from different perspectives in recent years[1] and Robert Stevens' historical account, in particular, surveys the period covered by this guide and makes use of the LCO papers. In fact for the most part the papers are a disappointing source of information on the operation of the Lords and shed little light on important issues such as the selection of judges to hear politically sensitive cases and the working relationship among the Lords of Appeal, despite the claim that "it is almost impossible to overestimate the influence of Lord Chancellors".[2] Again, the Lord Chancellor's Permanent Secretary may have been an "eminence grise" but he remains an uncommonly elusive one, whose handiwork is seldom to be detected. In part this is because there were few significant proposals considered by the LCO for legislative or rule changes affecting the Lords' jurisdiction, and it is those which tend to yield the best material on the workings of institutions. Thus there are instructive memoranda on the problem of unmeritorious appeals among the papers of the Hanworth Committee on the Business of the Courts, which led to the Administration of Justice (Appeals) Act 1934, whereby the appeal to the Lords as of right was replaced by the requirement of leave from either the Court of Appeal or a new Appeals Committee of the House of Lords. The more extensive papers of the Evershed Committee contain a good deal of information on the wasteful system of double appeals and the possibility of a "leapfrogging" facility, on the cost of appeals to the Lords and the possibility of public funding to secure the Lords' judgment on cases of exceptional public importance. There is also correspondence and notes of the meetings held with the Law Lords on the occasion of the constitutionally momentous creation of the Appellate Committee in 1948, brought about in a curiously oblique way as a result of the re-building of the Palace of Westminster after wartime bombing and fiercely opposed by Lord Simon.[4] In addition, there is interesting material on a few celebrated cases, notably on the trial of Lord de Clifford by his peers.[5]

Notes

1 *L. Blom-Cooper and G. Drewry,* ***Final Appeal*** *(1972); A. A. Paterson,* ***The Law Lords*** *(1982); R. Stevens,* ***Law and Politics; the House of Lords as a Judicial Body, 1800–1976*** *(1979).*

2 *R. Stevens,* ***supra****, 69.*

3 ***Ibid.****, 69 n. 191.*

4 *2/3458. Lord Simon,* ***In Retrospect*** *(1952), 259–60; L. Blom-Cooper and G. Drewry,* ***supra****, 111–13.*

5 *See W. T. West,* ***The Trial of Lord de Clifford*** *(1986).*

2 Organisation and Procedure

1/1	Unsigned memorandum on House of Lords appeals, pre 1875.
2/387, 365	Re-organisation of Judicial Office: memoranda by Muir Mckenzie and heads of agreement, 1917. State of business in 1918.
411, 2257, 4503	Notes on precedence among members, with notes on appointments, c. 1900 and 1917.
1007	Memorandum by Bankes L J on practice in applications for stay of proceedings in Court of Appeal pending appeal to House of Lords, with Haldane's reply, 1924.
1/46, 1/61; 2/292, 411, 545–6, 3459, 5230	Various minor points
2/3458	Meeting of law lords to discuss arrangements for sittings during "emergency works" 1946. Renewed discussions 1948, especially with Lord Simon.
2/3460–1	Correspondence with the Prime Minister on appointments, 1934 and 1947.

3 Jurisdiction

1/3	Appellate Jurisdiction Bill, 1884: discussions with T. S. Wortley and others on proposal to limit pauper appeals.
2/3337, 3340	Leave to appeal: approaches from Bar Council and counsel in *R v. Sims* (1946) and discussions with LCJ, 1947.
4620	Rushcliffe Committee papers on cost of Lords' appeals.
3989–96, 4047	Evershed Committee: papers of working parties 'L', 'M', 'N', 'O' and 'P' with draft reports, on "leapfrogging", printing costs etc. See also proposals by the Attorney-General in 4047 (1945).

4 Particular cases

2/173	Trial of Earl Russell, 1901.
471, 559	Lady Rhondda's claim to sit, 1922.
1325–6, 2571, 3345	Trial of Lord de Clifford, 1936.
3688, 4205	Baxter v. Baxter, 1946.

2
THE JUDICIAL COMMITTEE OF THE PRIVY COUNCIL

1 Introduction

The Judicial Committee of the Privy Council was an anomalous body both in its jurisdiction and its organisation.[1] Successive Australian governments repeatedly embarrassed their British and dominion counterparts with advocacy of a grandiose "Imperial Court of Appeal";[2] at the Imperial War Conference of 1918 it was "in particular pressed with great vigour and some bitterness by Mr. Hughes"[3] but among Lord Chancellors only Lord Haldane was converted to the cause, which Lord Finlay described as "really a superficial sentiment"[4] and there were at least covert objections from the other self-governing colonies. Schuster's memorandum of 1923 is especially useful in filling in the background to the published material, pointing out for example the Canadian Prime Minister's view that "in no circumstances could Canada contemplate a court in which Hindu or Mohammedan lawyers held an equal status with the other judges and might be called upon to decide a case from Canada."[5]

If this splendid vision could not be realised, the Committee was bound to become, in Haldane's own admission, "a disappearing body",[6] and its subsequent history is of the gradual erosion of its jurisdiction as most of the dominions severally took advantage of the Statute of Westminster to abolish the right of appeal.[7] The Irish Free State predictably took the lead, passing retrospective legislation to deny the benefit of judgments to successful appellants until it was able to deny them the right of appeal itself. It is clear from the LCO files that the British government preferred to keep the issue under wraps but Schuster expressed the disgust which was common in the legal establishment at the unscrupulous actions of the Irish government and Hailsham always advocated a firmer stand;[8] perhaps it is time that the political dimension of the Judicial Committee's decisions received a full examination from an English perspective. The Dominions Office was so set on not precipitating similar action on the part of Canada and South Africa that it effectively vetoed Hailsham's modest proposal to strengthen the dominion element in the court and the inability to do this was partly responsible for the post-war difficulties in manning the Judicial Committee.

Criminal appeals from the colonies had long been a bone of contention, since if the Privy Council was prepared to receive them the manipulation of its own leisurely procedures, quite unsuitable for criminal appeals, by lawyers acting on behalf of capitally convicted criminals (particularly from India) might create a delay of such dimensions as to make the execution practically impossible. For this reason alone such appeals were not normally entertained and when, exceptionally, they were, it was apt to cause great offence in the territory concerned. Lord Simon took particular interest in this problem,[10] which became acute in 1946 when Parliament interested itself in the plight of six men sentenced to death for sacrificial murders in the Gold Coast.[11] The Privy Council continued to reject Colonial Office pleas for a time limit and an end to the "inconvenient expensive and, at times, inevitably slow"[12] procedure by way of special leave, and departmental discussions highlight the awkwardness caused by South Africa's offer of her courts as an alternative for the African territories and the reluctance of the Judicial Committee to allow itself to become a criminal appeals court.[13] As usual, the upshot was a committee, under Dallas Waters, whose proceedings are also to be found here.[14]

The organisation and composition of the Committee also presented peculiar problems. Even a Treasury proposal to evict it from its highly unsuitable premises in Downing Street, and to relocate it within the Houses of Parliament, would have involved "the acquiesence or the opposition of the Lord President, the Leader of the House of Lords, the First Commissioner of Works, and some of the ex-Chancellors and Law Lords who . . . will take a lively interest in it."[15] Moreover, Schuster described the staff of the Committee as "to a great extent uncontrolled" because they were appointed by the Lord President and the Lord Chancellor "by courtesy" only exercised "a certain amount of control".[16] It was outside the scope of the Tomlin Committee's investigations and no serious attempt was made to integrate it with the House of Lords or the Supreme Court. Its membership also created headaches, for despite an act of Parliament which enabled it to sit in divisions[17] and others which increased its size,[18] its dependence on "volunteers", usually superannuated and sometimes of doubtful value, and the need for at least five members to sit on major dominions cases was highly inconvenient at times.[19] These problems are explained in several interesting memoranda, especially of the late 1940s when it was necessary to clear the final backlog of Indian appeals without increasing permanently the size of a body whose workload would obviously diminish once Indian cases, which were its staple diet, were no longer forthcoming.[20]

Notes

1 *For the history of the Judicial Committee in its modern form see P. A. Howell,* ***The Judicial Committee of the Privy Council, 1833–76*** *(1979) and R. Stevens,* ***op. cit.****, 72–6, 186–8. There are contemporary descriptions of its operations in (1923) 1 CLJ 143 (Lord Haldane) and (1939) 7 CLJ 2 (Sir George Rankin). There is much interesting material in Sir A. Fitzroy's* ***Memoirs*** *(1925).*

2 *C. G. Pierson,* ***Canada and the Privy Council*** *(1960) 38, 42–3.*

3 *2/3464: memorandum by Schuster, 10.7.1923, p. 7.*

4 ***Ibid****: memorandum to cabinet, 1918, p. 7.*

5 *2/3464, at p. 8.*

6 ***Supra****, n. 1, p. 154.*

7 *See E. M. Campbell (1959) 33 ALJ 196, which usefully reviews the literature.*

8 *2/910, 1190. The cases are discussed from an Irish perspective in N. Mansergh,* ***The Irish Free State*** *(1934), 320–8.*

9 *See Pierson,* ***op. cit.****, 31, 45, Howell,* ***op. cit.****, 523, and 1/2, 2/4508, 3454.*

10 *2/3454: to O. Stanley, 3.2.1944.*

11 *2/3231.* ***Parl. Debs.****, 1946–7 (H of C) vol. 434 cols. 37–51, 484–91, 958–62, vol. 435 cols 320–1. Sir K. Roberts Wray,* ***Commonwealth and Colonial Law*** *(1966), 437–47.*

12 *2/4508: P. Gordon Walker (Commonwealth Relations Office) to Lord Chancellor, 4.1.1951.*

13 *2/3231, 4508.*

14 *2/4509–13. Waters was the Registrar to the Judicial Committee, transferred from the LCO in 1940.*

15 ***Supra****, n. 3, at p. 2.*

16 ***Ibid.****, at p. 18.*

17 *Judicial Committee Act 1915.*

18 *Judicial Committee Amendments Act 1895, Appellate Jurisdiction Act 1908.*

19 *See e.g. 2/3460: Lord Chancellor's memorandum, 13.2.1934.*

20 *2/3461, 4506. From an average of about 60 cases a year in wartime, the Privy Council's workload rose to more than 100 in 1945 and 1946 before falling sharply again.*

2 Organisation and Procedure

2/552 Views of Lord Cave and others on proposal to end the reading of judgments, 1922.

553 Meetings of judges, views of Law Officers, and notes on precedents re Beck (the US Attorney-General)'s right of audience, 1922.

911 Schuster's memorandum on accommodation difficulties, 1923; Balfour's proposal for a new courthouse, 1925.

3458 Arrangements for sittings in 1940; post-war accommodation questions.

4626, 4682 Correspondence with J. D. Waters over legal aid, 1949.

33 Opinions of members of the JCPC on proposal to give separate opinions, 1888.

3 Composition and Reform Proposals

2/908 Notes on membership, to W. R. Wallace, 1926.

1444 Order under Government of India Act 1935 to correct error on eligibility, 1937.

3453, 3455–7, 3460–1, 5227 Appointments of overseas judges, especially retiring Indian judges recruited to assist disposal of Indian appeals after independence: correspondence with Privy Council Office, India Office; memo from V. Goodman and J. D. Waters on position in 1946; correspondence with Sir John Leach and others, and with Treasury on expenses claims.

179, 287, 292, 798, 813, 3464–5 Proposed Imperial Court of Appeal: report of 1901 Imperial Conference and draft bill by Ilbert. Appellate Jurisdiction Bill of 1912 with memoranda on current caseload. Law Officers' opinion on sitting in divisions; correspondence with Foreign and Colonial Offices, cabinet papers and correspondence with Privy Council Office on Judicial Committee Bill, 1915. Draft proposals, correspondence and cabinet papers on Administration of Justice Bill 1928. Collected papers on Australian proposals of 1916, proceedings of Imperial War Conference 1918 and memoranda by Lord Finlay *et al.* Schuster's memorandum of 1923 and correspondence with Dominions Office in 1929.

1596–7 Schuster's proposals and comments by Tomlin LJ and Lord MacMillan, 1931.

4 Jurisdiction

1/2 Canadian criminal appeals: Law Officers' opinion of 1885 on admissibility.

2/910, 1190 Irish Free State: discussions with Dominions Office, cabinet papers and memoranda (1923–31) and correspondence with Archbishop of Dublin. Cabinet memorandum and correspondence on cases in the 1920s and on the Statute of Westminster.

3462, 3465 Discussions with Dominions Office on abolition proposals in Canada and South Africa, 1935–47.

4488–90, 4506–7 India (Consequential Provisions) Bill 1949: discussions on judges' pensions, and correspondence on post-independence appeals.

4491 Medical Bill 1949: JCPC given appellate jurisdiction after prolonged departmental discussions.

4345 Suggested as forum for courts-martial, 1950 (*infra*, 156).

5 Colonial Criminal Appeals

2/909 Discussions with India Office, 1921.

3231 *R. v. Asare Apietu and others:* Parliamentary questions, correspondence with Colonial Office and Attorney-General, and cabinet papers; departmental discussions on possible time limits for appeals 1946–7; Home Office memorandum on "Parliament and the prerogative of mercy".

3454, 4508–12 Discussions with Colonial Office on problems of delay, 1943. Resumed discussions in 1950: memoranda on procedures, correspondence with Colonial and Commonwealth Relations Offices; discussions with LCJ and Lord Porter; and see 4509–12, Waters Committee papers (1952–3).

3336 Questions of bail in Indian appeals, 1945.

6 Particular Cases

2/551 Archdeacon Wakefield (1921), with notes on precedents, transcript of evidence, petition.

2964 R. A. and Dr. N. A. Cooper: voluminous petitions and papers, 1943–68.

Chapter 2

THE SUPREME COURT OF JUDICATURE

1 ORGANISATION

1 Introduction

As an institution the Supreme Court of Judicature has not received the attention that it deserves. This series of small, largely self-contained departments generating a highly technical business under rules largely of their own devising, presents an object of considerable interest to students of bureaucracies; as the point of contact between two influential dogmas — Treasury control of the public service and judicial independence — it raises important questions about the boundaries of each, and the influence on the cost and duration of litigation of the court's organisation and practice has been much less thoroughly examined than the role of the judges and the legal profession. Yet materials are not wanting, and the reports of successive committees and commissioners and the departmental papers of the Treasury and the LCO are a good starting point.[1]

The outline of events over the period is clear — the gradual conversion of a motley collection of almost independent fiefs in which patronage was controlled by the judges of the several courts and remuneration was provided by the hapless suitors, into a branch of the civil service governed by the same terms and conditions of service (save in the case of the quasi-judicial officers) as other departments, under the supervision of the LCO and within the control of the Treasury. The process was far from complete when Jowitt left office, and the reputation of the courts' administrative departments with the public and the profession was still not good.

Reforms in the conduct and organisation of business in the courts did not begin with the Judicature Acts, but they made a more drastic rearrangement necessary. The reports of the Childers Committee and the Lisgar Commission emphasised the need for changes, and during the next decade the Treasury and Lord Chancellor were busily engaged in effecting a complicated series of re-organisations, retirements and transfers.[2] The reconstruction of the courts' administration was not as thoroughgoing as it might have been, however. The establishment of a Central Office concealed the fact that Chancery and PD & A maintained separate structures, Bankruptcy and Lunacy went their own ways and there was no unified taxing office.[3] Not surprisingly, the supposed economies in manpower proved to be disappointingly small[4] and it soon emerged that the new structure fell far short of the ideal. The Central Office was overmanned with masters,[5] the Principal Probate Registry baffled the public by its short working hours[6] and the rituals of the Chancery Pay Office kept up the best traditions of Circumlocution.[7] Since the "Controller" that the Select Committee had advocated had not materialised there was no-one with the authority and the knowledge to oversee the several officers; an ill-advised Treasury Bill enabling the Lord Chancellor and the Treasury to regulate the SCJ and thereby eliminate the patronage and direction of the heads of divisions was so badly received (especially on the score that it did not adequately distinguish between purely clerical and judicial officers) that it had to be withdrawn, effectively ending the prospect of such changes for twenty years.[8] All that could be done was to deal piecemeal with the offices which were attracting particular criticism[9] and even then, when they were not within the direct control of the Lord Chancellor, great tact had to be exercised towards the head of the division concerned.

Once again, the impetus for change came from an investigation into the general civil service, which highlighted the peculiarities of the legal offices.[10] Nominations to masterships and clerkships by the judges, which had tended towards nepotism, were condemned in uncompromising terms and there was justifiable criticism of the excessive compartmentalisation which blocked avenues of promotion and encouraged divergent and undesirably complicated practices; not for the first time, nor for the last, the separate existence of the Chancery Registers came under threat and a retiring age for all officers was said to be a necessity. A small committee comprising the late and current Permanent Secretaries to the Lord Chancellor, the Senior Master in the KBD (T. W. Chitty), a prominent solicitor (Sir Roger Gregory, sometime President of the Law Society) and a Treasury representative went quickly to work and produced a scheme which embodied most of the Royal Commission's proposals and would have cut the separate offices in the courts to five,[11] but the exigencies of the war overtook it and action was postponed until 1919 when a similarly constituted committee, but with Tomlin KC as chairman, was set to work.

The Tomlin Committee produced a series of reports which are highly informative both as to the workings of the offices and on the thinking that informed their staff. Out of it came legislation on salaries, pensions, retirement etc.,[12] and in 1925 the Lord Chancellor was given statutory power to direct the organisation of the Central Office, though the Probate and Admiralty registries escaped his grasp.[13] Remarkably, the patronage question was not tackled. Pending legislation, the LCJ and MR had agreed in 1915 to appoint to clerkships only candidates approved by a selection board composed as recommended by the Royal Commission but Trevethin, "dressed in a little brief authority", was "only induced to abide by the arrangement after a desperate struggle"[14] and by an oversight it was not explained to Sir Ernest Pollock when he became MR in 1925. The appointment of Hewart as LCJ made legislation to supersede this secret and unsatisfactory arrangement much more difficult and as it was it did not extend to the PD & A, nor to the masterships, though the difficulty in finding a suitable candidate for them had generally obliged the person whose turn had come by rotation to seek help from the Lord Chancellor.[15]

Even apart from the problem of patronage however, the Lord Chancellor was not in a position to exert a continuous and effective superintendence over the courts. His establishment officer (a post created in 1919)[16] was a relatively junior official scarcely able to contend against the weight of authority wielded by masters and registrars. The Permanent Secretary had strengthened his position by becoming Accountant-General of the Supreme Court but Schuster found that even with Sankey, who was a determined reformer, on the Woolsack, the unco-operativeness of Hewart and, to a lesser extent, the Presidents of the PD & A, were formidable obstacles while attempts to stir the Council of Judges into action were failures. Not surprisingly, few initiatives came from the court staffs. The heads of department were mostly untrained in administration and prone to regard the convenience of the judges, rather than the public, as the principal consideration, and the masters saw themselves as judicial officers not civil servants.[17] The authority of the Senior Master in the KBD over the departments in the Central Office was not always readily conceded,[18] and while in some, such as the Scrivenery, a placid conservatism held sway, in others it could be plausibly maintained that "there is a tendency for the staff to control the Master and not for the Master to control the staff".[19] The White Book remained unpruned, the practice in divorce remained needlessly complicated, delays in drawing orders were a matter of course and the Peel Commission's call for a KBD 'business manager' was not just a condemnation of the then LCJ's management of his division.

After the war the Evershed Committee began a much more sustained and thorough investigation into the workings of the courts than had yet been undertaken. At the same time the Treasury's O & M team had been at work, though with greater haste and, the investigated departments alleged, little understanding.[20] A disgruntled clerk leaked one of its reports to the press and under "scandal" headlines the embarrassingly short working day in some of the offices became public knowledge, compelling the setting up of a committee.[21] Nevertheless the resistance to change within the SCJ remained deeply entrenched.

Notes

1 *The most useful Treasury classes are T 15 (General Law, Out Letters) and T 162 (Establishment Files).*

2 *See* **supra**, *19–21.*

3 *S.C.J. (Officers) Act 1879. This was based on the report of a committee under the Master of the Rolls: PP 1878 (Cd 2067) XXV, 5, and the detailed scheme was the work of the Official Solicitor (1/27).*

4 *The Treasury's efforts to secure economies and the contrary claims of the clerks, backed by the masters, can be followed in 1/27–35.*

5 *PP 1887 (181) LXVII, 179: report of a committee on the Central Office, chaired by Lord Coleridge.*

6 *2/26: report of Lord Chancellor's committee, 1893.*

7 *1/75.*

8 *2/91,93; 2/138: judges' resolutions, 29.4.1895, printed in (1895) 99 LT 165.*

9 *e.g. Taxing Offices, lunacy administration, Chancery Registrars*

10 *Report of Royal Commission on the Civil Service, PP 1914–16 (Cd. 7832) XII, 1; (Cd 8130) XII, 91. See e.g. 2/1012: Bonner to Schuster, 19.6.1928: "it is common ground that the appointment of Coleridge and Lawford . . . was a public scandal, solely directed to finding an occupation and livelihood for two of LCJ Coleridge's relations".*

11 *2/370.*

12 *SC (Officers) Act 1920.*

13 *SCJ (Consolidation) Act 1925 s.105(1).*

14 *2/938: Schuster's memorandum. The correspondence is in 4/300.*

15 ***Ibid.***

16 *4/221.*

17 *See e.g. Master Hulbert's protest at their inclusion in the annual "census of civil servants". 4/160 (1930).*

18 *In 1934 Master Bonner approached the Associates Department about spare capacity and was challenged by the head of the Crown Office, Master Romer. 4/69.*

19 *Sir Roger Gregory on the Lunacy Office, 4/48.*

20 *4/55 (Court of Protection), 4/236 (Scrivenery Dept), 4/297 (SCJ General).*

21 *4/297. The committee's report was not published.*

2 General Series Files

1/13	Correspondence with Treasury and memoranda on fate of clerks in the Associates' departments, 1876–80.
1/21–4	Papers on bankruptcy staff salaries and organisation 1872–88 (see *Bankruptcy*).
1/57	Correspondence with Treasury on re-arrangements after courts vacate Lincoln's Inn, 1883.
1/59	Reconstruction of divisions: correspondence of Lord Chancellor with Lord Chief Justice, 1880.
1/60	Muir McKenzie proposes a 'Controller' of the RCJ, 1883.
1/65	Suggestion by Fry LJ for a Lunacy Division, 1885.
1/70	Correspondence with Treasury re masters' salaries, 1885–6.
1/45	Removal of Durham registrar, 1886.
2/25	Scrivenery Department: report of departmental committee, 1889; correspondence on re-organisation with Official Solicitor and comments by heads of divisions.
2/47	Lord Esher's memorandum with plea for a royal commission 1890.
48	Attendants' regulations, correspondence with Treasury and complaint by LCJ on patronage, 1879–86.
50, 98	Report of departmental committee on accommodation for Bankruptcy Department, 1886. Re-organisation of business in 1894.
91, 93	SCJ Bill: correspondence with President, Senior Master etc., on staff qualifications and tenures, and correspondence with Treasury, 1893–4.
138	SCJ (Officers) Bill 1895, resolutions of judges' meeting and President's notes on draft regulations.
139	SCJ (Consolidation) Bill 1895: print with amendments.
188	Draft staff regulations sent to Treasury, 1902.
264	Report of committee on transfer of Lunacy masters (1908), correspondence with and memorandum by Official Solicitor, draft scheme, views of Visitors in Lunacy, H. J. Theobald, Treasury and others; draft bill (1911) with notes.
370	Muir McKenzie Committee papers, including notes on 6th report of RC on Civil Service, draft reports, papers on taxing masters, 1916.
420	Correspondence with Treasury and attendants' association on pay increases, 1918.
421	Discussion with Office of Works on offers of pictures for the RCJ, 1916.
464	SC Officers Bill, 1920; correspondence with PCO on drafting and with Master Fox *et al.* on contents (retirement and pensions).
489–506	Tomlin Committee papers, 1919–22. General correspondence (489) including memoranda on departments, preliminary report and correspondence on membership; some minutes and circulated papers (490) including draft reports; Schuster's papers (491) including papers on lunacy and bankruptcy administration; reports (492–500) with minutes of evidence, memoranda and correspondence; papers on Probate and Admiralty registries and minute book with précis of evidence (506).
507, 3214	Devolution conference, 1920: LCO evidence to judiciary sub-committee;

correspondence with Sankey J and Bankes LJ. Schuster's correspondence with Treasury on similar discussions in Machinery of Government Committee (1944).

666–70 Formation of Whitley Councils in RCJ and Land Registry; minutes of meetings on constitution, memoranda on position of various officers, 1920.

723–5 SCJ Bill, 1925; correspondence with PCO and Chitty, drafts, notes by A. Pulling, T. Matthew, memorandum for cabinet and other papers.

726–34 Administration of Justice Bill, 1925, including general files of correspondence and memoranda, on e.g. powers of the Rule Committee, jury trials, eligibility for offices, staff qualifications and promotions; observations by (*int. al.*) Law Society and Liverpool Law Society, T. W. Chitty, Treasury, President, Judge Bray, Master King; cabinet and Parliamentary papers. Particular files on administration bonds (732) deputies in SC (733), assizes (734).

820 Pensions for staff at Central Criminal Court: discussions with City Corporation and L.C.C. on private bills, 1920–33.

798, 800 Administration of Justice Bill, 1928; general file of correspondence with PCO and cabinet papers, Clauson LJ's clause on assignment of bankruptcy cases.

877 Amalgamation of Preston District Registry with County Court Registry, 1925.

1596–1609 Hanworth Committee papers, including discussion on fate of the PD & A, 1930–33. Papers and correspondence on membership (1598) county court limits (1600) second report (1602) assizes (1603) memoranda (1606); group minutes (1604). Administration of Justice (Miscellaneous Provisions) Bill (1599, 1601).

1610–17 Peel Commission papers, 1934 (see *King's Bench Division, infra*).

1618–27 Administration of Justice (Miscellaneous Provisions) Bill, 1938: general files (1618, 1620, 1626) of correspondence and notes, and files on clauses including quarter sessions, Mayor's and City Court, taxation of costs.

1918 Correspondence with Bank and Treasury on payment arrangements for staff, 1932.

1919 Schuster's examination before H of C Select Committee on Supreme Court Vote, 1932.

1920 Wartime economies, 1939.

3075 Correspondence with PCO (1939 and 1945) on proposed Consolidation Bill, especially on unsatisfactory statute law on SC establishment

3843 Discussions with LCJ on nominated judge for town planning legislation, 1946.

3826 Brief for Sir A. Herbert's amendment to King's Speech, on defects in the courts, 1943.

3876 SCJ (Amendment) Bill 1944; clause on transfer of judges discussed in cabinet and Parliament.

3929–3945, 3966–4040 Evershed Committee papers: including

3929 Discussions on terms of reference

3930, 4015–21 Minutes

3931–2 Correspondence with members

3937 "Bees" (the name given to a file in which all suggested reforms were collected)

3966–4011 Working Parties' papers:

'A' Personal Injuries & County Courts

'B' Interlocutory Procedure

‘C’ Documents
‘D’ Despatch of Business
‘E’ Chancery
‘F’ Costs and Fees
‘G’ Law of Evidence
‘H’ R.S.C.
‘I’ Counsel’s Fees
‘K’ Powers of Masters etc.
‘L–P’ Appeals, including ‘‘leapfrogging’’, public funding
‘Q’ Divisions of the High Court
‘R’ King’s Bench Masters, Execution, Third Party Procedure
‘S’ Durham Palatinate Court
‘T’ Trial Procedure
‘U’ Solicitors’ Bills

4012–4 Chairman’s correspondence
4022–9 Memoranda
4030–5 Evidence.

3 Establishment Files (LCO 4)

1 Inquiries and legislation

4/1–5, 64–5 Committee and working party on Official Solicitor (*infra*).
47–52 Committee on M & A Department (*infra*).
70–3 Committee on Circuit Officers (*infra*).
85 Atkinson Committee on Shorthand Writers. Negotiations with Association of Official Shorthand Writers Ltd, heads of divisions; PQs, directives and circulars. Also Finlay Committee on Court of Appeal; appointment after discussions with MR on *Bradford Third Equitable B.S. v. Borders*, 1939; PQs etc.
133–48 Herbert Committee on Manpower and Hours of Work in the Supreme Court: 133 includes correspondence on its setting up, 1951. The three reports (1952) were not published.
235 Inquiries into the conduct of attendants following complaints in 1924, 1949.
236 O & M Report on Scrivenery Department, 1950 and correspondence.
297 Inquiry into working hours at the RCJ, 1947 following Treasury circular. Ridley’s correspondence with departments, Treasury O & M report (1948) and further discussions with staff associations, masters and Treasury. Discussions following press leak of the O & M report, 1949.
309–11 Destruction of SC documents under the Public Records Acts, including minutes of Committee, 1928–9.
312–5 Committee on catering in the RCJ, papers 1907–14 (315) and various later dates to 1961.
327 Committee on accommodation: recommendations of 1938 and action.

2 Staffing questions

4/25 Admiralty Registry complement, 1924–53.
33 Appointments of QB Masters and Registrar of Court of Criminal Appeal.
35–6 Appointment and training of Associate for Revenue Cases, 1947–52.
40 Chancery chambers complement.

68–9	Various questions re circuit officers.
107	Appointment of Taxing Master for Ecclesiastical Fees.
131	Appointments without a civil service certificate.
149	Appointments of officers with abnormal rates of pay, hours etc., 1931–54.
150	Salaries fixed by statute, 1921–48.
151	Salaries of certain judicial officers, 1921–37.
176	Administration of Supreme Court Officers Act 1921.
179	Claims under Administration of Justice (Pensions) Act 1950.
192	Medical Certificates of masters etc.
234	Principal Probate Registry complements, 1920–46.
237–8	Pay Office, 1935–45.
240	Taxing masters' appointments, 1920–54.
246–51	Circuit officers (*infra*).
300	Appointment of masters and clerks, 1921–5. Schuster's correspondence with Chitty, Theobald; LC's correspondence with Treasury, MR and LCJ; correspondence with PCO on draft clause in Administration of Justice Bill 1925.

3 Fees, funds, Supreme Court vote etc

17	Admiralty Writs in Prize (*infra*).
21	Prize rules account (*infra*).
211–12	LCO and Prime Minister's memos on finances of the Supreme Court, 1947.
254–60	Fees questions on shorthand transcripts.

4 Other

6	Refreshments at the RCJ, 1918–22.
74	Specimen forms for circuit officers, 1945.
162–6	Civil Judicial Statistics, 1947–51.
184–5	Preservation of court records in wartime, 1939–46.
193	Shorthand notes for cases held *in camera*, 1942.
214	Protection of the RCJ in wartime.
217	Lowery bequest of pictures, 1942–50.
296	Case of smallpox in the RCJ, 1929.
307	Complaints of misbehaviour by the public in the RCJ, 1931–54.
329–30	Statuary etc. in the RCJ.

2
RULES

The Judicature Act 1873 included rules of court as appendixes but also perpetuated the statutory power of the judges to regulate procedure in their courts through rules having the force of law. The Judicature Act 1881 s. 19, however vested this power in the Lord Chancellor and a rule committee comprising the LCJ, the MR, the President of the PD & A and four judges selected by the Lord Chancellor; this arrangement was preferred by Jessel MR to the original proposal which envisaged nine judges.[1] The new body got off to an unfortunate start when it passed a large and controversial set of rules to simplify pleadings which were laid before Parliament at the end of the session of 1883, giving the Bar too little time to mount an effective protest,[2] and although Halsbury declined to grant the professional bodies formal consultative status in 1888, he did in fact consult them on major proposals and in 1894 a clause in the Supreme Court of Judicature Act put onto the committee representatives of each.[3] In 1909 the professional representation was increased,[4] and the composition of the committee remained constant thereafter throughout this period, although between 1940 and 1947 it was suspended by statute and rules were made by the Lord Chancellor with the concurrence of the LCJ and the MR. As a matter of practice, the judges of the KBD and PDA were nominated by their chiefs, subject to the Lord Chancellor's veto, and it is characteristic of Hewart's attitude to the LCO and all its works that on one occasion, when his first choice (Branson) declined because he lived well outside London, he did as Napier feared and named Charles—whose unsuitability was manifest and who had to be turned down by Maugham—instead of the obvious choice, Travers Humphreys.[5] The Lord Chancellor picked the Chancery judge himself and Clauson's claim that the senior in the division should be a member *ex officio* was rejected.[6]

Although the Committee is serviced by the LCO the available information about its functioning is in some respects less complete than for the junior body, the County Court Rule Committee.[7] Presumably because the chairman was readily at hand and the majority of members were in regular contact with each other, there is less preliminary correspondence, and of course unlike the county court rules, those made by this committee need no approval from a higher body. There are no general files for most years in the 1920s however, and most of those for the 1930s are unrevealing, so that for most years the proceedings have to be reconstructed from the files bearing on individual items. When meetings resumed in 1947 the LCO was caught out rather badly and the first meeting was "disastrous" because, as Coldstream wrote

> "it was evident that wholly insufficient preparation had been done on the three sets of rules under consideration. The brief on each of the rules was only circulated eight days before the meeting of the Rule Committee and . . . in the result there was really no opportunity for members such as Sir Douglas Garrett, Gerald Gardiner and others to send their criticisms to this office before the meeting. It followed that when the time of the meeting arrived neither the substance nor the drafting had been agreed of any of the rules under consideration . . . I have had no experience of the Rule Committee before. I had imagined that the Committee were prepared initially to take the form and substance of the Rules from the head of the division concerned. This is quite obviously not the case and in future there must be a far longer period of time between agreement of the rules with the head of the department (and of course the Masters and Registrars concerned) and the time when the rules are submitted to the Committee, so that members of the Committee . . . can make their comments on the drafts before they are ready for the Committee".[8]

The Evershed Committee's second interim report stated that "this committee, although impressive in point of distinction, is somewhat far removed from the workaday affairs of administration of the Rules"[9] and proposed to constitute separate authorities for rule reviews and rule making. Like many of its recommendations, this has been shelved and the rule committee's work has since been more flatteringly described by Sir J. H. Jacob.[10]

Nevertheless, since unlike the County Court Rule Committee it is very much a judge dominated body, it would be instructive to compare their workings from these papers. Certainly the absence of masters and registrars from the committee is striking, given the prominent role which the registrar played on the CCRC,[11] and it often necessitated lengthy correspondence with them in advance of the meetings in order that a draft rule might be presented in workable form, this can be seen particularly in Napier's correspondence with Master Chitty in the 1920s. An impression which the papers create, that the LCO received fewer suggestions to alter the detail of High Court rules than county court rules, may be accounted for in part by the greater curative facilities available to the High Court judges by way of Practice Directions made under their inherent jurisdiction: the Chancery Direction of 1936 on mortgage actions[12] is a well-known example, and Schuster noted in 1939 that ''Merrivale P, having lost the power to make Rules, got into the habit of issuing Directions which were in some cases not committed to writing and were not declared to the public. The resulting confusion was very great. I am far from suggesting that we should make any more RSCs than can possibly be helped. But even worse than voluminous Rules is a mass of unrecorded practice of which the public have no precise knowledge.''[13] Certainly the combination of the ''voluminous rules'', which were still based on those of 1883, and the Practice Directions and notes which swelled the White Book to forbidding dimensions and attracted the criticism of the Evershed Committee,[14] does suggest that the Rule Committee was not attempting to play a very ambitious role in making High Court litigation intelligible and streamlined.[15]

The rules made by the Committee were, of course, enormously varied in their subject matter, but three special types of rule require separate consideration. The first concerns the fees charged to suitors in civil cases, which were fixed by the committee with the concurrence of the Treasury. The policy underlying these was agreed at the time of the Judicature Acts, that only the cost of the judges should fall on the taxpayer, the remainder (court buildings, staff, heating and lighting etc.) being borne by the litigants, and this was broadly embodied in the Fees Order of 1883, after negotiations in which the Treasury had insisted that even the new Courts of Justice in the Strand should ''properly speaking'' cost it ''nothing''[16]. The fees in fact produced a handsome surplus until after the Great War, when the MacNaghten Committee was set to up to increase fees to combat the increased costs of administration, and its papers show the reluctance with which Chitty, in particular, was persuaded to the increases.[17] Although fees were a significant factor in the cost of litigation, there was no possibility of persuading the Treasury to a reduction which would send the account into the red so they were not included within the Hanworth Committee's terms of reference and no systematic consideration was given to them until the Evershed Committee began its deliberations.[18]

The second area is the Supreme Court Funds Rules, which Schuster described as a complete muddle.[19] Suitors in Chancery were still confronted with the rituals of the Chancery Pay Office, whose registrars are found in the 1880s doggedly obstructing elementary simplifications in the machinery for paying out money,[20] and the accounting arrangements in other offices, such as that of the Admiralty Marshal, were eccentric and unsatisfactory.[21]

Among these funds were those described as ''dormant'', i.e. unclaimed balances not dealt with in fifteen years, principally inherited from the Court of Chancery. In some cases they were claimed after a very long period (for instance **Re King Leopold of the Belgians** (1927) where a fund lodged in 1879 had awaited the death of the tragic and insane Empress of Mexico for forty-eight years), but others were beyond redemption; in 1947 Dack gave as an example the account of **Greenhill v. Chauncey**, opened in 1743 with a balance, now much swollen by interest, of £251.9s.8d.[22]

In 1869 the government had appropriated these funds to be used for the building of the law courts against a guarantee to meet claims, but very large claims were subsequently made, which rendered the expedient rather unsuccessful. Two committees of inquiry sat between the wars (both headed by Tomlin) the first in 1925, which found 4,300 accounts totalling £1.6 million (excluding those under £50), the second in 1932, but they rejected Schuster's plea for a limitation period and merely recommended discontinuing to pay interest on them.[23] After the war, Lord Samuel made an attempt to have them diverted to charitable purposes but the appointment of the Nathan Commission neatly sidetracked that initiative. New deposits were constantly being made, of course, and in some cases under new statutes which required them of e.g. insurance companies and traffic operators as guarantees of probity. These too generated difficulties due to the poor liaison between the ministries immediately concerned and the officials of the Pay Office, exacerbated by a marked lack of real comprehension within the LCO of the court's machinery.

The third area is the taxation of costs. Here the most interesting material concerns the attempt to create a unified taxing office, which was begun in 1889 after much discontent at what Kay J described as "the organised plunder of all estates which are being administered by the Court of Chancery [*sic*]"[24].

A departmental committee found clear evidence that Chancery practice was more generous to solicitors (hence, it was alleged, attracting nisi prius business) and recommended not only reductions, but also that the separate taxing masters' offices should be abolished and their work integrated with that of the registrars and chief clerks. Not surprisingly, this proposition failed to commend itself to the Chancery judges or their officers, and a second committee appointed by the Lord Chancellor in 1891 to consider the feasibility of a single taxing office for Chancery and the QBD pronounced it impracticable. Yet when Alverstone LCJ revived this call in 1901 the obstacles were found not to be so great, though the PDA still had to be excluded on account of the high cost of buying out vested interests, and the bankruptcy and lunacy establishments protested shrilly.[25] The new arrangements were not found very satisfactory by the Tomlin Committee, and the increased delegation of responsibility to the taxing masters' clerks authorised by Master King's scheme was unpopular with the profession. The taxing masters, too, were often the subject of complaints in the late 1940s and especially in the early days of the legal aid scheme, but the Senior Master (Gibbon), though he admitted to being "somewhat shocked at evidence of negligence of taxing officers" emphasised that their discretion was, within the limits of their powers, unchallengable.[26] Because of its influence upon the conduct of business by the legal profession, their peculiar role in the administration of justice deserves fuller investigation than it has received.

Notes

1 *1/76: MR to Lord Chancellor, 11.6.1881. The Rule Committee's operations are*

described by Sir J. H. Jacob in ***The Reform of Civil Procedural Law****, p. 323 and there is a detailed history in S. Rosenbaum,* ***The Rule Making Authority in the English Supreme Court****. Rosenbaum's material is more accessible in journal articles, which are therefore cited in preference.*

2 *S. Rosenbaum (1914–15) 63 University of Pennsylvania Law Review, at 293. The rules were based on the report of the Lord Chancellor's Legal Procedure Committee.*

3 *2/29; 57–58 Vic c. 16 s. 4.*

4 *Judicature (Rule Committee) Act 1909.*

5 *2/6109: Napier's minute of 5.12.1938.*

6 ***Ibid.***

7 ***Infra****, 123 ff.*

8 *2/4081: Coldstream's minute, 31.7.1947.*

9 *PP 1950–1 (Cmd 8176) XVI, 661, paras 132–9.*

10 ***Supra****, n. 1.*

11 ***Infra****, 124.*

12 ***Infra****, 237.*

13 *2/1929: to Master Jelf, 17.11.1939.*

14 *Prompted by Evershed's working party 'H' the LCO finally undertook to get the White Book revised. The work was begun by M. L. Gwyer, aided by Master Burnand, and completed after Gwyer's death by the PCO. In 1932 Sankey had told the judges "that something might have been done with regard to the White Book if Tom Chitty had lived, but that there was nobody now, and that it would take such a long time to do, that it was quite impossible to make any such alterations as suggested to it" (2/1703).*

15 *For criticism along these lines see e.g. (1947) 10 MLR 58.*

16 *1/84: W. E. Gladstone to Lord F. Cavendish (copy), 1.3.1882.*

17 *PP 1922 (Cmd 1565) X, 607; 2/1014–16.*

18 *2/1702 Schuster to Lord Chancellor, 27.2.1930. The Evershed Committee was, however, precluded from considering "free" litigation at the Chancellor of the Exchequer's insistence (2/3929). 2nd interim report, PP 1950–1 (Cmd 8176) XVI, 661, para. 141.*

19 *2/398: to R. S. Meiklejohn (Treasury), 10.7.1917.*

20 *1/85, where Muir McKenzie describes them as "always obstructive and old-fashioned".*

21 *2/1023.*

22 *2/2826: to Napier, 9.6.1947.*

23 *PP 1931–2 (Cmd 4152) VII, 969; 2/1645: Schuster to J. Rae (Treasury), 28.9.1931.*

24 *2/9: to Lord Chancellor, 18.2.1889.*

25 *PP 1886 (92) L111, 127: Report of the Esher Committee. RSC (Taxing Offices) 1901.*

26 *2/5485: R. Thesiger to T. G. Lund (Law Society), 25.7.1951.*

1 The Rule Committee

1 Composition and appointments

1/76 Jessel MR and Manisty J on proposed composition of Rule Committee, 1881.

1/80 Appointment of committee under Judicature Act 1881 s. 19, 1889.

2/91 Supreme Court Bill, correspondence on proposal to add representatives of legal profession, 1893. See also 2/29 for proposals in 1888.

250–1 Members suggested by Law Society and Bar Council, and London Chamber of Commerce request for representation, 1909.

6109 Correspondence with prospective members and others, 1921–50.

4073, 4319 Coldstream on need to revive it. Administration of Justice (Emergency Provisions) Act Expiry Order 1947.

3941–2 4014 Evershed Committee working party 'H': revision of the rules, correspondence with Lord Evershed MR and others. Revision by Gwyer and correspondence with him until his death (1952), thereafter with Johnston (PCO).

2 Meetings

1/49 Minute of 31 March 1885 with draft rules, and circular on Court of Passage procedure.

1/43 Lindley LJ's comments on Crown Office (QBD) Rules for next meeting, 1885.

2/43 Meeting of 21 May 1891: draft rules, especially under Partnership Act, and observations.

79 1892–93: twelve files, with agendas, draft rules, and correspondence, especially on Chancery registrars and QB Associates.

80 Meetings of January and September 1894: agendas, correspondence, rules.

125 Four meetings of 1895: agendas, draft rules, minutes and papers.

126 Four meetings of 1896: usual papers and several memoranda, especially arising out of report on consolidation and amendments by sub-committee under Lindley LJ.

127 Four meetings of 1897, usual papers.

128 Two meetings of 1899, one of 1900: usual papers.

174, 192 Two meetings of 1901, usual papers.

175 Two meetings of 1902: includes papers on proposal to dispense with probate grants on certain very small estates and Bar Council's claim to see proposals in advance.

176 Two meetings of 1903: includes F. A. Stringer on evidence for foreign tribunals.

177 Meetings of December 1903 and August 1904: papers include Phillimore J's memorandum on execution of judgments abroad.

178 Meeting of 1905: usual papers, including several suggestions for alterations to rules.

243–4 Meetings of March and April 1906; Crown Office rules, county courts rules, Merchant Shipping Act rules etc.; discussion of writs in revenue cases.

245 Meeting of December 1906 on commissions rogatoire rules, slander rules.

246–7 Meeting of July 1907: proposals re opening hours of registries, Law Society complaint re *Re Mercantile Lighterage Co*. Correspondence with Board of Trade on shipping rules.

248 Meeting of March 1908, including proposals to extend masters' jurisdiction, criminal appeals rules, Patent Act rules.

249 Two meetings of 1908 and one of March 1909, including draft poor persons rules by W. R. Bousfield.

250 Meeting of July 1909, including correspondence with the Official Solicitor on poor persons rules.

251 Meeting of October 1909.

253 Meeting of March 1910.

252	Two meetings in July, November 1910, including draft poor persons rules, and discussions and papers on rules under Finance Act 1910.
315	Meeting on 5 May 1911, including discussion of poor persons' rules.
316	Meeting on 20 December 1911: papers on actions by debenture holders.
317	Meeting on 2 April 1912.
318	Meeting on 24 July 1912.
319	Meeting on 18 December 1912, including papers on Finance Act appeals; see also Law Society letter in 2/252.
320	Meeting on 3 March 1913, including much material on poor persons rules; also Law Society representations on o.XXVII, o.XIV, Finance Act rules. 320(2) and (3) deal wholly with poor persons' rules, including meeting on 4 March 1914.
321	Meeting on 27 June 1913, including representation by Newspaper Society on payments into court.
322	Meeting on 18 December 1914, including report of sub-committee and other papers on poor persons rules.
323	Meeting on 26 January 1915, including Scrutton J's note on Emergency Powers Rules.
314, 392	Meeting on 10 April 1916, including discussions on rule on settlements out of court of poor persons cases, Friendly Society rules.
391	Meeting on 6 July 1916: correspondence on service out of the jurisdiction of foreclosure orders in actions.
394	Meeting on 5 September 1916.
395	Meeting on 19 February 1917, including report on obsolete rules and discussion on juries.
396	Meeting on 12 April 1917, including arrangements for reproducing documents.
397	Meeting on 6 November 1917.
400	Meeting on 13 May 1918, including position of N.H.I. Commissioners in litigation, solicitors' remuneration.
401	Meeting on 17 June 1918, including solicitors' costs, rules under Representation of the People Act.
402	Meeting on 22 July 1918, including consideration of Scrutton Committee proposals (see 422).
403	Meeting on 11 October 1918, material on rules under Juries Act 1918.
404	Meeting on 3 February 1919.
510	Meeting on 4 February 1920, considering rules on solicitors' remuneration and service out of the jurisdiction.
511	Meeting on 15 March 1920; mostly county court rules.
512	Meeting on 14 May 1920, including report on women jurors rules.
513	Meeting on 10 December 1920; agenda and memoranda on poor persons rules and inferior courts rules.
572	Meeting on 21 April 1921. Memorandum, correspondence with Chitty, draft rules.
1026	Extracts from meeting on 16 July 1926.
1027	Meeting on 22 June 1925; agenda and correspondence.
1680	Meeting on 2 February 1931; agenda, correspondence, rules (RSC(1) 1931). See 1068 (Matrimonial Causes).
1701	Meeting on 1 February 1932, including discussion on cost of litigation.

Satellite files are 1709 (service out of the jurisdiction) 1685 (counterclaim and set-off) 1682 (order XXIX rule 8) 1700 (Admiralty Marshal's fees) 1723 (change of solicitor) and especially 1703 (New Procedure Rules).

1728, 1724 Meeting on 11 July 1932 leading to RSC(2) 1932; see 1729 (divorce rules); 2803 (solicitors' remuneration) and 1706 (New Procedure amendments).

1745 Meeting on 25 April 1933; Hanworth Committee proposals, see files 1738 (payments into court) 1746 (order XIV), 1748.

1754 Meeting on 29 May 1933; see files 1748, 1744, 1766 (printed pleadings) 1750 (Town Planning Act 1932). RSC(1) 1933.

1757 Meeting on 26 June 1933; see files 1733 (Chancery procedure) 1749 (removal of actions) 1753 (Carriage by Air Act rules) 1729 (matrimonial causes) 1817 (default judgments). RSC(2) 1933.

1778 Meeting on 16 March 1934 and RSC(1) 1934. Satellite files include 1779 (payments into court) 1775 (Foreign Judgments Act 1933) 1774 (order XXII rule 8) 1773 (Local Government Act 1933) 1772 (order XXVIII rule 2) 1771 (costs in actions for recovery of land) 1770 (New Procedure rules) 1768 (security of receivers) 1747 (court expert) 1732 (Chancery rules) 1700 (*supra*) 1780 (patents) 1717 (order XI rule 9 (4)) 1777 (taxation).

1784 Meeting on 23 April 1934; see 1747 (*supra*) RSC(2) 1934.

1790 Meeting on 6 July 1934; see 1787 (order LV^{B}) 1785 (long vacation) 1783 (time limit on notices to appeal) and RSC(3) 1934.

1796 Meeting on 26 November 1934; see files 1717 (*supra*) 1743 (poor persons rules) 1781 (proceedings by mortgagees) 1789 (Arbitration Act 1934) 1791 (New Procedure judges) 1794 (matrimonial causes rules) 1735 (orders LVII, LIX) 1290 (county court rules); RSC(5) 1934. Also discussion of order LIV r 21.

1800 Meeting on 1 April 1935, including notes of meeting. See files 1781 (*supra*) 1793 (exhibits rules) 1802 (transfer of actions in Chancery Division) 1803 (Official Solicitor). RSC(1) 1935.

1817 Meeting on 23 March 1936; see files 1770 (New Procedure rules) 1792, 1805 (judgment for land recovery) 1808 (order XXII rule 2) 1809 (poor persons rules) 1810 (Law Reform Act). RSC(1) and (2) 1936.

1823 Meeting on 25 June 1936 (RSC(3) 1936); see files 1781 (*supra*) 1815 (ships' papers) 1684, 1816 (patent actions) 1824 (matrimonial causes) 1280 (county court rules) 1288 (county court venue rules).

1832 Meeting on 16 March 1937 (RSC(3) 1937); see files 1826 (order LVB rule 12) 1827 (order XXXV rule 5) 1829 (Official Referees) 1782 (*supra*) 1833 (patent actions) 1630 (court sittings) 1208 (county court rules).

1846 Meetings on 8, 29 November 1937 (RSC(3) 1937); see files 1814 (Peel Commission report) 1825 (order LXV) 1834 (Government of India Act 1935) 1840 (order LV) 1841 (carbon copies) 1844 (refresher fees on circuit), 1831 (change of solicitor).

1861 Meeting on 12 December 1938 (RSC(2) 1938); see files 1760–2 (Crown Office Rules) 1773 (*supra*) 1801 (county court counterclaims) 1849 (Chancery forms) 1850 (proposed amendment to RSC(3) 1937) 1854 (appearance by post) 1856 (remitted poor persons cases) 1862 (patent appeals) 1855.

1868 Meeting on 9 June 1939 (RSC(1) 1939); see files 1776 (discovery in actions against the crown) 1850 (*supra*) 1858 (Interheritance Act rules) 1866 (transfer of cases from county courts) 1869, 1632 (long vacation) 1865.

3922, 4083, 4089, 4148 4414, 4416 Two points noted for discussion (1944); various proposed rule changes (1947–50).

4082 Meeting on 30 July 1947 (RSC(4) 1947); documents and agenda. See files 4079 (masters' jurisdiction) 4081 (matrimonial causes) 4066 (Exchange Control, Prescribed Court Order).

4086–7 Meeting on 18 November 1947; agenda, documents; Crown Proceedings Rules 1947. See file 4080 (crown proceedings).

4093–4 Meeting on 24 March 1948 (RSC(1) 1948) with pencil notes of discussion; correspondence on Denning Report, Vaisey J's memorandum on wards of court. See files 4091 (order LXI) 4090 (bail) 3964 (Denning Report) 1494 (Middlesex Deeds Registry) 1804, 4166 (payment into court, order XXII).

4101–2 Meeting on 21 June 1948 (RSC(2) 1948); with documents and correspondence and draft rules. See files 4098 (divorce) 4100 (N.I. Act appeals).

4104–5 Meeting on 22 July 1948, correspondence. See RSC (Companies) 1948 and (Companies)(2) 1948, also 3257, 4092.

4112–3 Meeting on 15 December 1948 (RSC(4) 1948), including report of discussion. See files 3916 (service out of the jurisdiction) 3921 (taxation of costs) 4042 (change of solicitor) 4075 (vouching of counsel's fees) 4107 (congestion in Lancashire) 4212 (matrimonial causes rules).

4124–5 Meeting on 11 April 1949 (RSC(1) 1949). Correspondence, agenda, Criminal Proceedings Rules, 1949. See files 4118 (defamation) 4123 (interpleader).

4127–8 Meeting on 25 July 1949 (RSC(2) 1949). Documents and draft rules. See files 4109 (Veterinary Surgeons Act) 4120 (Town and Country Planning Act appeals) 4130 (Master Burnand's suggestions).

4136–7 Meeting on 21 December 1949 (RSC(3) 1949). Documents and draft rules. See files 4134 (Official Referees) 4135 (wards of court) 4138 (assizes) 3618, 3620 (crown proceedings in local courts).

4143–4 Meeting on 3 April 1950 (RSC(1) 1950). Documents and draft rules. See files 4138 (*supra*) 4139 (Patents and Designs Act) 4140 (appeals from Lands Tribunal) 3837.

4152–3 Meeting on 22 July 1950, including correspondence with Law Society. See file 4681 (legal aid).

4163–4 Meeting on 27 November 1950 (RSC(2) 1950). Documents, including brief to Lord Chancellor. See files 4162 (time limit on appeals from quarter sessions) 4157 (legal aid and transcripts) 4080 (*supra*) 4165, 4222 (maintenance orders) 4220, 4223–4 (matrimonial causes).

5926–7 Meeting on 9 June 1951 (RSC(1) 1951). Documents and draft rules. See file 5924 (time limits on appeals).

2 Rules

(see also under particular subject headings)

1/86 Various rules, including RSC 1883, 1885, 1887 and 1888, and comments by various judges on individual proposals, e.g. from Bowen and Hannen.

1/43 1885 Crown Office (QBD) Rules, amended copy.

1/47 1881 Fry LJ sends amended drafts of various rules.

1/81 1882 Settled Land Act Rules, signed copy.

1/44 1888 Deeds of Arrangement rules.

1/80	1888–9 Signed copies of various rules.
2/17, 19	1888–90 Escheat rules 1889, RSC December 1889, Bankruptcy rules 1890.
37	1889 Draft RSC on taxation, with m/s alterations, signed by Rule Committee.
52	1891 Signed print and note from G. F. Pollock.
125	1895 Rules re petitions under Local Government Act 1894, appeals under Finance Act 1894, costs proposals and others.
126	1896 Proposals on costs, rules on interpleader, order XLVI, Court of Passage rules, service abroad (order XI) rules, summons for directions (order XXX) *et al.*
127	1897 includes summons for directions, summons out of the district and other county court rules, workmens' compensation appeals.
128	1899 includes county court rules.
174	1901 includes solicitors' costs rules.
175	1902 includes order XXII rule 18^{A} (small estates).
176	1903 includes Court of Passage, Mayor's Court and county court rules.
177	1903 includes companies rules, order XIV rule 7, and appeals under Midwives Act.
178	1904 various proposals by Kekewich, Jelf JJ *et al.*
189	1902–9 correspondence on rules under Foreign Tribunals (Evidence) Act 1856 with Colonial and Foreign Offices.
243	1906 Middlesex CC Act 1898 rules.
248	1908 includes Patent Act rules (see also 268), Crown Office rules (criminal appeals), extended jurisdiction for masters.
249	1908–9 includes summonses in KBD, poor persons rules.
250	1909 includes service overseas (order XI), damages awarded to persons of unsound mind (order XXII).
252	1910 Finance Act rules, Hull Court of Record rules, county court rules.
279–80	1913–14 Bankruptcy Act rules.
315	1911 includes rules to reduce delays in Chancery.
317–9	1912 includes appeals under National Insurance Act and county court rules, Finance Act rules.
320–1	1913 includes Finance Act rules, poor persons rules, orders XXII and XXXIII amendments.
322	1914 poor persons rules.
291, 323	1915 Emergency Powers Acts rules.
293	1915 Trading with the Enemy Act rules.
337	1915 rules under Legal Proceedings Against Enemies Act 1915.
314	1916 rules under Friendly Societies Acts.
373–4	1916 rules under Emergency Powers (No. 2) Act 1916.
344	1917 Grand Juries (Suspension) Act rules.
391	1916 amendment to order XI rule 1 (foreclosure actions).
392	1916 includes poor persons rules.
394	1916 includes order on court vacations.
395	1917 includes county court rules.
399	1917 includes amendment to service of documents rules.
382–3	1918 emergency powers rules consolidated.
400	1918 includes amendment to National Health Insurance Act rules.
401	1918 includes county court rules, Court of Passage rules, rules under Representation of the People Act.

345	1918 rules under Non-Ferrous Metals Industry Act 1918; correspondence with Chitty and Bray J.
402	1918 includes RSC(Costs)(No. 2).
403	1918 includes Jurors Act 1918 rules.
422	1919 committee on rules revision, proposals implemented.
510	1920 includes solicitors' remuneration (see also 561), service out of the jurisdiction.
559	1920 women jurors rules, correspondence with Home Office, LCJ; report of the Avory Committee.
557, 564	1920 Poor Persons Rules.
555	1920 RSC(3) includes service out of the jurisdiction; memorandum and correspondence with Lord Sumner, objections by Lord Advocate to order XI r 1.
560	1920 rules under Patents Act 1919.
566	1921 National Health Insurance Act appeals rules; correspondence with Ministry of Health, and with Chitty on drafting.
568	1921 Unemployment Insurance Act rules (RSC(1) 1921); correspondence with Ministry of Labour and Chitty.
569	1921 proposed rule under s. 17 Administration of Justice Act 1920; correspondence with President of the PDA.
571	1921 Indemnity Act 1920 rules; correspondence with Bankes LJ, War Compensation Court, and Irish LC's secretary.
572	1921 amendment to order LV (Chancery judgments) and others in RSC 1921; correspondence with Chitty and others.
573	1921 proposed amendments to poor persons rules.
574	1925 Patents Act 1919 rules; correspondence with Sargent J, Treasury Solicitor, opinion of Law Officers, drafts etc.
575	1921–2 vacation sittings rules in RSC(1) 1921, (1) 1922.
576	1921 Treaties of Peace (Examination of Witnesses) Rules.
577	1922 matrimonial causes at assizes rules; correspondence with the President, Law Society, Treasury and others.
578A	1922 jury rules. Report of sub-committee, memoranda by Lord Atkin, Council of Judges report etc.
578B	1922 reciprocal enforcement of judgments: RSC (Administration of Justice Act) 1922.
581	1923 RSC(2): railway company actions rules.
582	1924 Industrial Assurance Act rules; notes by P. O. Lawrence J.
586	1923 Infanticide Act 1922 rules; drafts and correspondence with LCJ.
1026	1929 RSC (Third Party); sub-committee report, drafts and correspondence.
1027	1925 RSC(1), including agenda of SCRC meeting.
1028	1925 National Health Insurance rules, draft by Chitty, correspondence with SCRC members.
1029	1925 shipowners' negligence rules, drafts by Chitty.
1030	1925 infants' damages rules (RSC(3)), correspondence with Chitty.
1034	1925 RSC(2), juries; correspondence with Chitty.
1035	1925 RSC (Law of Property); correspondence with PCO and Ministry of Agriculture.
1037	1926 RSC(4), powers of attorney rules; correspondence with Chitty and discussion at SCRC meeting, 16.7.1926.

4415 1926 Supreme Court (Production of Documents) rules: correspondence with Chitty.

1058 1928 Landlord and Tenant rules: correspondence with Chitty, MR, C. H. Morton, Master Bonner.

1061 1929 RSC(1). Agenda, correspondence and report of sub-committee on rules revision, memorandum for SCRC meeting 15.5.1929, views of various members and memorandum by Napier.

1065–6 1929 RSC(3). Poor persons rules discussed at SCRC meeting, 14.3.1930. Moneylenders rules passed.

1068 1931 Matrimonial Causes (Amendment) Rules, 1931.

Rules already referred to under SCRC meetings after 1930 are not noticed separately in this section.

1730 1932 RSC(3): printing charges reduced; correspondence with British Federation of Master Printers and HMSO.

1734 1932 RSC(4): rules under s. 1 Administration of Justice Act 1932; correspondence with senior Official Referee.

1758–9 1933 RSC(3): notice of trial (order XXXVI); correspondence with Master Bonner and Rule Committee.

1788 1934 Registrars' query re order XXXVI sent to Bonner.

1793 1934 RSC(4): Administration of Justice (Appeals) Act 1934; correspondence with Master Bonner on county court appeals.

1818 1936 RSC forms changed.

1842–3 1937 Matrimonial causes rules (see under *Divorce, infra*, 111–2).

1845, 1853, 1857 1938 RSC(1): printing charges increased; appeals rules under Cinematograph Film Act 1938, and general file including correspondence with C. H. Morton and D. T. Garrett.

1852, 1864 1938–9 various forms modified.

1767 1940 RSC(8): specially endorsed writs, rule amended.

1835 1941 RSC(3): advertisements of unclaimed stock; correspondence with PCO and Farwell J in 1937–8.

1839 1941 RSC(1): trade marks rules (see under *Patents, infra*, 230).

1909 1939 Courts (Emergency Powers) (No. 1) rules; correspondence with masters.

1872 1939 SC (Military Forces) rules: correspondence with Master Ball.

1776 1939 RSC(1): corrections to Administration of Justice Act 1938.

1875 1939 RSC(2): service of documents rules; correspondence with Master Jelf and others.

1867 1940 RSC(2): rules under Coal Act 1938; correspondence with Farwell J and Coal Commission.

1871 1940 RSC(2): jurisdiction of district registrars enlarged.

1874 1940 Shorthand Writers Rules: report of committee, correspondence with Association of Official Shorthand Writers Ltd., MR, Goddard LJ, Treasury, Clauson LJ, Law Society and others.

1876 1940 RSC(6): Trading with the Enemy Act; correspondence with Board of Trade, Masters Holland, Willmott and others.

1767 1940 RSC(8): changes to 1933 rules re specially indorsed writs.

1885 1940 RSC(9): amending barristers' fees vouching rules; correspondence with Master Gibbon, Law Society, Attorney-General, Bar Council.

1887 1940 RSC(1): Farwell J's proposal for order XIII (recovery of land).

1891	1941 RSC(1): pleadings in poor persons' divorces; correspondence with President, PPR, Law Society.
1892	1940 RSC(2): general file. See files 1867, 1871 (*supra*).
1894	1940 RSC(3): Clauson LJ's proposal for better notice to mortgagees' wives.
1895	1940 RSC(4): Master Jelf's proposal to extend order XXVII rules 7, 17 (possession actions).
1896	1940 long vacation: see Judges' Council (*infra*, 90).
1897	1940 rules under Public Order Act 1936 s. 2(3).
1900	1940 RSC(5): rule under Defence Regulation 18^{A} para. 4, aimed at the B.U.F.
1890, 1898	1940 Courts (Emergency Powers No. 2) Rules: correspondence with Master Holland and Lambeth CC Registrar.
1901	1941 Courts (Emergency Powers No. 1) Rules: transfer of actions to enforce judgments.
1903	1940 RSC(8): time limits altered; correspondence with masters.
1904	1940 Matrimonial Causes (EP) Rules.
3890-1	1940 RSC(7) and various subsequent orders to December 1945, on arrangements for court vacations.
3890-2, 4619, 4088	1940-50 various rules on public holidays and sittings in the RCJ.
1905	1941 RSC(1): minor amendment to order LIIIA rule 3.
1906	1941 RSC(1): general file; see 1839, 1891, 1905 and 1907 (trustee securities).
1908	1941 RSC(2)(4): long vacation, correspondence with division heads.
1910, 1913	1941 RSC(3): amendment to order LV (advertisements for creditors) and XII; report of sub-committee.
1911	1941 RSC(6): Pharmacy Act rules; correspondence with PCO, masters, Ministry of Health.
1912	1941 RSC(6): general file and rules under War Damage Act; correspondence with Treasury Solicitor, War Damage Commission, Farwell J and others. See also files 1911 and 1913 (order XII rule 6).
1916	1941 RSC(8): printing charges raised.
2835, 2839	1942 RSC(2): obsolete rules revoked, correspondence with Dack and Master Jelf.
2837	1942 Courts (Emergency Powers) (No. 1) Rules: correspondence with Master Jelf and others on proposed strengthening of 1941 rules.
2838	1942 Courts (Emergency Powers) (No. 2) Rules: drafts by Farwell J.
2840	1943 RSC (Address for Service): masters' conference and Law Society views on complaints; extensive correspondence.
2843-6, 2848, 2854-5	Various poor persons rules (see Legal Aid, *infra*, 191), in RSC(8) 1941, RSC (Poor Persons) 1942, RSC (Poor Persons) 1943 and (No. 2) 1943, RSC(1) 1945.
2857	1942 RSC(3): paper serving measures discussed with masters and others.
3892	1942 RSC(3): correspondence with LCJ, MR on long vacation.
3897	1943 High Court Writs (Service Abroad) Order: correspondence with Foreign Office and Master Jelf.
3903	1942 Courts (Emergency Powers) and (Amendment) Rules: extensive correspondence with masters and registrars.
2721	1943 RSC(3): American Forces Court Martial.

3905 1943 RSC (Deposit of Powers of Attorney): correspondence with PCO, masters and Treasury Solicitor.

3909 1943 Courts (Emergency Powers) (No. 2) Act: notes of meeting, correspondence with registrars and judges.

3920 1944 RSC (Patents) (see *Patents, infra*, 230).

3911 1945 RSC(1): Prize Courts rules.

3924 1945 RSC(1): general file, see 3923 (time limits) 3926 (Trustee Securities) 3911 (*supra*).

4045 1945 RSC (Patents) (see *Patents, infra*, 230).

4041, 4044 1945 RSC(3): transfer of certain functions to Minister of National Insurance, also order XVI.

4052 1946 RSC(1): correspondence with LCJ, C. T. Carr on a procedural omission.

4053–4 1946 RSC(2): order LIX and War Damage (Valuations Appeal) Act rules.

4055 1946 RSC(3): Public Trustee applications, amendment suggested by Master Mosse; also nominated judge under various statutes (3843).

4058, 4062 1946 complaints re o.XXXVI, o.XXXXVI.

4067 1947 RSC(1): general file. See files 4063 (order LIX, appeals), 4065 (order LXIV(1), removal of wartime rule).

4070, 3672, 4069 1947 RSC(2): order LVB amendments; mother to act as guardian *ad litem*; continuation of actions against Coal Commission.

4072 1947 RSC(7): Acquisition of Land Act and other Acts.

2736 1950 Courts (End of Emergency Powers) Order.

5162 1951 Reserve and Auxiliary Forces (Protection of Civil Interests) Rules: correspondence with masters.

3 Fees Rules

(for Probate fees, see under "Probate", infra, *105)*

1 *Investigations and reports*

1/44, 83–4 Papers 1882–7, including Fees Order 1883, departmental committee, correspondence and drafts, including objection by Fry LJ. Bill to amend Courts of Justice Building Act 1865, Law Society observations and deputations, Muir McKenzie's notes and briefs on new fee scale, and correspondence with Treasury.

2/514–6, 1117 MacNaghten Committee, 1921. Minutes, memoranda, drafts, and correspondence with Treasury, divisional heads and others.

661 McCardie Committee on Sheriffs' and Bailiffs' Fees: memorandum by Sheriffs' Officers Association, correspondence with Chitty. Report and orders, 1921.

1014–6 MacNaghten Committee on use of adhesive stamps, 1928. Correspondence (1922 onwards) with MacNaghten J, Treasury and Chitty; minutes, preliminary correspondence and report; see Fees Order 1930 (1017).

3976–80 Evershed Committee working party 'F'; papers and correspondence on fees and costs.

2 *Orders*

2/190 1903.

276 1908: correspondence with Treasury and Winding up Fees Order.

352 Emergency powers fees amended after questions from masters; drafted by Sargent J.

397 1917 debenture holders' actions; opinion by J. H. Stamp, correspondence with Sargent J and Master Chandler.

426, 428, 431–2 1920–2 Bankruptcy and Winding-Up fees (see *infra*, 233).

562 1920 Trinity Masters' fees and correspondence on proposal to increase fees on summonses adjourned into court.

567, 4156 Surveyors' fees, 1916–20 and 1950 onwards; claims by professional bodies, views of masters and others, memorandum by Master Willmott on testing of Chancery practice on these fees.

678 1923 contempt fines; correspondence with registrars and list of recent fines.

1009 1924 order; correspondence with Chitty.

1634 1934 order under Foreign Judgments Act 1933.

1635 1934 order (2) under Administration of Justice (Appeals) Act.

1917 1934 abolition of officers' fee on unstamped documents, following negotiations with Treasury and IRC.

1830 1936 proposed order on fees of court expert.

1637–9 1938 including s. 17 Married Women's Property Act, short cause fees.

1641 1941; prerogative writs.

1644 1941, Liabilities (Wartime Adjustment) Act.

2822 1942: correspondence with Law Society and Brighton Registrar on mode of payment.

2823 1942: cash payments in Liverpool and Manchester Registries.

2824 1943: correspondence with President over fees in 'blameless' collision cases.

2825 1943: consolidating fees to relieve congestion in divorce registry.

3851 1946: photocopies and first Denning Committee report, correspondence with PPR, Treasury.

3853 1947: second Denning report, negotiations with Treasury and PPR.

3854 1947 (2): Official Referees.

3855 1948: suggested by E. F. lwi to stop a 'ramp' in PDA.

3858 1948 (2): correspondence with Treasury on fees for photocopies.

3859 1948: correspondence on a point in the Fees Order, 1930.

4068 1950: photocopies; correspondence with Master Simner, and see 'Evidence' (*infra*, 78).

4517 1949: fees in civil jury trials; correspondence on policy with Treasury, division heads.

3 Remitted Fees

2/1013 Treasury inquiry on practice when government departments litigate, 1928.

2793, 3849–51, 3857 Applications for revision, various dates. 3849 (Boynton Estates, 1941) includes correspondence on divergent practice between Pay Office and Chancery, raised again in 1949 but left unresolved.

4 Funds Rules

1 Dormant Funds

1/20 Correspondence with Treasury following report of committee on unclaimed dividends in bankruptcy.

2/1018, 1645–8 Tomlin Committee report: memorandum by Master Hulbert, correspondence and report. Draft orders. Correspondence with Pay Office and Treasury leading to second Tomlin Committee: memoranda, minutes, correspondence and report. Discussions on county court funds and on action (see Finance Act 1936 s. 26).

2826 Dack (SC Pay Office) on publication of lists, suspended in 1942. Further correspondence of 1946–8.

4646–8, 5891 Samuel's motion and Nathan Commission (see *Charities, infra*, 223–4).

2 *Investments*

1/72 Correspondence with Treasury on Chancery funds and National Debt Bill, 1881.

1/80, 2/11–2 National Debt Reduction Act 1889: correspondence with Treasury, Pay Office judges; draft rules by Official Solicitor; correspondence with Chancellor of Exchequer on concessions.

393 Status of 5% Exchequer Bonds discussed, 1916.

397 War stock rule: correspondence with Pay Office, 1917.

558 Rules of 1919 on brokerage commission.

565 Rules 1921, on commission rates and lodgment certificates: correspondence with Pay Office and others.

1024 Broker Committee 1930 (Schuster): minutes and correspondence only.

1649–50 War loan conversion: draft rule amended by Lord Chancellor to waive fees on 'continuance applications'.

3862 1944 Rule (1): wartime practices regularised at wish of Simonds J.

3 *General*

1/75, 85 Includes discussions on 1883 and 1884 rules, with observations by Law Society, M. Muir McKenzie, Bar Committee, Official Solicitor and others; also papers on Chancery Pay Office and funds rules (see *'Chancery' infra*, 96–7) and suggestions for rules amendments (1884–7) from Official Solicitor, Treasury, Fry LJ, and amended rules 1888. Also District Registries Funds Rules, 1887.

2/70 1892 report of departmental committee on suitors' funds; correspondence with Treasury.

102 1896 amendment to rule 41^{A} following Life Assurance Act 1896.

338 1911 new rules, correspondence with Pay Office and masters.

1019 1925 Rules: infants' damages and other matters; correspondence with Chitty.

2829 1926 Treasury minute on Official Solicitors' balance account and correspondence with Official Solicitor, 1959.

1022 1925 memorandum on working of the Pay Office, by J. A. Longley.

1021 1926 Railways and Canals Rules: correspondence with McCall (R & C Commission) and Pay Office.

1023 1928 Admiralty deposits.

1651 1932 minor modification of procedure.

1653–4 1933 Rules(2): correspondence with Pay Office, minor changes and correspondence with Master Bonner on an omission in these rules.

1655	1934 Rules(1) to meet *Meeson* v *Meeson*: correspondence with masters and registrars on practice.
1656, 3872	1935 Rules(2): various minor matters, mostly payments into court by Official Arbitrators, regularised by Funds Rules 1950.
1660	1941 Rules(2): Wartime Liabilities Act monies in court.
2827	Correspondence with S. Dack and Master Holland on various matters leading to Funds Rules (1) 1942, County Court Funds Rules 1942, Funds Rules (1) 1943 and discussions on position in Liverpool District Registry.
2828	Proposals by Dack for changes to r. 47(1) and (2), discussed with Master Holland, 1942.
3866	1947 Rules with Pay Office proposals on divorce lodgments.
3867	1947 Pay Office memorandum on "the account of the sale of the Land Tax".
3869–70	Exchange Control Act Rules 1947: drafts by Miller (Pay Office) and correspondence.
3871	1948 correspondence with Audit Department and Treasury on contempt fines.
4368	1950 Pay Office question re Lands Clauses Consolidation Act 1845.
3873	1950 Pay Office proposal to re-organise accounting system.
5606	1951 discussions with Pay Office and others on use of Administration of Justice Act 1928 s. 15 re charitable funds in court.

4 Deposits

2/1020	1927 Rules: memorandum by Roscoe (Admiralty Registry), correspondence with Treasury, Pay Office *et al.*
1025	Road Traffic Act 1930 deposits: discussions with Board of Trade, Treasury, Pay Office, Ministry of Transport.
1658–9	1938 Rules(1): deposits under various acts and investment rules; correspondence with Pay Office and Treasury; interest reduced in rules of 1941(1).
3074, 3863–4, 3868	1946 Assurance Companies Act: correspondence with PCO on position of Accountant General under Assurance Companies Act 1909. 1944 Rules (2): Prevention of Fraud Act 1939 deposits; draft by Board of Trade, correspondence with Pay Office; and their 1946 proposals discussed with Chancery judges. Master Holland's query of 1947. 1946 Pay Office proposal for easier withdrawal, with Chancery judges' views.

5 Payments

2/563	Enemy Funds in Court Rule, 1920: opinion of A. Cartmell, views of Eve J and Pay Office, drafts.
1652	Rules(3) 1935: to facilitate payments for lunatics; correspondence with Pay Office and Treasury.
4158	RSC(2) 1950, after correspondence with Pay Office on payments to legally aided parties.
4417	1937 correspondence with Air Ministry and draft rules by Board of Trade for deposits under Air Navigation Act 1936 (not made).
4208	1947 Law Society protest at practice direction on costs.

6 Local Acts

2/3145 1946 Banbury Corporation Bill: correspondence with Treasury, Pay Office and Parliamentary agents on objections to lodgment proposal.

3148 1945 Rushden District Gas Bill.

3149 1946 Newport (Isle of Wight) Corporation Bill: similar objections by Pay Office, discussed with Agents.

3865 1944 complaints by Pay Office on anomalies in local and private bills, noted for action, 1950.

5 Costs

(see also under "Legal Aid", "Legal Profession" infra, *especially 181–3, 185, 192–3)*

1 The machinery of taxation

2/9, 37 Reports on assimilation of costs between QBD and Chancery, correspondence with Kay J, masters, taxing masters on Chancery and lunacy taxation. Draft of new rule, 1889.

46 Report, 1891 and comments of committee on taxation, especially by Master Langbourne.

192 Committee on taxation 1901. Report; correspondence with LCJ, Treasury; representations by staff, Law Society; notes of meetings and comments by Board of Trade, Rule Committee papers.

489–91, 497 Tomlin Committee, 5th report on Taxing Office, correspondence and papers.

1064 Taxation of Costs (Principal Clerks) Order 1930. Doubts on existing practice (*King* v *Alfred Dawson (Rushmere) Ltd.* 1929 Ch D), report by Tomlin LJ and Master Drury; SCRC papers and correspondence with Law Society.

1625 Proposal to give taxing power to district registrars in Administration of Justice (Miscellaneous Provisions) Bill, 1924.

3921 Law Society proposal to widen taxing powers of Liverpool and Manchester district registries discussed, 1944.

4168 Circular to district registrars on practice in remitted actions, 1950.

4815–6, 5485 Complaints re taxation of counsel's fees under Legal Aid Act 1949 discussed with Master Gibbon.

2 Costs in particular actions

1/69 Complaint about costs in actions removed to High Court by certiorari, 1884.

2/567, 4156 Surveyors' costs: correspondence with their Institute, masters, Chancery judges 1920–3; revived 1950, views of masters etc.

802 Clause to put crown on same footing as subjects discussed, 1928.

1049 Parliamentary questions and London Chamber of Commerce proposals on costs in Inland Revenue appeals 1926; briefs and I.R. memoranda. Correspondence especially on *Seymour* v *Reed.*

1702 Cost of litigation; London Chamber of Commerce memorandum 1930, and see 1598–1603, Hanworth Committee papers.

1724 Discussion and rule change on taxation in matrimonial causes, 1932.

3913 Table of costs, 1932.

1756 Master Bonner's complaint of evasion of taxation by solicitors, 1933.

1771	Complaints re costs rule in land recovery actions 1926, 1933; practice defended by Masters Chitty, Ball, Gibbon.
1777, 1825	RSC(1) 1934, RSC(3) 1937: minor changes to order LXV.
3060	Costs in libel actions: specimens for Porter Committee, 1939.
1860	Law Society complain of inadequacy of costs in Court of Appeal, especially after Practice Direction of 1943.
2655	Coal Bill 1943; discussions with Ministry of Fuel and Master Gibbon on costs proposals.
4096	Law Society complaint re order XXII r 14, discussed with Master Gibbon, 1948.
4099	Discussion of *Wright* v *Bennett* with Master Gibbon, 1948.
4468	Law Society proposal to change rule on taxation in actions against bankrupt solicitors, 1950.
3325	High Court and county court costs in debt recovery discussed with Lynskey J, 1949.
2813–4	Commissioners for Oaths (Fees) Orders 1944 and afterwards.

6 Miscellaneous points of practice

2/799, 1060, 1067, 1124, 1432–3, 1679, 1804, 1890, 2858, 3351, 3835, 3906, 3910, 4062, 4083, 4089, 4106–7, 4114, 4121, 4126, 4149–50, 4154, 4166, 4193, 4331, 4351, 5167, 6198.

3
EVIDENCE AND PROCEDURE

1 The Jury

The decline of the jury in civil cases since the Judicature Acts is one of the most notable changes in the litigation landscape but one which has been obscured by controversies over the functioning of the jury in criminal trials.[1] Lord Mersey's committee in 1913 pronounced the unfettered right to jury trial in civil actions undesirable[2] but its recommendations were not implemented and although the wartime manpower shortage brought about restrictions, they were removed in 1925. It was soon noted that plaintiffs were becoming alive to the more generous damages to be had from juries in personal injuries cases,[3] and this aggravated the delays in the King's Bench Division. The deliberations of the Hanworth Committee, which led to a new curtailment of jury trials, are therefore of some importance in view of the course of subsequent judicial decisions on the measure of damages. The LCO was enthusiastically behind this move, for when the King's Bench masters prepared a set of guidelines on whether to order a jury which Schuster found "cuts down the effect of the section to an extent which never occurred to any of those who discussed the question before the bill became law, and will frustrate the hopes, which had been formed by those who were party to preparing it", he wrote to Hanworth that "it makes my hair stand on end".[4]

Not all the judges, let alone the Bar, welcomed the curbs on jury trials, and when the question of removing the further restrictions imposed during the second world war came under discussion, there were advocates of a wider right to a jury, notably the LCJ and Humphreys LJ as well as the Bar Council.[5] The Labour Party, however, was more interested in democratising the jury by providing for the payment of expenses and for loss of time (this had been done only in exceptionally protracted cases and on an *ex gratia* basis)[6] and by abolishing the special jury. The special jury became a particular target not only because it was almost overtly a replication of class distinctions but also by virtue of the verdict of one such jury in the Laski libel case; this virtually sealed its fate, apart from the London commercial list for which the LCJ pleaded successfully.[7] There are full papers on the Juries Act 1949, which implemented these changes, and on the Treasury's "specious and dishonourable"[8] bid to set the fees for jury trials at an economic level, regarding them as a luxury which the state should not finance.

The period also saw the end of that "expensive farce"[9] the Grand Jury, which was summoned to every assize and quarter sessions formally to find a true bill of indictment. The antiquity of the institution, and perhaps the fact that MPs were largely drawn from the same class, earned it such respect that it was able to survive one onslaught in the Criminal Justice Bill of 1922–5, before it too went under in the wake of the Hanworth committee.[10]

Notes

1 *W. R. Cornish,* ***The Jury*** *(1968); P. Devlin,* ***Trial by Jury*** *(1956); R. M. Jackson (1937–8) 1 MLR 132.*
2 *PP 1913 (Cd 6817) XXX, 403 and (6818) 463.*
3 *2/1703: Automobile Association to Maugham J, 2.2.1932.*
4 *2/1759: Schuster to Bonner and to MR, 17.10.1933. Perplexities on the interpretation of the rule were only set at rest by* ***Hope*** *v.* ***G.W.R.*** *(1937) HL.*
5 *2/3468.*
6 *2/3467 gives examples.*
7 *The LCJ's explanation of the Laski verdict is in his letter of 16.12.1946 to the Solicitor-General (2/3470) and a full record of the case (****Laski*** *v.* ***Newark Advertiser & Co. Ltd****) was published in book form.*
8 *2/4517: Coldstream's note, 4.11.1948.*
9 *2/583: A. H. Bodkin (DPP) to Schuster, 23.3.1922.*
10 *Sir Sidney Rowlatt was one of its staunchest defenders: see memoranda in 2/1599.*

1 Restrictions on jury trials

2/395	Discussions in the SC Rule Committee.
347–8, 354, 365, 389, 403	Juries Act 1918: views of KB judges, correspondence with PCO and draft bill; report by Avory J, amendments discussed. Rules for High Court, county and coroners courts.
442	Administration of Justice Act 1920: drafts and correspondence with PCO.
465–6, 473, 559, 578A	Juries (Emergency Provisions) Bills, 1920, 1922; correspondence with Home Office, LCJ, judges on jury lists; RSC (Women Jurors) 1920 after report of committee under Avory J, and Rules 1920 after report of SC Rule Committee and committee under Bray J.
726–31	Administration of Justice Bill: correspondence with PCO; Parliamentary proceedings (especially on county court juries).
1596–9, 1605–6	Hanworth Committee papers, and Administration of Justice (Miscellaneous Provisions) Bill 1933.

1759 Discussions with Master Bonner and Roche J on 'guidelines' to masters on juries in "running down" cases.

4073 Administration of Justice (Emergency Powers) Act (Expiry) Order, 1947.

2 *Juries Act 1949*

2/3109, 3467–70, 3412, 4516–7, 5275, 4122 Discussions of wartime problems; Jowitt's response to PLP resolution 1946; circular to clerks of assize and masters, answers to PQs; minutes of meeting with LCJ, December 1945 and meetings of 1946 with legal departments; papers on special juries, payments, etc. Resolutions from constituency parties and cabinet discussions on special juries; consideration of jury provisions in Companies Bill; correspondence with PCO on draft Juries Bill, especially on inferior courts; Parliamentary proceedings. Discussions with Treasury on fees in civil actions and with masters, clerks of assize, heads of divisions (see SC Fees (Amendment) Order, 1949), and with Home Office, Under Sheriffs Association and clerks of assize on allowances regulations. Consequential RSC changes.

3471–3, 5271 Discussions with Home Secretary on recent jury leaks (1950) and meetings with court officials on Geoffrey Crowther's campaign to improve the jury system, 1951. Other minor queries.

3 *The Grand Jury*

2/578A, 583, 612 Minute of Council of Judges on restoring Grand Jury (1920); DPP's criticism. Law Officers' opinion and correspondence with Home Office on S. Rowlatt's view of Grand Juries Suspension Act 1917.

712–7, 720, 873 Criminal Justice Bill: cabinet papers, S. Rowlatt's pamphlet, correspondence on Parliamentary tactics; discussions on abolition in Mayor's and City Court. Rules (1927) passed by Indictments Act committee.

1596–9, 1605–6, 1959–60 Hanworth Committee papers. Abolition clause in Administration of Justice (Miscellaneous Provisions) Act 1933: correspondence with PCO, DPP and Indictable Offences Rules 1933.

2 Evidence

1 *General*

2/1718–22 Evidence Bill. Maugham J's proposal, discussion in Judges' Council (1931); views of Lord Atkin, Russell, Greer LJJ, Avory J, Attorney-General. Minutes of Greer Committee (1931). Negotiations with Law Society and Bar Council and correspondence with PCO, 1931. Correspondence with PCO, 1938; discussions with Home Office, Law Society and Lord Atkin on amendments.

1747 Proposed "courts expert". Discussions with judges, masters and in SCRC, 1933–4. RSC(2) 1934 and applications from various bodies.

1961–5 Evidence (Foreign Documents) Act (see "International Law" *infra*, 285).

1671 Notes on the preservation of judges' notebooks.

3358–9, 3363 Crown Proceedings Bill (*infra*, 203), and especially 3363, criticisms of the clause on discovery in the 1947 bill.

3970, 3981–2, 3997–9 Evershed Committee, papers of working parties 'C' 'G' and 'Q'.

1819, 4068 Photographic copies. Correspondence with Treasury, Master Bonner and Scrivenery Office leading to Napier Committee 1936. Minutes, evidence and report (1937). Practice direction revised (1947) and complaints referred to Evershed Committee.

2 *Wartime expedients*

2/1878–84, 1893, 2635, 2639 Evidence (Wartime Facilities) Committee set up 1939 under Lord Maugham; correspondence on RCJ practice, draft bill, notes of interviews with departments, views of LCJ and Lord Atkin, notes of meetings. Also Criminal Evidence Committee under Humphreys LJ, with correspondence, notes of meeting and report. Discussions on both reports with Law Officers, PCO, Scottish departments and cabinet papers. Evidence and Powers of Attorney Bill: correspondence with PCO, with H. M. Cohen on his amendments, Parliamentary proceedings and Order in Council. Correspondence with Lord Maugham, Cohen and others on re-drafting RSC order LX1A (1940).

4277–8, 3905, 3052 Evidence and Powers of Attorney Act 1943: long correspondence with Master Burnand and services departments on use of airgraphs, etc.; with Law Society and Foreign Office on facilities for prisoners of war. Draft bill from PCO (1942) on prisoners of war and internees' documents and further extensive correspondence with interested departments; cabinet papers and Parliamentary proceedings. Correspondence with Foreign Office on Foreign Representatives (Proof of Notarial Acts) Order, 1943, and with Supreme Court officers and Treasury Solicitor on problems with the Act. See RSC (Deposit of Powers of Attorney) Rules, 1943. Isle of Man Bill sent by Home Office 1944.

1929 Discussions on possible relaxation of rules on execution of powers of attorney under Trustee Act 1925; views of Uthwatt J and H. Cohen. Draft bill from PCO, cabinet papers, Parliamentary proceedings. Subsequent discussions with Supreme Court officers on interpretation of the Act and rules, 1939–43.

2774–5, 2820, 2836, 2842, 3022, 3895, 3914, 4279 Proposals to relax rules in particular cases and minor queries.

3 *Welsh language*

2/4418–20, 4422 Correspondence with Board of Education on departmental committee recommendation and Home Office brief on the issue, 1927. Previous letters from Welsh language advocates and Attorney-General's memorandum on Administration of Justice (Wales) Bill 1937. Meetings with Artemus Jones and E. H. Parry (1939), and discussions with ministers and deputations of Welsh MPs 1942. Draft bill discussed with PCO, Attorney-General; correspondence with Morrison and Welsh Parliamentary party, cabinet papers, Parliamentary proceedings. Papers of 1906, 1911, 1923 and after on interpreters at assizes and in county courts and on oaths. Notes of conference with Home Office and DPP on Welsh Courts (Oaths and Interpreters) Rules, especially on fees, and with LCJ (1943).

4 *Oaths*

(see also 'Solicitors', infra, *181)*

2/238	Oaths Act 1908: correspondence with F. A. Stringer (RCJ) and others on drafting practice.
2635–6, 2638–9, 2669, 6698	Correspondence with armed service ministries and SCJ officials on Armed Forces (Administration of Oaths) Order, 1940.
2631–4, 2670, 3245–6, 3248, 3251, 3254	Appointment of High Commission officials and others as Commissioners.
482, 1132, 2585, 2641, 2628, 2813, 3248, 3250, 3252, 3255	Various minor questions.

5 *Law reporting*

2/1151–3, 2821	Judges' anxiety over proliferation of reports, leading to Simonds Committee. Correspondence on terms and composition, evidence and memoranda, report (1939). Correspondence with Admiralty on censoring wartime reports.

6 *Particular aspects*

2/624	Medical witnesses: Ministry of Health and B.M.A. seek privilege for documents; discussed with heads of SCJ divisions and in cabinet and rejected, 1921.
801, 4204	Suggested change in divorce rules (1927); solicitor's complaint against hoteliers (1946).
2957–8	*Fletcher* v *Platts*: application for discovery of LCO documents; internal memoranda and discussions on disclosure, 1945.
2780, 3699, 3708, 3733, 3740, 3053	Questions on discovery and evidence in Pensions Appeal Tribunals 1944. Discussions with Ministry of National Insurance on aspects of evidence rules in Industrial Injuries Tribunals, 1944.
3437, 3896, 5999	Minor questions on evidence.
4051	Witnesses Allowances Regulations, 1948: correspondence with masters, meetings with BMA, report of departmental committee (1947) and Rule Committee papers.
4979	Administration of Justice Bill 1951: Inland Revenue objections to admissibility of unstamped documents.
3351	Correspondence with Home Secretary and LCJ on contempt of court and the press, 1949, especially the *Haigh* case.

3 The Official Referees

The Official Referees were created in 1876 and survived until the next great re-organisation in 1971 without ever becoming a really valuable part of the High Court. The correspondence on their creation is interesting for the Treasury attempt to restrict tenure 'during good behaviour' to judges proper and the strong opposition to that restriction from the senior judges,[1] and when J. Anderson QC retired in 1886 the Lord Chancellor simply overrode Treasury objections to appointing a successor, although in the previous four years they had each disposed of only about 18–20 cases a year. H. W. Hemming, the new referee, was interestingly described as "not only not a Gladstonian, but that his Liberal friends consider him now a Tory".[2] Thereafter their future was secure enough but the Lord Chancellor's 1888 initiative to persuade the judges to give them more work had little success.[3] They felt themselves undervalued and underpaid and, besides attempting to publicise their work in legal journals, made persistent demands for increases in salary and improvements in status.

Notes

1 *1/73.*

2 ***Ibid**: Muir McKenzie to Lord Chancellor, 12.11.1887.*

3 *2/28: the correspondence with Edward Ridley in this file suggests that his temperamental unsuitability for the High Court judgeship to which he was controversally appointed in 1897 (see R. F. V. Heuston, **Lives of the Lord Chancellors** (1964), 50–51) might have been foreseen.*

1/73	Papers on the appointment of the ORs, discussions with Treasury and division heads on tenure, staff and fees (1875), on pensions (1886) and new appointments (1886–7).
1/84	Fees Order, 1887.
2/28	1888: discussions with judges on Dowdeswell's report on extended functions, and with E. Ridley on taking debtors' examinations.
5735, 1829, 3940, 4134	Transfer of actions *inter se*: orders under RSC o.XXXVI; general file (1921–56) proposals to simplify and their enactment in 1949.
1702	Scandalous legal costs, cases cited in Newbolt's memorandum to Hanworth Committee, 1932.
1710, 1734, 2771	Administration of Justice Act 1932 s. 1 restricts appeals; discussion in Judges' Council, drafting correspondence, rules and proposal to widen appeals, 1941.
1740, 3666, 5928	Other proposals for wider powers.
4/152, 2/1829, 2/6670	Proposals to style themselves judges; warrant of precedence (1938).
4/59, 2/4506	Appointment of Sir L. Leach as temporary OR (1948) and his transfer to Privy Council (1949); LCJ's views on other ORs.
3988	Evershed Committee Working Party 'K' papers.

4 The Official Solicitor

"The position of the Official Solicitor, indeed, appears in many respects to be extremely obscure", wrote a puzzled Danckwerts in 1946, giving his opinion on the first substantial negligence claim made against this strange officer (on account of Egyptian bonds which had gone missing in 1910),[1] and although the Official Solicitor later achieved a brief notoriety when he "appeared on the scene unexpectedly, like a good fairy, and wafted the recalcitrant three men away from the 'dungeon'" where they were confined for contempt of the short-lived National Industrial Relations Court in 1972,[2] the comment still has some force. His role in earlier contempt proceedings can be studied here, in two cases in which the Lord Chancellor was confronted with the prospect of the indefinite and fruitless imprisonment of wilful individuals and sought the Official Solicitor's help to extricate himself; the Pedrick case[3] is particularly interesting on the shifts to which the authorities were driven.

In the time of Lords Cairns and Selborne, however, the Official Solicitor, R. Leigh Pemberton, figured very prominently in carrying out the extensive reorganisation which followed the Judicature Acts. These papers show his activities in settling the fee structure, the bankruptcy business and the use of stamps; in particular he was given the delicate task of preparing a scheme for the distribution and organisation of work among the clerical staff of the Supreme Court, a scheme which could not fail to arouse vocal dissatisfaction among the office holders if it came anywhere near meeting the Treasury's requirements. It was a difficult and ill-defined role and as Muir McKenzie pointed out, the Official Solicitor had not the authority or position to be the business manager that was really needed.[4] This consideration, and the establishment of the LCO on its modern footing reduced the scope for him to play this part and Leigh Pemberton's successor Winterbotham (nicknamed "the botham" by Muir McKenzie) though he freely offered his advice, was kept at arm's length. On his retirement in 1919, the recommendations of the Tomlin Committee that the Official Solicitor should not practise privately and should become a regular salaried official were carried out and the business organisation of his office can be instructively studied in the papers of the Fass Committee of 1939.[5] On the basis of its report, the Lord Chancellor put an end to Gilchrist's enterprising attempt to obtain business under the Judicial Trustees Act 1896 and also told the Master in Lunacy to restrict his growing recourse to the Official Solicitor for reports and receiverships in lunacy.[6] At the end of the 1940s Gilchrist was faced with further threats from the new adoption rules which threatened to remove adoption business from the High Court to a large extent, and by the Law Society's endeavour so to frame the legal aid scheme that his role on behalf of prisoners would be severely curtailed.[7]

Notes

1 *2/3669.*

2 *R. M. Jackson,* **The Machinery of Justice in England** *(6th ed.), 412.*

3 *2/1546.*

4 *2/262: "Points connected with the Chancellor's Office"; 1/61: "Pemberton's statement of his duties".*

5 *The Committee was set up because of concern in the rapid increase in his lunacy receiverships (1,865 in February 1939): 4/1.*

6 *4/3.*

7 *2/4695.*

1 *General*

1/22, 27–36, 67, 75–6, 83–4 — Correspondence with LCO and Treasury on aspects of the clerical and administrative organisation of the Supreme Court, and on fees, 1875–88.

1/61	General statement of duties, n.d. (c.1884).
2/1554	Proposal to be a corporation sole, 1932.
1545	Questions on ceremonial dress etc.
489, 492	Tomlin Committee papers; memorandum on his office and 2nd report.
133	Correspondence with Treasury on staffing arrangements, 1896.
2829	His balance account; Treasury minute of 1926 and discussions in 1959.
262	Memorandum on Lord Chancellor's office, 1885, discussing his position.
4/1–5, 64–5	Fass Committee (1938–9), including preliminary correspondence with Treasury, minutes, evidence, memoranda, and report with notes of 1945. Meetings of working party on staff reorganisation (1946).

2 Particular aspects

2/141, 3674, 3676	Judicial Trustee: discussions on rules, 1896; position considered after Fass committee, 1948.
757, 1159, 3670, 4457, 3668, 3143, 3671	Views on Guardianship of Infants Bill 1920, on adoption records, 'taking up' wards, on new adoption rules, 1949; on enforcement of solicitors' costs as guardian *ad litem*.
264, 330, 415, 416, 1541, 3651, 3675, 3653, 3673	Protests against re-organisation of lunacy administration (1909, 1913); quarrel over fees; made *ex officio* receiver (1917); objects to new Patients Estates Rules (1934); in negotiations for new structure (1948–50); on *Rice* v. *Rice*.
4/63	Correspondence with Master in Lunacy on the "Treasury guarantee", 1920, 1932.
2/957, 3677, 4090, 4683, 4695, 1546, 1697, 1764, 1800, 1803, 3667	Correspondence with Home Office (1923) on visiting arrangements, revised after discussion on Crown Office rules (1931); RSC (Crown Proceedings) 1938; Pedrick's case (1938–42); Corcoran's case (1950); Law Society's attempt to curtail his role (1949); discussions on various aspects.
3669, 6676	Correspondence with Treasury on Re M. M. Keatinge deceased (1946) and on improving precautions against loss, and on F. W. Slater's claim (1950).

5 Arbitration

2/611	MR raises defects in arbitration appeals for reform in Administration of Justice Bill, 1920. Consultations with R. A. Wright, F. D. MacKinnon, W. Clifton, S. Garrett.
1197–1204	Arbitration Act 1934. Committee set up after memoranda by London Chamber of Commerce and others (1926). Committee papers, memoranda and report. Discussions with Board of Trade and trade bodies; PCO bill (1928), dropped. Correspondence with Askwith MP on his bill (1934), drafting correspondence with PCO and others; memorandum of Bar Council/Law Society joint committee; Parliamentary proceedings. Comments by MacKinnon and others on Asquith's further bill of 1936.
1789, 1683	Discussions with masters on interpretation, see RSC(5) 1934. Further criticisms and proposed changes (see also '*Private International Law*', *infra*, 284).
3086	Draft consolidation bill sent by PCO, 1945.

4
THE JUDGES

1 Introduction

1 Appointments

The higher judiciary has become a popular area of academic study in recent years but the custom of preserving a discreet reticence over the failings and foibles of living judges, the bland tone of many memoirs and biographies and the impenetrable nature of the selection process leaves much still to be learned.[1] It cannot be said that those LCO files which are at present open to inspection do very much to fill in the missing details in the picture but they furnish some interesting fragments nevertheless.

Thus there are discussions of the candidates for appointment on the occasion of particular vacancies and a defect in the selection process is revealed in a letter from Jowitt to Lord Clarendon, explaining that Wynn-Parry J had been appointed without it being known that he was divorced: ''If I had known I do not say I should have regarded it as an absolute bar, but I should certainly have regarded it as a point which told very strongly against his appointment. It was only after I had appointed him that I learned these facts and I now ask every judge whom I have to appoint, 'is there anything about your private life which you think you ought to tell me?' ''[2] It is also interesting to have Jowitt confirming in a private letter to the Lord Chief Justice his public boast that his appointments were entirely non-political, and adding that the Prime Minister had followed his wishes in every case.[3] Fear of the ''red judges'' who might be appointed under a future Labour government had probably done as much as anything to reconcile the other political parties to the depoliticisation of judicial appointments and few traces of it are to be seen in these papers.[4] There are also stray references to the characteristics of individual judges, such as Crossman J's slowness ''amounting almost to a disease'', Fry LJ ''sorely beset by technicalities'', and Charles J as ''a most indiscreet judge''.

What the papers do highlight is the difficulty regularly experienced in making appointments to the PDA division. Schuster explained the essence of the problem in 1922:

> There is no connection in the subject matter or in procedure between the Admiralty work, on the one hand and the divorce work on the other. The two bars engaged do not mix. Training required by a judge to sit in Admiralty is by no means the training required to sit in divorce and vice versa. The result has been in the past that judges have been appointed to the Division who were not specially suited for the Admiralty work. Sir Francis Jeune was trained as an ecclesiastical lawyer; Sir Samuel Evans, though his great quickness of mind enabled him to master the Admiralty work, was at first wholly unfamiliar with it. Mr. Justice Bargrave Deane had no previous experience in Admiralty, and never became specially suited for the trial of Admiralty cases. The divorce work is no doubt easier to learn when once the peculiarities of the practice have been mastered. But probably a leading counsel who has never been in the Admiralty, has received a training more specially suited to try the issues of a divorce case than a man who has spent the best years of his life in Admiralty . . .

and it remained substantially true until the break-up of the division in 1971. Moreover, as he continued ''note must be taken of the reluctance of many of those members of the bar who are best fitted for the bench, to accept appointment in a division which is solely confined to Admiralty and divorce''.[5] The reluctance of certain judges to endure a diet of unrelieved divorce even temporarily remained—Bennett J pronounced it ''loathsome''[6]—and divorce at assizes was said by Humphreys J to be ''adding a new terror to circuit life''[7]; Uthwatt J probably summed up a general feeling among the puisnes in the other divisions when he said that Denning was ''wasted in divorce''.[8] Roman Catholics, Schuster's memorandum indicates, were particularly liable to experience scruples of conscience; thus Lynskey declined appointment to the PDA, but he, Wallington and the Master of the Rolls (Lord Greene) were all on the bench at the end of 1949 when Jowitt became disturbed and indignant at reports of a speech of the Pope in which he seemed to rule that Roman Catholic judges should not normally grant divorces. Jowitt claimed to feel misgivings about appointing any new RC judges to the Bench and he was not satisfied until he had secured what he rather misleadingly called ''a complete climbdown'' from the Apostolic Delegate.[9]

Replacing retired judges was comparatively straightforward, but adding to their number was a much more difficult business because it required a resolution by Parliament and that gave critics of the courts a splendid opportunity. Moreover there were, of course, financial implications but it was seldom that the LCO was in the position of pressing action on a reluctant cabinet and Treasury because Lord Chancellors and the higher judiciary shared a general reluctance to increase their numbers for fear of diluting the quality. As late as 1950 the LCJ maintained that twenty four was as many as his division could cope with, and the judge-dominated inquiries into the courts always rejected mere expansion in numbers as a solution to delays.[10] Even the LCO, however, felt that the rigidity of the statutory provisions was an inconvenience (they were also not without ambiguity, and it was strongly argued at one time that Farwell J's appointment was *ultra vires* and invalid)[11] and several attempts were made to gain greater freedom from Parliamentary control. The SCJ (Amendment) Act 1944 gave the Lord Chancellor power to re-arrange the manpower of the divisions but the price was acceptance of Lord Maugham's amendment requiring the consent of the judge in question. The statutory maximum number of judges was progressively increased, but the need for Parliamentary approval could not be dispensed with until 1971.

2 *Salaries and pensions*

Three times during this period the emoluments of the judges became a matter of major concern, leading in 1931 to a minor constitutional crisis. In the 1880s Childers warned Selborne that ''Gladstone has often said to me that the judges are too well paid. . . . I well remember how strongly he insisted on this when it was a question of calling down the cost of the non-judicial officers eleven years ago and now £1 buys more than it did then''.[12] The last argument was not one that could be employed very often thereafter, and Gladstone did not, in fact, risk an attack on the £5,000 which they had been granted in 1832. There was, however, considerable discontent on the bench over the question of allowances and expenses for going on assize, especially as the common law judges reckoned their Chancery brethren better off by £500 p.a. because they were almost never obliged to go.

The Treasury declined to grant an allowance for circuit duty in 1878 but in 1884 renewed negotiations in which they sought a *quid pro quo* in reductions of the pomp and circumstance attending assizes did bring forth an offer, though Selborne got little thanks for his trouble from his brother judges.[13] Thereafter matters remained quiet until the end of the Great War, when the judges petitioned for an increase in salary to offset inflation and a bill was actually drawn up which foundered in the economy measures of 1921. Ten years later came the celebrated episode of the 10% cut in public service salaries, which was foolishly imposed on the judges without adequate consultation and in a form whose validity was open to question. The resulting row has been carefully described by Heuston,[14] and his account can be supplemented from the LCO files; they contain the opinions of the Law Officers, Parliamentary counsel, the Lord Chancellor and several judges on the constitutional position, notes of meetings with judges, notably Clauson and Luxmoore, MacNaghten (''definitely unbalanced'')[15] and the heads of divisions, and correspondence with McCardie J (whose especial indignation may have sprung from pecuniary embarrassments) and with Roche and Maugham who were threatening to resign over their income tax assessments during the reduction. There are also papers on Lord Rankeillour's Judiciary (Safeguarding) Bills and the legislation proposed by the government as part of the attempts to pacify the judges.

Even at that time Sankey claimed that many leading counsel were refusing the bench an account of the small rewards[16] and by the end of the second world war the restiveness of the entire judiciary, higher and lower, was reaching an embarrassing pitch. Early in 1949 Jowitt told the cabinet he had met two refusals for the High Court that year and that only ''burnt-out'' barristers would take county court judgeships.[17] He was coming under particular pressure from the Scottish judges, who were said to be ''perfectly wild''[18] on the subject but there was predictable and fierce opposition from within the Labour party and the trade unions to any increase and in August 1949 the Chorley report ''froze'' public sector salary increases and thereby condemned the higher judiciary to wait likewise. Frustrated there, the LCO and Home Office concentrated on securing increases for the less well paid county court judges and stipendiaries (who were also less obviously ''top people''), and for lower judges in Northern Ireland and Scotland, and attempted to pacify the others by concocting a widows' pension scheme. Both of these eventually become realities, the latter at the end of 1950 and the former only after the change of government, but in each case only after the most strenuous and uncomfortable battles with the cabinet. When Jowitt tried to revive the case for higher salaries in December 1950, for instance, Gaitskill (Chancellor of the Exchequer) was able to retort that ''nothing has caused more trouble with trade union circles recently than the increases in salaries of, for example, senior local government officials'',[19] yet these were of course the very increases that made the judges most angry. The absence of any independent review machinery and of any generally agreed basis of comparability made bargaining an uncomfortable process and was bringing some of the judges, especially those in Scotland, to the verge of campaigning publicly for an increase, and the LCO materials give an excellent account of the difficulties in settling salaries when they were thus 'at large'.

3 *Conduct*

If the judges' case did have to be presented to the public, it would certainly be through the medium of a press which was generally uncritical of their work. Few complaints were made in the press, and fewer still in Parliament, against individual judges after about 1900, and of these the more serious, e.g. Grantham's election case, and the 'Daily Worker' libel, are noticed not in these files.[20] An exception is the Prime Minister's complaint in 1924 against McCardie J's remarks in a libel case arising out of the Amritsar riots, where the file contains a sharp exchange between the unrepentent judge and a critical Lord Chancellor.[21] In general the LCO followed the familiar policy of not washing its dirty linen in public, as can be seen in their unwillingness to expose Lord Merriman's opposition to divorce reform to Parliamentary criticism. Even in the case of Hewart it was maladroitness, not calculated provocation, that drove him into his notorious attack on the Permanent Secretary, though Hewart had given plenty of scope for criticism, his journalistic activities being widely reprobated[22] and his unjudicial style on the bench notorious. But although the cabinet might be told that the King's Bench arrears were largely due to his incompetent management,[23] it was left to a Royal Commission to make this public in suitably guarded language.[24] Certainly of some interest in view of future events, however, is Jowitt's mild rebuke to Denning J over his first book "Freedom under the Law", unavailingly advising him to steer clear of controversial issues.[25]

4 The Judges' Council

Under the Judicature Act 1873 s. 75 the Council of Judges, comprising all members of the Supreme Court of Judicature (but not the Lords of Appeal in Ordinary, save the Lord Chancellor), was to meet annually to discuss matters relating to the administration of justice or the structure of divisions and to report to the Home Secretary, while under the Judicature Act 1875 s. 17 changes in the long vacation could be made only on the recommendation of a Council including at least five of the heads of divisions and Lords of Appeal and a majority of the puisnes.[26] It was envisaged therefore that the judges as a body would, for example, settle the rules of court and arrange the circuits, and they did meet annually, and sometimes more often, for at least fifteen years afterwards, although there is little material on the 1870s and the meetings of the 1880s are not minuted in regular form. Although other issues were discussed—there was, for instance, a lively discussion on the desirability of laying down guidelines in sentencing at a meeting in 1885—the meetings were dominated by the intractable problems of the assizes, and showed the unsuitability of the council as a law reforming body. For one thing, after the creation of the enlarged QBD in 1881, its judges were numerically dominant and could, in theory, pass resolutions against the views of the other divisions, so that it was not surprising that Butt J "did not think that the reference of such a question [at his liability to go on circuit] to the periodical meeting of the judges would be conducive to harmony and co-operation between the members of the judicial body".[27] Again, there was the awkward prospect of a head of division being outvoted on matters peculiarly within his province, and when this happened on the report of the judges' own committee on circuit arrangements in 1886 (by 17–5, and the rest of the minority was hardly impressive—Hawkins, Grantham, Day and Stephen JJ) Coleridge LCJ refused to bow to the majority verdict, insisted on publishing his dissent and extracted from Halsbury what was, in effect, an admission that majority decisions would not be binding.[28] It may have been that experience that decided Halsbury that the council was a waste of time: at all events, there is no record in the LCO of further meetings after 1889 during his long tenure of office, with the doubtful exception of a judges' meeting in 1895 to protest against the erosion of judges' control over court officers.[29]

When a meeting was next held in 1907, it was on the initiative of Alverstone LCJ, who wanted to make some changes in the circuit system; Schuster noted "the proceedings on each occasion have not been such as to encourage those present to come together again with any lively hopes for any good result''.[30] So after another brief flicker into life between 1920 and 1922, when reports were made to a surprised Home Secretary,[31] it lapsed again, although its statutory existence was perpetuated by s. 210 of the SCJ Act 1925. Sankey made a gallant effort to make use of it, although confronted with a good deal of scepticism, and in the early 1930s it discussed Maugham's evidence proposals, the Hanworth Committee reports, shorthand writers and other current issues, but the results were discouraging (no doubt the lack of enthusiasm on Hewart's part did not help) and during the latter part of the decade it met, when it did so at all (and never under Hailsham) only to settle the dates of the long vacation. It was again brought back to life in 1950, but by this time the judicial body was far larger and more unwieldy than Selborne's Act had envisaged, and an old difficulty re-emerged when the judges split 28–15 on no longer closing the courts on the King's Birthday. Jowitt wanted to override Evershed MR and the minority (including the entire Chancery division) but was prevailed upon to delay.[32]

Notes

1 *S. Shetstreet,* ***Judges on Trial*** *(1976) assembles much of the available information. R. F. V. Heuston,* ***Judges and Biographers*** *(1967) outlines some of the difficulties.*

2 *2/4618: Jowitt to Lord Clarendon, 11.7.1947.*

3 *2/3889: letter of 3.10.1950.*

4 *A newspaper suggestion to the contrary brought a detailed rebuttal by Schuster: 2/601: memorandum of October, 1917.*

5 *2/1008: memorandum of 24.12.1924.*

6 *2/1628.*

7 *2/1606: memorandum of 12.2.1933.*

8 *2/4198: Napier's note, 28.9.1945.*

9 *2/4228: Jowitt to J. Chuter Ede, June 1950.*

10 *2/3889: LCJ to Jowitt, 5.10.50.*

11 *2/601.*

12 *1/11: 21.12.1883.*

13 *1/11.*

14 ***Lives of the Lord Chancellors*** *(1964), 513–9.*

15 *2/1666: Schuster to Attorney-General, 6.4.1933.*

16 ***Ibid****: memorandum to cabinet, 25.9.1931.*

17 *2/3881: Jowitt's note, 8.7.1949; 2/4609: CM(50) 38th conclusions, 22.6.1950.*

18 *2/6342: Jowitt to LCJ, 13.10.1950.*

19 *2/4610: 11.12.1950.*

20 *S. Shetstreet,* ***supra*** *n 1, 163–78.*

21 *2/961.*

22 *e.g. 2/1549.* ***Cf.*** *R. Jackson,* ***The Chief*** *(1959), 327–8.*

23 *2/1610: CP (226) 34, 17.10.1934.*

24 *Peel Commission report, PP 1935–6 (Cmd 5065) VIII, 105, paras. 149–160.*

25 *2/4617. It was Coldstream, however, who was really responsible for the intervention. The book comprised Denning's Hamlyn Lectures.*

26 *S. Rosenbaum (1914–15) 63 Penn. Univ. Law Review, 160–2. See also C. Mullins,* ***In Quest of Justice****.*

27 *1/11: to Lord Chancellor, 10.4.1884.*

28 *1/9: LCJ to Lord Chancellor 21.6.1887 and draft reply 28.6.1887.*

29 *2/138. But see e.g. the reference to proposals of 1892 in LJ 13.8.1932, 526.*

30 *2/442: Schuster to LCJ, 23.6.1919.*

31 *2/602.*

32 *2/5925.*

2 Documents

1 Appointment, promotion and retirement

(see also "House of Lords", "Privy Council", ***supra****, 45 ff., "Court of Appeal"* ***infra****, 91 ff.).*

2/269	Draft of bill for additional judges, 1910.
442, 556	Administration of Justice Bill 1920: memoranda to cabinet for extra judges; correspondence with President.
601	Notes on authority for the number of judges and Schuster's memorandum on appointments; also discussions with MR on appointment of a Chancery judge in 1918.
604	Memoranda on the appointment of women judges, requested by foreign governments, 1922, 1925.
605	Correspondence and cabinet memorandum on vacancies and number of judges needed, 1923.
1008	Shipping interest campaign for extra PDA judge, including correspondence with President, and with Sir Leslie Scott, memorandum by Schuster on PDA judges, cabinet memorandum 1925.
798, 810	Administration of Justice Bill 1928: correspondence with PCO and cabinet papers, including clause to modify the Parliamentary sanction to new appointments.
1672, 1675–6	SCJ (Amendment) Bill 1934: correspondence with PCO on the 'Parliamentary sanction' and cabinet papers on extra judges.
1628	SCJ (Amendment) Bill 1937: discussions with President, and in cabinet and Parliament on need for extra judges to handle divorce.
1617–8	Administration of Justice Bill 1938: Peel Commission proposal on retiring age rejected; cabinet memorandum.
1677	Judges' memoranda on state of High Court, need for judges etc., mostly for cabinet; various dates, 1932–9.
3875–6	SCJ (Amendment) Bill: discussions with President on extra judge (1942), cabinet papers and further discussions, 1943.
3830	Discussions with LCJ on filling vacancies in KBD, 1947.
3238	Promotion of Denning J to Court of Appeal, 1948.
4605, 3887, 3889	High Court and County Court Judges Bill 1950: correspondence with LCJ on arrears; cabinet papers and further correspondence on number and persons to be appointed.
5884	Discussions on possible appointment of extra judge in Ch. D., 1951.
4228	1948–50: position of Roman Catholic judges: cabinet papers and correspondence with Foreign and Home Offices on Pope's speech and implications.
4618	Correspondence with Lord Clarendon on appointment of divorcees as judges, 1947.

2 Salaries, pensions and honours

1/5–6, 11	1877–84: circuit expenses and allowances; judges' resolutions and correspondence with them and with the Treasury.
2/168	1901–5: grants of pensions, formal correspondence.
467	Judges Salaries Bill 1921: memorandum of the judges, correspondence with Chancellor of the Exchequer, cabinet papers.
1663, 1666–9, 1678B	1931–5: reduction in judges' salaries, including minutes and papers from Judges' Council (1663), cabinet papers, opinions on the legality of the cut, correspondence with judges, memoranda, correspondence with PCO on draft legislation, and on Lord Rankeillour's Judiciary (Safeguarding) Bills (1667–1669). Cabinet and Parliamentary proceedings; correspondence with Attorney-General, Treasury and notes of meeting on income tax assessment complaints of Roche and Maugham (1678B). Statutory Salaries (Restoration) Bill 1934, draft and Parliamentary proceedings.
1670	1920, 1932: memoranda and correspondence on knighthoods for Russell and Lawrence JJ.
5789	Membership of Privy Council for puisne judges: correspondence with PM's office on patronage and practice, 1932–57.
6691	Papers on judicial salaries 1944–6, and discussions with IRC 1947–9 on possible tax reliefs (see also 4613).
3881–2, 4483, 4608–14, 6341–2, 6692	Salaries and pensions, 1949–51. Correspondence with Treasury, Lord President, judges (including Scottish and Northern Ireland judges), cabinet papers and meetings, Parliamentary proceedings, and Judicial Officers (Salaries) Bill. Also on pensions, including Administration of Justice (Pensions) Bill, with judges' replies to circular and detailed correspondence on the scheme.
4/241	Proposed scheme for judges' officers, 1925–52.
2/3003	Collar of the LCJ of Common Pleas: correspondence with Master Bonner, MacKinnon J, opinions of law officers and others on ownership, 1940–3.

3 Conduct

1/6	Criticism of Fry LJ by Muir McKenzie, 1884.
2/961	Parliamentary complaint against McCardie J (1924) with Schuster's memorandum on removal of judges and correspondence of Haldane with McCardie and Darling.
1549	Parliamentary criticism of Hewart LCJ's journalism and draft replies, 1935.
3877	Schuster's opinion of Crossman J, 1940.
4617	Correspondence with Denning LJ on his book "Freedom under the Law", 1949.
5789	Criticism of Charles J, 1947.
6672	Complaints of Bar Council against judges, 1950.
5901	1951 Vaisey J: apology from a solicitor.
2967	1945 Discussion with Foreign Office on "New Times" attack on Birkett J.

4 The Council of Judges

1/4	Resolutions of June 1874 on circuits, and December 1881 on long vacation.

1/59	Resolution of November 1880 on amalgamation of divisions (see PP 1881 (C 2781) LXXVI, 409).
1/5	Minutes of December 1883, on long vacation.
1/1, 6, 7	Resolutions on circuit arrangements, June 1884.
1/54, 76, 77	Resolutions and discussions on circuits, Inns of Court appeals, Provincial Sittings Bill, sentencing and other matters, March and December 1885.
1/7, 1/54	Meetings of March and December 1886.
1/9, 54	Meetings of April and November 1887 discussing circuits.
1/54	Meetings of January 1889 on circuits and sentencing.
2/138	Meeting of April 1895 to discuss SC Officers Bill.
242	Meetings of January, April of 1907 on Long Vacation.
442	Meetings of July 1919: correspondence with LCJ and PCO.
578A, 602	Meeting of July 1920, discussing grand juries, salaries, long vacation.
603	Meetings of June 1921, 1922: preliminary correspondence and reports to Home Office.
708	Meeting of December 1930; agenda, minutes, notes on sub-committee on appeals from Official Referees.
1266, 1661, 1714, 1718	Meeting of June 1931; correspondence with LCJ and others, agenda, minutes, report to Home Secretary (see also files on county court appeals (1266, 1714) and evidence (1718)).
1662, 1707	Meeting of June 1932 on long vacation and shorthand writers; correspondence, agenda, minutes.
1663	Meetings of March 1933: minutes and correspondence with Mackinnon J and Attorney-General on salaries.
1664A, 1807, 2604	Meetings of April 1934: preliminary correspondence, minutes; long vacation discussed.
1664B, 2604	Meeting of May 1935: *ibid.*
1630	March 1937: Order in Council on sittings and the coronation, dealt with by correspondence.
1665	Meeting of June 1938: correspondence with LCJ and other judges, agenda.
1632	Meeting of April 1939: correspondence with LCJ and judges, minute on long vacation.
1364, 1896	Meeting of July 1940 on long vacation; briefing paper by Schuster and minutes.
3874, 4607	Meeting of January 1950 on long vacation, hours of business, revenue list, with minutes and note on previous meetings.
5925	Discussions on observance of the King's Birthday in the RCJ, 1950–7, including note of judges' meeting 1951 and memorandum by MR.

5 *In other capacities*

2/2832	Correspondence with Board of Trade and Chancery judges over company law committee, 1943.
2792	Lord Atkin invited to chair committee on Welsh reconstruction, 1942.
3760	LCJ complains about KBD judges' quarter sessions duties, 1946, 1950.
3877	The Royal Commission on Patents: discussions with Treasury on chairman, 1940, 1945.
3888	Correspondence with Board of Trade and LCJ on chairman for copyright committee, 1940.

4262–5 1940: War Zone Courts (see Emergency Legislation, *infra*, 267).

3880 Evershed J assists Admiralty in review of Fleet Air Arm, 1945.

3234 Radcliffe's mission to London for the Boundary Commission, 1947.

4500 Requests to several judges to chair royal commission on capital punishment, 1948.

3240 Proposal to appoint a judge to arbitrate in the case of the North Borneo Chartered Company, 1945.

4563 Discussions on a successor to Uthwatt J on the leasehold committee, 1949.

4660, 4662 General and Shipping Claims Tribunals (see *infra*, 165–6) 1939–58.

5784 Correspondence with Foreign Office on appointment to Court of Arbitration at the Hague, 1949.

5787 Simonds LJ appointed to preside over Privy Council committee on two London University appeals, 1951.

5902 Correspondence with Ministry of Health on arbitrator in dispute over NHS terms, 1951.

5904 Discussions on Board of Trade proposal for a judge to head Monopolies Commission, including Thesiger's memorandum on judges' extra-judicial functions.

4762, 5905 Correspondence with Treasury, MR and Vaisey J on chairman of royal commission on income tax, 1950; also with Treasury on proposed 'independent panel' under Finance Act 1951 s. 22.

5

THE COURT OF APPEAL

The Judicature Acts established a new Court of Appeal for civil matters, with the Master of the Rolls at its head (from 1881) and staffed by full-time Lords Justices of Appeal appointed by the Prime Minister.[1] The court sat in divisions from the outset to cope with the considerable number of appeals and the arrangement of judicial manpower was primarily the Master of the Rolls' concern, though Lord Jowitt certainly intervened on at least one occasion to ensure that a case of great importance to the government was heard by a 'strong' court, and Lord Greene MR seemed to think this perfectly proper.[2] Attempts to reconcile the profession and the judiciary to courts manned by only two Lords Justices failed[3] and from time to time the Master of the Rolls found it necessary to approach the Lord Chancellor either for temporary assistance from the House of Lords or the puisne judges, or for a permanent addition; as the files show, Treasury consent to the appointment of three extra Lords Justices in 1938 was only obtained on condition that the liability of Lords Justices to serve in the High Court on request was made no longer conditional on their own consent.[4] As in the other appellate courts, the rising demand for senior judges to undertake extra-judicial duties sometimes denuded the court and it is interesting to have Greene's account of the trying circumstances under which the judgment in the celebrated case of Caleb Diplock's will had to be written. His own idea for improving the quality of judgments, that the court should only sit four days a week, had already found no favour.[5]

Criticism of the multiplicity of appeals which were possible under the changes to which Selborne's scheme had been subjected and their consequence in increasing costs and delays has been a staple ingredient in legal journals and a standby of critics ever since 1876 and the consideration of reform proposals by the Hanworth and Evershed Committees is therefore of considerable interest. The former made suggestions, which were forthwith enacted,[6] that county court appeals should by-pass the "antediluvian fatuity" of the divisional court and that leave should be necessary for appeals to the Lords, and was persuaded by Talbot J to adopt his idea of abolishing separate Lords Justices altogether in favour of puisne judges hearing appeals from their own number.[7] Schuster had been floating something similar in outline[8] but agreed that Talbot's scheme was "all wrong".[9] It was strongly opposed by most of the judges[10] and was never heard of again. The Evershed Committee in its turn considered appellate questions in several working parties and in exhaustive detail and though the recommendations were to be disappointingly modest, the evidence and minutes are informative on the plight of the litigant.

Mention should also be made of another clause in the Administration of Justice (Appeals) Bill, because it provoked the celebrated outburst in which Hewart denounced Schuster to an astonished House of Lords. The clause enabled the Lord Chancellor to nominate a vice-president of the Court of Appeal to preside over one of the divisions. By tradition the senior Lord Justice had presided over one division (the Master of the Rolls, of course, presided over the other) and the clause was interpreted by Slesser LJ, next in line of seniority to Greer LJ who was ailing and likely to retire shortly, as a personal slight, and possibly a political one too, since he was a former Labour politician. Hewart gave it a more sinister interpretation as another step in Schuster's campaign to create a Ministry of Justice controlled by the civil servants and accordingly launched his remarkable attack. Certainly Schuster and Sankey had been guilty of a grave discourtesy to Slesser and the LCO papers do nothing to explain or extenuate what was a tactical blunder of major proportions.[11]

Notes

1 *See 1/76. There are articles on the workings of the Court by Lord Cohen in (1951) 11 CLJ, 3 and Lord Asquith in [1950] JSPTL, 350 (also in 2/4514), and see R. M. Jackson,* ***Machinery of Justice****, 94–99.*

2 *2/4285. The case was* **Franklin v Minister of Town & Country Planning** *[1948] AC 87.*

3 *This was permitted under SCJ Act 1899, but only with the parties' consent.*

4 *2/1633. SCJ Amendment Act 1938 s. 2(1).*

5 *2/3846; 2/1633.*

6 *2/321: Muir McKenzie to H. A. McCardie, 11.7.1913; Administration of Justice (Appeals) Act 1934.*

7 *2/1605: Lord Wright to Schuster, 29.9.1933.*

8 *2/1596: this contains the response of Lords Atkin and Tomlin.*

9 *2/1605: to Lord Wright, 30.9.1933.*

10 *2/1602: report of judges' meeting, 7.2.1934.*

11 *2/1672–6; R. Jackson,* ***The Chief*** *(1959) 258–70; R. F. V. Heuston,* ***Lives of the Lord Chancellors*** *(1964) 519–20; H. A. Slesser* ***Judgment Reserved*** *(1941) 256–64.*

1 Organisation

1/76	Discussion on Master of Rolls as head: correspondence of A. Kekewich and Jessel MR, 1881.
2/140, 270	Bills to enable "two judge" sittings: 1899 and 1907 drafts with views of Bar Council, Law Society, Lindley MR.
1606, 1633	Hanworth Committee memoranda. Memoranda from MR and Schuster on state of business in 1938; correspondence with Treasury and PCO; cabinet papers on additional judges.
1672–6	Supreme Court of Judicature (Amendment) Bill, 1934: correspondence with PCO on drafting, with LCJ, President, MR and others; cabinet papers and Parliamentary proceedings.
3845	MR's memorandum on need for appropriate balance in courts, 1945.
3847, 3461, 5884	MR's warning on critical shortage of manpower; memoranda on new appointments, 1947; correspondence on MR's demand for an extra judge, 1951.
4514	Asquith LJ's article on the work of the court of Appeal, 1950.
4285	Discussions on the composition of the Court for the *Stevenage* case, 1947.
3846	Discussion of problems in forming a court for the *Diplock* case, 1948.

2 Jurisdiction and Proposed Reforms

2/1596–7	Schuster's proposals and judges' comments, 1931–2.
1598–1606	Hanworth Committee papers, especially 1604 (minutes) 1606 (memoranda).
1266, 1635, 1661, 1793, 1795, 1714	Administration of Justice (Appeals) Act 1934; correspondence with PCO, notes of discussion in Council of Judges; cabinet papers; notes on 'improper' appeals, Parliamentary papers, rules and fees order under the Act.
4063	Extension of appeals v. refusal of mandamus, RSC (1) 1947.
3842, 3848	Proposals by the LCJ for reforms re revenue and county court appeals, and discussions with LC 1946, 1949.
3989–95	Evershed Committee working parties 'L–P' on various aspects of appeals, including 'leap-frogging' and publicly funded appeals; correspondence, memoranda, notes of discussions and draft reports. 3994–5 show the evolution of the report of the working parties on appeals.
5924	Rules on time limits amended: correspondence with G. Paull KC and Registrar, 1950.

6
THE COURT OF CRIMINAL APPEAL

It was only in 1907, when the outcry over the wrongful conviction of Adolf Beck forced the government to act, that a satisfactory appeal court for criminal cases was established[1] and it was principally a Home Office undertaking. It figures very seldom in the LCO files and even its rule committee did not meet for forty years after its initial deliberations in 1907.[2] Its operation was essentially the responsibility of the LCJ and there is no indication that any Lord Chancellor was unhappy with it until Goddard's regime, when the government had to withdraw a proposal in the Criminal Justice Bill 1948 to give it the power to order a new trial in the face of attacks on the court in the House of

Commons. The Attorney-General explained the background to these attacks to Jowitt, admitting that "in the common or garden everyday cases . . . it does seem sometimes that the scales appear to be weighted against appellants" and "there is a feeling that also the appellants are dealt with in a rather summary way".[3] This no doubt was Goddard's way of discouraging the "futile" appeals of which he complained,[4] but there is nothing to suggest that Jowitt took the matter up with him.

Notes

1 *2/232.*

2 *The LCJ curiously cited this as evidence of the unwisdom of including on committees provincial persons, 2/3330: LCJ to Skyrme, 3.6.1948.*

3 *2/3341: 19.7.1948. Goddard's own description of the court in operation is in (1952) 2 JSPTL (n.s.) 1.*

4 *2/5588: Thesiger's note of 2.3.1951.*

2/232–4	Criminal Appeal Act 1907: bills of 1882–3, 1890; Judges' Council report, 1892; memoranda by Home Office; Amendment Bill, 1908 and meeting of Rules Committee, 1907.
491, 500	Tomlin Committee, 12th report, on Criminal Appeals Office, 1919.
1324	Proposed amendments to rules: memoranda and discussion with Criminal Appeals Office, 1938.
3329, 5588	LCJ and Humphreys LJ, proposals to reduce futile appeals, 1945, 1950.
3330	LCJ seeks reconvening of Rule Committee, 1948.
3340–2	Criminal Justice Bill 1948 papers, including memoranda on appeals.
4345–9, 5250	Courts Martial Appeals Act 1951 (*infra*, 156).

7
THE HIGH COURT, CHANCERY DIVISION

The Lord Chancellor remains the nominal head of the Chancery division although he never sits or exercises any personal superintendence. In 1971 the office of Vice-Chancellor was restored to provide an equivalent post to the heads of the other divisions, but for many years before that, the senior puisne in the division had routinely been treated as the head and consulted on proposed changes and complaints, and as the division was small (originally five strong, a sixth judge being added in 1899) and centralised enough to enable its judges to consult easily and regularly[1] no serious inconvenience had been felt.

In many respects Chancery retained its distinctiveness despite the administrative fusion of law and equity. Even the Chancery masters made their re-appearance in 1897 in recognition that, under the style of chief clerks, they had been performing their traditional role in making inquiries and taking accounts. Lord Bowen pointed out that unlike the QBD, Chancery administration had not been altered very much by the Judicature Acts and that each judge still held a virtually independent court.[2] Even when the "grouping" of judges was adopted, it was still felt that the Chancery judges lacked the "sense of cohesion''[3] that distinguished their counterparts in the KBD. Delays in the drawing up of orders by the registrars and in the taxing of costs by masters continued to be a source of complaint and the costs which were incurred through the insistence on formality, that, for example, ''every trumpery detail has to be verified by affidavit, which when made (often at very serious expense) is of no more value than a signed statement would be''[4] still meant that ''it not infrequently happens that the whole of an estate is eaten up by the costs of administering it, and that there is nothing left for the wife and children of the deceased man''.[5]

Inquiries instituted by the Lord Chancellor and the judges highlighted the problems but also seemed to demonstrate their intractability. A commentator on the most recent report on Chancery practice asserts that ''the fact that so much Chancery practice remains largely unpublished encourages the notion that the Division regales on its traditional mystique, and is content that its complicated, sometimes inconsistent, and cumbersome methods shall, except to the esoteric few remain in obsidian darkness''.[6] The report noted disapprovingly that recommendations of the Harman Report of 1960[7] had not been implemented, so that for example the independent existence of the registrars continued, although fifty years before Muir McKenzie had described their doings as ''magnificent, but it is not business''.[8] The conclusion of the Review Body in 1981 was that ''within the headquarters of the LCD not even in the most rudimentary manner at all, has the work of the officers of the Chancery Division ever been supervised''.[9]

One reason why the division was allowed to continue its old, unsatisfactory ways is that in the inter-war period the pressures for reforms which commercial and personal litigants generated in the KBD and PD & A divisions were not generally felt in relation to Chancery business. The exception is the patent business and that, significantly, was the only jurisdiction which was the subject of a specific departmental inquiry.[10] On the whole, Chancery kept abreast of its work by its own criteria and was even (reluctantly) able to take in bankruptcy and winding-up actions and eventually the revenue list. Moreover its conservatism in method and organisation did not preclude significant initiatives in practice, the most notable being the 1936 Practice Direction on mortgages described elsewhere.[11]

Nevertheless, the persistence of old and unsatisfactory procedures and their remarkable tenacity deserves to be studied more fully by those concerned either with the process of law reform or with the workings of institutions, and there is useful material in the LCO papers. For example, the Evershed Committee dragooned the division into experimenting with fixed dates and it was recognised that the outcome of the experiment was of some importance in determining whether it would be regarded as a feasible proposition in the KBD. However, the experiment was hardly given a fair trial: the judges, some of the masters, the judges' clerks (who stood to lose prestige) and the bar were hostile, and this, assisted by the incompetence of the master charged with arranging the dates, ensured that its benefits were not fully realised, to the great annoyance of Gerald Gardiner and others on working party 'D'.[12]

Notes

1 R. E. Ball (1961) 77 LQR 331. *The restoration of the Vice Chancellor was suggested by Lord Tomlin in 1932: see 2/1596, memorandum of 25.2.1932.*

2 *(1886) 2 LQR 1. This independence was emphasised by the practice of the Chancery bar practitioners of attaching themselves to a particular judge's court.*

3 *2/3940: Coldstream's note 3.4.1951.* **Cf.** *Lord Tomlin, n. 1* **supra**.

4 *1/35: J. W. Langbourne's memorandum, 3.10.1886.*

5 *1/35: Pearson J to Lord Chancellor, 6.11.1885. This file is a valuable source of complaints and defences.*

6 *R. Blackford, in LSG, 27.5.1981. The Oliver report is Cmd 8205 of 1981.*

7 *Cmd 967.*

8 *2/201: evidence to the Kekewich Committee, 1907.*

9 *R. Blackford,* **supra, n. 6**.

10 **Infra**, *228–9.*

11 **Infra**, *237.*

12 *2/3971: note by Boggis-Rolfe, 16.3.1949. See the Evershed Committee's first interim and final reports.*

1 Jurisdiction

2/107 Proposed transfer of winding-up and bankruptcy 1900–02.

268 Patent actions under Act of 1907.

373 Emergency Powers (No. 2) Act 1916; discussions with MR on rules, correspondence with Sargent J.

1631, 696 Transfer of bankruptcy 1921: correspondence on appeals with T. W. Chitty and registrars; arrangements among Chancery judges 1921–38; query by Chitty in 1926.

1224 Reporting of Estate Bills removed from Chancery, 1941: correspondence on standing order.

1781–2 Mortgage actions transferred, 1934 (*infra*, 229).

2756–8, 3427 Settled Land and Trustee Acts, 1942–3 (*infra*, 214).

4607, 3874 Revenue actions transferred, 1950: Judges' Council meeting, correspondence with judges.

5929 Distribution of Enemy Property (no. 2) Order 1951 gives jurisdiction over appeals from the Administrator, after correspondence with Board of Trade and Vaisey J.

5994 Correspondence on suggested transfer of lunacy to Chancery, 1951.

2 Organisation and Procedure

1/75 Extensive papers on Chancery Pay Office and new Funds Rules, 1883, including Treasury report, draft rules, objections by Law Society, views of Official Solicitor, M. Muir McKenzie.

1/83–5 New Stamp Rules 1884, objections by Chancery registrars.

1/5 Judges discuss delays and possible transfer of judges, 1883.

1/35 Various papers on Chancery, including Pearson J on small estates' administration, solicitors' petition on delays in taxation, Master Langbourne's proposals, proposal of the "Amalgamation of Chancery Offices Committee", Master Bloxam on delays.

2/192–3 Report of committee on taxation of costs, 1901; correspondence with LCJ, Treasury; notes of meetings, Law Society observations etc.

32, 48, 79	Reports on taxation of costs and Chancery offices, 1889; comments by Kay J, registrars and others; new taxation rules, and objections by Law Society; correspondence with Treasury 1895, 1901 on economies; 1892 Rule Committee discussions on registrars' offices; proposals by Chitty, views of judges; report on amalgamation of taxing offices, 1891, with note by Master Langbourne.
107	Discussions on organisation of business, 1900: views of Master Hewlett and judges.
201	Minutes of Kekewich Committee on registrars, 1906; representations of registrars, views of judges; correspondence with Treasury.
464	Supreme Court Officers Bill, 1920: correspondence with Master Fox on registrars.
489–92	Tomlin Report, 1920: including minutes, papers on Chancery chambers (494), 3rd report (495).
578A	Rule Committee's sub-committee on juries, 1922: correspondence on Sargent J's views.
1031	New practice directions, 1927; report of judges, LC's comments, correspondence with Clauson J.
1732–3	Master Hulbert's proposed economies; judges' views and rules made in RSC(1) 1934.
1800, 1802, 3837	RSC(1) 1935: new rules on assignment of actions discussed by judges; see also discussions leading to RSC(2) 1950.
1871	Clauson's proposal for extension of district registries' geographical limits in mortgage actions, 1927; correspondence with Master Holland and LCJ and rule made in RSC(2), 1940.
1961–62B	Recognition of foreign register entries, 1924–32 (see *infra*, 285).
560, 3886, 3920, 4059–60	Organisation of patent business (*infra*, 230).
4457, 4459	Adoption rules, 1950: general discussion with Vaisey J, and correspondence with him, Master Holland and Home Office on interpretation of s. 3(2)(3) of 1949 Act.
5935, 6191	Law Society complaint of delays in drawing up orders, 1951; Ministry of Town and Country Planning on costs (1950).
1752, 1840, 3838, 4044, 1849, 2000	Minor procedural changes and proposals, various dates.
3406, 3670,	Wardship proceedings, (*infra*, 253).
4135	Rules under Law Reform (Miscellaneous Provisions) Act 1949 c-9. Discussions with Vaisey J and Master Holland. RSC(3) 1949.
3934, 3971–3	Evershed Committee working party 'D': correspondence and papers; interim report on fixed dates with comments.
3974	Working party 'E' (Chancery): memoranda, correspondence etc.
3829	Request for additional judge, 1947; correspondence with Vaisey J and Solicitor-General.
4/40	Chancery Chambers, staff complements.

8
THE HIGH COURT, KING'S BENCH DIVISION

The incorporation of the Exchequer and Common Pleas divisions in 1881 made the Queen's Bench by far the largest division in the High Court. Moreover, whereas the

Chancery and PDA judges were static, the judges of the QBD bore the burden of assize work and many of the problems which reformers of the division encountered stemmed from the assizes, and in particular from the differing patterns and requirements of the civil and criminal sides which had to be accommodated.

As early as the 1880s Coleridge LCJ was complaining of the difficulty in meeting the obligations to London suitors during the assizes,[1] and the mercantile community was expressing its dissatisfaction with the delays and expense of the High Court in the most effective way, by taking their disputes to alternative fora for settlement. So potent was the threat posed by the London Chamber of Arbitration[2] in particular, that the judges responded with unusual speed and flexibility in establishing the Commercial List which succeeded at least in containing the threat.[3] It was an initiative with which the Lord Chancellor seems to have had nothing to do, but it was the last significant initiative to come from within the division for some years, though the judges were alert enough in opposing extensions to county court jurisdiction, as they had earlier opposed provincial sittings. Renewed complaints of delay led to a royal commission in 1913 but the government showed no disposition to act on its more important recommendations, about assizes, and the Treasury blocked its proposal for judges' pensions.[4] One extra judge was appointed, but even that obvious expedient for meeting arrears, though it had to be resorted to again at regular intervals, was adopted only with reluctance.

The character of the division's work was undergoing significant changes which were to increase the pressure on the judges. Personal injuries claims were enormously multiplied by the growth in numbers and speed of motor vehicles; by the end of the 1920s arrears were serious, and this was the division that was the focus for most of the criticism which followed the publication of the London Chamber of Commerce's indictment of judicial proceedings in 1930.[5]

Sankey became convinced that "we have *got* to do something"[6] to meet the criticisms but was faced with the awkward circumstance that the Lord Chief Justice did not accept that there was any need for serious changes in his division, notwithstanding the fact that many of the criticisms were direct reflections on his management.[7] Hewart had already shown himself to be obstructive in smaller matters[8] and the course of the response to the reformist agitation set on foot in 1930 is only intelligible in the light of his attitude and his almost pathological dislike to Schuster ("Shyster" as Hewart called him). He was absent from the Rule Committee meeting at which one of Sankey's initiatives—the "New Procedure" rules—was discussed and again, pleading illness, from the meeting of King's Bench judges which the Chancellor summoned to discuss them. In essence the rules were a tentative approach to fixed dates which, Sankey nervously told the judges, all his correspondents wanted, and they were initially popular with litigants, but instead of being nurtured they were almost surreptitiously amended out of existence under the more conservative Hailsham because they wasted judicial time.[9]

Sankey persuaded Hewart to agree to the appointment of a Business of the Courts Committee limited to lawyers,[10] and was able to enact their recommendation restricting jury trials.[11] This was particularly aimed at the running down cases which were overwhelming the division, but even then the interpretation proposed by the masters confined trial by judge alone to 'simple' cases. Schuster wrote "If the statute is run on these lines there will be practically no relief".[12] Clearly something more than this was needed to satisfy the critics and the cabinet was persuaded to set up a royal commission solely on "the dispatch of business at common law" with a view to outflanking Hewart. So predictable was his view that "the intended enquiry is wholly unnecessary"[13] that the LCO neglected the mere courtesy of consulting him on its membership and it was that slight, almost as much as the one to Slesser that goaded him into his outburst.[14]

The Commission under Lord Peel (the first choice, Austen Chamberlain, had declined) took a good deal of evidence from the legal profession, local authorities and commerce and came up with the sort of "reform on conservative and constitutional lines"[15] that had been wanted of them, including a proposal to appoint a "business manager" for the KBD, a direct hit at the LCJ's management. But Hewart was thick skinned and Peel was told that although Hailsham intended "to make a push for it . . . he realises that he cannot force it in the face of opposition because the opponents could frustrate the whole venture by obstructing the man appointed".[16] In other words, as long as Hewart remained, it could not be done.

The immediate fruits of the Peel Commission were meagre and mostly comprised in that "ill assorted medley"[17] the Administration of Justice (Miscellaneous Provisions) Act 1938. However, the evidence accumulated by it and the Hanworth Committee was extensively used by the Evershed Committee.

Notes

1 *1/7: to Lord Selborne, 29.7.1884.*
2 *See (1893) 9 LQR 86 for a fulsome description by E. Manson.*
3 *For its origins see (1944) 60 LQR 313 (FDM) and S. Rosenbaum (1914–15) 63 Pen. Univ. LR, 417–20.*
4 *2/324.*
5 *2/1702. B. Abel-Smith & R. Stevens,* **Lawyers and the Courts** *(1967), 102–3.*
6 *2/1703: notes of meeting with judges, 3.3.1932.*
7 ***Ibid.**, at p. 3.*
8 *e.g. 2/1012: Schuster to Hailsham, 19.6.1928: "the difficulty is that whatever we propose, the CJ will refuse to help".*
9 *(1937–8) 1 MLR 311.*
10 *2/1598: Schuster to Attorney-General, 14.12.1932.*
11 *Administration of Justice (Miscellaneous Provisions) Act 1933 s. 6.*
12 *2/1759: summary of masters' conclusions; Schuster to MR, 17.10.1933.*
13 *2/1610: to Schuster, 27.11.1934.*
14 *See* ***supra**, 92.*
15 *2/1610: Schuster to MR, November 1934.*
16 *2/1616: Schuster to Lord Peel, 29.5.1936; LC's memorandum to cabinet, 22.10.1937 in 2/1618.*
17 *(1938) 2 MLR 307.*

1 Jurisdiction

2/3874, 4067 Transfer of revenue list, 1951.
107 Transfer of winding-up, 1902.

696, 1631 Transfer of bankruptcy, 1921 (see 'Chancery' *supra*, 96).

1781–2 Transfer of mortgage actions, 1934 (*infra*, 238).

1266, 1635, 1661, 1793, 1795 Administration of Justice (Appeals) Act 1934; transfer of county court appeals (see 'Court of Appeal' *supra*).

2 Organisation and Procedure

1/7 LCJ complains of lack of available judges in London, 1884.

2/9 Committee on equalizing costs, 1888.

2/126 Commercial list rules discussed by Rule Committee, 1896.

269 Bill for appointment of an extra judge: memorandum by LCJ, correspondence with Treasury and PCO, 1910.

324 Correspondence with Treasury on Royal Commission report; memoranda by Chancery masters, F. A. Stringer, Pickford J, and KBD judges' committee.

489–506 Tomlin Committee papers (see *supra*, 54).

520, 556, 603 Arrears: discussions of 1919–21 with LCJ and President of the PD and A, cabinet papers, discussion in Council of Judges.

442 Administration of Justice Bill, 1920: correspondence with Treasury, PCO; comments by judges and LCJ, cabinet and Parliamentary papers.

570, 575 Correspondence with LCJ on Saturday sittings; complaints by solicitors' and solicitors' clerks organisations, 1921.

602 Council of Judges discusses jury trials, 1920.

605, 798, 810 Correspondence with LCJ and cabinet papers on need for extra judges, 1923–4. Administration of Justice Bill, 1928: instructions to PCO, memorandum by Schuster.

1012 Memorandum by Schuster on judgment debtors' examinations and attitude of the LCJ generally, and correspondence with Master Bonner and others, 1927–9.

1596–7, 1703–6, 1791 Schuster's "review of the present system" and comments by Atkin, Tomlin, MacMillan *et al.* 1931 Rule Committee papers leading to "New Procedure" rules 1932, including minutes of meetings, views of LCJ, Avory J, Roche J and outside bodies. Minutes of meeting of KBD judges, March 1932, observations by several judges and Law Society. Brief for Attorney-General on jury trials and Parliamentary questions. Amendments by Master Bonner, Swift, MacNaghten JJ; rule committee papers on appointment of New Procedure judges, 1934.

1738 Payments into court in defamation cases (see *infra*, 245).

1598–1618, 1675 Business of the Courts Committee and Administration of Justice Act 1934 papers. Peel Commission papers, including preliminary papers on terms of reference and membership, memoranda, minutes, evidence, report and comments. Discussions on implementation.

1813–4 Rules to effect Peel Commission recommendations: correspondence with PCO, LCJ, masters and commission members; RSC(3) 1937.

1677 Cabinet papers on state of business in KBD and need for more judges, 1934 and 1938; memoranda by Schuster.

1628, 1632 Correspondence with LCJ, and PQs on arrears and availability of judges, 1937–9.

2831 LCJ warns of shortage of judges, 1943.

3927–44, 3966–4040	Evershed Committee papers (*supra*, 55–6).
3887, 3889, 4605	Discussions with LCJ on need for more judges, 1949–50; cabinet papers, correspondence with PCO and Treasury on High Court and County Court Judges Bill.
1804, 2858 3840, 3906, 3921, 4063, 4091, 4107	Various points of practice.

9
THE HIGH COURT, PROBATE, DIVORCE AND ADMIRALTY DIVISION

1 General

"Generally I think organisation and procedure want constant watching and examination. They can never be perfect, and if left alone for long they tend to lose flexibility and to crystallise and become incapable of adapting themselves to changing conditions".[1] Lord Tomlin might have given as an example of this tendency the divisional structure of the High Court after 1881, and in particular the continued co-existence of Probate, Divorce and Admiralty work in a single division, which requires an historian to explain and a sophist to justify. It was almost literally a law unto itself, for until 1925 the President made his own rules[2] and the Lord Chancellor possessed only "a kind of suzerainty"[3] over the officers in the three registries of the division and the district probate registries, the President retaining the patronage and responsibility even after the Lord Chancellor's Permanent Secretary became Accountant-General to the High Court.[4]

Schuster had formed the view that the division itself should be broken up. One of his reasons was that each vacancy on the bench proved difficult to fill, so that even the post of President had sometimes to be hawked around; it is not surprising that the holders were not always of the highest calibre.[5] Schuster's ideas, which were common currency,[6] found some support among judges in other divisions and he was able to sell them to the Hanworth Committee, which proposed that probate work should go to Chancery, and the rest to the KBD, though with the nomination of particular judges in Admiralty and Divorce respectively to preserve the specialised practice in these areas.[7] Lord Merriman, the newly appointed President, accused Schuster of a breach of undertakings given to him on his appointment but it was not mainly his opposition that defeated the proposal:

"The scheme was wrecked

1 By the novelty
2 By the attacks made upon it before it had been published by Raeburn, leading the shipping community . . . Raeburn obtained his assumed knowledge of what the report was to contain from Merrivale, who, in his turn, had obtained it from a conversation between himself and the Master of the Rolls.
3 By the opposition, open and covert, of the Bar employed in probate and divorce work."[8]

That was the end of the most serious attempt to alter the structure of the division until the end of the 1960s, for the Evershed Committee, though they took up the evidence submitted to their predecessors, surprisingly decided that it was impracticable to detach the Admiralty side and combine it with the Commercial List in a new division.[9]

Notes

1 *2/1596: memorandum of 26.2.1932 at p. 8.*

2 *By the Administration of Justice Act 1925 s. 18 the President kept the power to make rules for non-contentious probate. For Lord Merrivale's tendency to issue Practice Directions see* ***supra****, 59. For an instance of the President's (Evans) reluctance to come into line with other divisions see 2/320.*

3 *2/938.*

4 *2/3630: Schuster's memorandum, 1943.*

5 ***Supra****, 83–4. 2/1008: Schuster's memorandum, 17.7.1924, in which it is said that H. E. Duke, Lord Merrivale, was only persuaded to accept the Presidency "upon an appeal to his public spirit" after he and all members of the Court of Appeal had refused it. Muir McKenzie called him "A pompous oaf" (2/747: to Schuster 8.11.1923).*

6 ***Cf.*** *Lord Phillimore in 2/460.*

7 *2nd report, PP 1933–4 (Cmd 4471) XI, 1, paras. 18–24.*

8 *2/1628: Schuster's memorandum, headed "Fusion", 18.11.1937.*

9 *2/3997–9, and Final Report, PP 1952–3 (Cmd 8878) para. 895.*

2/460	Lord Phillimore's memorandum on the future of the division, 1920.
320, 1929	President objects to imposition of poor persons rules. Schuster on use of practice directions, 1939.
726	Administration of Justice Bill, 1922: correspondence with PCO includes opinions on state of the division.
1008	1922–5: agitation for extra judge from shipping interest and President; cabinet papers and Schuster memoranda on future of the division and selection of judges; PQs and correspondence with Sir L. Scott.
747	Judicature Consolidation (PDA) Bill, 1923: correspondence with Lord Muir McKenzie.
1596–7	Memoranda by Schuster and judges on possible reforms in structure, 1931.
1598–1605	Hanworth Committee papers, especially 1602.
1610–14	Peel Commission papers (*supra*, 100).
1628	SCJ Amendment Bill, 1937.
3828, 3875–6, 4175	Schuster suggests amalgamation with KBD (Wedgwood Committee papers), 1943 Discussions on successor to Langton J.
3997–9	Evershed Committee: working party 'Q' on future of the PDA: minutes, evidence, correspondence.

2 Probate

Probate proceedings in the division were non-contentious, that is to say administrative rather than judicial, and were conducted either in the principal probate registry in Somerset

House or in district registries. As the number of wills rose towards the end of the nineteenth century, arrears in London mounted and temporary staff had to be grudgingly sanctioned by the Treasury.[1] This was necessary because the office still worked short hours and was generally inefficient, as was revealed by the report of a committee set up by the Lord Chancellor in 1893.[2] The situation uncovered by the Civil Service Commission in 1914 was little changed, and the Tomlin committee charged with implementing its recommendations found it "a tremendous job"[3] and deferred consideration for a remodelled committee which sat separately on the probate registries.[4] Schuster was sceptical "that the Reports should be brought into effectual operation unless the President will provide himself with some efficient person who has some knowledge of business organisation and government methods, and he appears unwilling to adopt this course".[5] The district probate registrars were found to be "overpaid and underworked, and . . . the clerks are grossly underpaid and in many cases overworked"[6] while the distribution of registries was no longer convenient. The most obvious defects were removed by legislation in the 1920s,[7] but the unfavourable impression of the probate establishment was confirmed by a scandal at Lancaster and a fraud in the principal registry,[8] to which the response of the President and his senior staff was felt by Hailsham to be lacking in vigour.[9]

Indeed the conservatism of the officials and their indifference to the public interest are clearly shown in the history of a quite minor reform embodied in the Non-Contentious Probate Fees Order 1933, which "needed very strenuous efforts and a great deal of patience".[10] The efforts in fact extended over six years before the "troublesome, dilatory and expensive"[11] method of registering probate by sending the original grant successively to each company or institution holding the deceased's assets could be improved. The solicitors were opposed because the costs of circulating the grant were "the real piece of fat"[12] in the business, the biggest companies were reluctant to accept mere certificates instead of a sealed grant and Hailsham himself was ultra cautious, but even when these obstacles had been overcome—two years after the original proposal from the Association of British Chambers of Commerce—it took a further three years (including two and a half months when the Senior Registrar put his own letter to Napier into a drawer and forgot it) before the PPR was finally forced into the modern world. Meanwhile "at the beginning of the slump some estates had fallen in value by 50% while the probate was on its leisurely rounds".[13]

Perhaps it was not entirely undeserved that the principal probate registry should be exiled to Llandudno for most of the war, though the public suffered more than the officials. Even the disposal of the old probate records was not accomplished without difficulty and a rather silly but acerbic dispute between the Master of the Rolls (as Keeper of the Public Records) and the President, whom he described as "suffering from some kind of persecution mania",[14] on the question of ultimate responsibility.

Notes

1 *1/76.*
2 *2/26.*
3 *2/489: Schuster to E. W. H. Millar (Treasury), 1.4.1919.*

4 *2/501–5.*
5 *2/938: Schuster's memorandum, p. 8.*
6 ***Ibid.**, at p. 19.*
7 *Administration of Justice Acts, 1925, 1928.*
8 *2/989–90.*
9 *See Pereira Committee report in 2/994. Merrivale's response to the criticism was to complain that Schuster had breached protocol in writing direct to C. T. A. Wilkinson in the Principal Probate Registry.*
10 *2/1736: Napier to Sankey, 13.6.1933.*
11 *2/1735: Public Trustee to Schuster, 14.2.1927.*
12 ***Ibid.***
13 *2/1736: Napier to Cunliffe (editor of 'The Solicitors Journal'), 11.12.1933.*
14 *2/5792: Evershed to Coldstream, 3.8.1953.*

1 The Principal Probate Registry

1/76 Various papers, 1881–8, including list of staff (1882); Treasury proposals for reductions, observations by Sir James Hannen P, Senior Registrar, Official Solicitor and clerks; correspondence with Treasury on arrears and temporary staff, 1886–8, reports.

2/26 Report of Lord Chancellor's committee, 1893; comments by Sir F. Jeune P and Senior Registrar, and discussions with Treasury on proposals.

489, 501–3 Tomlin Report, 1922: minutes, papers (including observations by staff) reports.

4/234 Staff complement, 1920–46.

2/994 Correspondence with Registrar and Treasury on inquiry into stamp frauds; report and Schuster's memorandum; correspondence with DPP, 1927–8.

725 President concerned about his "illegal" assistant registrar, 1924.

1010 Memoranda by Treasury and Schuster and correspondence with Audit Office on gratuities in PPR, 1926.

2788, 3743, 3891 Evacuation to Llandudno, 1940–6. Orders in Council and correspondence with President, Senior Registrar, Ministry of Works and Treasury on its return. Complaints from solicitors on inconvenience and opening times.

2 District Probate Registries

1/69 Miscellaneous correspondence over appointments to Manchester DPR, 1884–8.

2/646 Tomlin Report and correspondence with Treasury and President. See Schuster's summary in 938.

737–8, 740–6 Boundary changes, 1925. Correspondence with registrars, law societies etc.

991, 798 Correspondence with Treasury, Senior Registrar, PCO and Law Society on Supreme Court (DPRs) Bill, 1927. Cabinet papers and Parliamentary proceedings on Administration of Justice Bill, 1928.

992 PQs and correspondence with MPs and Treasury on clerks' pension rights, 1925.

989–90, 995 Correspondence with President and Treasury on removal of the Lancaster registrar, 1924. Inderwick Committee report on accounting arrangements, 1925.

1552, 5790 Correspondence with PCO on proposed alteration in districts, 1938. Further changes in 1940 (Canterbury), 1951 (York).

3 Rules

2/175, 1036, 1870, 2587, 2719, 2807, 3860–1, 3904, 4044, 4074 4141–2 Non-contentious probate rules, 1902–51.

4 Fees

2/85, 811, 1011, 2587, 1636–7, 1640, 1642, 1735–7, 3852–3, 3856, 3861, 3898, 6002 Fees orders, 1892–1947: correspondence with PPR. Note especially 3852, 6002 (1947), containing discussions with the Treasury on policy and with Law Society on effect on solicitors' costs.

1643 1941 Order, following discussions with PPR and other registries on remission of fees for documents destroyed by enemy action.

1014–7 Correspondence with Law Society, Treasury and IRC on use of adhesive stamps, leading to MacNaghten Committee (1928). Minutes, correspondence and report; correspondence with officials on implementation in SC Fees Order 1930 (1017).

5 Practice and records

2/1735–7, 1769, 3154 Registration of probates and use of office copies; memorandum from Association of British Chambers of Commerce (1927), correspondence with PPR, Public Trustee and Law Society. Negotiations with PPR, Inland Revenue and President leading to Fees Order, 1933 (for summary see Napier's memorandum in 3154). Correspondence on application to DPRs and (1769) on validation of Scottish Certificates of Confirmation in England.

1160 Dispute with Chancery division over adoption records, 1926.

1242 Inderwick encourages trust corporations, 1933.

1712–3 Defective grants: discussions with PCO, PPR on inclusion of a provision in Administration of Justice Bill, 1932.

2789 Proposal to amend s. 11 Administration of Justice Act 1928 (1942).

3747, 4046 Effect of death duty changes on probate fees; departmental discussions, clauses in local bills, 1946. Also re waiver of need for probate on war gratuities, 1945.

3896 Discussions with President and LCJ on interpretation of Execution of Trusts Act 1943. Non-Contentious Probate Rules, 1943.

2790, 3164, 3747, 4046 Proposals of various dates to exempt small estates from formalities.

3904 Correspondence with PPR and President on problems of evidence of death in wartime, and Law Officers' opinion and Public Trustee memorandum, 1943.

736, 4049	Correspondence with President and Law Society on problems in re-sealing grants, 1925, and problems with Northern Ireland, 1945.
4047	Evershed Committee's working party 'T': Master Willmott's proposals for administration of intestate estates.
993	Pereira Committee on custody of records, 1926, copy report only.
3744–61, 3749, 3751–, 3, 5791, 5851	Removal of DPR records to repositories, various dates 1946–51.
5792	Departmental committee on ancient records: discussions with President and MR, and report of 1953.
732, 739, 808–9, 1812, 2789, 3578, 3590, 3598, 3748, 4047, 4071, 4129, 6198	Other points of practice.

3 Divorce

The battle to keep divorce jurisdiction exclusively within the High Court in London despite recurrent waves of pressure from outside the judiciary was fought so effectively by the Presidents and puisnes of the division, the divorce bar and their other allies (principally the Church of England) that it lasted well beyond the period covered here, but these files provide a splendid insight into the interplay of the three branches of government, especially in the years immediately after World War II.

The story of divorce administration over this period is of a series of small concessions grudgingly yielded to prevent greater evils, especially the ultimate threat of devolution to the county courts. Substantive law and jurisdiction and procedural questions were intimately bound up together throughout: thus the Gorell Commission was appointed to consider both the grounds for divorce and the means of obtaining it, and the opposition of the Church generally extended to any material widening of either. The more technical and arcane divorce law was, the more plausible was the argument which the divorce bar and the PDA judges regularly advanced, that it needed the specialist attention and consistent practice that only a high degree of concentration could give it. The fragility of the argument was often exposed but it was never abandoned.[1]

Some form of decentralisation became unavoidable at the end of the Great War, when Lord Buckmaster's bills for widening the grounds of divorce and giving the county courts jurisdiction were seen to have such a head of public and Parliamentary support that the government's hand was forced.[2] The President and the Lord Chief Justice were both unenthusiastic about the hearing of divorce on assize, but it met the great anxiety of the Bar over rights of audience and the limitations of the Act (Administration of Justice Act 1920) to certain types of case (poor persons and undefendeds), to certain towns (only ten initially) and to the trial only (interlocutory business stayed in London) were sufficient to persuade them. Indeed, the concession succeeded in fending off any further changes for almost a decade, and then the changes recommended by the Schuster Committee amounted only to an addition to the assize towns where divorce could be heard and a limited degree of devolution in interlocutory matters.[3]

At the end of the 1930s, however, the situation deteriorated so badly that the Law Society was able to persuade the LCO to press for an extension of jurisdiction to all assize towns, to defended divorces and to all district registries. The President of the PD & A was proof against this, even when urged by a Law Society deputation and by the Lord Chancellor himself, and offered only a piecemeal extension of district registry jurisdiction; but by early 1939 he had become convinced that "the only real solution is for this division to become responsible for the trial of divorce in this country on lines independent of the existing circuit system . . . I should regard the trial of all classes of case in the country and a corresponding extension of jurisdiction to District Registrars, subject to the overriding control of the PPR as an integral part of such a scheme".[4] Faced with the possibility of a breakdown in the poor persons' scheme on the one hand,[5] and a President unwilling to take effective steps on the other, the LCO attempted to undermine his resistance by the usual device of a committee set up in May 1939[6] under one of his puisnes, Hodson J.

The war put an end to the Hodson Committee's deliberations but it had to be reconstituted in 1942 under Lord Wedgwood because of the volume of servicemen's cases pressing on a depleted number of divorce solicitors in the provinces. As Schuster's papers suggest, the option of the county courts was never seriously considered by a committee which was clearly set up only to streamline the existing arrangements. Merriman was placated by the recommendation that divorce judges should go on circuit and by restricting the "divorce" registries to those considered sufficiently responsible, but all classes of divorce might now be heard on assize. It was essentially a holding operation, and disappointed those like the Attorney-General who had more ambitious ideas.[7]

These people included the new Lord Chancellor and most of those who formed the Labour government in 1945. Divorce and legal aid were to be the legal reforms to which Jowitt wished the cabinet's law reform committee, set up in October 1945, to give priority.[8] They had already thrown out the feeble bill which was all that Simon had been able to persuade Merriman to, which would have enabled registrars appointed from the PPR to sit as "Commissioners" (Sir Granville Ram's term).[9] Merriman lost no time in informing Jowitt of the judges' opposition to county court divorce and other reforms, and now came up with a scheme for fostering reconciliation which was supported by the Archbishop of Canterbury and initially welcomed by Jowitt as "a really great idea"; others were less impressed and Jowitt had to withdraw his support.[10] In April, 1946 he decided on yet another committee, the problem being made urgent by Parliamentary pressures, and although laymen (including four women) were included, it was the chairman, Denning J (a recent appointment to the Bench when the first choice Lynskey refused the vacancy in the PD & A) who dominated the proceedings.[11] He got three reports issued with commendable speed: the first proposed to reduce the period of the decree nisi, as had already been agreed by the cabinet committee, and that was comparatively uncontroversial. The second, however, (October, 1946), proposed a large number of procedural reforms and the appointment as divorce commissioners of county court judges. Merriman was outraged, and not without reason for it was admitted by Jowitt that Denning had behaved discourteously to him in almost dismissively rejecting his own cherished scheme. The President had worked himself to the verge of a nervous breakdown trying to prove that the existing structure could cope; now he accused Denning of "selling the fort" and the latter had to be excused from going with him on assize.[12] Merriman railed against the Denning Committee's "amateurish blunders",[13] grumblingly accepted only twelve of its forty procedural reforms, and announced his intention to oppose publicly the proposal about county court judges.[14]

A memorandum by Coldstream's neatly sets out the difficulties which Merriman's stance posed:

> "normally speaking, neither the rule committee nor the LC would (I suggest) think of making a matrimonial causes rule against the wish of the President . . . I do not know what weight to give to the Denning Committee's recommendations on the one hand and the President's assertions on the other. Nor do I know to whom the Lord Chancellor can go for independent advice. The lesson to be learned is that no such enquiry ought to be allowed to be started unless we are quite sure that it is one which is likely to have the approval of the head of the division concerned".[15]

The immediate problem was the debates in Parliament on the recommendation for commissioners, to which the government was publicly committed, and to avoid the embarrassment of an open row, solicitors' interests were sacrificed and the Bar's exclusive audience in divorce maintained despite the additional cost to the parties and the state; this enabled Merriman to claim that the check which the Bar and High Court bench imposed on collusion between spouses would be maintained; in his view solicitors, not alive to the "very high standard of honour in this matter which is habitually observed by the Bar",[16] might prefer the interests of their clients to upholding the solemn farce by which Merriman set such store.

The procedural proposals were referred in secret to a small departmental committee under Hodson J which reported in February, 1947.[17] It rejected many of the most important proposals and the difference in approach can be summed up by Hodson's own comment on one proposal to save fourteen days where a respondent had appeared and said he did not intend to defend: "I see no reason why he should not have a locus poenitentiae or what the particular need of haste is supposed to be in this class of litigation. One cannot normally obtain a judgment until the time for appearance has expired".[18] The existence of the Hodson Committee leaked out and when it was seen that the new rules enacted only about half the Denning recommendations, Terence Donovan (one of the Denning Committee) moved the Commons to annul them for failing to give effect to the report.[19] The Attorney-General made a spirited defence but promised that these rules were only "something on account". Everyone knew where the problem lay, so much so that one MP openly threatened a motion for the President's removal.[20] He in the meantime had been forced by his doctors to take a rest.

When Parliament returned in the autumn of 1947 demands for the balance of the Denning proposals and for the court welfare service proposed in its final report (March, 1947) were certain and the LCO attempted to use Hodson J to persuade the President to give further ground. Hodson, however, had a new argument to oppose to the changes, that since uniformity was desirable in the High Court, many of them should await the Evershed Committee's findings on e.g. evidence, documents. This was gratefully accepted by the Lord Chancellor and although a few minor changes were made administratively, on the whole the PDA succeeded in holding the line, much to the disgust of the Attorney-General, who wrote "the administration of divorce in this country has become something of a racket''.[21] The subsequent Morton Commission on divorce refused the LCJ's suggestion to consider procedure as well as law and all that was done was to enlarge progressively the number of district registries having jurisdiction, usually overruling Merriman's view that it was unnecessary. As in the case of Hewart's opposition to the KBD reforms, the strength of the divisional structure and the curiously ill-defined position of the heads vis-à-vis the Lord Chancellor produced a situation with potentially far reaching implications, and which deserves fuller study.

Notes

1 *For a general account see O. R. McGregor,* ***Divorce in England*** *(1957), and see* ***infra****, 425–8.*
2 *2/556.*
3 *2/1055–7, 2066; PP 1929–30 (Cmd 3375) XVII, 265.*
4 *2/1837: to Schuster, 13.3.1939.*
5 ***Infra****, 188.*
6 *2/1837: Schuster to Merriman, 8.5.1939.*
7 *2/3876, 4171–7.*
8 *2/3927: Jowitt to Attlee, 15.10.1945.*
9 *2/4197: 34th cabinet conclusions, 20.9.1945.*
10 *2/3928: RLP Committee meeting, 3.4.1946.*
11 *Denning's verdict is ''no committee has ever worked so quickly or so well''. (****The Due Process of Law****, (1980) 191).*
12 *2/3951: Coldstream's note of a ''somewhat painful'' meeting with Merriman, 24.10.1946.* ***Cf.*** *Denning's own account,* ***supra*** *n. 11.*
13 *2/3957: to Napier, 6.11.1946, and Skyrme's note of 18.11.1946.*
14 ***Ibid.***
15 ***Ibid.***
16 ***Parl. Debs.*** *(H of L) 1946–7, vol. 144 cols. 475–82.*
17 *2/3957.*
18 *2/3964: ''Outstanding Points of Difference between the Committee and the Judges'', p. 3.*
19 *2/3958:* ***Parl. Debs.*** *(H of C) 1946–7, vol. 437 col. 363.*
20 *2/3964: Coldstream's note, 9.2.1948.*
21 *2/5481: to Jowitt, 5.1.1951.*

1 *Jurisdiction and organisation*

1/76 Jessel MR's proposal on appeals accepted by Sir J. Hannen P, 1881.

2/556 Proposal for divorce at assizes, 1919: correspondence with President, cabinet memorandum by LC and discussions with judges and LCJ; renewed proposals 1920, 1921.

2/77 SC Rules (Trial of Matrimonial Causes at Assizes) 1922: Representations from MPs and Law Society; drafting correspondence with President, registrars and Chitty. Protests from Bristol at exclusion.

2/644, 32/1–5 Lawrence Committee (*infra*, 190), including Law Society proposals for wider divorce facilities.

2/878–9, 1050, 2595 Correspondence with district registrars on 1925 circular re their duties in divorce petitions, and with A. O. Jennings, the President, and PP Registry. Manchester DR clerk appointed Commissioner for Oaths, 1928.

1055–7 Schuster Committee papers (*infra*, 190), including proposals from Law Societies and individuals and report (1929).

1066 Poor Persons' Rules (Matrimonial Causes) 1929; meeting of Rule Committee, correspondence with district registrars and with PPR on drafting and implementation.

1836–7 Correspondence leading to the Hodson Committee 1939, including LCO and Law Society proposals for extending jurisdiction and responses of President and PPR. Matrimonial Causes Rules 1937; further representations from Law Society and others and discussions on legal aid situation; correspondence on setting up committee.

1665 Judges Council 1938; views of LC, MR, President and others on divorce hearings on circuit.

4171–7, 3876 Wedgwood Committee papers, including membership and terms (4171) minutes (4174) evidence (4175) and recommendations (4176). Proposals discussed with Treasury and cabinet; correspondence with PCO on drafting SCJ (Amendment) Bill 1944, and Parliamentary proceedings; note from Law Society on costs of divorce.

3892 Correspondence on long vacation 1942 and use of KBD judges to assist PDA: views of MR, LCJ, President.

4179–80, 4209 Discussions with LCJ, judges and under sheriffs on facilities. Matrimonial Causes at Assizes Order, 1944.

4178, 4181, 4192 Applications for divorce jurisdiction in various district registries (1944–50); correspondence with President and orders of 1946, 1949, 1950, 1951.

4197 Matrimonial Causes (Divorce Commissioners) Bill 1945: correspondence with President, meeting with Attorney-General; cabinet papers; representations by Archbishop of Canterbury and Henn-Collins J, drafting correspondence with PCO and further cabinet discussions.

3831, 3879, 4198 Statistics on divorce cases and interventions by the King's Procter 1944–5; correspondence with President on divorce problems, 1947–50.

3927–8 Cabinet committee on legal reform (1945), including President's report on various proposals, cabinet committee's interim reports on divorce and service cases. Proposals by the President discussed, opposed by Attorney-General, Treasury Solicitor. Memoranda from Archbishop of Canterbury, Haldane Society and Parliamentary Labour Party. Briefs for PQs (1946).

2856, 4203 Treasury O & M report on the Divorce Registry 1946. E. F. Iwi's complaint re congestion, 1945.

4462–3 Assizes (Matrimonial Causes) Order 1946: discussions with LCJ and President, especially on whether to confine commissioners to service cases; discussions with officials on arrangements; list of special commissioners.

3946–64 Denning Committee: including notes on membership (3946) minutes (3947) evidence (3948); 1st interim report (3949) 2nd (3950), correspondence and meetings with the President and LCJ on 2nd report. Cabinet and Parliamentary papers (3951), replies to circular to county court judges, draft scheme, correspondence with registrars, professional bodies etc. on organisation of scheme to the end of 1950 (3952–6, 3961). Matrimonial Causes Rules 1947: correspondence with the President, PPR, registrars; Hodson Committee report on 2nd Denning report; drafting correspondence (3957), correspondence with T. Donovan MP on his prayer for annulment, and Parliamentary proceedings (3958). Denning's critique of Hodson report, and further negotiations for rule changes (3959). Amendment Rules 1947: correspondence with MR and Hodson and memoranda from PPR on decree absolute and other points (3960). Final Denning report, with comments from President, Registrar-General, Senior Registrar; cabinet papers, correspondence with Home Office on welfare proposals and meeting with welfare organisations (3962–3). Briefs for PQs, memoranda for Rule Committee meeting and Amendment Rules 1948 (3964).

4200 Matrimonial Causes (Amendment) Rules 1946, including material on the prayer for annulment (*cf.* 3958).

4201 MC (Amendment) (no. 2) Rules 1946; drafts by Denning and Norbury (PPR); complaint by Law Society of unavailability of rules.

4202 Matrimonial Causes (Decree Absolute) Order 1946: *cf.* 3960.

4081 Matrimonial Causes (Amendment) Rules 1947: memorandum on Rule Committee.

4212, 6161–2 Extensions to venues for divorce assizes and district registries with divorce jurisdiction; various applications and orders; correspondence with President and County Courts branch approvals (1948–52).

6159 *Ambler* v *Ambler* (1951): correspondence with the President and PPR on implications for special commissioners.

5481 Attorney-General's complaint on divorce costs, 1951; LCO memoranda on possible transfer to county courts.

6163 Morton Commission rejects LCJ's invitation to discuss divorce trials, 1951.

3965, 4642–3 Denning Committee final report, welfare and conciliation proposals: file on privilege question, raised by Bishop of Norwich and others, with discussions of case law etc. Discussions with Home Office on use of probation officers by divorce courts with their reports on the scheme; discussions with the President, briefs for PQs etc, to 1953.

2 *Evidence*

2/801 Proposal from Bournemouth Law Society referred to PCO, Attorney-General and President, 1927.

4204 Complaint re hoteliers and evidence, 1946.

4210 Query on differences between English and Scottish practice, 1948.

4221 Complaint from justices' clerks about wasteful practices, 1950.

3 *Financial provision*

2/1619, 1842 Proposal to increase courts' powers, see Matrimonial Causes Rules 1937.

1725, 4207 Problem of enforcing orders discussed; use of bankruptcy 1725 (1929); judgment orders 4207 (1947).

1813, 3651, 3675, 3914, 4211 Various minor aspects.

3046, 6160 Impact of taxation discussed.

3918, 3925, 4165 Enforcement of Scottish orders; extensive papers of 1944, 1950 (3918) following *McNaghten* v *McNaghten*, including correspondence with Treasury Solicitor and Law Officers, memorandum by Master Ball, report of a departmental committee, draft bills, meetings with Home Office and Scottish departments. Revived, and cabinet papers 1948–9. Also on attaching salary of a Scottish MP (3925).

4485 Married Women (Maintenance) Bill 1949: Home Office and President at variance on appeals forum.

4222–4, 4227 Rules made under Maintenance Orders Act 1950.

4 Service cases

2/2847–9, 2850–52 (delays), 3415, 3416–7 (G.I. Brides), 3908 (wife's allowance and separation proceedings), 4098.

5 Matrimonial Causes Rules

2/577 Trial at assizes rules, 1932.

1066–9 Rules 1929 (Poor Persons) and Amendment Rules 1931.

1724 Taxation Rules, 1932.

1929 Rules (3) 1932.

1786 Law Society proposals, 1934.

1794 Amendment Rules 1934.

1824 Amendment Rules 1936.

1842–3 Matrimonial Causes at Assizes Order 1937.

4180 *Ibid.* 1944.

3853 Fees Amendment Order 1947.

4183–4, 4209 Amendment (1 and 2) Rules 1947.

4182, 4195 Rules 1944 (Consolidation) and (Amendment) Rules 1944.

4191 Discussions with Law Officers, Treasury Solicitor on effects of *Cohen* v *Cohen* and other cases.

4201 Law Society complains re Rules (Amendment) (2) 1946.

4206 Rules(3) 1946.

4217, 4220, 4223 (Amendment) Rules 1950, including Rule Committee discussion on notification of decrees, notes of meetings, proposals and correspondence on drafting.

6158 (Amendment) Rules 1951.

3835 Complaint about late publication of lists, 1950.

4 Admiralty

The Admiralty section, succeeding the old High Court of Admiralty, was self-contained and esoteric to a degree.[1] Its clients were a politically powerful lobby, strong enough to press the cabinet to give them another judge in 1925 to relieve congestion in the court, and to defeat the Hanworth proposals to amalgamate it with the Commercial List. After that episode the LCO was content to let it go its own way.

Notes

1 *See F. L. Wiswall,* ***The Development of Admiralty Jurisdiction and Practice since 1880*** *(1970).*

1 Jurisdiction and organisation

1/7, 14 Correspondence with Butt J on request to send an Admiralty judge to Lancashire, 1884 and on liability to go on circuit.

1/87 Re-organisation of Wreck Commission.

2/150 Correspondence with President and Registrar (1906) on rules under Mailships Act 1891.

503–5 Tomlin Committee reports, minutes of evidence and memoranda, including analysis of proceedings 1900–21 by Hill J.

4/25 Staff complement, 1924–53.

2/733 Administration of Justice Bill 1925: deputy for Admiralty Registrar.

1598–1602, 1607 Hanworth Committee papers, including 2nd report (1602) and protests from Admiralty Bar, President and the shipping interest, and (1607) 3rd report and papers of Ships Papers sub-committee.

6694 Ownership of the Admiralty Silver Oar of the Cinque Ports discussed, 1951.

2 Rules, fees and funds

2/333–4 Trinity House masters' fees, 1913–14.

278 Fees order 1915, correspondence with Treasury.

1023, 1700 Funds Rules 1928: reorganisation of Admiralty Marshal's accounts after irregularities; correspondence with Audit Office and Registrar, and drafting correspondence. Fees Rules 1934.

1283 Registrar replies to queries on county court rules, 1935.

1682 Minor rule changes in RSC(1) 1932.

3248 Law Society question fees in bail applications, 1944.

3945 Correspondence leading to rules of 1953.

4/21 Deposit account under Supreme Court prize rules, Great War.

3 Prize courts

2/60 Discussions with Admiralty, PCO on proposed new commission, 1898.

146 Naval Prize Bill: extensive papers including drafts, cabinet papers, draft rules and correspondence with Admiralty and Registrar. For the history of the bill see Holland to Lord Chancellor, 2.2.1906.

1375 Discussions with Admiralty on a new Prize Commission, 1933–8.

1157 Disagreement between Registry and Ministry of Shipping over procedure.

4/17 Advertisement of Prize Writs, question on accounting, 1942–3.

2/3844 Complaints of delays in collecting fees, 1944.

3036, 3912 Prize Salvage Bill: correspondence with President, Registrar, PCO, Foreign Office *et al.* on the bill to prevent recaptured allied ships being claimed as prizes. Rules (1944): draft by Registrar, criticism by TSO.

10
THE ASSIZES

The circuit system and the future of the assizes was the subject which dominated the annual judges' meetings for twenty years after the Judicature Acts and figured largely in the wider public controversy on the administration of justice, and it was one on which no satisfactory agreement could be reached. To combine the demands of criminal justice, which necessitated regular gaol deliveries in all counties, with those of civil justice, where the business which did not go to London was increasingly concentrated in a few large provincial towns (some of which, like Sheffield, were not even assize towns), proved impossible, while any complete separation of the two functions was too determinedly opposed by vested interests, including the judges themselves, to gain support.[1] What therefore transpired was twenty years of schemes and projects put forward by the Judicature Commissioners,[2] the Home Secretary, the Lord Chancellor and the judges, which rang the changes on the number, dates and duration of assizes, the number of judges on circuit and the structure of the circuits. The judges emphatically denounced the Home Secretary's proposed fourth assize and the grouping of counties[3] but their own efforts to produce an agreed scheme were notably unsuccessful. The strong pressure from Manchester and Liverpool for continuous sittings, which eventually took the threatening shape of a Provincial Sittings Bill, did encourage them to greater efforts, and in December, 1886 they set up a committee to draw up a scheme which would extend grouping for civil cases (removing the civil assize from thirty-five towns) but end it in criminal ones and would revert to three assizes a year. At a contentious meeting in April, 1887 the committee's scheme was carried by 17 to 5 but with Grantham J denouncing it as "unconstitutional, ill-conceived and most injurious to the interests of those most concerned—suitors, jurymen, bar and public at large",[4] it was hardly an agreed measure. More serious was that the Lord Chief Justice was also in the minority, and he described the scheme as "altogether revolutionary".[5]

The Lord Chancellor was obliged to reply that "the fact that a judge holding the position of the Lord Chief Justice of England entertains such grave objections to the scheme recommended by the committee, though adopted by a majority of the judges, is quite enough to prevent it being finally adopted without much fuller debate than the subject has yet received".[6] In fact, without the concurrence of the LCJ any scheme which involved removing certain towns from the assize was unlikely to be practical politics. In June, 1888 the judges agreed that "grouping of civil business is the only answer but is at present impracticable".[7] Changes in personnel among the judges, and the continuing decline in civil business on circuit made them willing to propose bolder schemes for reducing the assize towns in the 1890s,[8] but the contradictory needs of criminal justice precluded any reforms.

Pressure from the provinces extended to demands for an Admiralty judge to try cases in Liverpool, which led to an unseemly dispute with Butt J over the liability of PD & A judges to go on circuit, in which he insisted on the division being "judges in our own cause" and called the Lord Chancellor's bluff when threatened with legislation to impose the obligation.[9] After 1884, in fact only QBD judges went on circuit and that strengthened the hand of the LCJ in opposing any suggested reforms. It was Alverstone LCJ who initiated the only worthwhile change before the Great War, instilling some element of 'elasticity' by allowing a judge to omit a visit when it would be completely pointless.[10] The Gorell Committee recommended grouping for civil cases but the cabinet was not prepared to risk the inevitable opposition[11] and that decision set the tone for the inter-war period. Though the Administration of Justice Act 1925 carried out the Swift Committee's recommendation that the Lord Chief Justice might re-organise a judge's circuit before the assize, even that was opposed both by local interests and by some judges, probably those who, "really do like . . . their progress through the little towns" with all the pomp and circumstance that could be mustered.[12] With the added complications of divorce on assize, Hewart's unco-operativeness and the fact that civil business picked up again between the wars and so diminished the sense of futility which some judges had experienced on their travels, ambitious proposals like those of Lord Wright[13] had no chance and even the modest proposals made successively by the Hanworth Committee, the Peel Commission and the Finlay Committee (its specially set up off-shoot), which amounted to little more than removing the least popular assize towns, amalgamating the Welsh circuits and making Sheffield an assize town, were not enacted.[14] The Evershed Committee, in its turn, considered the assizes, but chiefly on the possibility of fixed dates for hearings, since any radical changes would bring into question rights of audience and other issues of professional organisation which were excluded from its remit.[15] So the assizes remained inviolate, encumbered by divorces, and staggering under an increase of criminal business which relegated civil causes to hasty dispatch at the end of a judge's stay or to lengthy postponements.

A similar failure is not surprisingly to be found in the history of the circuit officers who serviced the assizes. The clerks of assize and their subordinates ought to have been integrated into the central office organisation in the 1870s but considerations of public finance (they were not pensionable full-time officers) and the sensitive issue of patronage combined to prevent it.[16] As a result the Associates Department in the RCJ had clerks idling away their time while the judges were on circuit, while the judges, in a complicated scheme of their own devising, continued to share the appointments of clerk of assize.[17] The MacDonnell Commission noted with disfavour the consequence, that five out of eight clerks were the sons of judges,[18] and their suitability was often questionable.[19] Nevertheless, since nothing could be done through Hewart, it was not until 1944 that action was taken and a committee under the more reasonable Lord Caldecote made the inevitable recommendation that these officers should become full-time and be controlled and managed from the RCJ; patronage should be transferred to the LCJ in the case of clerks of assize and to the Lord Chancellor in the case of their clerical staff.[20] The papers of this committee and on the SCJ (Circuit Officers) Bill 1946 reveal the usual discussions on qualifications and remuneration, and material on the idiosyncrasies of the elderly clerk at Lancaster reveals quite plainly how overdue the reform was.[21]

Notes

1 *B. Abel-Smith and R. Stevens,* ***Lawyers and the Courts*** *(1967) 84–6, 211–12.*

2 *1st report, PP 1868–9 XXV, 1.*

3 *PP 1878 (311) LXIII, 1.*

4 *1/9: to Lord Chancellor, June 1887.*

5 ***Ibid.*** *to Lord Chancellor, 21.6.1887.*

6 *1/9: 28.6.1887. The correspondence was published at Coleridge's insistence.*

7 *1/54: resolutions of meeting of 30.6.1888 on the committee's revised report of 14.12.1887.*

8 *See (1894) 10 LQR 10.*

9 *1/14. Butt's absence from the Admiralty court had occasioned criticism ((1884) 77 LT 21). Chancery judges had occasionally been sent but proved unsuitable, see A. G. C. Liddell,* ***Notes from the Life Of An Ordinary Mortal*** *(1911), 192.*

10 *2/242. Loreburn opposed his original, more drastic, proposals.*

11 *2/442: Schuster to LCJ, 14.6.1920. The Prime Minister's opposition probably owed something to the fact that most of the "rotten boroughs" on the circuits were in Wales.*

12 *2/690: Schuster to S. Coleridge, 30.7.1925. An example is the fictional Barber J in Cyril Hare [Judge Clark]'s* ***Tragedy At Law*** *(1942).*

13 *Hanworth Committee, appendix to 2nd report, PP 1933–34 (Cmd 4471) XI, 1. This precluded Wright from being chosen for the Peel Commission.*

14 *2/1618: CP 255(37) 22.10.1937.*

15 *2/3931.*

16 *See 2nd report of the Legal Departments Committee, PP 1874 (C-1107) XXIII, 583 and 1/12, 13.*

17 *4/69, 70.*

18 *Sixth Report, PP 1914–16 (Cd 7832) XII, 1.*

19 *4/70: Schuster to Simon, 4.2.1944.*

20 *At the request of the Treasury, the report was not published.*

21 *2/2643, 4/59–73.*

1 Organisation and Circuits

(see also Crown Office).

1/4–10, 54 Reorganisation of circuits 1874–6; resolution of judges and their report, memorandum by Brett MR; papers of Lord Chancellor's committee of 1878; minutes of Judges Council 1881 (all 1/4). The other files contain proceedings of the annual meeting of judges on assize proposals (1883–8), with numerous proposals and comments by individual judges, correspondence with Home Office and Treasury, representations and presentments from law societies, grand juries.

1/54 Duplicate reports, minutes etc. of the Judges Council which fill in some gaps.

1/14 Correspondence with Butt J on his liability to go on circuit, 1884.

2/55, 690 Proposal to unite the Welsh circuits, by S. Coleridge 1893; comments by LCJ, Vaughan-Williams and Cave JJ. Revived 1924, with comments from the circuit bars (especially T. Artemus Jones) and representations from various Welsh towns.

56 Standing order for winter and spring assizes, 1894.

100, 691 Changes in Surrey assizes, 1899; proposals from the Bar, comments by LCJ, Sir F. Jeune P, and others. Also removal to Kingston: correspondence with LCJ, local authorities etc., 1926–30.

242 LCJ's proposals for flexibility discussed in SCRC; deputation from Liverpool and Manchester and Order in Council of 1910 on Lancashire sittings.

442 Administration of Justice Bill 1920: proposal to abolish some assize towns dropped in cabinet.

2198 Correspondence with Treasury *et al.* on suggestions and need for commissioners, 1920–1.

521A Horridge Committee on detention of persons awaiting trial (1921): discussions with Home Office on composition, complaints from Howard League, draft report.

522–3, 734 Swift Committee on circuits, 1923: preliminary correspondence, Schuster's papers, draft report, cabinet paper. Clause in Administration of Justice Act 1925, correspondence with PCO.

692 Report of Committee of Judges proposing more facilities for civil business, 1930.

1603, 1606	Hanworth Committee: lists of complaints and protests, memoranda by judges, schemes by Schuster and J. Foster, presentments by grand juries etc.
1167–71	Finlay Committee papers: correspondence on membership, representations, memoranda, minutes, draft scheme and comments by LCJ and judges; interim report of LCJ's committee on circuit arrangements, 1939.
1618	Administration of Justice (Miscellaneous Provisions) Bill 1938: drafts, correspondence, cabinet papers: see HAC40(37), LC's memorandum.
2602, 2604	Autumn Circuit (1934) Order, minute of Judges Council and correspondence with LCJ; 1935 Order, long vacation.
2603, 2606, 2644	Civil Business (Autumn Circuit) (No. 1) Order 1940: representations of 1934, 1939 for civil business at Chelmsford and quarrel over precedence in 1943 (2044). Likewise 1939 orders for Lincoln, Durham, Bodmin, Stafford.
2605, 2607	Transfer of assizes from Monmouth to Newport: correspondence with LCJ.
2959, 2961–2	Representations on proposed changes in assizes from local authorities in North Wales, Durham and Devon, 1931–6.
4802	Sheffield assizes, 1933–55: petitions and representations, correspondence with LCJ, and with local authority on accommodation to 1940. Revived 1953, and see N.E. Circuit (Sheffield) Order 1955.
4418–20	Welsh Courts Act 1942 (see *Evidence, supra*, 78).
4804, 2794	Wartime savings on ceremonial and advertising, correspondence with LCJ.
4180, 4460	Ipswich assizes: correspondence on resumption in 1944–5 and see 1944 Matrimonial Causes (Bury St Edmunds) Order.
4461, 4786	Circuit (Wales and Chester) Order 1945; correspondence with LCJ and on arrangements at Newtown leading to Montgomeryshire Assizes Order 1949.
4787	1951 Assizes (S. E. Circuit) Order: proposed by LCJ and agreed.
3971–2	Evershed Committee working party 'D' on fixed dates: papers, including several memoranda on fixed dates on circuits.
3540D	List of ex-colonial judges suitable as commissioners agreed with LCJ 1948.
521B, 1172, 1806, 2960, 3468, 3641, 3834, 4078, 4138, 4516, 5275	Various points of practice.

2 Staffing and Expenses

1/11	Judges' allowances and expenses: correspondence with Treasury and memoranda and resolutions by judges, especially in 1884. Other papers in 1/5 (1883 resolution).
1/12, 13	Negotiations with Treasury on salaries and appointments to various clerkships and subordinate offices, 1876–88. 1/13 deals with clerks in the Associates Department of the QBD.
2/2643	Clerk of the assize at Lancaster's delayed accounts: long correspondence on complaints against him (1942–7), especially with the Clerk to the Duchy and the Home Office.
4608	Responses of clerks of assize to Judges' Widows Pensions Scheme 1950.
6652	Appointment of recorders from other circuits.
1563–6, 2794–5, 3475, 5302	Sheriffs: discussions (1920–41) on expense and shortage of candidates (1563), especially Howarth's memorandum. Wartime economies and minor matters.

4/69–73 Circuit Officers Committee. Discussions with Master Bonner, 1934 on control of SC staff. Preliminary meetings of 1944 and Lord Greene MR's complaint re drafting of orders. Correspondence on membership of committee, minutes, evidence, Schuster's papers (including discussions on patronage) interim report. Draft report discussed with Treasury and publication considered.

2/4471–2 SCJ (Circuit Officers) Bill 1946. Caldecote report considered in cabinet. Drafting correspondence with PCO.

Chapter 3

THE COUNTY COURTS

1 INTRODUCTION

The Judicature Acts were a major setback to the further development of the new-style county courts. The controversial recommendations of the Royal Commission[1] for a single civil court with central and local branches were quietly dropped, the Supreme Court of Judicature was installed in the place of honour and the county courts firmly confirmed in their inferior position. Henceforth, although the county courts continued to acquire important and burdensome new functions under statutes (notably the Rent Acts and the Workmen's Compensation Acts), repeated attempts to give them a much wider general jurisdiction, notably in several bills of 1877–78, foundered. These failures owed something to a genuine fear that the courts would thereby become less efficient as machinery for processing small debts, something also to government fears of additional expenditure on accommodation and salaries, but perhaps most to the implacable hostility of the Bar and most of the higher judiciary.

Jurisdiction was modestly extended in 1903 but further attempts promoted by the Law Society met with effective opposition and the LCO files make it possible to study the process picturesquely described by Schuster: "the proceedings of Parliament for the past few years are strewn with the wrecks of County Court Bills which have never reached harbour because they were overloaded".[2] Loreburn was prepared to support the proposals but not to persevere with them in the face of this hostility and his party's own weakness in the Lords.[3] The Gorell Committee report, recommending only a modest extension of jurisdiction,[4] was a further blow to the reformers and after the Great War county court jurisdiction was never again considered on its merits but "through the wrong end of the telescope"[5] by successive inquiries into the civil courts. Even then, the strength of the resistance to their expansion was clearly shown in the debates on the Bill embodying the Peel Commission's modest proposal to raise the upper value limit for county court actions from £100 to £300, which accordingly had to be compromised at £200. It is significant too that after World War Two this question was remitted not to the Austin Jones Committee on County Courts but to the Evershed Committee on the Supreme Court.[6]

The most notable and controversial aspect was the continued refusal to entrust the divorce business which overwhelmed the High Court to county courts, though by the enactment of the Denning Committee's recommendations their judges were miraculously transformed by putting on the majestic garb of commissioners of assize. Moreover by the end of this period, the LCO was having to contend against the preference of other government departments for specialist tribunals, e.g. on rating appeals. Nevertheless, the county courts did grow busier as credit buying became ever more popular and easy, as motor accidents multiplied and possession actions increased.

In 1899 Judge Selfe emphasised the well known weaknesses of a system in which 55 judges served 502 courts grouped into 54 circuits, and which ranged in business from

Birmingham, with over 50,000 cases in 1897, to Bellingham with 16. "With regard to the smaller courts, no-one who has not had practical experience of the county courts in country districts can adequately realise the waste of judicial time and public money which is involved in their maintenance".[7] Selfe was anxious to abolish the smallest courts, partly in order that the savings might be used to increase the salaries of the busiest judges, but also to improve the efficiency of the system; but any change which involved recompensing redundant registrars or clerks was difficult to sell to the Treasury, nor was there general acceptance of the principle of salary differentials among the judges. It was not until the Swift Committee reported in 1921[8] that the LCO had sufficient leverage to move the Treasury, and a more rational "grouping" of registries was brought about by rule in 1921. The same Committee was firmly in favour of ending "an anomaly to which I believe there is no parallel"[9]—the direct role of the Treasury's county courts department, which exercised day to day control over their administration and staff. This was deeply resented by the LCO, and the more so because the Superintendent, Bridgman, was a quarrelsome, punctilious and obstructive person who had dissented from the main recommendations of the Swift Committee and had "done everything possible to obstruct the deliberations of the committee".[10] He was persuaded to retire at the height of his civil service war bonus to pave the way for the transfer of the county courts department to the LCO in 1922, and thenceforth the Office had effective control of county courts administration through its own County Courts Department. Schuster ranked this a major gain,[11] and the next investigation of the county courts found little to criticise in the organisation: indeed, as Coldstream noted "Mr. Justice Jones has got it firmly into his head that there is nothing whatever wrong with the County Court system, and that the less interference there is, the better for all concerned".[12]

Most of its recommendations were therefore minor matters of detail,[13] but it is ironic in view of the chairman's attitude that one of them did cause a storm. As suggested, the LCO requested quarterly returns of the state of business and circularised those courts which seemed to be in arrears for an explanation. Not surprisingly, the judges and registrars objected to a scheme which was admitted to be "bureaucratic in the extreme and . . . an attempt at central interference in the administration of the courts" and thereafter the returns were tactfully not pursued.[14]

Notes

1 *2nd Report, PP 1872 (C 631) XX, 217, "potentially a revolutionary document" P. W. J. Bartrip in D. Sugarman and G. R. Rubin,* ***Law, Economy and Society*** *(1984) at p. 366).*

2 *2/434: to E. R. Cook (Secretary of the Law Society), 13.5.1919.*

3 *e.g. 2/207: Muir McKenzie to President of Law Society, 28.7.1909.*

4 *PP 1909 (71) LXXII, 311.*

5 *The phrase is R. M. Jackson's:* ***Machinery of Justice****, 29.*

6 *There is, unfortunately, no account of the history of county courts over the whole period, though see A. H. Manchester,* ***Modern Legal History****, (1980), 120–3 and G. R. Rubin in D. Sugarman and G. R. Rubin,* ***op. cit.****, 321–48.*

7 *2/111: memorandum of April, 1899 on County Courts (Extension of Jurisdiction) Bill.*

8 *PP 1920 (Cd. 1049) XIII, 307.*

9 *2/525: Lord Chancellor to Sir R. Horne (Treasury), 6.7.1921.*

10 ***Ibid.*** *memorandum of 10.1.1923.*

11 *2/938, which contains a good summary of the background to, and actions upon the Swift report. The capture of the County Courts Department was, of course, particularly valuable in strengthening the LCO's position against any attempts to create a "Ministry of Justice" centred in the Home Office: see G. Drewry, (1983) 61* ***Public Administration****, 396–415, especially at p. 406.*

12 *2/3295: to Napier, 17.1.1948.*

13 *For a summary see (1949) 12 MLR 354 (D. Lloyd).*

14 *2/3307: Rieu's note, 1949. The returns are not without interest, though. Of one judge "it is said that if anyone coughs in court it is mentioned in the judge's notes" (2/3311).*

2

JURISDICTION

1 General

1/64–5 Proposal to give them role in lunacy committals, 1885.

1/49 Nield and Stephen JJ on defects in jurisdiction, 1885.

2/111 County Courts (Extension of Jurisdiction) Bill 1899: Judge Selfe's bill, with his extensive notes.

153–5 County Courts (Jurisdiction Extension) Bill 1903: correspondence with the sponsor, Sir A. Rollit, with the Treasury, results of a questionnaire to county court judges on likely effects of proposed changes, and summary by Judge Selfe; memoranda from Bar Council, County Court Judges Society; Parliamentary papers.

156–8 1904 Bill: draft, comments by Judges Chalmers, Selfe, Greene; memorandum by Law Society and Liverpool ILS; resolutions of county court judges, High Bailiffs Association; correspondence with Selfe and the Treasury.

160 1905 Bill: notes by parliamentary counsel and Selfe; correspondence with Judge Smyly and Treasury; memorandum by Liverpool ILS.

204–10 1906 Bills: notes by Selfe, parliamentary counsel; drafts, correspondence with Judges Selfe and Woodfall, Registrar Whitelock; resolutions of county court judges, report of Bar Council.

210, 214 Gorrell Committee, preliminary correspondence on composition and terms 1909; resolution of county court judges.

285 County Courts Bill 1909: draft, correspondence with Judge Selfe; memorandum by Judge Graham on imprisonment for debt; report of Law Society.

434–6 County Courts Bill 1919: extensive correspondence with Judges Bray and Selfe, Sir T. W. Chitty, PCO, Treasury, Law Society, Registrar Lowe, Treasury Superintendent of County Courts, Home Office, Attorney-General; cabinet and Parliamentary papers; correspondence after the assent with Registrar White and Association of Trade Protection Societies.

12/42 Correspondence with Judge Parry, especially on fees, 1928.

2/803 Administration of Justice Bill 1928: correspondence with PCO on minor amendments to County Courts Act.

1252 Judge McLeary's Consolidation Bill 1929: drafts and correspondence with him and PCO.

1253–61 County Courts Amendment Act 1934: correspondence with PCO, Treasury;

observations by Judge Linley, metropolitan registrars, Law Society, county court judges, Bateson and Langton JJ, Judge McLeary, Master Romer, Lord Hailsham, Attorney-General, Judge Clements, Eve and Clauson JJ; drafts, cabinet and Parliamentary papers. Notes and correspondence with judges and departmental officials on particular topics, including dormant funds, equity and admiralty jurisdiction, Duchy of Lancaster, forfeiture of leases. See also 859 on warrants outside the jurisdiction. Parliamentary proceedings.

1262–4 County Courts Consolidation Bill 1934: correspondence with PCO; observations from various judges, registrars and officers; notes on amendments and Parliamentary proceedings.

1292 County Courts Bill 1936: brief for Attorney-General and notes.

1600, 1308 LCO papers for the Hanworth Committee on possible extensions of jurisdiction, 1933. Administration of Justice (Miscellaneous Provisions) Act 1938: correspondence with Registrar Hicks, Law Society.

3293 Austin Jones Committee, 1947: discussions on terms of reference.

3934, 3968 Evershed Committee, interim report on county courts and papers of working party 'A', 1947.

2 Particular Subjects

2/1, 2 Correspondence with Board of Trade on county court judges as Wreck Commissioners, 1889.

57 Married women and credit; Heywood's proposals discussed with judges and others, 1893.

112 County Courts Jurisdiction Order (Bankruptcy): discussions on descriptions of courts, 1899.

776 Moneylenders Bill: discussion on jurisdiction, 1926.

1208 Barking Corporation Bill 1933: discussions with Home Office and Ministry of Health on duties imposed by local acts.

806, 1266, 1714 Administration of Justice (Appeals) Act 1934 (see '*Court of Appeal*', *supra*, 89). Proposed appeal to assizes in Lancashire rejected, 1928(806).

1269 Special procedure for extended jurisdiction abolished, 1932.

1291 Non-enforceability of judgments in Scotland confirmed, 1935.

1516 Inheritance (Family Provision) Act 1938: Solicitor-General on proposal to confer jurisdiction on county courts.

3289 Widening of registrars' jurisdiction (1947) to include Married Women's Property Act 1882.

3586 Local Government Act 1947: discussions with Ministry of Health and Home Office on rating appeals.

4172 Wedgwood Committee papers, 1942; proposal to give divorce to county courts. *cf.* 5481 (1951).

4333 Coal Mining (Subsidence) Act 1950: correspondence with Treasury, Treasury Solicitor's Office, and opinions of Judges Stewart and Gamon on the best forum for actions.

4473 Children's Act 1949: discussions with Home Office, PCO, Registrar Hicks and interested parties on extended jurisdiction.

3
ORGANISATION

2/111, 115, 156–7, 159–60	Memoranda by Judges Selfe, Smyly, Chalmers and others on re-organisation of circuits, abolition of small courts etc.
210	Gorell Committee: correspondence with LCJ.
294	Report of Committee on Distribution of County Courts in Lancashire, 1914; correspondence with Treasury and others.
670	Proposed Whitley Council, memorandum by Ministry of Labour, opposed by Bridgman, 1919.
525–7	Swift Committee report, 1921: correspondence with Treasury on reform of administration, with proposals.
534	Rule Committee papers on "grouping" of registries; correspondence with members; sub-committee report on "branch courts", draft rules, 1921.
830	Law Society proposal for Central County Court, 1920; with Rule Committee members papers relating to proposals of 1893.
3293–3305, 3312–7	Austin Jones Committee papers: correspondence on terms and membership, list of suggestions, memoranda, minutes, evidence (written and oral), correspondence and draft reports. Summary of recommendations; correspondence on possible legislation, rules, observations by County Courts Branch and others.
3306	Publication of cause lists: circular and correspondence with Registrar Freeman-Coutts, 1948.
3307–11	Quarterly returns: correspondence with judges and registrars, returns (1949–53), complaints and investigations into delays, 1949–53.
4/121	Royal Commission on the Civil Service, 1929–30: Martin's evidence on county court staffs.
8/1–6	Treasury circulars (1846–1906), departmental circulars (1932–53) and various documents on work of the county courts.
8/52	Registrars' salaries and re-organisation.
8/57	Pensions for clerks and bailiffs, 1922–38.
8/63	Reorganisation and clerks' pay.
8/44	Committee on County Court Accounts (H. P. Boland). Report and notes, 1925.
8/58	Swift Committee on "Walking Possession" 1927: report, Superintendant's memorandum, circulars and observations by registrars. Also correspondence of 1938 on *Day* v *Davies*.

4
RULES AND PRACTICE

The County Court Rule Committee consisted of five county court judges nominated by the Lord Chancellor. Its functions were similar to those of the Supreme Court Rule Committee but since 1884 its rules have been required to be confirmed by that body, and although in many cases this was a matter of form, they were occasionally objected to, as in November, 1921 when the SCRC objected to two new forms as not in harmony with their practice and oppressive to defendants.[1]

The Permanent Secretary to the Lord Chancellor acted as secretary to the committee, a practice which they endorsed in 1915 on Muir McKenzie's retirement,[2] although later the duty was delegated to less senior officials in the department. The records of the earlier meetings are disappointingly thin however, and it is only from 1911 that a more or less regular series exists.[3] Thereafter each suggestion of any substance from within the department or the Committee or from outsiders was made the subject of an individual file and these were collated at intervals into the general file prepared for meetings. Meetings took place on average twice a year and the general files usually contain correspondence with the chairman and other members on meeting dates and on the agenda, the agenda itself, with explanatory notes, minutes of the meeting (settled with the chairman) and papers on the preparation of the rules, including correspondence with the Treasury where its approval was necessary. Sometimes memoranda, usually by members of the committee, are also to be found. The record of the Rule Committee's deliberations is valuable for the material it contains on the actual practice of the courts and the concerns of the more public-spirited and articulate judges and registrars: thus, for example, default summonses were extensively discussed in 1921 and the vexed question of venues in 1934.

The original composition of the Committee was not really suitable for its job, and for some years before his retirement Muir McKenzie had taken to consulting informally the Registrar of Birmingham (the busiest court), A. L. Lowe. In 1919 this practice was regularised by the addition of a registrar to the Committee (Lowe had to resign as chairman of the Association of County Registrars to achieve this 'ambition of a lifetime'),[4] and at the same time the Law Society's request for representation, made at least as early as 1905, was acceded to with the addition of a London and a provincial solicitor; the Bar also had to have a representative, enlarging the Committee to nine.

The registrar, in fact, became one of the most important figures, especially Lowe (who died in 1928) and Gilbert Hicks, Registrar of Shoreditch, chosen in 1934 and re-appointed after the war. The solicitor members too were often helpful, but the Bar representative was something of a dead weight; indeed the first one chosen, H. M. Giveen, treated it so lightly that he attended only one meeting before his appointment as a junior Treasury counsel in 1929, when he was asked to resign. The material on selection of members is interesting, showing that at least two registrars were passed over in 1934 on the basis of being "not a gent", and describing Judge Ormerod as "a star turn" (1947); generally the judges were recommended by the chairman, successively Sir W. L. Selfe (1894 to 1920), Sir Walworth Roberts (1920–1), Sir Edward Bray (1921–6), Sir William Cann (1926–31) and Sir S. A. Hill-Kelly (1931–9).[5] Although the Committee had continued to function throughout the Great War, it was suspended in 1939 and the Lord Chancellor was given power to make rules himself, although the LCO continued to consult leading members of the committee, such as Judge Hancock and Hicks. It was reconstituted in 1947 with Hancock as chairman, and he gave way to Gerald Hurst in 1950.

The Rule Committee, at least between the wars, interpreted its functions narrowly and to Napier's irritation, refused to offer opinions on the interpretation of the County Courts Acts.[6] Even so, its work was diverse enough. The appointment of Selfe and Chalmers in the 1880's inaugurated "a period of unexampled activity"[7] in rule making and thereafter a steady stream of rules flowed forth, sometimes required by the passage of new legislation which was to be implemented by the courts (e.g. the Adoption Act 1926, a good example of a role foisted upon them by Parliament against the wishes of the LCO) but more often by the discovery of flaws or gaps in existing rules. Not all county court rules were made by the Committee even in peacetime: occasionally, and for no apparent reason, statutes (e.g. the Rent Act 1923) would nominate the Lord Chancellor himself as the rule making authority, though even where this happened the leading figures on the Rule Committee tended to be consulted on the drafting. The vast majority were made by the Committee, however, and they are far too numerous and heterogeneous to be listed separately; some, indeed, cannot easily be explained in a sentence or two. Consequently, in the list below, the only matters particularised are those covered by an individual ''satellite file'' or which form the greatest part of a general file. As previously stated, the importance of procedural rules in the administration of civil justice can hardly be exaggerated, least of all in the 'poor man's courts', where many defendants, and some plaintiffs, were people of small means. The great tussle over venues in the 1936 rules shows very clearly how the balance of advantage between the parties might be tilted by rule changes.[8]

The fees rules deserve special mention. The Treasury principle was that while the salaries and pensions of the judges and the cost of maintaining the buildings would be met by the taxpayer, the litigants must meet the remaining costs through court fees.[9] Fees also provided the income of the registrars and out of them they paid their clerical staffs; this practice, so antediluvian and unexpected in courts of such recent creation, would have endured longer than it did but for the strong condemnation of the Swift Committee. Faced with the need to meet the cost of court staff out of the consolidated fund the Treasury insisted on a fees rise to restore the county courts to their pre-war ''profitability'', a demand that was the harder to resist as the proposed divorce of registrars' remuneration from the fees in any case necessitated a reconstruction of the scales. The MacNaghten Committee was accordingly set up and the fees were duly raised, but it was strongly felt in some quarters, not least among registrars, that the new fees were too high, and since they yielded a handsome surplus, Sankey was able to persuade the Treasury to a reduction in 1931. Nevertheless the difficulty of balancing the need to avoid hardship to the poor, given that legal aid was not available in these courts (where solicitors' costs were charged on a scale that was acknowledged to be unfairly low) with the need to raise sufficient revenue re-asserted itself again after the 1939–45 war.[10]

Notes

1 *2/534: Napier to Lowe, 17.11.1921. For the earlier history of this body see S. Rosenbaum in (1915) 31 LQR 304.*

2 *2/307: meeting of 3.5.1915.*

3 *It is not clear whether this is the result of destruction of files.*

4 *2/5094: Schuster to Judge Roberts, 25.3.1920.*

5 *2/5094. For Selfe see S. Rosenbaum,* **supra** *n. 1, at 310. Biographical details of the other judges can be found in the successive editions of* **Debrett's House of Commons and the Judicial Bench**.

6 *2/1267: to A. Jennings, 18.11.1931.*

7 *S. Rosenbaum,* **supra**, *n. 1 at p. 310.*

8 *2/1280, 1288–9.*

9 *See the correspondence with Judge Parry (1924) in 12/42. Parry was the best known county court judge of his day, and a prolific author of books*

*critical of the courts and the law, such as '**The Law and the Poor**' (1914).*

10 *B. Abel-Smith and R. Stevens, **Lawyers and the Courts** (1967) 247–8.*

1 The Rule Committee

1 Composition and procedures

2/307 Discussion on secretaryship, May 1915.

434–5 County Courts Bill 1919: correspondence and discussions with PCO, Treasury; Law Society memorandum on representation on the Rule Committee.

4319 Correspondence with Treasury on making of rules etc., 1946.

5094 Appointment of members, 1915–50: correspondence and papers, including material on the revival of the Rule Committee in 1947.

308 Memorandum on procedure, 1915.

2 Meetings

8/14 H. Nicol's covering notes with rules from meetings of 1870, 1875.

2/67 Meeting of November 1894: extensive correspondence with Judge Selfe, Law Society and various judges, and memoranda on rules, 1895.

113 Meeting of February 1895: correspondence with Law Society, complaints from registrars. Meeting of November 1896 and rules.

114 Meeting of May 1898, agenda. Meeting of February 1899: minutes and papers on Bankruptcy Act 1883 s. 122. Meeting of November 1900: agenda and various rules.

162 Meetings of April, May 1903: correspondence with Treasury, memorandum by Judge Harrington.

295 Meetings: March 1911.

296, 297 February 1912.

298 July 1912.

299 November 1912, includes discussion of *Re Millar* (1912).

300 February 1913.

301 May 1913.

302 November 1913, including memorandum "points for consideration in the committee on consolidated county court rules".

303 February 1914.

304 April 1914.

305 May 1914.

306 July 1914, including discussion on poor persons' rules.

307 May 1915, including discussions on the position of National Health Insurance Commissioners in appeals, and solicitors' charges in workmen's compensation.

308 November 1915, including proposals on judgment summonses out of the district.

310 February 1915: including Emergency Powers Rules.

358 February 1916.

359 May 1916, including papers on poor persons' cases.

360 November 1916, including workmen's compensation funds in court.

361 May 1917.

362	November 1917.
363	February 1918.
364	June 1918, including opinions of the judges and others on solicitors' remuneration.
365	October 1918: rules under Juries Act 1918.
366	February 1919: electoral registration appeals rules.
528	November 1919: on County Courts Bill.
529	February 1920, includes papers on summonses out of the district.
530	March 1920.
531–2	October 1920: includes sub-committee on s. 138 County Courts Act 1888.
533	January 1921: difficulties in agreeing the minutes.
534	October 1921: memoranda on default summonses; SC Rule Committee object to new forms; report of Examiners on "grouping", and of sub-committee on "branch courts".
535	January 1922: SC Rule Committee's objections discussed.
536	June 1922: Bar Council plea for higher scale fees.
537	February 1923: discussion on ejectments.
538	November 1923.
543, 842	1924: meeting on Fees Committee report (see A. Napier to Jennings, 5.9.1924).
845	March 1925 and June 1925: infants' damages.
848	October 1925.
852	February 1926: poor persons' rules and workmen's compensation questions.
854	March 1927: extensive papers on legitimation rules.
855	November 1927: including moneylenders' claims.
856–7	February, March 1928: Landlord and Tenant Act (1927) rules, extensive correspondence and memoranda.
860	May 1928.
862	November 1928.
864	March 1929.
866	July 1929: lump sum payments in workmen's compensation.
869, 941	February 1930: proposal to widen discretion on costs and bankruptcy fees discussed.
870	November 1930.
1250	April 1931.
1267–8	November 1931, with Napier's criticisms of the committee.
1272	July 1932.
1274	January 1933: includes discussion on possession orders.
1275	March 1933: consideration of referees' suggestions for amending rules under Landlord & Tenant Act 1927.
1287	April 1934.
1290	October 1934.
1279–80, 1282	February and December 1935 and March 1936: extensive discussions and papers on new rules under County Courts Act 1934, including papers from sub-committee; especially full on venue question.
1296	December 1936: see 1280 (*supra*) on venue.
1298	March 1937.
1300	December 1937, includes discussion on legitimacy rules.
1304	June 1938.

1309	November 1938.
1313	July 1939.
3321–4, 4681	December 1949, February, April, May, July 1950: extensive correspondence on rules implementing Austin Jones report. Also (4681) on legal aid proposals.
4496–8	November 1950, including digest of criticisms of County Courts (Amendment) Rules 1950.
4990–2	June 1951.

2 Rules

1/49	1884 rules discussed by High Court judges.
1/80	1889 rules and fees order.
2/65	1892 Rules.
67	1895 Rules, discussions in CCRC.
113	1896 Rules.
127	1897 Rules discussed in SCRC.
103	1898–9: rules under Workmens Compensation Act 1897.
110	1899 Rules: execution of warrants under County Courts Act 1888 s. 158; correspondence with Board of Trade, Law Officers' opinion.
161–2, 176, 178	1903 Rules, including amended rules for administration orders. Discussed in SCRC.
295	1911 Rules.
296–301	1912–13 Rules and rules under Workmens Compensation and National Insurance Acts.
302	1913: revised rule on administration orders under s. 122 Bankruptcy Act 1883.
306	1914: consolidated rules and workmen's compensation rules.
309	1914 rules under Mental Deficiency Act 1913.
310, 307, 290–91	1914 rules under Postponement of Payments and Courts (Emergency Powers) Acts, 1914: correspondence with Treasury, judges, registrars etc.
310	1915 rules under Trading with the Enemy Act.
357, 360, 372–3, 375–7, 381 382–4	1916–18 rules under Courts (Emergency Powers) Acts, including consolidation rules (1918): correspondence, especially with Judge Selfe.
357	1915 Rent Act rules: also rules under Rent Act 1919. Correspondence with Judge Selfe and the Lord Chancellor.
359	1916 Rules, also rules under Bankruptcy Act 1914 s. 41.
307, 358	1916 Rules under National Insurance Act 1911.
360	1916 Rules and Emergency Powers Rules.
361–3	1918 Rules: discussions with Treasury on Workmens Compensation Act funds in court.
364	1918 Rules(2).
365	Rules under Juries Act 1918.
345, 366	1918–19 rules under Representation of the People Act 1918: extensive correspondence with Local Government Board; meetings, various memoranda and notes.
528, 539	1920 Rules under County Courts Act 1919.
534	1921 Rules: grouping of courts and 'branch courts'', extensive correspondence.

534	1921 Rules: grouping of courts and "branch courts", extensive correspondence.
536	1922 Rules.
537	1923 Rules(1): on admissions.
538	1923 Rules(2).
544	1923 Rent Act rules, made by Lord Chancellor.
672	1923 Workmen's Compensation Rules, on medical assessors' fees; correspondence with Treasury and Home Office.
842	1924 Rules: costs in possession actions.
843	1924 Rent (Restrictions) Rules.
1077–8	1924 Workmen's Compensation Rules and (No. 2) Rules.
845–6	1925 Rules(1), including juries rules.
847	1925 Infants Damages Rules.
848	1925 Rules(2).
1079	1925 Workmen's Compensation Rules.
850	1925 Guardianship of Infants Rules.
852	1926 Rules(1) including (849) new Form of Summons in ejectment.
1080	1926 Workmen's Compensation (Amendment) Rules.
1120	1926 Adoption of Children (County Courts) Rules.
1084	1927, 1929 Workmen's Compensation (Silicosis) Rules.
851, 853	1927 Rules(1) including (851) security for costs.
854–5	1927 Rules(2), including Moneylenders Act rules and correspondence with Attorney-General, Home Office, Principal Probate Registry, Treasury Solicitor and others on Legitimation Act rules.
858	1928 Poor Persons Rules, remitted actions.
856, 860	1928 Landlord and Tenant Rules and Rules (2).
862	1928 Rules (3).
862, 1127–8	1926–29 Tithe Rent Charge Recovery Rules: correspondence with Ministry of Agriculture, Tithe Commissioners, Queen Anne's Bounty etc.
861, 864	1929 Rules(1) including (861) witness allowances and fines on judgment debtors.
866	1929 Rules (2), including rules under Companies Act 1929.
869	1930 Rules (1).
870	1930 Rules (2).
1250	1931 Rules (1).
1081–2	1930 Workmen's Compensation (No. 1) Rules and (No. 2) Rules.
1251, 1268	1931 Rules (2), including extensive correspondence on service abroad rules.
1265	1932 Rules (1): revision of order XXV r. 14.
2804	1932 Memoranda and correspondence on solicitors' remuneration rules.
1271–2	1932 Rules (3), including (1271) chancel repairs rules.
1922, 1926–7	1932–7 Tithe rentcharge recovery rules.
1273–4	1933 Rules (1).
1270, 1275, 1277	1933 Rules (2) including service abroad (1277) and remitted actions (1270).
1276	1933 Adoption of Children Rules.
1275, 1278, 1286–7	1934 Rules (1) including Landlord and Tenant Act Rules (1275, 1278).
1290	1934 Rules (2).

1279–83, 1288–9	1936 Rules under County Courts Act 1934: extensive papers, including CCRC drafting sub-committee, and correspondence with trading companies and organisations on venue rules (1288–9).
1294	1936 Administration orders rules.
1296	1936 County Courts Amendment Rules.
1298	1937 Rules (1).
1299, 1300	1938 Rules (1), including Legitimacy Act rules and judgment summonses.
1302, 1304	1938 Rules (2), including security for costs (1302).
1301, 1307–9	1938 Rules (3), including hire purchase rules (1307), increase of registrars' jurisdiction (1308), judgment creditors (1301).
1305, 1318	1938, 1939 Rent (Restriction) Rules.
1310, 1313, 1316	1939 Rules (1).
1315	1939 County Courts (Military Forces) Rules.
1355–60	1939 Emergency Powers Rules and (No. 2) Rules and (Consolidation) Rules 1940, including numerous complaints and representations from building societies, registrars and others.
1319	1940 Emergency Powers (No. 2) Rules.
1322	1941 Emergency Powers (No. 1) Rules.
1321, 1310	1942 Rules (1), including warrants of delivery.
1320	Draft rules under War Damage Acts: correspondence to 1942.
2679, 1312	1942 Rules (1).
2678	1942 Emergency Powers Rules (1).
2680–1	1943 Correspondence and suggestions for rules to assist creditors.
2682	1943 Rules (1).
3274, 3280	1944 Service Rules.
3279, 3282	1945 Rules (1). Coal Act (3282), Admiralty matters (3279).
3286	1946 War Damage Rules.
3288	1947 Exchange Control Rules.
3289, 3290, 3292	1947 Rules (1).
3327	1947 Crown Proceedings Rules.
3315	1949: Austin Jones Committee recommendations requiring rules.
3321–4	1950 Amendment Rules, CCRC meetings.
4496–7	1950 Amendment (2) Rules, with comments on Amendment Rules.
4996, 5001	1951 Suggested amendments.
4989, 5002	1951 Amendment Rules.
6223	1951 Workmen's Compensation Rules 1951.

3 Fees Orders

2/194	1903 Winding-up Fees Order.
540	1921 Fees Order: correspondence with Treasury and Registrars' Association.
541–2	1921 McNaghten Committee: correspondence, evidence, draft report.
543, 832	1924 Fees Order: correspondence with Treasury, registrars; Rule Committee papers.
833	1924–6 "agreed costs" (Fee 51), discussions and questions on interpretation.
834–5	1925 Fees (Amendment) Order.
836	1926 Fees (Amendment) Order.

837 1927 Fees Order, includes fees on legitimacy, new trustees, winding up.

839 1928 Fees (Amendment) Order, including Landlord & Tenant Act 1927, remitted actions.

697 1928 Bankruptcy Fees Order.

838, 840 1929 Fees Order: mortgagees' possession actions and "walking possession" fees.

841, 865 1930 Fees under Companies Act 1929 s. 142 and fees on abortive executions discussed.

1248 1931 Fees Order: correspondence with Treasury on reducing fees.

1249 1936 Fees Order: correspondence with County Courts Branch, Hicks and other registrars on revision, especially on judgment summonses.

2675 1941 new forms for fees 59, 63.

2672–3 1942 Fees (Amendment No. 2) Order: recovery of land; and (No. 3), War Damage Amendment Act fees.

2674 1942 Fee 83 ("agreed costs"), anomalous cases.

2676 1943 Fees Order, mostly consolidation.

3262 1947 Fees (Amendment) Order: auctioneers' fees.

3263–5 1949 Fees Order: discussions on policy.

3266 1950 Fees (Amendment) Order: interpleader and hire purchase recovery actions.

3267 1951 Fees (Amendment) Order: appeals.

3318–9 1949–50 Austin Jones Committee discussions on solicitors' remuneration (see 'Legal Professions', *infra*, 175–6).

4 Funds Orders

2/1645, 1257 1931: proposed rules on dormant funds; Tomlin Committee papers, discussions with Treasury.

1323 1934 Rules.

2677 1942–3 Funds Rules: transfers from High Court simplified.

3268 1945 Funds Rules: deposits under Liabilities (War-time Adjustment) Acts.

3269 1946 Savings Banks (Limits of Deposits) Order.

3270 1947 Funds Rules: reduction of interest rate. See also 4978, applications to invest in higher yield securities, 1951.

3271 1949 Funds Rules: consolidation.

3272 1950 Funds Rules: withdrawals by post.

5 Practice

2/1063, 4168 Proposed inquiry under Talbot J into costs in High Court actions within county court jurisdiction; correspondence with Talbot, Judge Crawford and inquiry abandoned, 1929. Also costs in remitted actions.

1297, 1306, 3276, 3278, 4979, 1311, 1317 Judgment debtors: proposed register of regulations, 1936 (1297), practice on committals for contempt (1306, 3276, 3278, 4979); form of summons (1311, 1317).

3320, 4324, 1284 Forms: Austin Jones report and protest by H.M.S.O.; complaints re forms under the Law Reform Act 1935.

4995 Taxation of costs under order V rule 19(5) discussed with Judge Wethered (1939), Registrars White and Hicks and revived 1951.

1293, 1303, Other points of practice and suggestions for changes.
630, 3228,
3273, 3283,
3291, 4243,
4206, 4252

5
JUDGES AND REGISTRARS

County court judgeships lay wholly within the gift of the Lord Chancellor but these papers offer no assistance in determining the criteria by which judges were appointed, though one file does carry a list of candidates for appointment as assistant judges to carry out the heavy, temporary work of hearing appeals against refusals to register voters under the Representation of the People Act 1918.[1] Likewise, although they might be removed for 'inability or misbehaviour', there are no instances recorded here, although there are scattered complaints against particular judges, such as Judge Lefroy in the 1880s and Judge Archer in the 1940s. In 1946 several judges in the London courts, especially those at Ilford, Edmonton, and Bromley, came under a sustained attack from the local authorities and Labour MPs for their handling of possession cases, and the Ministry of Health asked the LCO to point out to them the problems faced by housing authorities. A circular was issued with some reluctance but the LCO sternly maintained its inability to interfere with the judges, an especially sensitive subject in the first year of a Labour government.[2] In fact the county court judges, although generally improved in quality, were too numerous and far from the centre to be amenable to control, and a strong minded individual such as Judge Gamon could cheerfully admit to bending the law without much fear of retribution, since he had no hope of promotion (such mavericks were never even selected for the Rule Committee) and only appeals to the superior courts to curb him;[3] on at least one occasion, however, the weight of his brethren's unanimous disapproval was successfully brought to bear on an errant deputy judge.[4]

Although there was no official equivalent to the statutory Council of Judges for the county courts, the judges soon formed their own society, later styled 'Council'. This enabled them to put forward representations when they were sufficiently in accord, usually on the favourite question of their salaries, but sometimes in favour of increased general jurisdiction or particular powers. Their campaign for a rise from the £1,500 fixed in 1850 in lieu of fees failed to win government support in the 1900s, even after the increase in their workload imposed by Rollit's Act: in terms familiar to public servants today Muir McKenzie told them "it is impossible for [the Lord Chancellor] to close his eyes to the fact that a county court judgeship with its present salary is regarded as a desirable office by a very large number of most competent men at the bar".[5] They did succeed in obtaining a pension scheme in 1919, which enabled their retirement at seventy-two to be put on a statutory footing, although it is clear from the files that for some years an undertaking to retire at seventy "if called upon" had been extracted from appointees. A rise in salaries to £2,000 was conceded in the 1930s and their post-war agitation for increases was eventually successful, while as an interim measure they received the sop of a widows' pension scheme. In addition to their primary role, county court judges were sometimes chosen for other duties, most notably to act as divorce commissioners, and at other times they sat on committees and tribunals.

The author of a recent study of the office of registrar in the mid-nineteenth century describes the period as "the making of a judicial official" and contrasts unfavourably the "era of stagnation" which followed.[6] It may be fairer to describe it as an era of consolidation in which the main feature was the establishment of registrars' courts in 1919 and the recognition of their professional status in 1924 when they were finally removed from the undignified and precarious dependence on fees receipts for their livelihood, a reliance which had brought some of the full-timers to the brink of bankruptcy by the end of the war owing to the precipitous falling off in small debt litigation.[7] It was a recommendation of the Swift Committee, which also espoused the putting onto the civil service establishment of the lesser court officials, the clerks and bailiffs, who had hitherto held an ambiguous place in the system, being treated for pension purposes as the private employees of the registrar. This short-sighted and undesirable economy, endorsed by Bridgman in his minority report, had the natural consequence that many clung to their place long after they ceased to be fit to occupy it, and they could hardly be turned adrift entirely unprovided for.[8]

Schuster described the current state of the post-Swift negotiations with the Treasury in his memorandum for Haldane,[9] and the office papers afford an excellent insight into the difficulties of getting even a minor and politically uncontroversial institutional reform in legal administration enacted. By 1924 the establishment of the county courts was at last on a more satisfactory footing and the Lord Chancellor also obtained the power to appoint the registrars and move them around the courts. The judges woke up rather late to the loss of their patronage but failed to defeat it in Parliament: "there have in the past been disgraceful cases of nepotism on their part" wrote Schuster.[10]

The registrars had long had their own Association, whose president had been regularly consulted on rule changes. Now there was a registrar on the Rule Committee where he always played an important part, and when the rule committee was suspended in World War II, Gilbert Hicks, a London registrar, was indispensable to the hard-pressed Napier as a draftsman and adviser on the various wartime legislation rules. The Association itself was consulted on major rule and fee changes and individual registrars such as Glanfield and Freeman-Coutts were also in regular communication with the LCO.

Notes

1 *2/356.*
2 *2/3284.*
3 *2/3429: Judge Gamon to Dobson, 11.11.1950.*
4 *2/1301 (Deputy Judge Raglan Somerset at Pontypool).*
5 *2/204: to Judge Roberts, 26.2.1906. Their grievance was real enough, for as long ago as 1878 a select committee had recommended that they should be paid £2,000 p.a.: PP 1878 (267) X, 1345.*
6 *P. W. J. Bartrip in D. Sugarman and G. R. Rubin,* **op. cit.**, *at 49, 367. Proposals to increase the registrar's jurisdiction in the various County Courts Bills of the 1900s were unpopular with the Bar and some judges, see 2/209–11.*
7 *2/938.*
8 *2/709: Schuster's memorandum, 26.3.1923. A departmental committee had previously*

investigated this matter in 1898, see A. G. C. Liddell, ***Notes from the Life of an Ordinary Mortal*** *(1911), 318–19.*

9 *2/938.*

10 *2/709: Schuster to Attorney-General, 1.11.1923.*

1 Judges

1/41–2	Complaints: Nicol's notes on procedure (1873) and many and repeated complaints (1874–80) against Judge Lefroy.
2/111	Judge Selfe's proposal for salary increases and re-organisation.
153–60, 204–10	County Courts Bills (1903–06) and Gorell Committee: various proposals from judges, including Society of County Court Judges, for salary increases and pension rights.
211–3	Views on imprisonment for debt given to the Pickersgill Committee, 1909.
356	List of possible candidates for nomination as assistant judges, with comments on suitability (1919).
436, 606	Pensions Bill 1919: correspondence with Treasury; notes on the position of existing judges.
671	Opinions sought on Parliamentary amendments to Workmen's Compensation Bill, 1923.
607	Ruling on whether they can be subpoenaed, 1920.
608	Discussions with Ministry of Transport on appointment as arbitrators under Road Transport Regulation Order 1921.
609	Explanation of why they do not take an oath on taking office, 1921.
12/40	Representations from Judges' Council on salaries and discussions with Treasury, 1920–34. See also 2/955 on comparisons with police magistrates.
12/44	Correspondence with judges on arrangements during the general strike, 1926.
2/1063	Judge Crawford's campaign on costs under order XIV, 1929–30.
1253	Report of their Council on County Courts Amendment Bill, 1932.
1511	Views sought on Hire Purchase Bill amendments, 1937.
1301	Council persuades a Deputy Judge to alter his view of the law, 1938.
2680–1	Suggest assistance to creditors where property has been evacuated, 1941.
1408	Correspondence on the role of certain judges in tribunals under the Allied Powers (Maritime Courts) Act 1941.
3055	Appointment of Judges Hancock and Dale to committees set up by the Ministry of National Insurance, 1944.
3284	Criticisms of London judges in possession actions, 1946.
3299, 3968	Evidence submitted to Austin Jones and Evershed Committees, 1947–8.
3950–6	County court judges as divorce commissioners: Denning Committee papers, circulars, correspondence, 1946–8.
6225	Complaints re the practice of withholding payment of lump sums in court, 1944–51.
12/53	Correspondence with solicitors and Judge Hurst on procedure in a case part heard on death of deputy judge, 1944.
2/4298	Judge Hunter at the War Damage Tribunal, 1945.
4496, 4498	Suggestions by various judges for amendments to the rules, 1950.
3881, 4609–11	Salaries: correspondence, especially with Treasury, cabinet papers, statistics, memoranda and representations, 1948–51.

4608–10, 6341–2, 6691	Widows' pensions scheme: summary of views of judges, correspondence with Judges Council, Treasury and other departments, cabinet papers 1950–51.
5486	Council raises a question on judgment summonses in matrimonial causes, 1951.

2 Registrars and Other Staff

2/205, 285	Memoranda on proposed extensions of registrars' powers, 1907, 1912.
1954	Regulations in Courts of Survey in Blackpool and London; correspondence with Home Office 1906 and changes noted to 1946.
306	Observations of their Association on consolidation of rules, 1914.
311	Correspondence on the position of the registrar when the judge orders (*ultra vires*) a fine to be remitted, 1913.
525	Correspondence with Treasury on Swift Committee report, 1921.
526–7, 831	"Scheme of future remuneration"; drafts, meetings, correspondence with A.C.C.R., Clerks and Bailiffs Association etc., 1923–4.
709	County Courts Bill: extensive correspondence with Treasury, PCO; cabinet and Parliamentary papers, 1923–4.
539	A.C.C.R. observations on draft rules on their extended jurisdiction, 1920.
540	Comments on Fee Order 1921.
541–3	MacNaghten Committee: evidence to, comments on draft report etc. 1921–3.
610	Complaint of registrar bringing an action in his own court; correspondence with judge, and with President of A.C.C.R., 1922.
878–9	Registrars' complaints re circular of 1925 requiring their attendance at assize divorce trials; correspondence (1925–30) especially with Nottingham, Swansea and Cardiff DRs and PDA officials.
1253	Observations of several registrars on County Courts Amendment Bill, 1932.
1279	Observations on draft new rules under County Courts Act 1934.
1249	Comments on proposed fees order, 1936.
1288–9	Venues: correspondence with Westminster Registrar on practice of Judge Turner; correspondence with registrars on new rules, 1929–36.
1358	Suggestions to amend Courts (Emergency Powers) Rules 1939.
1400	Views of various registrars on Liabilities (War-time Adjustment) Bill, 1941.
2726	Appointment of certain registrars as custodians under Defence (Evacuated Areas) Regulations 1941.
3287	A.C.C.R. proposals to alter status and conditions of service of assistant registrars, 1946–56.
3289	Jurisdiction extended (see Jurisdiction, *supra*).
3298, 3300	Evidence to Austin Jones Committee, 1948.
3319	Views on proposed new scale of costs, 1950.
4177	Claim to remuneration for work suggested by Wedgwood Committee, 1943.
4249	Correspondence with Bolton Registrar and judge on complaint over workmen's compensation, 1944.
4496–8	Observations on County Courts (Amendment) Rules 1950.
587, 1295, 1919, 1921–3, 2724, 3298, 3300	Bailiffs: petition for pay rise (587); High Bailiff Court Order, 1936 (1295); role in tithe cases (1921–3), submissions to Austin Jones Committee (3298, 3300). See also "walking possession", *supra*, 117.

Chapter

4

THE MAGISTRATES' COURTS

1
INTRODUCTION

1 Appointments

Responsibility for the magistrates who performed the great bulk of criminal work, a considerable amount of civil business and a good number of administrative functions was divided between the Home Secretary and the Lord Chancellor.[1] The Lord Chancellor was responsible for making appointments and for taking any disciplinary action that was found necessary, while the main administrative burden, the day-to-day supervision of magistrates' courts, lay with the Home Office. Magistrates' courts were therefore perceived as "belonging" to the Home Office in much the same way as the county courts "belonged" to the LCO and when questions of status or jurisdiction arose the LCO tended to favour the latter: thus it never conceded that metropolitan police magistrates had a compelling claim to salaries equal to those of county court judges,[2] it resisted when it could attempts by local authorities to give themselves the right to bring their debtors before magistrates,[3] and it tended to favour the county courts rather than the magistrates as the forum for matrimonial causes if the High Court's exclusive jurisdiction was to be removed.[4]

Discontent with the magistracy in this period gave rise to two Royal Commissions, in 1910 and 1946. The first was set up chiefly because of dissatisfaction within the Liberal and Labour parties over the selection of county magistrates by the Lord-Lieutenants. The Liberal Chancellors, Herschell and Loreburn, came under intense pressure from their party to 'job the magistracy' in such a way as to counter the Conservative bias which had become apparent, but each in turn strongly resisted it. It may be characteristic of the organisation of the LCO at that time that no papers are preserved relating to this Commission, which led to the establishment of County Advisory Committees.[5] The Committees went a long way towards achieving a political equilibrium but at the price of blatant political jobbery and LCO 2/3481–3, 3494–5 give a glimpse of the unsalubrious outcome in London.

The multiplication of criminal offences in the twentieth century, especially motoring offences and innumerable wartime regulations, brought numbers of the middle classes into direct contact with magistrates' justice for the first time, where they encountered failings which might have been predicted from the mode of selection of justices and their lack of training but which had not been regarded with much concern as long as the magistrates remained principally an agency for policing the lower classes.[6] A second Royal Commission was appointed in 1946 and its report carried sufficient weight for the principal recommendations to be given scarce government time.[7] Under the Justices of the Peace Act 1949, the Advisory Committee system was retained in only slightly altered form. The majority of the Royal Commission had acknowledged that the political loyalties of candidates were a legitimate, though not decisive, factor in making appointments, and this was the view which Jowitt had already expressed in public and which the Labour party has understandably maintained, having most to gain from it; one of Lord Simonds' first acts however, was to drop Jowitt's paragraph to this effect from the handbook for Advisory Committees.[8] These papers give only a few indications of official policy on appointments: they illustrate, for example, the "settled practice of successive Lord Chancellors in modern times" in excluding beneficed clergymen[9] and reveal that in 1943 Lord Simon, on the advice of Leo Page, extended the policy of excluding senior public employees to embrace all levels of the public service, a "fallacious and untenable" measure according to Howorth and one which was immediately dropped under Jowitt.[10]

The ranks of the justices were swollen by "ex-officio" appointments, notably of mayors and ex-mayors (for a year after the end of their term of office) and chairmen of district councils. These people were obviously out of place if a trained magistracy was the goal and the Royal Commission recommended their removal, but as the files show, the cabinet demurred under strenuous lobbying. The Secretary for Commissions wrote that "the whole issue seems to turn on the question whether or not the transfer of all ex-officio Justices to the Supplemental List will tend to decrease Labour support in the country",[11] and the government evidently decided that it would, for only ex-mayors were deprived of their right to be ex-officio justices by the subsequent legislation.

2 Conduct and Disqualification

Complaints against the decisions of justices properly went to the Home Office, so few are to be found here, though one concerning the blatant non-enforcement of minimum wage levels for labourers by Welsh farmers sitting on the bench underlines the weakness of magistrates' justice in matters inimical to their own interests.[12] Of more general interest is the Home Office summary of complaints and proceedings against magistrates who were alleged to have given countenance in various ways to the General Strike of 1926, one of the few national events which tested their impartiality to the limit: nine persons were removed from the bench or from the advisory committees in the nearest approach this century to a purge.[13]

The case which most exercised the office, however, was that of the indomitable Mrs Esther Iwi, who drew Jowitt into her intractable dispute with the rest of the Hendon bench which culminated in her High Court libel action against its chairman. The voluminous papers on this episode are an enlightening and entertaining sidelight on the problem of an appointment which turned out badly but where none of the traditionally recognised forms of misbehaviour could be shown.[14]

A few of the files on complaints against individuals are worth mentioning here: the case of Ben Greene, whom Simon had removed "against my better judgment"[15] in deference to local opinion and refused to reinstate, merges into the more important episode of his detention and law suit against the Home Secretary, but that of William Dent is more interesting as an example of the conflicts inherent in the Lord Chancellor's peculiar office. Dent was an active and influential Liberal in Yorkshire who refused to pay the Education Rate as a "passive resister" and whose political opponents in the county manoeuvered his removal by petitioning the new Lord Chancellor. Haldane's action brought down upon him the wrath of the government's nonconformist supporters but despite heavy pressure from the Prime Minister he held to it.[16] Simon and Jowitt later came under similar, but less severe, pressure to reinstate one of three Monmouth councillors convicted in 1938 of fiddling expenses, especially after he had received an O.B.E. Like Haldane, they also resisted firmly.[17]

Even where there was no corruption among councillors, their presence on the bench posed awkward problems because of the increasing involvement of local authorities in bringing and defending actions. The LCO tried to restrict serving councillors to one-third of the membership of a bench but that was often impracticable,[18] and concern about bias led to the passing of s. 3 Justices of the Peace Act 1949, which placed on a statutory footing the exclusion of councillors from sitting in cases where they might have a bias, going indeed beyond what Napier considered really necessary.[19] The undesirable appearance of a conflict of interests which arose when a solicitor appeared before a bench of which a partner in his firm was a member, an occurrence particularly common with ex-officio justices, had already been dealt with in an earlier statute (Justices of the Peace Act 1906 s. 4) though the provisions were not free from ambiguity, and in fact the Law Society imposed its own curbs, which were more restrictive than those the LCO deemed necessary.[20]

More often than bias, the weakness of magistrates' justice was simply caused by incompetence, and this was often the result of advancing years. The lack of any obligatory retiring age led naturally to many magistrates holding onto what they regarded as being as much a personal honour as an office of state, well after they ceased to enjoy their full faculties; indeed it was often a real convenience in a locality to have a sufficient number of persons able to administer oaths, witness documents etc. It was the insistence of some who were blind, many who were deaf and even more who were not mentally alert on exercising their judicial functions that was the scandal, and one that was at last sought to be remedied by administrative means in 1938. Unfortunately the exhortation to retire in what came to be known as the ''resurrection circular'' proved a two-edged weapon which actually encouraged some moribund justices to exert themselves,[21] and legislation had to be resorted to in 1941 to make the Lord Chancellor's ''Supplemental List'' statutory. Not all Lord-Lieutenants welcomed it, and Schuster considered it badly drafted, but it proved its worth, especially when coupled with an undertaking extracted from all new justices to retire at seventy-five unless invited to stay on.[22]

3 Recorders, Stipendiary and Metropolitan Police Magistrates

The Royal Commission report and the 1949 Act were an endorsement of the system of amateur, unpaid justices and ensured that the few existing paid magistrates who complemented it would not be very much expanded. These fell into three classes, recorders, stipendiary magistrates and metropolitan police magistrates, and until 1950 the Lord Chancellor had little to do with them. All were appointed through the Home Secretary and his practice was to consult the Attorney-General, as head of the Bar, since all these posts were limited to barristers (a restriction which the Lord Chancellors vigorously defended).[23] The Attorney-General, however, usually consulted the LCO, probably because they had information on likely candidates gathered in connection with other offices, such as county court judgeships. When the du Parcq Commission proposed that the appointment and supervision of these officials should pass to the LCO the Home Office resisted strongly, and initially successfully, but pressure in Parliament obliged them to accept a compromise whereby full responsibility for recorders was transferred, along with the appointment of stipendiaries.[24] Besides the files dealing with the transfer of business and consequent administrative arrangements, a number of Home Office files on various matters connected with these officials was handed over to the LCO and merely re-registered in the general series. Among the more interesting are those which reveal the (largely ineffective) campaign to persuade elderly recorders who had been appointed before 1916—when undertakings as to retirement were first exacted—to retire gracefully,[25] the running feud between the Liverpool Recorder, Hemmerde and the corporation,[26] and the controversy surrounding the appointment of the first woman police magistrate, Miss Sybil Campbell, and subsequently her severe sentences.[27]

4 Quarter Sessions

The criminal jurisdiction of magistrates was performed at petty and quarter sessions, and the latter dealt with the more serious cases, including some felonies. It was therefore particularly important that the quarter sessions should be chaired by a responsible person with some legal training, but while the borough sessions were chaired by the recorder, county justices elected their own chairman. Legislative action was made necessary by the Bodkin Committee's report, which endorsed the Peel Commission's recommendation of an extension to the range of offences triable at quarter sessions in places where they had legally qualified chairmen.[28] Official pragmatism produced a "horrid piece of legislation" in the Administration of Justice (Miscellaneous Provisions) Act 1938 which encouraged counties rather than coercing them, by giving wider jurisdiction to those which had a legally qualified chairman.[29] The qualification was defined so generously that very few had difficulty in complying, and the LCO was able to resist pressures to make it compulsory.[30]

The borough benches presented a different problem, that of size and distribution. In fact the superimposition of the criminal justice administration on the out of date administrative units of county and borough made for vast inefficiency and the Home Office proposal (which was taken up by the Royal Commission) to abolish the separate quarter sessions of the smallest 58 boroughs (out of 126) was a very timid measure. Nevertheless it raised up a predictable storm of opposition, not only from the boroughs and the Bar Council but unexpectedly from the Lord Chief Justice, who felt it would overburden the assizes.[31] In Parliament the government had to concede that some might be saved by order in council (s. 10(5)) and in January, 1950 a small committee under the Attorney-General with Home Office and LCO representatives was formed to investigate the claims of each threatened borough; in the event several were reprieved.[32]

5 Juvenile and Licensing Business

Two special types of magistrates' work also deserve mention: the first is the juvenile court, because the Juvenile Courts (Metropolis) Act 1920, which introduced the system in London, is covered by an interesting file showing how the irreconcilable claims of the 'children's' and 'females' lobbies respectively, threatened to halt all progress on the bill,[33] and because the files which cover the implementation of the Childrens and Young Persons Act 1933 give a lively picture of the lobbying tactics of women's organisations.[34]

Licensing matters are also of interest because they showed many benches at their worst. Both party political interests and the activities of the temperance movement influenced many of the decisions, and Jowitt and the Attorney-General agreed that some London sessions were a disgrace.[35] Little could be done about the party politics but Jowitt took a strong line against the Rechabites, whose oath bade them use of any lawful means to discourage the drink trade, and he barred them from sitting on licensing benches, despite very vocal opposition from the temperance movement.[36]

6 Reforms

Since the Home Office was principally responsible for the administration of magistrates' courts, it was the natural official source for any reforming proposals, but the LCO could, and did, offer enthusiastic support to any reforms which it favoured. Thus in the 1930s it was Schuster who pressed the Home Office to set up a committee on justices' clerks, being himself a strong advocate of full time clerks appointed by a central authority and qualified as solicitors.[37] He unsuccessfully opposed the selection of Lord Roche as chairman on the grounds that he was too conservative, and the proposals of the committee did not go far enough to satisfy him,[38] but the changes which were proposed were given full backing by the LCO and did much to improve the organisation of magistrates' courts generally. The LCO was also the driving force behind the appointment of the Royal Commission. Jowitt told the cabinet that he was anxious to improve the number and quality of magistrates sympathetic to Labour and agreed readily enough that its terms should not extend to a consideration of magistrates' jurisdiction. The secretary was R. M. Jackson of the Home Office,[40] but the LCO papers on the Commission's proceedings are a valuable source on the manoeuvering over its composition and for the implementation of its recommendations, both by administrative action and, after prolonged discussions on cabinet and with the Treasury, through legislation.[41]

Notes

1 *For a general account see Sir Thomas Skyrme,* ***The Changing Image of the Magistracy*** *(2nd ed., 1983).*

2 *2/955: Schuster to C. Chapman, 1.5.1924.*

3 *see* ***infra****, 288–9.*

4 *see* ***supra****, 101 ff.*

5 *PP 1910 (Cd. 5250) XXXVII, 647; R. F. V. Heuston,* ***Lives of the Lord Chancellors*** *(1964), 114–17, 153–8; P. G. Richards,* ***Patronage in British Government*** *(1964) 154–77. The phrase quoted is Sir Almeric Fitzroy's (****Memoirs****, (1925) 346).*

6 *B. Abel-Smith and R. Stevens,* ***Lawyers and the Courts****, (1967) 103–4.*

7 *PP 1947–8 (Cmd 7463) XII, 733.*

8 *2/3500.*

9 *2/3480: Howorth to Lord Hazlerigg, 11.5.1945. The Royal Commission's recommendation to lift this ban was accepted:* ***ibid.****: Skyrme to J. W. Robertson Scott, 24.5.1954.*

10 *2/3501: Howorth's memorandum, January, 1946.*

11 *2/4475: Skyrme to Morgan Phillips, 1.4.1949; Home Policy Committee 13th meeting, 4.4.1949.*

12 *2/919.*

13 *2/918.*

14 *2/5306, 6677–88. See* **Iwi** *v* ***Montesole*** *[1955] Crim LR 313. Mrs Iwi was the wife of a well-known lawyer and writer on constitutional questions, E. F. Iwi, one of the LCO's most indefatigable correspondents. Her quarrel with the rest of the bench began when she took a joke made by a fellow magistrate literally.*

15 *2/1454: Simon's note, 19.1.1942. See* ***infra****, 259.*

16 *2/917.*

17 *2/1462. The Lord-Lieutenant admitted that there was "a good deal of corruption among Labour Councillors" on this council.*

18 *2/3131: Howorth to L. Blake-Odgers (Home Office), 21.1.1947.*

19 *A summary by L. Brass (Home Office) of the reported cases on bias is in 2/1455. Napier saw dangers "in letting the maxim about justice being manifestly seen to be done run riot and thereby do more harm than good": note of November, 1949 in 2/3514.*

20 *2/5301.*

21 *R. M. Jackson,* ***The Machinery of Justice in England****, 219–21.*

22 *2/1456. Rumours that it was intended to retire all JPs over seventy (Sir D. Hacking, chairman of the Conservative Party, to Simon, 28.2.1941) had to be countered through the B.B.C.*

23 *2/3658.*

24 *2/4475. Justices of the Peace Act, 1949 s. 29(3).*

25 *2/6655.*

26 *2/4376. See Inskip to Hutchinson, 10.10.1934 for an outline of Hemmerde's well-known quarrel with his erstwhile friend Lord Birkenhead.*

27 *2/4596–8.*

28 *PP 1935–6 (Cmd 5065) VIII, 105; PP 1935–6 (Cmd 5252) VIII, 265.*

29 *2/1622–3. R. M. Jackson,* ***supra****, 134.*

30 *2/6514, 6517, 3343.*

31 *2/3520.*

32 *2/3521–4.*

33 *2/463.*

34 *2/1955, 3227.*

35 *2/4479: Jowitt to Home Secretary, 19.10.1948; Attorney-General to Jowitt, 25.10.1948.*

36 *2/3517, especially Jowitt's memorandum of 21.7.1950. See also PP 1947–8 (Cmd 7463) XII, 733 at para. 150.*

37 *2/1449: Schuster to E. R. Cook, 29.9.1936.*

38 *2/1449–51. Leo Page also sat on the committee and favoured more radical proposals.*

39 *2/3481.*

40 *The author of "****The Machinery of Justice in England****". His chapters on magistrates are therefore particularly authoritative.*

41 *2/4475–8.*

2
APPOINTMENTS

1 Policy and Politics

2/3481–3 Du Parcq Commission, preliminary correspondence, Cabinet papers, discussions on membership, especially with Home Office; evidence and memoranda, especially from the LCO.

3500	Parliamentary question on Jowitt's speech to Magistrates' Association, 1945.

2 Particular Occupations etc.

2/350, 615	Justices of the Peace (Women) Bill, 1919: includes discussions on policy towards the bill, list of recommended candidates.
3474	1936–43: PQs and complaints about non-appointment of teachers; correspondence with R. H. Morgan MP and Lord Harewood.
3480	Correspondence with local authorities and others on beneficed clergymen as JPs, explaining LCO policy, 1945.
3501	Correspondence on "fallacious and untenable" bar on public employees imposed by Lord Simon, with Harewood and A. Moyle MP; also with C. R. Attlee (1947) on local councillors as JPs.
3475, 3496	Sheriffs and sheriff officers as JPs.
89, 414, 3510	Other cases.

3 The Advisory Committees and Lord-Lieutenants

2/3487, 3529, 5281	Scottish Central Advisory Committee: correspondence and meetings with Scottish departments on proposed transfer of responsibility, and on composition; also with Lord Exeter, with the secretary (P. J. Rose) and members, 1948–9. Further correspondence with Rose on agendas etc. to 1951.
3494–5	London: correspondence and meetings with Lord-Lieutenant, political organisations and Home Office on changes in composition and approach; Skyrme's papers include minutes of meetings, lists of candidates etc., 1949.
3493	Correspondence of 1947–8 with Morgan Phillips on the role of political parties in the selection of JPs.
3643	Query by Lord Strabogli re Deputy Lieutenants, 1950.
3640, 1155	Notes for Prime Minister's Office on their functions etc. (1946) and correspondence with Scottish Home Department. Discussions, papers etc. on possible retirement age, with Lord Exeter for the Association of Lord-Lieutenants; materials on the relationship of the office of Custos Rotulorum with that of Lord-Lieutenant. Notes on peculiarities of the post of Custos Rotulorum of Haverfordwest (1939).
5692	Correspondence with P. J. Rose and A. Bevir on political role of Lord-Lieutenants, 1949.
6340	Prime Minister asks Lord Chancellor to procure resignation of Duke of Sutherland after divorce scandal, 1944. Correspondence with Sutherland and Deputy Lieutenants. Attempts to re-instate him, 1950.

4 Ex-officio JPs

2/3505	Correspondence on the proposal of the London Labour Group of MPs to make all MPs *ex-officio* JPs, and on the subsequent LCO suggestion that the range of documents which MPs may witness for official purposes be expanded, 1946–7.

4475	Cabinet discussions on the proposal to end *ex-officio* appointments of mayors etc., 1948–9.

5 Particular Jurisdiction

2/2746	(Isle of Man) 2747 (Romney Marsh) 3479 (Holyhead Harbour Master) 3507 (Orkney and Zetland), 5304 (closure of Filey court).
2286, 2345, 3477	Soke of Peterborough: Holdich's case (1920) with Law Officers' opinions of various dates and other papers on the scope of the jurisdiction and validity of Crown Office practice on appointments.

6 Appointments under the Lunacy Act 1890 ss. 10(3) (4)

2/2859–2955, 4380–95	Mostly formal correspondence but some contain queries about the construction of the Act; see 2938 (Wells) for one instance where magistrates purported to make the appointments themselves and the appointees made a committal.

7 Formalities

2/332, 912, 914	Questions about the oath.
943, 1458, 5716	Miscellaneous questions.

3
CONDUCT AND DISQUALIFICATION

1 Solicitors

2/265	Justices of the Peace Bill 1906, notes.
266	Law Officers' opinion on Justices of the Peace Act 1906 s. 4, 1907.
616, 913	Mayor of Wisbech's case, 1922, with notes of precedents. J. L. Gillespie's case, 1925.
617, 1448, 3497, 3502–3, 3506, 3509	Other cases.
1447, 5301	Policy of LCO and Law Society explained in replies to complaints and questions, 1932–4 and 1951.

2 Local Authorities

2/267	Winchester, 1907, correspondence and Law Officers' opinion.
618	Croydon and Chester-le-Street complaints, 1923.
1455	Memorandum by L. S. Brass (Home Office) on precedents in decided cases, 1932.
3512	Wokingham complaint, 1949.
3535	Correspondence with HO on scope of s. 3 Justices of the Peace Act 1949.

3 Other Complaints

2/915, 918	General strike; correspondence with chairman of West Riding of Yorkshire quarter sessions on the "Doncaster Hold-Up"; general file (918) includes summary of complaints and disciplinary measures arising out of the strike, 1926–7.
919	Complaint by National Union of Agricultural Workers (1929) of leniency of JPs towards violations of wages legislation, especially in *Hughes* v *Davies*; correspondence with Ministry of Agriculture and abstract of prosecutions.
5315	1943–9: complaints that magistrates in Croydon and Brighton are unduly severe on conscientious objectors; correspondence with magistrates and others.
4211, 5300, 3514	Other complaints, including alleged bias in lunacy cases (3514).

4 The Removal of Justices and the Supplemental List

2/51, 1459	Effect of bankruptcy: case of Hadley.
1460	Cases of dishonesty, 1934.
1463	Effect of divorce scandal in case of Captain Heber-Percy.
1454	Removal of Ben Greene and correspondence on his request to be reinstated, 1939–42.
917	Removal of William Dent for refusal to pay the education rate; correspondence with Lord-Lieutenant of the East Riding, Prime Minister and others, 1924.
1462	Removal for dishonesty of several Monmouth JPs, and petitions for reinstatement, 1938–45.
1464	Reprimand to J. Green, convicted under wartime regulations, 1941.
1461	Reprimand for Mrs S. Noble for criticising a decision of her own bench, 1936.
2769	Correspondence with Home Office on power to remove metropolitan police magistrates, especially on the case of Metcalfe, 1931, and complaint that LCO not consulted.
5299	T.U.C. complaint re inability of state employed JPs to obtain adequate leave, 1951.
3478, 3513	Requests for notification to LCO of criminal convictions of magistrates: correspondence with Home Office on procedures, 1944–50.
5306, 6677–88	Extensive documents on the case of Mrs Iwi and the Hendon bench, 1949–55.
1456–7	Justices of the Peace (Supplemental List) Act 1941: cabinet papers, drafting correspondence, memoranda on elderly JPs; Parliamentary correspondence, especially with Lord Exeter and other Lord-Lieutenants.
3508, 3515–16, 3533, 3536–7	Sundry questions on interpretation of the supplemental list rules.
3527, 3531,	Supplemental List Rules 1950, drafting correspondence.
3515	Requests for deferred retirement, 1951–5.

4
RECORDERS, STIPENDIARY AND METROPOLITAN POLICE MAGISTRATES

1 Recorders

2/4373, 5726	Transfer of responsibility from Home Office: memoranda on HO practice and on proposed LCO practice, 1949–50.
4377	List of recorderships abolished under Justices of the Peace Act 1949 s. 10(1).
6652	Eligibility of barristers from other circuits: Law Officers' opinion (1886) correspondence with Bar Council, McCardie J, Law Officers *et al.*, various dates.
6654	Compatibility of recordership with county court judgeship; correspondence with Home Office, 1905–41.
4374, 6651, 6655–7	Attempts to remove recorders: general note on power to remove (4374) and cases in Bury St. Edmunds (4374), Cardiff (6651) Grantham (6657), Poole (6656), all in transferred Home Office files, and (6655) several cases after 1950.
4378	Home Office file on effect of bankruptcy on recordership, 1911.
4376	Home Office file on G. Hemmerde (Liverpool) and his disputes with the corporation, 1934–9.

2 Stipendiary Magistrates

2/3490, 4475, 5726	Transfer of appointments from Home Office 1948–50: memorandum on law and practice.
4594, 4599	Consolidated Home Office files on salaries and superannuation, including discussions with Society of Stipendiary Magistrates on superannuation schemes and retirements.
956	Correspondence with Home Office and Admiralty on abolition of stipendiary at Chatham and Sheerness, 1926.
3659, 3660	Appointment of Cardiff and Staffordshire stipendiaries: lists of candidates sent by Law Officers' Department and comments, 1939–51.
3663	Applications for posts by W. Purchase, 1927–41.

3 Metropolitan Police Magistrates

2/955	Discussions on salaries with Home Office, 1924.
3657	Correspondence with Home Office on salaries, with Home Office files on 1937 Statutory Salaries Bill and subsequent claims.
4609–11	Cabinet papers, memoranda and departmental correspondence leading to the Tribunal Salaries Bill, 1951.
5723, 5726	Correspondence with Home Office and Chief Metropolitan Magistrate on raising retiring age, 1951.
3658	LCO oppose proposals to make solicitors eligible, 1946.
2769	Correspondence with Home Office on power to dismiss, 1942.
2770	Lists of candidates for appointment sent by Law Officers' Department, with LCO comments, 1943–50.
3661	Home Office files on Sir Bertrand Watson, 1928–36, 1937–48.

4596–8 Home Office files on the appointment of Miss Sybil Campbell in 1945 and the press and Parliamentary campaign against her sentences.

6341–2 Salaries discussed (see under '*Judges*', *supra*, 89).

5
QUARTER SESSIONS

1 County Sessions

2/1620, 1622–3 Administration of Justice (Miscellaneous Provisions) Bill 1938: Parliamentary papers; memoranda by DPP, Bar Council, Law Society; correspondence with Home Office, PCO, Lord Roche, clerks of the peace, Middlesex CC etc.

3343, 3763, 6514, 6517 LCO memorandum (1947) on current position, correspondence on HO suggestion to introduce compulsion; lists of appointments, Parliamentary questions etc.

4601 Home Office files on chairman and deputy of London QS.: correspondence with them, L.C.C., Treasury on salaries, pensions etc., 1931–54.

3761, 3762 Particular issues in Lancashire and Hertfordshire, 1946–7.

816, 1212, 1214–5, 3138 Local bills empowering appointment of salaried chairmen reported by Home Office and considered, various dates.

3760 LCJ complains of the participation of High Court judges in quarter sessions work, 1946–50. See also 3499.

3765 E. F. Iwi's memorandum on need for Middlesex sessions to be held in long vacation, 1949.

6649 Correspondence with Clement Davies on proposal to remove solicitors' rights of audience at Montgomery QS, 1951.

2 Borough Sessions

2/3520–6, 4475–8 1948–51: proposed abolition of certain borough quarter sessions and commissions of the peace; correspondence with the LCJ, Association of Municipal Corporations, PCO, Bar Council, Attorney-General, Home Office etc; cabinet and Parliamentary papers; papers of Attorney-General's committee on applications for reprieve; Justices of the Peace Act 1949 (Saving of Borough Quarter Sessions) Orders, various.

4375 Home Office files on Halifax's application for separate quarter sessions, 1921.

84 Grant of quarter sessions to Dundee, 1894.

6
JUVENILE AND LICENSING BUSINESS

1 Juvenile Courts

2/463 Juvenile Courts (Metropolis) Bill 1920: correspondence with Home Office; notes of meetings with interested parties; memoranda by welfare and women's organisations, Parliamentary papers.

1453 Truancy complaints in London to go to juvenile courts, 1938.

1955–7, 3226 JCs (Constitution) Rules under Children and Young Persons Act 1933: drafts by Home Office, representations by women's organisations and others; amendments and wartime extensions of panels.

3227 Amendment Rules 1950: correspondence of 1946 on agitation by women's organisations on composition of panels; discussions (with PCO and Home Office) on provisions for minimum and maximum age for serving justices, 1950.

2 Licensing

2/3072 Licensing Planning (Temporary Provisions) Bill, 1945: Home Office brief for Lord Chancellor, and correspondence.

3131 Civic Restaurants Bill, 1947: petitions from church and brewers' organisations, correspondence with Ministry of Food, and with Home Office on the difficulty of constituting unbiased benches.

4479 Licensing Bill, 1948: representations from temperance bodies, discussions with Home Office and London Labour Party on London sessions, Parliamentary papers.

3517 Discussions on the ban on Independent Order of Rechabites sitting on licensing benches; deputations, memoranda, discussions with Scottish departments, and with magistrates' associations on proposed new form of undertaking, 1948–51.

3518 Complaint against the Abergele justices: correspondence with Home Office.

5318 Questions on the propriety of members of co-operative movement sitting on licensing benches: memorandum by Howarth on the Barnsley bench and correspondence on political considerations.

7
REFORMS

1 General

2/1453 Report of the Metropolitan Courts Committee, 1937: LCO objections sent to Home Office.

3037, 5285 Magistrates' Courts Bills (Consolidation): correspondence with PCO on abortive bill in 1943, and preliminary discussions on 1952 bill.

3481–95 Royal Commission on Justices of the Peace: general correspondence (3481) evidence (3482) report (3484) advisory committees (3486–7, 3494–5); rules committee (3489), proposed legislation (3485, 3488). 3487 deals with the reorganisation of Scottish advisory committees, including correspondence with Scottish departments and the secretary to the Scottish Central Advisory Committee.

4475–8 Justices of the Peace Bill: preliminary discussions with Home Office on transfer of responsibility; cabinet papers, discussions with departments and PCO on bill; cabinet discussions on *ex-officio* JPs, especially in London; representations from Justices Clerks Society, Law Society, local authorities, LCJ; Parliamentary papers.

3519–30, 3534, 5279, 5289 Justices of the Peace Act 1949: general correspondence on commencement orders (3519), on abolition of certain borough quarter sessions (3530–4) and various other particular aspects (3525–9); compensation regulations (5289), Parliamentary questions (5279).

2 Training, Expenses etc.

2/3142 Warrington Corporation Bill, 1945: discussions on proposal to pay expenses.

5291 Justices of the Peace Act 1949 s. 8: representations by various (mostly labour) organisations that it should be brought into effect.

5286 Discussions with Home Office and Magistrates' Association on "model scheme" of training, 1948.

3354 Appraisals of the training film "Four Men in Prison", 1950.

3 Magistrates' Clerks

2/1449–51 Roche Committee: Schuster's papers and departmental correspondence 1936–48 on its establishment and composition, and on its report, especially on Schuster's reservations.

1452 Note on dismissal of clerks, 1946.

1594 Summary Jurisdiction Rules (Money Payments Act 1935): correspondence on Justices Clerks Society proposal to levy fees, 1935.

3519 Compensation for part-time clerks and other proposals. Cabinet papers, correspondence with Home Office, Treasury etc; Lord Merthyr's campaign in Parliament.

3165 L.C.C. Bill giving power to appoint clerks discussed with Home Office, 1947.

3532 Justices of the Peace Act 1949 4th schedule: representations by Justices Clerks Society, Society of Clerks of the Peace and Clerks of County Councils on appointments of clerks to magistrates' courts committees.

5283 PQs, correspondence and Law Society, Home Office and cabinet papers on compensation for part-time clerks 1951. Negotiations continued and settlement reached 1954.

8
RULES AND PRACTICE

(see also under particular subject headings)

2/191, 1160–1, 1590–5, 4258, 5280 Summary jurisdiction rules, various dates, and attendant correspondence with Home Office.

1216, 2820, 3476, 3511, 3766 Questions of practice, including availability of justices' notes for appeals. (2820).

Chapter

5

LOCAL, MILITARY AND CORONERS' COURTS, AND COURTS OUTSIDE GREAT BRITAIN

1
LOCAL COURTS

1 Introduction

Recent scholarship has rescued the local courts of the nineteenth century from "the enormous condescension of posterity" and stresses their quantitative and qualitative significance in English legal administration.[1] These courts suffered two major blows in the course of that century however; the first, and more severe, was the establishment in 1846 of a nationwide network of county courts which were intended to supersede local courts of requests; the second was the Judicature Acts, which by creating a single, centralised Supreme Court of Judicature, left no scope in the new scheme of things for those local courts of record which were still active, though few of them were. As Henry Nicol wrote, they should all have been swept away at that time "and it would have been done but for the Lord Mayor's Court, confound it".[2] The LCO were to rue that omission, for although a further forty-two borough courts were abolished in 1886 as a by-product of local government reform, the following decades saw the attempted revival of several moribund ones, such as those at Worcester and Plymouth, presumably encouraged by the delays at assizes and the low financial limits of county court jurisdiction.[3]

In order to be profitable, which was a prerequisite of their continuance, they had to attract suitors directly, by offering these positive incentives in the form of speedier or less protective process, or indirectly by allowing higher costs to solicitors. Since most of them operated under antiquated rules, in some cases made before the Common Law Procedure Act of 1852, they also needed to remodel them and to obtain some of the rules of the Supreme Court, notably for interpleader, default summonses and the right to serve process on defendants residing outside the jurisdiction. By virtue of an Act of 1872 the Lord Chancellor had the power to grant them such powers by order in council, and in 1873 and again in the 1880s and 1890s, Lord Chancellors were persistently importuned to do so,[4] while corporations also attempted to circumvent him by inserting the enlarged powers into local bills. There was therefore the alarming possibility that the present handful of busy courts (the Lord Mayor's Court, the Salford Hundred Court, the Liverpool Court of Passage and the Bristol Tolzey Court)[5] might become the nucleus of a whole network of "branches of the High Court of Justice" which would compete seriously with the county courts.

In view of the continuing dissatisfaction with the availability of justice in the provinces, it was politically undesirable to attempt to abolish the local courts and not easy to resist pressure to give them adequate powers; for example, the Court of Passage had eventually to be given interpleader, which by a "*ne plus ultra* of legal anomaly"[6] it had purported to exercise until brought up short by the judgment of Wills J in **Speers** v. **Daggers** (1885).

At first therefore, the Supreme Court Rule Committee, to whom Selborne had committed the task of examining proposed new rules, was disposed to base them on the county court rules, but a sub-committee set up in 1894 reported that if the courts were to continue at all their rules should be based upon the RSC.[7]

In fact only a few succeeded in attracting and retaining a significant volume of business: among those in the provinces Salford, Liverpool, Derby, Bristol and Norwich were the only significant ones, and the LCO had no hopes of abolishing them while they remained busy. Their popularity, however, was more likely to be among suitors and solicitors than defendants: thus the Derby Court of Record had repeatedly been complained of and depended largely on Nottingham moneylenders who found it easier than the county court,[8] while of Salford (whose jurisdiction had been narrowed by a local act in 1911) Napier noted that "I do not think that the Salford Court tempers the wind to the shorn lamb" and Schuster, concurring, said "under its present judge the court is something in the nature of a scandal".[9]

The LCO missed a trick by not referring the future of these courts to the Evershed Committee. Indeed they were badly outmanoeuvered over the now ailing Salford Court, for having fended off a bid by Manchester Corporation to raise the financial limits of its jurisdiction by making the conventional concession of an inquiry, they found that its report unexpectedly endorsed the corporation's claim.[10] The LCO had squashed attempts to revive moribund borough courts, and viewed with satisfaction the decline of others, such as Norwich, but it was left to the Beeching Commission to chop down the more firmly planted, leaving only the Mayor's and City Corporation Court (the two had been amalgamated in 1920) to survive, and that in name only, for it became essentially a county court.[11]

Two other local courts merit separate treatment, for the Palatinate Courts of Lancaster and Durham were local chancery courts, which also perished in the 1971 reorganisation.[12] In neither case were appointments in the Lord Chancellor's gift, but belonged to the Chancellor of the Duchy and the Home Secretary respectively and it was the location of the former within the Duchy that ensured its survival. The Durham court was much less important, its geographical limits being both peculiar and narrow, and the Chancellorship really almost a sinecure even after it was reorganised in the 1880s on the lines of Lancaster. Once again, Napier was disconcerted in the post-war period when an enquiry into Durham, this time an offshoot of the deliberation of the Evershed Committee, came out with "a conclusion the opposite of what I had hoped for", recommending retention and a modest expansion of boundaries.[13]

Notes

1 *H. W. Arthurs,* **Without the Law** *(1984). The phrase quoted is from the preface to E. P. Thompson's* **The Making of the English Working Class** *(1963).*

2 *2/75: to Muir McKenzie, 8.5.1894.*

3 **Halsbury's Laws** *(4th ed.) vol. 10, paras 969–88. The* **Civil Judicial Statistics** *give numbers of plaints issued in each court.*

4 *Borough Courts of Record of Act 1872 s. 3. 1/48: Lord Chancellor to Lord President*

and to Home Secretary, both 20.1.1873; 1/49. Lord Chancellor's circular, 8.3.1884.

5 *PP 1888 (187) LXXXII, 169 lists the active courts.*

6 *1/49: Wills J to Lord Chancellor, 26.3.1885.*

7 *2/76: report of 12.6.1894.*

8 *2/1089–90.*

9 *2/1821: notes of 25.3.1936.*

10 *PP 1950–1 (Cmd 8310) XV, 637 (the Upjohn report).*

11 *PP 1969 (Cmd 4158) XXVIII. 2/4898: minute by Dobson, 14.4.1953.*

12 *For Durham see K. Emsley and C. M. Fraser,* ***The Courts of the County Palatine of Durham*** *(1984).*

13 *2/4645: minute of 10.7.1952. PP 1950–1 (Cmd 8364) XI, 55.*

2 General

1/48–50 1873–83: pleas for wider jurisdiction from various local courts, especially Hull: correspondence with Lord President, Home Office and Rule Committee papers.

2/76 Report of committee on rules for inferior courts of record, 1894.

3468 Correspondence with PCO on juries in local courts, 1948.

3 Particular Courts

1 Barmote Court of Wirksworth

2/4516 Correspondence with Duchy of Lancaster on juries, 1948.

2 Bideford Court of Record

2/24 Draft rules 1891.

3 Bristol Tolzey Court

1/48 Attempt to obtain wider powers, 1873.

2/23 Correspondence with Judge Prideaux on new rules, 1890.

1091 Correspondence with Registrar and Town Clerk on exemption from Moneylenders Act 1925 s. 11 and costs in the court.

4626 On application of legal aid scheme, 1948.

4 Chipping Wycombe Court of Record

2/1154 Correspondence with Town Clerk on proposed revival, 1939.

5 Deal Court of Record

2/2687 Correspondence with Town Clerk on rules and threatened lawsuit in 1945.

6 Derby Court of Record

1/50 Complaint from Derby County Court about its activities: comments of H. Nicol, 1885.

2/121	Complaint by county court judge, 1900.
303	Complaints discussed by County Court Rule Committee, 1914.
1089–90	Law Society complaint 1924: history and constitution of the court; memorandum on local courts; correspondence on revised rules with PCO, Recorder, Nottingham CC Registrar *et al.*

7 *Durham Palatinate Court*

1/50	Correspondence about appointments and rules, 1885.
2/22	1887–92: eight files relating to the appointment of Gainsford Bruce as Chancellor (1887) and the Durham Palatinate Court Bill. Correspondence with PCO, Bruce and A. O. Smith (Registrar) and memoranda from local law societies.
134	1895–98: six files on Durham Palatinate Bill: correspondence with Home Office and other departments and summaries of cases in the court.
3382	1879–1955: Home Office files (transferred 1950) on appointments of Attorney- and Solicitor-General; correspondence on the transfer.
880	Correspondence with Prime Minister's office on appointments, 1930.
2688, 4005–6, 4645	1936–52: proposals to reform and expand jurisdiction. Evershed Committee working party 'S', papers, correspondence and report.
3381	Questions raised by the new registrar, 1950.

8 *Hull Court of Record*

1/48, 50	1873–88: petitions for wider powers; correspondence with H. A. Bruce MP, Town Clerk.
2/75	Hull Corporation Bill: correspondence with Sir A. Rollit MP, Home Office and Treasury, 1894.
252	SCRC discuss new rules.

9 *Lancaster Chancery Court*

1/61	Memorandum opposing increased powers for Lancashire district registries, with comments by Muir McKenzie.
2/21	1888–90: correspondence on Chancery of Lancaster Bill, with Board of Trade and Liverpool Law Society.
81	Revised rules: correspondence with Vice-Chancellor, report of Kay J, 1894.
406	Lord Derby complains about costs, 1916.
554	New costs and fees orders approved, 1920.
795, 922	Memoranda and correspondence on Duchy of Lancaster Bill 1918. Correspondence of 1926 with Treasury and Vice-Chancellor on costs and tenure of officers. Proposals for economies, 1925.
923–6	1925–30: various rules and fees orders; Rule Committee views, especially on proposed consolidation of 1927.
1473–4	Rules applying Inheritance Act 1938 and RSC(3) 1941.
3363	Order in Council under Crown Proceedings Act 1947: correspondence with Treasury Solicitor and Registrar.
3542	Correspondence on rules consolidation, 1949.
4133	1949–52: Court of Chancery of Lancaster Act 1952; correspondence with

Kyffin Taylor V-C., PCO, Inland Revenue, Vaisey J on transfer of actions from High Court. Cabinet papers and correspondence on amendments.

10 Liverpool Court of Passage

1/49, 51	1885: Rule Committee papers on Wills J's judgment in **Speers** v **Daggers**. Proposals for wider powers by Judge Baylis (1876–83) with comments by county court judges, H. Nicol. Correspondence on Liverpool Corporation Bill, 1886.
2/18, 73–4, 122	1893–9: extensive correspondence on bills and rules to give wider jurisdiction. Memoranda from county court judges, correspondence with Judge Baylis, Home Office, Sir W. R. Greene MP, Registrar; meetings with deputations; Rule Committee papers.
176, 240	Rule Committee report 1903; further deputations etc. 1906; rules passed 1909; rule amendment 1915.
548	New costs order, and rules (1922); correspondence with Treasury on possible abolition.
932	Rules under Moneylenders Act 1927 s. 11; correspondence with J. A. Tinne MP, statistics on business; brief to Attorney-General.
1517, 3363, 3617	Given jurisdiction under Hire Purchase Act 1938, Exchange Control Act 1947, Crown Proceedings Act 1947.
3618, 3621–2	Crown Proceedings (Torts) Order 1950: correspondence with Registrar, Treasury Solicitor; Rule Committee papers. Transfer of patronage to LC (1950) and later appointments.
3619	Correspondence with Home Office, Attorney-General on candidates for the judgeship, 1948.
3620	Rules(1) 1950, correspondence with Registrar.

11 Mayor's and City of London Court

1/48	Petition to serve process outside jurisdiction, 1873.
1/36	City Court, 1873–81: appointment of assistant judge (1873), statistical returns and another appointment (1880).
2/14	Memorandum on the constitution of the City Court, 1890.
108	Rule Committee approve new fees structure in Mayor's Court, 1899.
152	Discussions on style and precedence of City Court judges.
202	Rule Committee approve new Mayor's Court rules, 1907.
389	Rule Committee approve Mayor's Court rules under Juries Act 1918.
461, 550	1919–21: Amalgamation Bill, 1920; discussions and correspondence with the Corporation on reduction in judges, and on business of the courts; papers on compensation for officers.
549	New costs order and rules, 1921: correspondence with T. W. Chitty.
524, 679	Sir Ernest Wild, Recorder: memoranda and correspondence on his position as an MP, 1921–2.
1288–9, 1624	Correspondence with Registrar on application of new county court venue rules to the Court, 1936.
1624	Administration of Justice (Miscellaneous Provisions) Act 1938: correspondence with PCO, Slesser LJ and others on clause re appeals from the Court.

2666 Correspondence on new rules (made 1944) with Registrar, H. Pickford, Judge Thomas and Law Society. Validity questioned by E. F. Iwi, 1947.

3228 Correspondence on Funds Rules, 1947.

5729–30 Correspondence with Corporation on salary and appointment of Common Sergeant, Recorder and Judge, 1951.

12 Newcastle Burgess Court

1/52 Petition for increased powers; correspondence with their agent and C. E. Pollock, 1883–6.

2/1207 Correspondence on saving of jurisdiction in Gateshead Extension Bill, 1932.

13 Norwich Guildhall Court of Record

2/123, 547 Correspondence with Registrar on revival and proposed rules, 1897. Also correspondence with County Court Registrar and others on Norwich Corporation Bill, 1920.

3468, 3665 Proposed new fees order, 1948; correspondence with County Court Judge, Town Clerk.

4627 Legal aid facilities, 1949.

14 Oxford Vice-Chancellor's Court

2/77 Correspondence with T. E. Holland on new appeals procedure, 1894.

241, 390 New rules approved by Rule Committee, 1907, 1918.

15 Plymouth Civil Court

2/71, 124 Proposed new rules; correspondence with the Recorder and County Court Judge, 1892–5.

16 Salford Hundred Court

2/72 Heywood and Rochdale petition for exclusion from jurisdiction in small claims, 1893.

776, 1092 Moneylenders Bill, 1925; report of joint select committee on Salford; correspondence with draftsmen and promoters; rules (1928).

1288 Complaints from solicitors on its proceedings, 1935.

1821 Correspondence with Master Bonner on *ultra vires* practices and possible remedies, 1936.

1517, 3363, 3783–4 Given jurisdiction under Hire Purchase Act 1938, Crown Proceedings Act 1947, Exchange Control Act 1947.

3207, 3785–6, 4898 1950–2: Manchester Corporation Bill, 1950 and proposal to increase jurisdiction, with supporting correspondence; considered with PCO and Davies (County Court Registrar); correspondence on setting up Upjohn Committee, its evidence and report; cabinet papers and correspondence with Duchy of Lancaster.

17 Stannaries Court

2/136–7, 3256 Abolition Bill, 1895: correspondence with PCO, Treasury and Board of Trade report by Official Receiver; correspondence with Judge Granger about transfer of business to Truro County Court; memoranda by Truro Registrar and others.

18 Worcester Court of Pleas

2/78 Correspondence with Earl Beauchamp, Rule Committee papers on proposed new rules, 1894.

2
MILITARY COURTS

1 Introduction

For most of this period, the armed forces were able to conduct their disciplinary proceedings with a minimum of publicity and interference from civilians, but in 1937 awkward questions were asked in Parliament about the conduct of certain courts-martial and the government responded in conventional fashion by setting up an inquiry under a High Court judge.[1] The report of the Oliver Committee made recommendations which were so unwelcome to the service departments, particularly to the notoriously independent Admiralty, that its publication was deferred for some months while attempts were made to bring them into harmony with each other on a modest reform package, and the Lord Chancellor and Sir Thomas Inskip were given the unwelcome task of ''adjudicating'' between them.[2] It was a relief to all concerned that the outbreak of war enabled this awkward subject to be shelved.

It could not be evaded when peace returned, however, if only because the permanent presence in the forces of large numbers of civilians on national service ensured that grievances would be widely ventilated, and since the Oliver report had not met the services' wishes, another judge was appointed to head a second committee, limited to the army and R.A.F. The Lewis report[3] in its turn was not altogether palatable, although the majority had rejected the suggestion most abhorred by the services, that other ranks should sit on courts-martial, and the Admiralty was proving so resistant to any change that it had to be placated with yet another enquiry, with a different membership under Pilcher J as they feared that the Lewis Committee would have preconceived notions.[4] Meanwhile a committee of officials under Sir Albert Napier was set to work adapting the Lewis proposals for legislation which would be acceptable to the service departments, the principal outstanding difficulty being the proper forum for appeals from courts-martial. At the same time arrangements were put in hand for the re-organisation of the office and department of the Judge-Advocate General and the transfer of responsibility for appointments and establishment matters to the LCO, as recommended by Lewis. That was accomplished in 1948 and in 1950 the Judge-Advocate of the Fleet was likewise transferred.

Progress on the more important changes was held up by the slow pace of the Pilcher Committee (largely dictated by the Admiralty), which had been set up in 1949 but whose final report did not reach the Lord Chancellor until November, 1950.[5] Not surprisingly, its recommendations differed in certain respects from the Lewis Committee so that to produce the desired legislation (which the cabinet had now decided to confine to the most politically sensitive area, appeals) yet another committee of officials was assembled: as Napier explained to the Attorney-General "the report will be confidential and can never be published, and even the fact of its existence will be treated with caution, as it is *prima facie* open to criticism that two published reports should be the subject of a report by a third committee, and that a committee of officials and not ministers".[6] Urgency was injected into these dilatory proceedings by public concern over the case of Private Linsell, sentenced to death for shooting a German civilian while on sentry duty, and with some difficulty Chorley drafted a bill which the service departments could all accept and which was passed in May, 1951, whereby appeals went to the Court of Criminal Appeal, despite the reluctance of the Lord Chief Justice to accept an extra burden.[7] This modest bill was the fruit of three departmental committees plus two committees of civil servants.

Notes

1 ***Parl. Debs*** *(H of C) 1936–7 vol. 322 cols. 935–63. Birkenhead's largely uncritical account of Great War courts martial is in* ***Points of View*** *(1922) II, 1–28.*

2 *PP 1939–40 (Cmd 6200) IV, 49; 2/4335: CP 71(39) and RCM (39) 1st meeting, March 1939.*

3 *PP 1948–9 (Cmd 7608) XIV, 61.*

4 *2/4343: First Lord to Lord Chancellor, 27.1.1949.*

5 *PP 1950–1 (Cmd 8094) XI, 55.*

6 *2/4345: 13.6.1950.*

7 ***Parl. Debs*** *(H of L) 1950–1, vol. 170 cols. 1095* ***et seq.****; 2/4346. The service departments had favoured the Privy Council for this purpose. The modern law is summarised in* ***Halsbury's Laws****, 4th ed., vol. 10, paras. 952–6.*

2 The Reform of Courts Martial

2/4335 The Oliver Committee, 1937–8: correspondence with service departments; cabinet papers including the "adjudication" by the Lord Chancellor and Inskip; notes of meetings, correspondence on publishing the report, and with the Judge-Advocate General on his salary.

4336–42, 5260 The Lewis Committee and interdepartmental (Napier) Committee. Evidence and report of Lewis Committee; memoranda by Sir F. Cassel and Sir H. McGreagh (past and present J-AGs), cabinet papers, papers on J-AG's establishment, correspondence on establishment of "interim committee" and its report (July 1948, papers in 4338). Napier Committee papers (4336, 4338–9, 4341); summary of Lewis Committee recommendations and notes of action taken (4341–2). Departmental and cabinet discussions on the reports (4337) to the end of 1948. Note on Blackburn's minority report (5260).

4343, 5256 The Pilcher Committee: correspondence with Admiralty on setting up and publication of report; discussions on a statutory definition of mutiny (5256).

4345–9 Courts Martial (Appeals) Bill, 1951: correspondence with service departments and J-AG, J-AF on Lewis and Pilcher proposals; report of interdepartmental committee (4345); cabinet papers and extensive correspondence with PCO and departments (including Colonial and Home Offices) on draft bill; notes on clauses and amendments and Parliamentary papers including briefs for Lord Reading's motion (4348).

5250–2, 5255 Rules and forms under Courts Martial (Appeals) Act: discussions with service departments and Criminal Appeals Office, and with Bar Council and Law Officers on rights of audience. Discussions on provision of summaries of evidence (5255).

4336, 4340, 4343–4, 5267 Transfer of judicial departments of J-AG and J-AF to LCO (1948, 1950): correspondence with Treasury and service departments, establishment sub-committee papers (4340). Correspondence with Treasury Solicitor on demarcation, and with Law Officers' Department on recourse for opinions.

3 Other papers

2/3636 Officers on staff of J-AG given right to take affidavits: correspondence with Attorney-General, J-AG and Master Jelf, 1939.

2682, 2981–2 Correspondence with J-AG on War Crimes Bill and trials of major war criminals, 1943–5.

3031 Temporary use of solicitors on staff of J-AG, 1945.

5253 Correspondence with Air Council on the case of F/O J. K. Smith, 1951.

5254 W. J. H. Carter's petition to the Admiralty, 1951.

3009 Admiralty seek opinion on effect of s. 62 Naval Discipline Act on irregularly constituted courts, 1945.

5256 Discussions (1951) on definition of mutiny: meeting with Law Officers.

3
CORONERS' COURTS

That peculiar officer of state the coroner came within the purview of the Lord Chancellor directly because it fell to him to remove an incapable or delinquent one under the Coroners Act 1887 s. 8(1) and indirectly because the Home Secretary was certain to consult him on any proposals for substantially altering the rather archaic process of the coroner's inquest. Thus there are scattered papers both on allegations against individual coroners (with useful memoranda detailing precedent and policy[1]) and on reform proposals, notably the response to the Wright Committee's report of 1936 and the papers of the Rules Committee which was belatedly set up after the war on its recommendation.[2]

Notes

1 *Especially valuable is Schuster's memorandum (33 pp.) in 2/1244, which details all complaints received in the office over 40 years and the action taken upon them.*

2 *PP 1935–6 (Cmd 5070) VIII, 1. The LCO was not represented on the Committee and although the Home Office was disappointed at its lukewarmness in recommending full-time coroners Schuster was less concerned: "some of the very worst things . . . have been done by full-time coroners" (2/1245: to A. Maxwell (HO), 3.3.1936).*

2/353–4, 748–9, 826–7 Correspondence with Coroners Society on rules and forms under Indictments Act (1915); with Home Office, PCO and several coroners on Juries Act 1918;

Home Office and Chitty on drafting of Coroners Bill, 1924; on Parliamentary stages of Amendment Bill, 1926 and rules thereunder; with Home Office on abolition of Admiralty Coronership, 1927.

1244–5, 4958–62 Wright Committee: correspondence with Home Office on setting up, memorandum on Lord Chancellor's jurisdiction; cabinet papers on report and views of DPP, Home Office; memoranda and correspondence. Coroners Rules Committee: draft rules sent by Home Office 1937, revised 1950 and personnel discussed. Memoranda, list of recommendations to the Committee, draft rules, correspondence with secretary, draft report, evidence, minutes, report (1952).

61, 203, 355, 829, 1247, 4964 Removal of coroners at Scarborough (1893) and in Montgomeryshire (1908). Home Office memoranda on removal of coroners (1919). PQs on the Reading coroner (1929); complaints by Medical Defence Union (1951).

518–9, 828, 3261, 3498 Correspondence with Privy Council Office on forms of writs, alteration of districts (1922); correspondence on right of appointment of Ampthill coroner (1928); office held incompatible with Sheriff (1950); suggested as chairmen of justices' benches (1945).

4
COURTS OF JUSTICE OUTSIDE GREAT BRITAIN

1 Northern Ireland

2/796, 2647 S.C.J. (N.I.) Bills, 1926, 1942: formal correspondence only.

1442 Knighthood for LCJ (NI) 1941: correspondence with Home Office.

3461, 5900, 3005 Irish judges: promotion of MacDermott in 1947 (3461); position of LCJ's permanent secretary (3005); Labour party complaints re political appointments (5900).

5910 Discussions with Attorney-General, Home Office in 1949 on transfer of judicial appointments to Lord Chancellor and establishment of advisory body. Correspondence with Black LJ (chairman) and appointments.

2 India

2/2970 Vacant Indian judgeships: India Office seek advice, 1941 and candidates discussed in correspondence. Further requests 1942 (for Chief Justice) and 1946.

3040 India (Attachment of States) Bill 1944 sent by India Office with memorandum on effects of the *Bhadua Taluka* case.

4494 Judges Pensions (India and Burma) Bill 1948 sent by PCO. Cabinet and Parliamentary proceedings.

3 Colonies

(see also 'King's Counsel', infra, *179–80)*

2/3235, 3233, 3242 LCO opinion on recommendations of Colonial Office's Battershill commission, 1947, on removability of judges; reversion to older method of appointing judges in Malta; disputes in the Seychelles and Malaya (1949–50), including PQs, note by Sir K. Roberts-Wray and papers on the case of M. D. Lyon (Chief Justice in the Seychelles) to 1956.

3463 Federal Courts (Enlargement of Jurisdiction) Bill 1947 [India].

Chapter

6

ADMINISTRATIVE TRIBUNALS

1

GENERAL

The proliferation of administrative tribunals and the exclusion of the courts from reviewing administrative decisions both stemmed mainly from the dissatisfaction of government departments with the slowness and expense of the courts and with the quality of their decisions, especially in areas removed from their normal business. It gathered pace during the second world war and under the Attlee government tribunals became a prominent feature of the juridical scene.[1]

The creation of tribunals to undertake judicial functions which might have been allotted to the courts was one element in the conservative dissatisfaction with trends in ''administrative law'' which found voice Lord Hewart's crude polemic '**The New Despotism**' in 1929 and later found more sophisticated expression in the writings of Sir Carleton Allen, George Keeton and others. As the minister with responsibility for the administration of civil justice, the Lord Chancellor might be expected to show particular concern at the tendency of legislation to oust the courts, either by substituting tribunals or excluding any judicial review of administrative actions, but in fact the papers of his department are unrewarding on this issue. In particular, although Schuster took a prominent part in the deliberations of the Committee on Ministers Powers which was set up to examine and to refute the criticisms about overmighty civil servants, the only files on the subject throw little new light on its deliberations,[2] though they are of interest in showing how its composition was determined. Schuster's papers as a member of the Committee are not among the office records. Although it was generally LCO policy to prefer the courts, particularly the county courts, to new tribunals, and although there are isolated expressions of concern at the growth of the latter,[3] the Office does not seem to have been able to oppose the determination of those ministries chiefly concerned to by-pass the courts. When tribunals really began to increase under Attlee's government it was the Attorney-General, more closely in touch with the Bar's antagonism, who took up suggestions for a general inquiry into their constitution and operations, and the Jowitt showed little enthusiasm.[4] In general, the role of the LCO was limited to assisting in finding suitable chairmen and personnel.

Notes

1 *A comparison between the first and second editions of W. A. Robson,* ***Justice and Administrative Law*** *(1928, 1947) conveniently illustrates their expansion.*

2 *For Robson's criticism of Schuster's performance see* ***Justice and Administrative Law*** *(2nd Ed., 1947), 330–1.*

3 *e.g. 2/3586: discussions with Ministry of Health on replacing quarter sessions for rating appeals, 1946–8.*

4 *2/4288. But* ***Cf.*** *Shawcross's defence of the government's policy in (1947–8) 11 MLR 1.*

2/1133–4	Papers on the Donoughmore Committee, 1932, including correspondence on membership, memorandum on LC's power to make rules and regulations, copy report and LC's memorandum for cabinet; PQs and representations.
1873	Discussions with Board of Trade on CIPA demands for a patent appeal tribunal, 1939.
3776	Alternative Remedies (Monckton Committee) 1944: LCO opposition to tribunals.
4284	LC's concern at exclusion of judicial review from Acquisition of Land Rules, 1945.
3069	Special Procedure Bill 1945: discussions on clause restricting prerogative writs.
3586	LCO concern at proliferation of "*ad hoc* tribunals", 1946.
4288	Bar resolution hostile to tribunals and Attorney-General's proposed committee, 1948.
4625	Cabinet decides to exclude them from legal aid scheme (see *Legal Aid, infra*, 185) 1948.
4434	Professor Robson's proposal for reporting tribunal cases, rejected by Jowitt, 1948.

2
WARTIME TRIBUNALS

1 Pension Tribunals

1 Introduction

A very interesting collection of files concerns the administration and organisation of an appeals procedure from decisions of the Ministry of Pensions on eligibility for war disability pensions. At the end of the Great War this became a question which greatly inflamed public opinion, for while the Ministry regarded the tribunals which had been set up as incompetently manned and biased against them, disappointed ex-servicemen and their friends were equally convinced that they acted as tools of the government.[1] The LCO resisted attempts to establish a further tier of appellate tribunals both in 1922 and again in 1924, but Schuster was deeply impressed by his experience of the depth of public feeling: he had "personally read the papers in every case in which there was a serious complaint made of a decision reached"[2] and was dismayed to find in the next war that the Ministry of Pensions, having already rejected 110,000 claims, nevertheless continued to defer the establishment of appeal tribunals and proposed to restrict appeals to those who had served a certain term in the forces.[3] Schuster's conviction that, whatever the formal constitutional position in relation to the exercise of the prerogative power to award pensions might be, the Parliamentary reality was that a satisfactory procedure must be proferred at an early date, was amply borne out by the Parliamentary history of the Pensions Appeal Tribunals Bill in 1943, when Sir Walter Womersley "had virtually to withdraw the bill and substitute (in effect by amendment) a different measure".[4] Among the concessions which had to be made was to allow an appeal on points of law to a nominated High Court judge, and Coldstream wrote that only he and Sir Reginald Hankey realised "how much law was involved in the interpretation of the various pensions instruments".[5]

Finding good men for these tribunals, especially to chair them, was difficult, as the papers testify, and mediating between the rather narrow constructions of their successive

Presidents (first A. S. Ashby then Sir Owen Beasley), and the sometimes cavalier attitude of the Ministry of Pensions was difficult work.[6] The intention had been that they should be as informal as possible and that the fate of the Workmen's Compensation Acts (to which disability pensions had obvious similarities) which had become immersed in case law, should be avoided.[7]

What actually happened is interesting as an excellent illustration of the familiar tendency of English courts to impose their own conceptions of judicial process upon tribunals and as an early forum for Denning J to display his robust paternalism. It also provides, within a relatively small and manageable corpus of documents, an opportunity to examine the interaction between judges and civil servants.

Denning succeeded Tucker J as the nominated judge in the winter of 1945 and promptly endorsed his view, put forward in the *Moxon* case,[8] that the Tribunal must act in a judicial manner, noticing only evidence (in the sense understood by the courts) which was before it; the medical member was not to supplement such evidence but only to interpret it.[9] The 'dethronement of the medical member' and the insistence also that the new Royal Warrant of December, 1943 placed on the Ministry the onus of negativing the claim by "a real preponderance of probability",[10] transformed proceedings before the Tribunals. The Ministry had to be more "pugnacious" in its presentation,[11] and the need to conform to the rules of evidence inevitably slowed down its preparation of cases and made proceedings more elaborate. The chairman, for his part, had to take greater pains to ensure the availability of all the evidence needed.[12]

The consequence of *Moxon* was that virtually all earlier decisions unfavourable to the claimant were seen to be vitiated by procedural errors, though most of the claimants were now out of time for an appeal to the nominated judge. However, the British Legion (which represented many of the claimants) "could not believe that the Government would wish to stand on the legal position"[13] as it had declared in Parliament, while Denning promptly circumvented the obstacle and began to allow appeals out of time;[14] this encouraged the Legion to prepare a "mass attack" by bringing some seventy appeals with the disconcerting prospect of thousands of time-barred cases to be revived.[15] Press headlines and Parliamentary pressure brought the 'crisis' to a head and the Ministry was obliged to concede the establishment of 'Special Arbitration Tribunals' to handle appeals which were out of time and which the Minister was not prepared to admit.[16] A bargain was struck with the Legion, who promised to do their best to dissuade such applicants from appealing to the judge, and the four Special Reference Tribunals (the dangerous word 'arbitration' was hastily dropped) were manned by the best available doctors and lawyers.[17]

Not content with his achievement Denning, to the horror of the Ministry, first ruled that an Appeal Tribunal had to be unanimous in rejecting an appeal,[18] thereby casting doubt on an unknown number of decisions, then did "not agree with the view that as a matter of ethics the legal principle that you take the law as you find it at any given moment should be applied to pensions appeal cases. He has recently expressed the view that if in a judgment on a pensions case the case is decided by a P.A.T. on grounds which subsequently appear to have been wrong it ought to be re-heard".[19] Such a view opened up the prospect of innumerable appeals, for the Legion representatives were freely citing Denning's judgments to the Tribunals where, as the President grumpily remarked, "the medicine has to a very large extent been swamped by law''.[20] Denning's final stroke was to undermine the Special Reference Tribunals by ruling that he would consider granting leave to appeal from a P.A.T. decision out of time even if the appellant had already been found against by an S.R.T.[21] The result, not surprisingly, was greatly to diminish the value and popularity of the S.R.Ts.

The Ministry of Pensions, whose competence was criticised by the LCO on several occasions, naturally found Denning's decisions highly annoying, but he was loyally supported by the LCO and the Law Officers.[22] Nevertheless, it was admitted that an appeal to a single judge whose decisions were final was not a satisfactory procedure;[23] no doubt the Ministry of Pensions drew stronger conclusions about judicial review.

Notes

1 *War Pensions Acts, 1919, 1921. 2/971.*

2 *2/2780: minute of 16.4.1943. See also his account in 2/938.*

3 *2/2646: memorandum of 22.7.1942. There was fierce Parliamentary criticism of the decision and the reason given, that it was impossible to obtain enough doctors, was widely regarded as a front for the Treasury's refusal to sanction the expense; see* **Parl. Debs.**, *1942–3 (H of C), vol. 385, cols. 425–9, 462–8; vol. 387, cols. 1490–1585.*

4 *2/3714: Coldstream to Napier, 9.9.1947. The debates are in* **Parl. Debs.**, *1942–3 (H of C), vol. 390, cols 1333–1428, 1818–54, vol. 391, cols. 1114–1220.*

5 **Ibid.**

6 *For an example, on the definition of ''war risk injury'', see 2/3702.*

7 *2/3711: Coldstream's memorandum, 1.5.1946. For this reason, the Attorney-General had promised the House of Commons that there would be no right to legal representation before the tribunals, 2/3695.*

8 **Moxon** *v* **Minister of Pensions** *[1945] KB 490, discussed by W. A. Robson,* **supra** *(2nd ed.) 403–6.*

9 *On this question, and on several others, the Court of Session took a different view:* **Taylor** *v* **Minister of Pensions** *[1946] SC 99. This divergence was embarrassing for the government; see 2/3711.*

10 *per Denning J in* **Starr, Nuttall, Bourne** *v* **Ministry of Pensions** *[1946] KB 345 at p. 351. These cases are discussed in Coldstream's memorandum of 1.5.1946 in 2/3711.*

11 *2/3711: notes of departmental meeting, May 1946.*

12 *2/3711: Ashby's memorandum, 11.6.1946; Coldstream to Ashby, 18.6.1946. One result was a tendency to play safe and seek medical specialists' testimony, which increased costs and delays: 2/3709.*

13 *2/3711: Minister of Pensions to Lord Chancellor, 16.7.1946.*

14 *Tribunals after the Great War had consistently taken a firm line against out of time appeals: 2/978.*

15 *2/3711.*

16 **Parl. Debs.** *(H of C) 1945–6, vol 426 cols. 202–5; 2/3711–2.*

17 *2/3711: Coldstream's memorandum, 3.10.1946.*

18 **Brain & Wilkes** *v* **Ministry of Pensions** *[1947] KB 625.*

19 **James** *v* **Ministry of Pensions** *[1947] KB 867;* **Higham** *v* **Ministry of Pensions** *[1948] 2 KB 653. 2/3719: Coldstream to Napier, 9.9.1947.*

20 *2/3713: Sir O. Beasley to Rieu, 8.9.1947.*

21 ***Gillibrand** v **Minister of Pensions** [1947] WN 320: "she shall not be forced to go before a Tribunal from which there is no appeal".*

22 *e.g. 2/3711: Coldstream to Ashby, 18.6.1946. **Cf.** Coldstream to Napier, 9.9.1947.*

23 *2/5610: note of meeting, 13.4.1951.*

2 *Great War*

2/640 Appeals Tribunal (War Pensions) Rules 1919: correspondence on drafting with Griffith-Jones (PAT) and Treasury.

641 Proposal by Ministry of Pensions to restrict appeals: correspondence with Griffith-Jones, Law Officers, Ministry of Pensions, 1919.

642 War Pensions Act 1921, correspondence on regulations.

643 Correspondence with Ministry of Pensions and H. Bailey (PAT) on appeals machinery abroad, 1922.

971 Proposed "supreme tribunal" discussed with Ministry of Pensions, Solicitor-General, A. Chamberlain; draft schemes and memoranda; notes of conference with British Legion (1923) and cabinet papers (1924).

974, 978 Conferences and correspondence with Ministry of Pensions and PATs on proposed bill to relax time limit on appeals (1924). Validity of restrictions questioned by F. L. Ratto (PAT), 1929, and correspondence leading to *Price* (1931).

972–3 Representation before PATs: Parliamentary questions on expenses, complaints about "touting", 1921–4.

976 Extract from draft report of departmental committee on the St. Dunstan's Homes, 1926.

969, 975, 977 Negotiations with PATs and Colonial Office on overseas appeals, leading to regulations of 1926. Arrangements for West Africa Frontier Force and Indian Army Officers.

970 PAT (England & Wales) Regulations 1926: drafting correspondence with PAT Secretary.

2787 Parliamentary questions, 1921–5: discussions with Chief Whip on departmental responsibility.

3 *World War II: Pension Appeals Tribunals*

2/1551 Canadian appeals: correspondence with PAT secretary 1941.

2646 Pensions (Mercantile Marine) Act 1942: discussions with Ministry of Pensions, Parliamentary papers.

2780–1 Pensions Appeal Tribunals Act 1943: correspondence from 1941, with cabinet and Parliamentary papers; discussions on the bill and composition of tribunals with Ministry of Pensions, Treasury, PCO, Treasury Solicitor and Attorney-General.

2782, 2784–5, 3704, 3739 Appointments Committee: correspondence with T.U.C., General Haining (chairman), and report (1943). Reconstituted committee of 1946: correspondence with Newton Anderson (Northern Ireland) and Lord Normand President of the Court of Session) on arrangements for Ireland and Scotland. Complaints and correspondence with civil service Whitley Council on civil servants on appeals committees. 1950 query re pacifists on tribunals.

2783, 3708 Pension Appeal Tribunals Rules, 1943: long correspondence with Treasury Solicitor, Ministry of Pensions, President of the Tribunals etc. Suggested changes, especially on anonymity of doctors; correspondence with Ministry of Pensions, Attorney-General, Ministry of Health, and Amendment Rules, 1946.

2786 Lengthy discussions with departments on terms of the new royal warrant and on questions of entitlement, 1943.

3694, 3700, 3703, 3707 Appeals to the High Court 1943–6, including attempts to avoid diversity between England and Scotland (3694), form of notice (3700), practice on costs (3703), form of case stated (3707).

4600 Production of "notes for the guidance of claiments" (1943) and revises to 1952; views of Ministry of Pensions, Ashby, Beasley and others; representations from R.A.F. Association, T.U.C. and others.

3699, 3705 Disclosure of documents (medical service reports, police reports); correspondence with departments.

3697–8 Special cases: Indian appeals and naval reservists.

3695 Legal representation: correspondence with Ministry of Pensions and Attorney-General on terms of pledge to Parliament (1943).

3701 Correspondence with Ashby and L. H. Elphinstone on interpretation of s. 4 and on Schedule 3.

3702, 3732 Mercantile marine cases 1944, 1949; correspondence with Ashby and Ministry of Pensions on divergent interpretations of "war risk injury".

3706 Ministry of Pensions complaint about tribunals 'backdating' awards, 1945.

3709 Treasury concern at rising costs of medical specialists (1947).

4 *Special Reference Tribunals*

2/3713 Correspondence with B. M. Cloutman (President of SRTs) *et al.* on publication of digest of decisions, 1946.

3711–2 Correspondence and Parliamentary papers on the effect of Denning J's judgments on 'out of time appeals' and on setting up of SRTs, 1946.

3714 Effect of Denning J's decisions in *James* and *Revely*, 1947.

3715 Memorandum from Ministry of Pensions on problems with decisions on the Act; correspondence with Sir O. Beasley, Cloutman *et al.*, 1947.

3716 Reduction in SRTs: statistics of business, correspondence with Ministry of Pensions and SRT President (Sir H. Braund), 1948–9.

4/266 Correspondence with Secretary on allegations against Edsall, a clerk, and the case against Massey, another clerk, considered with CPSA and Secretary, 1947–9.

5 *Pension Assessment Tribunals*

2/3718, 3734 Interim assessments and assessment tribunals: correspondence and meetings, 1946–50.

3725 Meetings on doubtful points of procedure, and changes, 1947.

3726 Problem of Eire cases discussed, 1947.

3727 Memorandum on post-Great War procedure, 1947.

6 *Particular aspects*

2/3717, 3735 Alleged contempts in "Daily Mail", "Daily Despatch", 1946, 1950; views of Law Officers and DPP.

3719, 3738-9	Correspondence on deceased claimants and appeals by widows and children, 1946, 1950.
3720-3733, 3740, 3742, 3696, 4085, 3737	Various points on tribunal procedure, 1946-50.
3723, 3728, 3731, 3736	Modification order (1947); proposed amendments to the Act; Amendment Rules, 1949. Northern Ireland Amendment Rules, 1950.
3724	Correspondence re publication of a book of practice by Sir L. Elphinstone, 1946. *Cf.* 5769, pamphlet by H. J. Knapman (1953).
3730	Appeals procedure: discussion on 'sign post cases'.

2 War Damage Compensation (Valuation Appeals) Tribunals

Complaints from the War Damage Commission about the incompetence of the Official Arbitrators in dealing with appeals from their determinations led first to proposals for further appeals, perhaps to the Railway and Canal Commission, and then to an insistence that valuation appeals, which they estimated might run into thousands, be taken to a new body, consisting mainly of surveyors with a legally qualified chairman.[1] Accordingly, the Valuation Appeals Tribunal was established under a county court judge, Trevor Hunter. In fact its projected business scarcely materialised, and it had heard only 209 appeals by the end of July, 1948 against an initial estimate of up to 10,000, leading one official to comment acidly "it is a mystery how [Hunter] manages to pass the time".[2] He did so in fact by doing the clerical work of the office, and it was only after a long battle that he was persuaded back to his proper post. The remaining work of the Tribunal was transferred to the Lands Tribunal in 1950.

Notes

1 *2/4666. For the Official Arbitrators see* ***infra****, 163.*

2 *2/4299. E. C. Martin to Coldstream, 20.6.1947.*

2/4666	Correspondence with War Damage Commission, Treasury on need for a better tribunal than Official Arbitrators, 1944.
3092	War Damage (Valuation Appeals) Bill 1945: cabinet papers and correspondence with WDC, Treasury and Law Society on composition.
4299	1945-50: discussions over chairman and members; correspondence with Judge Hunter and County Courts Department; appointment of Tribunal for Northern Ireland (1949); arrangements for transfer to Lands Tribunal 1950.
4300-4, 3054	Rules of the Tribunal 1946, Amendment rules 1947, 1948: correspondence with Hunter, WDC *et al.*; complaint about costs discussed (1949).
4668	Lands Tribunal (War Damage Appeals) Jurisdiction Order 1950 (see *Lands Tribunal, infra*, 163).

3 Claims Tribunals

Under the Compensation (Defence) Act 1939, a tribunal was to be established to determine appeals against compensation offered for compulsory acquisition of property for war purposes and a separate one for shipping so acquired. The files detail the preliminary stages, especially the problem of drafting rules and of obtaining suitable members (the latter exacerbated by the insistence, contrary to practice in the Great War, on requiring legal members to give up their Bar practice[1]). They also give some insight into the working of the Tribunals, such as the attempt to avoid embarrassment from Sir Sidney Rowlatt's (President of the General Claims Tribunal) impaired faculties[2] and complaints at its reluctance to sit outside London. As with the Valuation Appeals Tribunal, there was much less business than had been anticipated.[3]

Notes

1 *2/4662. As a result, H. U. Willink had to be replaced by H. C. Gutteridge.*
2 *2/4660: Schuster to Asquith J, 7.10.1941.*
3 *2/4660, 4662.*

2/4660	Correspondence with LCJ, Treasury and others on appointment of President and members to General Claims Tribunal, 1939 and on changes in membership and remuneration to 1950.
4662	Similar file for Shipping Claims Tribunal.
4661, 4663, 4271, 4276	Correspondence on rules, with Presidents, draftsmen, Treasury Solicitor; also on further rules, 1942, and on reports.
4272–3	Complaints against Tribunal practices and Treasury attitudes: correspondence with solicitors, Law Society, Scottish Claims Tribunal and Treasury Solicitor, 1943–9.
4274	Correspondence with Home Office and Treasury (1939–43) on position of the Isle of Man.
4275	Tribunal under Shipping (War Risks) Insurance and Tonnage Replacement Scheme: correspondence with Ministry of Shipping on adapting SCT, 1940.
4371	Proposed amalgamation of tribunals if Compensation (Defence) Acts revived: correspondence with Treasury and Ministry of Transport, 1950.

4 Alien Internment Tribunals

2/1377	Correspondence with Home Office on membership, with notes on candidates, and instructions circular, 1940.

5 Allied Powers (Maritime Courts) Act Tribunals

2/1406	Correspondence with Home Office, Attorney-General and meeting of departments (1940) on the proposed courts. Drafting correspondence with PCO and record of meetings with governments in exile; Parliamentary papers.
1408–9	Correspondence with county court judges, reports from Police Commissioners, 1941.

See also 2707, discussions on proposals for allied powers prize courts, 1942; 3418, discussions on French maritime court (1943–4).

6 The Foreign Compensation Commission

This file, which has detailed discussions on the rules, may be of interest in the light of the celebrated **Anisminic** case,[1] which brought the Commission into unlikely prominence on the question of the exclusion of judicial review of its determinations.

Notes

1 *Anisminic Ltd v Foreign Compensation Commission* [*1969*] *2 AC 172.*

2/4379 Correspondence with F.C.C., Foreign Office on rules, 1950.

3
TRANSPORT

1 The Railway and Canal Commission

The Railway and Canal Commission represents one of the most interesting experiments of the nineteenth century in creating a judicial body with both legal and professional expertise to decide on questions involving commercial contracts and practices.[1] The LCO papers only deal with the Commission when it had already "fallen on evil days"[2] and when much of its railway business had been taken over by the Railway Rates Tribunal created in 1921;[3] Mackinnon J, the presiding judge, claimed to have heard only two railway cases in his first two years. Confusion over the respective jurisdictions of the two bodies led the Ministry of Transport to ask for a departmental inquiry and Schuster headed a small committee which found that the Rates Tribunal had almost finished its major task and the Commission had too little to do to justify the salaries of its members.[4] Against the wishes of the Lord Chancellor a bill to abolish the latter was presented to Parliament in 1933 but it foundered because the Lords, led by Hailsham and Hanworth, would not countenance the refusal of the Treasury to compensate one of the judges, the popular Kyffin Taylor.[5] His longevity remained an obstacle when the Bill was revived in 1948, and he had to be raised to the peerage as Lord Maenon at the age of ninety-four.[6]

Notes

1 *O. Kahn-Freund,* ***The Law of Inland Transport*** *(2nd ed., 1949) 68–76.*
2 *2/1004: Sankey J to Napier, 5.12.1923.*
3 *Railways Act 1921. W. A. Robson* ***supra*** *(2nd ed.), 93–6.*
4 *2/1556: Schuster to MacKinnon J, 27.11.1929.*
5 *2/1559.* ***Parl. Debs.****, 1932–33, (H of L) vol. 88 cols. 945–57.*
6 *Railway & Canal Commission Abolition Act 1949. See the obituary in (1951) 212 LT 178, 182. Taylor had also been judge of the Court of Passage from 1903 to 1948.*

2/3 Court of Appeal rules under Railways Act 1889 s. 17.
368 Draft rules under Defence of the Realm (Acquisition of Land) Act 1916: comments by service departments.
470 Railways Act 1921: representations from various interested bodies.
1004–6 1923–5: new Fees Order and consolidated rules; correspondence with the Registrar, Sankey J, Treasury; also on rule making powers in connection with Mines Act 1923.

1561–2 Railway Rates Tribunal (Amendment) and (Amendment) (No. 2) Rules 1934, drafts.

1021 Funds Rules 1926, correspondence with Registrar.

1556–9 Schuster Committee papers, including views of departments, MacKinnon J, Registrar; cabinet papers; correspondence with PCO on drafting Bill of 1933; memoranda on work of the two Tribunals.

2656 Suggested by Treasury for war damage appeals, 1943: discussions on judges.

4286, 4290 Town and Country Planning (Modification of Mines Act) Regulations 1948, discussions with M.T.C.P. and Registrar on forum for appeals.

3767, 3769 New Rules and Fees Order, 1945.

3770–2 Abolition Bill, 1948: correspondence with Ministry of Transport, departmental views, cabinet papers; discussions on compensation; Parliamentary papers.

3773 RSC(1) 1949: draft rules and correspondence.

3774 Discussions on disposal of records and library, 1949.

2 Other Transport Tribunals

2/3024 1921–51: appointment of county court judges as arbitrators under the Ministry of Transport Act 1919.

4301 Law Society points to evils of lay representation before Road Traffic Tribunal, 1946.

3768 Appointment of chairman of tribunals under Railways (Valuation for Rating) Act 1930: correspondence with department and with J. Scholefield, and subsequent correspondence re his salary and re-appointment.

1958, 4355 Road and Rail Traffic Act (Appeals Tribunal) Rules 1934 and (Amendment) Rules 1950, drafts.

1560 Chairman of Traffic Commissioners (Tenure of Office) Bill, 1937: correspondence with Ministry of Transport, Treasury from 1932 on pensions for them and for chairman of Railway Rates Tribunal and Road and Rail Traffic Act (Appeals) Tribunal.

4350–2 Transport Arbitration Tribunal Rules 1947 discussed with B.T.C. and correspondence on RSC o. XVIII r 7A. Transport Tribunal Rules 1949: correspondence with Registrar and with the Scottish departments on their objections to a single machinery for Britain.

3 Wreck Commission

1/87 Correspondence with Treasury on appointment of H. G. Rothery and on his establishment, 1878.

2/1, 2 Correspondence with Board of Trade on their proposal to appoint certain county court judges as Wreck Commissioners, 1889.

4257 Correspondence with Ministry of War Transport and K. Carpmael on proposal (1942) to transfer to Wreck Commission powers under s. 471 Merchant Shipping Act 1894 to inquire into officers' competence.

4
PROPERTY

The Official Arbitrators were surveyors appointed by a Reference Committee under the Acquisition of Land Act 1919 to determine compensation for compulsory purchase and cognate matters.[1] When their functions were extended during the second world war by war damage and reconstruction measures their inability to get to grips with this complicated legislation, which led them to 'split the difference' or to seek advice on legal points from friends at the Bar, caused increasing dissatisfaction to the government departments concerned, especially in view of the great quantity of public money which would be in issue under the new town and country planning legislation.[2] However, several ministries were anxious to an almost phobic extent that the ordinary courts should not acquire jurisdiction over compensation questions.[3] Consequently, from 1944 onwards, proposals for a much strengthened forum which would not be arbitral but would have judicial competence were considered, the original suggestion emanating from Sir Arthur Capewell KC.[4] This was the genesis of the Lands Tribunal, which was set up in 1950 to perform a variety of functions in relation to property questions and which comprised a mixture of surveyors and lawyers presided over by Sir William Fitzgerald, a former colonial judge. The LCO files on the establishment of the Lands Tribunal contain interesting material on the tensions between what the Franks report[5] was to describe as the ''administrative'' and the ''judicial'' models of a tribunal, evident in discussions on such questions as rights of audience and the regulation of procedure by formal rules.

Notes

1 *For the proceedings of the Reconstruction Committee in relation to compensation see 3/28–33.*

2 *2/4666: minute of 5.5.1948.*

3 *See e.g. 2/3370, on the attempt by the Ministries of Town and Country Planning and Agriculture to exclude the courts from any role in determining compensation for mineral rights taken by the state.*

4 ***supra**, n. 2.*

5 *PP 1957 (Cmd 218) VIII, 1.*

1 The Official Arbitrators

2/4421 1934–7: Acquisition of Land Act 1919 s. 1(2); Parliamentary questions and correspondence with the Secretary to the Reference Committee and Treasury on the requirement of a Welsh speaking Arbitrator.

3043–4, 4666, 3101 Discussions with Ministry of Town & Country Planning on OAs' role under Town and Country Planning Bill; complaints of their ineptitude by War Damage Commission and Treasury and proposals to replace them, 1944. Resumed discussions 1948 re conduct of Arbitrator in a case at Croydon.

4284 Discussions on respective roles of War Damage Commission and OAs, 1946.

4356 Given jurisdiction in disputes over Ashdown Forest, 1947.

3556, 4294 Atomic Energy (Assessment of Compensation) Rules 1947: correspondence with Ministry of Supply.

2 The Lands Tribunal

2/4286 Notes of departmental meeting proposing a ''general'' tribunal, 1948.

4666–7, 4367, 4371	Discussions with departments on inadequacy of existing arrangements re Town Planning Acts. Resumed 1948 with Treasury, Reference Committee, RICS, PCO; also on composition and jurisdiction; Parliamentary papers and draft bill. Further papers on possible jurisdiction.
5569, 4140, 6325	Rules 1950, Appeals Rules 1950 and Amendment Rules 1951: extensive discussions with departments and interested parties, especially on rights of audience, pleadings.
4299, 4668	Given jurisdiction over War Damage Valuation Appeals, 1950. Correspondence with Treasury and Treasury Solicitor's Office.
4297, 4364	Given jurisdiction over compensation to statutory undertakers under Town and Country Planning Acts (1952).
4372, 6191	Correspondence with departments on transfer of jurisdiction under s. 81(3)(a) Town and Country Planning Act 1947 to vary mineral leases, 1950; correspondence on proposed Mineral Workings Bill, 1951.
4850	Forestry Bill papers 1951, including discussions on jurisdiction over compensation.
4365, 4370	Possible establishment of Scottish and Northern Ireland Lands Tribunals, 1950.
4366, 4368	Fees Order 1950 and problem of fees under Lands Clauses Consolidation Act 1845 s. 58.
4369, 4295	Correspondence on alleged defect in jurisdiction over rating appeals (Pengelly's case) 1950. Appeals (Local Valuation Courts) Regulation 1949.

3 Patents

(*see* infra, *220ff.*)

2/149, 268	Patent Law Amendment Bill 1907; correspondence with Board of Trade on proposed transfer of appeals to High Court; report by Kekewich J on working of the Act, memo by Parker J, draft rules, memos, and Law Society criticisms.
1062	Rule Committee sub-committee on patent actions 1929: memorandum by Tomlin J, comments by D. W. Kerley, W. A. Greene *et al.*; draft rules, criticised by other experts.
1192	Patents and Designs Act 1932: cabinet papers, proposals by Clauson J, Parliamentary papers.
1629, 1684, 1780, 1876, 1833, 1862	1932: correspondence on constituting a tribunal, on fees, rules and forms, with Treasury, Board of Trade, Law Officers' Department; protest by CIPA. Minor rules revisions 1934, 1936, 1937, 1938, 1940.
1873	Proposals by CIPA and Trade Marks etc. Federation for a tribunal: departmental memoranda and discussions with Board of Trade about an inquiry, 1939.
4045, 4059	RSC (Patents) 1945 to implement Swan Committee interim report: correspondence with Board of Trade and Chancery judges; also amendment in RSC (4) 1947.
4060–1	Patents and Designs Bill, 1948: preliminary discussions on Swan report proposals; cabinet and Parliamentary papers.
4139, 4147	Patents Appeal Tribunal Rules, 1949: correspondence with Board of Trade, Lloyd-Jacob J and Chief Registrar.

5
WELFARE

The important decision to remove the scrutiny of decisions on entitlement to benefit under the expanded body of welfare legislation from the courts was much influenced by the unhappy history of the administration of the Workmen's Compensation Acts and was prefigured in the Beveridge Report, Simon's protests being brusquely rebuffed.[1] In consequence of that decision, the Lord Chancellor had little to do with the new tribunals, over which he did not have the patronage nor any disciplinary functions. Consequently these papers contain little of importance, though the undesirability of a situation in which the ministry responsible for appointments was also directly interested in the tribunals' decisions is clear from the course of action followed in the case of Haggen, chairman of a local appeals tribunal under the National Insurance Acts, whose style and decisions made the Ministry of National Insurance anxious not to re-appoint him.[2]

Notes

1 *2/3776.*
2 *2/5577: Coldstream to E. M. King, 27.4.1951.*

2/307, 400, 566, 568, 582, 1027 5610	Appeals from Commissioners under National Health Insurance, Unemployment Insurance and Industrial Assurance Acts. Discussions on form and forum with Ministry of Health, Chitty and in rule committees. See RSC and County Court Rules (*supra*). 1951 discussions on appeal from medical boards.
3776	Simon's objections to creation of tribunals for industrial injuries: correspondence with Home Office, 1943.
3100	Correspondence with Ministry of Health on appointment of tribunal chairmen under Furnished Houses (Rent Control) Act 1945.
3053, 3056	National Insurance (Industrial Injuries) Act 1946: cabinet and Parliamentary papers; representation on rights of audience, notes on legal points; applications for posts.
3102–3	National Insurance Act 1946: correspondence with Treasury and Ministry of National Insurance on position of Insurance and Friendly Societies; Parliamentary papers.
4252	Proposal to ensure conformity between county courts and National Insurance Tribunals, 1946.
5610	Ministry of National Insurance propose higher tier of Medical Appeal Tribunals, 1951.
5577	Ministry complaint about a local appeal tribunal chairman, and correspondence on decision not to re-appoint him, 1951.

6
NATIONALISED INDUSTRIES

The welfare tribunals were intended to be permanent, but many others were established by the Attlee government for purely temporary purposes, such as valuing property in the industries which were being nationalised, and in these cases the Lord Chancellor did appoint the chairmen (mostly ex-colonial judges), but their business was generally uncontroversial, and in at least one case non-existent.[1]

Note

1 *2/4329: tribunal appointed to hear appeals under Coal, Industry Nationalisation Act 1946 ss. 24–5.*

2/3115 Electricity Act: notes by Ministry of Fuel and Power on proposed Tribunal, 1948.

4329 Appointment of Tribunal under Coal Act 1946: correspondence with Ministry of Fuel and Power, Law Society, Vaisey J on procedure and representation and with Treasury on financial questions. Correspondence with prospective members, to end of 1950.

4350, 4353–4 Transport Arbitration Tribunal: correspondence with British Transport Commission, Ministry of Transport and C. M. White (draftsman) on rules and proposed statutory amendment, 1947.

4357–61, 5199 Electricity, Iron & Steel and Gas Arbitration Tribunals: correspondence with Ministry of Supply on composition and rules, 1948.

7
DOMESTIC TRIBUNALS[1]

Of particular interest are the files on the Medical Disciplinary Committee for the discussions they contain on the role of the legal assessor which, as Coldstream pointed out, raised similar issues to those encountered in regulating the role of the clerk to the justices and the judge-advocate before courts-martial.[2]

Notes

1 *For disciplinary proceedings by the Inns of Court see* ***infra****, 178.*

2 *2/4491: to Lord Chancellor, 19.10.1949.*

2/4453, 4491, 4708 Medical Disciplinary (Procedure) Rules, 1951: discussion on role of the "legal assessor" with Ministry of Health; meetings with professional bodies, discussion with Scottish departments, Attorney-General *et al.* on appeals. M.D.C. (Legal Assessor) Rules 1951: correspondence with PCO, C. P. Harvey, Law Officers; notes on case of Dr J. M. Sinclair.

1205, 3023 Architects Registration Tribunal: correspondence re appointment of chairman and arrangements for sittings; correspondence on *R* v. *Architects Registration Tribunal, Ex p. Jaggar*.

1911, 2651 Pharmacy Act 1941, Nurses Act 1943: correspondence with PCO and Master Romer on appeals rules (RSC (6) 1941).

8
MISCELLANEOUS

(for the Legal Aid Complaints Tribunal, see *Legal Aid*, *infra*, 186)

2/1165 City of London (St Paul's Cathedral Preservation) Act, 1925: appointment of Trustram Eve to head tribunal, 1935; also draft regulations, 1937.

3050 Brief on Lord Teviot's amendment to Food and Drugs (Health and Dairies) Bill to make tribunal independent, 1944.

4119, 4473 Children Act 1949: correspondence with Home Office on proposed tribunal, and on rules.

2657 Education Act 1944: Simon's opposition to High Court appeals from Appeals Tribunal.

9
TRIBUNALS OF INQUIRY

The Tribunals of Inquiry Act 1921 was hastily passed by Parliament to meet the difficulty that their own committees of inquiry were not empowered to examine witnesses on oath. Neither the bill itself nor the early tribunals set up under its provisions[1] are the subject of important LCO files, but there is potentially valuable material on the Lynskey Tribunal of 1948.[2] This arose out of the activities of an enterprising Polish jew who usually called himself Sidney Stanley and who enmeshed J. W. Belcher MP, Parliamentary Secretary to the Board of Trade, in a web of favours and expectations which became the subject of a police investigation and press reports. The Home Secretary was prudent enough to pass to the Lord Chancellor the task of appraising the preliminary findings with a view to government action and the papers relating to his investigation and to the cabinet discussions which followed survive, and include correspondence with the Attorney-General on his important and controversial decision to take a leading part in the proceedings of the Tribunal set up in October, 1948.[3]

Various other inquiries, not held under the 1921 Act, are also documented in the LCO. In particular, there are extensive papers on the celebrated case of Inspector John Syme, dismissed from the Metropolitan Police in 1909. The Labour party rashly espoused his cause and when MacDonald formed his ministry in 1924 he found himself obliged to take action, so Syme was persuaded with difficulty to accept an inquiry headed by Talbot J.[4] Its findings left him dissatisfied and he, and after his death in 1945, a tireless busybody named Wilfred Platt, continued to plague successive Lord Chancellors for many years with demands for justice. Another persistent correspondent with a grievance was H. B. Spiller, who pursued complaints arising out of the effect of the Devonshire Agreement of 1923 and a subsequent order in council on the North Charter Land Exploration Company (1910) even after the High Court had rejected a Petition of Right in 1931 and Maugham J had made a further adverse report in 1932. Again, every incoming Chancellor found Spiller awaiting him.[5]

The LCO was also involved in the creation of a panel to conduct investigations into civil aviation accidents. Early disasters had been made the subject of *ad hoc* inquiries, such as Simon conducted on the R101 in 1931, but in the late 1940s there was a spate of serious passenger aircraft crashes. The Newton Committee report of 1948[6] recommended a permanent panel somewhat akin to the Wreck Commissioners but some of its recommendations were unacceptable to the Ministry of Civil Aviation and protracted inter-departmental discussions were overtaken by another crash at Prestwick. The Ministry's rejection of the findings of its own investigating tribunal (the McDonald report) into that accident was hotly debated in Parliament[7] and the files contain interesting background material on the government's handling of the affair and on the creation of the new statutory tribunals.[8]

Notes

1 *For an account of the background to the Act and the tribunals up to 1959 see G. W. Keeton,* ***Trial by Tribunal*** *(1960).*

2 ***Ibid.****, 152–82; PP 1948–9 (Cmd 7616) XVIII, 425.*

3 *See J.Ll.J. Edwards,* ***The Law Officers of the Crown*** *(1964), 295–306.*

4 *2/4698A.*

5 *2/4699. See [1931] 1 Ch. 169.*

6 *PP 1948–9 (Cmd 7564) XI, 183.*

7 *2/3691.* ***Parl. Debs.*** *(H of C) 1948–9, vol. 470, cols. 1335–42, 2039–2178.*

8 *2/5572, 6356.*

1 Under the Tribunals of Inquiry Act 1921

2/468 Memorandum from PCO, notes on amendments, Parliamentary papers and representations from legal profession on audience.

1678A Budget Leak Tribunal, 1936, correspondence with prospective participants.

3597, 3883–4 Lynskey Tribunal 1948: statements, police reports, correspondence with Board of Trade, Attorney-General, R. Boothby MP. Meetings of ministers, report and Treasury circular on practice.

2 Other Inquiries

2/4698A-B Inquiry into case of ex-Inspector John Syme. Correspondence with Home Office, Talbot J and other members of the inquiry; notes and papers, including evidence, transcript of proceedings and report. Correspondence with Syme, W. Platt and Archbishop of Canterbury (1925–60).

4699 Maugham inquiry into affairs of North Chartered Concession Exploration Company. Correspondence with H. B. Spiller (1928–58).

4759–61 Gambia poultry scheme inquiry. Correspondence with Colonial Office, Lord Trefgarne, Upjohn J; inquiry papers, and report.

6347–8 Case of Sir Christopher Bullock. Jowitt's report to Prime Minister (1947); correspondence with Bullock and Bridges and Jowitt's denunciation of "a mere essay in appeasement" (1950).

3 Aircraft Accidents

2/6356, 3691, 4702, 5572 Prestwick inquiry report 1949: discussions with Attorney-General, Treasury Solicitor and Ministry of Civil Aviation on inquiry procedure, and Parliamentary papers. Newton report: discussions with Ministry and Treasury on personnel for panel, 1948–51; applications, list of inquiries. Correspondence on Monckton's appointment to conduct Viking air crash inquiry, 1951.

THE LEGAL PROFESSION AND LEGAL AID

1
THE LEGAL PROFESSION

1 Introduction

During the period covered by this guide, relations between the governing bodies of barristers and solicitors, especially the Law Society, and the government and Lord Chancellor's Department became much closer. The Law Society was granted extensive powers of discipline and regulation over solicitors (including those who are not members of the Society) akin to those long enjoyed by the Inns of Court over their members; the Bar Council and the Law Society obtained representation on the rule committees for the Supreme and county courts and came to be consulted as a matter of course on proposed changes in law and practice. Perhaps the most significant development, however, has been the government's delegation to the professional bodies of the administration of the legal aid scheme. The legal profession has continued to emphasise the importance of its own independence of state control but the financial dependence of many lawyers on the legal aid fund and the close involvement of the governing bodies with the Lord Chancellor's Department has created tensions within the profession; the Law Society, in particular, has often been criticised by solicitors for giving undue weight to its "regulatory" as distinct from its "representative" or trade union function.[2] In general, however, the advantages which the profession has derived from the arrangement have been perceived by most lawyers as outweighing these drawbacks. It is, accordingly, of considerable interest to follow the steps by which it was brought about and for this purpose the LCO papers are of great value.

Notes

1 *H. Kirk,* ***Portrait of a Profession*** *(1976) is an admirable short history of the solicitors' branch and M. Birks,* ***Gentlemen of the Law*** *(1960) is also useful. The bar is less well served but R. Cocks,* ***Foundations of the Modern Bar*** *(1983) is interesting.*

2 *This contributed to the formation of the British Legal Association in 1964; see H. Kirk,* ***supra****, 44–5.*

2 Solicitors

1 Introduction
Conduct and discipline

One of the Law Society's cherished aims was to establish itself as the arbiter of alleged misconduct on the part of solicitors, whether or not they were members of the Society. Responsibility for disciplinary matters lay with the courts and the active co-operation of the Lord Chancellor, or at the very least his benevolent neutrality, was necessary if the Society was to succeed in interposing itself between the court and the alleged miscreant.

A major step was taken with the Solicitors Act 1888, which removed the initial investigation of complaint from a master to a committee chosen by the Master of the Rolls from the Council of the Law Society.[1] This however fell well short of the Society's ambitions; for the original bill had empowered it to hear and determine the issue, subject to an appeal to the court, and it is disappointing not to have a file recording the role of the LCO in the legislation. The Society continued to press for wider powers and Loreburn gave ready support to bills for this purpose, but it was not until 1919 that one passed into law. By the Solicitors Act of that year a Disciplinary Committee was set up and significantly, it was the Lord Chancellor not the Master of the Rolls who was to nominate its members, to be drawn from past and present members of the Council.[2] The Committee was empowered to determine allegations of professional misconduct, subject to appeal to the High Court, and where its findings were adverse to the solicitor, it was the practice of the Society to ask for his commissionership of oaths to be removed by the Lord Chancellor through a writ of *supersedeas*. Some of the files dealing with these requests survive and furnish interesting information about the operations of the more shady practitioners, some of them in Chancery Lane itself.[3]

The disciplinary process, however, was an inadequate safeguard for the public against solicitors' misconduct in relation to clients' money. One knowledgeable observer remarked on the "dislike of figures and incapacity to deal with accounts which have become almost a professional condition"[4] and it extended to a cavalier attitude to clients' money which made defalcations fatally tempting and simple. There was no obligation to keep separate accounts for client and office monies, nor to have the accounts audited, and the inability of the Law Society to deny practising certificates to undischarged bankrupts was symptomatic of the lack of regulation which enabled misconduct to flourish.[5] Public indignation came to a head at the turn of the century, fuelled by several spectacular and scandalous bankruptcies (including that of B. G. Lake, the first chairman of the Disciplinary Committee); government legislation was threatened and the Law Society attempted to head it off by putting its house in order; its own members, however, rejected the compulsory imposition of separate bank accounts for client and office monies and receding public interest and government preoccupations enabled them to do so with impunity.[6]

Another rash of defalcations in 1928[7] however, gave rise to a renewed agitation for regulation, which assumed the threatening shape of a private member's bill, the Agents (Deposit) Bill. Some action now seemed unavoidable and Schuster, who was broadly sympathetic to the Society's difficulties with its own members, made himself an intermediary between it and the bill's sponsors, with the result that the course of negotiations can be clearly charted in these files.[8] Schuster preferred separate accounts and a compulsory annual audit to the Law Society's pet scheme for a compensation fund financed by a levy on all solicitors[9] (who would be obliged to become members of the Society, thereby fulfilling another of its long standing aims), and when the membership again flatly rejected any regulation of their accounting methods, he gave encouragement to Sir John Withers, who resigned from the Council in disgust and introduced a Solicitors (Clients' Accounts) Bill in July, 1930. The Society had a bill of its own to consolidate the combined mass of statutory provisions regulating the profession and the reformers ensured that it stayed becalmed until the current issue was resolved; nevertheless the compromise which emerged is an illustration of the favour with which the LCO regarded the Law Society.[10]

Schuster wrote to Lord Haldane that "the Law Society have done so much for the Lord Chancellor in the past that they have a claim to be kept straight"[11] and for the small price of being required to make rules obliging solicitors to keep separate accounts it was given a remarkably wide power to make rules "for regulating in respect of any other matter the professional practice, conduct and discipline of solicitors".[12] The power was quickly exercised to curb "touting" by "ambulance-chasers" and, more controversially, to prevent practitioners from "undercutting" scales of conveyancing charges set by local law societies.[13] The LCO defended this extensive delegation of authority from Home Office and Parliamentary criticism and in return plainly expected the Law Society to enforce high standards of conduct and to find enough willing solicitors to keep the poor persons' scheme afloat.[14]

However, in the absence of any effective sanction, the new accounts rules were widely disregarded and this led to another spate of frauds in 1938.[15] The Society thereupon produced a bill which provided for compulsory audit but "made proposals which seemed ineffective for the purpose intended, and of such a nature that there would have been a danger that either House of Parliament would require them to be greatly strengthened"; their timidity was said to be caused by the fact that "an audit would disclose a lack of financial stability in places where it would least have been expected".[16] The bill also included a proposal for a contributory compensation fund, although Schuster still felt this was unnecessary and likely to encounter serious practical difficulties, being obviously inadequate to meet "such a defalcation as was disclosed in the case of Sutton and Ommaney's in which Courtauld alone lost some £5,000".[17] Progress of the bill was delayed because the Law Society added a clause aimed at strengthening their existing practice rules against undercutting in conveyancing matters,[18] and this was determinedly opposed by a group of twenty-seven large London firms, whose activities were co-ordinated by an unofficial body known as the Simmons committee. Eventually the Society had to abandon its controversial clause and the bill passed into law in 1941; Schuster's correspondence with Lord Wright, chairman of the joint select committee on the bill, is particularly illuminating.[19]

Remuneration

The remuneration of solicitors was naturally a matter of great concern to the Law Society. They were dependent upon LCO support for any improvements in their position because proposals to alter the scale charges for contentious business had to pass the two rule committees, each subject to the Lord Chancellor's veto, while for most non-contentious matters the scales were fixed by a committee set up under the Solicitors Remuneration Act 1881 and had to be approved by the Lord Chancellor. When the scales were originally fixed they were based on detailed, itemised bills of charges in the case of contentious matters, and on a rather complicated *ad valorem* scale in the case of conveyancing.[20] Neither was calculated on any clearly intelligible principle; hence subsequent committees tended to adopt the crude practice of altering the entire scale by a fixed percentage, rather than the laborious one of re-ordering it in detail. These scales were not only difficult to interpret, they were out of keeping with the growing practice of delivering a lump sum bill, which under the existing law ran the risk of being challenged by the client unless he had agreed to that course in advance. The Russell Committee was set up in 1921 to consider removing this limitation but the Lord Chief Justice was opposed to a change and the Law Society was willing to settle for a percentage increase instead.[21] The papers in this series are a valuable source of information for the various increases of remuneration granted between the wars, particularly for the hard bargaining to produce an acceptable level of remuneration for registered conveyancing without demolishing its claim to cheapen land transfers,[22] and for the temporary "voluntary" decrease which was forced on solicitors in 1931 to parallel the public service salary reductions.

The skimpy and unsystematic evidence the Society provided in support of its claims, and the evident haziness of the committees which considered them about the profitability of solicitors' practices, does not show the LCO in a favourable light, and when more detailed evidence *was* gathered, it was not by the LCO but by the Treasury. This was in 1948, when Sir Stafford Cripps not only vetoed any increase in the non-contentious scale on the ground that it would conflict with the government's prices and incomes policy, but justified himself further by reference to Inland Revenue figures on solicitors' incomes. This veto exposed the anomalous position occupied by the Lord Chancellor, who alone on the remuneration committee was also a member of the government; the Master of the Rolls and the Lord Chief Justice wrote to dissociate themselves expressly from his decision to support the Treasury and although the Revenue's figures exposed serious weaknesses in the solicitors' case, Jowitt was acutely embarrassed by the whole affair.[23]

Other matters

The Law Society also maintained a vigilant watch on questions of audience and eligibility for appointments, though it had little success in breaching the Bar's established claims to exclusivity, nor in preventing government departments from appointing barristers to the highest legal positions.[24] However, its representations were by no means confined to purely professional questions, and it regularly suggested changes in law and practice, particularly the latter. Quite often, it is true, the Society's views were strongly influenced by self-interest; the long rearguard action against title registration, which actually succeeded in reducing it to an adjunct of the conveyancing process and so preserved a profitable line of business largely intact, is the best known example, and another which can be profitably examined is their resistance to the routine use of office-copies of grants of probate.[25] Sometimes too, the Council of the Society was merely passing on the views of members without any expectation, or real desire, for action, but in other important branches of law, such as crown proceedings legislation, the Society's pressure was sustained and important. Schuster acknowledged that it was a much more helpful body than the Bar Council,[26] while Birkenhead declared (in relation to the property legislation) that "the claim of the Law Society to have initiated reforms for the benefit of the community at large is completely justified".[27]

Notes

1 *H. Kirk,* ***supra****, ch. 4, especially pp. 76–82. The Master of the Rolls explained and defended his special position in relation to solicitors in 1/76: Jessel to Selborne, 11.6.1881.*

2 *H. Kirk,* ***supra****, 78–9; 2/288.*

3 *e.g. 2/596: W. K. Styles to T. Hickman, 22.2.1923.*

4 *E. B. V. Christian,* ***A Short History of Solicitors*** *(1896) 216.*

5 *This was remedied by the Solicitors Act 1906; H. Kirk,* ***supra****, 97–101.*

6 *H. Kirk,* **supra**, *97–103.*
7 **Parl. Debs.** *1930–1 (H of C) vol. 237 cols. 2897–8; vol. 238 cols. 656–7.*
8 *2/1567, especially note of a meeting on 10.3.1930.*
9 ***Ibid.***; *Schuster to Withers, 30.1.1930.*
10 *H. Kirk,* **supra**, *103; 2/1567–73.*
11 *2/1567: 23.1.1931.*
12 *Solicitors Act 1933 s. 1. The rules were subject to the consent of the Master of the Rolls.*
13 *H. Kirk,* **supra**, *81, 146. The existence of "rings" to prevent undercutting had been noticed critically by the Chief Land Registrar during discussions on solicitors' remuneration in 1925 (2/1073).*
14 *2/1568. Schuster was sometimes disappointed with the Law Society's attitude to unscrupulous solicitors, see e.g. 2/1756.*
15 *M. Birks,* **supra**, *274.*
16 *2/1581: Schuster to Attorney-General, 7.11.1939.*
17 *2/1581: Schuster to Lord Wright MR, 29.6.1939.*
18 *H. Kirk,* **supra**, *146.*
19 *2/1581–2.*
20 *H. Kirk,* **supra**, *143–6.*
21 *The Russell report (2/472) was not published but is interesting on the changes taking place in solicitors' practices.*
22 *2/1073 is very instructive on this struggle. See also A. Offer (1977) 40 MLR 505 at 521.*
23 *H. Kirk,* **supra**, *93. Not surprisingly, the accuracy of the Inland Revenue figures was hotly debated (2/5858).*
24 *See e.g. 2/729: Schuster to Cook, 27.2.1924, explaining the determination of successive Lord Chancellors to uphold the Bar's monopolies. For the Law Society's unsuccessful challenge to the appointment of barristers as departmental "solicitors" see 2/1074.*
25 *See* **supra**, *103.*
26 *2/3565: to Sir D. Somervell, 24.2.1933.*
27 *Quoted by H. Kirk,* **supra**, *153.*

2 *Training and qualifications*

2/90	Draft regulations under Solicitors Act 1894.
424	Solicitors (Articled Clerks) Act 1919: correspondence with Law Society and PCO on draft bill.
462	Solicitors Act 1922: memoranda and correspondence with Law Society, Board of Education, PCO, Lord Chief Justice, Managing Clerks Association.
1573	Regulations under Solicitors Acts 1932, 1936: drafts sent by Law Society and Master of the Rolls, 1936–46.
1575–6	Regulations concerning exemptions and syllabuses, formal correspondence, 1933–50.
1579	Solicitors Bills, 1935–6: Law Society proposals on articled clerks and memoranda thereon.
1586, 2637	Solicitors (Emergency Provisions) Act 1940: correspondence with Law Society and PCO, cabinet papers, evidence of A. C. Morgan, Parliamentary proceedings. Also assurances on computation of war service for qualifications of Commissioners for Oaths, 1940.
791–3, 3803–4, 5819, 5821	Various regulations on law schools and examinations; formal correspondence only, 1946–55.

3794 Public Notaries (Articled Clerks) Act 1946: correspondence with Registrar of Faculties, PCO and Solicitor-General; cabinet and Parliamentary papers.

3801 Correspondence with MR leading to Law Society's Examinations (Fees) Regulations, 1948.

3 *Discipline, accounts and practising certificates*

2/288 Solicitors Bill, 1912–19: drafts, memoranda and correspondence with
1075 C. A. Coward. Solicitors Act 1928: correspondence with Law Society, Home Office, Lord Darling, Attorney-General.

1567–9, Agents (Deposit) Bill, Solicitors (Clients Accounts) Bill, Solicitors Bill,
1571 1929–33: correspondence with Law Society, A. Somerville and Sir J. Withers MPs, PCO; briefs on Parliamentary questions, memoranda by A. Burrows, G. Hicks, and solicitors in government employment; departmental meetings and correspondence. Solicitors' Act 1933: correspondence with PCO; cabinet papers, circular to High Court judges, draft report from joint select committee, Parliamentary proceedings.

1572, Solicitors Act (Disciplinary) Appeal Rules, 1932, 1943; case of C. H. Smith
1577–8 (1933) correspondence with Official Solicitor and Law Society; correspondence with Law Society, PCO, Scottish Office on Solicitors Act 1934.

1193 Road Traffic (Compensation) Bill 1933. Law Society clause to outlaw 'touting' by solicitors and others discussed.

1570 Solicitors' Accounts Rules 1935.

1585, 5818 Complaints about rules against "undercutting", and Law Society's defence, 1939. Brief for PQ on Evill's case (1951), fined for breach of these rules.

1584 Solicitors (Disciplinary Committee) Bill 1939; explanatory memorandum, correspondence with Law Society.

1581–3 Solicitors Act 1941: correspondence with Law Society from 1938 on defaults, Parliamentary questions, draft bill, correspondence with MR, Attorney-General, Treasury; memoranda on proposed amendments, Parliamentary papers, including evidence to joint select committee.

2797–8, Draft rules under 1941 Act re allegations of dishonesty, and arrangements for
3789 notification to Law Society of writs against solicitors. Disciplinary regulations and orders to 1948.

2796 Complaint of J. L. Smith-Ward against compensation fund rules, 1941.

3788, 3790 Order bringing insurance fund into operation; further discussions with Attorney-General, PCO, and Law Society (1944) on operation of s. 1.

3798 Protests of Association of International Accountants at exclusion from recognition for this purpose, 1947.

3795, 3797 Discussions on need of metropolitan police solicitors to take out practising certificate, 1947.

3796 Solicitors Act 1949: correspondence with Law Society, IRC, Treasury on stamp duty on certificates, with PCO on drafting; cabinet papers.

3805–6 Queries in 1922 and 1949 about the position of Irish and Australian solicitors.

3808 Solicitors Act 1950: correspondence and meetings on bill to raise fee on practising certificates.

3026	Bankruptcy amendment rules 1943: solicitors' bankruptcies to be notified to Law Society.
3807	Grant in aid: correspondence with Law Society, Lord Advocate on Treasury proposal to withdraw it, 1949.

4 Solicitors as Commissioners for Oaths

2/2640	Memorandum by Schuster on policy, 1940.
2625–7, 2629–30	Complaints against abuses by commissioners, 1924–33.
2586, 2588–9, 2592–4, 2596–2601, 2640, 2668, 3253	Writs of Supersedeas, various dates, usually with information on offences, and some with correspondence with the defaulter.
2590–1	Discussions with Law Society on action against commissioners with lapsed certificates, 1927.

5 Remuneration

General

1/82	Solicitors' Remuneration Order, 1883.
2/423	Deputation to Lord Chancellor, 1917. Discussions among heads of SC Divisions and others and increases agreed 1918. Drafting correspondence. Application of 1919 by Law Society, with evidence. Discussions with LCJ and MR and further order 1919.
472	Solicitors' Remuneration Bill: report, minutes and precis of evidence of Russell Committee, correspondence with PCO, Law Society and LCJ (1921–3).
561, 662	Solicitors Remuneration Order, 1920: correspondence with departments; discussions on 'lump sum' bills and proposed order, with Law Society, MR, LCJ.
1071	Remuneration Order, 1925: appointment and report of committee under the 1881 Act; discussions with Tomlin J and Law Society.
2800–3	Remuneration Orders 1932, 1936, 1944: papers of Solicitors' Remuneration Committee, 1932 and 1936; memoranda on earnings, representations and Parliamentary questions, meetings with Law Society and SC Rule Committee; correspondence with MR (1943).
2815	Solicitors Remuneration (Gross Sum) Order 1934; SR Committee meeting, views of Master Gibbon.
2804–12	1932, 1936, 1944: remuneration orders for specific courts and subjects.
4008–10	Evershed Committee, working party 'U': papers, correspondence, minutes, 1951–2.
5858	Law Society claim for increase (1948): correspondence with MR, LCJ, Master Gibbon, Chief Land Registrar; Treasury veto, IRC figures on profits; further claim (1950) and correspondence with Treasury.

Contentious business

2/546	Complaints against disallowances of country solicitors' costs attending House of Lords appeals, 1923.

364 County Court Rule Committee discussion and judges' opinions on proposed increase, 1918.

1308 Discussions in CCRC, 1938, on remuneration.

1860–1 Discussions on costs in Court of Appeal, 1938; renewed 1943 and 1944 after new practice directions.

3318–9, 3321 Austin Jones report, 1947: discussions on Law Society proposals with Bar Council, CCRC; investigations into cost levels, including specimen bills.

Conveyancing

2/259 Law Society complaint against proposed land transfer fees order, 1908.

1072 Remuneration under Law of Property legislation on copyhold enfranchisement: correspondence with Law Society, B. L. Cherry, Ministry of Agriculture; proceedings of SR Committee and draft order, 1926.

1073 Remuneration under Land Registration Act 1925: correspondence with CLR and Law Society including memoranda from both; SR Committee proceedings and correspondence with members; draft order.

2816 Solicitors Remuneration (Manorial Incidents) Order, 1935: correspondence with Ministry of Agriculture, Law Society; SR Committee proceedings; correspondence of 1944 on proposed increase.

3810–4 Investigation into H. A. Holland's complaint re scale fees, and 1949 complaints of high charges; Law Society proposals on registered land rejected, with memoranda from Chief Land Registrar; correspondence with Ministry of Health on fees on compulsory purchases, 1949.

3800 Law Society's attempt to obtain exclusive rights to draw up land contracts, 1948.

3802 Solicitor's complaint re 'touting' by costs draftsmen rejected, 1948.

Other

2/482 Commissioners for Oaths Fees Order, 1921: report of Law Society Committee, correspondence with Treasury, MR, LCJ *et al.*

1735–7 Supreme Court (Non-Contentious Probate) Fees Order, 1933: Law Society objections to effect on solicitors.

3021 Correspondence (1944) with Home Office, registrars, and departmental discussions on solicitors' charges under Adoption of Children Act 1939.

2818 Discussions with Law Society and Treasury leading to Coal (Costs of Valuation) Order 1940, amended 1944.

2813–4 Commissioners for Oaths Fees order, 1944: discussions of 1932; renewed discussions with MR, LCJ, Registrars; also Clergy Discipline Rules (1944), omitted from main order in error.

3668 Law Society protests v. the Official Solicitor's practice in demanding solicitor's undertaking for costs before acting as guardian *ad litem*, 1945–9. Policy investigated and upheld.

6 *Taxation of costs*

2/9 Law Society resolutions and deputation against new costs order, 1889.

1064 Taxation of Costs (Principal Clerks) Order 1930: correspondence with Law Society and Rule Committee papers.

1756	Complaints about evasion of taxation in 'running down' cases, especially *Vanner* v *West Ham Corporation*; Law Society action, 1933.
2833–4	Bills of costs in wartime. Proposal to amend s. 65 Solicitors Act 1932 dropped after discussions with PCO, Attorney-General.
3921	Law Society complaint re limited taxing powers of district registrars discussed with masters, 1944.
4096	Law Society complaint re practice where one plaintiff is under disability; discussions with Master Gibbon, 1948.
4208	New practice in divorce cases: correspondence with Probate Registry on complaints, 1947.
4468	Law Society object to practice in actions against defaulting solicitors: discussions with Gibbon, Board of Trade, 1950.
5475	Correspondence with masters and registrars on diversity of practice in legal aid cases, 1951.
3248	Question as to bail fee in Admiralty actions 1944.

7 *Rights of audience*

2/149, 2653, 4301, 4329, 5569, 5574	Protests against proposals to give it to Patent Agents (149), to laymen, in Catering Wages Bill 1943 (2653); before War Damage (Valuation Appeals) Tribunals 1948 (4301) Coal Industry Nationalisation Tribunal 1946 (4329) Lands Tribunal 1949 (5569) Legal Aid Panel Complaints Tribunal 1950 (5574).
3799, 4286, 4360	Attempts to secure rights of audience in: divorce cases *in camera* 1948 (3799) tribunal to deal with minerals questions 1948 (4286) Iron and Steel Arbitration Tribunal 1950 (4360).

8 *Appointments*

2/727, 729, 1622–3, 3092, 3031, 3658, 3565, 4471–2, 4/71	Claims for eligibility for: Official Referees (727) Master in Lunacy (729), both 1924; "legally qualified" chairmen of Quarter Sessions 1938 (1622–3); War Damage (Valuation Appeals) panel 1945 (3092); posts in Judge-Advocate General's office (3031); Metropolitan Stipendiary Magistrates 1946, 1951 (3658); Law Revision Committee 1934 (3565); Clerks of Assize 1946 (4471–2); President of Lands Tribunal 1949 (4667); Circuit Officers 1946 (4/71).
2/1074	Law Society protest re appointment of barristers as solicitors to government departments, 1920, discussed with Treasury. Revived 1923, cabinet papers, opinions of Simon and Law Officers (1926) and Law Society case rejected then and again in 1933.
277, 4259	Claims to exclude from eligibility the Clerk to County Council as Deeds Registrar (277, 4259), clerks in Probate Registry from appointment as District Probate Registrar (991).

9 *Miscellaneous*

2/685	Law Society refused permission to celebrate centenary in Westminster Hall, 1925.
3630	Law Society support plan for a Ministry of Justice, 1918.
1436	Correspondence on certificate to enable a lawyer to practise in Japan, 1936–9.

3809 Law Society concern at position of solicitors in a general mobilisation, 1950. Discussions with Law Society.

5817 Query from Joynson, Hicks & Co. re duty to disclose whereabouts of a deserter referred to Home Office, 1951.

1996 Papers read at Provincial Law Society meetings, 1937. Receipt acknowledged of three papers.

1580 Correspondence with county court judges and Law Society on women solicitors' attire in court, 1936.

2841 Wartime proposals for salvage: MR and LCO protest to Ministry of Supply re lack of consultation, 1942. Appeal substituted for regulation.

3 Barristers

In contrast to the Law Society, the Bar Council makes a poor showing in these papers. The comparison is, however, unfair, for the two bodies, though superficially similar, differed very widely in their powers, functions and objectives. The Bar was a far smaller, more homogeneous group than the solicitors, and its members had a readier informal access to authority for the redress of grievances and the promotion of reforms. In particular, the Attorney General as head of the Bar could be relied upon to defend its interests and barristers were so strongly represented in Parliament throughout this period that they could effectively defeat almost any bill which was inimical to their interests.[1] Furthermore, the cult of individualism was strongly developed and the ethos of the Bar was unfavourable to any form of collective discussion or representation. It should be remembered too that barristers' fees, unlike those of solicitors, were not regulated by statute or rules, so that the Bar Council was neither dependent on nor suppliant to the Lord Chancellor in the same way that the Law Society was periodically obliged to be. Again, the nature of the profession was such that disciplinary proceedings against members of the Inns of Court were infrequent and hardly a matter of public concern since any malpractice did not usually involve the disappearance of clients' money. The few files which do deal with appeals from the benches are however of some interest in showing how the profession brought its own domestic tribunals up to the levels of natural justice which were demanded from those appointed under statute.

The Lord Chancellor was, however, responsible for appointing King's Counsel, by an occult process which was already being criticised at the beginning of this period[2] but which remained practically unchanged throughout and is currently under fire once again. There are interesting files on the moratorium on creations which was imposed during the Great War to protect the careers of barristers who had volunteered for military service and the Crown Office papers offer potted biographies of the successful candidates for a few years in the 1920s, as well as a scattering of memoranda bearing on their selection. For the post-second world war period there is interesting correspondence with the Colonial Office on the difficulties in applying conventional criteria in the smaller colonial territories where the profession was undivided or at least where functional separation was very imperfect.[3]

Notes

1 *2/1254: Sankey to Judge Clements, 20.2.1934.*

2 *(1885) 1 LQR 314 (E. S. Roscoe)*
3 *2/5338.*

1 *Discipline*

1/54 Council of Judges, discussions on procedure in appeals from Benchers, 1886, 1888.
2/707–8 Case of I. A. Reuben (1929), disbarred by Lincoln's Inn: proceedings and memoranda.
1182 H. W. Wickham's appeal (1932): correspondence with J. Rolt KC.
1183 E. Duvivier's Appeal (1937): correspondence with Middle Temple, notes of hearing, general memorandum.
6072 Bar Council complaints of judges' criticisms of barristers, with report of disciplinary proceedings against W. R. Rees-Davies, 1950.

2 *Fees*

2/536 Claim for higher scale of County Court fees, discussion in CC Rule Committee 1922.
4815–6 Correspondence with Bar Council (1932) on proposal to modify the "two thirds rule", on proposal to increase fees for preparatory work (1936), on proposal to abolish two thirds rule (1950) and on the exercise of the Taxing Masters' powers (1950–2).
1844 Rule Committee discuss proposal on refresher fees, 1937.
1885, 4075 Wartime arrangements for signing vouchers 1940, 1947.
3318 Bar Council criticism of Austin Jones Committee proposals, 1949.
3980, 3984–7 Evershed Committee, working party 'F': Bar Council opposes costs proposals, 1948. Extensive papers of working party 'I' on counsel's fees to 1951, including minutes, evidence, papers.
5521 Proposal to raise minimum fees, 1951.
4688 Counsel's fees in legally aided divorce cases, see *Legal Aid* (*infra*, 186).

3 *Rights of audience*

2/4301 (War Damage Valuation Appeals Tribunals) 4819 (salaried barristers) 5250–1 (Courts Martial Appeals).

4 *Appointments*

1/79 Revising Barristers: correspondence with Treasury, Home Office, Attorney-General re appointments under the Redistribution of Seats Act 1885 and responsibility for them, 1885–7.
2/6652 (Recorders from other circuits) 6654 (County Court Judges as Recorders) 277 (Deeds Registrars) 1934 (taxing masters in KB given to solicitors) 2799 (Coal Commission solicitor).

5 *Other subjects*

2/680 Arrangements for visit of American Bar Association, 1924.
705 Costume of barristers before the International Court. LCJ's decision 1924.

1184	Question of alien refugees called to the Bar, 1938.
1863	Proposal to allow an arbitrator to reply to criticism, 1938.
3444	Discussion on which international law association Bar Council should join, 1947.
3630	Views on "Ministry of Justice" proposals 1918.
3931, 4028, 4031	Deputation on terms of reference for Evershed Committee, 1947. Memoranda submitted to the Committee.
4817	Request for deferment of call-up for certain reservists, 1951.
4818	Complimentary copies of student magazine, 1951–5.

6 *King's Counsel*

2/135	Correspondence with Scottish Office on need for Scottish law officers to be QCs, 1896.
328, 405	Wartime appointments: policy memorandum (1915), lists of candidates, and post-war discussions; also memoranda on exceptional cases, including Muir McKenzie.
619	Licences to plead against the crown abolished at request of Home Office, 1920.
2229–30, 2514–22	Crown Office papers, 1917–23, including biographical notes of new KCs and memoranda on wartime policy.
605	Schuster's notes on candidates, 1923.
1466	Offer of silk to A. Bremner on his retirement: papers on precedents, 1932.
1468, 1472, 3540C, 3540E	Colonial cases, various dates: H. V. Perera, H. G. Morgan, ex-colonial judges, L. A. Rajakapse, L. W. deSilva.
3540	KCs for ex-colonial judges to facilitate appointment as Assize Commissioners, 1948.
1469	Application by Isle of Man Attorney General, 1937.
1465	Allegations against J. A. G. Smith KC in Jamaica, with notes on precedents in revocation of patents, 1931.
1467	Use of Patents of Precedence, correspondence and memoranda from Duchy of Lancaster, 1933.
1471	London chambers rule suspended, 1941.
3539	Explanations of procedure for applicants, 1944.
3540B	LCO reject proposal to make the Queen a KC, 1948.
5338	Correspondence with Colonial Office on their policy towards applicants practising as solicitors, with notes on various territories, 1947–57.
3540A	Query on appearance of K. Carpmael KC in a Northern Ireland case, 1947.
920–1, 1470, 2956	Queries on precedence among KCs, judges etc., use of the title by judges and in dominions, various dates.

4 Legal Education

The dispiriting tale of English legal education between the failure of Lord Selborne's initiative in the 1870s and 1950 has been admirably summarised by L. C. B. Gower, whose severe verdict on the proceedings of the two Atkin committees which sat in 1927 and 1932 is fully borne out by the documents in this series.[1] Schuster was inclined to attribute some of their failings to the chairman, Lord Atkin, whom he described as "a very bad chairman, the last man in the world to keep a committee together and full of whimsies of his own''.[2] The first Atkin Committee had a sufficiently modest objective, the establishment of an ''Imperial Law School'' (an institute of advanced legal studies), yet, as Schuster later told Edward Jenks, a leading advocate of the reform of legal education, ''it simply came to an end. I do not know why the chairman, in whose hands the matter practically lay, let it die, unless it was that he saw that it would have no practical outcome''.[3] The fact that it was allowed to peter out in this way however, presumably reflects the low priority which Schuster and the Lord Chancellors of the day afforded to legal education.

Sankey was an honourable exception and he appointed a second committee in 1932, again under Atkin, to review legal education, but its report was ''a thoroughly disappointing document''.[4] One recommendation, for a committee to co-ordinate legal education, was met with great suspicion by the Law Society and the Council of Legal Education, while consideration of the other, for a research institute, was remitted to a further committee under Lord MacMillan whose proceedings were interrupted by the war. Such was the prevailing apathy that it was only in 1947, when a Parliamentary question was put down, that the matter was considered again and then both the proposed institute and the co-ordinating committee were dismissed as unnecessary or inexpedient.[5] ''Anyone in the past who had touched the subject has burnt his fingers'',[6] wrote Schuster and neither he nor Napier was sufficiently interested to risk following suit.

Notes

1 *(1950) 13 MLR 147. For Selborne's initiatives see B. Abel-Smith and R. Stevens,* ***Lawyers and the Courts*** *(1967) 70–6.*
2 *2/1138: to Napier, 20.6.1932.*
3 *2/1138: 2.6.1934.*
4 *L. C. B. Gower,* ***op. cit.****, 147.*
5 ***Ibid.****, 148. See also 2/1144.*
6 *2/1138: A. Napier, 20.6.1932.*

2/623	Proposed Imperial Law School: correspondence with Law Society, 1921.
706	Atkin Committee: preliminary correspondence on Institute of Advanced Legal Studies, minutes, report of sub-committees 1926.
1138–49	Second Atkin Committee 1932. Discussions on membership, replies to questionnaire on university teaching, draft reports, correspondence on composition of proposed advisory committee; 1143–4 on proposed Institute, MacMillan committee, memoranda and draft report of 1947.
3565–6	S.P.T.L. proposals for Law Revision Committee, 1950.

2
LEGAL AID

1 Introduction

The history of modern legal aid in England is well known in outline but the LCO papers are an indispensable source for a detailed study, especially of civil legal aid. To obtain a full picture of criminal legal aid, the Home Office papers must be consulted too.[1]

It is possible to trace through the papers the early discussions on the development of the *in forma pauperis* regulations from the beginning of the Great War. At first, debate on these matters was largely confined to the Rule Committee.[2] The resistance of the legal profession and the Lord Chancellor's Office to large scale extensions of the procedure, based as it was on charitable contributions by members of the legal profession, was a prominent feature of such debate during the period to the beginning of the Second World War, the difficulties of providing adequate legal services for the increasing numbers of divorces is particularly clearly shown. Between the two wars a succession of committees—the two Lawrence Committees, the Finlay and Schuster Committees, the Rule Committee's own committee and the Hodson Committee—had the procedure under examination: the minutes and evidence of the earlier committees are remarkably full and give considerable details about the administration and working of the poor persons' procedure. Of particular relevance is the close working relationship which developed between the LCO and the Law Society which administered the procedure. After the second Lawrence Committee the Society began to play a much larger role in helping to keep the procedure working and it understandably shared a mutual concern with the LCO that demands for a state-run scheme did not come to fruition. Schuster often found himself with conflicting demands being made upon him: engaged in keeping constant pressure on the Law Society to assist in finding enough volunteers to deal adequately with the work, he faced demands from the Society and practitioners for changes in procedure which would enable poor persons' cases to be dealt with more simply and expeditiously. This in turn brought him into conflict with the judiciary, anxious to maintain a formal and centralised control over High Court business.[3]

By 1939 the system appeared to be on the verge of breakdown. The increase in divorce business following the Herbert Act of 1937 had put considerable pressure on solicitors, especially in areas affected by the recession. By mid-1939, the South Wales Law Societies had declared a "strike" in relation to the poor persons' business.[4] Confronted with an unyielding attitude from the President of the P. D. & A. Division, the Hodson Committee was created to produce proposals designed to alleviate the position without yielding to demands for increased government grants, adequate remuneration and changes in divorce administration.[5]

Although the Second World War brought the deliberations of the Hodson Committee to a halt, the huge number of broken marriages which resulted from the social upheavals caused by the War was the force which ensured that those charitable measures which had sustained the poor persons' procedure became inadequate for the scale of the problem[6] During the war, a salaried services legal aid scheme supplemented the newly formed poor persons' Law Society's civilian department, but these were clearly intended to be no more than temporary measures. In 1944, the government set up the Rushcliffe Committee and their report in the following year, largely dictated by Law Society interests, recommended a comprehensive government-funded legal aid scheme whose administration would be in the hands of the profession and which would provide remuneration for individual practitioners.[7]

The files on the Rushcliffe Committee provide a rich source of material for the long deliberations of the Attlee government on the proposals and the decision to implement them in an amended form through the Legal Aid and Advice Act 1949, which came into force in October, 1950 in a truncated form. The Lord Chancellor's Office was responsible for the complicated negotiations with the Law Society and the Bar Council as well as with other government departments, which led to the establishment of the scheme. The official responsible, Richard Thesiger, was the central figure in this process and the papers are particularly interesting in showing the tensions between the two branches of the legal profession and the pressures on the government in the course of formulating the scheme. The papers for the period under review also contain important material on the interpretation of the legislation and contain some criticisms from judges, both on and off the bench, about the operation of the new scheme.[8] The development of this important social service under the aegis of the Lord Chancellor's Office, must also be seen in the light of developments in the administration of the courts and undefended divorce procedure as well as providing, for the first time, legal services on a subsidised basis for a considerable proportion of the population. Although the files relating to pre-war developments in legal services have been looked at by some historians, the post-war history has not been the subject of any proper examination. In view of the crucial importance of legal aid to the subsequent history of legal institutions and the profession and the marked and significant contrast between the administration of this form of state financial provision and others introduced or enhanced at the same time, the papers on this subject provide a unique insight into the development of this important service to the community.

Notes

1 *R. Egerton,* ***Legal Aid*** *(1945) remains the best account of the history and operation of the early arrangements, and J. M. Maguire,* ***Poverty and Civil Litigation*** *(1923) 36 Harvard LR 361 is also useful.*

2 *See especially 2/249–50, 252, 315.*

3 *R. Egerton,* ***supra****, 11–16.*

4 *There had always been particular difficulty in finding enough volunteers in South Wales, R. Egerton,* ***supra****, 16–17.*

5 *See* ***supra****, 102–3.*

6 *G. Rowntree and N. H. Carrier,* ***The Resort to Divorce in England and Wales, 1858–1957*** *(1958) 2 Population Studies 188–233.*

7 *PP 1944–5 (Cmd 6641) V, 187.*

8 *See e.g. 2/5588, which contains discussions with the LCJ and Lords Justices on their complaints of unmeritorious appeals to the Court of Appeal (March, 1951).*

2 Before 1914

1/3 Plea by solicitors to restrict paupers' appeals to House of Lords, 1876.

2/148 Poor Prisoners Defence Act 1903: correspondence with Attorney-General, W. R. Bousfield MP, Sir H. Poland. Resolutions of various bodies hostile to the bill. Correspondence with Home Office, Attorney-General on rules with observations from interested organisations and individuals.

249, 250, 252, 315 1909–11: Rule Committee meetings; draft scheme, objections from Bar and some judges, discussions on proposed committee.

320, 322, 392 1913–14: extensive papers on new rules; correspondence on drafting, observations of Rule Committee members (especially President of PDA, MR, Parker J) masters and registrars, Treasury, law societies, Bar Council; meetings of Rule Committee and sub-committee; reports from London

Prescribed Officers (Archibald and Fox); discussions on proposed rule of 1916 on settlements out of court.

3 Inter-War Committees and Reforms

32/8	List of poor persons' cases in which the Procurator-General has intervened, 1919 and short list of cases with expenses etc.
2/491-2, 499	Tomlin Committee 10th Report (Poor Persons' Department): evidence and further hearing of Hassard Short, 1919.
32/1-5	First Lawrence Committee, 1919: index to evidence and minute book.
2/557, 564	Correspondence on Poor Persons' Rules 1920 and Lawrence report with A. Hassard Short, Pay Office etc.
573	Suggested amendments, and views of P. O. Lawrence J; correspondence with Hassard Short and Chitty, 1921.
644	Second Lawrence Committee, 1923; correspondence with Hassard Short and Law Society on defects in the scheme; cabinet papers and discussions on terms of reference and membership; report.
852, 858	County Court Rule Committee: discussions on poor suitors (1926) and Poor Persons' Rules (1928).
879	Poor persons' divorce at assizes, complaints from solicitors about the organisation; correspondence and circular to Clerks of Assize, 1926.
962, 979-87	Conferences, briefs for Parliamentary questions, memorandum on growth of legal aid, memoranda from voluntary organisations, correspondence with Home Secretary, LCJ and Finlay J on composition of committee; minutes, evidence and correspondence of Finlay Committee, 1924.
988	League of Nations inquiry into legal aid: correspondence with Chitty, 1924.
1032	Matrimonial Causes (Poor Persons) Rules: memoranda by President of PD & A and Chief Registrar of PPR, 1925.
1033, 1055-7, 1059	Poor Persons' Rules 1925: correspondence with Law Society, Hassard Short and conference to settle new arrangements; reports and discussions on finances. Schuster committee papers: correspondence, minutes, evidence and memoranda; report. Poor Persons Rules 1928, discussions on "old" cases.
1068	Matrimonial Causes (Amendment) Rules 1931: correspondence with Law Society, Official Solicitor *et al.* on liability of solicitors for fees.
1764	Correspondence with Official Solicitor, Treasury and others on legal aid in extradition cases, 1933.
1743-4, 1838	Rule Committee meetings 1933: establishment of sub-committee under Merriman P to investigate Law Society complaints re non-award of costs where successful plaintiff is under Poor Persons Rules. Evidence, minutes, correspondence and report. RSC (5) 1934. Correspondence (1940) with Law Society and Merriman on *Jackson* v *Jackson*.
1809, 1626	Criteria for refusing legal aid; Rule Committee discuss relevance of defendants' means, 1935; Attorney-General's undertaking on cases within county court limits, 1938.
1195, 1836-7	Hodson Committee: Law Society's concern at impact of Herbert Act; discussions with Law Society and President of PDA on extension of divorce at assizes and other reforms; reports and statistics on provincial position, especially in South Wales; meetings with President and establishment of Committee, 1939.

1856, 1859, 1869, 1888	Minor questions on legal aid, 1938–40.
3067 B:	Memorandum of Oswald Hickson on abuses in legal aid.

4 The Second World War

2/2843–4	Complaints from MPs, Law Society *et al.* about delays; papers on the *Lemon* case; correspondence on setting up the "tame solicitor" scheme and RSC (8) 1941. Correspondence with Law Society, President and Principal Probate Registrar on "limited certificates" and RSC (Poor Persons) Rules 1943.
3245	Secretary of Manchester Law Society's poor persons committee made a Commissioner for Oaths to expedite proceedings, 1942.
2845–6, 2848	Services legal aid schemes: papers of Schuster Committee, correspondence and conferences with services departments' President, Treasury. RSC (Poor Persons) 1942, RSC (Poor Persons) (2) 1942, RSC (Poor Persons) (No. 2) 1943. Discussion on problem of servicemen overseas.
2847, 2850, 2853, 2854	Particular aspects of army scheme including separation orders, 1942–5. Correspondence with War Office, Home Office, President; see RSC(1) 1945.
2851	Problems with operation of navy scheme, 1944.
2852	Law Society complaint re inadequate deposits, 1944; correspondence with President, memorandum by Haldane Society.
2849, 2855	Legal aid conferences with service departments 1943–6. RSC(3) 1945, extension of scheme over demobilisation; correspondence with Master Burnand on drafting and interpretation.
3416–7	G.I. brides: conferences with departments (especially Home Office and Foreign Office) and Law Society, arrangements for "special legal aid", 1946.
5843	Treasury and Law Society discussions on writing off bad debts, 1947.

5 The Rushcliffe Report

2/3899–3901	Rushcliffe Committee 1944–5: evidence and analysis of views presented, and minutes.
3902, 3927	Correspondence on implementation (1945) with Treasury and Law Society. Representations from Haldane Society and others, cabinet papers. Cabinet committee papers on priorities in legal reforms.
3764, 4090, 5105	Criminal legal aid: queries over scope, especially for bail applications (4090); correspondence with LCJ, Home Office, Treasury; and RSC(4) 1948. Law Society and Bar Council complain re judges' interpretation of s. 44 Criminal Justice Act 1948 (payment of defence costs from public funds); discussions with Attorney-General and LCJ, and Home Office circular considered.
4057	Law Society proposal that counsel should be paid in poor persons' divorce cases; correspondence with LCJ and President, brief for Attorney-General. Rule made 1947, and correspondence on interpretation.
4098	Services Divorce Dept. of Law Society takes over all divorce cases *pro tem* on Law Society's initiative, 1948.

6 The Legal Aid Scheme

1 The 1949 Act

2/4620–30 Extensive material on departmental and cabinet discussions on Rushcliffe, on the drafting of the bill and the modification of the original proposals. It includes Law Society estimates, report of its Special Committee and proposals; discussions with service departments on integrating their schemes; Scottish departments' objections to original proposals, and modifications; correspondence with PCO on instructions for the bill; cabinet discussions; correspondence with Ministry of National Insurance on the role of National Assistance Boards; memoranda from voluntary organisations, T.U.C. etc.

4631–5, 4674 Law Society's Legal Aid Committee: minutes and Thesiger's correspondence, 1948–9.

4636–41 Legal Aid Services Committee (Schuster Committee) papers 1946–7; correspondence, minutes, evidence, report; discussions on implementation.

5511 Legal Aid Advisory Committee, annual reports (1951–7): correspondence with members on drafting.

2 The regulations (1949–51)

2/4678–9 Minutes of Law Society's drafting sub-committee with Thesiger's correspondence, 1949–50.

4680–1 General regulations: drafting correspondence with Law Society (E. McDougall) Master Burnand, and others; memorandum by Judge Hurst; discussions in Supreme and County Court Rule Committees, 1949–50.

4675 Legal Aid (Scotland) Regulations and other material sent by Scottish Home Department, 1950.

4677, 5475 Financial arrangements: correspondence with Treasury and Audit Office on accounts and estimates 1950–1. Discussions with Audit Office on scheme for audit under s. 9.

4682, 4694 Appeals: legal aid in Privy Council, and amendment to rules on costs, 1950.

4683, 4695 Official Solicitor: discussions with him, the Law Society, PCO on his role in legally aided criminal cases, and on his practice in requiring costs undertakings with him, the Law Society, PCO, 1950.

4684, 4697, 5515, 5580 Scope of the scheme: cuts discussed with ministers and Law Society, memorandum on Evershed Committee recommendations for County Court jurisdiction, and discussions on provision of legal advice; correspondence with PCO and Law Society on bringing parts of the Act into effect by Legal Aid Orders.

4685 Trade Unions: correspondence with the T.U.C. and N.C.B. on draft regulations, 1950.

4163, 4225, 4686, 4688–9, 4693, 5481, 5485, 5514, 5517–21 Costs and fees: correspondence with Pay Office and masters on machinery for recovery by Law Society (4689). Attorney-General's complaint re divorce costs; county court divorce discussed with G. Hicks and R. Gregory (5481). Taxations in Supreme Court (5485), correspondence with Pereira and Gibbon on Law Society's complaints. LCO attempt to end divergent practices on security for costs (4225, 5517). Taxation problem raised by Law Society after *Pemberton* v *Pemberton* (5518). Bar Council proposals to raise minimum fees (5521). Principal Probate Registry raise question of costs incurred after taxation (5514).

4687 Assessment of resources: discussions on position of persons acting in a representative capacity, on the discretion of the National Assistance Board, tax position and servicemen. Correspondence on drafting of Legal Aid (Assessment of Resources) Regulations 1950.

4690–1, 5499, 5509–10, 5522, 5544 Eligibility: discussions with Treasury on Emergency Certificates (4690); discussions on Anglo-Scottish mutual eligibility (4691, 5222); inquiry on legal aid for uncontested probate application (5499); collected correspondence with Law Society and National Assistance Board on persons acting in a representative capacity (5510); correspondence with Foreign Office, Home Office and other departments on eligibility of overseas residents, paper to Lord President (5544); discussions with N. A. Board about anomalies in resources regulations (5509).

4692, 5536, 5583 Contributions and charge on recovered property: proposed guidelines on enforcing charge discussed with Law Society and registrars (4692); brief on the case of Mrs Wilson (5536); proposed amendments to regulations (5583).

4696 Publicity arrangements, 1950.

5480, 6276 Confidentiality: complaints against area and local committees through MPs and correspondence with Attorney-General (5480); correspondence with Ministry of National Insurance on frauds disclosed on legal aid forms (6276).

5482, 5487, 5491, 5571 Panel Complaints Tribunal: discussion on rules with Law Society's rule committee, and minutes; Law Society's objection to lay advocates on appeals rejected. Advisory Committee: correspondence on selection of chairman and members, minutes and papers, draft reports, agendas.

5495, 5501 5519, 5588 Criticisms: twenty-seven judicial criticisms, mostly press cuttings (5495); copies of Law Society's report on legal aid, 1951, sent to certain judges (5501); Court of Appeal criticisms of unmeritorious appeals, and judges' proposals, correspondence with Law Society, LCJ, President (5588); complaint by Devlin J investigated (5519).

5516 Services Legal Aid: interim reports of Law Society "overseas" sub-committee; correspondence with service departments on transfer of responsibility; conference of July, 1951.

5534 Legal Advice: representations from local authorities and voluntary agencies for government funds; discussions with Ministry of Health, 1951.

5581, 5583–4 Proposed amendments to general regulations: from Law Society, LCJ, President, Principal Probate Registrar and many others (to 1953). Specific proposals in 5583, mostly from Law Society, but also includes discussions with Chief Taxing Master, notes of registrars' meetings. Papers from Law Society's drafting sub-committee to 1953.

4676 Amendment Scheme 1951. Thesiger's correspondence with Treasury on defects; Law Society's committee reconvened and revised scheme issued.

6275 Correspondence on appointments to Area and Local Committees with Law Society and Treasury; on salaries, eligibility, some applications and complaint about Law Society's requirements.

4157 Supply of free transcripts outside the scheme under o LXVI[A] proposed to be curtailed. Correspondence with Master Burnand and Treasury and SCRC discussions 1950.

REFORMS IN THE LAW

THE PROCESS OF LAW REFORM: THE LAW REVISION COMMITTEE

1 INTRODUCTION

One of the main planks in the case for the creation of a Ministry of Justice as it was argued at the end of the Great War was the need for a department with general responsibility for promoting legal reforms in those areas which were not clearly and naturally within the province of existing ministries. As has been mentioned already, Birkenhead and Schuster made determined efforts to refute that proposition by emphasising the paramountcy of Parliamentary, rather than administrative, obstacles to legislative reforms and also by demonstrating that the LCO was already capable of performing that function.[1] At that time, the tendency was very much to think of law reform in terms of codification and consolidation[2] but the defeat of the Frauds Bill, which effectively ended Loreburn's initiative in the piecemeal codification of the criminal law, the unexpectedly protracted progress of the Law of Property Bill and the paralysis of the Crown Proceedings Committee emphasised the difficulties which major initiatives were likely to encounter. Moreover Birkenhead's immediate successors showed little interest in such projects and, Schuster later explained, "since the end of the chancellorship of Lord Birkenhead (during which, as you will remember, we dealt with the Law of Property) no Chancellor has ever been in office for a sufficient time to permit any advance on such a subject. The times have also been very unpropitious and we have certainly not found in such attempts as we have made any disposition in the bench or bar to render assistance as was likely to encourage us".[3]

Clearly, it needed a fresh stimulus from outside to revive the reforming spirit, and the upsurge of dissatisfaction with the delays, expense and uncertainty of the law which surfaced in the early 1930s, along with the promotion of Sankey to the Woolsack duly provided it. The opportunity was taken to make a major breakthrough by creating the Law Revision Committee, a standing body which would be able to work methodically and without deadlines on whatever subjects were remitted to it, and which did not depend upon the fitful attentions of the Lord Chancellor and his senior staff. Somervell, the Attorney-General, had proposed "a panel of legal MPs" but Schuster envisaged instead "a standing committee comprising judges, members of the Bar and members of the Law Society as well as one or two persons of experience from the outside world."[4]

This represented a significant shift away from the Statute Law Committee[5] and indeed away from the emphasis on codification, the holy grail of many law reformers. Schuster's view was that the value and difficulties of that course were greatly misjudged by those without personal experience, such as Inskip, who, "was under the impression that codification and consolidation were extremely simple things and that all that was wanted was to take some young gentlemen from the Bar and set them to prepare, for example, a Bill codifying the law of libel and slander."[6]

Sankey was found to be sympathetic to Schuster's proposition and when Hanworth concluded his labours on the Business of the Courts Committee he was straightaway pressed into service as chairman. The selection of members can be followed in these files and the small representation of academic lawyers reflects the low regard in which their contributions were held by the permanent officials.[7] A more important feature is that Schuster and Hanworth stiffened Sankey's resolve against attempts to make the body more 'representative' by adding a provincial solicitor and a woman.[8]

The work of the Committee, which produced eight reports before the war put an end to its operations, has been described elsewhere[9] but a more detailed study of the law reform process in action, examining the intentions and effect of the enacted reports with the aid of these papers, would be of considerable interest. The first four reports, dealing respectively with *actio personalis*, interest on civil judgments, contribution between joint tortfeasors and the liability of a husband for his wife's torts, were rapidly produced and embodied in Law Reform Acts with impressive speed, though only Hanworth's insistence prevented the second bill from sharing the unrevealing and uninspiring "Miscellaneous Provisions" label of the first.[10] Those subjects were the Committee's original references but the success of the enterprise emboldened Hanworth to seek more and weightier topics and his suggestions—limitations, consideration in contract and the Statute of Frauds—were accepted. Lord Wright, who succeeded him as chairman in 1935, held academic lawyers in higher regard than most of the judges and strengthened the Committee by adding Percy Winfield and W. T. S. Stallybrass for their formidable expertise in tort law.[11]

The report on limitations met with objections from the Board of Trade about its effect on the ownership of the foreshore and from local authorities anxious to preserve their privileged position intact,[12] and the Act which followed was perhaps rather unambitious in failing to provide a common standard for actions in tort and contract, but it was certainly a worthwhile measure.[13] It is convenient to mention at this point the proceedings of the Tucker Committee on Limitations. It was set up because the Monckton Committee had expressed dissatisfaction with the limitation period in cases of personal injury[14] (six years, subject to important statutory exceptions in favour of certain public authorities) and the Labour government's nationalisation programme made this a question of particular concern. Napier represented the LCO and Dobson was secretary, but E. C. S. Wade seems to have been as influential as anyone. At all events, the report,[15] proposing a two year period for personal injuries, and six years for other actions in tort and contract, was strongly and predictably opposed by most government departments and found little favour in the cabinet, where it was accordingly given a very low legislative priority.[16] Even among the government's legal luminaries (the Lord Chancellor, the Law Officers and the Treasury Solicitor) there was no unanimity either on the desirability of a common period for tort and contract or on the retention of the privileged position of public authorities, and the Treasury Solicitor's advice to do nothing therefore prevailed.[17]

The Law Reform Committee's proposals on consideration and the Statute of Frauds did not go so far in altering the law as Lord Wright would have wished but nevertheless went far enough to arouse a good deal of opposition. Maugham approved legislation on two of the recommendations—the reform of consideration and the modification of the rule that there was no *ius quaesitium tertio* in English contract law—but it was noted that its Parliamentary prospects in 1939 were poor and it was shelved. After the war Jowitt was not prepared to try to fit it into an already crowded legislative programme and (alone of the Committee's reports) it has remained unimplemented.[18]

Whereas the outbreak of war ruined the chances of that report, it ensured that the seventh, on frustrated contracts and in particular on the rule in **Chandler v. Webster**,[19] became urgently topical. That legislation did not follow very quickly can be seen to be due partly to the draftsman being withdrawn to undertake more pressing tasks but mainly to the Attorney-General's argument that it ought to await the government's policy decisions on contracts affected by war.[20] Caldecote gratefully concurred because disagreements over the theoretical basis of the doctrine had ''impressed [him] with the difficulties and danger of legislating at all on frustration''.[21] It was 1941 before discussions with the PCO were resumed, but decisions in the courts soon quickened the pace, and Simon set a clutch of judges to work on it before the Lords had even decided **The Fibrosa**, the most important of the wartime cases.[22] The papers show an unusually extensive judicial contribution towards this bill, which was finally passed in 1943.

Simon had originally intended to implement in the same bill the Committee's ninth report, on contributory negligence. That report, however, had by far the longest and most complicated passage into legislation, because the common law rules of contributory negligence were politically controversial in a way that most of those considered by the Committee were not. Together with the equally controversial doctrine of common employment, their elaboration in the nineteenth century had done much to make a statutory regime of workmen's compensation necessary. Now the Beveridge report proposed to replace workmen's compensation with a system of ''social insurance'' and to remove the common law ''alternative remedy'' from workmen altogether.[23] The implications of that proposal were still being digested, and acceptance of the LRC's recommendations would, in many instances, make recourse to the common law a more hazardous option for the injured party. The issue had to be confronted: either a Contributory Negligence Bill must await the cabinet's decision on ''alternative remedies'' or it must exclude workmen's actions. The Monckton Committee[24] was already struggling with ''alternative remedies'' and Simon's persistent pressure on the harrassed chairman rapidly to produce an interim report on the contributory negligence aspect[25] and his efforts to ensure the passage of the Bill, albeit in its rather imperfect form, before the coalition broke-up, are fully documented.[26]

Jowitt's unwillingness to revive the Law Revision Committee after the war is surprising. His explanation was that it would only arouse frustration to let them pile up reports which could not be given government time for legislation.[27] However, his own interest in statute law revision and codification suggest that he preferred to give priority to that, and after Schuster's departure neither Napier nor Coldstream had any particular fondness for his creation. Once again, it was outside pressure that led to its revival under the style of the Law Reform Committee.

Notes

1 *See* **supra**, *22ff.*
2 *See e.g. Lord Birkenhead,* ***Point of View*** *(1922), 1, 151–90.*
3 *2/3565: Schuster to Somervell, 24.2.1933.*

4 ***Ibid***

5 ***Infra***, *297–8.*

6 *2/3565: Schuster to Somervell, 13.1.1933.*

7 *e.g. by Coldstream: 2/3565, note of 10.3.1950.*

8 *2/3565.*

9 *John Foster (the secretary, later Sir John) reviewed the first four reports in (1938) 2 MLR 14. The same journal carried notes on the later reports.*

10 *2/1977. See also N. Hutton in (1961) 24 MLR 18.*

11 *2/1989. On the abortive proposal to extend its activities to the criminal law see* ***infra*** *259.*

12 *2/1971, 1982–4.*

13 *(1941–2) 4 MLR 45.*

14 *PP 1945–6 (Cmd. 6860) XIII, 281.*

15 *PP 1948–9 (Cmd. 7740) XVII, 727.*

16 *2/4591.*

17 ***Ibid***.

18 *2/1985: Schuster to A. Ram (PCO), 28.11.1938; 2/3565: Napier to Lord Chancellor, 14.4.1949.*

19 *[1904] 1 KB 493.*

20 *2/1991: Attorney-General to Schuster, 14.9.1939.*

21 ***Ibid***: *note of May, 1941.*

22 *[1943] AC 32.*

23 *See A. Russell-Jones (1944) 7 MLR 13.*

24 *See* ***infra***, *244.*

25 *This course was agreed at a meeting on 26.11.1943 (2/3775). The interim report was presented on 15.12.1944.*

26 *2/3563, 3775–7.*

27 *2/3565: meeting of 3.10.1946.*

2
GENERAL

2/3565, 1968, 1979, 1971, 5442 — Schuster's correspondence with Attorney-General and Master of the Rolls. Discussions on membership and subjects and on replacing and adding members. Discussions on extended terms of reference, especially on criminal law. Minutes, including discussions of draft reports and suggestions. Discussions with Attorney-General and Treasury Solicitor on revival (1946), suggested members and replies to PQ, and other approaches.

3
FIRST REPORT: "ACTIO PERSONALIS . . ."
(Cmd 4540 of 1934)

2/968, 1972 — Early drafts and report. Cabinet papers on Law Reform (Miscellaneous Provisions) Bill and correspondence with PCO; conferences and memoranda, especially from Lord Wright, and Parliamentary proceedings. Complaints on working of the act by insurance companies in 1938. Correspondence with W. H. Thompson, 1942.

4

SECOND REPORT: INTEREST IN CIVIL JUDGMENTS

(Cmd 4546 of 1934)

2/1970, 1974–5 — Memorandum by chairman and other papers, draft report. Files on Law Reform (Miscellaneous Provisions) Bill (***supra***).

5

THIRD REPORT: CONTRIBUTION BETWEEN TORTFEASORS

(Cmd 4637 of 1934)

2/1967, 1976–8, 1820 — Correspondence with the PCO, cabinet papers on legislation (see Law Reform (Married Women and Tortfeasors) Act 1935). Correspondence on rules and interpretation with Masters Bonner and Simner.

6

FOURTH REPORT: LIABILITY OF HUSBAND FOR WIFE'S TORTS

(Cmd 4770 of 1934)

2/1969, 1976–8, 1810 — Various suggestions for changes in law of husband and wife, including lobbying from women's groups. Draft report and subsequent proposal re restraint upon anticipation; correspondence with Stationery Office on printing delays. Correspondence, cabinet papers and Parliamentary proceedings on Law Reform (Married Women and Tortfeasors) Bill, with notes of discussions with women MPs, views of committee members. Correspondence with Masters Ball and Simner on rules and interpretation.

7

FIFTH REPORT: LIMITATIONS OF ACTIONS

(Cmd 5534 of 1936)

2/1279–80, 1982–4, 1988 — Correspondence, draft consolidation bill sent by PCO, committee memoranda by, *inter alia*, A. F. Topham, D. S. Dannreuther, H. C. Gutteridge, H. S. Kent. Report and draft bill; representations by local authority organisations, correspondence with PCO, cabinet papers; objections of Board of Trade and Ministry of Health discussed; negotiations on particular clauses, and criticisms e.g. by A. H. Withers; correspondence with Post Office on effect of *Johns and Hunt* v. *P.O. Savings Bank*.

3585 — Act discussed in connection with nationalised industries bills, 1946.

4586–92 — Limitations Committee (Tucker): preliminary discussions (1947), notes on possible members and discussions with H. Morrison, Scottish Office. Minutes, evidence, correspondence, draft report and drafting correspondence. Memoranda from government departments and discussions with Treasury Solicitor and departments on proposed legislation; cabinet papers and views on local authority and government contracts and torts.

8

SIXTH REPORT: THE STATUTE OF FRAUDS AND CONSIDERATION

(Cmd 5449 of 1937)

2/1979, 1985, 3565 Terms of reference extended, various memoranda, drafts of report, observations by Porter LJ, dissent by Goddard LJ, marked copy for PCO to prepare legislation; office memorandum (1949) on prospects of enacting it.

9

SEVENTH REPORT: FRUSTRATED CONTRACTS

(Cmd 6009 of 1938)

2/1990–1, 1993 Draft report and memoranda, correspondence on amendments and Goddard LJ's dissent; cabinet papers, correspondence with PCO, draft bill and comments. Representations from interested parties, PQs and objections by Attorney-General; discussions with PCO. Board of Trade urge bill after the *Fibrosa* case. Judges asked for assistance; meetings and correspondence, report of Association of British Chambers of Commerce; discussions on scope, especially re insurance contracts, and on suggested amendments, especially by E. O. Walford. Parliamentary proceedings of Law Reform (Frustrated Contracts) Bill, 1943.

10

EIGHTH REPORT: CONTRIBUTORY NEGLIGENCE

(Cmd 6032 of 1939)

2/1973, 1992, 3563, 3775–80 Memoranda and report of sub-committee and final report. Notes by A. L. Goodhart on Ontario legislation; cabinet papers authorising a bill, and PCO draft views of judges and others and reservations of Home Office. Bill dropped pending Beveridge Report. Meetings on 'alternative remedies' (1943) and setting up of committee (Monckton) on alternative remedies. Draft bill for committee and extensive committee papers, including notes of meetings, agendas, Napier's papers, memoranda, evidence and draft reports. Cabinet papers and correspondence on recommendations, discussions on Parliamentary tactics and drafting, especially on objections by TUC and services departments. Law Reform (Personal Injuries) Bill discussed extensively and Parliamentary proceedings.

11

CRIMINAL LAW

2/3565, 1937, 1995 Suggested by M. Gwyer and Lord Wright, and committee appointed; correspondence with Home Office on terms of reference.

12

OTHER SUGGESTIONS

2/1148, 1986–7, 2755, 3565–6, 5611

Marriage laws (1148), various questions (1986–7), powers of appointment (2755), defamation (3565), animals on the highway (3565, 5611), innkeepers' liability (3566), various (3565).

Chapter

2

CROWN PROCEEDINGS

Schuster's long memorandum to Lord Haldane[1] outlines the tortuous and difficult path followed by the committee set up in 1921 to lay the foundations for legislation placing proceedings brought by and against the crown on an intelligible and consistent footing. The Law Society had made the running and Birkenhead and Hewart had been ready enough to comply with their wishes, but the committee that was chosen was too unwieldy and heterogeneous to be effective and at length Schuster was given a sub-committee of officials to put together a draft bill and notes for discussion. For reasons which Schuster does not explain, Hewart did his best to kill the committee by inanition and when it did finally meet again (October, 1923) both Hewart and the Master of the Rolls opposed the officials' scheme. Indeed, there was no general measure of agreement on any of the main issues, viz. (1) should the position of the crown in litigation be brought closer to that of a subject? (2) if so, should this extend to liability in tort? (3) how extensive should be the crown's protection against discovery of documents? Despite Schuster's "Fabian tactics" the deadlock persisted for years and the Admiralty tried to prevent even the publication of the report, though it only embodied the unhelpful conclusion that, if the principles underlying the draft bill which it incorporated were to be accepted, the bill would adequately implement them. The advocates of the bill had to contend against the embattled resistance of the Inland Revenue, the adamant opposition of the Attorney-General (Sir Douglas Hogg) and, most of all, the Admiralty. When Sankey wrote to Laski of the discouragements and disappointments which beset the law reformer,[2] he might have taken this bill as his model, for the papers give ample chapter and verse to his view.

In particular the Admiralty behaved with an unscrupulousness which caused him to write to the First Lord in restrained but angry terms.[3] Despite the strong and persistent pressure of the Law Society and the shipping lobby the bill was not introduced, largely because of fears that the clauses granting discovery of documents, which already "went to the extreme limit of concession"[4] and terrified senior civil servants, would be widened in the Commons, and because of the unknown cost of assuming liability in tort. It was not picked up again even when the Hanworth Committee recommended that actions be capable of being brought against the crown in the county court,[5] and Hailsham's known views made its reactivation impossible during his chancellorship.

Various expedients were adopted in order to mitigate the hardships which flowed from the crown's immunity from suit in tort. One which can be studied in these papers is the nomination of an "independent person" to whom reference might be made in cases where the driver of a government vehicle caused an injury attributable to his negligence (an occurrence which the black-out and the expansion of the armed forces made much more frequent) but where it was debatable whether he was driving in the course of his employment at the time. Until 1942 government departments would meet damages awarded against the tortfeasor only if this was the case, and acted as judges in their own cause. The "independent person" called into existence to decide this single—but often difficult — point of law represents one of the more curious wartime expedients.[6] It was hardly satisfactory, and in 1944 the House of Lords deliberately exploded another such expedient with a view to forcing the issue; in **Adams v Naylor**,[7] where a child had been injured in a minefield, they blew away the convenient crown practice of nominating a representative defendant to contest liability.

After this judgment action could no longer be delayed, and the Attorney-General promptly bespoke a new bill from the PCO, but it was left to Jowitt to force this long overdue reform through. A new argument could now be suggested, too: "at the present moment it is doubly important that legislation should be brought in for this pupose because it is clear that the government will pass a good deal of legislation which will impose restrictions upon things which citizens have been free to undertake in the past. It would therefore be a wise action to disarm criticism, and to show that the government intended to maintain the rights of citizens even against the state".[8] There was still great opposition to be overcome though, both from the Lord President, who grudged the bill room in the legislative programme, and from government departments (the Admiralty were again the worst offenders, "trying to sabotage the bill").[9] The files are interesting on the wide consultations which Jowitt undertook and on the sensitive issue of discovery of documents, where a new directive had to be prepared, although since the **Thetis**[10] case it had been clear that the government would be able to rely upon the judges not to inconvenience it in that regard. Perhaps the advocates of a Ministry of Justice might draw on the saga of the Crown Proceedings Bill for support; certainly it is a textbook instance of the difficulty of persuading government departments to relinquish powers and immunities, and deserves a full study.

Schuster had more success in modernising the Crown Office rules which governed the prerogative writs, criminal informations, *quo warranto* proceedings and a whole host of antiquated, abstruse and mostly little-used procedures brought on behalf of the crown. With the expansion of government activity and the proliferation of bodies to whom decision-making powers were delegated, the prerogative writs which enabled their activities to be challenged by the private citizen recovered much of their importance but the 1906 rules needed drastic revision.[11] "Sooner or later", wrote Schuster, "and I hope sooner, I intend to launch an attack on the forms of procedure under the prerogative writs".[12] A sub-committee of the Hanworth Committee undertook this important task and their papers include interesting memoranda on particular aspects, such as *ex-officio* informations. Not surprisingly, the process of overhauling these venerable actions was slow and highly technical (even Kent, the draftsman, described his draft rules as "a repulsive document")[13] and in the later stages Schuster had to give a good deal of his time to it. The results were embodied in that "rather ill-assorted miscellany"[14] the Administration of Justice (Miscellaneous Provisions) Act 1938 and the RSC (Divisional Courts) 1938, and made a worthwhile and necessary improvement, ending anachronisms such as outlawry and sensibly restricting informations.

Notes

1 *2/938. Lord Rushcliffe explained the genesis of the committee in* ***Parl. Debs****. 1942–3 (HL) vol. 122 cols. 540–3.*

2 *R. F. V. Heuston,* ***Lives of the Lord Chancellors*** *(1964), 823.*

3 *2/3359: 21.11.1929.*

4 *2/3358: cabinet paper, 17.10.1927, Sir D. Hogg.*

5 *2/1600.*

6 **Parl. Debs.** *1942–3 (HL) vol. 122 cols. 533–63. The cases submitted to the "independent person" are listed in 2/2684, but the files dealing with them are not in the PRO.*

7 *[1944] KB 750.*

8 *2/3361: Douglas's memorandum, 22.8.1945.*

9 *2/3362: Treasury Solicitor to Napier, 30.1.1947.*

10 **Duncan v Cammell Laird & Company** *[1942] AC 624.*

11 *2/1608: memorandum by J. Rowlatt (PCO), February, 1934.*

12 *2/1699: to E. J. Maude (Ministry of Health), 5.12.1931.*

13 *2/1761: to Napier, 7.10.1938.*

14 *(1938–9) 2 MLR 307 (E. Wyndham White).*

2/1093–1101, 3358–61	Crown Proceedings Committee (Hewart). Proposal by Law Society, 1920. Views of Law Officers and preliminary correspondence on terms and membership; correspondence with members; minutes, memoranda, correspondence with departments, draft bill and comments thereon; correspondence on drafting the report. Report and draft bill and correspondence with Admiralty on publication. Cabinet and committee papers; memoranda by departments, representations from shipping and commercial associations, Bar Council, Law Society and others. Discussions in cabinet resumed 1929; further departmental memoranda, meetings of officials and correspondence with Admiralty. Renewed proposals 1932, 1936.
1598, 1608	Hanworth Committee (see first and third reports); memoranda on Inland Revenue proceedings (1606); Crown Office rules and sub-committee papers.
1753	Rules under Carriage by Air Act 1932 s. 2; draft and correspondence with Treasury Solicitor and Foreign Office; see RSC(2) 1933.
1/43, 2/1699, 1760–3	Crown Office (QB) Rules, draft with manuscript alterations by Lindley. Crown Office Rules: correspondence with Ministry of Health (1931) on Public Health Act 1875 ss. 225, 262; drafts by J. Rowlatt; notes of meetings of officials and with Attorney-General; protracted drafting correspondence leading to Rules 1938, Criminal Proceedings Rules 1938 and Change of Venue Order 1938.
2/1776	Discussions with GPO, IRC and Treasury Solicitor on effect of Administration of Justice (Miscellaneous Provisions) Act 1933 s. 4(1), and draft rules following amendments in Administration of Justice Act 1938.
1380	Correspondence with Attorney-General on likely test cases on effect of Courts (Emergency Powers) Act 1939 on the crown.
2683–5	PQs on road accidents involving crown servants, especially soldiers. Correspondence with Treasury Solicitor, and discussions of cases where liability denied. LC's memorandum leading to appointment of the "Independent Person". List of cases submitted to him 1946–8, correspondence with J. W. Morris KC, mostly on fees, and discussions on his successor (F. W. Beney) 1945.
4661–3	Treasury Solicitor's objections to discovery provisions in Claims Tribunals Rules, 1939.

3095–6, 3115, 3104	Discussions on limitation periods and litigation privileges in Coal Industry Nationalisation Bill, Electricity Bill, Borrowing Bill, 1946.
3361–6	Crown Proceedings Bill revived by Attorney-General 1944 and correspondence with Home Office, PCO in 1945. PQs, cabinet papers, meeting of legal departments, discussion of cases, especially *Adams* v. *Naylor*; IRC and Admiralty objections, comments of judges and others, detailed correspondence with Treasury Solicitor on discovery; Parliamentary proceedings, especially notes on insurance companies' objections, and Treasury Solicitor's directive on discovery, 1947.
4080, 4091	Correspondence on drafting High Court rules; employment of C. Pearson, comments on draft by masters, and discussed in SCRC, November 1947. Order LXI discussed March 1948 (RSC(1) 1948) after difficulties raised by Attorney-General.
3327, 3618, 3784	Correspondence on rules for county and inferior courts.
3370	Minutes of meetings of committee (Colonial Office) on application of Crown Proceedings Act to the colonies (Dobson's papers).
3368–9	Queries on the scope of the Act in relation to National Insurance Act and bankruptcy proceedings, negligence by fellow soldiers, 1948–9.
3699	Discussions with Home Office. Treasury Solicitor on discovery of police reports, etc. in pension cases, 1943–5.
3841	Petition of right in case of *M. V. Delphincula* heard by Lord Chancellor on application for transfer between divisions, 1946.
3910, 4076	Two points of practice raised by LCJ, 1943, 1947.

Chapter
3

THE LAW OF PROPERTY

1
THE LAND LAW

1 The 1925 Legislation

In a series of acts which are collectively known as "the 1925 legislation" or "the Birkenhead Acts" the English law of real property, which a leading conveyancer had described as "a barbarous system", was brought into harmony with the values and needs of the post-war world.[1] Sir Claud Schuster described this as 'the largest measure originating in the department'[2] and it was no exaggeration, for there were formidable obstacles, both technical and political, to be overcome. The making of the Acts has been described by Avner Offer, drawing freely on the LCO papers, and they afford an excellent insight into the stages by which the legislation achieved its final form.[3]

Substantial files record the deliberations of the Ministry of Reconstruction's sub-committee on land transfer (the "Scott Committee") in 1919, including its minutes, evidence and correspondence, and reveal the way in which the eminent conveyancers Sir Benjamin Cherry, Arthur Underhill, A. E. Russell and Charles Sweet put together the scheme which emerged in the second phase as a giant Law of Property Bill.

The series of files which take the bill from its early drafts in 1919 to its passage in 1922 cover the negotiations in which interested parties such as the Law Society, the Land Union and the Institute of Conveyancers, and Parliamentary critics, in particular Lord Cave, were bought off, won over, or disarmed; they deal also with specific questions such as compensation for copyhold enfranchisement, settled land and commons.

In the third phase the unwieldy bill, which had passed in 1922 but had not been brought into force, was handed over to a small committee under Romer J to be broken up into more manageable parts, so that the final legislation assumed a complicated form of consolidation, postponement and amendment acts, carefully described by Cherry in LCO 2/766. Many significant changes were made by the committee, e.g. on co-ownership and mortgages, but inevitably the end product did not satisfy everyone, and representations from the various local law societies are particularly valuable on the impact of the search requirements imposed by the Land Charges Act on conveyancing practice. Some obvious flaws, such as Settled Land Act provisions concerning family charges which threatened havoc on recently broken up family estates in Bournemouth and elsewhere,[5] were remedied by an Amendment Act in 1926 and a further problem by government legislation thinly disguised as a private members bill, in 1932[6].

In general, considering their complexity and importance, the 1925 Acts were a remarkable success and despite academic criticisms,[7] experience did not suggest that many amendments were necessary until the system had to accommodate the challenges posed by matrimonial co-ownership and marriage breakdown after the war. Particular aspects of the law of property did, however, create difficulties, as shown in the files listed below.

Notes

1 *Charles Sweet in (1912) 28 LQR 6, at p. 24. See R. E. Megarry and H. W. R. Wade,* ***The Law of Real Property*** *(5th ed., 1984), 1144–54 for a brief assessment of the legislation. Underhill's account is in* ***Change and Decay*** *(1938).*

2 *2/3630, at p. 13.*

3 *(1977) 40 MLR 505. See also his book,* ***Property and Politics, 1870–1914*** *(1981).*

4 *2/788.*

5 *2/780–1.*

6 *2/1496.*

7 *e.g. A. H. Withers (1947) 62 LQR 167, H. Potter (1944) 8 Conv. (N.S.) 147,191.*

1/55–6	Reform proposals from various individuals including Lord Davey, E. P. Wolstenholme, H. E. Elphinstone.
2/198	Law Society's Conveyancing Bill, 1910: correspondence with J. Hills MP, B. L. Cherry, Parker J and notes of conference with the Building Societies Association.
14, 19, 1125	Escheat rules 1889 and discussions with Home Office and Treasury Solicitor's Department on Escheated Estates (Northern Ireland) Rules in 1927.
2/508–9, 3/40–5	Land Transfer sub-committee: agenda, correspondence, documents, minutes. Includes draft bills and proposals from the CLR and eminent conveyancers.
2/443–52	Law of Property Bill, 1920–22: drafting correspondence, negotiations with various interest groups and individuals, Parliamentary papers and correspondence.
459	Amendments to the Bill: mostly duplicates of papers in main series.
450–6	Particular subjects in the Bill: title registration, royal manors, lunacy and intestacy, commons, copyhold enfranchisement.
763–72	Law of property legislation 1924–5, including proposed amendments to L.P. Act 1922 (763), files on the various Consolidation Bills, 1924 and Law of Property (Postponement) Bill 1924; papers of the Romer Committee.
779–94	Amendment proposals on particular subjects e.g. aspects of the Settled Land Act, obligations of trustees for sale, lost probate grants, local land charges, copyhold enfranchisement in the Honour of Clitheroe. 788 and 791 contain suggestions of a more wide ranging kind, from Local Law Societies and A. V. Alexander MP respectively.
1087	Statutory will forms under L.P.A. 1925 s. 179; papers and correspondence of Clauson Committee.
1088	Correspondence with the Treasury on Law of Property Restrictive Covenants (Discharge and Modification) Fees Rules, 1925.
688	Discussions with IRC, B. L. Cherry on tax treatment of trusts for sale, 1926.
1123	Law of Property (Amendment) Bill, 1929: correspondence with Cherry, A. H. Withers, PCO on bill to remedy an omission raised by British Bankers Association.
1496	Law of Property (Entailed Interests) Act 1932. Drafted by Cherry and introduced as a private member's bill by Lord Blanesburgh, principally to reverse the inconvenient decision in *Re Price* [1928] Ch. 579. Correspondence on drafting and Parliamentary scrapbook.

1497 Correspondence with the Ministry of Agriculture, Cherry and others on the power of the crown to grant concurrent leases (Crown Lands Act 1927 s. 21, Settled Land Act 1925 s. 42(1), Law of Property Act 1925 s. 198(3)), together with opinions of the Law Officers.

1805 Amendment to RSC o XXI r 21 by RSC(2) 1936 to avoid the consequences to tenants of *Kisch* v *Hawes* and *Barton* v *Reed*.

3076 Complaint by the Law Society re the Welsh Church Burial Grounds Act 1945, which created an exception to the structure of legal estates in land; correspondence with its promoters, the Home Office.

2816–7, 3560 Solicitors remuneration on copyhold enfranchisement, 1935–50 (see *supra*, 182).

2 Registers of Deeds and Titles

1 *The Middlesex Deeds Registry*

The Middlesex Registry, created by an Act of 1707, had become an embarrassment by the 1880s, partly because its practice was inefficient and doubtfully in conformity with the statute[1] but chiefly because of "the fine old sinecure"[2] which netted the Registrar, Lord Truro, over £4,700 a year out of the fees and attracted fierce Parliamentary criticism.[3] The various bills prepared in the early 1880s both by private individuals and by the government came to nothing, largely because of the lack of general agreement on whether the Registry should be reformed, abolished or replaced by title registration but also because the Lord Chief Justice objected to the expedients proposed to deal with the Registrar's emoluments.[4] Truro's death in 1891 facilitated the transfer of the administration of the registry to the Chief Land Registrar without resolving its fate, and it was not until 1937 that further action was taken.

The extension of compulsory registration of title to Middlesex in that year inevitably produced a loss on the fees account of the deeds registry and in October, 1939 the Land Registry Rule Committee under Farwell J (with the addition of a Treasury representative) recommended closure.[5] This was effected by the Middlesex Deeds Registry Act 1940, and when the LCO was pressed to re-open it temporarily after the blitz to aid solicitors in tracing lost deeds, Schuster was furious to discover that many of its records had been destroyed, and others saved only by the intervention of the London County Council. Legal responsibility was "a frightful tangle"[6] and necessitated a conference with representatives of the Land Registry, the Public Record Office and the local authorities.

Notes

1 ***Munton** v **Lord Truro*** *(1886) 17 QBD 783.*
2 *2/40: Muir McKenzie to G. F. Pollock, 1.4.1891.*
3 *e.g.* ***Parl. Debs.*** *1881 (H of C) vol. 260, cols. 825–34.*
4 *1/71: Coleridge to Treasury, 13.9.1881.*
5 *2/1493.*
6 *2/1491: Schuster to Chief Land Registrar, 9.9.1941.*

1/71, 88 Hopwood's Bill (1881) (sponsored by the Building Societies' Protection

	Association), Gifford's Bill (1884) and the LCO's bill; observations and correspondence with the Treasury and the Lord Chief Justice.
2/40, 44, 53	Middlesex Deeds Registry Bill (1891). Memoranda on fees, staff and practice, schemes for reform by Holt (Chief Land Registrar), Munton and Ansell (Deputy Registrar); correspondence with Treasury on the Bill and establishment, petitions from clerks etc.
257	Correspondence with Chief Land Registrar and Treasury on proposed new fees orders 1910, 1914.
1485–6, 1491, 1493–5	Middlesex Deeds Registry Act 1940 and Rules 1948. Correspondence with Chief Land Registrar and Treasury report of Land Registry Rules Committee, December 1939. Correspondence with PCO and the Attorney-General on the bill, Parliamentary scrapbook (1943). The rules were made following a claim for indemnity: correspondence with Treasury Solicitor, and draft approved by Vaisey J and Master Holland (1494). Correspondence with solicitors and the Law Society, the Master of the Rolls, the London CC, Middlesex CC, Public Records Office and CLR on records disposal (1491). Middlesex Deeds Rules, 1936.

2 *The Yorkshire Deeds Registries*

The three ridings each had their own deeds registry and local sentiment, especially in the legal profession, was strongly in favour of their retention or, in the event of the imposition of title registration, of a title registry run along similar lines by the county councils. Consequently there was particular alarm at the Scott Committee's proposal to abolish the county veto on extensions of compulsory title registration, and long and difficult negotiations ensued, especially with the West Riding (by far the most populous and important of the three).[1] A compromise was agreed and embodied in the Law of Property Act 1922 s.181(6) but the extra complications and expense caused by the duplication of searching in the deeds registries and the Land Registry (under the Land Charges Act) dissatisfied both the law societies and the promoters of the 1925 legislation.[2] The outcome was the Tomlin Committee, which the Chief Land Registrar sought to 'pack' with supporters of a *centralised* title registration. The evidence given to the committee is interesting on contemporary conveyancing practice and the changing practice of the Land Registry (see especially that of A. H. Withers, a member of the Committee, which also included Schuster and Rae of the Treasury), but its report[3] is an anodyne affair which admits that district land registries, perhaps to the number of half a dozen, will ultimately be necessary, but rejects decentralisation of control to local authorities; Yorkshire is admitted to be a special case because of the existing registers and the prevalence of mineral rights, but not one justifying a wholly distinct system. It was another forty years before the deeds registries were in fact closed and compulsory title registration reached Yorkshire.[4]

Notes

1 *2/1491; A. Offer (1977) 40 MLR 505, at 520.*
2 *2/793.*
3 *PP 1929–30 (Cmd 3564) XV, 539.*
4 *Law of Property Act 1969 s. 16.*

1/88	Correspondence with the clerks of the peace in Yorkshire on procedure for making rules, 1884–5.
2/277	East Riding County Council Bill, including a proposal to allow the Clerk of the Council to be appointed Deeds Registrar. Objections from Hull Law Society, Bar Council and other bodies, correspondence with Lord St Aldwyn (chairman of the Royal Commission on the Land Transfer Act) and with the bill's sponsors. It was enacted in 1910.
4259	A similar (temporary) proposal from the West Riding CC, opposed by local law societies and the Law Society but supported by the LCO and enacted in 1944.
450, 457	Negotiations with West Riding CC on the abolition of the county veto and the land registration provisions in the Law of Property Bill, 1920–2.
793	Petitions and correspondence from Yorkshire county and district councils on their proposal to make land charges in Yorkshire registrable only in the deeds registrars; comments by Cherry, 1925.
1106–8	Tomlin Committee 1926: correspondence with the CLR and others on its establishment and membership; evidence to the Committee (1108), minutes (1107) and report (1106).
1109, 1111, 1953	Correspondence with West Riding CC, Cherry and others on Land Charges Rules 1925, and on fees orders in 1927 and 1941.
4260	North Riding CC attempts to recover registry building, 1948.

3 H.M. Land Registry

1 Introduction

The Land Registry was for many years the LCO's problem child. Lord Chancellor Westbury had fathered it in 1862 and Lord Chancellor Cairns had attempted to give the sickly infant a new lease of life in 1875 but in the face of the implacable hostility of solicitors it languished and few of Cairns' successors were enthusiastic supporters of the principle of title registration. There is considerable material in the LCO files on various bills and proposals made during the 1880s and 1890s, especially the Land Transfer Act 1888, and on the registry staff, salaries and organisation, but there is nothing on the Act of 1897 which foisted compulsory registration on London county. The strength of the opposition is clearly seen, however, in 2/182–3, which deals with its extension to the City of London. Sir Charles Brickdale's various attempts to promote registration by offering financial inducements and relaxing the registry's rigorous standards for the grant of absolute titles were generally disapproved by the Treasury, while the LCO remained benevolently neutral. [1]

The principle of registration was endorsed by a royal commission in 1911 [2] but its progress continued to disappoint its supporters and to provide ammunition for its many critics. Brickdale made strenuous efforts to persuade the Scott Committee of the need to abolish the county veto, which effectively prevented the extension of compulsion, and to rebut the usual criticisms of the registry, e.g., in relation to restrictive covenants and mortgages, [3] but the eminent conveyancers who dominated the Committee were no friends to title registration and Birkenhead was prepared to sacrifice any immediate progress in registration in order to enact the law of property legislation, and even to pay the price of a ten year moratorium exacted by the Law Society. [4] Brickdale and his more emollient successor Stewart-Wallace had therefore to come to terms with the profession and to concede a more profitable scale of costs for dealings with registered land[5] which, during the moratorium, gradually reconciled the profession to title registration.

Apart from an extension to Eastbourne in 1925 and to Hastings in 1927 no significant expansion could be contemplated within the moratorium period. The full-scale comparative investigation into the respective merits of the two systems of land transfer which had been promised never did take place, for the second Tomlin Committee which was set up in 1933 did the job that Schuster had clearly intended that it should by recommending an extension to Middlesex, but made only a superficial enquiry;[6] when a further extension to Croydon and Surrey was recommended in 1939 in response to persistent demands in Parliament, the only issues which were seriously discussed were the problems of mapping and solicitors' remuneration.[7] The policy of a gradual extension outwards from London was challenged by the ''egregious recommendation'' of the Scott Committee on rural land (1942) for an extension of compulsory registration to all rural land within five years.[8] The LCO had to respond in haste to this cavalier and impracticable recommendation by concocting another committee sitting under Lord Rushcliffe and chosen and tutored specifically to reject the proposal.[9]

Hence, when the post-war manpower shortage eased sufficiently for further extensions to be contemplated, it was to Surrey that the land registry turned again. Delays were occasioned first by the refusal of the Treasury to sanction extra staff and then by the demand of the local law society for an enquiry,[10] but the Gray report[11] of 1951 marked the end of serious resistance to registration and the beginnings of a period of more rapid expansion. This was given added impetus by the Roxburgh Committee in 1956,[12] which condemned the other part of the land registry, a central charges registry created in 1888 and vastly extended in 1925, as ''a kind of conveyancing of Frankenstein's monster'',[13] incapable of being made to work satisfactorily.

The land registry rules and fees are settled by an *ad hoc* committee under a Chancery judge subject to the approval of the Lord Chancellor and, in the case of fees, the Treasury.[14] The rule making power is very wide and the fees orders have had to be made quite frequently in order to keep the accounts in broad balance in conformity with the statutory requirement to break even. The fees can be used as a policy instrument e.g. to discourage voluntary registration, but the Treasury has not usually been prepared to countenance the registrar's bolder schemes. Solicitors' charges for registered transactions are also fixed by rules, and successive registrars have usually opposed increases which would narrow the differential between registered and unregistered land.[15] The discussions in 1925 are especially full and valuable on contemporary practices.

They also throw interesting light on the working of the indemnity fund which supported the ''state guarantee'' of the register's accuracy, much touted as an advantage over the existing private conveyancing system. High standards and low pressure of work enabled claims occasioned by errors in the registry to be kept to a very low figure until after 1925, but inevitably, there was a tension between security and speed.[16] The receipt of several substantial claims impelled the departments concerned to settle the procedure[17] and also contributed to a review of the fund itself; by the Land Registration Act 1936 the separate fund formed out of the fees was appropriated by the Treasury in exchange for a guaranteed £100,000 change on the Consolidated Fund.[18]

Notes

1 *e.g. 2/185.*
2 *PP 1911 (Cd 5483) XXX, 1.*
3 *e.g. his memoranda in 3/45.*
4 *See A. Offer (1977) 40 MLR 511–7.*
5 *2/1073.*
6 *PP 1934 (Cmd 4776) X, 395.*
7 *2/1481–5, 1489.*
8 *2/2749: Schuster to Lord Chief Justice, 15.9.1943; PP 1941–2 (Cmd 6378) IV, 421.*
9 *PP 1943 (Cmd 6407) V, 21; 2/2749: Schuster's minute to Lord Chancellor, 2.11.1942.*
10 *2/3811: CLR to Napier, 28.6.1951.*
11 *2/5369–72.*
12 *PP 1955–6 (Cmd 9825) XXII.*
13 *H. W. R. Wade (1956) 14 CLJ, 216.*
14 *The committee was established by the Land Transfer Act 1897 s. 22(2).*
15 *e.g. 2/1073, 1102, 1489, 3811, 5858.*
16 *"Sir John Stewart-Wallace has always taken the view that safety mattered very little as long as expedition could be obtained", 2/1491: minute by Coldstream, June 1941.*
17 *2/929: Notes of conference on 1.7.1926.*
18 *2/1487.*

2 The Land Registry before 1925

1/55–6, 2/8 Land Transfer Act 1888: various papers on land registration by e.g. Lord Davey, the Building Societies' Association, E. P. Wolstenholme, H. E. Elphinstone, C. F. Brickdale and Holt; drafts of the bill and correspondence with C. P. Ilbert (draftsman).

1/61, 71; 2/4, 53 Questions of organisation and salaries, c. 1881–93: petitions etc. by staff and correspondence with Holt and the Treasury.

1/82 Rules under Agricultural Holdings Act 1892 with protest by Law Society.

2/27 Rules 1898, with observations by the Law Society on the draft.

181 Report of a committee on organisation, with Brickdale's observations. Extension of compulsory registration to the City of London: correspondence with the CLR and with the City Corporation, petitions, postponement orders etc., 1900–3.

180 Proposal by the CLR to compel the Post Office to register title to its London premises, rejected by the Treasury, 1906.

184–5, 259 Land Registry rules committee proposals on rules and fees, 1902–4: correspondence with Treasury, CLR and Kekewich J (chairman). 1908 Rules & Fees Orders: correspondence with Treasury and Kekewich.

182, 256 Report of committee on mapping and the CLR's proposals for changes in "Report on Compulsory Registration". Correspondence with CLR and Treasury, 1905–6.

258 CLR's scheme for a general registration consequent on the Finance Act 1910; notes of discussions with Inland Revenue, 1910.

260	CLR's memoranda to the St. Aubyn Commission, 1908.
2/407-8, 450, 508-9, 4/45	Brickdale's papers on the county veto and extension of registration, and evidence on registration to the Reconstruction Committee, 1918-21.
2/620	Memorandum by the CLR on title examination policy within the Land Registry, 1919.
3/40-5	Scott Committee papers (*supra*, 206).
2/668	Whitley Council papers.

3 Proposals to extend compulsory registration

2/927	Eastbourne extension order: correspondence with CLR and East Sussex Law Society, 1924.
1104-5	Hastings extension order, 1927 and committee on Land Registry-Ordnance Survey relations, 1928.
1106-8	Tomlin Committee, 1928-9 (*supra*, 202).
1481-4	Second Tomlin Committee, 1933: correspondence on setting up, evidence, minutes, report.
1486, 1488	Land Registration Act 1935: correspondence with CLR, Treasury, PCO, Middlesex CC *et al.*, and Parliamentary scrapbook.
1489	Croydon extension order, 1938: answers to PQs, correspondence with CLR, Law Society, Treasury.
2749-53, 3547-8, 3351	Rushcliffe Committee, 1943: correspondence on Scott Report and on membership of Committee; minutes, evidence, report; correspondence on the report with CLR, Association of Municipal Corporations, A. H. Withers *et al.*
3549	Staff side deputation press for speedier extension of compulsory areas, 1950.
5369-72	Surrey extension order. Correspondence with CLR, Treasury, Law Society. Arrangements for inquiry by J. N. Gray KC, Land Registration (Conduct of Public Inquiries) Rules 1951; correspondence with Ministries of Town and Country Planning and Local Government.

4 Rules and fees

2/5	New scale proposed by CLR, 1889.
256	CLR's proposals to re-structure fees, 1906.
927	Eastbourne extension order: negotiations on solicitors' costs between CLR and Law Society, 1924.
1072-3, 1102	Discussions with CLR, Law Society, Ministry of Agriculture, on solicitors costs, 1925; meeting of committee and subsequent correspondence; draft order and memoranda on contracts, 1925.
1103, 1110-1	Rules and Fee Orders 1926-30: memoranda by solicitors, notes on priority notices by CLR, discussions on fees strategy.
1126	Agricultural Credits Act 1928 rules.
1480	Rules, 1936: committee report, correspondence with CLR and Treasury Solicitor.

1485 CLR proposals for fees changes, 1935.
1489 Discussions on Law Society's claim for higher scale costs, 1937.
1490 Fees Order 1939: draft and official letters.
2802 Correspondence on solicitors' remuneration, 1938.
3552, 3554 Fees Orders, 1948, 1950; correspondence with CLR; rule committee approvals.
3811, 5858 Solicitors' remuneration 1948–51; correspondence with CLR, Master of the Rolls, Law Society and Chancellor of the Exchequer, rejecting any increase.
4330 Correspondence on liability of Coal Commission and other nationalised industries to pay fees, 1946.

5 *The insurance fund*

2/256 CLR proposals and Treasury views on liability of the fund, 1906.
929, 5385 Bermondsey claim, 1926: discussions on procedure with CLR, Treasury and Treasury Solicitor.
930 Kensington claim papers, 1930.
931, 5385 *Chowood's claim*, ([1930] 2 Ch. 156), papers.
1485–9 Land Registration Act 1936: papers and correspondence on the fund from 1928, discussions with Treasury, report of Dormant Funds Committee; Cherry's explanation of s.75(4) L.R. Act 1925.
1492 Russell's claim papers, and general correspondence on claims, 1931.
5384 Reviews of value of securities comprising the fund, 1939–66.
5382 Norman's claim, 1950 (the "Haigh Case") papers.

6 *Other registration matters*

2/1376 Registration under the Essential Buildings and Plant (War Damage) Act 1939.
2652, 3137 Requisitioned Land Act 1944.
3095–6, 4330 Nationalisation of coal mines.
3573–4 Limitation Acts 1939, 1944 and registered land.
3611, 3616 Liabilities (War-time Adjustment) Acts.
3550 Registration of local authority purchases considered, 1946.
4626 Registration of statutory charges under Legal Aid Act 1949.
3553 CLR invited to sit on Scottish Registration Committee, 1948.
4519 Complaints about operation of Land Charges Act 1925.
5351 Law Society proposal to register company mortgages under Land Charges Act discussed with Board of Trade, Chancery judges and subsequent correspondence, 1950–4.
5381 Annual reports, 1948–57 with correspondence with CLR.
4/264 Chief Land Registrar, appointments and salary, 1923–47.
2/3687 Delays: complaints and PQs, 1946. Meetings and correspondence.

3 Landlord and Tenant

1 *The Rent Acts*

Departmental responsibility for this notoriously controversial and unsatisfactory legislation lay with the Ministry of Health, but besides the Lord Chancellor's position as a cabinet minister, he was concerned because landlords' claims for possession were made in the courts, and the material in the LCO reflects both of these functions.

2/379	Courts (Emergency Powers) Bill 1917: correspondence on the proposal to facilitate recovery of overpaid rent.
385	Increase of Rent (Amendment) Bill 1918: correspondence with other ministers on scope of protection.
478–9	Rent Act 1923: reports of Ministry of Health and cabinet committees, discussion papers and briefing papers.
762	Protection from Eviction Bill 1924: papers and correspondence.
3006, 3275	Ridley Committee, 1943: county court evidence and selection of county court judge as member; suggestion from G. Hicks.
3100	Furnished Houses Bill 1945: correspondence with Ministry of Health on responsibility for appointments to tribunals.
3275, 3583, 5605A	Various suggestions for alterations to the Acts, 1943–51.
3599	Evidence from Principal Probate Registry on the effect of the decision in *Thynne* v. *Salmon* [1948] 1 KB 482.
4480	Landlord and Tenant (Rent Control) Act 1949: cabinet papers, briefs for Parliamentary proceedings, etc.
4570–1	Cabinet discussions on proposals to deal with "hardships" in the Landlord and Tenant (Temporary Provisions) Bill 1950.
357	Making of rules under the Rent Acts 1915–19: correspondence with Sir W. L. Selfe.
544, 843, 1305, 1318, 1285	Rules under later Rent Acts.
863	Birmingham Corporation (General Powers) Bill 1929: correspondence with Ministry of Health over clauses giving wide power to protect sub-lessees in the county court.
853	*Dunkley* v *Knight* (*R.* v *Registrar of Lambeth CC, Ex p. Dunkley*): correspondence with the Registrar, Judges Parry and Cluer and memoranda on county court practice on possession orders.
3284	Large file of complaints by local authorities, MPs and others, about the making of possession orders by county court judges, especially in London; circular to the judges and correspondence with Home Office and Ministry of Health, 1946–7.

2 Leasehold reform

The respective rights and duties of landlord and tenant were mostly outside the scope of the 1925 legislation, but there had for many years been recurrent bouts of agitation for change emanating mainly from two types of tenant, those in business premises and residential tenants on long leases.[1] A measure of assistance was given to the former in 1927, and a particular abuse by corporate lessors in South Wales was tackled with impressive rapidity by the LCO in the Landlord and Tenant (Leasehold Repairs) Act 1938,[2] but as soon as the war ended the shortage of business and residential accommodation and the lifting of temporary restrictions on possession actions led to rapidly rising rents, evictions and a renewed clamour for reform. The government was confronted with vociferous demands for leasehold enfranchisement by its own supporters, particularly in South Wales, and was further embarrassed when the Scottish Office took independent remedial action.[3] The LCO tried to evade responsibility, arguing that the question was essentially political rather than legal,[4] but Jowitt reluctantly agreed that something would have to be done and the Uthwatt Committee was set up to examine the complaints both of business tenants and homeowners on long leases. The coupling of two distinct issues proved unfortunate and the Committee had a most unhappy history, handicapped by uncertainty about which of its tasks was to have priority, hamstrung by irreconcilable differences of opinion among its members and further hampered by the untimely death of its chairman.[5]

Not surprisingly, its reports lacked authority and conviction and the cabinet discussions which produced the Landlord and Tenant (Temporary Provisions) Bill show equal uncertainty over what Jowitt called "a perfectly revolting subject".[6] The papers on this episode are, however, a valuable source of material on both the political and the legal dimensions of leasehold reform.

Notes

1 *For the historical background see D. Englander,* ***Landlord and Tenant in Urban Britain, 1838–1918*** *(1983), and see the summary of official reports in 2/4566.*

2 *2/1498.*

3 *2/4545–6.*

4 *2/4546: Napier's minute, 16.10.1946.*

5 *2/4563 is particularly interesting on the attempt to find a suitable successor to Uthwatt.*

6 *2/4570, to Morrison, 11.10.1950. The bill was "fathered at the official level by a scratch team of civil servants" (2/4571, Coldstream to Sir H. Lascelles, 4.12.1950) after great difficulties and prompted one scholar to comment "it is melancholy to reflect that every fresh enactment on this topic seems only to render more distant than ever the day when some comprehensive measure may be introduced to rationalise this branch of the law" (D. Lloyd in (1951) 14 MLR 465 at p. 467).*

2/1498–9 Landlord and Tenant (Leasehold Repairs) Act 1938: complaints from MPs and others; correspondence with Attorney-General, PCO etc.; cabinet and Parliamentary papers on the bill.

856, 860 County court rules (1928) under Landlord and Tenant Act 1927; extensive correspondence with members of the rule committee, especially Judge Cann and C. H. Morton. The rules had to be amended in the same year (860).

1278 Further rule changes at the instance of the Referees Association, 1934.

1987 Judge Konstam suggests the doctrine of waiver as a subject for the Law Revision Committee, 1934.

3584 Parliamentary questions and departmental correspondence on the colour bar in leases; legislation opposed by the LCO 1946–9.

4546 Departmental correspondence, especially with the President of the Council, on the setting up of a leasehold committee, its membership and terms of reference. Correspondence on the actions of the Scottish Office, 1946–7.

4547–67 Uthwatt-Jenkins Committee 1948–50.

4551–60 Evidence; with index in 4551.

4561–2 Minutes and papers.

4547–50, 4563 Correspondence.

4564, 4567 Interim and final reports.

4566 Summary of findings of previous committees.

4568–79, 4989 Leasehold Property (Temporary Provisions) Act 1951. Lengthy correspondence at ministerial and official levels with departments, especially Ministry of Health, Board of Trade, Scottish Home Department, Attorney-General; report of working party under Sir B. Gilbert (July, 1950); correspondence with PCO on drafting; cabinet papers (4568–71). Representations from MPs and others, briefs for Parliamentary proceedings, notes and discussions on amendments (4571–9); correspondence on application to crown lands (4574), and on county court rules (4989).

4580–1 Scottish Leasehold Committee (Guthrie) and Long Leases (Temporary Provisions) (Scotland) Act 1951; discussions with Scottish Office and Attorney-General.

3562, 3580, 4545, 4582–5, 5609, 5466 Representations on leasehold reform from various quarters, 1945–53.

5450 Correspondence with Treasury and PCO on drafting of Shops Order under the 1951 Act.

4993 Discussion of Lady Reading's proposal to educate tenants in domestic management, 1951.

3 *Wartime emergency legislation*

Consideration of the probable effects of another European war began well before hostilities and three particular problems were anticipated: the requisitioning of land, leasehold property damaged by enemy action and the inability of tenants to meet their obligations. The last was, of course, part of the wider problem considered by the Schuster sub-committee on civil liabilities, and was dealt with by the Courts (Emergency Powers) Acts and the Liabilities (War-time Adjustment) Acts.[1] Requisitioning was the subject of two Acts, in 1941 and 1943, and the problem of war damage, which arose chiefly from the refusal of insurance companies to offer cover against war risks, was met by the War Damage Acts. Not surprisingly, this novel and intricate mass of legislation, drawn up under great pressure, gave rise to many difficulties of interpretation and complaints of unfairness.[2] A particular problem arose out of the House of Lords decision in *Lace* v *Chantler*,[3] which declared leases whose term was defined by reference to the duration of the war void for uncertainty, disconcerting several ministers (and Coldstream) who had granted or taken property under such leases, and requiring legislation to undo its effects.

Notes

1 ***infra**, 271ff.*

2 *See e.g. 3/2729: H. S. Kent to Coldstream, 8.6.1942 on "these terrible landlord and tenant statutes".*

3 [1944] KB 368.

2/1391–9, 1412–5 Civil liabilities sub-committee, 1939–40 papers, especially 4th report (1392), and papers on ground leases.

1374 Courts (Emergency Powers) (No. 2) Bill 1939: various papers on leasehold aspects.

1421, 2663 Requisitioned Land Acts 1941 and 1943: Morris Report on the Compensation (Defence) Act 1939, Parliamentary papers on the 1941 Bill; extensive drafting correspondence with PCO on 1943 Bill, dealing principally with repairing obligations.

1416–8, 1500–2, 2729, 2731, 3422 War Damage Acts 1939, 1943: 1939 correspondence with PCO, Uthwatt Committee and Ministry of Health; cabinet papers, Parliamentary briefing papers. Correspondence of 1941 on a "sweeping up measure", with PCO, various MPs and professional bodies, and extensive cabinet and Parliamentary papers, especially on ground leases and mortgages. Amendment Bill 1943 to deal with anomalies and hardships; representations from various persons and bodies, correspondence with PCO and War Damage Commission, especially on disclaimers. The bill was dropped.

1320 County Courts (War Damage) Rules: lengthy correspondence, mostly with the Treasury and Inland Revenue, on the employment of assessors.

3568–9 Wartime Leases (Validation) Act 1944: correspondence with Attorney-General and Law Society and re establishment of Committee under Evershed. Evidence gathered for it, minutes, cabinet papers, drafting correspondence and Parliamentary papers. Correspondence with Law Society, PCO, government departments, and PQs on orders under the Act.

4 Town and Country Planning

1 *Introduction*

Responsibility for town planning lay with the Ministry of Health until the Ministry of Town and Country Planning was created in 1943 to implement the ambitious proposals for a comprehensive and nationwide system of planning controls. The LCO had a direct concern with two aspects of planning however; first, in the provision of a form of adjudication for the inevitable disputes between citizen and state which would arise out of the exercise of these revolutionary powers; second, in providing a means of enabling the existence of planning restrictions and land charges to be ascertained by purchasers, mortgagees and other interested parties.

The town and country planning legislation which was being contemplated envisaged a much wider interference with rights of user than hitherto, and a much more widespread use of compulsory purchase, as well as novel and severe taxation on landowners, all of which were certain to generate a large volume of complaint. Moreover, the amount of public money at issue in disputes over compensation and valuation would in the aggregate be very large, so the Treasury, as well as the new ministry, was concerned about the procedures to be adopted.[1]

Compensation and valuation questions had been considered in great detail by the Reconstruction Committee at the end of the Great War, but under very different circumstances. The files on their deliberations are particularly interesting on the vexed question of "betterment" taxation and on the possibility of penalising landowners who held up private development, but neither of these found a place in the subsequent legislation[2] and the Official Arbitrators, to whom it fell to determine disputed financial questions, were considered not to be up to the tasks which lay ahead at the end of the second world war. The hostility to their informal and unjudicial procedures manifested by the departments concerned was only exceeded by the determination of those departments not to resort to the courts. The Lands Tribunal, which was the outcome of long deliberations, was intended to be more judicial than arbitral, without being as formal and costly as the courts.[3]

The courts did become involved, however, when the Minister's exercise of his decision making powers under the new acts was successfully challenged at first instance after inquiries at Stevenage and Plymouth.[4] It is indicative of the importance which was attached to the Stevenage case that it affords the only instance in these papers in which the Lord Chancellor approached the Master of the Rolls to ensure that the composition of the Court of Appeal would be "satisfactory".[5] In the event its decision avoided a clash between the government and the judges on an issue of great importance and on which the cabinet had already decided to legislate if necessary.[6]

The financial scheme of the 1947 Act was fiercely assailed by expert opinion from the outset. Land prices showed an incorrigible tendency to exceed the "existing use value" at which it had been naïvely assumed sales would take place once the "development value" had been appropriated by the state and this led that unpopular creation the Central Land Board to threaten to stretch the statutory powers to their limit and perhaps beyond in an effort to keep prices down. In fact, as the files reveal, the Law Officers' opinion on the extent of the Board's powers (from which both Jowitt and the draftsman differed) had been unfavourable, and a sharp protest followed the Minister's "disingenuous" authorisation to the Board to use the s. 43 powers in the very way which the Law Officers had pronounced *ultra vires*.[7] Lack of any appeal procedure, which had made Jowitt uneasy from the outset, also contributed to the Board's unpopularity. Jowitt had to meet allegations of "hardship" made in debates in the Lords first by acting as a go-between for the complainants and the Ministry, then by helping to set up a "Development Charges Committee" of the cabinet. Grievances were redressed but the impression of dictatorial bureaucracy was hard to efface.[8]

The imposition of the 1947 Act also made unavoidable a review of the system of local land charges registers. The Law Society rightly claimed that the proliferation of assorted charges and notices made registrable under various statutes had made searches for incumbrances a tedious and protracted exercise, and Coldstream agreed: "I do not think that there is any public business which is in such a muddle as that . . . concerning local land charges".[9] The departments principally concerned were anxious to avoid a "full dress enquiry" and naturally opposed any sanction arising out of a failure to register, so they had to be dragooned into accepting an enquiry under Sir John Stainton (February, 1949).[10] The Stainton Committee did not report until early in 1952, and found the "ghastly subject"[11] every bit as intractable and unappealing as they had feared, but its papers contain interesting and valuable material.[12] Meanwhile, of course, orders had had to be made to accommodate the new legislation.

Notes

1 *2/4666: Coldstream to Napier, 31.8.1944.*

2 *3/28–33. PP 1918 (Cd 8998) XI, 1; 1918 (Cd 9229) XI, 59; 1919 (Cmd 156) XXIX, 51. Acquisition of Land (Assessment of Compensation) Act 1919.*

3 ***Supra**, 169–70.*

4 ***Franklin** v **Minister of Town & Country Planning** [1948] AC 87; **Robinson** v **Ministry of Town & Country Planning** [1947] KB 702. See H. W. R. Wade (1949) 10 CLJ 228.*

5 *2/4285: Master of the Rolls to Napier, 19.3.1947.*

6 *2/4285: cabinet minutes (47) 25th meeting, 27.2.1947.*

7 *2/4292: Attorney-General to Minister of Town and Country Planning (copy), 8.10.1948. See (1948) 1 JPL 507–8 for the text of the Minister's letter. This episode is not discussed by Edwards in his book on the Law Officers, which was written before these documents became open to inspection.*

8 ***Parl. Debs.** 1948–9 (H of L) vol. 165, cols. 713–66; vol. 166 cols. 383–444; 2/4296.*

9 *2/3544: to P. H. See (PCO), 25.9.1945.*

10 *2/4579.*

11 *2/4519: minute by Napier, 9.12.1948.*

12 *The report is PP 1951–2 (Cmd 8440) XVI, 287.*

2 Planning law

2/2650, 2658 Ministry of Town and Country Planning Act 1943, and Town and Country Planning (Interim Development) Act 1943: Parliamentary briefs.

3043–5 Town and Country Planning Act 1944: Parliamentary briefs, also correspondence on appeals forum.

3071 Town and Country Planning (Scotland) Bill 1945. Lord Chancellor arbitrates between Scottish ministers in dispute over rule-making power.

3101 Betterment Bill 1945: discussions on appeals.

4286–7, 4293 Town and Country Planning (Minerals) Regulations 1947: discussions on tribunals; criticisms in 4293.

4289, 4296–7 Town and Country Planning (Development Charge) Regulations, 1948, 1950: correspondence with Minister of Town & Country Planning and Lord Llewellin on exemptions and policy; Parliamentary papers; correspondence and reports on 'hardship' allegations; report from Central Land Board on reforms.

4292 Town & Country Planning Act 1947 s. 43: discussions over construction, 1948.

4285 Stevenage and Plymouth (T & C.P.) Orders: government reactions to judicial decisions, 1946–7.

4291 Orders and regulations 1948, no correspondence.

4298 R.I.C.S., Law Society and Chartered Auctioneers etc. Institute proposals for changes, 1950.

3 Land Charges

2/1113 Correspondence with Ministry of Health and Law Society, on complaints about operation of local land charges and rules, 1927.

3077 Distribution of Industry Bill 1945: correspondence with Board of Trade and Ministry of Health on registration of C.P.Os.

1112–3 Rules and Fees Orders 1925, 1927: correspondence with Ministry of Health and representations from interested organisations.

1475–9, 3543–6 Various local land charges amendment rules 1931–46 and correspondence on consolidation (3544).

2652, 3137 Requisitioned Land and War Works Bills, 1945, 1947: correspondence with PCO, Chief Land Registrar, Ministry of Town and Country Planning on registration of charges.

4541, 4543–4 Local Land Charges (Amendment) Rules and (no. 2) Rules 1948. Discussions, queries from local authorities and correspondence with Ministry of Town and Country Planning.

4540 Correspondence with N. Ireland PCO on their proposed local land charges registers, 1950.

4519–42 Stainton Committee, 1949–52: correspondence with departments; Enever Committee (1948) report; members and terms of reference (4520–1) correspondence (4522) evidence (4523–5) minutes (4526) memoranda by members (4527–30) draft reports (4531–6, 4541), summary and prospects for legislation (4537, 4542). Articles from law papers (4539).

4538 Chancel repairs: correspondence on F. Crowder's suggestion for registration, with CLR, Tithe Redemption Commissioners, 1949.

4 Compulsory purchase and compensation

3/1–39 Reconstruction Committee, 1917–19. Correspondence and papers on setting up and work of Acquisition and Valuation of Land Committee; agendas, minutes, documents and reports; similar papers of the Compensation Committee and Mining Sub-Committee. The evidence and documents are particularly extensive.

2/4283 Acquisition of Land (Owner-Occupier) Regulations 1944: correspondence with PCO, Uthwatt J, Judge Davies and government departments; queries on meaning of the regulations.

2791 Suggested inquiry into machinery discussed, 1944.

4297, 3813 Correspondence with Ministry of Town and Country Planning on machinery for assessing compensation to statutory undertakers etc. 1949, and on solicitors' costs.

6191 Correspondence with Ministry of Town and Country Planning, cabinet papers etc. on compulsory purchase powers in the Mineral Workings Bill, 1951.

2
TRUSTS AND INHERITANCE

1 Private Trusts

1 Introduction

The law of trusts went through a phase of vigorous judicial and legislative activity for about thirty years after c. 1880, but apart from the files relating to the creation of the Public Trustee and to the Judicial Trustees Act 1896, this is not very fully reflected in the LCO papers. Thereafter there was a period of relative quiet until the combined effects of taxation and inflation on fixed trusts became serious enough to produce calls for trustees to have wider powers.[1] The war made their problems more acute in many instances, and a bill was drafted at the instance of the LCO in 1941 to enable the High Court to authorise the release of trust capital for immediate needs, but because "no-one who has thought about this subject at all has any real enthusiasm for it",[2] it was replaced by a much narrower bill limited to charging certain expenses to capital. The only general legislation on trusts under the Labour government came about fortuitously when the Mountbatten Estate Bill (a private bill aimed at removing a restraint upon anticipation) ran into a Parliamentary storm engineered by the supporters of women's rights and had to be withdrawn; a public bill was substituted which abolished those restraints which had survived the (non-retrospective) Law Reform Act 1935.[3] A later proposal to enable capital to be used to preserve ancient family documents failed to attract the sympathy of the Chancery judges.[4]

Pressure on trust incomes naturally led to attempts to widen the range of "trustee securities" in which trustees whose trust instrument did not give them a wide discretion might safely invest. Here, however, the LCO recognised the overriding interest of the Treasury in not devaluing government stock by expanding the list,[5] and the Lawrence Committee in 1928 recommended few significant changes.[6] After the war there were questions in Parliament, and Jowitt had a rough ride on at least one occasion, but the Chancellor of the Exchequer maintained an unbending opposition to any liberalisation.[7] The existing list was not only narrow, but riddled with inconsistencies: in particular, the statutory list was actually narrower than the list of those recognised by the Court, yet the latter could hardly be narrowed in conformity lest it devalue the securities concerned.

A feature of the inter-war period was the rise of the trust corporation. They were recognised by the 1912 Public Trustee (Custodian Trustee) Rules, which were revised in 1925 and 1926, and which required them to obtain a certificate from the Lord Chancellor before they could act as charitable trustees. In 1936 discussions were held with the interested departments to simplify this process for local authorities although in one case the "wide form" was withheld where a county's finances were "not all that could be desired".[8] Persistent attempts were made by the commercial trust corporations to put themselves on the same footing as the Public Trustee by empowering them to charge for their services where there was no specific charging clause in the trust instrument, but this was never conceded.[9]

Notes

1 *See G. W. Keeton,* ***Modern Developments in the Law of Trusts*** *(1971).*

2 *2/2756: Coldstream to Schuster, 2.4.1942. Settled Land and Trustee Acts (Courts General Powers) Act 1943.*

3 *2/3204, especially Lord Chancellor's memorandum to cabinet, June 1949.*

4 *2/3605.*

5 *For this "unwritten convention" see 2/1731: Schuster's memorandum, 21.1.1932.*

6 *PP 1928 (Cmd 3107) XII, 497. The committee seems to have made no attempt to collect evidence from trustees, other than the Public Trustee (2/1045).*

7 *2/3917. See e.g.* ***Parl. Debs.*** *1946–7 (H of L) vol. 149, cols. 375–80.*

8	*2/1932: note on Kent CC application, 1947 (referring to Monmouthshire).*
9	*e.g. 2/769.*

2 General questions

2/94	Rules made under Trustee Act 1893.
141	Judicial Trustees Act 1896: correspondence and drafts of rules.
283	Trustee (Bodies Corporate) Bill 1911: correspondence with Treasury, Public Trustee etc.
447, 786	Law of Property Bill: correspondence with B. L. Cherry on power of trustees to charge, and on s. 26(3) LPA 1925.
1657	Anderson Committee report on unit trusts, 1936, sent to LCO.
2756–8, 3045, 3907, 3427	Settled Land and Trustee Act (Courts General Powers) Act 1943: extensive correspondence from 1939 with Attorney-General, PCO, Chancery judges, Treasury, Inland Revenue *et al.*; cabinet and Parliamentary papers. Discussions with Chancery judges on making it permanent, 1949.
3204, 3601	Mountbatten Estate Bill: cabinet papers, representations from women's organisations, correspondence with Mountbatten solicitors.
3605	Proposal to use capital to preserve estate documents 1950: views of Chancery judges, D. B. Buckley, Law Society.
3646	Law Reform (Miscellaneous Provisions) Bill 1949 s. 8, reversing *Re Custance's Sett.* (1946) Ch. 42: correspondence with Master Poyser, PCO, Treasury, Chancery judges.
4230	Trading with the Enemy Acts: correspondence with Board of Trade, Custodian of Enemy Property, Simonds J on effect on protective trusts, 1942–52.
4856	Trustees and Liquidators (Emergency Provisions) Bill 1951; consultations with experts.
3674, 3676	Official Solicitor as judicial trustee. Report of Fass Committee, correspondence with Official Solicitor, Vaisey J and Master Holland on fees, 1948.
784, 1310, 1928, 1930, 1986, 3594, 3604, 4231	Miscellaneous minor points.

3 Trustee securities

2/1043–7	Lawrence Committee 1926: minutes, evidence, correspondence, report. 1043 includes Sir H. Jenkyns' history of trustee securities (c. 1890).
1731, 3917	Proposals to widen, 1930–46: correspondence with Treasury; memorandum by Schuster (1932) on policy.
1914, 4064	Discrepancies in trustee securities: discussions with Pay Office, 1941, 1947. For particular types of security see 2/393, 476, 481, 583, 1217, 1907, 1848, 3082, 3926.

4 Trust corporations

2/283, 447	*supra*
769	Trustee (Consolidation) Bill: correspondence with B. L. Cherry, Public Trustee.

997–9 Custodian Trustee Rules 1925: discussions with Public Trustee, Cherry, H. Cohen and various bodies on definitions and drafting.

818 Royal Exchange Insurance Bill 1930: correspondence with Treasury etc. on policy.

1932 Lord Chancellor's certificate: correspondence with Charity Commissioners, Board of Education; Law Officers' opinion, 1936. Further correspondence of 1940, 1947.

1115–6, 1931, 1933, 3750, 3758, 4232–3 4235–6, 4238–9, 6693 Particular corporations.

2 Public (Charitable) Trusts

Although the legal definition of charity was generally acknowledged to be a fearful tangle, there was no enthusiasm in official circles to tackle it, perhaps partly because it was the acknowledged responsibility of no department and the one official body directly concerned, the Charity Commission, formed "a sort of 'imperium in imperio'" and was under no effective superintendence.[1] It was only when a series of well publicised cases (particularly the **Diplock** case and the **Oxford Group** case)[2] during and after the second world war highlighted its unsatisfactory condition and Lord Samuel and others proposed to divert dormant charitable funds to meet pressing social needs that the government was persuaded to set up a royal commission under Lord Nathan. The LCO was not represented on the Commission, which reported in 1952 but Coldstream sat on the Barnes Committee which considered that part of the report which dealt with "Imperfect Trusts", and which produced the Charitable Trusts (Validation) Bill 1954, while Rieu was on the Playfair Committee, also composed of officials, which examined the other recommendations in the Nathan report.[3]

Notes

1. *2/4646: Jowitt to Morrison, 4.7.1949. For confusion over the Lord Chancellor's position vis à vis the Commissioners; see 2/3636, correspondence with Lord Morton, 1950.*
2. *See G. W. Keeton (1949) 2 CLP 86.*
3. *PP 1952/3 (Cmd 8710) VIII, 5 (Nathan report); the officials' reports were not published.*

2/5838–9 St. Katharine's Hospital papers, 1889–1917, include discussions with Charity Commissioners and on its charitable status.

59 Rules under Charitable Trusts (Recovery) Act 1891: draft by Charity Commissioners annotated by Ilbert, Heywood, 1892.

104, 4470 British Museum Bills; correspondence with Treasury on bills of 1898, 1900 and with MR on bill of 1946.

1130 Memo by Judge Jones on disaster funds and discussions with Public Trustee and Attorney-General on Gresford Relief Fund, 1934.

1221	St. Bartholomew's Hospital Bill 1938: conventions on Parliamentary sanction for variation of charitable trust by private bill discussed.
2648	Universities (Trusts) Bill 1943, widens investment powers.
3185	LCO on longer requires to scrutinise charities' private bills, 1949.
3636, 3576	Minor complaints and queries.
4646–8	Correspondence with Morrison and others on terms and membership of Nathan Commission 1949; minutes, report.
4649–52	Barnes Committee report. Charitable Trusts (Validation) Act, correspondence and Parliamentary papers, 1952–4.
4653–6	Playfair Committee: minutes, correspondence, evidence, 1953–4.
4657	Briefs for debate on dormant funds, 1953.

3 The Public Trustee

1 Introduction

Like the Land Registry, and also under the supervision of the Lord Chancellor, the Public Trustee Office was essentially the product of public dissatisfaction with the conduct of business by solicitors, in this case the service they provided as trustees, and the 1906 Act which established the office was the brainchild of Sir Howard Vincent, who battled for twenty years to secure its passage. Like the Land Registry too, the Public Trustee's services were to be voluntary, but their histories diverged, for the Registry's inability to attract business led to compulsion being introduced, whereas the Public Trustee has never sought any monopoly position.

In the first phase of its history, the Public Trustee Office, under Sir Charles Stewart, was a vigorous, adventurous and aggressive institution, actively seeking to expand its powers and maximise the business on which its future depended, for like the Land Registry its obligation to be self-supporting (though not profit making) had been written into the Act by the Treasury.[1] For this reason too, its fees had frequently to be adjusted, but this was a much more complicated task than it was for the Land Registry, as the level of fees would influence the volume of new business; there was also the added complication that it was debatable whether any degree of 'cross-subsidisation' between trusts was permissible.[2]

The Great War ended Stewart's honeymoon period, for the pressure of the greatly increased business which it almost inevitably produced (and which was further increased by the imposition on the Public Trustee of the role of Custodian of Enemy Property) proved altogether too much for an office which was first denuded of its experienced men by the needs of the war, and then hampered by internal feuding as its ailing chief lost his grip on its affairs.[3] Costs rose fast once the office became established within the civil service, delays and (less noticeably) mistakes gave ammunition to its many critics in the legal and banking professions and before its fees could be raised to the level needed to wipe out its deficit, it was deemed prudent to hold an inquiry under Sir Gilbert Murray, late of the Treasury: as Schuster wrote to him "the office is at the parting of the ways".[4] The papers of that Committee—and those of the Branson Committee[5] which reported on the vexed question of the awards to infants under the Workmen's Compensation Acts which were being expensively administered by the Public Trustee—are splendidly informative on the problems of running what was essentially a private business operating within the structure of a government department, and other files dealing with particular issues such as investment policy,[6] the disclosure of breaches of trust[7] and the almost inadvertent acquisition of profits[8] suggest interesting reflections on the paradoxical position which the Public Trustee occupies.

The Murray Committee could not produce an unanimous report because the solicitor representative, Sir Samuel Garratt, insisted on the view that the Public Trustee should be little more than a custodian trustee, putting out legal and professional business to the private sector, and also maintained the principle that each trust should bear its own expenses. Garratt made sure his dissent received publicity and his criticisms of inflated administration costs and an unwieldy bureaucracy probably prevailed in the public mind over the majority report, which cautiously endorsed most of the office's practices.[9]

After an uncomfortable few years in the limelight, however, the office settled down to a humdrum existence, in which it seldom attracted public attention. The coolness of the Permanent Secretary and the downright antipathy of the more "Chancery minded" Lord Chancellors, like Cave and Maugham, encouraged Stewart's successors to opt for a lower profile and they presided over a gradual decline in business; since the Public Trustee had ceased to be a threat either to solicitors or to the trust corporations which were taking an increasing share of trustee and executorship business, the Kingsway office became a quiet backwater, which it remained until the rude shock administered by the Holmes Committee in the mid-1950s.[10] For all that, its history is an interesting and curious one, which can be followed in some detail in the LCO papers and those of the Public Trustee Office itself, though the files belonging to individual trusts are, of course, not open to inspection.

Notes

1 *See e.g. 2/340: Stewart's proposals for additional powers, 1911.*
2 *This is discussed in the Murray report (PP 1919 (Cmd 422) XXVIII, 341) at paras 15–20 and in Garratt's dissenting note.*
3 *2/485.*
4 *2/484: 26.2.1919.*
5 *2/648.*
6 *2/1001.*
7 *2/419.*
8 *2/1553. Public Trustee (General Deposit Fund) Act 1939.*
9 *See 2/659 for the "very irregular post-mortem combat" on the report in the columns of* **The Times**.
10 *PP 1955–6 (Cmd 9755) XXVII, 253. 4/88–101 deal with the report and its implementation.*

2 *General questions*

2/39 Public Trustee Bill, 1890: drafts, notes, views of Law Society, Treasury; memoranda from Parker J, Law Society, Official Solicitor.

271–3, 275 Public Trustee Act 1906 and rules: drafts, correspondence and memoranda on the bill; Parliamentary proceedings. *Ad hoc* rule making committee, correspondence and organisation; new premises; audit regulations and irregularities.

286, 340	Public Trustee Bills, 1911–2: correspondence with Public Trustee, Treasury, Law Society.
339, 342	New premises in London; appointment of Deputy Public Trustee at Manchester, 1915.
484–7	Murray Committee, 1919. Preliminary correspondence with Public Trustee, Treasury; evidence, memoranda, correspondence and report.
659	Correspondence with Murray Committee on Garratt's letter to *The Times*, 1921, and draft replies.
488, 669	Establishment papers, including minutes of re-grading committee (1920) and creation of Whitley Council.

3 Fees

272	Fees Order 1908.
341	Fees Order 1912.
418	Fees Order and effect on existing trusts.
647–52, 658, 660	Orders of 1920–3: correspondence with Public Trustee and Treasury on policy; memorandum on compensation funds; acceptance fees on sales of settled land, Treasury Solicitor's opinion. Branson Committee papers (648); memorandum on prospects (1921) by Public Trustee.
1003	Fees Order 1926: correspondence with Public Trustee, and with Cherry on effects of Law of Property legislation on Public Trustee.
3757	Fees Order 1948: report by Public Trustee, discussions with Treasury.

4 Particular questions

2/274, 419, 674, 1130, 3646, 275, 419, 544, 654, 996, 3162, 3646 3755–6, 3759	Particular trusts, mostly errors and legal difficulties.
1130, 3756	Policy towards "disaster funds".
3277	US servicemen's bastards: policy on acceptance of small trusts explained.
1553, 4230	Public Trustee as Custodian of Enemy Property 1924, 1942. Includes correspondence on the "General Deposit Account" from 1924, leading to the Act of 1939.
4647	Evidence to Nathan Commission, 1950.
274	Jurisdiction over Irish trusts: Law Officers' opinion, 1909.
417, 652, 655, 657	Various legal questions.
653	Receipt of brokers' commission: report by Younger J and correspondence, 1919.
1000	Three cases involving questions about Public Trustee's duty to disclose information to other government departments 1922–6.
1001	Discussions with Treasury on investment policy, 1927.
1002	Trotter Committee papers, 1929, on security in stock transfers by the PTO.

4 Wills and Intestacy

The principle of unfettered testamentary freedom which had become strongly entrenched in English law began to come under serious attack in the 1920s as a result of the agitation for increased rights for women and the wider spread of home ownership. Before long the pressures of taxation and inflation also highlighted the possible inadequacy of the existing rules for distribution of an estate upon intestacy, laid down as recently as 1925 in the Administration of Estates Act.

The agitation of women's rights groups led to a series of bills in Parliament in 1928 and through the 1930s, for the subject "excites a good deal of interest among that wing of the professional feminists who belong to the upper and middle classes"[1] wrote Schuster. Sankey was sympathetic to the general idea of making some reserved provision for spouses, but Hailsham was sternly opposed and the Chancery judges, although they initially and tentatively suggested the course which was eventually adopted, were equally hostile to the whole idea by 1937, when the government resignedly came to accept that the principle could no longer be opposed directly but only by the familiar Parliamentary tactics employed against popular but unwanted private members' bills.[2] In the event a bargain had to be struck with the promoter of "this obnoxious bill",[3] which left provision for the aggrieved relative in the discretion of the High Court rather than making any fixed allocation as of right. The episode is fully covered in these papers.

The 1938 Inheritance (Family Provision) Act did not extend to intestacy and shortly after the end of the war the Law Society made its own inquiry into the intestacy rules and began to campaign for a change which would give greater rights to the surviving spouse and children at the expense of more distant kin. The Attorney-General was keen to set up a committee and the Lord Chancellor agreed, although as usual Morrison was able to insist on a larger, more politically weighted one than Jowitt wanted.[4] Its terms were to consider the rights of the surviving spouse on intestacy and whether the 1938 Act should be extended to cases of intestacy.

The Morton Committee's papers in the LCO include valuable statistics for earlier years collected by the revenue departments. The Committee was easily persuaded, especially by the Bar Council's evidence, of the need to improve the widow's position, and M. J. Albery eventually won over the chairman on the question of the 1938 Act; the only major disagreements were on the rights of siblings to share in the estate.[5] The report was accepted and its recommendations put into effect by the Intestate Succession Act 1952.[6]

In wartime an aspect of wills which was normally of only esoteric interest came into prominence, *viz.* the informal (nuncupative) wills of servicemen. First the Law Society discovered that a sub-section in the 1925 legislation, which Uthwatt described as "pure nonsense",[7] seemed to have inadvertently deprived those who were infants of their power to dispose of realty in this fashion, then several court decisions on the scope of "actual military service" seemed to invalidate numerous servicemen's wills made under the inaccurate advice given in their paybooks, and finally the view of the Law Officers had to be taken on the applicability of this informal will-making procedure to women in the armed forces. The attempts to deal with these points do not show the LCO or the service departments in a favourable light; the first remained unresolved throughout the war, and the second was only partly cured by the President's Practice Direction of 1944, based on his own decision in *Anderson.*[8]

Notes

1 *2/1187.*
2 *2/1189.*
3 ***Ibid.**: per Lord Hailsham.*
4 *2/4440.*
5 *2/4448.*
6 *PP 1950–1 (Cmd 8310) XV, 637. See J. D. B. Mitchell in (1951) 14 MLR 478.*
7 *2/5635: to Schuster 14.3.1940, on s. 51(3) Administration of Estates Act 1925.*
8 *[1944] P. 1.*

2/1185–9 Inheritance (Family Provision and Dependants) Bill 1938 and its predecessors from 1928. Correspondence with promoters and supporters; views of the Chancery judges, cabinet and Parliamentary papers.

2968 Query by Public Trustee on recent decisions on Finance Act 1941 s. 25. Revived by Treasury, 1946 after *Berkeley* v *Berkeley* (HL). Consultations with Law Society and Public Trustee on possible legislation.

3557 Concern at effect of *Grosvenor* v *Peace* (1944) 1 Ch. 138.

3588 Correspondence with R. K. Law MP on time limits under the Act and "hard cases", 1947.

3559 Information on inheritance law sent to Iceland, 1946, 1954.

4440–1, Morton Committee papers, including correspondence with Morrison, the LOD

4443, 4445–50 and others on terms. Discussions on composition (4441) evidence, statistics (445) correspondence with members (4446) memoranda by reform groups, Law Society, Bar Council, M. J. Albery *et al.* (4447) minutes (4448) report (4449) and comments and criticisms by the Treasury Solicitor and others.

4450–1, 6671 Intestate Succession Bill: correspondence, drafting papers, Parliamentary proceedings, 1951–2.

5635 Problems of servicemen's wills, 1940–52: PQs, correspondence with service ministers, Law Society, President of the PDA, Uthwatt J etc.

5607 Wills etc. (Publication) Bill 1951. PQ of 1951 and cabinet discussions, 1953–4.

3
INTELLECTUAL PROPERTY

The law of intellectual property was sufficiently profitable, as well as sufficiently esoteric, to have generated its own specialist bar, and the substantive law was the departmental responsibility of the Board of Trade. However, the role of the Lord Chancellor and of the lawyers and judges who sat on several committees on the adjudication process was the subject of some of Professor Robson's most trenchant criticisms and that alone makes the record worth examining.[1] Thus it is of interest to notice that the removal of appeals against the decision of the Comptroller-General from the Law Officers — a rather unlikely forum — to the Patents Appeal Tribunal (really a nominated judge of the High Court) which was implemented by the Patents and Designs Act 1932 on the recommendations of the Sargent Committee,[2] and much criticised by Robson, had actually been proposed by the Board of Trade in the Patents and Designs Bill of 1907, when the Lord Chancellor complained that he had not been consulted and that he would oppose the change.[3] Other patent cases were heard in the Chancery Division and dissatisfaction with the cost and length of actions and with the insufficient expertise of the judges grew loud during the 1920s and was not silenced by the palliatives recommended by a small committee set up in 1929 on the initiative of Tomlin J.[4] With the Sargent Committee itself the LCO appears to have had little involvement, nor were they the prime movers in the Hanworth Committee's decision to set up a sub-committee to consider delegating judicial functions to the Comptroller, but Robson's strictures on the "loose and unsubstantial . . . fashion"[5] in which the Committee went to work can be tested against its minutes and evidence. Nothing that came out of any of the committees satisfied those engaged in patent work (other than the lawyers) but although the continuing agitation for a tribunal and a restriction on appeals made some impression on the Board of Trade, it made none on Lord Maugham, whose attitude is neatly summed up in a letter to the President:

> the establishment of a special tribunal for this particular type of work might have most serious results upon our judicial system generally. If a special tribunal is to be set up for this business I can easily imagine that there may be other industries of importance which might make a similar demand, and could not in logic be denied. Why should not the property owners in this country, seeing this precedent established, demand a tribunal specially set up to deal with questions of real property; or those interested press the demand which has often been made, that all matters arising from the use of mechanical power on the highway both civil and criminal be determined in special courts?[6]

The reluctance of the Chancery judges and Lord Chancellors to admit that the jurisdiction over patents demanded specialist knowledge persisted, leading them to oppose the recommendation of the post-war Swan report for the appointment of two specialists to hear patent cases, as well as any devolution to the Comptroller.[7] In the event the LCO was able to veto the latter and restrict the former to one new judge, Lloyd Jacob.

Notes

1 ***Justice and Administrative Law*** *(2nd ed., 1947), 410–20. For a history of modern patent law see W. R. Cornish,* ***Intellectual Property*** *(1981), 79–84.*

2 *PP 1930–1 (Cmd 3829) XVI, 709.*

3 *2/149: Muir McKenzie to H. Llewellyn Smith, 16.7.1907.*

4 *2/1062 (no report published).*

5 ***Op. cit.***, *p. 416.*

6 *2/1873: July, 1939.*

7 *PP 1944–5 (Cmd 6618) V, 421; 1945–6 (Cmd 6789) XIV, 155; 1946–7 (Cmd 7206) XIII, 457. The outcome of the reports was the Patents and Designs Act 1949.*

1/54, 77 Home Office send complaint re refusal of Manisty J to try a patent case on assize, 1885.

2/21	Correspondence with Board of Trade on proposal to give jurisdiction to Lancaster Chancery Court, 1888.
149, 268	Patents of Inventions Bill 1901: draft with notes; correspondence with Board of Trade, representations from Official Solicitor and Law Society. Draft rules and memoranda by Law Society and J. W. Gordon; correspondence with Chancery judges on organisation, 1908.
437	Patents and Designs Bill 1919: memoranda from Patents Office, Federation of British Industries and others; Parliamentary proceedings and correspondence.
560, 574	Rules, 1920, 1924, 1925: correspondence with Sargent J, Law Officers, Board of Trade.
1062	Correspondence with Tomlin J re committee on patent actions; comments on his memorandum by D. W. Kerley, W. A. Greene, W. T. Watson and J. Swinburne; draft rules and comments by Maugham J.
1192, 1629	Patents and Designs Act 1932: correspondence with Board of Trade, Clauson J; cabinet papers and Parliamentary proceedings. Correspondence with Luxmoore J, Patents Registrar on the new tribunal 1932, and with Treasury on fees, 1932–6.
1684	RSC o. LIIIA: SC Rule Committee papers on proposed change (Comptroller's costs) and protest by C.I.P.A., 1933.
1609, 1614	Hanworth Committee papers: sub-committee on patent actions (1934) and Committee minutes.
1780, 1816, 1833, 1862	Rule changes 1934, 1936, 1937, 1938; rule committee papers.
1839, 1906	Rules under Trade Marks Bill 1938: correspondence with Board of Trade, Clauson LJ, Patent Office and W. K. Watson (draftsman), then with Lloyd Jacob; RSC(1) 1941.
1873	Resolutions by C.I.P.A. and Trade Marks etc. Federation for inquiry, 1939; correspondence with Board of Trade.
3877	Correspondence with Treasury on chairman for royal commission, 1940, revived 1943, 1945. Correspondence with Radcliffe J and appointment of Cohen J. Correspondence with Attorney-General on Heald's complaint re crown brief distribution, 1947.
3878, 3888	Correspondence with Board of Trade, MR, LCJ on chairman for Patents Committee, 1944, and on chairman for Copyright Committee, 1950.
3886, 3920	Correspondence with Vaisey and Morton LJJ on arrangements within Chancery division, and RSC (Patents) 1944.
4060–1	Swan Committee reports: correspondence with MR, Board of Trade, Chancery judges, Comptroller; cabinet papers, correspondence with PCO on implementation, 1946–9. Parliamentary proceedings on Patents and Designs Bill 1949; correspondence with Sir K. Swan and Scottish departments on clause 7.
4045, 4059, 4139, 4147	Rules 1945 (implementing Swan Committee first interim report) discussed with Uthwatt LJ, Lloyd Jacob and others; 1947 rules discussed with Vaisey J and Board of Trade. Appeal Tribunal Rules 1950.
4108, 4151	Miscellaneous queries and suggestions.

Chapter 4

DEBTOR AND CREDITOR

1
INSOLVENCY

1 Bankruptcy

1 *Introduction*

The law on insolvency was primarily the responsibility of the Board of Trade, which even had to give formal approval to rules of court on the subject. However, any project for reforming the law necessarily involved the LCO closely, and the organisation of bankruptcy business in the courts was the Lord Chancellor's direct responsibility. The law had been transformed in the 1840s, when bankruptcy ceased to be applicable only to traders and became a generally available recourse to the insolvent debtor, while an Act of 1883 introduced the administration order (s. 122), intended to provide a similar resort to the poor.[1] In the third quarter of the century insolvency questions achieved a prominence in public and Parliamentary affairs that they have never again been accorded. One outcome was a reorganisation of the bankruptcy courts in which the London Bankruptcy Court was absorbed by the SCJ in 1883.[2] Bankruptcy law and administration remained in the forefront of public affairs beyond the end of the last century but after a committee chaired by Muir McKenzie's brother had reported that it was generally in reasonable shape,[3] and especially after legislation to implement that report, bankruptcy law entered a quiescent phase in which the principal aspect to which official attention had to be given was the fees which were charged.

The Chancery division finally succumbed to pressure to take over bankruptcy business in 1921, and apart from a small amending Act of 1926 arising from a departmental committee report, it receded from its prominent place in law reform agitation. By 1952 Dobson was remarking that "a drastic revision of the Bankruptcy Act itself . . . is indeed long overdue" and the rules had only been imperfectly consolidated at the instance of the editor of "Statutory Instruments".[4] This may indicate there was a tendency for the division of responsibility between the LCO and the Board of Trade to lead to slackness in the absence of outside pressures.

Notes

1 *G. R. Rubin in D. Sugarman and G. R. Rubin,* ***Law, Economy and Society*** *(1984), 241–9; J. Cohen (1982) 3 JLH, 153.*

2 *PP 1874 (C. 1107) XXIII, 583: 2nd report of Committee on Administrative Departments of the Courts of Justice. Bankruptcy Act 1883 s. 93(1).*

3 *PP 1908 (Cd 4068) XXXIV, 1. The law was consolidated in the Bankruptcy Act 1914.*

4 *2/4467: minute of December, 1952.*

2 *Legislation*

1/15	Bankruptcy Act 1883: memoranda, especially on s. 122, by M. D. Chalmers, Judge Selfe; memorials by traders' associations; correspondence with Board of Trade.
1/16	General file 1874–87, including correspondence on *Re Sager*, memorial from Mercantile Law Amendment Society with various proposals.
2/195	Departmental committee on various aspects proposed by Board of Trade, 1906.
211–3	Opinions of county court judges on imprisonment for debt, including views on s. 122.
284–5	Bankruptcy bills 1911–2: observations by Phillimore J, M. Muir McKenzie, Tindal Atkinson, A. H. Bodkin. Correspondence with Treasury Solicitor and Board of Trade.
289	Bankruptcy Act 1914: drafts, observations of Horridge J, PCO and others.
444–6	Correspondence with Board of Trade on bankruptcy provisions in Law of Property Bill, 1920–2.
695, 626, 1069	Report of departmental committee and Bankruptcy (Amendment) Bill 1926; briefing papers from Board of Trade, representations from Liverpool Inc. Law Society, registrars; memorandum on case of *Wigzell* [1921] 2 KB 835. Correspondence on Registration of Unsatisfied Judgments Bill (1930); representations from chambers of commerce, and Law Society; brief for Attorney-General.
1725	Enforcement of maintenance orders in bankruptcy: proposed by Clauson J, discussions with Merrivale P. and Attorney-General, 1929–32.
3610	Questions on the impact of the Liabilities (War-time Adjustment) Acts on bankruptcy actions, 1942.

3 *Rules and orders*

1/17	"Original rules and orders", includes London Chamber of Commerce proposals, 1882, consolidated rules 1886 (draft), proposed amendments and further rules of 1887, 1888.
2/86	Deeds of Arrangement Rules 1887; letters from judges and others.
30, 101, 161	Rules 1890, 1895: r. 101 amended (right to representation of debtors of unsound mind).
279–80	Bankruptcy Act 1914: correspondence on rules with County Courts Dept, Board of Trade etc.
151, 196, 875, 1340	Deeds of Arrangement Rules revised to prevent fraud: views of Law Officers, M. Muir McKenzie, Board of Trade etc. Later rules.
1180	Amendment Rules 1940, restricting employment of solicitors.
4464–7	Rules 1953: correspondence from 1949 with Board of Trade on need for consolidation, notes for interdepartmental conference, opinions by K. Muir Hunter, C. R. Waterer, Bankruptcy Registrar etc.
358–9, 427, 693, 698, 700–1, 703, 841, 1174–5, 1177–80, 1294, 3026	Various minor rules including county court rules, 1916–43.

4 *Fees and costs*

1/17	Various fees orders, 1882–8.

1/18	Solicitors' costs; proposals by law societies, Board of Trade and others; views of Official Receivers and others, 1883–6.
2/343, 426, 428, 694	Fees orders 1918, 1920, 1922: correspondence with Board of Trade and Treasury on policy on fees and cost of bankruptcy administration. Deposits on petitions also raised.
432	Economy (Miscellaneous Provisions) Act 1926: correspondence with Treasury, Board of Trade, and conferences on amalgamating Bankruptcy and Winding-Up accounts to enable the latter's surplus to be transferred to Treasury.
697, 341, 876, 144, 429, 433, 1173, 1176, 1240, 3025, 3028, 4468, 1181	Minor matters and fees.

5 Organisation of business

1/19	Future of London Bankruptcy Court: discussions with City traders on taking of affidavits in the City, 1874–7.
1/53	Nicol's report on Insolvent Debtors Court, correspondence with Treasury, W. Hazlitt (Senior Registrar, London Bankruptcy Court) and several officers about duties and posts, 1879–81.
1/16	Memoranda and correspondence (1874–87) on various subjects, including unclaimed dividends, vacation business, bankruptcy registrar's jurisdiction in High Court.
1/20	Unclaimed dividends: report of committee and correspondence on action, 1875.
1/21–4	Staffing and organisation, 1872–6; including salaries of registrars and clerks, effect of Bankruptcy Act 1881 on London Bankruptcy Court, filling of clerical vacancies, classification of clerks, including taxation masters' clerks. Reports of Treasury committees 1883–6, correspondence with Board of Trade, Bacon VC, Treasury, petitions by clerks etc.
2/50	Report of departmental committee on bankruptcy departments' accommodation, 1886.
95, 98	Appointment of Vaughan Williams J as bankruptcy judge 1892. Memoranda on proposal to combine bankruptcy and winding-up administration; correspondence with registrars on amalgamation, 1894.
107, 1631	Chancery judges' memorandum on proposal to transfer bankruptcy actions to them (1902) and revived proposal, 1921.
491–2, 496	Tomlin Committee: 4th report and memoranda and evidence on bankruptcy administration.
92, 1178–9, 3027	Minor matters.

2 Winding-up and Company Law

1 Introduction

Dissatisfaction with the "abominable" costs of winding-up of actions in the Chancery division led to a change in 1892, when it was transferred to the KBD bankruptcy judge by an order under s. 2 of the Companies (Winding Up) Act 1890, with interesting results.[1] However, the pressure of work on him caused a reversion to the old arrangement in 1902, when the rules were consolidated and fees adjusted. Following the report of the Tomlin Committee (1921) the respective departments of winding-up and bankruptcy were recommended to be amalgamated and the accounts were combined to obviate the difficulties in settling fees. These had been the subject of lively discussion with the Treasury and Board of Trade, it being widely felt that the winding up fees were too low in comparison with those of private liquidation whereas in bankruptcy they were rather high.[2] Thereafter there was little to concern the LCO until the major overhaul of company law undertaken by the Board of Trade in the 1940s, and even then it was only peripherally involved.

Notes

1 F. Evans (1900) 15 LQR 86.

2 2/428: Schuster's minute, 17.7.1923.

2 Company law and partnership

2/42-3 Partnership Act 1890 and rules. Report of Bar Committee, comments by judges and PCO; Lindley's draft rules discussed by SCRC.

3109-14 Companies Act 1947: correspondence, mostly with the PCO and Board of Trade, with Cohen, Uthwatt and Vaisey LJJs, and various interested bodies and individuals. Extensive Parliamentary briefs and papers.

3256-9 Companies Act 1948: correspondence with the PCO on consolidation, and on rules and fees orders, 1949.

3 Organisation, rules and fees in winding up

2/9 Costs in Chancery: mem. by Kay J 1889.

87, 95-8 Transfer of business 1892-5; reorganisation among registrars, new rules and fee scales. Reports by Board of Trade, Bar Council and Law Society; drafts and correspondence; report on Official Receiver's position vis à vis Board of Trade by committee under the Solicitor-General (1893) and Law Officers' opinion.

107, 194 Winding-up re-transferred to Chancery division: consolidated rules and fees, drafts and correspondence with M. Muir McKenzie, Board of Trade, Byrne and Buckley JJ *et al.*

431-4 Registrar Stiebel's memorandum on a Winding-Up Court, 1921.

496 Tomlin Committee 4th report, 1921.

45, 110, 142, 276, 430, 421, 886, 1240-1, 1847, 1890, 3593 Rules, 1890-1940 and (3593) proposed change in the law, 1948.

428, 431-2 Discussions on fees with Treasury and Board of Trade, 1921-4; consolidation of accounts.

194, 428, 699 Fees orders, various dates: correspondence with Treasury; rule committee papers.

2806 Solicitors' remuneration orders, 1932-44.

2
MONEYLENDERS AND HIRE PURCHASE

The Act of 1927[1] which gave debtors significantly enhanced protection in actions brought by moneylenders was a private member's bill but Schuster was involved in discussions over government assistance, principally on the question of jurisdiction. The local courts of record were particularly problematical, since moneylenders tended to turn to them to escape the restrictions which might be imposed in the county courts.[2] These safeguards had to be strengthened by further rules in 1930, and how effective the legislation proved may have depended on location, for while a London registrar wrote that "the Moneylenders Act and Bills of Sale Acts have practically driven moneylenders out of business", Judge Gamon at Middlesborough pleaded for wider powers to protect debtors.[3]

However, if the moneylender was an increasingly old-fashioned figure, he was being replaced as a county court suitor by the hire purchase firm and since debt collection was the primary source of county court business, the growth in instalment and hire purchase transactions, increasing the ability of all classes to contract debts, was sure to be a matter of concern. The county court judges' opinions given to the Pickersgill Committee in 1906[4] are an interesting commentary on the habits of the poor as well as the practices of the courts but they reflect the wide division of opinion about the desirability of hire purchase, and it is not surprising that no specific legislation was enacted until 1938. It took the form of a private member's bill introduced by Miss Ellen Wilkinson after a series of well publicised scandals to which the government were still sluggishly contemplating their standard response of a departmental committee. The cabinet decided not to oppose the bill and the LCO became deeply involved in putting it into a workable shape, consulting a dozen county court judges on the way: the files on this subject give a full account of the Parliamentary agitation which preceded the bill, the cabinet discussion on tactics, drafting papers, extensive materials on the Parliamentary proceedings (including the concessions secured by particular trades) and some subsequent complaints on the working of the Act.[5]

In the war that began soon after, the hire purchase companies experienced a problem peculiar to themselves, for in the blitzed areas many families simply locked up their houses, with "hire purchased" furniture inside, and decamped, defaulting on the instalments. The hire-purchase companies had no address for service and could not gain entry to re-possess their goods. They were able to convince the council of county court judges of the urgent need for legislation but Schuster was not persuaded until he had circularised all the county court judges for further information, by which time the emergency was over; when it recurred in 1944 during the 'V'-weapon attacks on London the cabinet decided that the political effects of action on behalf of creditors in the 'furniture' cases were too adverse to contemplate it. After the war the LCO received a number of complaints about the defective state of the law, but action did not take place until after 1951.

Notes

1 *See P. V. Baker in (1967) 83 LQR 196 for an outline of the 1906 and 1927 Acts.*
2 ***Supra**, 149–50.*

3 *2/3295: G. Hicks to Coldstream, 15.3.1946; 2/3429: Gamon to Coldstream, 21.5.1950.*

4 *2/205, 211–3. Discussed by G. R. Rubin,* ***op. cit.****, 278–81.*

5 *For the Act see (1938) 2 MLR 51 (R.S.T. Chorley).*

2/776	Moneylenders Act 1927: Schuster's evidence to joint select committee on local courts, notes on amendments to the bill etc.
855, 932, 1091–2	Jurisdiction under the Act: correspondence and memoranda re Liverpool Court of Passage, Salford Hundred Court and Bristol Tolzey Court. County Court Rules 1927 after meeting of CCRC.
1089–90	Derby Court of Record: complaints and investigation into abuses by moneylenders, and Order in Council, 1927.
864	County Court Rule Committee discusses moneylenders' plea on default summons, 1928.
1065, 1268	New rules 1930, drawn by Tindal Atkinson and Master Bonner; views of Clauson and Luxmoore JJ, Supreme Court Rule Committee discussions.
3285, 3429	Views on the need for protection legislation: Hicks and Judge Gamon, 1946, 1950.
205, 211–3	Views of county court judges and others on the effects of credit and the desirability of restricting it, 1905–6.
1280, 1288–9, 1307, 1349	County Court Rules 1936, 1938 on venue: representations of traders' organisations discussed by County Courts Rule Committee.
1511–3, 1517	Hire Purchase Act 1938: complaints and PQs on alleged abuses, 1936–7 and correspondence with Attorney-General on tactics. Representations of interested parties on the Wilkinson Bill, cabinet papers and departmental views; observations from PCO and county court judges; extensive notes on Parliamentary proceedings and drafting correspondence. Complaints of abuses and of "Hire Purchase Trading"; appraisal of the Act by G. Hicks, 1945. Also Order in Council giving jurisdiction to Liverpool and Salford Courts.
1355, 1401, 2680–1, 2726, 3570–1, 3274, 4126	Wartime problems: complaints from lenders re County Courts (Emergency Powers) Rules 1939 considered with registrars and changes made; definition of hire purchase in Liabilities (Wartime Adjustment) Act 1941; criticisms over exclusion from Evacuated Areas Regulations; discussions on problem of "locked up furniture"; evidence to McNair Committee on Limitations. Renewed complaints re rules about service of documents, 1944.
3266, 3276, 3285	County court hire purchase questions, on fees, remedies and practice.
4110	Law Society press for orders of specific restitution: views of High Court masters and County Courts Department, 1948.
5628	Suggestions for changes to the Act, 1947.
5604	Finance Houses Association urge claim to be consulted on proposed changes, 1951.

3
MORTGAGES

The LCO papers provide an interesting starting point for a little studied topic. The expansion of the Building Society movement and the provision of mortgage finance to an increasing number of home owners created new tensions, especially as the necessity to tap ever lower income groups to continue the expansion led inevitably to an increasing risk of default. The worst abuses, especially the so-called ''pooling agreement'' with speculative builders, which had become public knowledge in the **Borders** case, were met by the Building Societies Act 1939, on which there is a curious lack of material in these papers.[1]

However, the growing tendency of mortgagees to make use of their right to possession as a preliminary to exercising their power of sale, and the complete vulnerability of the mortgagor in this situation, had been exercising the judges and masters in the High Court from about 1933 onwards[2] and after discussions, and a sub-committee of judges, practice directions were made in 1936 transferring all mortgagees' possession actions to the Chancery Division and empowering the court to ''temper the wind to the shorn lamb'' by giving the mortgagor time to make good his default and discharge the mortgage. The directions also sought to end the practice of 'open judgments' whereby an occupier, usually a tenant of the mortgagor, might find himself subjected to an immediate possession order without having any advance notice or opportunity to state his case.[3] The *vires* of the practice direction were soon challenged and the judges anxiously watched the outcome of the **Hinckley** case,[4] but by that time the war had brought a new dimension to the problem.

The evacuation of the coastal areas, the bombing of the cities and the flight of many homeowners ensured that mortgagees would be resorting to the courts in vastly greater numbers, and the Civil Liabilities Sub-Committee had to devote a good deal of time to it.[5] The Building Societies Association gave voluntary undertakings in order to stave off more severe restrictions on possession and the files relating to the Courts (Emergency Powers) Acts and Rules are filled with dissatisfaction about their practices and the effects of several judicial decisions;[6] the Societies, for their part, had complaints about the Liabilities (War-time Adjustment) Acts and the problem of serving documents.[7]

Notes

1 *E. J. Cleary,* ***The Building Society Movement*** *(1965) is a good general account of these developments. The* ***Borders*** *case is discussed by L. C. B. Gower in (1939) 3 MLR 33. See however 2/1585 on some aspects of the question.*

2 *Master Bonner wrote ''our experience here, and that of many county court judges with whom I have spoken, is that . . . the Building Societies or some of them — are almost as extortionate as moneylenders''. 2/1792: to Schuster, 19.7.1934.*

3 *The practice is explained in 2/1792: Bonner to Schuster, 17.7.1934 and see RSC (2) 1936.*

4 ***Hinckley and South Leicestershire P.B.B.S.*** *v.* ***Freeman*** *[1941] Ch. 32. 2/1782: Attorney-General to Schuster, 31.7.1940.*

5 ***infra****, 271 ff.*

6 *e.g.* ***Woolwich Equitable B.S.*** *v.* ***Heywood (1942) 1 All E.R. 284****; 2/2714: Napier's minute, 26.4.1942.*

7 *It is interesting to consider these complaints alongside the rather complacent accounts given in Cleary* (**op. cit.**) *and H. Ashworth,* ***The Building Society Story*** *(1980).*

2/1781–2, 1792, 1894	Discussions on practice in Rule Committee (1934); sub-committee report (1935); discussions with leading building societies; Rule Committee papers (1936) leading to RSC (3) & (4) 1936. Masters' meeting (1934) on 'open judgments' and Rule Committee papers leading to RSC(2) 1936 (notice), amended in 1940.
1871	Mortgage summonses in district registries, correspondence with Clauson LJ, Master Holland, and Rules (2) 1940.
1357, 1359, 1378, 1381, 1898, 1915	Courts (Emergency Powers) Acts and Possession of Mortgaged Land Emergency Powers) Acts and rules; drafting correspondence, cabinet papers, memoranda by masters, building societies.
1392, 1413, 1419	Civil Liabilities sub-committee (1940), third report and papers. Meetings with building societies, discussions with Treasury and masters on complaints and case law, 1940–1.
2714, 2730, 2838	Proposed amendments to Courts (Emergency Powers) Acts and Rules to meet case law developments; correspondence with Farwell J, Holland and the PCO; cabinet and joint select committee papers. Courts (E.P.) Act 1943.
1401, 2759–64, 3611	Liabilities (War-time Adjustment) Acts: various papers on administration of the acts.
4103, 4155, 5162	Various post-war proposals from Master Willmott and others.

4
REMEDIES

1 Introduction

Legislation of 1888[1] attempted to remedy some of the abuses to which the ancient remedy of distress had succumbed at the hands of unscrupulous landlords by requiring the employment of certificated bailiffs only, but it continued to generate friction because it was both harsh and inefficient. After 1924 the county court high bailiff (usually the registrar) had to account to the Lord Chancellor's Office for the fees derived from "possession" cases, which brought it directly up against the convenient but legally doubtful practice of "walking possessions" (i.e. notional possession) which was extensively used and on which practice as to fees varied widely. In 1927 a committee under Swift J found, like its predecessor the McCardie Committee, that walking possession had become indispensable and ought to be regularised,[2] but the new fees structure which was painstakingly put together was blown apart by the decision in **Day** v. **Davies**[3] in 1938 that no fee might lawfully be charged for walking possession even with the occupier's express agreement. Yet another Committee was set up, under Judge Lilley, but by this time the hostility of tenants' organisation to distress *per se* led some of them to decline to give evidence to a Committee whose terms of reference excluded any possibility of abolishing it and by the time the Committee was ready to report protective wartime legislation was already in place which superseded its recommendations *pro tem*. It never did report but Napier's papers contain the minutes and evidence.[4]

An even more drastic remedy, and one which has received recent attention for the earlier part of this period,[5] was imprisonment for debt. Technically, of course, there was no such thing, the Debtors Act 1869 having abolished it, but under the guise of contempt of court in wilfully disobeying orders to pay sums judged due, it remained a regular feature of county court practice and in the twentieth century its use became increasingly frequent in magistrates' courts for contempt of maintenance orders. It was investigated by select committees in 1893 and 1908,[6] which succeeded only in establishing the problematical effectiveness of any alternative means of coercing debtors and their connections. In the 1920s the Home Office began to manifest uneasiness about the numbers of debtors in prison, especially those who were juveniles,[7] and in 1933 set up a committee on the subject (restricted, however, to magistrates' courts) which led to the Money Payments (Justices Procedure) Act 1935.[8] The fuller consideration of cases imposed on magistrates by this Act was not matched by any similar initiative in relation to county courts; the number of debtors committed by the county courts was in any case much smaller and in some cases judges and registrars were disposed to bend the law to be lenient,[9] though the discretion of individual judges was no substitute for a more effective means of executing judgments.[10]

Notes

1 *Law of Distress Amendment Act. See D. Englander,* ***Landlord and Tenant in Urban Britain, 1838–1918*** *(1983), 22–7.*

2 *8/58.*

3 *(1938) 2 KB 74.*

4 *The Committee was uncertain whether it was empowered to consider hire-purchase as well. It met nineteen times and adjourned* **sine die** *in July, 1939. Transcripts of oral evidence and written submissions are preserved in 2/1344–5.*

5 *G. R. Rubin,* **op. cit.** *241 ff.*

6 *PP 1893–4 (HL 156) IX; PP 1909 (239) VII, 281.*

7 *See 2/868 for instances.*

8 *PP 1934 (Cmd 4649) II, 69. R. M. Jackson,* **Machinery of Justice**, *401–2.*

9 *See e.g. 2/3317: O. J. Cole to R. Rieu, 25.8.1949 on the practices followed in the Doncaster court since 1930 and attempts by the County Courts Department to regularise them.*

10 *The report of the Payne Committee on the Enforcement of Judgment Debts (Cmnd 3909 of 1969) contains a valuable review of the remedies and practice. The records of the Committee are open to inspection (LCO 31).*

2 Distress

2/587	Rules 1920: representations from Association of Metropolitan Town Clerks and Certified Bailiffs Association, 1921.
2/807, 844, 838, 8/58	Swift Committee on "Walking Possession", 1927. Evidence from Scotland and overseas; county court practice notes; discussions on chairman for committee; report and discussions with registrars and Superintendent on new fees structure. Fees Order 1929.
2/865, 867, 1341–2	Various rule changes and proposals, including discussions with local authorities on their claim to priority.

1343–5 Lilley Committee on distress, 1938: Napier's papers, including evidence, minutes and correspondence, draft majority report (1939).

1355–7 County Courts (Emergency Powers) Rules 1939, including Rules (no. 2) to repair an omission on distress for rates.

1921–3 Tithe agitation: problems in execution of orders (see "Ecclesiastical Affairs" *infra*, 316).

3380 Discussions with Customs and Excise on fees and auctioneers' fees, 1948.

3787 Brief for PQ on "the Reading trouser case", 1950.

3 Judgment Orders and Imprisonment for Contempt

2/66 Select committee (Lords) on Debtors Act: evidence of county court judges and offers from other persons; pamphlets by Judge Stonor and F. K. Munton. Summary of judges' views.

211–3 Pickersgill Committee: judges' views, 1906.

868 Correspondence with Home Office on imprisonment of minors, 1925 onwards.

1012 Correspondence with Master Bonner on re-organisation of debtors' examinations, 1928.

1145, 1147 Correspondence with Home Office, Judge Parry and with Judge Cann, J. J. Wontner. Briefs for PQ and correspondence re Committee on Summary Jurisdiction. Correspondence with Home Office on Money Payments Bill.

1069 Registration of Unsatisfied Judgments Bill 1930. PQs and correspondence with Attorney-General and Master Bonner.

1725 Alimony defaults: discussions with Clauson J and Merrivale P on remedies and on possible amendments to Debtors Act. Notes on *Re Blanchard*.

3281 Correspondence with county court judges and Home Office on the role of the police, 1924, 1926, 1930, 1945.

3278 County court judges discuss interpretation of Money Payments Act 1935, including note from Judge Hunter, 1942 and report of judges' committee 1943.

1146 Chancery judges' practice statement (*re a Judgment Debtor (1935) 51 TLR 524*); correspondence with Clauson J.

4000–4 Evershed Committee working party 'R' on enforcement of judgments, 1951: memoranda, correspondence, minutes.

4979 Proposal to extend county court judges' contempt powers in Administration of Justice Bill 1951 dropped as too controversial.

3362 Crown Proceedings Bill 1947: IRC protest at omission of power to imprison for non-payment of taxes.

3317 Austin Jones report: County Courts Department comments on excessive protection of debtors by some judges, 1949.

299, 301, 308, 539, 1306, 1311–2, 1317, 3265, 3822 Points of county court practice, 1912–49.

4 Bills of Sale

1/2 Proposals for rule changes by Association of Chambers of Commerce, 1883; draft by C. E. Pollock, observations by Lindley MR.

1/26 Memoranda by Muir McKenzie, M. D. Chalmers (1887), and correspondence with H. Jenkyns, M. Muir McKenzie on Law Society's bill to save bills avoided by *Re Barber* (1886).

2/58 Bills of Sale Bill 1893: observations by Bar Council, law societies and others, correspondence with draftsman.

5 Miscellaneous

474 Discussions with Chief Whip and memorandum from Ladbroke's on *Sutters* v *Briggs* [1922] 1AC 1. Cabinet papers and Gaming Bill, 1922.

4167 Customs practice in condemnation cases considered after *Hennig* (1950) by LCJ and LCO.

Chapter

— 5 —

TORTS AND ACCIDENT COMPENSATION

1

INTRODUCTION

The main changes in the law of torts effected by statute in this period were the product of the Law Revision Committee's deliberations, and as has been noticed already[1] it was the recommendations on contributory negligence which proved most difficult to enact, not because they were controversial in themselves (the 'all or nothing' approach of the common law was widely regarded as unfortunate) but because they impinged on the Beveridge proposals for a new scheme of industrial injuries insurance. That scheme was itself a reflection of the disenchantment which the administration of the Workmen's Compensation Acts had engendered with the use of the courts as a forum for dealing with "social" legislation of this kind,[2] and the opposition of Lord Simon and his department to the creation of tribunals where legal representation would not normally be allowed, and whose decisions would be as immune from judicial review as possible was roundly rejected by the Home Office. As we have seen, the Monckton Committee was set up to consider the interaction of tortious remedies with compulsory accident insurance and Simon made frantic efforts to hustle the chairman into producing an early interim report which would enable his Contributory Negligence Bill to go on; the unsatisfactory terms and conditions under which the Committee had to operate is evident from the LCO papers and in its reports.[3] Jowitt, as Simon's successor, then had to push through a Personal Injuries Bill which would give effect to the rather uneasy compromise which the government had decided upon, whereby one-half of the benefits which an injured employee could count upon under the new state scheme would be deducted from his common law damages if he brought an action.[4]

As the files show, it proved an uncomfortable undertaking, for the TUC "frightened of communist pressure"[5] were unwilling to adhere to concessions they had made and the cabinet reached an utter deadlock on the position of benefits received under the various supplementary benefit schemes in the newly nationalised industries, especially in coalmining, where the fuel shortage placed miners in a strong position to dictate terms.[6] Outside the difficult area of industrial injuries, however, the Law Reform (Personal Injuries) Act, which also ended the discredited doctrine of 'common employment', completed the rationalisation of the tort of negligence begun by the Law Revision Committee.[7]

This was fortunate in view of the boom in negligence actions brought about by the motor car. There are only scattered materials in these papers on the problems which they created, but there is an interesting foretaste of the future in Jowitt's proposal to Morrison for a no-fault compensation scheme for running down cases; both Morrison and the Ministries of Transport and National Insurance were predictably discouraging.[8]

Other branches of the law of tort still needed to be tackled, and defamation was at once the most in need of reform and the most difficult to deal with, largely because of the peculiar position and problems of the national press. It was the newspapers who were the leading advocates of change, and they could cite numerous instances of opportunistic and unmeritorious actions against them. The deliberations of the Porter Committee, which had been set up in 1939 as an expedient concession by a government which wanted to kill A. P. Herbert's Bill, were suspended on account of the war before they had really begun. The discussions on the composition of the Committee make entertaining reading; E. M. Forster was chosen from nominees put forward by Society of Authors (Hugh Walpole and Ernest Raymond were the others) and Lord Ridley "was taken to represent the point of view of the man in the street" (*sic*).[9] It received ample evidence from the newspaper proprietors and, interestingly, from the B.B.C. on its own special difficulties;[10] the evidence is also revealing on the methods adopted by publishers and newspapers to deal with allegations of libel and on the strong Jewish lobbying for the creation of an offence of 'group defamation'—this gained added point after the failure of the Public Order Act prosecution of William Caunt in 1947.[11]

However, the Porter report when it finally emerged fell somewhat flat. The Attorney-General commented that "the mountain has produced rather a mouse"[12] and particularly regretted that the assimilation of libel and slander was not recommended. Because Jowitt was similarly unenthusiastic, he was not unduly concerned that there was no immediate prospect of government legislation. As a result, the drafting of the bill was an uncharacteristically leisurely process, and was brought to a halt by Morrison's insistence that newspaper proprietors should set up a Press Council as a *quid pro quo* for the benefits they would receive from legislation.[13] Morrison's antipathy to the press, fuelled by the outcome of the Laski libel trial,[14] also ensured that defamation would be the only tort to be excluded absolutely from the scope of the Legal Aid Act. The draftsman's difficulties with the Defamation Bill are splendidly documented, and his efforts were not to be wasted, for although Lord Simonds disliked it, the Conservative government was prepared to support a private member's bill and passed the official draft over for adoption.[15]

Notes

1 ***Supra***, *196.*

2 *e.g. W. A. Robson,* ***Justice and Administrative Law*** *(2nd ed., 1947), 195–7; A. Russell-Jones (1943–44) 7 MLR 13. On the development of the "ugly sisters of the common law" see A. H. Manchester,* ***Modern Legal History*** *(1980), 286–97.*

3 *The original chairman was R. G. Hetherington and when he resigned in December, 1943, the first choice as his replacement, W. L. McNair, refused the job. Jowitt suggested Denning or Lynskey JJ but Morrison insisted on Monckton. 2/3777 shows what a thankless task he found it.*

4 *2/3782: HPC (47) 23rd meeting, 7.11.1947.*

5 ***Ibid.*** *Jowitt's note, 21.2.1948, and the "terrific discussion" in the Lord President's Committee, 23.4.1948.*

6 ***Ibid.*** *note of meeting, 5.5.1948.*

7 *Earning Jowitt the congratulations of A. L. Goodhart: 2/3782, letter of 1.12.1947.*

8 *2/3606: 5.5.1950.*

9 *2/3058: Schuster to Lord Porter, 8.3.1939.*

10 *2/3059–67. The Wholesale Newsagents' Association "Black List" of publications unsafe to handle (including "The Daily Worker")—is also of some interest.*

11 *See H. M. Hyde,* **Norman Birkett** *(1964), 532–5.*

12 *2/4858: to Jowitt, 16.2.1949. This reaction was common, see e.g. (1949) 12 MLR 217.*

13 ***Ibid.*** *Dobson's minute, 13.11.1951. The Attorney-General's invitation to the press to do so is in (1949) 12 MLR at 355.*

14 **Laski** *v* **Newark Advertiser Co. Ltd and Parlby** *(1946). The action was fought on Laski's alleged threat that Labour would resort to revolutionary means if their programme could not be carried through constitutionally.*

15 *2/4859: HA (51) 3rd meeting, 7.12.1951.*

2
PERSONAL INJURIES

1 Statutes

2/671 Workmen's Compensation Committee, 1920; cabinet papers and discussions with Home Office and MacNaghten (County Court Fees Committee chairman) on fees. Draft bill, briefs for Parliament.

1222 Monmouthshire and South Wales Mutual Indemnity Society Ltd's private bill, 1939 (see *Private Bills*, *infra*. 305).

1993 Contributory negligence clauses dropped from Law Reform Bill 1943 through Home Office concern at effects on workmen's compensation.

3775–7 Monckton Committee on Alternative Remedies: correspondence with Home Office on membership and terms; Lord Chancellor's protest at ousting of courts from industrial injuries scheme; cabinet papers; correspondence with chairman, draft reports, notes of meetings, memoranda and papers; reservations by F. W. Beney, J. S. Boyd and G. de G. Warren.

3563 Law Revision Committee report on Contributory Negligence (*supra*). See also 3564 (Isle of Man Bill).

3053–7 National Insurance (Industrial Injuries) Bill 1946. Correspondence with PCO on drafting, especially on appeals procedure; correspondence with Ministry of National Insurance on various clauses.

3781–2, 4254 Law Reform (Personal Injuries) Bill. Cabinet discussions on Monckton Committee final report; negotiations with TUC and Ministry of National Insurance and drafting correspondence with PCO; briefs for PQs, notes on clauses and recent cases. Parliamentary proceedings, further negotiations with TUC and discussions on supplementary benefit schemes in nationalised industries; correspondence with Attorney-General. See National Insurance (Industrial Injuries) (Colliery Workers Supplementary Scheme) Order 1948.

2 County Court Rules

2/103–4, 299, 303, 306–7, 310, 533, 542, 608, 672, 852, 866, 869, 1077–86, 1272–4, 1934–52, 4242–9, 4251, 4253–6, 6223 County court rules, including discussions in Rule Committee and drafting correspondence; subject matter includes the following:

307, 310	Allegations of excessive solicitors' charges.
866, 869, 1077–8, 1081–2, 1942–3, 1948–9, 6225, 4256	Rule 19: lump sum payments under agreements paid into court; questions of *vires* and discussions of the practice of withholding payment from persons *sui juris* especially 1943 with views of county court judges and registrars; correspondence with Home Office from 1926, draft bill 1934 and notes on *Embleton* [1947] KB 492.
1085–6, 1935–7, 4255	Transfer of actions to Irish Free State and Northern Ireland, and to the Dominions, following Imperial Conference resolution 1926; correspondence with Dominions Office, draft bill and Rule Committee papers.

3
DEFAMATION

2/321, 1738–9	Newspaper organisations seek changes in RSC on payments into court; memorandum by B. Odgers (1913); Swift sub-committee report (1933).
1812	Law Society complain re probate practice in actions to strike out 'libels' in wills, 1935.
3058–67B	Porter Committee papers, with views of Goddard LJ and Tucker J on Herbert's Bill (1938) and cabinet papers; correspondence on membership of the Committee (1939) minutes of meetings and of evidence, correspondence with members, memoranda and other papers, specimen writs, defences etc. from recent cases; draft report.
4118	Discussions with Lord Porter, with LCJ and MR on rule changes to implement the report. See RSC (1) 1949.
4625–7	Cabinet discussions on legal aid include decision on defamation.
3470	LCJ's comments on the Laski libel case, 1946.
4858–61	Cabinet and departmental discussions, especially on 'group libels' and unintentional libels; correspondence with Law Officers, PCO, Lord President, Lord Parker; drafting correspondence, especially on privileged reports of court proceedings; cabinet papers on this and Lever's bill (1951); Parliamentary proceedings.
5605B	Complaint by the editor of "The Greyhound Owner and Breeder" of the state of the law.

4
OTHER

2/3565, 5611–5	Liability for animals straying onto the highway; suggested as a topic for Law Revision Committee (1947–9). Revived 1951 and correspondence with LCJ and Law Society on membership of a committee; correspondence, minutes and memoranda.
1738–9, 1703, 3595, 3606	Swift sub-committee of S C Rule Committee discuss abuses in costs in settled running-down cases. Administration of Justice (Miscellaneous Provisions) Act s. 6. Discussions with KB masters on their guidelines; Automobile Association complaint (1932) on damages awards. Post-war suggestions for transferring burden of proof or a no-fault compensation scheme (3606).

1982–4, 3582	Proposal from Sir P. Harris to lengthen limitation period against local authorities (1945); local authority associations lobby against proposals in the Limitations Bill (1937–9).
4586–92	Tucker Committee on Limitations: correspondence on membership, and Scottish committee; minutes, evidence, correspondence, draft report. Proposed legislation: views of departments, cabinet papers, discussions with legal departments.
1548	Breach of promise: briefs for PQs in 1935.

Chapter
6

FAMILY LAW

1

MATRIMONIAL LAW

1 Introduction

The record of governments in the period covered by these papers on most questions relating to the legal ordering of family life is one of evasion wherever possible and reluctant activity when it was unavoidable. This is most striking in the case of divorce law, where the initiatives came from outside the government, from individuals and, increasingly, from pressure groups such as the Marriage Law Reform Committee. Significantly, they did not come from the judges of the PD & A Division, who on the whole were disposed not only to object to legislative changes in divorce practice, but to interpret restrictively the grounds upon which divorce might be granted. Lord Merriman's thirty-year presidency of the division, in particular, ensured that governments would not be got off the hook by judicial activism in divorce law in the way they were to be by Lord Denning's decisions on financial relief and matrimonial property.[1]

In 1912 the Gorell Commission recommended an extension of the grounds for divorce. This was taken up in Lord Buckmaster's bills of 1919 and 1920, and they attracted so much support that the government was compelled to offer concessions on adjectival law to fend them off[2]. There was then a lull, but agitation resumed in the 1930s and resulted at length in A. P. Herbert's Act in which some of the recommendations made by the Gorell Commission were finally enacted. As the papers show, Hailsham was firmly opposed to the bill and had to be pursuaded that the Law Officers' pragmatic view that it would relieve the pressure for government action was sound. The bill's backers were induced to drop their clauses relating to summary jurisdiction, which Schuster described as "a wild leap in the dark",[3] in return for the government's benevolent neutrality and the Act did permit the dissolution of some of the "Holy Deadlocks" that Herbert had described.[4] The disadvantages of legislation by a private member's bill which had to make compromises in order to pass were soon obvious, however. In particular, the controversial issue of refusal to consummate, which because of the Church's opposition to widening the grounds for divorce had been made a ground of nullity instead, came before the House of Lords in **Baxter** v. **Baxter**[5] and the well publicised efforts of the courts to define and distinguish among degrees and types of physical intimacy did not give general satisfaction. The Archbishop of Canterbury rashly pronounced that "our judges have not the slightest idea what the law of nullity by this time means; or how to administer it", which understandably sent Merriman "off the deep end".[6]

Of course, neither the Herbert Act, nor anything short of divorce on the grounds of separation could satisfy the more determined reformers and although the government of Attlee, backed by Merriman, repeatedly stalled the insistent demands for a royal commission, Irene White's bill for divorce on the basis of seven years separation ultimately forced their hand.[7] In March, 1951 the cabinet conceded a royal commission in order to get rid of the bill[8] and although its deliberations, amply covered in these files, fall outside the period under review, the material on the lengthy and delicate task of selecting the membership is an instructive study in the political arts. It reveals, for instance, that the first choice as chairman (Lord Eustace Percy) declined because of his christian beliefs and that Morton's name was put forward by Jowitt, rather late in the day. Jowitt also unsuccessfully pressed the actress Celia Johnson on his colleagues as a representative of the younger generation; not all of the numerous suggestions for members were well received, one eminent historian being described as "inclined to vulgarity"; the full cabinet had to decide on the most difficult question, the representation of the churches.[9]

The same reluctance which characterised the government (and the LCO) approach to divorce can be seen in the context of other proposals. For example, in the 1930s they recoiled from Sir Eric Beckett's demand for a committee on the law of marriage, to sort out the muddled position on recognition of foreign and polygamous marriages. Schuster sceptically predicted that it "probably will not result in any very effective recommendation"[10] and it was repeatedly put off on various pretexts before the Foreign Office finally forced Maugham to set it up under Sir William Graham-Harrison in January, 1939.[11] Likewise, when Jowitt was pressed to investigate the topical question of artificial insemination he called it "a beastly subject" and sought to postpone consideration of it.[12]

As mentioned above, it was often left to the judges to improve the property position of spouses and cohabitees in the post-war period, and this judicial activism was the more understandable in the light of the government's response first to the widespread indignation caused by **Blackwell** v. **Blackwell**,[13] in which a wife's housekeeping savings were held to belong to her husband, and then to a private member's Deserted Wives Bill 1951, which the cabinet treated as "rather a joke".[14]

Notes

1 *O. R. McGregor,* ***Divorce in England*** *(1957); Lord Denning,* ***The Due Process of Law*** *(1980), 187–93.*
2 ***Supra****, 106–7.*
3 *2/1195: minute of 18.11.1936.*
4 *Herbert described these manoeuvres in his book "****The 'Ayes' Have It****" (1937) and it is interesting to compare his perceptions of government attitudes with the materials in 2/1194–6.*
5 *[1948] AC 274.*
6 *2/4218: his speech to the Medico-Legal Society was reported in the press (20.1.1950); the Archbishop said he was unaware that reporters were present.*
7 *2/4213: The Marriage Law Reform Committee urged supporters to write to the Lord Chancellor, who received some 250 letters.*
8 *2/4855: CM (51) 18th conclusions, 8.3.1951.*
9 *2/6131–2.*
10 *2/1148: minute of 23.6.1936.*
11 *2/1149.*
12 *2/6361A.*
13 *[1943] 2 All ER 519. "We should not attempt to deal with this matter unless we are forced to": 2/2777: E. Bevin to Attorney-General, 29.12.1943.*

14 *2/4851: Rieu to Attorney-General, 22.1.1951. The minutes of HPC (51) 1st meeting, 16.1.1951 justify Rieu's interpretation.*

2 The Law of Marriage

2/120 Proposed Marriage (Amendment) Bill 1919 based on bill of 1900 sent by Chancellor of London diocese for LC's views.

1148–9 Committee on Marriage Laws: discussions with Home Office and Treasury Solicitor's Department on W. E. Beckett's memorandum on polygamous marriages (1932), with Law Officers' opinion. Correspondence on Committee's terms and membership, further discussions 1936–7 and finally set up 1939 under Graham-Harrison. Numerous Foreign Office papers, various Committee papers, discussions on new chairman.

1420 Marriage (Members of the Forces) Bill 1941, sent with letter from Attorney-General.

3039 Marriage (Declaration of Law) Bill (N.I.) 1944, sent by Home Office for information.

3163 Correspondence with Home Office, agreeing to oppose the Stevenson Marriage Bill (marriage to divorced husband's brother) 1947.

3609 Age of consent, differences between England and Scotland, letter from Home Office (1940), no action.

3 Rights of Married Women

2/57 Judge Heywood's paper on the wife's authority to pledge her husband's credit (1892) with comments by judges and others.

777 Married Women (Torts) Bill 1925: PQs on *Callot* v. *Nash*, correspondence with PCO on possible reforms.

2/2777, 3558 Repercussions of *Blackwell* v. *Blackwell*; representations and deputation from women's groups, discussions with Law Officers, note on French law by J. Foster, correspondence with Ernest Bevin. Discussions on Haldane Society proposals, 1945–6. See also 3558, resolution of Scottish Women's Co-operative Guild (1949).

3204, 3601 Mountbatten Estate Bill and subsequent legislation (see 'Trusts'', *supra*, 221).

4851 Deserted Wives Bill, 1951: cabinet papers, views of Judge Engelbach, meetings with sponsors.

4 Separation and Maintenance Orders and Magistrates' Jurisdiction

2/773 Summary Jurisdiction (Separation and Maintenance) Act 1925: cabinet papers on the bill, petitions from women's groups, Home Office notes on the bill, 1924. Correspondence with Mrs Hubback, further cabinet papers (1925) and correspondence on Parliamentary proceedings, especially on the "furniture" amendment.

1595 Rules (1937) under Summary Proceedings (Domestic Proceedings) Act, draft from Home Office.

2850 Time limit for filing information of adultery by men on war service discussed with War and Home Offices, and President. Defence regulation of 1944 and extension made permanent 1952.

3908 Meetings with armed services departments and registrars on wartime difficulties in bringing actions v. servicemen, 1943.

4214 Discussions with Home Office and President and representations from Justices Clerks Society and Magistrates' Association on role and powers of magistrates in custody cases, 1948.

3918 Enforcement of maintenance orders: discussions with Home Office, Treasury Solicitor's Office, Law Officers and others on *McNaughten* v *McNaughten* (1944) and legislation to facilitate reciprocal enforcement between England and Scotland, 1944–5. Revived in 1947 and cabinet papers to 1949.

4485 Married Women (Maintenance) Bill 1949. Cabinet papers, arguments between Home Office and President on the forum for appeals, Parliamentary proceedings and report on appeals by President.

665, 1619, 3046, 3825, 3919, 3925 Rules and points of practice on maintenance questions, 1920–50.

5 Divorce

1 General reform proposals

2/460 Lord Buckmaster's Bill 1919: observations by President, PCO, drafts and amendments; memorandum by Lord Phillimore on the PDA and Parliamentary papers.

1194–6 Matrimonial Causes Bills: Schuster's memoranda and correspondence on Knight's Bill (1931); cabinet papers and views of the President of the PDA, Schuster, Treasury Solicitor, Attorney-General and Home Secretary. Correspondence with Law Society on effect of Herbert's Bill on legal aid; Lord Chancellor's proposals for more judges. Files on proposed amendments to the Herbert Act, mostly on the problem of insanity; correspondence with Attorney-General, Treasury Solicitor, Hodson J, President and others. See also 4226.

4484, 4189–90 Law Reform (Miscellaneous Provisions) Bill 1949: discussions on inclusion of divorce law reforms, including *Russell* v *Russell*; cabinet papers, views of Bar Council, Archbishop of Canterbury, Lord Advocate and President and extensive Parliamentary proceedings. 4189–90 are files of suggestions for reforms and amendments to the 1937 Act.

4213, 4854, 6113, 6131–2, 6136 Marriage Law Reform Committee and other groups' proposal for a royal commission (1948). Correspondence with Attorney-General, cabinet papers rejecting a commission, discussions on Mancroft's motion. Cabinet papers on Matrimonial Causes Bill (1951) and correspondence leading to the appointment of the Morton Commission. Meetings with ministers on composition, on extension to Scotland and Northern Ireland and terms of reference, especially on the representation of church interests.

2 Particular reforms

2/775 Judicial Proceedings (Regulation of Reports) Bill 1925: correspondence with Home Office, H.M.'s Private Secretary; PQs, cabinet papers, memoranda.

349 Matrimonial Causes (Dominions Troops) Bill 1919: correspondence with President, PCO (especially on Phillimore's amendment) and others.

1673–4	Lord Merrivale's Bill and SCJ (Amendment) Bill 1934 discussed with President, PCO etc.
3099	Matrimonial Causes (Guernsey) Bill sent by Home Office, 1939.
2776	Brief for PQ on Croom-Johnson J's suggestion, 1943.
3688, 4205	Draft opinions on *Baxter* v *Baxter*, with discussions on response to Lord Meston's motion, and correspondence with Treasury Solicitor on possible appeal.
4191	Attorney-General's and solicitors' request to bring *Cohen* v *Cohen* on appeal to the Lords and correspondence with Treasury Solicitor, 1939.
797, 4196, 4185–8, 4199	Matrimonial Causes (War Marriages Act) 1944. Law Society proposals, discussions with Dominions Office, President, Attorney-General, and meetings of officials; draft bill from PCO and further correspondence with Home, Foreign and Dominions Offices and President. Representations from Colonial Office and Parliamentary proceedings. Matrimonial Causes (War Marriages) (Malta) Order 1946 and drafting correspondence; Orders in Council on counterpart Dominion legislation and drafting difficulties discussed with PCO. Matrimonial Causes (War Marriages) (Appointed Day) Order 1950 following discussions with Home Office and Scottish Home Department and drafting correspondence with PCO. Parliamentary discussions on domicile and departmental discussions on answers to PQs; Law Reform (Miscellaneous Provisions) Bill 1949. See also 797—Divorce Jurisdiction (Overseas Domicile) Bill 1927.
4218	Archbishop Fisher's speech on nullity and the responses of the Lord Chancellor and the President.
6361A, 6110	Artificial insemination: discussions following *R.L* v *E.L* and PQs; notes for Lord Brabazon's and Lord Reading's motion and consideration of government policy. Lord Rothschild's suggestion for a committee on gestation periods.
3445, 3448	Pleas for assistance by husbands of Russians and Polish wives discussed 1947, 1949.
3415, 3099, 3447, 4169, 4216, 4226, 5639	Various minor points.

2
CHILD LAW

1 Introduction

Whereas no ministry accepted general responsibility for the law of husband and wife, the law relating to infants came under the Home Office. The LCO was vitally interested, however, in all matters which pertained to the courts and to property rights and on one occasion complained strongly at not being consulted in advance when a committee was proposed to investigate an aspect of the law.[1] Consequently, there is a good deal of useful information on the LCO response to Home Office proposals and to private members' bills.

The most important phase in the statutory revision of child law was the mid-1920s when three major statutes, the Guardianship of Infants Act 1925, the Legitimacy Act 1926 and the Adoption of Children Act 1926 were all passed. The first two both originated in private members' bills soon after the war and neither was welcomed in the LCO. Cave objected in principle to the revolution in bastardy law brought about by the Legitimacy

Act[2] and was hardly less hostile to the idea embodied in the Guardianship Bill of giving "equal authority, rights and responsibilities" to each parent,[3] so the scope of the Legitimacy Bill at least was considerably narrowed. Schuster's own distaste for the measures was increased by the fact that they involved him in wearisome correspondence with sundry women's organisations lobbying for them, in particular with the intolerably persistent Mrs Hubback of the National Union for Equal Citizenship. Given the wide differences of opinion which had to be accommodated it is not surprising that the drafting of the Acts was unsatisfactory,[4] although as can be seen, several eminent persons contributed to the end product.

There are also extensive materials on the Adoption Act 1949, and of particular interest is the correspondence with the judges on the scope of the measure and on the interpretation of important provisions concerning disclosure of identity, where they obdurately adhered to a construction which left the draftsman very annoyed.[5]

Notes

1. *2/1162: Schuster to S. Harris (Home Office), 27.11.1935.*
2. *2/750: Schuster to J. Anderson (Home Office), 2.12.1922.*
3. *2/757: CP 3719 (1921).*
4. *See e.g. E. Jenks (1928) 44 LQR 314.*
5. *2/4459: N. Hutton to Dobson, 23.2.1950.*

2 Custody, Guardianship and Wardship

1/47	Rules under Guardianship of Infants Act 1886, with amendments by Stirling J.
2/757–9, 805	Guardianship of Infants Bill: cabinet discussions on 1920 bill, with views of Chancery judges and Official Solicitor. Resumed 1922 and correspondence with Home Office; draft report of select committee and conferences with the promoters (1924); drafting correspondence with PCO and Greer J, correspondence with Mrs. Hubback and H. Scott. The bill was split into two and further drafting correspondence and Parliamentary papers follow. Proposed amendments to the Guardianship of Infants Act 1925 discussed with Home Office and Scottish Office (1928).
812, 854, 1300	Legitimacy Act 1926: proposed amendment and county court rules discussed in CCRC. Discussion in CCRC 1937 on interpretation.
3600	Law Society suggestion on powers of putative fathers in bigamous marriages, 1949.
5608	Guardianship and Maintenance of Infants Bill. Correspondence with Home Office on *R.* v *Sandbach Justices, Ex p. Smith*; cabinet papers and Home Office brief for Lord Chancellor, 1951.
1427, 1828, 4131	Foreign Office request for clarification on execution of custody orders abroad (1937) following discussions of Passport Office practice. Denning J's concern with removal of children by mothers, 1945, and discussions on preventive measures.
10, 3670	Role of the Sergeant at Arms in securing wards from recalcitrant parents (1891); resumed 1946 when Vaisey J's request for Official Solicitor to exercise this function is discussed.

3292 County Court Rules 1947 allow married women to act as guardian *ad litem*.

3677 Case of D. J. Corcoran 1949: interviews with judges, press cuttings, correspondence with Home Secretary.

3821 Guardianship of Infants (Summary Jurisdiction) Rules 1944: discussions with Home Office on relaxation of 1925 rules for servicemen abroad.

4642 Assignment of Probation Officer to High Court in custody cases.

3406 Case of Miss M. Robertson. Correspondence with Danckwerts J and others, 1949.

4135 RSC(3)1949 (see *supra*, 97).

3 Bastardy and Adoption

2/750–4 Legitimacy Act 1925: correspondence with B. L. Cherry, Home Office, Ministry of Health and others from 1921 on bills; cabinet papers; drafting correspondence and Parliamentary proceedings.

1120, 1159–60, 1276, 3273 Adoption of Children Act 1926. Discussions on county court rules, especially on disclosure of adopters' identity, and summary jurisdiction rules, amending original rules; consultations with clerks to the justices and others, and further suggestions 1935, 1940. Discussions with Home Office, Chancery judges, Registrar-General, Official Solicitor; informal committee on format of adoption register (1928).

1162, 3020–1 Horsbrugh Committee on adoption societies; LCO protest to Home Office at not being consulted; Napier's evidence and views of county court judges. Adoption of Children (Regulation) Act Orders 1939 discussed with Home Office and (1944) with Law Society and Sheffield CC on costs and expenses.

3277, 1161 Bastards of U.S. servicemen: discussions with Home and Foreign Office from 1944 on "a serious social and political problem". Consultations with Public Trustee, G. Hicks, Uthwatt J and Home Office on administration of U.S. money payments via the courts. Also Adoption (Summary Jurisdiction) Rules, 1941, 1942 (1161).

4483, 4456–9, 4141, 4473, 4773 Adoption of Children Acts 1949, 1950: correspondence with Home Office, PCO, Vaisey J and cabinet papers on Nield's bill. Consultations with Law Lords, Judge Gamon and MPs and discussions on Parliamentary tactics. Lengthy papers on SCJ, county court and summary jurisdiction rules; discussions with Vaisey, Chancery masters, Official Solicitor and county court registrars, especially on the form of the mother's consent and on the issue of disclosing names. Also non-contentious probate rules necessitated by the Act (1950) and Lord Simon's query on use of police information about prospective adopters. Establishment of appeals tribunal. Brief from PCO on amendments to the Bill and meeting with interested parties on provision for religious objections.

4119 Children Act (Appeal Tribunal) Rules 1949 made after correspondence with Home Office, and discussions on secretaryship.

4 Other Matters

2/868 Infants imprisoned under judgment summonses: reports from Home Office (1925–9) and correspondence with judges.

5635 Testamentary capacity (see *Wills, supra,* 228).

5637 Complaints about infants as traders, 1928, 1954.

LUNACY

1
INTRODUCTION

The Lord Chancellor's special position as protector of lunatics involved him in a mountain of work which is not reflected at all in these files, for as several Chancellors wryly noted, lunatics were prone to solicit his intervention on their behalf at great length and with untiring frequency, and as Lord Herschell said "you cannot put them aside; there may be something that deserves enquiry"[1]; given the ease with which persons could be confined in the nineteenth century and the inadequate supervision which was exercised over asylums, especially private ones, he was no doubt right. The tensions inherent in locking up the mentally ill, between civil liberties and public safety and between the medical and legal professions, are admirably illustrated among those papers which relate to the bills introduced in the 1880s, particularly by Lord Selborne, and which sought to interpose the magistrate in the committal process.[2] It was conceded by the Home Office and the Lord Chancellor that county court judges or stipendary magistrates would have been more satisfactory, but they were too few, and no judicial intrusion would have been acceptable to the medical profession.[3] Selborne used all his arts to reconcile the veteran reformer Lord Shaftesbury, now Chief Commissioner in Lunacy, to the bill, or at least to persuade him not to resign his place even if he had to oppose it, but all in vain. Even after Shaftesbury's death the opposition was so strong that it was only in 1890 that the Act was passed, with the concession that jurisdiction over committal orders was to be vested only in specially appointed justices.[4] It was the last major initiative in lunacy law to come from a Lord Chancellor: the subsequent trend away from "legalism" stemmed mostly from the Ministry of Health and was endorsed by the MacMillan Commission of 1926.

The Lord Chancellor's position in the administration of the lunacy laws was uncomfortable and the structure unsatisfactory. Two Lord Justices in Chancery were appointed under an Act of 1851 to exercise the royal prerogatives in relation to lunatics and a master in lunacy carried out the painstaking commissions of inquiry by which lunacy must be established before the lunatic's property could be administered by the court.[5] Increasingly, however, this costly and tedious method of establishing legal insanity was being displaced by the statutory process administered by the Lunacy Commissioners and the Lord Chancellor's visitors, whose concern lay with the person of the lunatic rather than with his property.[6] The Commissioners were independently minded and not disposed to acquiesce quietly in changes they disliked, and the lunacy judges could be just as intractable, as Selborne had discovered when he came to implement the Legal Departments Committee proposals for the reform of the lunacy offices; he deeply wounded the *amour propre* of the Lords Justices by not consulting them in advance on the new rules, which Cotton LJ consequently refused to sign.[7]

The Act of 1890 empowered the incorporation of these several bodies into a single organisation, but the opportunity was not taken and the tangle of vested interests and divergent views would have made it a formidable undertaking. The Lunacy

Commissioners, re-named the Board of Control, were, however, given greatly extended functions by the Mental Defectives Act 1913 which followed the recommendations of the Radnor Commission,[8] and in 1919 they passed under the control of the Ministry of Health. The Radnor Commission also recommended the abolition of the separate masters in lunacy and the absorption of their business in the Chancery division but the proceedings of a committee which the Lord Chancellor set up to consider the proposal were acrimonious and the changes which were eventually agreed on fell far short of the original proposal.[9] This is unsurprising because what the papers reveal is that all the main protagonists tended to advance schemes which expanded their own roles and powers at the expense of the others. A few years later the Tomlin Committee on the structure and staffing of SCJ agreed that the Master's office must remain as a separate unit, though in 1925 it did formally become an office of the Supreme Court.[10]

The business of administering lunatics' property grew apace, the number of estates expanding six fold between 1890 and 1920, and exposed the deficiencies of an organisation which reflected the eccentric and obsessive working methods of H. S. Theobold, the dominant figure in lunacy administration for thirty years.[11] The Fischer Williams enquiry of 1934 revealed a conflict over principles of organisation similar to those the Murray Committee had found in the Public Trustee Office[12] and, supplemented by a Treasury O & M report in 1949, is instructive on the experience of a bureaucracy coping with unplanned expansion.[13] The papers also enable one to trace the evolution of euphemistic titles in line with the policy laid down by the mental health legislation, whereby the Master in Lunacy was metamorphosed, via the unfortunately titled Management and Administration Department, to the fanciful Court of Protection (Clauson LJ's suggestion).[14] The Ministry of Health then proposed the amalgamation with the Board of Control first mooted in 1890, but the LCO showed no interest.

Notes

1 *R.F.V. Heuston,* **Lives of the Lord Chancellors***, (1964) 115. The Lunacy Act 1890 increased the burden by obliging asylums to forward inmates' letters to* **(inter alia)** *the Lord Chancellor unopened.*

2 *The "triumph of legalism" is unsympathetically recounted in K. Jones,* **A History of the Mental Health Services** *(1972), and see also G. B. A. M. Finlayson,* **Lord Shaftesbury** *(1981), 590–3.*

3 *1/65: H. Fowler (HO) to Selborne, 25.3.1885.*

4 *The 1890 Act, drafted by H. S. Theobald, also effected a consolidation of the statute law.*

5 *T. C. S. Keely (1944) 8 CLJ 195, gives a brief outline of the history of lunacy administration.*

6 *K. Jones,* **supra***, 178–82.*

7 *1/67–8. Henry Graham, Cairns's former Principal Secretary, whom he had appointed Master in Lunacy in 1880, also protested at the changes.*

8 *PP 1908 (Cd 4203), XXXIX, 159.*

9 *2/264: report of 3.3.1910 (unpublished).*

10 *2/492: third and sixth reports. SCJ (Consolidation) Act 1925 s.124.*

11 *T. Keely,* **supra***. Theobald had drafted the rules of 1882 and the Act of 1890. He was Master in Lunacy from 1907 to 1922. On his working methods see the memorandum in 2/491.*

12 *See* ***supra****, 224–5.*

13 *4/47–52. The papers are particularly interesting on the amount of supervision exercised over receivers.*

14 *4/53. Both Jowitt and Napier waxed sarcastic at the adoption of euphemisms.*

2
LEGISLATION

1/62–8, 2/6–7, 41, 54, 83	Extensive papers and correspondence on the lunacy bills from 1883, including views of Cotton and Bagallay LJJ on consolidation bill, H. S. Theobald (draftsman) BMA, Lunacy Commissioners and others; numerous amended drafts and proofs of the Amendment Bill 1884–5 and copy report of select committee (1878). Long correspondence with Lord Shaftesbury, Home Office, Local Government Board and Theobald, with papers from various asylum boards, ending 1886. Observations of Home Secretary on bill of 1889 and correspondence with BMA, Royal College of Physicians and others. Drafts of rules under 1890 Act and draft rules of 1891 with comments of judges, Law Society, IRC, Theobald *et al.*; further rules of 1892 sent to Law Society.
2/132	Lunacy Bill 1900: correspondence with Home Office, Treasury and others on draft bill; suggested clauses from Lunacy Commissioners and Boards of Guardians and observations by LGB and others on proposed amendments. File on Lord Russell's PQ on the "St Pancras scandal", with Law Officers' opinion.
412	Correspondence with lunacy masters and LGB on applications for old age pensions, 1916.
475, 477	Lunacy Bills: 1919 memorandum and draft bill from Board of Control, and notes of conference with LGB; Master Romer's suggestions (1921) with Theobald's comments and notes on 1922 Bill, and cabinet papers.
636	Lunacy Rules 1921: correspondence with Treasury and Ministry of Pensions on tax concessions.
952	Notes on LCO evidence to Royal Commission and copy report, 1924.
953–4	Medical Treatment Bill 1930: correspondence with Board of Control and Ministry of Health on possible amendments. Rules made 1930 and revised 1940, 1942.
1840, 1842, 4190	Matrimonial Causes Act and Rules 1937: Board of Control views to Merriman Committee.
3644, 3648	Meetings and correspondence with Ministry of Health, PCO on lunacy provisions in National Health Service Bill 1946 and Parliamentary proceedings; NHS (Mental Treatment) Amendment Rules 1947, formal approval by LC.
3650–2	Correspondence with Ministry of Health, Official Solicitor, Home Office on various mental health rules, 1948.
3654–5	Memorandum from Society of Labour Lawyers, 1950, opposing the locking up of 'moral defectives', and protest by Board of Control at remarks of Croom-Johnson J.
3705	Discussions of the problem of mentally ill persons bringing pension claims

and other problems 1945; correspondence with Ministry of Pensions, Pensions Appeal Tribunals.

3334 Proposals of Humphreys LJ re criminal lunatics discussed with Board of Control and Home Office, 1945.

3646 Discussions on the effect of appointing a receiver on protective trusts, as in *Re Douglas* (1945). Discussions with Poyser, PCO leading to clause in Law Reform (Miscellaneous Provisions) Act 1949.

3
LUNACY ADMINISTRATION

9/1, 2–4 Office of the Lord Chancellor's visitors. Indexed reports.

10/1–7 Board of Visitors, agendas and other documents, 1879–1952.

11/1–6 Miscellaneous books relating to the LC's Visitors.

1/67–8 Negotiations with the Treasury over the position of Christopher James, the "secretary" to the judges in lunacy, and further correspondence with the judges, 1886–7. General Orders in Lunacy 1882; drafts by H. S. Theobald and correspondence with Cotton, Baggallay LJJ on the former's refusal to sign them.

2/13 Proposal from Irish Lord Chancellor for improving procedure where a lunatic has property in both countries; views of Cotton LJ, and other judges, correspondence with registrar in lunacy (Ireland) and PCO drafts and order of 1889.

9, 20 Taxation of costs: discussions with SCJ officials and Kay LJ on re-organisation, and draft rules, 1889.

84 Objections of the lunacy masters to proposed regulations (retirement etc.) for the legal departments, 1900.

192 Representations on report of committee on taxation of costs, 1901.

264, 282, 330 Arrangements for a committee to consider report of Royal Commission; resignation from committee of the Official Solicitor, correspondence with members, report, draft scheme for amalgamating some offices, with memoranda thereon and correspondence with Treasury. Draft bill 1911 and correspondence with PCO and Theobald; views of Lunacy Commissioners and others. Discussions on Theobald's draft rules with views of Farwell LJ, Buckley J, Official Solicitor, and conference with MR, Farwell, Buckley.

309 County court rules (1914) under Mental Defectives Act 1913, with memorandum by Board of Control.

331 Rule of 1913 made to obviate difficulties caused by National Insurance Act s.46(3).

413 Draft rules by Theobald, 1919.

635 Proposed re-organisation of Board of Control with dissenting note by L. L. Shadwell. Amalgamation of Chancery Visitors with Lunacy Commissioners proposed by Home Office and discussed with Theobald. Transfer of lunacy from Home Office to Ministry of Health.

489–95, 506, 975 Tomlin Committee "preliminary report" (1919) in 489; minutes and papers (490, 506) memoranda on lunacy administration (491); 2nd, 3rd and 5th reports (492); 3rd report and papers (495); Romer's scheme with Theobald's comments and draft bill of 1921 (975).

947	Report of Board of Control committee on clinical records and suggested new rules, 1922.
948, 1540	Problems of Irish Free State orders against English property: memorandum by Master Hildyard, explanation by PCO, 1924. Northern Ireland warrants discussed with Home Office, 1932.
949	Rules 1925, correspondence with Master Hildyard.
3652A, 2830, 3647, 3656	Complaints against Court of Protection, mostly of delays. Dispute between Pay Office and Lunacy Office on one complaint (1943), order for enquiry in case of E. H. Trapnell (1947) and complaint against a Visitor by Lord Exeter (1950).
3338	Discussions with Board of Control on transfer of Broadmoor from Home Office in Criminal Justice Act 1938.
3653	Correspondence with Ministry of Health, Court of Protection, Board of Control on proposed amalgamation of last two, 1950–1.
5994	Home Office queries need for new warrant on each appointment of a Lord Justice with lunacy jurisdiction (1947); notes on previous discussions, 1906; referred to Master Poyser 1951.
4/47–50, 52	Fischer-Williams report on the Management and Administration Department: evidence, memoranda, minutes, discussions on draft, 1934.
4/53	Discussions with T. W. Chitty (1925), Master Poyser (1934) and Chancery judges (1947), on change of name to Court of Protection (1947).
4/54	Solicitor's complaint re delays, 1947.
4/55	O & M Report, 1949 and discussions with Poyser.

4
FEES AND PAYMENTS

2/415	Voluminous correspondence with Theobald and Official Solicitor on their dispute over fees, with report of Duke and Warrington JJ (1919).
637, 950–1	Rules (Percentage) 1921; discussions with Treasury and Pay Office on levels; Rules (Percentage) 1927, minor changes; Personal Application Fees, 1928 with explanatory memorandum.
1541–2	Management of Patients Estates Rules 1934, and (Percentage and Fees) Order 1939; correspondence with Master Poyser, Treasury, Official Solicitor.
1652	Payments out of court to receivers eased by SC Funds Rules (3) 1934.
4064	Investment powers (see 'Trustee Securities, *supra*, 222).

Chapter 8

CRIMINAL LAW AND PROCEDURE

1 INTRODUCTION

The substance of the criminal law in this period was marked by a tremendous increase in the number and variety of statutory offences, but most of the new offences were essentially petty violations of prohibitions made necessary either by technological change, e.g. motoring offences, or by the increasing range of state activities, e.g. in the regulation of the economy. The statute book expanded remorselessly and the criminal law remained uncodified after the abandonment of the plan to enact Stephen's code. Lord Loreburn encouraged attempts at piecemeal codification which met with some success until the bill to codify fraud prepared by Avory's criminal law committee "was criticised out of existence".[1] When the possibility of codification was afterwards raised in Parliament the LCO produced briefs which were first temporising then downright discouraging.[2] Schuster pinned his hopes for reform instead on the Law Revision Committee, which was eager to tackle criminal subjects, only to find that those they proposed (the felony-misdemeanour distinction, evidence of spouses, the simplification of larceny, false pretences, conversion and embezzlement and changes in pleadings) met with an entirely negative response from the Home Office, without whose co-operation legislation was impossible.[3] However, when bills were put forward, either by private members or other government departments, the Lord Chancellor and his staff were usually involved and a few files on such bills contain interesting details on how they reached their final state: thus when the need to define the phrase 'newly born' in the Infanticide Act 1922 was raised by Humphreys J and in the House of Commons in 1936, Schuster admitted that he had been responsible for the words;[4] again, the anomalous defence available to a man under the age of twenty four accused of sexual offences against minors, that he believed the victim to be above the age of consent, is seen to have been a compromise between powerful lobbies on the Criminal Amendment Bill 1921 and the government's negotiations with them are laid open in 2/469.

The administration of the criminal law was in a much worse condition than the law itself and the Lord Chancellor's involvement was more direct. As stated earlier,[5] the central problem with serious offences was that the quarter sessions were considered unqualified to deal with them, while the assizes were too infrequent and geographically inconvenient, so that trials were frequently delayed for many months and prisoners on remand languished in gaol. This state of affairs was investigated by the Horridge Committee in 1921 and a further committee under the DPP was asked to recommend changes in procedure and whether any further offences could be made triable summarily. The Criminal Justice Bill which embodied some of their rather cautious recommendations is fully dealt with in the LCO papers; indeed it became something of a burden because it attracted a miscellany of proposals from government departments and had a tedious and troubled passage through Parliament. It did not help its progress to have the Lord Chief Justice suggesting a clause to enable blackmailers to be flogged, nor to have the Treasury wanting to stop the pledging of pension books to moneylenders, while anything which touched the grand jury was bound to be controversial. Cave took a keen interest in the bill and personally vetoed certain provisions which the DPP and the Post Office were anxious to have, but many concessions had to be made in Parliament and it was not until 1925 that it finally passed into law.[6]

Similarly, the Criminal Justice Act 1948, although it was much more speedy in its passage, involved the Lord Chancellor in animated discussions with his colleagues which are fully documented. They are of particular interest on the question of punishments rather than administration, however. Earlier files on sentencing are mainly interesting for the Lord Chancellor's suggestion that the Council of Judges should consider formulating guidelines in sentencing and their rejection of it[7] (one of the decisions which ensured that that body would not perform any worthwhile functions) and for discussions on the vexed question of criminal responsibility; these include the report of the Lord Chancellor's committee under Atkin to examine the Trial of Lunatics Act 1883 (with useful Home Office material on the working of the law)[8] and Lord Darling's bill of 1924, with a long background memorandum from Schuster.[9]

More generally, the files show traces of a widening rift between 'progressive' opinion in the Home Office and the 'reactionary' views of the judges, including the Lord Chief Justice and the Lord Chancellor. This was evident in their opposition to Home Office proposals for the widespread substitution of fines for imprisonment in cases of felony in an abortive bill of 1938, but became more important in the post-war years. Jowitt was deeply disturbed by the 'crime wave', particularly by juvenile crime, and the strength with which he resisted the case argued by the Law Officers, the Haldane Society and others for the abolition of the death penalty, and his hopeless but vigorous advocacy of corporal punishment, deserve emphasising as a corrective to the common over emphasis on Goddard LCJ as the principal obstacle to liberal hopes. Jowitt was well aware that the judges had a bad reputation among reformers: ''of course it will be said that the judges, amongst whom I number myself, are playing the traditional role which they have played since Romilly's time of obstructing every reform in the criminal law'' but he disliked the whole tenor of the Home Office proposals, which he stigmatised as ''sentimental sloppiness'' unworthy of a government which, unlike that of 1938, was no longer ''living a world of make believe.''[11] These files are of equal value on the question of criminal appeals, where the Lord Chief Justice's harshness was already causing unfavourable comment at the bar.[12] It is also to be noted, however, that alarmed as Jowitt was by the crime wave, he was at one with Shawcross (the more progressive Attorney-General) in condemning the Home Secretary's bill on ''offensive weapons'' designed to allay a panic over an outbreak of ''coshing''.[13]

Notes

1 *2/963: Schuster's memorandum, 1927. See also Lord Birkenhead,* ***Points of View*** *(1922), I, 177–83 which explains the working of this committee and envisages its further progress.*

2 *2/963.*

3 *2/1995.*

4 *2/1329.*

5 ***supra****, 113–5, 139.*

6 *2/715–6.*

7 *1/54: LCJ to LC, 26.3.1885.*

8 *2/585, especially E. Blackwell (HO) to Schuster, 6.11.1923.*

9 *2/761.*

10 *2/3340: to LCJ, 7.3.1947. The judges' comments on the draft bill are in the same file.*

11 ***Ibid**: draft and memorandum to cabinet, 1947.*

12 ***supra**, 93–4.*

13 *2/3356: to Attorney-General, 22.7.1950.*

2
GENERAL LEGISLATION

1/42 Proposed codification of criminal law. Holker (Attorney-General)'s correspondence with Lord Chancellor, 1877; arrangements with Treasury to pay J. F. Stephen; observations of F. S. Reilly. Correspondence on salary of secretary to Criminal Code Commission. Stephen's marked copy of the Code with notes and LC's side notes and correspondence; printed reports of the Commission.

2/200 Criminal Procedure Bill 1911: comments by judges and LCJ; meetings of indictments committee under Avory J and draft rules, minutes of evidence taken before joint select committee on the Bill, 1915.

521A, 583–4, 712–21 Criminal Justice Bill: extensive papers 1922–5, following Horridge Committee report on detention before trial and DPP's report on possible changes, especially on grand jury. Draft bill from Home Office, correspondence with PCO, DPP and Cave's observations; memorandum for cabinet; discussions on clauses by Lord Phillimore, Ministry of Health *et al.*, and on Parliamentary amendments in 1923 session. Representations from law societies, chambers of commerce and other interested bodies, cabinet papers (1924) and discussions on amendments and on suggestions for inclusion, by Treasury, LCJ and others. Correspondence with Home Office and conference on Parliamentary tactics. Drafts of reply to attacks by Atherley-Jones. Files also on F. Mead (a metropolitan magistrate)'s suggestions, Hertfordshire quarter sessions, grand juries at Central Criminal Court and on coercion of wife (on which see also 584, LC's Committee under Avory J to consider *R. v Peel*).

3338–9 Criminal Justice Bill: correspondence with Home Office, cabinet papers, LCJ's views, 1937–8.

963 Schuster's notes on history of codification for Griffiths' motion (1928).

1995, 3565 Law Revision Committee papers (*supra*, 199–200).

3827 Schuster's proposals for reform, 1943, and notes of meeting with Conservative party sub-committee.

2737, 3340–2, 5101 Large files on Criminal Justice Bill from 1946. Home Office proposals and draft bill, cabinet papers, extensive correspondence of Jowitt with LCJ on punishment; memoranda and correspondence on the death penalty and corporal punishment. Views of clerks of the peace on right of pre-empting challenge; notes on new clauses, especially on appeals, statistics on sentences. Dispute between Home Secretary and LCJ on commutation of death penalty and on Simon's amendments. See also 5105, discussions with Home Office,

LCJ, Attorney-General on interpretation of s.44 (payment of defence costs from public funds).

3823 Summary Jurisdiction Rules 1948, 1949, formal correspondence.

3
PARTICULAR OFFENCES

2/86 Draft bill of 1892 by PCO to remove doubts about Forged Transfers Act 1891.

469 Criminal Law Amendment Bill 1921, (Sexual Offences): discussions with sponsors, whips and cabinet on concessions to pass the bill; lobbying by women's organisations and Parliamentary proceedings.

471 Fraud and Falsification Bill 1921. Draft and notes to Avory's committee on criminal bills, their report, correspondence with Muir McKenzie and criticism by departments and DPP; Bill withdrawn.

476, 1329, 3591 Infanticide: Sir H. Thring's notes on 1922 Bill and discussions with PCO, DPP, Phillimore and Muir McKenzie. Discussions of 1936 with Humphreys J, Home Office; discussions with DPP on Jagger's Bill and Dawson's Bill, and Parliamentary proceedings on the 1937 Bill; solicitor's complaint of 1947 re publicity.

1325 Notes on case law of 'motoring manslaughter', 1933.

3346 Lord Cranbrook's complaint, 1947, about indecency prosecutions at the assizes, with Home Office, DPP comments.

3349 Complaint of jury acquittals in dockyard pilfering cases, 1948. (*Cf.* 4596–8, Miss Campbell's sentences).

3356 Discussions on Home Office Bill for ''offensive weapons'' offences.

1897, 1900 Public Order Act 1936: inquiry about rules, made in RSC (4) 1940.

3602 Motor Vehicles (Variation of Speed Limit) Regulation 1950 following complaints by LC and Attorney-General on the 'fantastic' definition of a ''goods vehicle''.

3104 Protests by LC and Solicitor-General re powers of officials under Borrowing Bill 1946; discussions on burden of proof and amendments.

4
OFFENCES AGAINST THE STATE

2/1383, 3073, 5755 Treachery Bill 1940. Conference with Home Office; memoranda, correspondence with Judge-Advocate General on possible bill for wartime treasons; draft bill and notes on clauses; cabinet papers. Treason Bill 1945: memorandum by DPP on procedure, draft bill and cabinet papers. PQs and discussions with Attorney-General on activity of British citizens in Korea, 1950–5.

197, 1206, 3219 Official secrets: draft bill (1908) by PCO circulated, correspondence with Admiralty meetings with Newspaper Proprietors Association. Select committee on Lord Snell's PQ on effect of Official Secrets Act 1939 on House of Lords. Discussions with Attorney-General on Sir James Grigg's memoirs, 1948.

5
THE ADMINISTRATION OF CRIMINAL JUSTICE

1 Bail

2/871, 3332, 4090, 2819, 4111 Home Office memorandum and correspondence with Magistrates' Association Discussions with other legal departments on ''casus omissus'' revealed in *R.* v *Sinnott.* Discussions with Official Solicitor, Home Office, Treasury, LCJ on legal aid to make bail applications (see RSC(4) 1948). Discussions with Home Office and Master King leading to RSC (Criminal Proceedings Act) 1949. Complaint by Sir W. Smithers MP on a refusal of bail, 1942.

2 Jurisdiction

(see 'Quarter Sessions', 'Assizes' supra, 108, 139)

2/1328, 3331, 3766

3 Other Aspects

2/148 Poor Prisoners' Defence Act 1903 (*supra*, 189).

1330 Discussions with Attorney-General, Law Society on attempts to restrict newspapers paying defence costs in exchange for stories.

3333 *Stirland* v *DPP*: investigations into a rule of evidence, 1944.

3355 Correspondence with LOD on newspaper criticism of judges' rules, 1950.

3915, 4436, 4853 Informers: *Green* v *Haymarket Capital Ltd* (1944) discussed on question of professional informer's ability to avoid publicity, and brief for 'planted' PQ. Parliamentary objections to payment of rewards under Exchange Control Act discussed in cabinet, with statistics (1949). Common Informers Bill discussed in cabinet, 1951 and correspondence with PCO. Correspondence with Home Office on Northern Ireland Bill.

1325–7, 2571 Trial of peers (see *supra*, 46).

1998 Special pardon for P. Bradbury, 1891.

4 The Director of Public Prosecutions

1/78 Regulations 1886: drafts and correspondence.

2/1627 Administration of Justice Act 1938 s.6: arrangements for DPP's committals in London.

3335 New regulations discussed with DPP and Home Office, 1945.

3348 Rejects criticisms of fines against local authorities, 1948.

3735 Rules on alleged contempt of a Pensions Appeal Tribunal.

4423 His report (with F. A. Newsam) on Control Commission Courts, 1947.

6
PUNISHMENTS

1/54	Council of Judges discusses issue of sentencing guidelines, 1886.
2/585	Discussions on possible repeal of Trials of Lunatics Act 1883, as proposed by H. Stephen; committee set up by LC under Atkin LJ and report (1922). Home Office list of cases under the Act.
147	Youthful Offenders Act 1901 rules sent by Home Office.
761	Criminal Responsibility (Trials) Bill 1924 (Lord Darling's) sent to judges and Parliamentary proceedings; long memorandum by Schuster.
3342	Collection of PQs and answers, 1946.
3352	Correspondence with Home Office on criticisms of sentencing, 1949.
3353	Suggestion by J. S. Henderson KC on conditional discharges, 1950.
3357	Sir Leo Page's memorandum on suspended sentences, 1950.
3446	Memorandum on loss of civil rights for convicted criminals, requested by FO, 1949.
3511	Memorandum by E. F. Iwi on pardons.
3824	Summary Jurisdiction (Children and Young Persons) Rules 1950.
5303	Discussions on practice of trade unions paying members' motoring fines, 1951.
1331, 3231	Argument between Home Office and Oliver J on mitigation of sentences, 1941. Home Office memorandum on the prerogative of mercy, 1948.
3351	Correspondence with Attorney-General and LCJ in 1949 and in 1953 on LCJ's proposal to restrict contempt proceedings to the Law Officers: *Haigh's case* and *R.* v *Hargreaves* (1954) Crim L. R. 54.
4500	Royal Commission on Capital Punishment: cabinet papers 1948, refusals to chair by several judges; a few papers.
5149	Theft of the Stone of Scone. Cabinet discussions on Attorney-General's decision not to prosecute and on possible changes in the law. Memoranda by LC and Law Officers on constitutional aspects; discussions with Dean of Westminster and meetings, 1951–2.

7
INDICTMENTS RULES

2/200	Committee under Avory J; discussions on members, Avory's comments and minutes of meetings, 1913.
353	Indictment Rules 1916.
586	Rules under Infanticide Act 1922: correspondence with LCJ and draft rules.
872	Indictable Offences Rules 1926: correspondence with Home Office.
873	Grand Juries (Dispensation at Quarter Sessions) Rules 1927.
1959–60	Indictments (Procedure) Rules and Indictable Offences Rules, 1933: correspondence with Home Office, DPP, Avory J.

8
POLICE

2/916, 2836, 3107, 3977, 3281, 4077, 4266, 3954	Various matters, including discussions on rules of evidence re police reports (2836), attendance at assizes (3954) and police legislation.

WARTIME EMERGENCY LEGISLATION

1
THE GREAT WAR

The contrast between the hasty improvisation of legislation during the Great War and the extensive and elaborate preparation which was made in anticipation of the next is very marked. However, even though the material in this source on the former is much smaller in quantity and rather unrevealing on some major aspects, such as the Rent Act 1915, it does contain some useful information both on the problems which arose in working out the clumsily conceived moratorium on payments, and the Courts (Emergency Powers) Acts which perpetuated it in a modified and discretionary form, and on the legal tightrope which the services departments walked in their requisitioning practices. There are particularly interesting memoranda on the impact of the Shoreham Aerodrome case,[1] on the scope of defence regulations and the prerogative power and on the concern of the Admiralty at the potentially enormous sums of compensation which might be payable if it was ruled that they had to give full current market value. The interaction of the demands of the Lord Chancellor and Law Officers for compliance with the law, the desire of the services departments for the widest discretionary powers and the unwillingness of the politicians to cast any doubt on past actions or regulations by the introduction of fresh legislation is highly instructive.

Notes

1 ***In re a Petition of Right*** *[1915] 3 KB 649, compromised in the House of Lords where the Crown would have lost, see 2/367: Lord Chancellor's memorandum, August 1916.*

2/290–1, 306, 310, 323, 352 — Emergency Powers Act and Postponement of Payments Act 1914; suggested by LCJ, draft bill, memoranda by Parker J, MacDonnell; draft rules, correspondence with county court judges (especially Selfe) and registrars; suggested rule amendments, new rules (1915); complaints, mostly from solicitors; discussions in rule committees (1915); fees amended (1916).

371–2 — Emergency Powers Act 1916. Draft from PCO with memorandum from Stock Exchange Committee on *Farnol Eades* (1915) and *Ziman* (1915); county court rules.

373–7 — Emergency Powers (No. 2) Act 1916: rules for Supreme Court and county courts and consolidation of county court rules discussed.

378–84 — Courts (Emergency Powers) Act 1917: suggestions from Registrars Association, Sargent J, discussions with Law Officers and War Trade Department. Amendments discussed, especially to clause on recovery of rents; lobbying by power supply companies, consultations with interested parties, extensive Parliamentary papers. Rules for Supreme and county courts and rules consolidation; correspondence with Chitty, Selfe and others.

293, 425 Correspondence with Board of Trade and Attorney-General on rules under Trading with the Enemy Act, and rules amended 1916 as suggested by Younger J.

312 Discussions with Admiralty, War Office and press bureau on draft defence regulations (censorship), with memoranda and cabinet memorandum, 1915.

337 Rules under Legal Proceedings Against Enemies Act 1915.

367–9 Lord Chancellor's memorandum on requisitioning power and the Shoreham Aerodrome case; proposals discussed and memorandum by R. E. Duke (Losses Commission); draft bill, cabinet papers. Rules under Defence of the Realm (Acquisition of Land) Act 1916 and lengthy correspondence with Treasury on fees. Cabinet and Parliamentary papers on 1917 bill, and Law Officers' opinion on Beans and Peas Order. Correspondence with Admiralty, PCO, A. C. Clauson on draft Defence of the Realm (Acquisition of Ships) Bill 1917.

385 Increase of Rent Amendment Act 1918: memoranda and discussions on amendments to meet gaps in Rent Act; Scottish Office draft bill, representations from Office of Works, MPs, Ministry of Munitions, county court judges.

674 Discussions with Lord Stamfordham, Law Officers and Custodian of Enemy Property on liability of Duke of Albany's reversionary interest to meet British claims, 1920.

438, 440–1 War Emergency Laws (Continuation) Act: Lord Chancellor's memorandum to war cabinet, summary of correspondence with departments, draft report by "Continuance of Emergency Laws Committee" to war cabinet and draft bill. Cabinet papers, views of judges, memoranda and discussions on tactics. Interdepartmental committee on indemnities, report and draft bill, especially on shipping claims and the judgments in *De Keyser* and *Newcastle Breweries*. Report of House of Commons select committee and Parliamentary brief for Lord Chancellor.

2
THE SECOND WORLD WAR

1 The Administration of Justice

This time there had been an opportunity to prepare for the coming of war, especially for the bombing which might dislocate London and other major cities. A war legislation sub-committee of the Committee of Imperial Defence was set up, which produced a draft Administration of Justice (Emergency Provisions) Bill in February 1939, and for some months beforehand a small committee under the Master of the Rolls had been meeting to consider the implications of war for the courts. An *ad hoc* committee under the Lord Chief Justice approved the outlines of the bill in April so the legislation was already in place and orders prepared in draft before the war began. The strategy which was first envisaged for civil actions was to scatter the High Court judges in towns distant from the capital, but the KBD judges were successful in modifying it and substituting an inner ring of five major home counties towns. Contingency plans had also been drawn up for a complete evacuation of the courts, but in the event it was only the Principal Probate Registry that left Somerset House for a long exile in Llandudno.

Criminal justice became a particular problem in the invasion year of 1940. Discussions with the Home Office and Humphreys LJ had produced the Defence (Administration of Justice) Regulations, which empowered the removal of assizes from threatened towns and otherwise facilitated flexible justice, but the military had by then produced circular ERHF 1/1079 (May 27th) an "amazing production"[1] which even the War Office admitted "went much further than it should have done"[2] and led to stiff exchanges with the LCO and Home Office. A short measure, the Emergency Powers (Defence) (No. 2) Bill 1940 was put together to reduce the military's powers and was approved by the Home Policy Committee in July. Under it, War Zone Courts were set up in eleven regions, each under a High Court judge as President, ready to be activated in the event of an area being designated a war zone, and maintaining as many as possible of the traditional safeguards of the criminal justice system.[3] Even then the military area commanders had to be restrained from recruiting for contingent "military courts" of their own.[4]

Notes

1 *2/4261: Lord Chancellor's note, 8.7.1940. Lord Cooper called it "a semi-permanent military dictatorship": to Lord Chancellor, 16.6.1940.*

2 ***Ibid**.: S. Stewart (Home Defence Executive) to Schuster, 19.6.1940.*

3 *2/3412. The original Home Office proposals were felt by the LCO to be too drastic, see Schuster's minute, 27.5.1940. The Act was described as "admirable" by W. I. Jennings (1939–40), 4 MLR 132 at p. 136.*

4 *2/4267.*

2/1373	Administration of Justice in War Committee, 1938: proceedings, memoranda, correspondence.
1361–2	Administration of Justice (Emergency Powers) Act 1939: correspondence with Home Office and PCO, meeting of *ad hoc* committee, cabinet papers, draft orders and notes, Parliamentary papers.
1363–8	Orders (drafts) under the above: meetings, memoranda, drafts and prints.
1369–71	Orders of 1939 for dispersal of High Court: drafts, correspondence, judges' meetings.
3412	Defence (Administration of Justice) Regulations 1940: correspondence with Home Office and Humphreys LJ, explanatory circulars etc.; supplementary regulation on jury detention.
4261–9	War Zone Courts: correspondence with Attorney-General, Home Office, War Office and other departments, cabinet papers; correspondence with PCO on Emergency Powers(2) Bill. Meetings of officials, correspondence with proposed Presidents, Humphreys LJ; draft rules; correspondence with Treasury on remuneration. Correspondence with Goddard LJ and Home Office on amendment by Order in Council 1942.
1372, 1405, 1875, 3423, 3426	Minor matters.

2 Internment

The only LCO papers of interest are those relating to the selection of personnel for the tribunals which administered the scheme, and on the celebrated case of the British fascist Ben Greene, in which the LCO became involved as a result of Greene's legal action against the Home Secretary.[1]

Note

1 *Greene* v *Anderson [1942] AC 284.*

2/1377 Alien internment scheme: correspondence with Home Office, notes on county court judges and other candidates for employment.

1454 Case of Ben Greene: correspondence with Home Office, report of advisory committee, internal LCO memoranda.

3 Compensation

1 Compulsory acquisition

The Compensation (Defence) Act 1939 settled the powers of the crown for the duration of the war and provided for the establishment of claims tribunals to which disputes might be referred. Two separate claims tribunals, one general and one for shipping, were constituted, as well as a separate one for Scotland, and as usual it fell to the Lord Chancellor to find suitable members. Much of the correspondence in the files is devoted to the search for suitable men, especially lawyers, and to subsequent changes in composition. The rules also gave rise to some difficulty, however, since the Treasury Solicitor proved very stubborn in opposing provisions enabling discovery of documents against the crown.

Once these preliminaries were dealt with, there was little in the operation of the tribunals to give rise to anxiety. The Shipping Claims Tribunal was virtually unused—so much so that, with slightly altered composition, it was able to double as the Valuation Tribunal under the Shipping (War Rules) Insurance and Tonnage Replacement Scheme, which proved equally superfluous. The General Claims Tribunal had more to do, and its unwillingness to sit outside London gave rise to complaints, but there is little material here on its operation.[1]

Note

1 ***Supra**, 165–6. For a summary see (1939–40) 4 Conv. (NS.) 54, 117 (R. H. Thorold Rogers).*

2/4660–3 Rules and appointments: correspondence on rules with draftsmen, Sir S. Rowlatt (President of SCT) and Treasury Solicitor; with Board of Trade and Treasury on members and terms, with the appointees, especially Rowlatt and McKinnon (President of GCT).

1506 New rules of 1942 and complaint re Treasury attitudes (1949) by Scottish solicitors.

4273 Law Society complaints of GCT and correspondence.

4275–6 Shipping Claims Tribunal and Valuation Tribunal: correspondence with Ministry of Shipping.

4371 Correspondence with Treasury and Ministry of Transport on emergency laws, 1950.

4284 Acquisition of Land (Compensation for War Damage) Rules 1945; discussions on exclusion of judicial review.

4271–2 Rules complaints, position of Channel Islands and Isle of Man.

2652 Requisitioned Land Bill: correspondence with PCO, Land Registry; cabinet and Parliamentary papers; Law Society representations, 1944–5.

2 *The War Damage Acts*

The impossibility of insuring against war risks threatened to add to the physical devastation of the cities which was forecast (''the bomber will always get through'') an impossible and unfair burden on owners of destroyed or damaged premises. Where the premises were leasehold (as was overwhelmingly the case in the towns) it also threatened to create injustice by obliging one party to the lease to reinstate without the benefit of insurance or risk losing his lease or paying huge damages. It was to meet these problems, for which the Great War provided no precedent, that the ''second Uthwatt Committee'' was appointed by the cabinet in March, 1939, with Napier representing the LCO. An interim measure, the Landlord and Tenant (War Damage) Act 1939, merely absolved either party to a lease of any duty to repair war damaged premises and enabled the party which did repair premises made unfit for occupation to become ''master of the situation''.[1] In 1941, after consultations with commercial organisations about the setting up of a compulsory contributory scheme, the War Damage Act was passed, and it is not surprising in view of the complexity of the subject matter and the novelty of the approach, that it proved to need repeated amendments.[2] Some of the hardships which were alleged arose out of basic policy decisions, especially the meanness of the ''value payment'' for total destruction, and the government was not helped by the fact that one of those aggrieved was Lord Hailsham, who had disclaimed the lease of his house in Bryanston Square under the first, less favourable Act. In consequence a measure intended as a ''sweeping up'' bill of a highly technical nature grew to be much more substantial and controversial. ''Mixed payments'', to be apportioned between landlord and tenant, were perhaps the most awkward of many unpleasant issues which had to be dealt with in the 1944 bill.

The Acts were administered by a War Damage Commission headed by Malcolm Eve KC and legal questions were referred to a nominated Chancery judge (Uthwatt) or, within financial limits, to the county court; proposals to simplify the question of ''fitness' by the written report of an assessor were unsuccessful.[3] Appeals against valuations were initially for the Official Arbitrators sitting under the Acquisitions of Land Act 1919 but the War Damage Commission quickly grew dissatisfied with their inconsistency and in 1944 persuaded the government to set up a Valuation Tribunal under Judge Hunter. As in other wartime legislation, the expected volume of business failed to materialise and only Hunter's unwillingness to return to his county court duties kept it in being until its work was transferred to the new Lands Tribunal in 1950.[4]

Notes

1 *B. A. Bicknell, (1939–40) 4 Conv. (NS.) 39, 264.*
2 *(1941–2) 5 MLR 54 (M. Finer) gives a useful summary.*
3 *2/1320: Napier to Judge Lilley, 12.2.1942.*
4 **supra**, *164–5.*

2/1376	Essential Buildings and Plant (Repair of War Damage) Act 1939: correspondence with Ministry of Health and Land Registry on registration of charges.
1502–4	Landlord and Tenant (War Damage) Act 1939: report of Uthwatt Committees and C.I.D. sub-committee. Cabinet papers, correspondence with Ministry of Health, Treasury and other departments; drafting correspondence, Parliamentary papers; report of "Weir Conference", 1939.
1418	Proposed amendments sent by Treasury to LCO; correspondence with Uthwatt J, Law Officers Department, President of Chartered Surveyors Institute *et al.*, mostly on ground leases.
1416–7	Amendment Act 1941: extensive correspondence with Attorney-General and draftsman on this "sweeping up" measure; memoranda from various organisations and individuals, notes on Parliamentary amendments etc.
1505, 1507–8, 1930	War Damage Act 1941: drafting correspondence with PCO; memoranda by Roche LJ, G. Benson MP and others, and Parliamentary papers. Trustees' powers to insure chattels, opinion of Danckwerts, extensive drafting correspondence, memoranda and Parliamentary papers.
2725	Amendment Act 1942: memoranda and general correspondence; with Uthwatt J, PCO, Treasury, and Parliamentary papers.
2729–31, 3422, 2656	Amendment Bill 1942–3: correspondence with Law Officers, War Damage Commission and draftsman on Law Society's proposals for problems of already disclaimed leases, and Parliamentary amendments; notes and correspondence on Lord Meston's motions in House of Lords. Correspondence with Treasury on appeals forum.
1912	Correspondence on rules 1941.
1320	County Court Rules 1940: correspondence with Treasury and others on use and payment of assessors.
3092, 4666	War Damage (Valuation Appeals) Act 1945: cabinet papers, correspondence with War Damage Commission, Parliamentary papers, departmental meetings.
4300–4	War Damage (Valuation Appeals and References) Rules 1946, and amendments 1947, 1948. Meetings of officials, drafting correspondence, representations against lay advocates by Law Society and Bar Council; complaint re costs in the Tribunal.
4299	1946–50: correspondence with War Damage Commission, Treasury *et al.*, re membership and terms of the Tribunal; changes in personnel; correspondence with Hunter and County Courts Department on its workload

and organisation; appointment of members for Northern Ireland; transfer of jurisdiction under Lands Tribunal (War Damage Appeals Jurisdiction) Order 1950.

3614, 3923, 3286, 4054, 4469 Various rules, regulations and queries under the War Damage Acts, 1940–6.

4 Civil Liabilities

1 *Introduction*

As mentioned above, the Second World War took no-one in authority by surprise and as early as 1935 the Treasury had approached the LCO for advice on a more sophisticated and less inflationary form of debtor protection than the 1914 moratorium.[1] The greatest difficulty was to decide on the extent to which the courts ought to be given powers to re-write contracts, the Lord Chancellor and the judges being hostile to any wide power of that sort. Thus the power was excluded from the Courts (Emergency Powers) Act 1939, which was the basic form of general statutory regulation of civil liabilities, in the hope that the common law doctrine of frustration would prove adequate. After questions in Parliament, mostly on the plight of business tenants with long leases, and the second report of the Uthwatt Committee on War Damage a civil liabilities sub-committee of the War Legislation Committee was set up with Schuster as chairman.[2] It gave particular attention to leases, to commercial contracts generally and to the special position of the "evacuated areas"—coastal towns in the south and east which had been partly evacuated in anticipation of the invasion. The papers of the sub-committee are an excellent source on the complicated problem of civil liabilities in a state at war and on the interplay of social, economic, political and legal factors in determining the policies adopted towards them.

The Courts (Emergency Powers) Act, as amended, remained the basic legislation. It was initially modelled closely on its Great War predecessors but had steadily to be extended to protect debtors against creditors' practices which rendered it ineffective. Mortgagors were especially badly protected by the original act, which also suffered (according to one experienced county court registrar) from "the Court of Appeal, who seem to take a wicked delight in making these provisions as useless as possible to a defendant."[3]

However, as the war progressed, two other approaches were tried to this difficult problem. The first was a crude reversion to the discredited practice of a moratorium on debt, which was applied to the evacuated areas by defence regulation in 1940. As early as December, 1941 the Lord Chancellor can be found arguing cogently that it should be ended without delay as being wrong both in principle, not discriminating between inability to pay and unwillingness, and in practice, since it was widely misunderstood by debtors as writing off debts altogether and was likely to leave the less provident with impossible arrears when it *was* lifted.[4] The Home Office view, based on considerations of civilian morale and a desire to halt the drift back to the coast by evacuees, not only prevailed then, but even in 1944 when the Jowitt Committee deliberated on the rehabilitation of these impoverished and neglected towns, and the moratorium was not finally ended until well after the war.[5] Not surprisingly, it was unpopular with creditors and several county court judges made their sympathies plain: Judge Archer in particular drove a 'cart and horse' through the regulations by one of his decisions.[6]

A more novel and interesting experiment was devised by Schuster's sub-committee and put into practice by the Liabilities (War-time Adjustment) Acts 1941–4. In a memorandum to the cabinet it was described as "a kind of preventitive and remedial bankruptcy without stigma"[7] and it was particularly designed to assist small traders whose livelihood was threatened by government controls on supply, as well as wartime shortages. A debtor who was unable to meet his liabilities might anticipate insolvency proceedings by calling on the district Liabilities Adjustment Officer (appointed by the Lord Chancellor) to negotiate with his creditors a "scheme of arrangement", rescheduling existing and recurrent liabilities to enable him to remain in business; the sanction was the power of the county court to impose an "adjustment and settlement" order on reluctant creditors.[8] It was a more sophisticated measure than the Courts (Emergency Powers) Acts and one which had the merit of anticipating the day of reckoning rather than postponing it. In 1944 it was strengthened considerably and its terms broadened in the hope of encouraging debtors under the evacuated areas moratorium to utilise it.[9]

One commentator wrote that "it seems unimaginable that the insolvency legislation should not take the experiences gained under the Act into account when the time for repeal of the emergency laws comes",[10] yet this imaginative legislation was both disappointingly little used in the war and forgotten in the peace. It deserves a better fate and although most of the records of the LAOs seem to have perished, enough remain to make an interesting study.

One of the reasons for its failure illustrates a problem encountered in all these attempts to assist the economic casualties of the war–the intransigence of public authorities, and particularly the Inland Revenue. The Revenue was implacably opposed to giving any judicial body the power to abate or re-assess tax liabilities, and its own practice was alleged to be inflexible to a degree.[11] Likewise the public utilities continued to resort to the threat of disconnection to secure priority for their claims over private creditors,[12] and with these examples before them, it was small wonder if the latter were not disposed to relinquish their own rights, and even (as was the case with some mortgagees) sought to evade the protective litigation by every lawful means.[13] Current interest in the experience of the civilian population during the Second World War should make a study of these attempts to mitigate the financial stresses of war while preserving the fragile credit structure rewarding.

Notes

1 *2/1353: F. Phillips to Schuster, 18.10.1935.*

2 *The terms were "to consider the problems arising from the inability of persons, owing to war conditions, to fulfil their contractual and other obligations, and in particular to consider the complaints already made to MPs and government departments".*

3 *2/3909: G. Hicks to Napier, 8.12.1942.*

4 *2/2726: memorandum of December, 1941.*

5 *2/2727: note of meeting at Home Office, 24.4.1942. 2/3420: memorandum by Home Office and Ministry of Home Security, 1944.*

6 *2/2726: Coldstream to H. S. Kent (PCO), 24.9.1941.*

7 *2/1400: memorandum of February, 1941.*

8 *A summary by M. Finer is in (1941–2) 5 MLR 120.*

9 *2/3419: R(C)(44)7, LCO memorandum, 14.5.1944.*

10 *M. Harnik jnr (1941–2) 5 MLR 127.*

11 *e.g. 2/3419: Napier's note of discussion with Sir C. Gregg, 30.5.1944.*

12 *e.g. 2/3613: W. T. Sansom's case, 1942; 2/1381: 2nd interim report of war legislation sub-committee, 31.1.1940.*

13 *e.g. 2/1381: memorandum of Chancery masters, 1940.*

2 *Home Policy Committee Civil Liabilities Sub-Committee*

2/1391–9, 1412–5 Memoranda, reports, minutes, evidence and correspondence. Memoranda to Lord Chancellor. 1939–40.

3 *The Courts (Emergency Powers) Acts and Rules*

2/1353, 1380 Treasury approach to LCO, 1935, discussions resumed 1936. Correspondence with PCO on draft bill. Lord Chancellor's views on re-writing contracts discussed in 1938; bill approved by war legislation sub-committee; rules drafted and bill passed, 1939. Discussions with departments on crown immunity.

1378 Possession of Mortgaged Land (E.P.) Bill 1939, drafted by PCO to meet Master Holland's request.

1354, 1356 Supreme Court Rules: correspondence with PCO and Master Ball; EP (no. 2) Rules to cover distress of rates, after query by Derby Town Clerk and correspondence with Home Office.

1374 Courts (Emergency Powers) (no. 2) Bill 1939: LCO notes on Uthwatt report, draft by PCO, cabinet papers, with memoranda on Great War measures. Bill not proceeded with.

1319, 1321, 1355, 1357–9, 2680–1 County court rules and correspondence on numerous complaints from creditors of difficulties of service, discussed especially with registrars. Complaints from mortgagees discussed with Master Holland. Service on enemy aliens discussed with Master Jelf. Draft amended rules discussed with Farwell J and Registrars.

1381 Amendment bill; second interim report of war legislation sub-committee discussed in cabinet and draft bill from PCO; views of judges and masters, revised draft, Parliamentary briefs. Proposals to extend relief, by Chancery masters *et al.*, especially on mortgages and return of goods, with statistics on re-possession, views on *Soho Square Syndicate Ltd* v *E. Pollard & Co. Ltd* [1940] 2 All E.R. 801 and views of departments on practices of public utilities.

1898, 1319, 1359–60 Rules (2) 1940, after discussions of recent cases on mortgages with Master Holland; County Court Rules (2), mostly on mortgages and County Court (Consolidation) Rules, including correspondence with Judge Gamon and complaints from creditors.

1901–2, 1909 Rules (1) 1941: on transfer of actions, after complaint by Newcastle District Registrar. Complaints about costs. County Court Rules (1) 1941, both sets mostly to deal with attempts to forestall Liabilities (War-time Adjustment) Act.

2837–8 Rules (1) 1942; correspondence with Master Jelf and others on various omissions, and Rules (2), drafted by Farwell J, on mortgages.

2678 County Court Rules (1) 1942, after approach by Registrar Hicks.

2714, 2730 Proposed amendments to the Acts. Notes on cases under the Acts and correspondence with Holland, with the PCO, with Farwell; cabinet papers; draft bill; correspondence with Judge Wethered on *Butcher* v *Poole Corporation* (1943) 59 TLR 56; further cabinet papers and minutes of evidence on mortgages.

3893–4, 3903, 3909 Complaints re practice of rating authorities and negotiations with Institute of Municipal Treasurers; questions on interpretation. Rules of 1943 and Amendment Rules and Amendment (2) Rules 1943. Suggestions from registrars and masters; questions on vires, note of meeting with Chancery judges.

3425–9 Repeal of the Acts discussed from 1946 with representations from registrars and masters; draft rules, 1947.

2736–40 Law Society representations and further agitation from Bar Council, legal press and others, opposed by Attorney-General; reviews, 1948–50 and decision to repeal the Acts, 1950.

4 The Liabilities (War-time Adjustment) Acts

2/1400–2 Proposal from Schuster sub-committee (*supra*), approved by cabinet. Draft sent to Uthwatt J; correspondence with Attorney-General, views of registrars, masters and county court judges, and of government departments and Law Society. Correspondence with PCO and others, especially on defining HP agreements; IRC views on crown debts; deputation from Building Societies' Association; memorandum from Senior Official Receiver on companies liquidation. Parliamentary proceedings on 1941 Bill.

1322 Emergency Powers Rules to forestall evasion.

1403–4 Rules under Part 1: correspondence with Registrar of Companies on registration of schemes, 1941, and with Law Society and others on registration questions.

2759–64 Correspondence of central office with Liabilities Adjustment Officers on the working of the Act; statistics, circulars, reports of cases, memoranda, copy articles, explanatory notes, 1941–8.

2728, 3610–1 Coldstream's list of possible amendments after meeting with moratorium areas MPs (1943), and notes on problems; proposals for changes from LAOs, judges; correspondence with PCO and with IRC, Customs and Ministry of Health on rates and taxes. Jowitt Committee papers. Notes of meetings of officials, drafts of 1944 Bill; correspondence with Law Society on protection of purchasers; deputation from clearing banks, protest from Association of Municipal Authorities.

2765, 3612–6 Rules 1942. Suggestions from LAOs and comments on draft rules by them and masters. Suggestions for further changes 1943, especially on Water Board's use of alternative remedies (3613 on W.T. Sansom's case, with Law Officers' opinion and correspondence with the Board). Correspondence with IRC on War Damage Act contributions, and on alternative remedies; correspondence with Chief Land Registrar.

3268 County Court Fund Rules 1945 and correspondence with PCO, Judge Gamon, Registrar Freeman-Coutts.

26/1–10 London Central district: registers of callers, proceedings books, adjustment proceedings books, moratorium order book, and moratorium settlement books, 1941–50.

11–16 London East: registers of callers, proceedings book, adjustment proceedings book, moratorium settlement book, 1941–5.

17–23 London South: registers of callers, proceedings books, adjustment proceedings book, moratorium book, 1941–7.

24–32 London West: registers of callers, proceedings book, adjustment proceedings book, moratorium settlement book.

33–336 Brighton: callers files, moratorium orders files, moratorium settlement files.

337–380 Bognor Regis: callers files and register.

381–408 Eastbourne: callers files and register.

409–37 Hastings: callers files and register.

438–76, 559–60 Portsmouth: callers files and miscellaneous documents, register of callers and adjustment proceedings book.

477 Folkestone and Hythe: index to cases, 1941–8.

478–558 Southampton: callers files, pending applications, returns of statutes, proceedings book and adjustment proceedings book.

561–2 Birmingham: proceedings book and adjustment proceedings book.

563–78 Scarborough: callers files, index and register, proceedings book, adjustment proceedings book.

579–82 Central Office: memoranda and rules, notes and reports of decided cases, forms and letters, circulars and instructions.

5 *Defence (Evacuated Areas) Regulations*

2/1387, 2726–8 Departmental discussions among legal departments, Home Office, PCO on policy; correspondence with Ministry of Home Security and with county court registrars on appointment of "custodians". J. S. Rowe on inadequate definition of HP arrangements; circulars to registrars and correspondence on interpretations, especially by Judges Archer and Hunter. LCO memorandum, December 1941 on future policy and brief for PQ. Meeting at Home Office, April 1942 and correspondence on complaints and questions. Meeting with deputation of MPs 1943; memoranda on problems and policy. Meeting to discuss M. T. Eve's opinion on War Damage Act payments, 1943.

3419 Interdepartmental committee on Rehabilitation of Coastal Towns (Jowitt) established March 1944; minutes, correspondence, memoranda by borough councils, departments and others. Discussions on Liabilities Bill (*supra*), on removal of defence works, planning law proposals. Draft report, October 1944.

3420 Discussions with Ministry of Home Security on ending the moratorium; circulars, memoranda, briefs for PQs; correspondence with PCO on means of ending it, and draft regulations with comments from departments and Liabilities Adjustment Officers, opinion of Attorney-General on legal issues. Discussions on date of termination.

6 *Limitation of Actions*

2/3570–5, 3081, 3428, 3608 Board of Trade representations on inconveniences, 1944. Departmental conference and McNair Committee established; terms widened. Minutes and evidence, report and comments; Limitations (Enemies and War Prisoners) Bill 1944 in cabinet and representations of Law Society considered. Correspondence with Attorney-General on tactics, especially re "Bethnal Green"-type cases. Other *casi omissi* remedied. Correspondence with Land Registry on G. Newsom's complaints (see 91 SJ p. 111). Foreign Office records of 'enemy territory' and discussions on anomalies, especially *'The Atlantic Scout'*. Isle of Man Bill 1945 sent by Home Office.

5 Other Defence Regulations

2/2733 War cabinet legislation committee sub-committee on classification of S.Is made under Defence Acts, and LCO memoranda, 1943, 1945.

1338 Defence (Regency) Regulations (*infra*, 289).

1379 Defence (Commencement of Enactments) Order 1939; collection of Orders in Council.

1382 Defence (Finance) Regulations: correspondence with Treasury Solicitor on circular to the courts, and with Pay Office.

1384–6, 2713 Emergency Powers (Defence) Regulations, rr. 2,62, draft from PCO 1939. Rule 54A (modifying the law of nuisance): correspondence with Treasury, Ministry of Supply on the *Hyganis* case, with memorandum by the Lord Chancellor. Rule 88(A) (1): draft circulars to JPs and chief constables on search warrants. Reg. 79C.

1876, 2732 Rules under Trading with the Enemy Act 1939; L. Burgin MP raises HL decision in *Sovfracht* (1943); memorandum from Treasury Solicitor.

1886 Arrest of S.S. 'Manzoni' referred to the committee on contraband and note on their findings, 1940.

1389 Defence (General) Regulations: discussions with PCO and meetings about proposed regulations authorising detention of suspected articles, 1940.

1388 Defence (Administration of Justice) (Scotland) Regulations 1940 approved.

1390 Emergency Powers (Defence) Regulations: 38A (looting) discussed with PCO and Humphreys LJ.

3413 Defence (General) Regulations 1939, 56AB, re-draft of 1946.

2708, 2724 Defence (Recovery of Fines) Regulations, 1942 (discussed with Home Office, PCO. Sale by Auction (Control) Order 1942: correspondence with Board of Trade, county court registrars and Chancery masters; circular to under sheriffs.

3414 Defence Regulations (6) Order 1950, discussed with PCO.

6 Ending the Wartime Restrictions

2/2734 Cease Fire (Europe) Book: draft schedule from cabinet committee on emergency legislation (1943) and plans for the "transition period"; views of local authorities and others on ending the moratorium and meetings of departmental representatives; drafts of the Book.

2735 Discussions among departments following Law Society representations, on a possible bill to declare an "end of the war" date, 1945–6, with notes of meetings, briefs for PQs.

2739 Execution of Trusts (Emergency Powers) Act (End of Emergency) Order 1948, made at request of Law Society.

3085, 3089 Emergency Powers (Defence) Bill 1945: brief from Home Office. Emergency Laws (Transitional Provisions) Bill: discussions with PCO, Home Office, representations from Law Society, Parliamentary papers.

3424 Supplies and Services (Transitional Provisions) Act 1945: draft from PCO, committee on emergency legislation papers, Law Officers' opinion on EP (Defence) Acts, discussions on Parliamentary tactics.

3427, 4328 Discussions on repeal of emergency legislation from January 1949, with Law Society, Law Officers, Chancery judges; further review 1950 with committee and cabinet papers, draft orders and Parliamentary proceedings. Order of 1950.

3431, 5162 Supplies and Services (Defence Purposes) Bill: draft by Emergency Laws Committee 1950 and correspondence; Reserve and Auxiliary Forces Rules 1951, drafts and opinions of masters and registrars.

Chapter
10

INTERNATIONAL LAW AND NATIONALITY

1
INTRODUCTION

Most of the Lord Chancellors of this period, and their permanent secretaries, shared with the majority of judges and lawyers a profoundly insular outlook towards the law which made them instinctively hostile towards almost any proposition which might trench on the sovereignty of the English courts. Bilateral treaties to facilitate the enforcement of private rights might be tolerated, though seldom encouraged, but multilateral treaties and conventions were anathema. Perhaps for this reason, the LCO regularly found that other departments (usually the Board of Trade or the Foreign Office) consulted it only after international negotiations had gone so far that this country was committed in principle, and when only the details remained open to discussion.[1] There seems to have been a marked lack of understanding in the LCO of the inevitability of increased international regulation in the wake of rapid developments in communications and trade and an unwillingness to initiate improvements in legal facilities.

Between the wars the pressure for such initiatives came mostly from the shipping and mercantile community, who were the principal sufferers from the undeveloped state of private international law, and the report of the Sumner Committee on British and Foreign Legal Procedure gave their campaigning a boost.[2] The first fruits came from the Geneva Conference in the shape of a protocol on arbitrations, threatening inroads into the supervisory jurisdiction of the courts which had only recently been decisively re-stated in **Czarnikov *v* Roth Schmidt & Co.**[3] Schuster "protested in season and out of season against any such protocol being entered into" but Cave was barely able to persuade the cabinet even to authorise revisions to make it less objectionable.[4] Another League of Nations initiative in the same field led to a 1927 convention on the enforcement of foreign awards, again pressed by the Board of Trade on a doubting LCO.[5] A small committee under Greer J approved the convention, however, and it was given statutory force in 1930.[6] Later in the decade an agitation developed for a relaxation of the courts' control over arbitrators and the Rome Institute produced a draft convention which predictably departed from the "Anglo-Saxon model". The draft found no favour with Hailsham but the papers on this episode are chiefly interesting in revealing the ignorance of his higher officials of the issues at stake.[7]

A similarly negative outlook pervaded attempts to improve the position of the suitor who wished to enforce English judgments abroad, although England could only be the gainer since most overseas judgments could already be enforced here.[8] The Board of Trade and Foreign Office made the running, while the Lord Chancellor referred first the general principle then the specific conventions which were negotiated with France and others to successive committees under Greer. A very useful measure, the Foreign Judgments (Reciprocal Enforcement) Act 1933 was ultimately passed.[9]

The moving spirit within the Foreign Office was W.E. (later Sir Eric) Beckett and his notorious prolixity ("if left to himself [he will] probably produce something so long and technical, and elaborate that none of those for whose benefit it is written would be very likely to read it")[10] may have dampened any enthusiasm Schuster and his subordinates possessed. For his part Beckett had some grounds for complaint: he was, for instance, dismayed at the almost neurotic suspiciousness shown by the Chancery judges when faced with a laboriously negotiated civil procedure convention with Belgium—five years in the making and only to enable foreign official register entries to be accepted as evidence of their contents without further proof—where once again England had all to gain and nothing to lose.[11] He was also put out at their view, accepted by the Lord Chancellor, that legislation (the Evidence (Foreign Documents) Act 1933) was required to implement the convention.

Sometimes there were sound reasons for caution, however. The Brussels maritime conventions of the 1920s, for example, were embarrassing because they pre-empted a decision on the deadlocked issue of crown liability in tort and consequently provoked opposition from the Admiralty.[12] As for the wider international movement for the unification of private law, Napier summed up the Office's view when asked by the Foreign Office whether the revival of the Rome Institute (to which the League had delegated this task) was to be encouraged:

> "On many subjects . . . our law is so different from that of other nations and so difficult to alter that an attempt at unification is apt to cause our lawyers a lot of trouble and expense in attending conferences with no result except inconvenience and embarrassment . . .
>
> Again I have sympathy for the restiveness of Englishmen when they are asked to alter their laws so as to follow the law of a foreign country which looks very just on paper but is vitiated in practice by the corruption and inefficiency of the foreign country's legal system."[13]

After the Second World War it was increasingly from new international organisations that initiatives came and the demands for information and comment from the U.N. and its offspring came so thick and fast that the Office was provoked into threatening to ignore one "ridiculous questionnaire" from UNESCO altogether,[14] while Rieu felt it "a waste of time for us to be represented on the I[nternational] O[rganisation] C[ommittee] to be sent the vast wads of paper which they circulate".[15] None of the projects espoused by these bodies appealed to the Office, least of all the proposed European Convention of Human Rights. Since the LCO had already objected to difficult questions like divorce and maintenance orders being discussed in the Council of Europe,[16] it was naturally displeased to receive a draft convention from the Foreign Office (July, 1950) with the brisk assertion that its rejection was not practical politics. Jowitt was "not prepared to encourage our European friends to jeopardise our whole system of law, which we have laboriously built up over the centuries, in favour of some half-baked scheme to be administered by some unknown court"[17] and if he could not get it rejected, he certainly laboured hard to remove the individual's right to petition and modify objectionably wide or vague "rights" in the draft. A similar rearguard action was fought by the LCO and the Law Officers against the Geneva Convention on War Crimes on which, again, they had not been consulted at an early stage. They could not persuade the cabinet to reject proposals which were "plainly inconsistent with the criminal law"[18] in putting foreign nationals involuntarily in this country in a favoured position, but they succeeded in retarding the UK's accession to the Convention.

Finally, mention should be made of the LCO files dealing with the punishment of war crimes committed in the Second World War, which have been used in a recent study of the Nuremberg trials.[19] They are of particular value in illuminating the inglorious history of the attempt to prosecute some of the lesser German offenders and on the conduct of "Operation Old Lace" (the trials of minor war criminals by German courts), which Jowitt described as "the most remarkable achievement in the whole of my legal experience".[20]

Notes

1 *e.g. 2/755: Schuster to Attorney-General, 28.6.1923; 2/4956: Lord Advocate to Lord Chancellor, 22.2.1951.*

2 *PP 1919 (Cmd 251) XXIV, 333.*

3 *[1919] 2 KB 478.*

4 *Arbitration Clauses (Protocol) Act 1924. 2/755: Schuster to Chitty, 25.10.1924.*

5 *2/1038: Schuster to Greer J, 7.5.1927.*

6 ***Ibid**: Greer report, 24.5.1927. Arbitration (Foreign Awards) Act 1930.*

7 *2/1789: Napier to J. G. Archibald, 10.12.1937, to Foreign Office, 1.3.1938.*

8 *See Cheshire, **Private International Law** (9th ed., 1974), 664–72.*

9 *2/1687: Schuster to Foreign Office, 12.7.1926. Greer Committee reports, June 1929 and 12.12.1932.*

10 *2/1091: Sir W. Graham-Harrison (PCO) to Schuster, 10.1.1933.*

11 *2/1961: Chitty to Schuster, 2.11.1927; 2/1962: Napier to Beckett, 18.6.1930.*

12 *2/1425: M. Gwyer to Schuster, 5.2.1927; Napier's minute, 25.5.1934.*

13 *2/3439: to Beckett, 1.11.1945.*

14 *2/4315: Dobson to Innes, 19.10.1951.*

15 *2/4316: minute of 28.4.1950.*

16 *2/4145: Newman's minute, 15.5.1950.*

17 *2/5580: to Dalton, 3.8.1950.*

18 *2/4311: Coldstream to Attorney-General, 19.9.1949.*

19 *J. and A. Tusa, **The Nuremberg Trial** (1983).*

20 *2/2991: to E. Bevin, 14.2.1949.*

2
PUBLIC INTERNATIONAL LAW

1 Diplomatic Privileges and the Diplomatic Service

2/1150 Committee on employment of women in the diplomatic and consular services. Schuster's correspondence as chairman, especially with Rae (Treasury) and Vansittart (FO), evidence and report (1936).

4280 Various enquiries from Foreign Office, 1931–9 on US and Chilean consuls subpoenaed at assizes; instructions to consuls on evidence and other matters.

722 Discussions with Foreign and Home Offices and PCO on amendment to law

on trial of British consular officials, with list of offences committed by them, 1923–6.

1410 Diplomatic Privileges (Extension) Bill 1940: copy Home Office and Foreign Office papers, memoranda of discussions with Attorney-General and others; draft bill with notes; cabinet papers and papers sent by Foreign Office for information.

4281 Diplomatic Privileges (Extension) Bill 1944: Foreign Office proposals, cabinet papers, Parliamentary proceedings.

4282 Consular Conventions Bill: cabinet papers and brief for Parliamentary proceedings.

4433 Lord Chancellor consulted by FO on whether Cavendish-Bentinck is entitled to a pension, 1947. His opinion and that of the Treasury Solicitor.

4664–5 Complaints of abuses by *Tass*: meeting of officials and briefs from Foreign Office for Vansittart's motion; interdepartmental meeting and committee papers.

4956 Cabinet papers and protests by Lord Chancellor, Attorney-General and Lord Advocate on FO proposal to extend immunity to NATO. Continuing discussions on scope of immunity.

2 United Nations

2/3247, 4281 1944 Privileges for UNRRA (*supra*).

3105 United Nations Bill 1946: brief from Foreign Office.

4305 UN league of lawyers: discussions with LCJ, Lord Normand, FO, 1946.

4307 Correspondence with Lord Cecil on his proposal for a permanent court to try international crime, 1946.

4308 Proposed convention on presumption of death, 1948: correspondence with Foreign Office, opposition from LCO and lobbying from Jewish and refugee organisations.

4315 LCO complains of questionnaire on status of women; correspondence with FO, 1949.

4316–7 Documents and discussions on draft convention on stateless persons.

4306, 4318, 4672 Miscellaneous matters connected with the UN.

3 Treaties and Conventions

2/313 Hague Convention: memoranda by Kennedy LJ (1913) and Lord Dunedin; correspondence with FO.

576 Treaties of Peace (Examination of Witnesses) Rules 1921, order drafted by PCO.

628 Interdepartmental conference (1923) on Foreign Office proposals, with memoranda and correspondence.

825 Correspondence with Foreign Office on ratification of the Kellogg Pact by Irish Free State and extensive copy FO papers. Report of legal sub-committee on "counsellors of state".

1237 Papers from Foreign Office on mode of accession to treaties by UK, 1939.

1424 Anglo-US Liquor Treaty (1924) and Napier's papers from committee on interpretation of the Treaty, 1931.

1438 Orders made under Domicile Act 1861 re estates of Britons abroad, after commercial treaties.

3443, 4160 Peace treaties with satellite countries; 1947 Orders in Council. Position of Isle of Man and Channel Islands under future treaties, memorandum by FO, 1950.

4435 Foreign Office cabinet paper on proposed convention on rights in the sea bed. Notes of meeting and of debates at International Law Association conference 1948.

4669–70, 5570, 6274 Council of Europe's proposed convention on human rights sent by FO 1950; cabinet papers and correspondence with other departments, especially on the right of individual petition; further cabinet and Parliamentary proceedings.

4 War Crimes and Post-war Germany

2/2662, 2972–6 Preliminary papers. Correspondence with J. H. Morgan (1940) on proposals for publicising atrocities; papers from "London International Assembly" and the (unofficial) McNair Commission 1943. Correspondence with Home Office and Sir Cecil Hurst on terms and procedure of Hurst Committee. Meetings of ministers, Lord Chancellor's correspondence with Foreign Secretary on proposed UN War Crimes Commission, and Simon's attempts to make it effective. Discussions on PCO draft War Crimes Bill and memoranda by Simon with his own draft bill (1944).

2977–8 Draft convention for surrender of war criminals; meetings of ministers and establishment of Finlay Committee; minutes and correspondence, 1944–6.

2980–3, 2985, 2988 Trials of major war criminals in Germany: cabinet papers on UNWCC report and discussions with Attorney-General, Foreign Office, War Office and Judge Advocate-General on process. Meetings with US's Rosenbaum delegation (1945), full discussions and agreement (Cmd 6668); war cabinet papers for judges' visit to Berlin, copy FO papers from war crimes executive (Nuremberg).

2984, 2989, 2990–1, 2993–6 Other trials in Germany: copy FO documents, memorandum on progress from Law Officers, notes on case against industrialists and generals. LC's visit to Germany (1947), documents on "Operation Old Lace" including correspondence with N. Macaskie and FO. LC's visit to French war crimes services at Baden-Baden. Meetings of legal departments on trial of generals, medical reports and correspondence on trial of Manstein, including appointment of Judge Collingwood.

2997–8, 3692 Discussions on "The Peleus" (1947), and Lord Cork's motion, (1950). Also on the request for extradition of Dr. Dering to Poland (1948).

2999 Italian war criminals: Italian request for remissions, Jowitt's investigation, meetings with FO, Judge-Advocate General, War Office.

2983, 2986, 3001–2 Japanese war crimes: copy documents on Far Eastern International Military Tribunal correspondence on nomination of a British judge; correspondence with Hankey on the trials, especially that of Shigemitsu; case of the SS "Suez Maru" discussed with Shinwell.

4426–8 Clemency for German war criminals. Discussions of 1951 with Law Officers and others.

4309–14 Geneva Convention: minutes of meetings of working party on war crimes, and cabinet committee on proposed conventions; discussions among legal departments of article 18, and lengthy departmental meetings (extending to 1957) on implementing the Convention.

3436, 6675 Attorney-General's proposals for legal administration in Germany; meetings of officials and opinion of Law Officers; cabinet papers and extensive material on drafting the occupation statute (1948), including correspondence with FO, meetings of officials and ministers, drafts, cabinet papers and copy FO papers on negotiations.

2979, 2990–1, 3000, 3250, 4423, 4425 Control Commission Courts: correspondence with Foreign Office and prospective appointees in 1944; report on conditions in Germany, 1947 and of committee set up in consequence (1948); queries over powers and correspondence with Judges Inglis and O'Sullivan and the Foreign Office on extensions of jurisdiction; also on complaints of executive interference, 1947–50.

5 Visiting Forces

2/2715–22, 3022 US (Visiting Forces) Act 1942. Cabinet and Foreign Office papers, Parliamentary papers; meetings and correspondence on enforcement of civil claims *v* allied servicemen; lengthy discussions in the "Bolero" committee and with departments and judges leading to Defence (US Forces—Administration of Estates) Regulations and Rules, 1942–3; meeting with Foreign Office and others on jurisdiction over UK forces in the USA; consultations with LCJ and others on Registrar Hayman's question re witness attendance at US courts martial, leading to RSC(3) 1943; discussions with FO, Treasury Solicitor on jurisdiction over US merchant seamen.

4432 Polish courts martial: query by E. F. Iwi leading to discussions with FO and a PQ, 1946–7.

5161 Visiting Forces Bill, 1949; minutes of meetings at Home Office, cabinet papers etc. Suspended until late 1951.

3277 US servicemen's bastards (see *supra*, 253).

3416–7 G.I. brides: interdepartmental meetings of 1946 on US divorces and possible legal assistance; discussions with Law Society and papers on its "American Divorce Department" to 1949.

6 Miscellaneous

2/3216 Foreign Office request for LC's opinion on sovereignty questions in the Sudan. Law Officers' opinion, copy treaties etc., 1946.

3217 Corfu Channel incident. Note, briefing papers from FO and correspondence, 1946.

3218 Cabinet papers and LC's opinion on interception of Jewish immigration ships; correspondence with Admiralty, notes of meetings, and of Privy Council hearing of *The Asyra*, 1946–8.

3441 Visit of Russian delegation, 1947. Biographical sketches, notes of meeting etc.

3220 LC's note on talk with Italians on Eritrea (1949), and memorandum by FO.

3222–3 Report of Makins Committee on status of the Korean conflict and copy correspondence from FO and Attorney-General on Foreign Enlistment Act, Army Act and other issues, 1950.

3438, 3442 Correspondence with FO and Attorney-General on proposed delegation of legal experts to Greece, 1945.

2654 Minor alterations to Foreign Service Bill 1943.

1509 International museums committee on stolen exhibits: correspondence with H. C. Gutteridge and Home Office, 1938.

1510 Query on arrestment of seamen's wages passed on by Home Office, 1936.

874 Committee on extradition suggested by Attorney-General; correspondence with FO but vetoed by Home Secretary, 1926.

5171 Approach by L. Heald on case of J. Abdu's extradition from Kenya to Ethiopia and FO opinion, 1951.

5191 Lord Chancellor's views on measures against Persia, 1951.

3
PRIVATE INTERNATIONAL LAW

1 Arbitration

2/594 Award by mixed arbitral tribunal, 1923: Order in Council for enforcement after correspondence with Chitty and PCO.

755 Arbitration (Protocol) Act 1924: correspondence with Board of Trade and F. D. MacKinnon on Geneva Conference, and MacKinnon's report and memorandum on draft protocol (1922). Cabinet papers and departmental correspondence on draft convention and bill.

1038–40 Views of MacKinnon and Chitty on draft convention on enforcement of foreign awards. Copy correspondence of Claughton Scott as UK representative on League sub-committee. Greer report (1927) and Chitty's dissent, with Committee papers. Draft Arbitration (Foreign Awards) Bill, 1930 from PCO and correspondence on Parliamentary proceedings.

1683 Correspondence with Master Bonner on rules, 1930, 1935.

1686 Orders in Council, 1930–9 and correspondence with Foreign Office on definition of reciprocal provisions.

1789 Correspondence with Foreign Office and representations from trade organisations re the "Rome draft", 1938.

3589 Anglo-French conference proposal on 'final' arbitrations rejected after discussions with FO, Board of Trade.

2 Service of Process and Law of Evidence

2/17, 19, 126, 172, 176, 178, 189 Practice change of 1889 discussed with PCO and FO, and Order drafted. SC Rule Committee discussions on difficulties and minor changes, 1896. Stringer's paper on evidence for foreign tribunals (1903); RSC Order XI applied to further countries by FO 1905–11. Discussions with Colonial Office on rules under Foreign Tribunals (Evidence) Act 1856.

391, 555 Rule Committee discussions on service out of jurisdiction in foreclosure proceedings, 1916. Rule withdrawn 1920 after Scottish complaints.

1041 Complaints against Russian companies by commercial bodies, 1925, discussed with Chitty and Board of Trade and meeting with representative of complainants.

1709 Proposal to extend order XI (1930): long correspondence with W. E. Beckett (FO) and Master Bonner and draft direction for LC; see Matrimonial Causes (Foreign Conventions) Rules 1932.

580 Discussions with Treasury and FO on possibility of reducing the costs of commissions rogatoires, 1922.

593 Complaints of delays in Spain and Belgium discussed with FO (1920) and draft convention with France.

704 Complaint that RSC are defective for service abroad on infants. Opinion of G. Beyfus and views of Chancery judges, 1930.

1238 Query on taking of evidence in England for an Indian action, 1940.

1251, 1277 1931 County Court (Services Abroad) Rules, and 1933 amendment.

3897, 4095 High Court Writs (Service Abroad) Order 1943 made at FO request; settled with Master Jelf.

1961–5 Anglo-Belgian convention on civil procedure. Approach by FO (1924); sent to Chitty; drafts by FO, meetings of officials, views of Chancery judges; draft bill from PCO; correspondence with FO and the judges, and officials' meetings; cabinet papers, Parliamentary papers on the Evidence (Foreign Documents) Act and Order in Council 1933. Correspondence with Colonial Office on extension to dominions and colonies, with views of Chancery judges.

1966, 4146 Extension to France proposed by Foreign Office (1933). Draft and views of Maugham J, draft report for Privy Council. Cmd 5476 of 1937 and proposals for revised Anglo-French convention, 1950.

3 Enforcement of Judgments

2/177, 252–3 Phillimore's memorandum to SC Rule Committee (1904); London Chamber of Commerce press for extension of Judgments Extension Act 1868 (1910).

483 Sumner Committee on Legal Procedure 1919, report.

578B 1922 SC Rules on enforcement of dominions judgments.

1051–2, 627 Committee on Arrestment of Foreigners' Property (1922), set up after pressure from Association of British Chambers of Commerce. Memoranda on foreign law, evidence, draft report, correspondence. See also (627) proposed legislation on Russian claims.

1687–96 Reciprocal enforcement of judgments. Correspondence with Chitty and Board of Trade and Foreign Office, 1926, and further on establishment of committee under Greer. Discussions on membership; draft treaty with Belgium sent by FO and considered. Officials' committee set up, and report (1931) with draft bill. Second committee under Greer, correspondence, minutes, report (Cmd 4273 of 1932) and draft bill. Memoranda on talks with foreign countries, draft convention. Foreign Judgments (Reciprocal Enforcement) Bill 1933, and Parliamentary proceedings. Correspondence on Orders in Council applying conventions to the dominions, and on conventions with Belgium, France, Czechoslovakia, Italy, Uruguay, Switzerland and Austria; questions on interpretation from solicitors.

1048 Complaint by Board of Trade, memorandum from Dominions Office on notes of official discussions with Irish Free State on reciprocal enforcement of warrants, 1926.

1291 Solicitors enquiry, 1935, re enforcement of county court judgments in Scotland.

3440 FO attempts to secure reciprocity on war damage legislation, 1945.

1726–7, 1741–2, 1799, 1822 Conventions with Netherlands and Italy and extension to colonies; also with Iraq, Greece, France, Switzerland.

4 Matrimonial Orders

2/665 Rules under Maintenance Orders (Facilities) Act 1920 made in 1922 after consultations with Home and Colonial Offices and Chief Magistrate at Bow Street.

2/1751, 4097, 4145, 6183, 4215, 4227 Notes of meeting of officials on proposed reciprocal enforcement of maintenance orders with Australia, 1927. Revived 1930, views of Lord Merrivale and Judge Hill-Kelly, further meetings and correspondence. Foreign Office presses for action or reference to Council of Europe, 1948 and 1950, and LCO memoranda and views of other departments. Proposed international convention 1950 discussed with Home Office, Principal Probate Registry. Problems of foreign marriages discussed in 1949; see also 6136 (Morton Commission papers).

1121–2, 1445, 3236, 5246–7 Indian divorce rules 1927 and correspondence with Colonial Office on proposed extension. Committee on amendments to the Indian and Colonial Divorce Act 1926 (1938) and bill. Applications to Kenya (1926), Jamaica (1932) and Ceylonese independence (1947).

1351 Marriages Validity Act 1939: validity of banns published in Eire challenged; memoranda on the law, draft bill and correspondence with PCO and government whips.

5 Legal Aid

2/1681, 1799 Convention with Belgium discussed with FO and Master Bonner; drafts and correspondence on ratification (Cmd 4639 of 1932).

1851 Discussions with FO on French convention (Cmd 5182 of 1936). Correspondence and draft convention with USA, 1937.

988 League of Nations report and questionnaires 1923–4; LCO replies and correspondence with Chitty.

5544 Discussions with FO on Lord President's wish to restrict legal aid for foreigners, 1948–50.

6 Other Aspects

2/199 Bills of Exchange: correspondence with Board of Trade re drafting new bill following Hague Conference; representatives from Council of Bankers, M. D. Chalmers and others, 1910–14.

1425–7 Brussels Maritime Convention on maritime liens. Discussions with PCO, Board of Trade, cabinet papers, towards making draft protocols and signing the convention, 1922–34. Maritime Conventions Bill and subsequent discussions with Admiralty and Law Officers on immunity of state owned ships, clause in Administration of Justice Bill, and Parliamentary proceedings.

1428–9 Conventions on Aircraft Damage and Cautionary Arrest: drafts from Air Ministry, 1933 and correspondence on possible legislation.

1433–4	Conventions on aircraft salvage and collisions (1934) circulated by Air Ministry with departmental notes.
1430–1	Proposed unification of sale of goods law: papers sent by Foreign Office (1934); LC's committee set up under Roche LJ, report (1936) and memorandum by H. C. Gutteridge.
1432, 3439	Draft from the Rome Institute on innkeepers' liability with report by Home Office and correspondence with Attorney-General and Treasury. Opinion from C. Asquith KC. Discussions on whether to renew support, 1945.

4
NATIONALITY AND ALIENS

2/595–6	Saunders and Blandy naturalisation bills, 1920, 1923; correspondence with Home Office on procedure, and on refusal of certificates.
664	Summary Jurisdiction (Aliens) Order 1920.
2649, 3232, 3241, 4474, 3432	Cabinet papers on British Nationality Bill (1938); cabinet discussions, 1942, and correspondence with Home Office, PCO and women's organisations. Committee set up 1946 and draft bill from PCO 1948; correspondence with Lord Pethick-Lawrence, briefs from Home Office and PCO, cabinet papers; Parliamentary papers and correspondence on individual cases, especially L. W. Boalth. Enrolment of Deeds (Change of Name) Regulations 1949.
4487, 3689	Ireland Bill, 1949: legal opinions of Lord Chancellor on doubtful points; correspondence with Foreign Office and Lord Simon especially on Passport Office practice; cabinet papers etc. Long correspondence with Simon and Commonwealth Relations Office on effect of British Nationality Act on Eire.
3221	Correspondence with Ministry of Health and Lord President, 1949 on foreign visitors seeking NHS treatment.
3690	Brief and correspondence on Vansittart's PQ on deportations, 1949.
874, 6294, 115, 239	Extradition: DPP suggests committee on treaties, 1926, rejected by Home Office. 1949 discussions with Home Office and meeting on practice of reciprocal execution of warrants with Eire. Appeals to the Lord Chancellor against extradition in 1896, 1906, 1914.

CHURCH AND STATE

THE CROWN, THE CONSTITUTION AND THE EMPIRE

1
INTRODUCTION

> "It has, however, for a long time been the habit of successive Private Secretaries to the King to ask for the view of the Lord Chancellor on matters which are not directly the concern or function of the Lord Chancellor's Office, in accordance with a general but undefined idea that in matters which raise semi-legal or semi-constitutional points the Lord Chancellor stands in a peculiarly confidential relationship with the crown".[1]

The Lord Chancellor was not often asked to exercise his function as the constitutional adviser to the sovereign. The only noteworthy instances recorded here are in 1924 and 1935, the former occasioned by Asquith's complaints about the use of the dissolution, the latter by rumours that the opposition might complain that the government was exploiting the Silver Jubilee, and in each case there is only a memorandum by Schuster of impeccable orthodoxy; the abdication crisis occurred during Hailsham's illness and is not dealt with directly at all in these papers.[2] There are, however, several files relating to the sovereign's incapacity, legal or medical, to perform his functions, which had been highlighted by George V's serious illness in 1928–9, and they cover negotiations with the Dominions and the Regency Act of 1937.[3] There is also a collection of memoranda by the indefatigable barrister E. F. Iwi, whose excessive concern for constitutional rectitude in the midst of war drove Simon to note "why does he not propose an Act of Parliament to render an invasion of this country unlawful?" There is also one interesting example of the King making a personal attempt to alter the law: both in 1922, when the Russell divorce case was in the news, and again in 1925 on the occasion of the Dennistown case he made known his "feelings of disgust and shame at the daily published discreditable and nauseating evidence".[5] Schuster made an excellent reasoned reply to his suggestion of trials *in camera* and Cave did not favour a government measure to restrict reporting, but did support generally a private member's bill, and the file records the inter-departmental discussions and the lobbying to which the government was subjected.

Notes

1 *2/1131: Schuster's minute, 28.5.1941.*
2 *For Schuster's role see F. Donaldson, **Edward VIII** (1974), 293.*
3 *See (1937–38) 1 MLR 66 (E. C. S. Wade).*
4 *2/1339.*
5 *2/775: Stamfordham to Lord Chancellor, 6.3.1925.*

2
ROYAL TITLES, REGALIA AND MARRIAGES

2/684	Royal title, seals etc. after creation of Irish Free State. Conferences convened by Home Office (1924–6) draft bill and orders, discussions with departments. Cabinet and Parliamentary procedures on Royal Titles Bill, Order in Council and Crown Office Rules (2) 1927.
1339	E. F. Iwi's memorandum on power to send regalia abroad, with Lord Chancellor's comments, 1941.
3371 B	Meetings with Dominions Office and India Office about change of title following Indian independence, 1946.
3374	Query from Garter King of Arms on the royal surname, 1947.
5145	Query from Hardinge on power to take the Imperial Crown out of the country, 1939.
4402	Consent to marriage of Prince Paul and Princess Frederica, 1938.
3371A	Foreign Office seek advice on Duke of Brunswick's request (technically an enemy alien) 1946.
3375, 3379	Royal warrants on Princess Elizabeth's and Lord Harewood's marriages 1947.
6352	Discussions with PCO, H. Lascelles *et al.* on the Royal Marriages Act (1949), renewed 1952, 1955.

3
DEMISE OF THE CROWN

2/145	Demise of the Crown Bill 1901: Sir C. Ilbert's brief to the Lord Chancellor and notes on demise of William IV.
255	"Diary" of the events on Edward VII's death, 1910.
2094	Court of Claims, 1910, with list of claims and some correspondence.
2686	Memorandum by Iwi, "not of any practical use", 1942.

4
REGENCY ARRANGEMENTS

2/825, 897	Reports of cabinet legal sub-committee on "counsellors of state", 1929, and Home Office question on the homage of bishops, with Lord Chancellor's memorandum.
1332–5	Regency Bill, 1937. Correspondence with Lord Stamfordham, 1930, on Imperial Conference. Resumed 1934, discussions with PCO, Dominions Office; notes of discussions; Law Officers' opinion on succession; draft bill (1935) and cabinet papers, copy telegrams to and from dominion governments; further drafting correspondence: further opinion of Law Officers (1937).
1338	Defence (Regency) Regulations 1941: correspondence with PCO, HO; cabinet decision to withhold them.
3034	Regency Bill 1943: Simon's amending bill; cabinet papers, correspondence with Dominions Office.
5133	Councillors of State Bill 1952, includes Coldstream memorandum of November, 1951 on previous bills.
6314	Query on royal tour to Australia, 1951.

5
THE ROYAL PREROGATIVE AND CONSTITUTIONAL QUESTIONS

2/2078	Lord Chancellor's opinion on the possibility of using the veto against a private bill not properly sanctioned in Parliament, 1907.
2199	Memorandum on rights of the sovereign in the choice of ministers.
1337	Visit to Canada: question from Dominions Office on mode of assenting to bills there, 1939.
2778	Brief for PQ on Roman Catholic disabilities (1943) and press cuttings of 1949.
3008	Schuster's view on procedure on petitions to be heard at the Bar of the House of Commons, 1943.
2650	Notes on the prerogative power to create new government offices, for cabinet discussion on Ministry of Town and Country Planning Bill 1943.
3377	Iwi's memorandum on allegiance, 1949.
3683	Discussions on whether the Queen should be on the electoral register, 1945.
4416, 1226	Two memoranda by Schuster on the King's right to dissolve Parliament, 1924, 1935. Brief for PQ on resignation of cabinet ministers, 1935.
4872	Napier's memorandum on procedure for procuring the royal assent, 1949.
4486	Censorship of Plays (Repeal) Bill 1949: discussion of survival of prerogative after Act of 1843; cabinet papers, Home Office and Lord Chancellor's views, Law Officers' opinion.

6
OTHER MATTERS CONCERNING THE CROWN

2/775	Judicial Proceedings (Regulation of Reports) Bill, 1925: correspondence with Lord Stamfordham on the King's wish to curtail prurient newspaper reports.
1229	Correspondence with Wigram on B.B.C. request to broadcast the King's Speech 1935.
3225	Correspondence on entrée to Buckingham Palace for judges, 1946.
2692	Confidential memoranda from PM's Secretary on King's views on the bishops' poverty, 1942.
3373	Correspondence with Privy Purse on Ministry of Labour suggestion of a "Whitley Council" for royal household, 1946.
3376	Office memoranda etc. on suggestion that Queen becomes Visitor of Girton College, 1948.
3540B	Correspondence with Lascelles on proposal that Queen should be made a KC, 1948.
5838–40	Queen Alexandra as patron of St. Katharine's Hospital. Extensive papers including discussions with Charity Commissioners 1889; reports of 1866, 1878, 1893; correspondence on changes in rules, 1912 and scheme of 1914, especially with Archbishop of Canterbury, H. A. White, Charity Commissioners. Discussions of 1928–9 on sale of site in Regent's Park, on new rules of 1934 and move to Hatfield in 1946.
681, 4437	Office of Lord Great Chamberlain. Schuster's comments on a proposal of 1924; appointments *ad interim* in 1901, 1928, 1936, 1946 after extensive correspondence with Office of Works, Law Officers, Home Office *et al.* on rival claims.

7

THE EMPIRE

(see also under 'THE JUDICIAL COMMITTEE OF THE PRIVY COUNCIL', *supra*, 46–50)

1 The Statute of Westminster

2/1190, 1234, 2667 Cabinet memoranda 1931; correspondence with Dominions Office especially on disputes with Irish Free State. Law Officers' memorandum (1934) on s.4; Iwi's memorandum (1942) on its effect on the Abbey.

2 Australia

2/1115, 1239, 1751, 1935-7, 3251, 3254

3 Canada

2/3239 Newfoundland 1949. Cabinet papers, Law Officers' opinion and Jowitt's contrary view; correspondence with Dominions Office.

1236, 1337, 2683, 3232, 3696 Other matters.

4 South Africa

2/905–6, 1233 (on use of seals), 3249, 3454, 3462, 4508

1235, 1237 South African Bills sent by Dominions Office 1934 and correspondence on accession to treaties, 1939.

5 India

2/1444, 1834, 2970, 3040, 3234, 4488–90, 4494

3093 Proclamations of Emergency Bill 1945, draft sent for comment.

6 Ireland

2/825, 2571, 5683

819 Boundary commission. 1924 cabinet papers, opinions of Law Officers and Lord Chancellor on position if no commissioner is appointed by Northern Ireland; proposed referral to Privy Council and arrangements for commission.

1231 Conference on disputes with Irish Free State, 1932: correspondence with Dominions Office and others.

3237–8,3689 Eire Bill 1949: sent for observations and referred to masters; legal opinions on effect of repeal of Eire Executive Authority (External Relations) Act 1936; cabinet papers, notes of meetings between English and Irish officials; correspondence with Commonwealth Relations Office on brief for Simon's PQ on nationality implications.

Chapter

2

PARLIAMENT AND LEGISLATION

1

PARLIAMENT

1 Introduction

Although the Lord Chancellor was Speaker of the House of Lords and in that capacity was likely to be closely involved in controversies and reform proposals for Parliament, these papers are not very revealing on the most important episode, for there is no material on the crisis of 1909–11. The Parliament Bill of 1949 is covered, and includes notes of discussions among the permanent officials and material on the influence of tactical considerations concerning the controversial legislation already in the pipeline, as well as the better known inter-party conferences and proposals.[1]

On less momentous topics one can follow the consternation of officials when a clergyman pointed out that the number of secretaries of state in the Commons exceeded that permitted by statute, and there are extensive files on the drawn out discussions following the report of a select committee in 1941 which recommended a limit of sixty on the number of ministerial office-holders in the Commons.

In the Lords the most disturbing question, apart from the great question of its future (if any) was the admission of women peers. These files contain some good background material on the decision in Lady Rhondda's case[2] and the Lord Chancellor's indignation when the peers' verdict was questioned, and also on the cabinet discussions in Attlee's government, which declined to act on the grounds that a further infusion of hereditary members was contrary to party policy. Likewise, the embarrassment over the position of the Irish representative peers after the creation of the Irish Free State is well illustrated, and the position of peers holding armed service commissions who made speeches hostile to the government, in particular Admiral Lord Fraser who spoke against the Parliament Bill 1949, is considered.[3] The Lords also experienced considerable difficulty in dealing with those who sought to disinter abeyant peerages, such as Lady St. Davids who "collects peerages as she might collect postage stamps"[4] and the background material to the committee which reported in 1926 is of some interest.

Notes

1 *PP 1947–8 (Cmd 7380) XXII, 1001 summaries the discussions and previous proposals.*
2 *[1922] AC 339.*
3 *2/4504; Lord Chancellor to First Lord, 24.6.1948.*
4 *2/598: Schuster to G. Proby, 22.1.1923.*

2 Composition

1 The House of Lords

2/31, 2259 Mar peerage case: correspondence with Ponsonby, 1889 and abusive letter from Lord Garisch, 1916.

2029 Lord Selborne's case, 1895

4503 Notes on appointment of Deputy Speaker (1900) with precedents, and letter to Lord Wright, 1948.

598 Abeyant peerages committee: notes by G. Proby, Schuster and others on the general law and pending claims (1921). Proposed committee discussed. Correspondence with Lord Stamfordham on its report, 1926.

2097, 965, 967, 335, 1446, 3693 Irish representative peers. Election of Lord Curzon (1908); formal papers on elections (1911–6); memoranda, Law Officers' and counsel's opinion, correspondence with Irish Office, Home Office and cabinet discussions on Lord Oranmore's campaign for continued elections, 1923–36. Also notes of 1949 on protocol.

386 Title Deprivation Bill 1916: correspondence with Lord Stamfordham, draft bill, and report of select committee.

388, 439, 599, 760, 966, 5764 Women in the Lords. Women's Emancipation Bill (1918) with notes of LC's opinion and cabinet papers; Sex Disqualification Bill (1919), correspondence with PCO, Attorney-General, Muir M^C^Kenzie and others, cabinet papers. Lady Rhondda's case: judgments, report and other papers. Memoranda on Parliament (Qualification of Peeresses) Bill (1924), and on Lady Clifton's petition (1925). Correspondence with Morrison and Attlee, memoranda by Iwi on need for legislation (1946); cabinet papers on Lord Reading's motion (1949).

968, 1550 Life peerages. Memoranda by Napier (1926), notes on Lord Strickland's Bill (1937) and Parliamentary proceedings.

1137 Schuster's notes on right of secretaries of state to sit in Lords, 1931.

2 *The House of Commons*

2/689 Revd. Skipton's complaint that too many secretaries of state were in the House (1929); correspondence with the Lord President, meetings with Prime Minister's office, draft bill and Parliamentary proceedings.

1135 Correspondence with Treasury on MPs holding offices of profit and on expenses etc., 1926 and 1931, with 1939 memorandum by Attorney-General.

1136, 1411, 3042, 3010–1 Select Committee on Offices of Profit under the Crown: draft evidence of Lord Chancellor, notes on Chiltern Hundreds (Schuster), copies of other evidence and memoranda, and report (Cmd 120 of 1940–1). House of Commons Disqualification (Temporary Provisions) Bill (1941): memorandum by H. J. Wilson, meetings and cabinet papers, draft bill. Similar bill of 1944 with brief from Law Officers' Department. Report by Lord Chancellor and Law Officers on possible infringements (1945), papers for select committee, cabinet papers and correspondence with PCO. Further (interdepartmental) committee 1949 and draft bill (1950), cabinet papers.

3032 Lists of MPs who are barristers, 1945–57.

3449 Brief for PQ on ministers holding company directorships, with note on Lord Annan's case 1945.

4706 Correspondence with Lord Nathan and others on the "History of Parliament" project, 1940–54.

3685 Notes on position of under-sheriffs as candidates for Parliament, 1950.

3 *Parliamentary reform*

2/4414 Livery Companies petition to retain their rights under the Representation of the People Bill 1917.

597 Committee on Lords reform. Lowther's bill, cabinet papers with memoranda by H. Cecil, H. A. L. Fisher *et al.*; instructions to cabinet committee, proceedings and conclusions (1921). Correspondence with MPs and others.

774 Copy of Parliamentary Reform Bill 1924.

817 Representation of the People (Equal Franchise) Bill 1928: notes on debates, Home Office briefs and notes, LC's memorandum to cabinet, petitions, resolutions etc. of interested organisations.

1443 Parliament (Reform) Bill 1934: correspondence with Lord Salisbury and Crown Office notes.

3078, 3130, 3682 House of Commons (Redistribution of Seats) Bills: briefs from Home Office (1944, 1947) and notes for debates. Draft Boundary Commission Order (1945) sent by Home Office.

3678 Lord Simon's correspondence on composition of conference on electoral reform 1944.

3680 Representation of the People Bill, brief from Home Office 1944.

3133–6 Parliament Bill. Cabinet papers 1946–7 and meetings of officials. Lord Chancellor's memoranda and correspondence, notes on proceedings on previous Parliament Acts. Coldstream's papers including minutes and papers of committee of officials and of the inter-party conferences, with memoranda and calculations of government business and the effect of various proposals.

2660, 3083 Prolongation of Parliament Bills, 1942–3: briefs for Lord Chancellor.

3240 Representation of the People (N.I.) Regulations, 1949: Parliamentary debates.

3 Procedure

1 House of Lords

2/824, 964 Ceremonial procedure, notes of 1929. Notes on procedure for Labour government, 1924.

600 Proposed broadcasts rejected, 1923.

3451 Memorandum by H. Badeley on duplicate motions, 1946.

4359 Correspondence with Lord President and PCO on Parliament Act procedure on Iron and Steel Bill, 1948.

4505 Proceedings of select committee on tied votes at committee stage with memorandum by Lord Badeley, the instigator, 1950.

4709–10 Signed orders (various dates), and notes of arrangements for early recall of House of Lords, mostly 1930s and especially full on 1931–2. Memoranda by E. F. Iwi, various dates.

4751 Requests to Lord Esme Gordon-Lennox for access to the Bar of the House for certain LCO staff (1934 and 1947). Most of the file concerns a dispute over this issue in 1956.

4504, 2743, 5206 Memoranda by Admiralty and Lord Salisbury on Parliamentary speeches by serving officers following Admiral Lord Fraser's on the Parliament Bill; notes by Napier on privilege; also questions by Lord Cherwell (1942). Lord Russell's query on his voting position as an Assistant Judge-Advocate General (1951).

824, 964, 2571, 2742, 2744–5, 5205 Miscellaneous minor points.

2 *General*

1/6	Proposed "Grand Committee" on law discussed with Attorney-General 1884.
2/638, 3450, 5201	Notes on procedure at the opening of Parliament 1920–3; other minor matters of 1946, 1951.
1119	Simplified pronouncement of royal assent to bills when given by Lord President: Crown Office Rules (1) Order 1920.
959–60	Correspondence with Hankey and Duff on the dissolution and means of obtaining ministerial resignations, 1929–30.
1156	Meetings of 1939 with Home Office, Whips, Speaker and cabinet papers on air raids; notes on constitutional position re meeting place of Parliament.
1444	List of money bills 1927–34 and Schuster's memorandum on interpretation.
4439	Arrangements for opening of new House of Commons 1950: correspondence with Speaker, notes of meetings and details of arrangements.
3435	Lord Chancellor's correspondence on proposed Parliamentary delegation to Russia 1944.
4711	Cabinet office query on prorogation, and notes by F. Mayall 1947.
3008, 3450, 3505	Various minor questions.

3 *The Machinery of Government Committee*

2/3211–3	Sub-committee on Parliamentary procedure 1944; Coldstream's papers, including memoranda by Sir G. Campion, C. T. Carr, draft reports.

4 *Parliamentary elections*

2/2661	Parliament Bill 1943. Discussions with PCO (1939) on service of writs and proposed simplification; correspondence with Attorney-General on proposed defence regulation (1940); cabinet papers (1941) on Prolongation of Parliament Bill and correspondence with Home Office on registration of voters. Resumed consideration of both questions, 1943.
2768	Lord Rosebery's question on electioneering by Lord-Lieutenants, 1942.
2772–3	Minor Home Office queries on registration 1943 and correspondence with PCO on issue of writs to Isle of Wight 1943.
3035	Writs order, drafting correspondence with PCO 1944.
3049	Parliamentary Elections (War-time Registration) Bill 1944: brief from Home Office.
3070, 5741–2	Sealing of writs in Northern Ireland: discussion of proposed defence regulation and Bill (Northern Ireland Miscellaneous Provisions Bill) with Home Office and PCO; further queries on personation and election rules, 1951.
3679	Observations of Coldstream and LCJ on report of committee on electoral law, 1945.
3083	Postponement of Polling Day Bill 1945, copy draft from PCO.
3097	Elections and Jurors Bill 1945, copy from PCO.
3681	Electoral Registration Regulations, correspondence with PCO on appeals procedure, 1945.
3684	Question on election expenses in Irish university seats and reply, 1945.
3686	Question from Law Officers' Department on issue of writs during the recess, 1950.

2
LEGISLATION

1 Introduction

It is notorious that in this century the leisurely process by which statutes are made has proved incapable of coping with the multiplicity of projects, often of a parochial or trivial character, which require legislative sanction. Governments have therefore resorted to the practice of enacting legislation which empowers ministers or public or statutory bodies to give it effect in detail by secondary or delegated legislation in the form of orders or statutory instruments. The seemingly unstoppable tide of delegated legislation has in turn given rise to sharp criticism for its tendency to enhance the power of the executive over the legislature and for exacerbating the purely practical problem of ascertaining, understanding and applying the law.[1] In view of the Lord Chancellor's position, one might expect these concerns to be reflected in official correspondence, but this is not really the case on any extensive scale before the Second World War.

Two great landmarks in the modern debate on the use and abuse of statutory powers to impose legislation are the Donoughmore Committee on Ministers' Powers, set up in 1929,[2] and the Franks Committee, whose deliberations (culminating in their report of 1957) lie beyond the end of the period covered here. The Donoughmore Committee was set up more or less expressly to rebut the melodramatic accusations made by Lord Chief Justice Hewart in "The New Despotism" and given wide publicity, and it is disappointing that the files are so uninformative on the background and working of the Committee. It is clear that the permanent staff of the LCO were not especially concerned at the proliferation of orders and instruments (mostly promoted by local authorities and public utilities) although, as became clear later, they were themselves unable effectively to police them even in defence of their own departmental interests.[3]

When this rather uninspiring subject next forced itself on the attention of government it was in consequence of the purely practical stresses imposed by the Second World War on the machinery of government, which led Parliament to institute a thorough re-examination of its own procedures. The Maxwell-Fyfe Committee on the Machinery of Government reported in 1944; Coldstream sat on its sub-committee on Parliamentary procedure, whose papers offer insights into civil service thinking, particularly in the discussions of Sir Gilbert Campion's proposals to extend the watchdog role of the Houses' joint Special Orders Committee on Satutory Instruments.[4]

These attempts to streamline the passage of legislation but also to strengthen Parliamentary scrutiny of delegated legislation resulted in the Statutory Orders (Special Procedure) Act 1945, and the Statutory Instruments Act 1946. They were the subject of lengthy discussions within and among government departments. In the LCO Coldstream asked rhetorically "is it not clear that we must approach the whole matter of making rules of court in particular and statutory instruments in general, in a very different frame of mind?".[5] A Parliamentary storm in a teacup over the Home Office failure to follow the correct procedure in making their Fire Service Regulations in 1944[6] had a most salutary effect, although it did not, of course, prevent oversights, including one by the LCO itself.[7] One particularly interesting outcome of the revised procedures is the row which broke out between the LCO and the clerks of the House of Lords on a comparatively minor procedural matter, the interpretation of Statutory Instruments Act 1946 s. 4 on the laying of documents before the House in the recess. The House of Commons standing orders had been amended in accordance with government policy, although the *vires* were felt to be doubtful, but the Parliament Office in the Lords proved so stubborn that "it had come to be regarded as something in the nature of a battle between the officials of the House and the Government". [8] Coldstream stigmatised the methods of the Parliament Office as "amateur and unbusinesslike in the extreme" and concluded that "the interaction between the functions of the Parliament Office and the Lord Chancellor's Office respectively seems to me to be far too uncertain for efficient administration"; nevertheless, they had to pass a "clarifying" Act. The impatience shown by the LCO in this episode reflects the natural tendency which the war had engendered in administrators to resent the resumption of peacetime practices. A reviving spirit of backbench resistance to merely "rubber stamping" legislation was also becoming evident which would hinder the rapid passage of complex legislation. [10]

Departments which had become accustomed to govern by circular and order with a minimum of delay and challenge were naturally loth to submit to a more protracted and better scrutinised mode of governing, and the Labour government's ambitious programme of social and economic reconstruction could not be implemented without an extensive resort to these means. [11] The Attlee administration therefore gave to an important constitutional debate a strongly political flavour, with the government cast as dictatorial, authoritarian and anti-Parliamentary and labelling its opponents as hypocritical and reactionary. Jowitt's own sensitivity to the "Gestapo" accusations of the opposition is very evident and the discussions on, for example, the Exchange Control Bill 1946 and the Full Employment Bill 1950 bring it out well. [12]

By 1950 even the government had begun to have misgivings at the avalanche of statutory instruments and in March the cabinet's legislation committee invited the Lord Chancellor to consider how the number of those in force and the volume of those being made, might be reduced. In a sweepstake to guess the number made in between 1st January and 26th April 1950 Jowitt (250) Coldstream (350) and Sir Granville Ram, former chief Parliamentary Counsel (150) all underestimated hopelessly (the true figure was 674), but they quickly established that nothing obvious could be done to curtail the flow. [13]

Jowitt did however make notable attempts to improve the form in which the ever increasing body of enacted law was cast and to encourage the systematic removal from the statute book of defunct and obsolete law. The principal agency for this was the Statute Law Committee, but it is clear from the papers on its activities in the 1920s that it was then a rather ineffective body. Because of its informal standing it was unable to command the services of the PCO draftsmen, who were constantly being purloined for more urgent duties, and as some of its own members admitted, it contained too many old men whose best days were past. Progress on consolidation was slow and disappointing, and codification had been more or less abandoned after the disastrous failure of the Fraud Bill, which had brought to an abrupt end Lord Loreburn's initiative in piecemeal codification of the criminal law. [14]

Credit for the re-invigoration of the Statute Law Committee seems to be due partly to the Attorney-General in the wartime governments, Sir Donald Somervell, to Sir Granville Ram and to Jowitt himself, for by the time (1941) that Somervell began to urge it Schuster had grown pessimistic[15] and there is little in the papers to suggest that Napier or Coldstream had any special interest. In July, 1944 Somervell urged Simon to seek cabinet approval for a consolidation programme with published annual reports to stimulate interest, but it was only after the change of government that action was taken. Jowitt was able to obtain the backing of the government's legislation committee (March, 1946) for the reconstruction of the Statute Law Committee and for a formal programme in which the revenue statutes, (especially the notorious state of the law on income tax), would have a high priority, along with the repeal of obsolete provisions to which Somervell had drawn attention.[16] To facilitate their labours it was necessary to pass the Consolidation of Enactments (Procedure) Act 1949 which enables minor amendments to be made in the law within the form of a consolidation act subject to certain safeguards. As the file shows, it was no mean achievement to overcome the ingrained conservatism and professional jealousy of the House of Commons and the touchy suspiciousness of Lord Simon and to produce an agreed measure; it was considerably removed from Ram's original scheme involving the use of Orders in Council, which Simon had dismissed as "cumbrous, artificial and really objectionable",[17] but nevertheless greatly facilitated this worthwhile if unglamorous work.

Inevitably progress on consolidation was slow, especially as the government was unwilling to make draftsmen available, and did not bear much fruit until the 1950s. Moreover the great prize, the income tax, posed special problems, which had once before defeated a codification committee; as predicted, it took almost three years to produce the giant Income Tax Bill and then there were further delays in the joint select committee; for they had to satisfy the "formidable intellectual conscience" of Lord Radcliffe, who had been pressed into taking the post of chairman , that no substantive changes had been made to the law.[18] Nevertheless it is fitting that Jowitt should have taken Statute Law Revision as the theme of his Holdsworth Club lecture and the 1949 Act and the work of the Committee stand as his memorial.[19]

As mentioned earlier, much of the subordinate legislation which was introduced was for the purposes of local authorities, but it still remained necessary for them to seek private bills, and these bills frequently contained matter of interest to the LCO, though it was often buried in a jungle of unrelated and miscellaneous clauses.

> "A good many years ago . . . [we] made an arrangement under which the Treasury were to draw our attention to any clauses in private bills which related to particular subjects in which the LCD might be interested. The reason for this was that we have not the staff to enable us to search through all the private bills for provisions to which we ought to take objection".[20]

This probably followed from the LCO's discovery in 1932 that it was becoming standard practice for local acts to impose extra duties on the county courts in housing and sanitation matters. Napier instanced lunacy and the jurisdiction of county and magistrates' courts as subjects for LCO scrutiny and in 1946, after objections from Miller of the Supreme Court Pay Office, added payments into court to the list.[21]

At about the same time it became obvious that LCO scrutiny arrangements were not working well. A problem arose over the persistent attempts of local authorities to recover their debts in magistrates' courts instead of through the county courts: E. W. Holderness of the Home Office explained how this had been allowed to come about:

> "It appears that from the early years of public health legislation Parliament has allowed local authorities powers to recover summarily as civil debts any charges or expenses which they have incurred in executing any works on behalf of owners and occupiers, such as fall normally within their governmental function. s. 293 of the PH Act 1936 was no more than a reenactment of earlier powers. So well established was this principle that a model clause regarding the summary recovery of expenses was included in the old series of model clauses as follows:—(see p 121 of H of Lords, model Bills and clauses as amended, 1921). As regards recovery of damages, the summary recovery of damages from an offender was conceded as far back as 1845 in s. 152 of the Railways Clauses Act which was later incorporated in the Gas Works Clauses Act and the Water Works Clauses Act of, approximately, the same date."[22]

It became a matter of greater concern as local authorities widened their activities into the trading field (thus the Manchester Corporation Bill[23] rang alarm bells in the Home Office because the power was to be used in relation to debts owed by purchasers of central heating equipment) and because they were now able to cite as a precedent the Water Act 1945, which had slipped through the net and which did not contain the upper limit of £20 habitually imposed on such powers. It is clear from Napier's response that the LCO was quite ignorant how widespread and ancient such powers were. In the following year the anomaly was made greater by the Crown Proceedings Bill, from which the Home Secretary got a similar provision deleted *in toto* as wrong in principle, and the LCO then sought to persuade the Lord Chairman of Committees "to disallow all future provisions in private bills conferring power to recover a civil debt summarily".[24] Stainton's response makes it plain that Napier badly underestimated the political strength of the local authorities and the difficulties of dealing with a very important question of policy at such a low level of decision making.[25]

Other private bills seldom caused much concern, though the Mountbatten Estate Bill[26] represents one notable exception. However, the existing private bill procedure was brought into question by two bills at the end of the 1930s, one of them "a most outrageous attempt to pervert the course of justice" in Schuster's view, and there is an interesting letter of his to Lord Kilbracken which outlines his fears on recent "attempts, such as have never been made within my experience, to use [private bill] procedure to upset private rights for private purposes".[27]

Notes

1 *Perhaps the best known examples of such criticisms are G. W. Keeton,* ***The Passing of Parliament*** *(1952) and Sir C. K. Allen,* ***Law and Orders*** *(1945).*

2 *PP 1931–2 (Cmd 4060) XII, 231.*

3 *Schuster was (almost inevitably) on the Committee and it is apparent from his questions to witnesses that he was unconvinced that any real problem existed. However, as early as 1921 he had admitted that "it is very difficult to keep pace with statutes imposing a duty to make rules, and we generally rely on the department more immediately concerned to keep us up to scratch": 2/571: to Bankes LJ, 3.3.1921.*

4 *For a summary of these developments see W. I. Jennings,* **Parliament** *(2nd ed., 1957), 489–516.*

5 *2/4319: Coldstream to Clarke (Treasury), 20.9.1946.*

6 **Parl. Debs.** *1943–4 (H of C) vol. 402 cols. 761–7.*

7 *2/4052.*

8 *2/4320: Coldstream's minute, 19.12.1947.*

9 **Ibid.** *Laying of Documents before Parliament (Interpretation) Act 1948.*

10 *H. S. Kent,* **In On The Act** *(1979), 154–9.*

11 *"It was the deliberate policy of the late government that bills should be drawn in a form that left as much detail as possible to be dealt with by subordinate legislation". 2/4326: Sir G. Ram to Dobson, 19.4.1950.*

12 *2/3098, 2/4320. There is an amusing exchange with the Ministry of Transport over a regulation which Shawcross asserted would need "the services of a senior wrangler with a tape measure": 2/3602.*

13 *2/4326. It is not surprising that Jowitt was uneasy at the proliferation of regulations: he had recently confessed that even after studying one set, the Coal Industry Nationalisation (Superannuation) Regulations 1950, for several days, he still did not understand them (2/4334).*

14 *There is a useful history in 2/3816: Ram to Somervell, 3.11.1941, Appendix 'B'. See also Lord Birkenhead,* **Points of View** *(1922) I, 159–76, admitting that "at present the work excites no enthusiasm".*

15 *2/3816: Schuster to Somervell, 13.11.1941.*

16 *2/3816.*

17 *2/4603: memorandum of February, 1948.*

18 *2/3818.*

19 *See also (1951) 14 MLR 320 (L. C. B. Gower).*

20 *2/3145: Napier to H. R. Jones, 1.6.1946.*

21 **Ibid.**

22 *2/3150: to Coldstream, 21.5.1946.*

23 *2/3147.*

24 *2/3151: 24.3.1947.*

25 *2/3151.*

26 *See "Trusts",* **supra**, *222.*

27 *2/1222: to Lord Kilbracken, December, 1939.*

2 Public Bills, General

1 Drafting and form

2/424 Treasury revive requirement of consent to employment of draftsmen, 1919.

625 Balfour's motion on legislation by reference (1920): correspondence with him and with PCO, especially on effecting Lord Chancellor's undertaking to provide more information in bills.

2969 Miscellaneous notes from PCO on citations of acts, 1942.

3577, 2659 Memoranda by Lord Chancellor and Attorney-General (1944) and cabinet papers re-affirming policy on provision for "joint ministerial responsibility" in statutes, with papers on H.E.P. (Scotland) Bill 1943.

4419 Correspondence with PCO over the addition of "and Wales" to description of England in bills.

4994 Long memorandum from PCO on s. 111 County Courts Act 1934 and on the misuse of the "Stainton formula" in bills (1951).

3378 Home Office request earlier notice of bills which affect the royal prerogative, 1949.

4855 Discussions with Statute Law Committee on improving procedure for consent of Crown to be bound by a private member's bill, 1951.

2 *Status of Bills*

2/1219–20 Discussions on National Trust Bill, 1939: opinions of H. H. King, A. Uthwatt, correspondence with the Trust and the PCO on private/public bill distinction in relation to their proposed acquisition of Knole Park.

3181 Discussions with Foreign Office on possibility of a private bill to make US Education Foundation free of income tax, 1948.

4481 Treasury send report of Select Committee on Hybrid Bills, approved by cabinet; memorandum by Badeley on effect in the Lords, 1949.

3 *Consolidation and codification*

2/663, 3814–6, 3818, 3581, 5864, 4604 Statute Law Committee. Papers 1920–2 including agendas and minutes of meetings, memoranda on various aspects and Schuster's correspondence with Chalmers, Ilbert, Liddell and Muir McKenzie. Correspondence on membership 1924–50, including notes of meeting in 1944 to re-vitalise the Committee. Formal minutes 1931–50 and correspondence with A. Ram on difficulties; Jowitt's memoranda and approach to cabinet and departments on revenue law codification. Attorney-General's initiative in 1944, briefs for PQs, correspondence with I.R.C. and Lord Radcliffe on the Income Tax (Consolidation) Bill 1951 following Somervell's and Jowitt's campaign from 1945. Reports of S.L.C.'s sub-committee on form in which S.Is annual volumes should be published. Minutes of meetings, and reports of sub-committees, 1947–50, and further papers to the end of 1954.

4603 Consolidation of Enactments Bill. Cabinet papers and correspondence with Morrison and Ram on the latter's scheme (1948); discussions with other political parties and modified bill; cabinet and Parliamentary proceedings.

963 Proposals for criminal law codification 1924, 1927, 1929 and memorandum by Schuster (1924) on history of Lord Loreburn's programme.

3466 Correspondence with Chairmen of the Joint Parliamentary Committee on Consolidation Bills, 1932–50, mostly on composition and chairmanship.

6674 Marriage Bill 1949; drafting correspondence with PCO, cabinet papers, representation from Union of Liberal and Progressive Synagogues.

4 *Revision and repeal*

2/1587 Question from Statute Law Committee in 1935 on value of 8,9 Vic. c.72.

1588 Correspondence with SLC (1937) on proposed repeal of parts of Habeas Corpus Act 1679.

1589, 3817 Statute Law Revision Bill sent by SLC 1938. Noted to be postponed "till after the crisis" (31.8.1939). Notes and correspondence of 1948.

3819 S.L. Revision Bill 1949, correspondence with PCO.

4169 SLC asks for repeal of s. 42 Matrimonial Causes Act 1857; President rejects, 1942.

4853 Common Informers Bill 1951: Jowitt suggests further acts for repeal.

3820 Preface to "Statutes Revised", written by Ram for Jowitt, 1950.

2734–9 Discussions on repeal of wartime emergency legislation (see under *Emergency Legislation*, *supra*, 276–7).

5 *Interpretation*

2/36 Interpretation Bill 1889. Correspondence with PCO, memorandum by R. S. Webster, comments from departments.

2646 Pensions (Mercantile Marine) Bill 1942. Correspondence with Ministry of Pensions, memoranda and notes for Parliamentary debates.

3 Subordinate Legislation

1 *Drafting*

2/856 Correspondence on Landlord & Tenant Rules includes Napier's view of the superiority of PCO drafting over judges', 1928.

1174 Correspondence with Board of Trade on Bankruptcy Rules includes general observations, 1931.

1279 Napier's advice to Hicks on the art of drafting, 1933.

4324 Memorandum by C. T. Carr (1939) and Treasury circular of 1949 on format for rules.

2 *Parliamentary procedure*

1/78 Error in laying Public Prosecutor Regulations 1886; correspondence with Attorney-General.

2/2733 War Cabinet Legislation Committee sub-committee on harmonisation of procedures 1943: LCO notes on its own practice and meetings of 1945 on the issue of explanatory memoranda.

3069, 3091 4319–21, 3211–3 Discussions on SIs, beginning in 1944 with Treasury circulars and correspondence on procedure and the new Select Committee on Scrutiny of SIs. Brief from PCO on Special Procedure Bill (1945) and cabinet papers, following Maxwell Fyfe Report on the Machinery of Government. Cabinet and Parliamentary proceedings on the Statutory Instruments Bill; departmental conferences on common forms and procedures, and on making regulations under the Act. Discussions on proposed legislation to facilitate 'laying' orders during the recess, especially disputes with Parliamentary clerks, leading to Laying of Documents before Parliament (Interpretation) Act 1948.

3051 National Fire Service Regulations (Indemnity) Bill 1946: correspondence with PCO, Parliamentary proceedings.

4080, 4184, 4283 Explanatory memoranda on RSC (Crown Proceedings) 1947, PQ on absence of same from Matrimonial Causes (Amendment) (No. 2) Rules, 1943; PQ on Acquisition of Land (Owner-Occupier) Regulations, 1944 with discussions with Treasury on policy.

4052 RSC (1) 1946, retrospective owing to "fearful error"; memorandum to Scrutiny Committee and brief to Solicitor-General.

3452 Discussion on Lord President's proposal that Orders in Council be annulled only by resolution of both Houses (1946).

4284, 4352 Scottish questions: *vires* of Acquisition of Land (Compensation for War Damaged Land) (Costs) Rules 1946 questioned by Scottish Reference Office; President of Court of Session insists on separate Scottish Transport Tribunal Rules 1949.

3736, 5872 Correspondence with Clerk to the LCJ of Northern Ireland on procedure over Pensions Appeal Tribunal (N.I.) Amendment Rules (1950), and Home Office questions (1951) on procedure under S.I. Act 1946.

3430 Cabinet discussions on Lord Chancellor's suggestions for stricter Parliamentary controls, 1950.

2971 Law Officers' opinion on whether Orders in Council are within Rules Publication Act 1893.

3 *Policy questions*

2/939 Evidence of LCO to Donoughmore Committee on Ministers' Powers, 1932.

3069 Discussion on clause in Special Procedure Bill excluding judicial review of certain orders, 1944.

3098 Discussions among ministers on Exchange Controls Bill, including tactics of delegated legislation 1946.

4326 Cabinet discussion on reducing number of SIs, and discussions with Ram and Morrison, 1950.

4 Particular Public Bills and Regulations

This includes only measures not discussed elsewhere. Most files relate to bills sent to the Lord Chancellor to be introduced or debated by him in the House of Lords and consist of prints of the bill with briefing documents and correspondence with the department responsible for the bill on amendments etc.

1 *Transport*

2/470 (Railways Act 1921), 1435 (Air Navigation Act 1936), 3121-8 (Transport Act 1947).

2 *Nationalisation*

2/3115–20, 4083 Electricity Act 1947, including correspondence re limitation of actions, notes of meeting with opposition, correspondence with PCO and discussions on appeals tribunal. Also regulations 1947–8.

3095–6, 4329–32, 4334, 4918 Coal Industry Nationalisation Act 1946, with correspondence on costs, limitations, registration, liability of directors, and with the opposition. Regulations under the Act, with discussions on registration, compensation, costs, superannuation and other questions. Also Coal Industry Act 1951, to correct valuation error by Central Valuation Board.

3090 (Bank of England Act 1946).

4362 (Gas (Staff Compensation) Regulations 1949).

3 *Labour*

2/3038 (Disabled Persons (Employment) Act 1944).
2653 (Catering Wages Act 1943, with discussions on the Truck Acts).
3087–8 (Trade Disputes and Trade Unions Act 1946, with cabinet papers and query on the position in Northern Ireland).
3079 (Wages Councils Act 1945).
3106, 3132 (National Service Acts, 1946–7, on position of conscientious objectors).

4 *Health and welfare*

2/3004 (Medical Act 1858 (Amendment) Bill 1944, to reverse *R. v G.M.C., Ex.p. Spackman*).
3084 (Family Allowance Act 1945).
3048 (Pensions (Increase) Act 1944).
3102–3 (National Insurance Act 1946, with discussions on the position of Friendly Societies).

5 *Finance and taxation*

2/3041 (Income Tax (Offices and Employments) Act 1944).
3047 (National Loans Act 1944).
3098 (Exchange Control Act 1947, described by Solicitor-General as "much more drastic than any Act which forms part of our legislation", important correspondence on tactics and drafting).
3104 (Borrowing (Control and Guarantees) Act 1946, with discussions on burden of proof).

6 *Other government measures*

2/3129 (Ministry of Defence Act 1946).
3108 (Licensing Planning (Temporary Provisions) Act 1946).
3094 (Chartered Bodies (Resumption of Elections) Act 1946).
3350 (Proposed extension to Prevention of Corruption Act 1916 discussed with departments, 1949).
3080 (Building Materials and Housing Act 1945).
4363 (Plant and Machinery (Valuation for Rating) (Amendment) Rules 1950).
4850 (Forestry Act 1951).
3019 (Roosevelt Memorial Act 1946).

7 *Private members' bills*

2/4486 (Censorship of Plays (Repeal) Bill, 1949: cabinet papers and opinions on the royal prerogative).
4857 (Fireworks Act 1951).

5 Local Bills

1 *General aspects*

2/1208 Correspondence with Home Office, Treasury and Ministry of Health on local bills putting extra duties on to county courts, 1932.

3145–6, 3148–9 Problems over local bills providing for payments into court: objections by Pay Office, correspondence with Treasury, Chairman of Committees, 1946.

3147, 3150–1 Local bills empowering recovery of debts in magistrates' courts: correspondence with Home Office, Chairman of Committees, PCO, 1946; resumed 1949.

3158 Correspondence with PCO and Parliamentary agents on Home Office request for marked up "precedent copies" of local bills, 1946.

3180 Procedure on objections explained by PCO, 1948.

2 *Particular Bills*

1. containing objectionable clauses on debt recovery or otherwise ousting county courts: 2/3147, 3150, 3166, 3178, 3188, 3193–4, 3196, 3198, 3201-2, 3207, 3209.

2. containing power to pay out monies without production of probates: 2/3154, 3164, 3173, 3177, 3192, 3200, 3210. See also the general discussion in 2/3747.

3. other objectionable or questionable clauses: 2/3138–42, 3159, 3165, 3170, 3174, 3179, 3208, 1212, 1213–7.

4. no LCO objections: 2/3152–3, 3155–7, 3160–1, 3167–9, 3171–2, 3175–6, 3182–4, 3186–7, 3191, 3195, 3197, 3203, 3205–6, 1207, 1209, 1211.

6 Private Bills

2/818 Royal Exchange Assurance Co. Ltd's Bill, 1930: correspondence with Public Trustee, PCO, Treasury and Parliamentary agents on trustees' "charging clause".

1210 Grosvenor Estate Bill 1923: nomination of Chancery judges to report.

1218 Tatton Estate Bill 1937: explanation to Simonds J of procedure, and report.

1223 Freemasons Lodges Bill 1939: notes of meetings with Home Office and masonic delegation, opinions on scope of legislation against secret societies and proceedings on threatened prosecutions by the Deputy Clerk of the Peace for Essex.

3143 Abergavenny Estate Bill 1945: correspondence with Official Solicitor on nomination as guardian *ad litem*.

1224 Standing Orders revision removing reference to judges, 1941.

1222 Monmouthshire and South Wales Mutual Indemnity Society Ltd's Bill to reverse *Wooding, James, Hawkins v the Society* (1939): correspondence with Board of Trade, Home Office; Schuster's observations on private bill procedure.

3144 Proposal to vest Lord Chancellor's "vetting" duty on private bills in Estate Bills Committee agreed, 1944; notes on cases of McGuffie and Smith.

3185, 3189–90 LCO advises Treasury it will no longer require to scrutinise charities bills, 1945.

3162 Nazeing Wood or Park Bill 1947: correspondence with PCO, Public Trustee, Treasury Solicitor's Office.

3163 Correspondence with Home Office on objections to Stevenson Marriage Bill 1947.

3199 Model clauses sent by PCO, 1949.

3204 Mountbatten Estate Bill.

3445 Kenward's case: attempt to obtain private bill divorce when Russian wife was refused exit visa; discussions with Attorney-General 1947.

1221 St. Bartholomew Hospital Bill, 1938.

4239 Hoare's (Messrs) Bill 1926, correspondence with Agents.

3
MISCELLANEOUS ASPECTS OF GOVERNMENT

1 Government and Civil Service

2/1225 Law Officers' opinion on retention and use of cabinet papers, 1934; cabinet paper and circular re old cabinet papers in LCO. Return of papers by successive LCs and Foreign Office circular re laxity over secret documents, 1938.

1227 Memorandum (1937) advocating concessions to appease Welsh nationalism.

3215 Script of Lord Hankey's broadcast on the cabinet system, 1946.

3224 Note on ministers' pension rights (1949) and advice to Addison (1951).

2 Finance, Rates and Taxes

2/634, 1164 Appointment of referees under Safeguarding of Industries Act 1921: negotiations with Treasury on fees, after requests by Board of Trade and Customs. Appointment of C. Atkinson KC, G. M. T. Hildyard KC and successors. Appointment of referee (E. M. Konstam), under Abnormal Importations (Customs Duties) Act 1931.

1594 Metropolitan Boroughs standing joint committee memorial re problems with rate defaulters under Money Payments (Justices) Act 1935.

3561 Meeting of departments (1949) to discuss remission of duty on Lord Gretton's estate.

3592 Question by Ministry of Health on position of Althorpe parish, Towcester under Rating and Valuation Act 1925 s. 64(2).

3596 Law Society complains of delays in Stamp Office, 1948, and Stamp Office rebuttal.

3747 Proposals to free small estates from estate duty, 1947. Correspondence with Norbury (PPR), Kinsley (Friendly Societies Registry) and others, and TUC pressure. See also *Local Bills*, *supra*.

3 Health and Welfare

2/2774 PQs (1942) on lost and stolen ration books: correspondence with Ministry of Health and Board of Trade on safeguards. Further complaints 1945 and correspondence with Ministry of Pensions.

3007 Royal Commission on population problems: correspondence with Ministry of Health (1943) on request to Lord Simon to act as chairman, on selection of an historian member, terms of reference etc.

3645 Counsel's opinion sent by Ministry of Health on B.M.A.'s opposition to National Health Service Act 1946.

4455 Attorney-General and Lord Chancellor criticise proposal for a "legal committee on medical partnerships" to consider N.H.S. Act 1946 ss. 35–7. Cabinet papers and report of committee under G. P. Slade (1948).

4 Industrial Relations

2/1514–5 Truck Acts: Treasury question re alleged infringement by savings bonds scheme (1939) and meeting with Home Office and Attorney-General on *Pratt v Cook* (1940). Draft Truck Bill 1940, Parliamentary proceedings.

639 Cabinet papers and briefing papers for Lord Birkenhead's PQ on T.U.C. political levies, 1923.

3411 S. Micklethwait's suggestion on how to stop unofficial strikes (1944); sent to Ministry of Labour.

5 Public Records

2/336 Meetings of committee on preservation of documents, on RCJ records, 1911. Correspondence with Treasury on documentary organisation and fire precautions.

565 Correspondence with Masters Chitty and Fox on destruction of certificates of lodgment, 1920.

3743 Correspondence (1942) with PP Registry on transfer of old documents to PRO.

4438 Dispute between Treasury and Master of the Rolls on storage of PRO records, 1950: proposed removal from deep storage shelters to Hayes, and subsequent purchase of Ashridge. Meetings of MR, Treasury and Ministry of Works.

27/29 Report of the Hanworth Committee on the Destruction of documents in the SCJ, 1929.

6 Other

2/3603 Royal Commission on Gambling seeks evidence on law from LCO, 1949. LCO evidence and representations from temperance societies.

3607 Tucker Committee on pension schemes: Treasury seek LCO views on terms of reference, 1950.

THE CROWN OFFICE

1

INTRODUCTION

The Crown Office papers in this series are for the most part of limited interest to the researcher, consisting in many cases only of files in standard form with formal correspondence on the preparation and sealing of grants of honours and dignities, offices, charters etc. which were required to pass under the Great Seal, as prescribed by the Great Seal Act 1884. The Seal itself gives rise to some more interesting material because it had to be renewed periodically and whenever there was a new sovereign, and lively discussions usually ensued on the artistic merits of the various designs, into which Lord Chancellors and Permanent Secretaries entered with notable vigour: thus Hailsham is found describing one such as "looking like a Pope in the family way"[1] while Schuster at one point "was preparing myself for a supreme struggle . . . if at any time a proposal was made that the Seal should be prepared by Eric Gill";[2] for his part the Deputy Master of the Mint regarded an existing Counter Seal as "the most awful thing of its kind that has ever seen the light of day".[3] The time and trouble which the Permanent Secretary was able to devote to this matter is perhaps a further illustration of his relatively light workload.

In the official correspondence with the Home Office on the preparation of warrants for the issue of Letters Patent conferring peerages and baronetcies there is seldom much of interest except for occasional discussions about unusual remainders, although the ripples from Lloyd George's peerage creations penetrated even these backwaters.[4] Likewise the files relating to a bizarre assortment of civil appointments, ranging from the election of a verderer under the rare writ "de viridario eligendo" to Lord-Lieutenants and the Commissioners of the Treasury, are almost purely formal. The appointment of High Court judges, however, does yield a few nuggets, because for at least a few years from 1918 it was the custom of the Crown Office to send to the King a potted biography of each appointee: for the most part these add little to what is already known but they establish, for example, that Talbot (appointed by Cave) had already been selected for the next vacancy by Birkenhead, explain why no county court judge before Acton had been promoted to the High Court bench and include a report of the health of Farwell LJ in connection with his pension.[5]

All these appointments proved expensive to the recipient, and the burden of the fees gave rise to frequent applications for remission. Several were reduced or abolished altogether, including the fees on judicial appointments, following a complaint by the Attorney-General; then in 1936 the Treasury decided on a departmental committee; since the total produce of these fees and stamp duties on honours and offices was barely £7,000 a year, the Treasury could afford to dispense with them. Schuster chaired the committee, and as a result of its two reports, most of the remaining fees were abolished, though fees on mortmain licences (mostly sought by foreign companies and city livery companies) remained in being until 1945, the licences themselves until 1960.

A variety of other documents emanated from the Crown Office, notably those in connection with Parliamentary elections, but few are of any importance, although at times they were a considerable nuisance.[6]

Notes

1 *2/1440: to Schuster, 19.3.1937.*
2 *2/905: to Deputy Master of the Mint, 1.2.1929.*
3 ***Ibid**: to Home Office (copy) 12.3.1927. Liddell recounts the inspection of new designs in 1904 (**Notes from the Life of an Ordinary Mortal** (1911), 346–7 and Fitzroy records friction between the Mint and the Lord Chancellor (**Memoirs** (1925), 115).*
4 *2/2570, 2572.*
5 *2/2537, 2/2539, 2/2171.*
6 *e.g. 2/4412, when the bags of ballot papers delivered there after the 1918 elections created chaos. The Clerk of the Crown was also Registrar of the Court of Claims, which involved him in considerable work in connection with coronations. On this court see Sir G. Woods Wollaston, **The Court of Claims** (1903).*

2
FEES

1 Accounts

2/2123 (1911–3), 940 (1923–7).

2 Alterations in Particular Fees

2/63, 165, 235, 2003–4, 941–2, 2006, 2289, 2292, 1531–2, 2126–7, 3631.

3 Remissions and Queries

2/613, 2004, 1528, 941, 2010, 2027, 2006.

4 Schuster Committee on Crown Office Fees.

2/1529–33, 2963 — Proposed by Treasury 1936, minutes, draft interim report (Cmd 5450 of 1937) and correspondence with Archbishop of Canterbury on Bishop's patent fees. Consequential Orders and final report (Cmd 5767 of 1938).

3
WARRANTS AND PATENTS

1 General

2/99, 1526 — Correspondence with Home Office on preparation of warrants, 1889–91, 1931.
2290 — Memorandum on preparation of Letters Patent (R. L. Overbury, 1923).
3629 — Use of warrants and patents explained for Princess Elizabeth, 1944.

2 Honours and Dignities

2/2094, 6/390–409 — List of claims, with notes, before Court of Claims 1910, 1937.

2/2135 — Law Officers' opinion (1902) and correspondence on Baronetcy of Perrott, form of patent 1911.

2138 — Notes on four disputed baronetcies, 1913.

2210 — Correspondence on special remainder to Hon. C. Russell's baronetcy, 1916.

2212 — Memorandum from Home Office on special remainders, 1918.

2256 — Memoranda on certain questions of the descent of peerages, 1919.

2237 — Revocation of patents of Roger Casement and Joseph Jones, 1916.

2433 — Discussion on unprecedented remainder in Hicking's case, 1919.

2566 — List of peers created after previous wars, 1919.

2567 — St. Aldwyn's case: discussions with Burke, 1919.

2570, 2572 — Briefs and papers on House of Lords debates on peerage offers to Vestey and Robinson (1922) including Robinson's explanation of *Randfontein v Robinson* [1921] S.A.C.A. 168.

2573 — Alteration to Lord Leith's patent, 1922.

169–70, 254, 2245, 2248–9, 2254 — Questions on the form of patents of membership of royal orders etc., various dates.

6/953–5 — Patents for the orders of knighthood.

2/1076 — Correspondence with G. Hewitt, H. Maxwell-Lyte and others on new design for peerage patent, 1924–9; Crown Office Rules (Preparation of Documents) Order 1927.

629, 1232 — Questions on acceptance and wearing of foreign decorations.

4/7–16 — New Year's and Birthday Honours Lists. Correspondence of various dates 1942–9, including recommendations by the Lord Chancellor and suggested honours for judges.

2/3433 — Conference with Home Office, MR, Master Simner, Ormerod J on unauthorised use of foreign titles and regulation on changes of name, 1950; case of "The Count of Torrigia" ("the son of a very untitled confectioner in Edinburgh").

1997, 2201, 2779, 4408, 4593 — General questions on form of patents, procedure and the patent roll. The last (4593) contains discussions from 1925 on the maintenance and form of the Hanaper Roll.

2008, 2059–63, 2136–7, 2139–41, 2177, 2211–6, 2431–54 — Patents of peerages, baronetcies and knighthoods; colonial knighthoods are in 2525–33.

3 Legal Appointments, Pensions etc.

1 *English judges and other legal posts*

2/2014, 2019, 2021–2, 2068–70, 2089, 2146–7, 2171, 2173–5, 2225–30, 2242–3, 2247, 2536–7, 2514–22, 2539, 2542–4, 2547–50, 2552–3, 2555–9.

6/861–946, 1197–1229, 1269–70, 1372–8, 1501, 1503–4, 1552–4.

2 *Indian judges*

2/2001, 2071, 2148–9, 2224–5, 2534–5, 2538, 2540–1, 2545–6, 2551, 2554, 2560. 6/1–3, 6–9, 847.

3 *Irish judges*

2/946, 2146 Alteration in Patent of Irish Master of the Rolls (1912).

4 Ecclesiastical Appointments

2/945, 2009–10, 2018, 2051–8, 2128–34, 2204–9, 2388, 2479–2514. 6/4–5, 535–810, 1520–1.

These files are mostly on presentations to crown livings, deaneries and canonries and Indian bishoprics.

2/2125, 4406	Orders for the prorogation of Convocation, 1911–8.
2357	Correspondence, including Law Officers' opinion, on a "canon" altering clergy representation in convocation.
2565	Dispute over Durham spiritualities, 1890 and 1902.
2254, 6/1301–67	Lambeth degrees, 1921–39.

5 Civil Appointments

These include Lord-Lieutenants, government offices in commission (e.g. Treasury, Commissioners for Sewers, Army Council) and offices in Channel Islands.

2/167, 517, 944, 2002, 2007, 2011, 2020, 2073–5, 2082, 2085, 2087, 2090, 2092, 2095, 2124, 2150, 2157–9, 2166, 2168–70, 2176, 2179–80, 2202, 2219–21, 2235, 2238–41, 2244, 2246, 2250, 2301, 2309–10, 2313–4, 2317–22, 2328–9, 2345 (curing ineffective appointments of JPs, 1920) 2346–8, 2352–3, 2355–6, 2363–4, 2374, 2379, 2390, 2396–7, 2399, 2410–1, 2413, 2419–20, 2428.

6/28–33, 38–47, 388–9. 410–69 (colonial governors) 476–84, 520–30, 819–25, 833–5, 848–60, 1092–1166, 1168, 1224–44, 1251–5, 1263–8, 1286–94, 1295B–1300, 1502.

4
CHARTERS, COMMISSIONS AND LICENCES

1 Charters

2/944, 2013, 2253, 6/1388–92, 1484–91	City charters.
2/4715	Proposal to make Cardiff the capital city of Wales, 1932. Discussions among officials, 1953.
2088, 2295–6, 2418	Grants of separate quarter-sessions.
2072, 2152, 2223, 2455–72, 6/179–387, 1261–2	Other grants, including supplementary charters.

2/2178 Grant of right to Durham to bear a sword before the Mayor 1913.

2005 Shortening of recitals, 1898.

1999 Dispute over Wellington College Charter (1893) including draft opinion.

2015–6, 2083–4, 2153–5, 2222, 2252, 2312, 2395, 2471–8 Colonial patents and charters, including (2015) revocation of Royal Niger Company's charter.

2 Commissions of Escheat

2/2086, 2172, 2236, 2323, 2333, 2337, 2350, 2361, 2370, 2383, 2392, 2394, 2405, 2409, 2412 and 2417 (revoked when a relative was found) 6/811–8

3 Commissions of Assize

2/2030–49 (1907–11), 2099–2118 (1911–6) 2181–2197 (1916–9) 2262–81 (1919–23), 6/1394–1459 (1924–39).

2/2198 Commissions of Assize 1918–9, including correspondence with Treasury.

2279 Schuster explains to Master Lawford that it is not policy to appoint Commissioners before knowing on which circuit they are to go as some circuits have been unlucky, which "provokes unfavourable and well-justified comment", 1923.

4401 A. Pilling (PCO) sends draft Order in Council in common form for assize commissions, 1923.

2263 Restoration of Taunton as an assize town, 1920.

4 Licences in Mortmain and Others

2/2064–7, 2142–5, 2217–8, 2303–8, 2324–7, 2329–30, 2332, 2334–6, 2340–4, 2351, 2354, 2358, 2360, 2362, 2365–7, 2369, 2371, 2373, 2376–8, 2381–2, 2385, 2387, 2391, 2393, 2400–1, 2403–4, 2406–8, 2414–5, 2421–7, 2429, 6/10–27.

2/1543 Correspondence with Home Office on amended form of instructions (1922) and further procedural changes, 1933 and 1937.

3576 Question from Red Cross on mortmain referred to Danckwerts KC, 1944.

3664 Correspondence with Board of Trade and Treasury on abolition of mortmain licences for foreign companies 1945; notes of previous discussions in 1928.

2/2093, 2156, 2331, 1368–71 Licences to alienate land in the Channel Islands.

6/1385–6 Licences to hold markets, 1924–30.

5 PROCLAMATIONS

2/2119–22 (1911–5) 4403-5 (1916–8, Great War subjects), 2282–4 (1919–23).

2200 Discussions (1916) on economies in distribution.

6
THE ROYAL FAMILY

1/74	Letters Patent on royal marriages; memorandum by Thesiger proposing simplification and correspondence, 1872.
2/2023, 6/1282	Annuities to royal family: appointments of new commissioners, 1900–31.
2/2027	Correspondence with Royal College of Arms on grant of "Royal Highness" to children of a Prince of Wales's eldest son.
2/166, 2091, 2293, 2316, 2368, 4398, 6/841–6	Authorities to the Prince of Wales, Duke of York and Duke of Connaught to confer honours on their visits abroad, 1900–34.
2/4396–7, 6/1393	Authority for members of the royal family to open the Parliament of Australia, 1901, 1926.
2/2294	Memorandum on procedure for ratifying treaties, 1933.
6/493–508	Coronation warrants, Edward VIII and George VI.
6/509–12	Council of State, 1925–39.
2/186, 6/513–6	Demise of the Crown.
6/517–9	Abdication of Edward VIII.

7
PARLIAMENT AND THE PRIVY COUNCIL

1 Elections

2/2024–5	1900 election papers—including correspondence on election petitions.
2/64, 2017, 2287, 6/1472–83, 1505–19	By-election writs.
2/4409–13	General election of 1918, including Liddell's memorandum on duties of Crown Office, correspondence with Office of Works on storing ballot papers.
2575	Correspondence on destroyed writs in Ireland, with Crown Office, Dublin, 1922.
2576, 2579–80, 2582	Election petitions, 1922.
2577	A personation case, 1923.
2581, 2583	Questions on procedure in Ireland.
958	Spoilt papers (1924), classification for PQ.
2288	Descriptions of MPs.
6/34–7	Appellate jurisdiction and general elections, 1921, 1935.

2 Commissions for Opening and Proroguing Parliament

2/2076, 2151, 2234, 2311, 6/1172–92

3 Commissions for Giving the Royal Assent

2/2077–81, 2160–2, 2231–3, 2561–4, 4400 (explanatory memorandum) 1119 (Crown Office Rules, 1926); 6/1271–81.

4 Other Commissions etc.

6/1193–6, 1285	Appointment of Clerk of the Parliaments and other officers.
2/2012, 2416	Authorising summons of Privy Council while the sovereign is abroad.
1114	Admission of Prince Henry to Privy Council, 1925.
2359	Approving choice of Speaker.
6/1387, 1492A	Appointments to the Privy Council.
2/2167, 2389	Appointment of Chairmen of Committees and Deputy Speakers in House of Lords; 2389 includes Schuster's explanation of recent omissions.
2255, 2258	Bishops entitled to sit in the Lords, correspondence.
2260–1, 2568–9	Formal papers on elections of Scottish and Irish representative peers.
6/1167	Appointment of Lord High Steward for the trial of Lord de Clifford.

8
CEREMONIAL OCCASIONS AND QUESTIONS

2/351, 823, 114, 821, 1228, 5201	Parliament and Privy Council.
2/106, 683, 686, 3225, 6292	Courts and Judges.
118, 1166, 4430, 5849	Local disputes over precedence.

9
THE HERALDS' COLLEGE

2/2163–5, 2251, 2297–300, 2302, 2375, 2380, 2384, 2402; 6/836–40, 947–52, 1256–60 Appointments.

2/164	Report of Committee of Enquiry, with Muir McKenzie's dissenting minute,
1525	1903. Correspondence with Garter King of Arms and Home Office on cabinet committee report (1928).

10
SEALS AND EMBLEMS

1 The Great Seal

Renewals, new designs etc: 1/59 (new purse), 2/16, 630, 905 (1930 minutes of standing committee, memoranda and correspondence) 1439 (correspondence with Mint on wax, boxes etc. 1935) 1440 (correspondence on new design 1936), 4502 (1947, minutes of Committee on Honours), 6317 (prices of resin).

2 Usage

2/327, 1129 (Irish Free State) 1233 (South Africa) 2741 (memorandum by E. F. Iwi) 3070 (Northern Ireland and Parliamentary writs) 4399 (use for dominions in peace treaty, 1919) 676, 903–4 (exemplification of documents) 907 (former usage in Chancery).

3 Other Seals etc

2/34 (Petty Bag Seal) 1236 (Wafer Seal, Canada) 1441 (Great Seal of Northern Ireland) 1811 (Seal of the Supreme Court) 906 (dominion seals) 2285 (use of wafer seal).

2/1158: meeting of standing committee on coins, medals etc. 1936; correspondence with Mint and discussions on proposed change in words on coins.

11
THE LORD CHANCELLOR

2/131, 2574	Commissioners appointed while the Lord Chancellor is abroad.
130, 187	Warrants to pass grants depending.
6/1283–4	Sergeant at Arms to attend Lord Chancellor, 1936–9.
6/826–32	Commissions under the Great Seal, 1928–39.

Chapter 4

THE CHURCH

1

INTRODUCTION

The Lord Chancellor was concerned directly in the affairs of the church by virtue of the patronage which he exercised over some 500 livings, mostly of small value. For this purpose each incoming Chancellor appointed a Secretary of Presentations but in the re-organisation of his staff in the 1880s this post was superseded by an Ecclesiastical Secretary who became a permanent official. The exercise of the patronage cannot be studied from the available files, but Schuster was emphatic that by the early 1920s it was entirely free from any political taint.[1] Liddell helps to chart the chronology of this state of affairs: "the notion that politics play a part in these appointments is now [1911] beginning to be less universal, but at the time of which I am speaking [c.1890] it was more widespread."[2] It was, nevertheless, steadfastly defended from attempted or alleged encroachments by the Prime Minister or by the church authorities.

In the 1920s the Church Assembly began to consider a series of measures designed to eliminate the irresponsible exercise of lay patronage, such as the sale of benefices which Cave agreed was a scandal.[3] The earliest of these proposals, in 1924, led to earnest consultations within the government as to how Measures from the Assembly ought to be handled, and Baldwin set up a cabinet committee under the Lord Chancellor for this purpose which recommended that they be given consideration first by the Prime Minister's office.[4] Despite the strenuous lobbying of the church's lay spokesmen, Lord Henry Cecil and Lord Wolmer (renewed when the devout Sankey became Lord Chancellor) they were, as these files show, unable to persuade the government to accept any obligation to consult Diocesan Boards on the disposal of crown livings, and a similarly firm line was taken on other measures which affected rights of patronage, such as the Benefices (Appropriation of Surplus Endowments) Measure and the post-Second World War diocesan re-organisation.[5] The Lord Chancellor refused to give a general consent to the suppression or amalgamation of crown livings after the bombing of the cities and therefore each diocesan measure had to be submitted for his approval. In 1948 Jowitt also refused to undertake to consult the bishop on proposed appointments within his diocese, a proposition he asserted to be part of an Anglo-Catholic attempt to reduce state control over the church.[6]

Of course, the conflicts over patronage were only one manifestation of the tensions between church and state engendered by the Church Assembly's reforming legislation. The best known is the Prayer Book controversy of the late 1920s, not covered in these files, though it is anticipated in a file of 1924,[7] which makes very clear the unsatisfactory position of Parliament with respect to Measures under the Church Assembly Act 1920. The impasse in church–state relations created by the rejection of the Prayer Book was partly defused by Randall Davidson's decision to set up a commission to study possible solutions and its first report was remitted to a departmental committee of officials chaired by Schuster, whose deliberations make interesting reading,[8] though nothing much came of them. The leaders of the church had shown little political aptitude in presenting their measures so it is interesting to see the care with which the Archbishop of Canterbury set about preparing the ground for the revision of canon law following the commission's final report in 1947, also documented here.[9]

William Temple, the leading figure among the reformers between the wars, professed three great aims: the revision of the system of appointing to livings, the reform of the liturgy and the imposition of effective discipline upon the clergy.[10] A few files on amendments to the Clergy Discipline Act 1892 relate to the last of these, but they are of little interest; indeed it is perhaps significant that a set of draft rules for the new dioceses of Guildford and Portsmouth was left unconfirmed from 1928 to 1940; "it is very fortunate for me", wrote Napier "that the Portsmouth and Guildford diocesan clergy have behaved so well in the last decade".[11]

Two other church matters may be mentioned because of the useful materials which the LCO papers afford for their study. One is the knotty question of the liability of landowners, usually laymen, to repair the chancels of parish churches, an unusual burden and one which is both onerous and difficult to discover. It became briefly notorious when the rare writ *de contumace capiendo* haled a fenland farmer into the High Court on his refusal to obey an order of the Ely Consistory Court,[12] leading to indignant questions in Parliament and to the inevitable government committee on which Napier sat and whose papers, including the critical observations of senior judges on the Bill which evolved, are open to inspection.[13] The Act was far from a satisfactory answer even to the problem of alerting a purchaser to this timebomb and it continued to elude solution.[14]

The other problem was tithe. The LCO was dragged into the "tithe war" of the 1930s via the county courts. The Tithe Act of 1891 had been causing acute difficulties for registrars and bailiffs in recent years[15] and the unsatisfactory execution of judgments, culminating in a minor riot at Ruckinge, led to complaints from tithe owners.[16] With extreme reluctance the LCO issued a circular to clarify the legal position—"an innovation, and a dangerous one".[17] Soon afterwards there was further trouble in the same area and a buyer, deprived of his purchase by a mob, threatened to sue the bailiff and had to be compensated out of public funds.[18] The legal position was further complicated by a judgment of Swift J which favoured tithe payers but this was rapidly discountenanced by the Court of Appeal.[19] The embarrassing rural disorder obliged the government to act but there are no LCO files in this series which cover the discussions and progress of the Tithe Act 1936; it resumes with files on the drafting of the 1937 rules and the teething troubles to which they were subject.

Notes

1 *2/885: to Bishop Ryle, 18.5.1922.*

2 ***Notes from the Life of an Ordinary Mortal*** *(1911), 279. This short account of the exercise of the Lord Chancellor's patronage stresses the emphasis given to preserving continuity of doctrinal position within a parish.*

3 *2/881.*

4 *2/882: Report of Church Assembly Measures Committee, CP 72(25).*

5 *2/890, 2/3401.*

6 *2/3409.*

7 *2/881: CP 209 (24) 7.5.1924.*

8 *2/1348.*

9 *2/5152.*

10 *F. A. Iremonger,* ***William Temple*** *(1948), 347.*

11 *2/1352: to I. Heath, 24.10.1940.*

12 ***Hauxton Parochial Church Council v Stevens*** *[1929] P 240.*

13 *2/902.*

14 *See the proposals in Law Commission Working Paper no. 86 (1983).*

15 *See 2/1127–8.*

16 *2/1921: Churchmen's Defence Union to Lord Chancellor, 1.10.1931.*

17 ***Ibid****: Napier to A. Jennings, 1931.*

18 *2/1922.*

19 ***Ibid. New College v Davison*** *49 TLR 579;* ***Queen Anne's Bounty v Thorne*** *[1934] KB 175.*

2
CONVOCATION AND THE CHURCH ASSEMBLY

1/38 LC's memorandum for the Prime Minister and the Primate on the right of convocation to alter its composition (see also 2/2357, Crown Office *supra*, 311), and copy of H. Matthews to Primate (1887) with Law Officers' opinion on new canons on marriage law.

2/645, 2125, 2357, 4406 Prorogation (see *supra*), and correspondence on dissolution, 1921.

591 Church Assembly (Powers) Act 1920. Extensive correspondence with Sir H. Thring and Sir C. Ilbert on promulgation of Measures.

592 Opinion of Law Officers (1923) on propriety of government assent to Measures not yet before Parliament.

589, 881–3, 885–90, 894 Proposals on ecclesiastical patronage. Union of Benefices Rules 1920. Reports of Church Assembly's patronage committee, memorandum by Sir Lewis Dibdin (1922). Notes of departmental conference (1924) and memoranda on tactics; meetings with Lord Henry Cecil and Lord Wolmer. Cabinet papers and proceedings of its Church Assembly Measures committee, 1925; correspondence and discussions with Cecil and Wolmer, 1926. Memoranda, correspondence and discussions on: Union of Benefices (Metropolis) Measure (1924), Benefices (Patronage) Measures (1926–31), Transfer of Patronage Measure (1926–30), Benefices (Appropriation of Surplus Endowment) Measure (1926), Cathedrals Measure (1928–31).

884, 893, 1346, 891–2 Arrangements for appeals in connection with Clergy Pensions Measure 1926, Benefices (Ecclesiastical Duties) Rules 1928 and other Measures and rules on the subject (1923, 1927); County Court Rule Committee discussions.

1348 Meetings of departmental committee on report of Archbishop of Canterbury's commission on Church and State, with memoranda and report, 1936.

2689–2708, 3383, 3388, 3391–3, 3398–3402, 3404–5, 3407–8, 3410, 4132 Various Measures sent by Treasury to LCO for examination, 1942 onwards. Many are Diocesan Re-organisation Measures on which see the general Pastoral Re-organisation Measure in 3388, 3401. A few contain material relating to the LC's patronage (e.g. 2694, 2705) or observations from other departments (e.g. 3400, 3402).

5152 Report of Law Officers (1948) on the Primate's memorandum on revision of canon law. Discussions in 1951 on mode of presenting the proposals to Parliament and proceedings and reports of the "legal committee" set up to consider them.

3
QUEEN ANNE'S BOUNTY AND THE CHURCH COMMISSIONERS

(see also *Tithes*, *infra*).

2/456 Draft clause to avoid double registration under Land Transfer Acts, 1920.

1921–7 Correspondence on tithe disputes and legislation, 1931–7.

3396–7 Amalgamation of Queen Anne's Bounty with Ecclesiastical Commissioners; Lord Chancellor as member, correspondence with the Primate on constitution and papers for meetings in 1948.

4
CLERGY

1 Discipline

2/68, 119, 236, 588, 1352, 2314, 3393 Rules under Clergy Discipline Act 1892, and correspondence with Law Society and others. Amendment to cover unbeneficed clergy (1898), including correspondence with PCO. Extension to new dioceses. Rules (1944) raising solicitors' remuneration.

2 Patronage and Emoluments

2/105 Benefices Act 1898: draft rules and correspondence with Solicitor-General, PCO and Central Office; establishment of Registrar's department.

117 Lord Chancellor arbitrates in dispute over a presentation, 1895.

118, 590, 1349, 2209 Discussions with Duchy of Cornwall and Prime Minister's Office over doubtful cases.

69, 237 Select committee of Ecclesiastical Commissioners (1908) on grants to retired incumbents: correspondence with Sir L. Dibdin, minutes and report. Fees altered from scale adopted in 1894.

1347 Benefices (Purchase of Rights of Patronage) Rules 1933: correspondence with secretary to Church Assembly, memorandum on the rule committee, drafts and rules.

1350, 3394 Correspondence with Official Solicitor on resignation of insane incumbent, 1938. Memorandum on practice, 1945.

896 Correspondence on Canon Boulter's claim that conditions attached to crown livings are simoniacal, 1928.

2706, 3385, 3387, 895 Presentations *sede vacante*: arrangements on death of Archbishops, and correspondence on Archbishop of Canterbury's claim re the period before an unpresented living lapses to the Crown, with authorities, including opinion of A. Hamilton Thompson (1943). Correspondence on fees, 1928.

3390 Correspondence with Air Ministry on loss of patronage in building Heathrow Airport, 1945.

3395 Statistics and notes on sale of advowsons under the Lord Chancellor's Augmentation Act 1864, and investment of funds (1928–50).

5/1-3, 2/3409 Returns of crown livings, 1793–1940 and general file of 1948.

5
WESTMINSTER ABBEY

2/261 Petition to King in Council and accompanying papers on dispute over interpretation of its statute, 1910, with Lord Chancellor's opinion.

4240, 4658–9, 6121–2 Extensive material on the proposed Measure of 1929, referred to Lord Chancellor as Visitor. His inquiry into objections and temporary sanction; correspondence on the renewal of the scheme in 1934 with report of an inquiry by Sir W. Graham-Harrison and Lord Plender. Amended scheme 1941 and discussions on *vires*. Revived dispute 1949; petition of canons to the Privy Council and counter-petition of Dean and Chapter; correspondence with the parties, notes of meetings and setting up of Privy Council committee under Simonds LJ, with notes on possible members, report (1951) and subsequent correspondence.

6
TITHES AND CHANCEL REPAIRS

1 Tithes

2/49 Selborne's suggested rules under Tithe Rent Charge Act 1891.

778 Church Assembly report, cabinet papers, lobbying by university colleges on Tithe Bill, 1925.

1127–8, 862 Tithe Rentcharge Recovery Rules. County Court Rule Committee papers and discussions, 1926–9; correspondence with Ministry of Agriculture, Tithe Commissioners, registrars on procedure, forms and service.

1921–3 Disturbances in Kent and Sussex, 1931 onwards. Memoranda on events, circular to High Bailiffs after discussions with Treasury Solicitor. Correspondence with Queen Anne's Bounty, Home Office, registrars. CC Rule Committee meetings and papers, 1932–3, draft rules discussed with Ministry of Agriculture, Q.A.B. Cases in Hythe C.C. discussed with Treasury Solicitor, Judge Clements, Q.A.B., leading to *R. v Clements, Ex p. Q.A.B.*, *New College v Davidson.* Correspondence with Treasury on compensation to New College.

1924–7, 1298 Opinions of Danckwerts and Law Officers on Tithe Act 1936 s. 20 (1937). Transcript of *Q.A.B. v T.R.C.* (1937). Tithe Rules 1937: correspondence with departments, CCRC meeting and papers. Amended rules after discussions with Q.A.B. and Law Officers on *T.R.C. v Rosser*. Tithe (Arrears Investigation Committee) Rules 1937 and correspondence with departments on drafts.

3403 Mrs. G. H. Thompson seeks permission to collect prebendial tithes, 1947.

4229 E. C. Martin asks for simplification of county court tithe fees, 1942.

4852 Papers on Tithe Act 1951 including cabinet papers, Treasury brief, Parliamentary papers.

2 Chancel Repairs

2/898–902 Correspondence and papers arising out of *Hauxton P. C. v Stevens*, leading to the Inskip Committee; Napier's papers including minutes, memoranda, draft bill, drafts and report (Cmd 3571 of 1930); Chancel Repairs Bill 1932 with memoranda by Diocesan Chancellors, correspondence with PCO, observations by judges, conferences with Attorney-General and Parliamentary papers.

3384, 3434 4538 Miscellaneous papers, including speeches in 1944 House of Lords cases, an exemplification of 1948 and discussions on registration as local land changes, 1949.

7
MISCELLANEOUS

2/116 (Proposed gift of property to National Trust), 897 (Lord Chancellor's opinion on homage in case of a Regency) 3406 (case of the Reverend Robertson).

Appendix

1

THE LORD CHANCELLORS AND THEIR STAFF, 1872–1951

1

LORD CHANCELLORS

October 1872 to	February 1874	Roundell Palmer, LORD SELBORNE
February 1874 to	April 1880	Hugh McCalmont Cairns, LORD CAIRNS
April 1880 to	June 1885	LORD SELBORNE
June 1885 to	February 1886	Hardinge Stanley Giffard, LORD HALSBURY
February 1886 to	August 1886	Farrer Herschell, LORD HERSCHELL
August 1886 to	August 1892	LORD HALSBURY
August 1892 to	June 1895	LORD HERSCHELL
June 1895 to	December 1905	LORD HALSBURY
December 1905 to	June 1912	Robert Thresher Reid, LORD LOREBURN
June 1912 to	May 1915	Richard Burdon Haldane, LORD HALDANE
May 1915 to	December 1916	Stanley Owen Buckmaster, LORD BUCKMASTER
December 1916 to	January 1919	Robert Bannatyne Finlay, LORD FINLAY
January 1919 to	October 1922	Frederick Edwin Smith, LORD BIRKENHEAD
October 1922 to	January 1924	George Cave, LORD CAVE
January 1924 to	November 1924	LORD HALDANE
November 1924 to	March 1928	LORD CAVE
March 1928 to	June 1929	Douglas McGarel Hogg, LORD HAILSHAM
June 1929 to	June 1935	John Sankey, LORD SANKEY
June 1935 to	March 1938	LORD HAILSHAM
March 1938 to	September 1939	Frederic Herbert Maugham, LORD MAUGHAM
September 1939 to	May 1940	Thomas Inskip, LORD CALDECOTE
May 1940 to	August 1945	John Simon, LORD SIMON
August 1945 to	November 1951	William Allen Jowett, LORD JOWITT
November 1951 to	October 1954	Gavin Turnbull Simonds, LORD SIMONDS

2
PERMANENT STAFF AND PRIVATE SECRETARIES

ALDERSON, Sir Edward H.
b. 1864, grandson of Baron Alderson. Brasenose College, Oxford. Inner Temple 1890. Private Secretary to Lord Chancellor and Secretary of Commissions 1895–1900. Reading Clerk (House of Lords) 1900–17, Clerk Assistant to the Parliaments 1917–30. Clerk of the Parliaments 1930–4. KBE 1925, KCB 1931. d. 1951.

BADELEY, Henry John Fanshawe, later **LORD BADELEY**
b. 1874. Radley and Trinity College, Oxford. Clerk in Parliament Office 1897. Private Secretary to the Permanent Secretary 1903–8. Clerk of the Parliaments 1934–49. KCB 1935, CBE 1920, FSA. d. 1951.

BANKES, Robert W.
b. 1887. Eton and University College, Oxford. Inner Temple 1911. War service, ending as ADC to Lord Allenby. Private Secretary to Lord Chancellor 1919–29. Assistant Secretary and (from 1935) Secretary to Institute of Chartered Accountants 1929–49. JP. High Sheriff of Flint 1945. d. 1975.

BOGGIS-ROLFE, Hume
b. 1911. Westminster School, Freiburg University and Trinity College, Cambridge. Middle Temple 1935. Army Intelligence Corps 1939–46 (Lt-Col.). Legal Assistant 1948, Private Secretary to Lord Chancellor 1949–51, Assistant Solicitor 1951–65, Secretary to the Law Commission 1965–8, Assistant Secretary and Deputy Clerk of the Crown 1968–75, Deputy Secretary from 1970. Retired 1975.

BUTLER, A. Hugh M.
b. 1873. Harrow. Clerk in House of Lords 1895–7. Assistant Librarian 1897–1914, Librarian 1914–22. Secretary to Statute Law Revision Committee 1902–22. Private Secretary to the Permanent Secretary 1902, Secretary of Commissions 1909–14. d. 1943.

CAIRNS, William McNeile
Secretary of Commissions 1877–80.

CARTWRIGHT, Major G. H. G.
b. 1889. Eton and New College, Oxford (MA 1914). Barrister 1913. Secretary for Ecclesiastical Patronage 1921–5. d. 1976.

CLAY, Sir Charles T.
b. 1885. Harrow and Balliol College, Oxford. Assistant Private Secretary to Lord Crewe 1909–14, Secretary for Ecclesiastical Patronage 1914–5. Assistant Librarian in House of Lords 1914–22, Librarian 1922–56. Hon. Litt.D., FSA, FRA. CB 1944, Kt. 1957. d. 1978.

COLDSTREAM, Sir George P.
b. 1907. Rugby and Oriel College, Oxford. Lincoln's Inn 1930, bencher 1954. Assistant to Parliamentary Counsel 1934–9. Legal Assistant 1939–44. Assistant Secretary and Deputy Clerk of the Crown 1944–54. Permanent Secretary and Clerk of the Crown 1954–68. On British War Crimes Executive 1944–6. KCB 1955, QC 1960, KCVO 1968.

DAVIDSON, Sir W. Edward

b. 1853. Balliol College, Oxford. Inner Temple 1879, bencher 1901. Assistant to Law Officers 1881–6. Private Secretary to Lord Chancellor and Secretary of Commissions 1886. Legal Assistant Under Secretary in Foreign Office 1886–1918. QC 1892. CB, KC, KCMG. d. 1923.

DOBSON, Sir Denis W.

b. 1908. Charterhouse and Trinity College, Cambridge. LL.B, MA. Solicitor 1933, Middle Temple 1951. Statute Law Revision Office. R.A.F. 1940–5. Senior Legal Assistant 1947, Assistant Secretary and Deputy Clerk of the Crown 1954–68, Permanent Secretary and Clerk of the Crown. 1968–77. QC 1971. OBE 1945, KCB 1969.

FLETCHER, Fitzroy

b. 1918 or 1919. Legal Assistant 1947–52.

FRANCIS, Carrington

Principal Secretary and Secretary of Commissions 1872–4, Secretary of Commissions 1880–2.

GIFFARD, Hardinge F.

Son of Judge Giffard, eldest brother of Lord Halsbury. Merton College, Oxford (MA), Inner Temple 1887. Private Secretary to Lord Chancellor and Secretary of Commissions 1891–2. Secretary to Commissioners in Lunacy 1895–1900, Commissioner in Lunacy 1900–8. d. 1908.

GRAHAM, Sir Henry J. L.

b. 1842. Inner Temple 1868. Principal Secretary 1874–80. Master in Lunacy 1880–5. Clerk of the Parliaments 1885–1917. KCB 1902. d. 1930.

HAMILTON, Charles G.

b. 1857. Eton and Trinity College, Cambridge. Private Secretary to Lord Chancellor and Secretary of Commissions 1892–5. In business thereafter. OBE. d. 1955.

HARINGTON, E. H. Vernon

b. 1907. Eton. Inner Temple 1930. Private Secretary to Lord Chancellor 1934–40. War service (Major, Coldstream Guards) 1940–5, War Office 1944–5, Austrian Control Commission 1945–6. Deputy Judge-Advocate 1946–54, Assistant Judge-Advocate General 1954–73. Crown Court Recorder 1972–5. JP.

HAVILAND, Major Leonard P.

Secretary for Ecclesiastical Patronage, 1928–50.

HOPE, Sir Herbert J.

b. 1851. Eton and Christchurch College, Oxford. Inner Temple. Private Secretary to Lord Chancellor and Secretary of Commissions 1885, 1886–91. Registrar in Bankruptcy 1891–1926. Kt. 1925. d. 1930.

HOWORTH, Sir Rupert G.

b. 1880. St. Paul's and New College, Oxford. Inner Temple 1903. Board of Education, then

Treasury 1915. Cabinet Office 1919 and Deputy Secretary 1938–42. Clerk of Privy Council 1938–42. Secretary of Commissions 1945–8. CB 1926, CMG 1931, KCMG 1933, KCVO 1942. FSA. JP. d. 1964.

HUMFREY, Bruce
Inland Revenue 1925. Treasury Solicitor's Office 1929–33, on loan to LCO 1932. Assistant Official Solicitor 1934. District Registrar (Croydon) 1937–56.

LEE, Percy
Clerk in HM Land Registry 1901–19. Establishments Officer 1919–25, Chief Clerk 1925–30.

LIDDELL, Adolphus G. C.
b. 1846. Eton, Balliol College, Oxford. Bar 1871. Revising Barrister 1884–6. Counsel to the Mint for NE Counties. Chief Clerk in Crown Office 1886, Assistant Secretary 1888, also Secretary for Ecclesiastical Patronage from 1893 to 1909. Private Secretary to the Lord Chancellor 1909–15. Retired 1919. CB 1908. d. 1920.

MACAREE, J. W.
Clerk in HM Customs 1909–12. Supervisory Assistant Clerk in N.H.I. Department. Staff Clerk (Registry) 1919–34, Chief Clerk and Establishments Officer 1934–48.

MARTIN, E. C.
Principal Officer, Treasury. Superintendent of County Courts, 1924–48. MBE.

MAYELL, F.
Executive Officer, Metropolitan Police and Senior Clerk 1940. Acting Private Secretary to Lord Chancellor 1940–5, Private Secretary 1945–9, Superintendent of County Courts 1949–59.

MUIR McKENZIE, Kenneth A. (later **LORD MUIR McKENZIE**)
b. 1845, son of Sir J. W. P. Muir McKenzie, Bart. Charterhouse and Balliol College, Oxford. Lincoln's Inn 1873, Treasurer 1917. Principal Secretary 1880, Principal and Permanent Secretary 1884. Clerk of the Crown in Chancery 1885. Retired 1915 with a peerage. KC. KCB 1898, GCB 1911, PC 1924. JP. A Lord in Waiting 1924, 1929. d. 1930.

MUIR McKENZIE, Montague Ronald Alfred
b. 1881, cousin of Kenneth Muir McKenzie. Barrister. Private Secretary to Permanent Secretary 1908, and Secretary for Ecclesiastical Patronage from 1909; Private Secretary to the Permanent Secretary and Secretary of Commissions 1914–5. Deputy Sergeant at Arms in House of Lords to 1916, Reading Clerk 1916–34, Clerk Assistant to the Parliaments 1934. d. 1937.

MUIR McKENZIE, William Montague
b. 1876, son of Kenneth Muir McKenzie. Barrister. Private Secretary to Permanent Secretary 1897–1901 (died).

MURRAY, Evelyn H.
Secretary of Commissions 1882–3.

NAPIER, Sir Albert E. A.
b. 1881, younger son of Baron Napier of Magdala. Eton and New College, Oxford. Eldon Law Scholar. Inner Temple 1909. Private Secretary to Lord Chancellor and Secretary of Commissions 1915–9, Assistant Secretary and Deputy Clerk of the Crown 1919–44, Permanent Secretary and Clerk of the Crown 1944–54. KCVO 1954. d. 1973.

NEISH, Sir Charles H. L.
b. 1857. Edinburgh University (MA). Middle Temple 1881. Private Secretary to Lord Chancellor and Secretary of Commissions 1906–9. Registrar of Privy Council 1909–34. CB 1911, KBE 1924. d. 1934.

NEWMAN, Karl M. H.
b. 1919. Ottershaw College and Christchurch College, Oxford. War service 1940–2. Gray's Inn 1946. Legal Assistant 1949, Senior Legal Assistant 1959, Assistant Solicitor 1962. Under Secretary (Ecclesiastical and International Division) 1972–82. Legal adviser to House of Lords E.C. Committee 1982.

NICOL, Henry
b. 1821. Superintendent of County Courts (Treasury) 1860–91. Assistant to Lord Chancellor from 1861. d. 1905.

NORMAN, Ronald C.
b. 1873. Eton and Trinity College, Cambridge. Private Secretary to Lord Chancellor and Secretary of Commissions 1901–6. Councillor (1907–22) and Alderman (1922–34) on LCC. Chairman of BBC 1935–9. d. 1963.

OVERBURY, Sir Robert L.
b. 1887. Clerk in Central Office 1912. Staff Clerk (Crown Office) 1919–23. Secretary of Commissions 1923–30, Chief Clerk 1934. Reading Clerk in House of Lords 1934, Clerk Assistant 1937, Clerk of the Parliaments (House of Lords) 1949. Retired 1953. KCB 1950. d. 1955.

PAGE, Sir Leo
b. 1890. Beaumont, RMA Woolwich and University College, Oxford. Inner Temple 1918. JP 1925. High Sheriff of Berkshire 1937. Secretary of Commissions 1940–5. d. 1951.

PALMER, Ralph Charlton
b. 1839, son of Col. George Palmer and cousin of 1st Lord Selborne. Winchester and Balliol College, Oxford. Lincoln's Inn 1884. Principal Secretary 1880, Clerk of the Crown in Chancery 1880–5. Visitor in Lunacy 1885–1910. JP. d. 1923.

PATERSON, Aylmer J. N.
b. 1902. Rugby and Clare College, Cambridge. Middle Temple 1926. Private Secretary to Lord Chancellor 1930–4, Staff Clerk 1934–9. Chief Clerk to the Privy Council 1939–54, Registrar 1954–63. CBE 1963. d. 1977.

RANKIN, Charles W. B.
b. 1910. Legal Assistant 1949, Private Secretary to Lord Chancellor 1951.

RIDLEY, L. C.
Clerk in LCO 1922, later Staff Clerk in Crown Office. Deputy Establishments Officer 1945–59. MBE.

RIEU, R. L.
b. 1915. Solicitor. Colonial service (Gold Coast) 1939. Legal Assistant 1944, Senior Legal Assistant 1947, Assistant Solicitor 1962. District Registrar (Hastings) 1962–73.

ROBERTS, Hon. Trevor
Assistant Secretary of Commissions, 1947–53.

ROBSON, Hon. Harold
Secretary of Commissions 1919–23.

ROMILLY, Charles
b. 1808, 5th son of Sir Samuel and brother of Lord Romilly MR. Barrister. Clerk of the Crown in Chancery 1851–85. d. 1887.

ROSS, Edward
Secretary of Commissions 1875–7.

SCHUSTER, Sir Claud (later **LORD SCHUSTER**)
b. 1869. Winchester and New College, Oxford. Inner Temple 1895. Secretary to Local Government Act Commission 1899–1902. Secretary to G.N.R. Co. Legal Assistant to Board of Education 1903, Assistant Secretary 1907, Principal Assistant Secretary to Legal Department 1911. Chief Registrar of Friendly Societies, Secretary and Legal Adviser to NHI Commission 1912, and legal member of the Commission 1913. Permanent Secretary and Clerk of the Crown 1915–44. Head of legal branch of Control Commission (Austria) 1944–6. High Sheriff of Dorset 1941. Kt. 1913, CVO 1918, KC 1919, KCB 1920, GCB 1927. Created Baron Schuster 1944. d. 1956.

SELFE, Sir W. Lucius
b. 1845, son of a Police Magistrate. Inner Temple 1870. Principal Secretary to Lord Chancellor 1880. County court judge 1883–1919 and chairman of County Court Rule Committee from 1895. d. 1924.

SKYRME, Sir Thomas (W. T. C.)
b. 1913. Rugby and Universities of Oxford (New College), Dresden and Paris. Inner Temple 1935. Royal Artillery 1939–45 (Lt-Col.), twice wounded. Legal Assistant 1944. Assistant Secretary of Commissions (S.L.A.) 1946. Secretary of Commissions 1948–77. JP. DL. TD 1949, CBE 1953, CB 1966, KCVO 1974. Chairman of Broadcasting Complaints Commission.

SMITH, Colin
b. 1881. Charterhouse and Christchurch College, Oxford. Inner Temple 1903. Private Secretary to the Permanent Secretary and Secretary for Ecclesiastical Patronage 1916–21. Deputy Clerk to Privy Council 1921, Registrar 1934–40. OBE 1929, MVO 1932. d. 1940.

SMITH, Lt-Col. Samuel H.
b. 1888. Leys and Caius College, Cambridge. Inner Temple 1913. Deputy Director of Army Welfare Services 1940–4, served on Rushcliffe Committee on Legal Aid 1943. Director of

legal division of Austrian Control Commission 1947–8. Temporary Assistant Secretary 1946. MC 1917, OBE 1943. d. 1971.

SNAGGE, Major Ralph
b.c. 1911. Assistant Private Secretary to Lord Chancellor, 1945–7.

STORR, Lt-Col. Lancelot
b. 1874. Harrow, RMC Sandhurst, ISC. Regular soldier 1893–1921. DAAG War Office 1914–16, Assistant Secretary to C.I.D. 1916–21, Assistant Secretary to War Cabinet 1916–18. Secretary to Shadow Cabinet of Unionist Party 1924. Secretary for Ecclesiastical Patronage 1924–8. Chevalier of the Legion of Honour 1917, CB 1919. d. 1944.

THESIGER, Sir Edward P.
b. 1842, son of 1st Lord Chelmsford. Eton. Clerk in Parliament Office (House of Lords) 1862, Clerk Assistant 1890–1916. Secretary of Presentations 1866–90. KCB 1911. d. 1928.

THESIGER, Richard E. K.
b.c. 1912. Winchester and Magdalen College, Oxford. Barrister 1936, army service (Lt-Col.). Served with Control Commission (Austria) 1944–6. Legal Assistant 1947, Senior Legal Assistant 1948. Assistant Solicitor. Retired 1973. d. 1984.

WATERS, Lt-Col. J. Dallas
b. 1889. Beaumont and Merton College, Oxford. Inner Temple. Private Secretary to Lord Chancellor 1929–30, Secretary of Commissions 1930–40. Registrar to Privy Council 1940–54. DSO 1918, CB 1936, KCSG. DL. JP. Chairman of Cheshire Quarter Sessions 1936–61. d. 1967.

Appendix

2

REPORTS OF COMMITTEES

These are reports of Royal Commissions, select, departmental and interdepartmental committees, and committees and sub-committees set up by bodies such as the Rule Committees, and which were the subject of consideration by the LCO, either with a view to their establishment and composition, the provision of evidence or the implementation of their recommendations. The list is not exhaustive.

1871	Royal Commission on St. Katherine's Hospital	PP 1871 (C 321) XVI,371	Hatherley LC	2/5838
1874	Judges' Council Committee on Circuits		Cockburn CJ	1/4
1875	Departmental Committee (LC) on Unclaimed Dividends in Bankruptcy			1/20
1876	Royal Commission on the Criminal Code	PP 1878-9 [C-2345] XX, 169		1/42
1876	Departmental Committee (Treasury) on Office of Assistant Taxing Master in Bankruptcy			1/21
1878	Select Committee on the Lunacy Law	PP 1878 (133) XVI, 43	S. Cave	1/63
1880	Committee of Masters to consider the re-organisation of the Supreme Court Central Office			1/27
1881	Inter-departmental Committee (Board of Trade/LCO) on London Bankruptcy Court Staff			1/22
1883	Inter-departmental Committee on Fees in the Supreme Court			1/84
1885	Inter-departmental Committee on the Distribution of Staff and Business in Chancery	PP 1886 (92) LIII, 127	Lord Esher MR	2/107
	Departmental Committee on Central Office of the Supreme Court	PP 1887 (181) LXVII, 179	Coleridge LCJ	1/31–2
1886	Inter-departmental Committee (Treasury/LCO) on Classification of Clerks in Bankruptcy			1/24
1886	Judges' Council Committee on Circuits (two reports)			1/9,54

	Departmental Committee (LC) on Bankruptcy Departments' Accommodation		T. H. Farrer	2/50
1887	Inter-departmental Committee on Revising Barristers		L. Cave	1/79
1888	Departmental Committee (LC) on Scrivenery Dept of the SCJ		R. P. Pritchard	2/25
1889	Departmental Committee (LC) on Chancery Practice		Bowen LJ	2/32
	Departmental Committee (LC) on Assimilation of Supreme Court Practice on Costs		H. H. Johnson	9
	Departmental Committee (LC) on Official Referees		G. M. Dowdeswell QC	28
1891	Departmental Committee (LC) on Taxing Offices of the SCJ		H. H. Johnson	2/46
1892	Departmental Committee (Treasury) on Suitors' Funds in the SCJ		K. Muir McKenzie	2/70
1893	Departmental Committee (LC) on Companies' Winding-up Actions	1893/4 (C 7221) LXXXI, 219	Sir J. Rigby	2/97
	Departmental Committee (LC) on Staffing in the Principal Probate Registry		R. P. Pritchard	26
1894	Departmental Committee (LC) on Rules for Local Courts		C. E. Pollock	2/76
1901	Departmental Committee (LC) on HM Land Registry organisation		Lord Monkswell	2/181
	Committee on Taxation of Costs in the SCJ		Alverstone LCJ	2/192
1903	Departmental Committee (Treasury) on Heralds' College			2/164
1905	Departmental Committee (LC) on HM Land Registry Mapping Department		S. Walpole	2/182
1906	Departmental Committee (LC) on Chancery Registrars	PP 1914–16 (Cd 8130) XII, 91 at p. 362	Kekewich J	2/201

1907	Departmental Committee (LC) on Rules under the Public Trustee Act 1906			2/272
	Committee of the Ecclesiastical Commissioners on Grants to Retired Incumbents		Sir L. Dibdin	237
	Select Committee on Imprisonment for Debt	PP 1909 (239) VII, 281	E. H. Pickersgill	213
1908	Departmental Committee (B of T) on Bankruptcy	PP 1908 (Cd 4068–9) XXXIV, 1, 49; PP 1911 (Cd 5483, 5494) XXX, 1, 65	M. Muir McKenzie	2/284–5
	Royal Commission on the Land Transfer Acts	PP 1909 (Cd 4510) XXVII, 733	Lord St. Aldwyn	260
	Departmental Committee (LC) on County Courts	PP 1909 (71) LXXII, 311	Lord Gorell	210, 214
1909	Departmental Committee (LC) on Lunacy Administration	PP 1914–16 (Cd 8130) XII, 91 at p. 755	H. H. Cozens-Hardy MR	2/264
1911	Departmental Committee (LC) on Preservation of Documents in the RCJ		H. H. Cozens-Hardy MR	2/336
1913	Committee on rules under Criminal Procedure Bill		Avory J	2/200
	Committee of KBD Judges on Report of the Royal Commission on Delays in the KBD			324
	Committee on Distribution of County Courts in Lancashire			294
1915	Royal Commission on the Civil Service, 6th Report	PP 1914–16 (Cd 7832) XII, 1; (Cd 8130) XII, 91.	Sir H. B. Smith	2/370
	Department Committee (LC) on Organisation of SCJ Staff		Lord Muir-McKenzie	370
1916	SC Rule Committee sub-committee on Revision of Rules		Scrutton LJ	2/395, 402, 422
1917	Report of the Machinery of Government Committee of the Ministry of Reconstruction	PP 1918 (Cd 9230) XII, 1	Lord Haldane	2/938

1918	Cabinet Committee on Continuation of Emergency Laws		Lord Cave	2/438
	Departmental Committee (LC) on British and Foreign Legal Procedure	PP 1919 (Cmd 251) XXIV, 333	Lord Sumner	483, 555
	Committee on Reconstruction: Acquisition and Valuation of Land Committee, four reports	PP 1918 (Cd 8998) XI, 1; 1918 (Cd 9229) XI, 59; 1919 (Cmd 156) XXIX, 51; 1919 (Cmd 424) XXIX, 89	Sir L. Scott	3/1–45, 2/508–9
1919	Inter-departmental Committee on Indemnity and Limitations for Wartime Actions		Lord Peel	2/440
	Select Committee (H of C) on the Indemnity Bill	PP 1920 (136) VII, 391	Sir S. Roberts	441
	Departmental Committee (LC) on the Public Trustee Office	PP 1919 (Cmd 421, 422) XXVIII, 337, 341	Sir G. H. Murray	484–8
	Departmental Committee (LC) on the Organisation and Staff of the Supreme Court (13 reports)		T. J. C. Tomlin KC	2/489–506
	Departmental Committee (LC) on Poor Persons' Rules	PP 1919 (Cmd 430) XXVII, 743	P. O. Lawrence J	2/557, 32/1–5
	Departmental Committee (LC) on County Court Staff	PP 1920 (Cmd 1049) XIII, 307	Swift J	2/525
	Committee to frame RSC (Women Jurors) 1920		Avory J	559
1920	Departmental Committee (LC) on Sheriffs' and Bailiffs' Fees		McCardie J	2/661
	Departmental Committee (HC) on the Workmen's Compensation Acts	PP 1920 (Cmd 816, 908–9) XXVI, 1, 87	Holman Gregory	671
	County Court Rule Committee sub-committee on County Courts Act 1888 ss 138–9		A. L. Lowe	534
	County Court Rule Committee sub-committee on "Branch Courts"		Judge Cann	534
	Departmental Committee (LC) on Supreme Court Fees	PP 1922 (Cmd 1565) X, 607	Sir M. MacNaghten	514–6

1921	Departmental Committee (LC) on Detention of Prisoners Awaiting Trial	PP 1922 (Cmd 1574) X, 405	Horridge J	2/521A
	Committee on Solicitors' Remuneration		Russell J	472
	D.P.P.'s Committee on Criminal Procedure	PP 1923 (Cmd 1813) X, 273	Sir A. Bodkin	583, 712–7
	Departmental Committee (LC) on County Court Fees	PP 1923 (Cmd 1856) X, 231	Sir M. MacNaghten	541–3
	Departmental Committee (LC) on Insanity and Crime	PP 1923 (Cmd 2005) XII (1) 787	Atkin J	585
	Cabinet Committee on the Reform of the House of Lords			597
	Departmental Committee (LC) on Crown Proceedings	PP 1927 (Cmd 2842) VIII, 193	Hewart LCJ	1093–1101, 1038
1922	Departmental Committee (LC) on Refreshments in the R.C.J.		Master G. A. Bonner	29/7
	Departmental Committee (LC) on Coercion of Wives	PP 1922 (Cmd 1677) VII, 219	Avory J	2/584
	Departmental Committee (LC) on Civil Judicial Statistics		Sir T. Willes Chitty	29/9
	Cabinet Committees on the Rent Acts, and on Minister of Health's Committee Report	PP 1920 (Cd 658) XVIII, 315		2/478–9
	SC Rule Committee sub-committee on Jury Rules		Bray J	578A
	House of Lords Committee of Privileges Report on Lady Rhondda's Claim			599
	Departmental Committee (LC) on Carriage of Goods by Sea Bill	[Report of U.K. delegates at Brussels published by the Board of Trade]	Sir L. Scott	756
	Board of Control Committee on Clinical Records in Lunacy			947
	Departmental Committee (LC) on Re-arrangement of Assize Towns	PP 1923 (Cmd 1831) IX, 925	Swift J	522–3

	Departmental Committee (LC) on District Probate Registries	PP 1923 (Cmd 1968) XII(2), 525	T. J. C. Tomlin KC	646
1923	Departmental Committee (LC) on Infants' Damages and the Public Trustee	PP 1923 (Cmd 1870) XII(2), 519	Branson J	2/648
	County Court Rule Committee sub-committee on the Seal of the Court			538
	Departmental Committee (LC) on Poor Persons' Rules	PP 1924–5 (Cmd 2358) XV, 313	P. O. Lawrence J	644
	Departmental Committee on the Law of Property Consolidation Bills	PP 1924 (Cmd 2271) XI, 363	Romer J	763–4
1924	Royal Commission on Lunacy	PP 1926 (Cmd 2700) XIII, 373	Lord Macmillan	2/952
	Departmental Committee (LC) on County Court Accounts		H. P. Boland	8/44
	Cabinet Committee on Church Assembly Measures		Lord Cave	2/882
	Supreme Court Rule Committee sub-committee on Third Party Procedure		Roche J	1026
	Committee of Inquiry into the case of ex-Inspector Syme.	PP 1924 (Cmd 2193) XII, 149	Talbot J	2/4698 A & B
	President of the PD & A Division's Committee of Inquiry into District Probate Registry Accounting Systems		W. A. Inderwick	989
1925	Committee on Statutory Will Forms under Law of Property Act 1925 s. 179		A. C. Clauson KC	2/1087
	Departmental Committee (Board of Trade) on Bankruptcy	PP 1924–5 (Cmd 2326) IX, 249	E. W. Hansell	695
	Joint Select Committee on the Moneylenders Bill	PP 1924–5 (Cmd 153) VIII, 31	Lord Darling	776
	President of the PD & A Division's Committee on the Custody of Probate Records	(Non-Parliamentary publication)	A. C. Pereira	993

	Inter-departmental Committee (LC & Home Office) on Legal Aid	PP 1926 (Cmd 2638) XIII, 195; 1928 (Cmd 3016) XI, 243	Finlay J	979–87
1926	House of Lords Committee on Peerages in Abeyance	PP 1926 (HL 189, 190) VI, 337	Lord Sumner	2/598
	Departmental Committee (LC) on Trustee Securities	PP 1928 (Cmd 3107) XII, 497	P. O. Lawrence J	1043–7
	Departmental Committee (LC) on Dormant Funds in the Supreme Court		Tomlin J	1018
	Departmental Committee (LC) on the Arbitration Acts	PP 1927 (Cmd 2817) VII, 157	MacKinnon J	755, 1197–1201
1927	Departmental Committee (LC) on Arbitration		Greer J	2/1038
	Departmental Committee (LC) on "Walking Possession"		Swift J	2/807, 844, 8/58
	Probate Registry Committee of Inquiry on Judicature Stamps		C. A. Pereira	2/994
	Departmental Committee on Welsh Language (Ministry of Education)	(1927, Non-Parliamentary)		4418
	Departmental Committee (LC) on Arrestment of Foreigners' Goods	PP 1928 (Cmd 3108) VII, 103	Hill J	1051–4
	Departmental Committee (LC) on Legal Education: sub-committee report		Atkin J	706
1928	Departmental Committee (LC) on Staff in the Taxing Office of the Supreme Court		Tomlin J	29/26
	Departmental Committee (LC) on HM Land Registry and the Ordnance Survey		Sir J. Stewart-Wallace	2/1105
	Departmental Committee (LC) on Adhesive Stamps in the SCJ		Sir M. MacNaghten KC	1014–7
1929	Departmental Committee (LC) on the Destruction of Public Records		Lord Hanworth MR	4/309–11, 27/29
	Departmental Committee (LC) on Poor Persons (Divorce Jurisdiction)	PP 1929–30 (Cmd 3375) XVII, 265	Sir C. Schuster	2/1055–7

	Departmental Committee (LC) on Reciprocal Enforcement of Judgments		Greer J	1687
	Supreme Court Rule Committee sub-committee on Rule Proposals		Swift J	1061
	Departmental Committee (LC) on Cost of Small Actions in the High Court	No report	Talbot J	1063
	Departmental Committee (LC) on Title Registration	PP 1929–30 (Cmd 3564) XV, 539	Lord Tomlin	1106–8
	Departmental Committee (LC) on Chancel Repairs	PP 1929–30 (Cmd 3571) VIII, 373	Sir T. Inskip	898–902
	Committee of KBD Judges on Business at the Autumn Assizes			692
	Departmental Committee (Ministry of Transport) on Railway and Canal Commission		Sir. C. Schuster	1556–9
	Departmental Committee (LC) on Ministers' Powers	PP 1931–2 (Cmd 4060) XII, 341	Lord Donoughmore	939, 1133–4
1930	Departmental Committee (LC) on the Scrivenery Department of the SCJ		Master G. A. Bonner	29/32
	Departmental Committee (LC) on the Supreme Court Broker		Sir C. Schuster	2/1024
	Cabinet legal sub-committee on the appointment of Counsellors of State			825
	Departmental Committee (Board of Trade) on Patents and Designs	PP 1930–1 (Cmd 3829) XVI, 709	Sargent J	1192
	Royal Commission on the Civil Service	PP 1930–1 (Cmd 3909) X, 517	Lord Tomlin	4/121
1931	Inter-departmental Committee on Codification of International Law			2/1424
	Inter-departmental Committee on Reciprocal Enforcement of Judgments	PP 1932–3 (Cmd 4213) X, 585	Greer LJ	2/1688–90
	Supreme Court Rule Committee sub-committee on Law of Evidence		Greer LJ	1718–9
1932	Departmental Committee (LC) on Dormant Funds	PP 1931–2 (Cmd 4152) VII, 969	Lord Tomlin	2/1257

	Departmental Committee (LC) on the Business of the Courts	PP 1932–3 (Cmd 4265) X, 561; 1933–4 (Cmd 4471) XI, 1; 1935–6 (Cmd 5066) VIII, 81	Lord Hanworth MR	2/1597–1609
	Departmental Committee (LC) on Legal Education	PP 1933–4 (Cmd 4663) XI, 197	Lord Atkin	1438–44
1933	Supreme Court Rule Committee sub-committee Order XXII (Payments into Court)		Swift J	2/1738–9
1934	Law Revision Committee "Actio Personalis"	PP 1933–4 (Cmd 4540) XI, 169	Lord Hanworth MR	2/1968
	Law Revision Committee on Interest on Civil Judgments	PP 1933–4 (Cmd 4546) XI, 179	Lord Hanworth MR	1970
	Law Revision Committee on Contribution Between Tortfeasors	PP 1933–4 (Cmd 4637) XI, 187	Lord Hanworth MR	1967
	Law Revision Committee on Liability of Husband for Wife's Torts	PP 1934 (Cmd 4770) X, 427	Lord Hanworth MR	1969
	Departmental Committee (LC) on Land Transfer	PP 1934–5 (Cmd 4776) X, 395	Lord Tomlin	1481–4
	Supreme Court Rule Committee's Committee on Poor Persons Procedure	(Non-Parliamentary, 1934)	Sir F. B. Merriman P	1143–4
	Royal Commission on the Despatch of Business at Common Law	PP 1935–6 (Cmd 5065) VIII, 105	Lord Peel	1610–6
	Supreme Court Rule Committee sub-committee on Mortgagees' Actions		Maugham LJ	1781–2
1935	Committee on Renewals of the Westminster Abbey Measure, 1929		Sir W. Graham-Harrison	2/6221
	Inter-departmental Committee on the Employment of Women in the Diplomatic and Consular Services	PP 1935–6 (Cmd 5166) XXVII, 21	Sir C. Schuster	1150
	Inter-departmental Committee on the Management and Administration Department of the SCJ		Sir J. Fischer-Williams	4/47–52

	Inter-departmental Committee on the International Law of the Sale of Goods		Lord Roche	2/1430–1
	Law Revision Committee on Limitations	PP 1935–6 (Cmd 5334) XIII, 37	Lord Wright MR	1979
	Departmental Committee (Home Office) on Law and Practice of Coroners	PP 1935–6 (Cmd 5070) VIII, 1	Lord Wright MR	1244–5
1936	Departmental Committee (LC) on the Shorthand Writers in the SCJ	PP 1936–7 (Cmd 5395) IX, 541	Atkinson J	4/85
	Departmental Committee (LC) on Circuit Towns	PP 1935–6 (Cmd 5262) VIII, 253	Finlay J	2/1167–71
	Departmental Committee (LC) on Quarter Sessions	PP 1935–6 (Cmd 5252) VIII, 265	Sir A. Bodkin	1328
	Departmental Committee (Home Office) on Adoption Societies	PP 1936–7 (Cmd 5499) IX, 1	Mrs. F. Horsbrugh	1162
	Cabinet legal sub-committee on Report of the Archbishop of Canterbury's Commission on Relations between Church and State		Sir C. Schuster	1348
	Departmental Committee (Treasury) on Fixed Trusts	PP 1935–6 (Cmd 5259) X, 521	Sir J. Anderson	1657
	Departmental Committee (LC) on Photographic Copying in the SCJ		Hon. A. Napier	1819, 4068
1937	Law Revision Committee on Statute of Frauds and the Doctrine of Consideration in Contracts	PP 1936–7 (Cmd 5449) XIII, 81	Lord Wright MR	2/1990–1
	Departmental Committee (Home Office) on Metropolitan Courts of Summary Justice	Non-Parliamentary	Sir A. Maxwell	1453
	Departmental Committee (Treasury) on Crown Office Fees	PP 1936–7 (Cmd 5450) XI, 751; 1937–8 (Cmd 5767) XII, 349	Sir C. Schuster	1529–30, 1533
	Supreme Court Rule Committee sub-committee on the Matrimonial Causes Rules		Sir F. B. Merriman P	1842–3
	Departmental Committee (India Office) on Indian Divorce Jurisdiction Act			1445

	Law Revision Committee on Frustrated Contracts	PP 1938–9 (Cmd 6009) XII, 679	Lord Wright MR	1990–1
1938	Hostilities Committee (LC) on Liability to Repair War-Damaged Property	PP 1939 (Cmd 5934) XV, 523	A. A. Uthwatt KC	2/1500–1
	Departmental Committee (LC) on Official Solicitor's Department		Sir H. Fass	4/1–5
	Departmental Committee (LC) on Accommodation at the Law Courts		Humphreys J	4/327
	Committee on Precautions in the Courts during Wartime		Maugham LC	2/1373, 1361–3
	Departmental Committee on Courts-Martial	PP 1939–40 (Cmd 6200) IV, 49	Oliver J	4335
	Law Revision Committee on Contributory Negligence	PP 1939 (Cmd 6032) XII, 691	Lord Wright MR	1992
	Departmental Committee (Home Office) on Distress		Judge Lilley	1343
	Departmental Committee (Home Office) on Justices' Clerks	PP 1944 (Cmd 6507) IV, 189	Lord Roche	1449–51
1939	Departmental Committee (LC) on Effects of War on Contracts	PP 1939 (Cmd 6100) XV, 573	A. A. Uthwatt KC	2/1503
	Departmental Committee (LC) on the Supply of Transcripts to the Court of Appeal in Poor Persons' Cases		Finlay LJ	2/1874
	Departmental Committee (LC) on Law Reporting	Non-Parliamentary	Simonds J	1151–3
	Departmental Committee (LC) on the Middlesex Deeds Registry		Farwell J	1493
	Departmental Committee (Foreign Office) on Marriage Laws		Sir W. Graham-Harrison	1148–9
	Select Committee (House of Lords) on Official Secrets Act and Parliament			1206
	Cabinet sub-committee on Civil Liabilities: six reports (1939–41)		Sir C. Schuster	2/1391–9, 1412

	Report of a Conference on War Damaged Property	PP 1939 (Cmd 6116) XV, 553	Lord Weir	1504
	Departmental Committee (LC) on Divorce at Assizes (suspended)		Hodson J	1836–7
	Departmental Committee (LC) on Rules of Evidence in Wartime		Lord Maugham	1878–81, 2638
	Committee on Defamation	PP 1948 (Cmd 7536) I, 559	Lord Porter	3058–68
1940	Departmental Committee (LC) on Rules of Criminal Evidence in Wartime		Humphreys LJ	2/1879–81
1941	Select Committee (H of C) on Offices of Profit under the Crown	PP 1940–1 (Cmd 120) III, 487		2/1136
	Supreme Court Rule Committee sub-committee on Advertisements for Creditors in Wartime			1910
1942	Departmental Committee (Ministry of Works) on Land Utilisation in Rural Areas	PP 1941–2 (Cmd 6378) IV, 421	Sir L. Scott	2/2749
	Departmental Committee (LC) on Land Transfer	PP 1942–3 (Cmd 6467) V, 21	Lord Rushcliffe	2750–3, 3547
	Departmental Committee on Divorce in the Provinces	PP 1942 (Cmd 6480) V, 659	Sir Ralph Wedgwood	4171–7
1943	Inter-departmental Committee on Rent Controls	PP 1944 (Cmd 6621) V, 499	Lord Ridley	2/3006
	Royal Commission on Population	PP 1948–9 (Cmd 7695) XIX, 635	H. D. Henderson	3007
	Inter-departmental Committee on Alternative Remedies	PP 1945–6 (Cmd 6860) XIII, 281	Sir W. Monckton	3775–80
1944	Departmental Committee (LC) on Effects of the Decision in *Lace* v *Chantler*		Evershed J	2/3568
	United Nations War Crimes Commission		Sir C. Hurst	2/2976–7
	Inter-departmental Committee on Rehabilitation of Coastal Towns in South-East England		Sir W. Jowitt	2/3419, 3610

	Departmental Committee (LC) on Amendments to the Limitation Acts	PP 1945 (Cmd 6591) V, 239	W. L. McNair	3570
	Departmental Committee (Home Office) on Enforcement of Judgment Orders		Sir D. Somervell	3918
	Joint Select Committee on the Machinery of Government sub-committee on Parliamentary Procedure		Sir D. Maxwell-Fyfe	3211–3
	Cabinet legal committee on Defence Regulations		Lord Schuster	3424
	Departmental Committee (LC) on Legal Aid and Advice	PP 1944–5 (Cmd 6641) V, 187	Lord Rushcliffe	3899–3902
1945	Cabinet legal committee on War Crimes		Sir D. Somervell	2/2980
	Royal Commission on Justices of the Peace	PP 1947–8 (Cmd 7463) XII, 733	Lord du Parcq	3481–3, 4475
	Select Committee (H of C) on Offices of Profit under the Crown			3010
	Committee on Electoral Law Reform	PP 1945 (Cmd 6606) V, 59; 1947–8 (Cmd 7286) XI, 727	Sir C. Carr	3679
	Departmental Committee (Treasury) on Civil Service Recruitment during Reconstruction	PP 1945–6 (Cmd 6824) VIII, 7	Sir A. Barlow	4/123
	Joint Select Committee on the Roosevelt Memorial	PP 1945–6 (Cmd 184) IX, 787	Lord Halifax	2/3019
	Royal Commission on Inventions (1st interim) report)	PP 1948–9 (Cmd 7586) XVII, 345	Cohen J	3877
	Committee on Patent Law	PP 1944–5 (Cmd 6618) V, 421; 1945–6 (Cmd 6789) XIV, 155; 1946–7 (Cmd 7206) XIII, 457	K. R. Swan KC	3877, 4045, 4060
	Cabinet Committee on the Reform of Legal Procedure		Lord Jowitt	3927
1946	Departmental Committee (LC) on Circuit Officers		Lord Caldecote	2/4471–2, 4/69–72

	Departmental Committee (Scottish Office) on Leasehold Shop Premises	PP 1947–8 (Cmd 7285) XVI, 257	T. M. Taylor	2/4546
	Committee on Procedure in Matrimonial Causes	PP 1945–6 (Cmd 6881) XIII, 789; (Cmd 6945) XIII, 795; 1946–7 (Cmd 7824) XIII, 187	Denning J	3946–64
1947	Departmental Committee (LC) on Leaseholds	PP 1948–9 (Cmd 7706) XII, 471; 1950 (Cmd 7982) XII, 703	Uthwatt J, Jenkins LJ	2/4546–67
	President of the PD & A's Committee on the Denning Report		Hodson J	3957
	Departmental Committee (Home Office) on Witnesses Allowances Regulations	Non-Parliamentary	F. C. Johnson	4051
	Committee on Army and Air Force Courts-Martial	PP 1948–9 (Cmd 7608) XIV, 61	Lewis J	4336, 4342
	Committee on Services' Aid Scheme		Lord Schuster	4636–41
	Report on Control Commission Courts		Sir F. A. Newsam, Sir T. Matthew	4423
	Committee (LC) on County Courts	PP 1947–8 (Cmd 7486) XI, 321; 1948–9 (Cmd 7668) XIII, 805	Judge Austin Jones	3293–3305, 3312–3
	Committee (LC) on the Supreme Court Practice and Procedure	PP 1948–9 (Cmd 7764) XIV, 1; 1950–1 (Cmd 8176) XVI, 661; 1951–2 (Cmd 8617) XV, 409; 1952–3 (Cmd 8878) XVI, 409	Evershed MR	3929–44, 3966–4040, 4645
1948	Royal Commission on Capital Punishment	PP 1952–3 (Cmd 8932) VII, 677	Sir E. Gowers	2/4500
	Committee on Air Accident Investigation Procedure	PP 1948–9 (Cmd 7564) XI, 183	C. M. Newton	3691, 6356
	Inter-departmental Committee on the Lewis Report		Sir A. Napier	4336–41
	Legal Committee on Medical Partnerships (Ministry of Health)	PP 1948–9 (Cmd 7565) XVII, 787	G. O. Slade KC	4455

	Select Committee on Hybrid Bills			4481
	Officials' Committee on Parliamentary Reform Discussions		N. Brook	3134–6
	Committee on Limitation of Actions	PP 1948–9 (Cmd 7740) XVII, 727	Tucker LJ	4586–91
	Departmental Committee (Scottish Office) on Leasehold Premises	PP 1948–9 (Cmd 7603) XIII, 513; 1950 (Cmd 7903) XIV, 192	H. W. Guthrie	4580
1949	Departmental Committee (Colonial Office) on Crown Proceedings in the Colonies			2/3370
	Cabinet Committee on Hardship Cases in Development Charges			4296
	Cabinet Committee on the Geneva Convention			4309
	Royal Commission on Betting and Gambling	PP 1950–1 (Cmd 8190) VIII, 625	Sir H. U. Willink	3603
	Committee on Local Land Charges	PP 1951–2 (Cmd 8440) XVI, 287	Sir J. A. Stainton	4519–42
	Royal Commission on Charitable Trusts	PP 1952–3 (Cmd 8710) VIII, 5	Lord Nathan	4646–8
	Committee on Procedure in Supreme Court of Northern Ireland		Black LJ	5910
1950	Departmental Committee (Foreign Office) on the Status of the Korean Conflict		Sir H. Makins	2/3222
	Attorney-General's Committee on Justices of the Peace Act 1949 s. 10(5) (Borough Commissions)		Sir H. Shawcross	3521–6
	Inter-departmental Committee on Naval Courts-Martial	PP 1950–1 (Cmd 8094, 8119) XVIII, 511, 569	Pilcher J	4343–5, 4347
	Inter-departmental Committee on the Lewis and Pilcher Reports	See PP 1950–1 (Cmd 8141) XXVII, 31 for recommendations		4345–7
	Officials Working Party on the Leasehold Property (Temporary Provisions) Bill		Sir B. Gilbert	4568–71

	Departmental Committee on the Salford Hundred Court	PP 1950–1 (Cmd 8364) XI, 55	G. R. Upjohn KC	3786
	Committee on Intestate Succession	PP 1950–1 (Cmd 8310) XV, 637	Lord Morton	4441, 4443, 4445–50
1951	House of Lords Select Committee on Tied Votes at Committee Stage of Bills		Lord Drogheda	4505
	Officials Committee on Judicial Salaries		T. Padmore	4610
	Privy Council Committee on Westminster Abbey Charter		Simonds LJ	4658–9
1951	Prime Minister's Legal Committee on Canon Law Revision		Sir T. Barnes	2/5152
	Report on the Extension of Registration of Title to Surrey (Lord Chancellor's Office)	Non-Parliamentary	J. N. Gray KC	5370–2
	Report on the Gambia Poultry Scheme	PP 1951–2 (Cmd 8560) IX, 433	Upjohn J	4759–61
	Committee on Abuses of State Immunity	PP 1951–2 (Cmd 8460) XXX, 197	Lord Somervell	4664–5
	Committee on Coroners Rules	Non-Parliamentary	Austin Jones J	4958–62
	Committee on Civil Liability for Damage Done By Animals	PP 1952–3 (Cmd 8746) XIV, 981	Goddard LCJ	5611–5
	Departmental Committee (LC) on Manpower and Hours of Work in the RCJ		Sir E. Herbert	4/133–8
	President of PDA's Committee on Ancient Probate Records			5792
1952	Committee on Colonial Criminal Appeals		J. D. Waters	2/4509–13
	Inter-departmental Committee on "Imperfect" Charitable Trusts		Sir T. Barnes	4649
	Inter-departmental Committee on the Nathan Report		E. W. Playfair	4653–6

Appendix

3

STATUTES AND BILLS

This list is highly selective. It includes only those Bills in whose preparation the LCO was consulted or became involved and those whose interpretation or consequences gave rise to significant activity on the part of the department.

1
PUBLIC ACTS

39 & 40 Vic		
c 59	Appellate Jurisdiction Act 1876	1/3
44 & 45 Vic		
55	National Debt Act 1881	1/72
45 & 46 Vic		
31	Inferior Courts Judgments Extension Act 1882	1/49
46 & 47 Vic		
52	Bankruptcy Act 1883	1/16
52 & 53 Vic		
41	Lunacy Act 1889	1/62–8, 2/6–7
47	Durham Palatinate Court Act 1889	2/22
63	Interpretation Act 1889	36
53 & 54 Vic		
5	Lunacy Act 1890	1/62–8, 2/6–7
23	Chancery Court of Lancaster Act 1890	2/21
39	Partnership Act 1890	42
54 & 55 Vic		
49	Tithe Act 1891	2/49
64	Land Registry (Middlesex Deeds) Act 1891	40
56 & 57 Vic		
58	Companies (Winding Up) Act 1893	2/65
57 & 58 Vic		
16	Supreme Court of Judicature (Procedure) Act 1894	2/92, 139
59 & 60 Vic		
21	Liverpool Court of Passage Act 1896	2/122
45	Stannaries Court (Abolition) Act 1896	136
62 & 63 Vic		
6	Supreme Court of Judicature Act 1899	2/140
63 & 64 Vic		
19	Land Registry (New Buildings) Act 1900	2/129

9 & 10 Geo V

7	Increase of Rent and Mortgage Interest (Restrictions) Act 1919	2/385
55	Courts (Emergency Powers) Act 1919	438
70	County Court Judges Act 1919	434–6
71	Sex Disqualification (Removal) Act 1919	439
80	Patents and Designs Act 1919	437

10 & 11 Geo V

20	War Emergency Laws (Continuance) Act 1920	2/438
48	Indemnity Act 1920	440–1
51	Duchy of Lancaster Act 1920	795
68	Juvenile Courts (Metropolis) Act 1920	463
78	Juries (Emergency Provisions) Act 1920	465
81	Administration of Justice Act 1920	611, 442

11 & 12 Geo V

7	Tribunals of Enquiry (Evidence) Act 1921	2/468
36	Juries (Emergency Provisions Renewal) Act 1921	473
55	Railways Act 1921	470
56	Supreme Court of Judicature Officers Act 1921	464

12 & 13 Geo V

11	Juries Act 1922	2/466
12	Solicitors Act 1922	462
16	Law of Property Act 1922	472, 443–59
18	Infanticide Act 1922	476
19	Gaming Act 1922	474
27	Solicitors (Articled Clerks) Act 1922	424
56	Criminal Law Amendment Act 1922	469
60	Lunacy Act 1922	475

13 & 14 Geo V

13	Rent (Notice of Increase) Act 1923	2/478–9

14 & 15 Geo V

17	County Courts Act 1924	2/709–11
18	Prevention of Eviction Act 1924	762
22	Carriage of Goods by Sea Act 1924	756
39	Arbitration Clauses (Protocol) Act 1924	755

15 & 16 Geo V

4	Law of Property (Postponement) Act 1924	2/763–72
5	Law of Property (Amendment) Act 1924	763–72
18	Settled Land Act 1925	763–72
19	Trustee Act 1925	763–72
20	Law of Property Act 1925	763–72
21	Land Registration Act 1925	763–72
22	Land Charges Act 1925	763–72
23	Administration of Estates Act 1925	763–72
28	Administration of Justice Act 1925	726–36
45	Guardianship of Infants Act 1925	757–9

21	Treachery Act 1940	1383
28	Evidence and Powers of Attorney Act 1940	1880–5
34	Middlesex Deeds Act 1940	1493
35	Indian and Colonial Divorce Jurisdiction Act 1940	1445
37	Courts (Emergency Powers) Amendment Act 1940	1381
38	Truck Act 1940	1514–5
45	Emergency Powers (Defence) (no. 2) Act 1940	4261

4 & 5 Geo VI

7	Diplomatic Privileges (Extension) Act 1941	2/1410
8	House of Commons Disqualification (Temporary Provisions) Act 1941	1411
12	War Damage Act 1941	1505, 1507–8
21	Allied Powers (Maritime Courts) Act 1941	1406
24	Liabilities (War-Time Adjustment) Act 1941	1400–4, 1909
27	Justices of the Peace (Supplemental List) Act 1941	1456
28	Trustee (War Damage Insurance) Act 1941	1930
41	Landlord and Tenant (War Damage) Act 1941	1416–7
46	Solicitors Act 1941	1581–4
47	Marriage (Members of HM Forces) Act 1941	1420

5 & 6 Geo VI

26	Pensions (Mercantile Marine) Act 1942	2/2646
28	War Damage Amendment Act 1942	2725
31	Visiting Forces (U.S.A.) Act 1942	2715
37	Prolongation of Parliament Act 1942	2660
40	Welsh Courts Act 1942	4419

6 & 7 Geo VI

2	Supreme Court (Northern Ireland) Act 1942	2/2647
5	Minister of Town and Country Planning Act 1942	2650
9	Universities (Trusts) Act 1943	2648
14	British Nationality and Status of Aliens Act 1943	2649
17	Nurses Act 1943	2651
18	Evidence and Powers of Attorney Act 1943	4277
19	Courts (Emergency Powers) Act 1943	2730
21	War Damage Act 1943	2731
24	Catering Wages Act 1943	2653
25	Settled Land and Trustee Acts (Courts General Powers) Act 1943	2756–7
29	Town and Country Planning (Interim Development) Act 1943	2658
32	Hydro-Electric Development (Scotland) Act 1943	2659
35	Foreign Service Act 1943	2654
38	Coal Act 1943	2655
39	Pensions Appeal Tribunals Act 1943	2780–1
40	Law Reform (Frustrated Contracts) Act 1943	1943–4
42	Regency Act 1943	3034
48	Parliament (Elections and Meeting) Act 1943	2660–1

7 & 8 Geo VI

5	Landlord and Tenant (Requisitioned Land) Act 1944	2/2663

7	Prize Salvage Act 1944	3036
10	Disabled Persons (Employment) Act 1944	3038
11	House of Commons Disqualification (Temporary Provisions) Act 1944	3042
12	Income Tax (Offices and Employments) Act 1944	3041
14	India (Attachment of States) Act 1944	3040
19	National Loans Act 1944	3047
21	Pensions (Increase) Act 1944	3048
23	Finance Act 1944	3046
24	Parliamentary Electors (War-Time Registration) Act 1944	3049
25	Law Officers Act 1944	3567
29	Food and Drugs (Milk and Dairies) Act 1944	3050
31	Education Act 1944	2656–7
34	Validation of War-Time Leases Act 1944	3568
35	National Fire Service Regulations (Indemnity) Act 1944	3051
40	Liabilities (War-Time Adjustment) (Amendment) Act 1944	3419, 3610–1
43	Matrimonial Causes (War Marriages) Act 1944	4185
47	Town and Country Planning Act 1944	3043–5

8 & 9 Geo VI

5	Representation of the People Act 1945	2/3078
15	Licensing Planning (Temporary Provisions) Act 1945	3072
16	Limitations (Enemies and War Prisoners) Act 1945	3573–4
17	Wages Councils Act 1945	3079
18	Statutory Orders (Special Procedure) Act 1945	3069
27	Welsh Church (Burial Grounds) Act 1945	3076
28	Law Reform (Contributory Negligence) Act 1945	3563
31	Emergency Powers (Defence) Act 1945	3085
33	Town and Country Planning (Scotland) Act 1945	3071
36	Distribution of Industry Act 1945	3077
38	Local Government (Boundary Commission) Act 1945	3477
40	Postponement of Polling Day Act 1945	3083
41	Family Allowances Act 1945	3084
42	Water Act 1945	3082
43	Requisitioned Land and War Works Act 1945	2652
44	Treason Act 1945	3073

9 & 10 Geo VI

2	Ministry of Defence Act 1946	2/3129
6	Chartered Bodies (Resumption of Elections) Act 1946	3094
8	War Damage (Valuation Appeals) Act 1946	3092
10	Supplies and Services (Transitional Provisions) Act 1946	3424
20	Building Materials and Housing Act 1946	3080
21	Elections and Jurors Act 1946	3097
23	India (Proclamation of Emergency) Act 1946	3093
26	Emergency Laws (Transitional Provisions) Act 1946	3089
27	Bank of England Act 1946	3090
28	Assurance Companies Act 1946	3074
34	Furnished Houses (Rent Control) Act 1946	3100
36	Statutory Instruments Act 1946	3091
38	National Service Act 1946	3106

51	Legal Aid and Advice Act 1949	4621–8
59	Licensing Act 1949	4479
63	Legal Aid and Solicitors (Scotland) Act 1949	4621–2
72	Iron and Steel Act 1949	4359
76	Marriage Act 1949	6674
87	Patents Act 1949	4060–1
92	India (Consequential Provisions) Act 1949	4488–9
98	Adoption of Children Act 1949	4483
100	Law Reform (Miscellaneous Provisions) Act 1949	3646, 4190, 4196, 4484
101	Justices of the Peace Act 1949	3489, 4475–8
103	Parliament Act 1949	3133–6

14 Geo VI

23	Coal-Mining (Subsidence) Act 1950	2/4333
29	Medical Act 1950	4491

14 & 15 Geo VI

11	Administration of Justice (Pensions) Act 1950	2/4609–10
25	Supplies and Services (Defence Purposes) Act 1951	3431
28	Long Leases (Temporary Provisions) (Scotland) Act 1951	4581
38	Leasehold Property (Temporary Provisions) Act 1951	4568–79
39	Common Informers Act 1951	4853
41	Coal Industry Act 1951	4918
46	Courts Martial (Appeals) Act 1951	4346–9
56	Guardianship and Maintenance of Infants Act 1951	5608
58	Fireworks Act 1951	4859
60	Mineral Workings Act 1951	6191
61	Forestry Act 1951	4850
62	Tithe Act 1951	4852

15 & 16 Geo VI & 1 Eliz II

49	Court of Chancery of Lancaster Act 1952	2/4133
64	Intestates Estates Act 1952	4451–2
66	Defamation Act 1952	4858–60
67	Visiting Forces Act 1952	5161

2
LOCAL AND PERSONAL ACTS

56 & 57 Vic

clxxxi	Liverpool Corporation Act 1893	2/73

57 & 58 Vic

lxxiv	Dundee Corporation Act 1894	2/62

10 & 11 Geo V

cxxxiv	Mayor's Court Act 1920	2/461

18 & 19 Geo V

xxx	Lancashire Quarter Sessions Act 1928	2/1207

20 & 21 Geo V

xxxviii	Birmingham Corporation (General Powers) Act 1930	2/863
cxviii	Royal Exchange Assurance Act 1930	818

22 & 23 Geo V

lxxvii	Gateshead Extension Act 1932	2/1207

20 & 21 Geo V

xxxviii	Birmingham Corporation (General Powers) Act 1930	2/863
cxviii	Royal Exchange Assurance Act 1930	818

22 & 23 Geo V

lxxvii	Gateshead Extension Act 1932	2/1207

23 & 24 Geo V

lxviii	Barking Corporation Act 1933	2/1208
lxxxii	Dover Harbour Act 1933	1209
1	(Private Act) Grosvenor Estate Act 1933	1210

24 & 25 Geo V

lxxviii	Tyne Improvement Act 1934	2/1213
lxxxix	Middlesex CC Act 1934	1212

25 & 26 Geo V

xxxiii	London CC (General Powers) Act 1935	2/1211, 1214
cxiii	Hertfordshire CC Act 1935	1215

26 Geo V & 1 Edw VIII

cxi	Wolverhampton Corporation Act 1936	2/1216

1 Edw VIII & 1 Geo VI

xlv	City of London (Various Powers) Act 1937	2/1217

1 & 2 Geo VI

1	(Private Act) Tatton Estate Act 1938	2/1218

2 & 3 Geo VI

lxxvi	National Trust Act 1939	2/1219–20

3 & 4 Geo VI

xxxii	Monmouthshire & South Wales Mutual Indemnity Society Ltd. Act 1940	2/1222

7 & 8 Geo VI

i	Yorkshire Registries (West Riding) (Amendment) Act 1944	2/4259

8 & 9 Geo VI

xli	Warrington Corporation Act 1945	2/3142

9 & 19 Geo VI

xxi	Newport (Isle of Wight) Corporation Act 1946	2/3149
xxxi	Rushden District Gas & Water Act 1946	4148
xxxviii	Manchester Corporation Act 1946	3147
xlix	Long Eaton UDC Act 1946	3150

liii	Tees Conservancy Act 1946	3146
lxii	Banbury Corporation Act 1946	3145
1	(Private Act) Abergavenny Estate Act 1945	3143
10 & 11 Geo VI		
xxvii	Dudley Corporation Act 1947	2/3154
xxxix	Nazeing Wood or Park Act 1947	3162
xliii	North Cumberland Water Board Act 1947	3164
11 & 12 Geo VI		
xxxv	Salford Corporation Act 1948	2/3179
xxxix	Birmingham Corporation Act 1948	3174
xli	Ipswich Corporation Act 1948	3173
xliii	Cumberland County Council Act 1948	3166
xlvi	Great Yarmouth Harbour Act 1948	3178
xlvii	Rochdale Corporation Act 1948	3170
liii	London County Council General Powers Act 1948	3165
12 & 13 Geo VI		
xv	People's Dispensary for Sick Animals Act 1949	2/3185
xxxvii	Huddersfield Corporation Act 1949	3198
xli	Crewe Corporation Act 1949	3188
xliii	Bolton Corporation Act 1949	3192
liii	Urmston UDC Act 1949	3193
14 Geo VI		
xxxix	L.C.C. (Woolwich Subsidence) Act 1950	2/3208
xlv	Ipswich Dockyards Act 1950	3209
lvii	Manchester Corporation Act 1950	3207

3
BILLS

1877, 1886	Indictable Offences and other criminal justice Bills	1/42
1881–4	Middlesex Land Registry Bills	1/71
1884	Courts of Justice Building Act Amendment Bill	1/84
1885	Provincial Sittings Bill	1/54, 77
1886–7	Land Transfer Bills	1/56
1887	Bills of Sale Bill	1/26
1888	Land Transfer Bill	2/8
1890	Public Trustee Bill	2/39
1892–3	Married Women Bills	57
1893	Bills of Sale Bill	58
1893–5	Supreme Court of Judicature (Officers) Bill	91–3, 138
1896–1900	Durham Palatinate Bill	134
1898	British Museum Bill	104
1899	County Courts (Extension of Jurisdiction) Bill	111
1899	Bankruptcy (Administration Orders) Bill	114
1900	Marriage Act (Amendment) Bill	120
1900	Lunacy Bill	132

1901	Judicial Committee of the Privy Council Bill	179
1901–6	Naval Prize Bill	146
1905–12	County Courts Bills	156–8, 160, 205–10, 285
1910	Conveyancing Bill	198
1910	Bills of Exchange Bill	199
1910	Criminal Procedure Bill	200
1911	Trustee (Bodies Corporate) Bill	283
1912–4	Public Trustee Bill	286
1912	Solicitors Bill	288
1917	Defence of the Realm (Acquisition of Ships) Bill	369
1918–9	Women's Emancipation Bill	350, 388
1919	Justices of the Peace (Women) Bill	350
1919	Conveyancing Bills presented to the Land Transfer sub-committee	2/508–9, 3/44
1920	Matrimonial Causes Bill	2/460
1921	Judges' Salaries Bill	467
1921	Fraud and Falsification Bill	471
1922	House of Lords Reform Bill	597
1922	Economy (Miscellaneous Provisions) Bill	525
1924	Criminal Responsibility (Trials) Bill	761
1924	Parliament (Qualification of Peeresses) Bill	760
1924	Parliamentary Reform Bill	774
1925	Married Women (Torts) Bill	777
1927	Crown Proceedings Bill	1093–1101
1927	Divorce Jurisdiction (Overseas Domicile) Bill	797
1928	Representation of the People (Equal Franchise) Bill	817
1929	Agents (Deposit) Bill	1567
1929	Solicitors (Clients' Accounts) Bill	1567
1930	Registration of Unsatisfied Judgments Bill	1069
1930–4	Maritime Conventions Bill	1425–6
1933	Bank of Ireland Bill	1554
1934	Parliament (Reform) Bill	1443
1934–7	Judiciary (Safeguards) Bill	1667–9
1936	Arbitration Bill	1204
1936	County Courts Bill	1292
1936	Peers Trial Abolition Bill	1326
1937	Administration of Justice (Wales) Bill	4418
1938	Criminal Justice Bill	3338–9
1938	St. Bartholomew's Hospital Bill	1221
1938	Law of Libel (Amendment) Bill	3058
1938	Statute Law Revision Bill	1589
1939	Freemasons' Lodges Bill	1223
1939	Courts (Emergency Powers) (no. 2) Bill	1374
1940	Parliamentary Writs Bill	2661
1943	War Crimes Bill	2662
1943	Justices of the Peace Bill	3037
1943	Landlord and Tenant (War Damage) (Amendment) Bill	2729
1944	Medical Act (1858) Amendment Bill	3004
1944	Judgment Summonses Bill	3918

1945	Matrimonial Causes (Divorce Commissioners) Bill	4197
1945	Arbitration (Consolidation) Bill	3086
1945	Supreme Court of Judicature Bill	3075
1947	Privy Council Appeals Bill	3482
1947	Stevenson Marriage Bill	3163
1949	Mountbatten Estate Bill	3204
1949	Statutory Instruments (Parliamentary Control) Bill	4323
1949	Landlord and Tenant (Colour Bar) Bill	3584
1949	Married Women (Maintenance) Bill	4485
1949	Censorship of Plays (Repeal) Bill	4486
1949–55	House of Commons Disqualification Bills	3011
1950	High Court and County Court Judges Bill	4605
1950	Offensive Weapons Bill	3356
1951	Deserted Wives Bill	4851
1951	Matrimonial Causes Bill	4854
1951	Administration of Justice Bill	4979
1951	Wills etc. (Publication) Bill	5607
1951	Trustees and Liquidators (Emergency Provisions) Bill	4856

Appendix

4

DECIDED CASES

A selective list of cases which are the subject of discussion in LCO files.

A & B Taxis Ltd v Secretary of State for Air	[1922] 2 KB 328	2/571
Adams v Naylor	[1946] AC 543	3361–2
Adamson v Union Cold Storage	(1932) 146 LT 172	1266(1)
Re Adey	(1931)	1174
All Souls College, Oxford v Middlesex CC	[1938] 2 All ER 586	5569
Allinson v Secretary of State for Air	(1946) County Court	4251
Re Alsop	(1945) CA	26/580
Ambatielos v The Foundation Company Limited	(1948) CA	2/4092
Ambler v Ambler	[1951] 1 All ER 980	6159
Re Anderson	[1944] P1	5635
Apted v Apted	[1930] P 246	1794
Duke of Argyll v I.R.C.	(1913) 109 LT 893	631
Arness v Robinson	(1932) KBD	1743
Arnold v Gates	[1933] 1 Ch 913	1986
'The Asya'	(1948) 81 Lloyds List 277	3218
Duke of Athol v Read	[1934] 2 KB 92	1783
"The Atlantic Scout"	[1950] P 266	3428, 3575, 3608
Attorney-General v Hancock	[1940] 1 KB 427	1357, 1380
Attorney-General v Odell	[1906] 2 Ch 47	256
Attorney-General of the Duchy of Lancaster v Moresby	[1919] WN 69	1380
Austerberry v Oldham Corp.	(1885) 29 Ch D 750	788
A. W. Ltd v Cooper & Hall	[1925] 2 KB 186	844
Bahia Tramway Light & Power Co.	(1946) Ch	2/3850
Bailey v Bailey	(1946) PD & A	4056
Re Barber	(1886) 31 Ch D 665	1/26
Barker v Wathes Cattell & Gurden Limited	(1925) KBD	2/1042
Barnett v Howard	[1900] 2 KB 784	244
Re Barringer, deceased	(1926/7) County Court	837
Barrington v Jennings	(1919)	32/1
Barton v Reed	(1932) 1 Ch 362	2/1805
Baxter v Baxter	[1948] AC 274	3688, 4205
Beaumont v Jeffrey	[1925] 1 Ch 1	764

Bell v North Staffordshire Railway Company	(1879) 4 QBD 205	1797
Re Bennett	[1896] 1 Ch 778	1930
Bennett v Bennett	[1934] WN 26	1813
Berkeley v Berkeley	[1946] AC 555	2968
Berton v Alliance Economic Investment Company Ltd	[1922] 1 KB 742	1792
Birmingham & Co. v Lang	[1904] 1 KB 35	244
Birt v Minister of Pensions	(1946) Denning J	3694, 3708
Blackwell v Blackwell	[1943] 2 All ER 579	2777
Blaikie v Halifax Building Society	'The Times', 14.7.1934	1792
Re Blanchard	[1932] WN 149	1725
Re Blewett	(1950) Ch	4468
Re Blow	[1914] 1 Ch 233	657
Boone v Williams	(1879) County Court	1/41
Bosch v Perpetual Trustee Company (Limited) New South Wales	[1938] AC 463	2/1189
Boswell v Partridge-Jones	[1941] 2 KB 300	4243
Boulton v Cattrall	(1916) Chancery Court of the Duchy of Lancaster	406
Bourne v Minister of Pensions	[1946] KB 345	3711
Bowater v Davidson	[1936] 1 KB 465	1624
Bowman v Secular Society	[1917] AC 406	2559
Re Boynton Estates	(1944) Ch	2849
Bradford Third Equitable Building Society v Borders	[1939] 1 Ch 520, [1940] 1 Ch 202	1874
Brain & Wilkes v Minister ofPensions	[1947]KB 625	3711, 3714
Brayshaw v Minister of Pensions	(1946) Court of Session	3721
Brazier v Minister of Pensions	[1945] SC 359	3703
Bridge v Minister of Pensions	(1946) Denning J	3711
Re Bridgett & Hayes' Contract	[1928] Ch 163	1713
Brown v Dimbleby	[1904] 1 KB 28	244
Brown v Wilkinson	(1942) 194 LT 24	24/582
Browning v Browning	[1951] 1 All ER 758	2/6158
Brydges v Brydges & Wood	[1909] P 187	4194
Bundy v Motor Association	(1917) 143 LT 334	1265
Burton v Holdsworth	[1951] 2 All ER 581	5517
Butcher v Poole Corporation	[1942] 2 All ER 572	2730

Callot v Nash	(1923) 39 TLR 291	2/777
Re Campbell	(1951) Ch	4230
Re L. Casey, deceased	(1919) High Court of Ireland	1124
Re Carroll, deceased	[1931] 1 KB 317	1048, 1124
Re Cathcart	(1944) 197 LT 97	26/580
"The Champion"	[1934] P 1	2/1258
Chandler v Webster	[1904] 1 KB 493	1374, 1971, 1991, 1993-4

Gallegher v Dorman Long & Co.	[1947] 2 All ER 38	3782
Garner v Garner	(1920) 36 TLR 196	624
Gay v Gay	(1940)	1888
Re Geneva Tramways Co. Ltd	(1906) KBD	276
Gerrard v Associated Newspapers Ltd		3067A
In re Gibson	[1941] 2 All ER 91	5635
Gilgan v Courtney	(1948)	3857
Gillibrand v Minister of Pensions	[1947] WN 320	3711
Glasgow Corporation v Bruce	[1948] AC 78	3782
Goodsell v Lloyds Ltd	[1914] 3 KB 1001	306
Gough's Garages v Pugsley	(1930) 46 TLR 283	1680
Re Gourju's WTs	[1943] Ch 24	4230
Graham v Glasgow Corporation	[1947] AC 368	3782
Green v Haymarket Capitol Ltd	(1944)	3915
Green v Heering	[1905] 1 KB 152	1792
Greene v Anderson	[1942] AC 284	1454
Greenhalgh & Bleakley Ltd v Barrow	(1939) County Court	1312
Griffin v Minister of Pensions	[1951] SLT 245	3739
Re Grosvenor SE	[1933] Ch 97	1497
Grosvenor v Peacey	[1944] 1 Ch 138	3557, 3578

Ex p. Haines	[1945] KB 183	2/3694
Halifax Building Society v Hardaker	(1948) Ch	4103
Halifax Building Society v Hill	(1940) Ch	1871
Hanne v Cox	(1874) County Court	1/41
Harnett v Bond	[1925] AC 669	2/952
Harnett v Fisher	(1925–6) 42 TLR 486	1971
Harriman v Harriman	[1909] P 123	4189
Re Harris	[1930] WN 190	703
Re Harris	[1931] 1 Ch 138	1241
Harris v Ball	(1913) County Court	311
Harrison v Liverpool Corporation	[1943] 2 All ER 449	1852
Hartley v Holden	(1946) KBD	1749
Hartz v Minister of Pensions	(1949) Ormerod J	3730
Re Hassop Estates	[1911] Ch 611	286, 417
Hatch v Hatch	[1951] 1 TLR 825	5583
Hauxton Parochial Church Council v Stevens	[1929] P 240	898,901,3434
Hawkes v Stewart	(1886) Liverpool Court of Passage	1/51
Hazzard v Smith	(1922) County Court	2/610
Re Hennig	(1950) 114 JP 650	4167
Henry v Galloway	(1928–33) 17 TC 470	1678B
Hickman v Peacey	(1945) AC 304	3457, 3578
Hicks v Hicks	(1943)	3908
Higgins v Scott	(1888) 21 QBD 10	320

Hill v Wm. Hill Ltd	(1949) AC 530	3603
Hillingdon Estates Ltd v Stonefield Estates Ltd	[1952] 2 Ch 627	4573
Hinckley & South Leicestershire PBBS v Freeman	[1941] Ch 32	1782, 2714
Hingston v Hingston	(1944)	3415
Hirst v Associated Newspapers Ltd		3067A
Hoare-Nairne v Langford	(1937) County Court	1293
Holmes v Cleaver	(1923) KBD	2576
Horsfall v Womersley	(1944) Tucker J	3694
Hubbard v Messenger	(1937) 157 LT 512	3602
Hughes v Davies	(1930) 28 LGR 11	919
Hughes v Justin	[1894] 1 QB 667	320
Hughes v Oxenham	[1914] 1 Ch 254	391
Re Hull	(1882) 9 QBD 689	355
Huxtable v Hope	(1925)	2589
Hyman v Empire Clothing Co. Ltd	(1930) KBD	1063

Ind v Midland Bank Executor & Trustee Co. Ltd	(1937)	2/1887
Inskip v Odhams Press Ltd		3067A
Irving v Minister of Pensions	[1945] SC 21	3703
Irwin v Liverpool Victoria Friendly Society		1988
Isaias v Marine Insurance Co. Ltd	(1923) 15 Lloyds List 193	1007
Iwi v Montesole	[1955] Crim. LR 313	6684–8

Jackson v Jackson	[1936] P 214	2/1838
Jackson v Jackson	(1947) 64 TLR 63	3965
Jacobson v Frachon	(1927) 44 TLR 103	1747
James v Minister of Pensions	[1947] KB 867	3711
Johns & Hunt v Post Office Savings Bank	(1934) Industrial Insurance Commissioner	1980, 1988
Re Johnson	[1939] 2 All ER 458	3756
Re R. W. Johnson Ltd	[1942] WN 29	2759
Johnson v Hill	(1944) 61 TLR 398	3563
Johnson v Johnson	[1952] 1 All ER 250	6159
Johnson v Taylor Brothers & Co.	[1920] AC 144	555
Johnston v Henry Liston & Co.	[1920] 1 KB 99	1943
Jones v MacAulay	[1891] 1 QB 221	320
Re a Judgment Debtor	(1935) 51 TLR 524	1146

Kempley v Poole	[1923] 1 KB 195	2/864, 1081

O'Dwyer v Nair	(1924) KBD	2/961
Re Orbit Trust Ltd's Lease	[1943] 1 All ER 373	2713
Ormerod Grierson v St. George's Ironworks	[1905] AC 505	178
Osborne v Waller	(1941) 6 LJCCR 157	2726
Oxenburg v Harding	(1880) County Court	1/41
Re Oxford's Application	(1946) Pensions Appeal Tribunal	2/3719

Re Palmer	[1944] Ch 374	2/3646
Re Panther	(1939) County Court	1180
Re Pavion Industries Ltd'sDebenture	(1950) Ch	3253
Payne v Watts	(1940) KBD	1749
Pearl Assurance Ltd v Government of the Union of South Africa	[1934] AC 570	3465
Pearson v Wilcock	[1906] 2 KB 440	246
Pemberton v Pemberton	(1951) PDA	5518
Re Pengelly's Appeal	(1950)	4369
Performing Rights Society v London Theatre of Varieties	[1924] AC 1	910
Perry v L.G.O.C.	[1916] 2 KB 355	360
Perry & Bridge v Osborn	(1880) County Court	1/41
Re a Petition of Right	[1916] 3 KB 649	2/367–8
Re Petty	[1929] 1 Ch 726	1930
Plymouth Estates Limited v Tithe Redemption Commissioners	[1944] AC 228	3384
Pole-Carew v Craddock	[1920] 3 KB 109	631
Pooley v Brying	[1940] 2 All ER 377	1749
Powell v Main Collery Company Ltd	[1900] AC 366	114
Poznanski v London Film Productions Limited	(1937–45) 107 MacG.Cop.Cas.	1693
Re Pozot S T	[1952] Ch 427	4230
Pratt v Cook	(1939–40) 56 TLR 363	5415
Re Price	[1928] Ch 579	1496
Prince v Prince	[1951] P 71	4224
Pryor v City Offices Co.	(1883) 52 LJ QB 962	1/49

Queen Anne's Bounty v Thorne	[1934] 2 KB 175	2/1923
Queen Anne's Bounty v Tithe Redemption Commissioners	[1938] 1 Ch 229	1925

R v Architects' Registration Appeal Tribunal, Ex p. Jaggar	[1945] WN 142	2/3023

Re Viscountess Rhondda's Claim	[1922] 2 AC 339	471, 599
Rice v Raynold Spring-Rice	[1948] 1 All ER 188	3673
Richardson v Minister of Pensions	[1945] SC 363	3711
Re Miss M. Robertson	[1949] 1 All ER 1042	3406
Robinson v Wilmington	(1925) County Court	833
Roe v Nix	[1893] P 55	5714
Rose v Ford	[1937] AC 826	1972
Roskill v Cook	(1932) KBD	1598
Rowing v Minister of Pensions	[1946] 1 All ER 664	3711
Re Royal Albion Hotel Limited	(1943) 195 LT 236	26/580
Re Royal Bank of Scotland's Application	[1940] Ch 857	2/1898
Royal Mutual Benefit BS v Neville		3518
Royster v Cavey	[1946] WN 8	3361
Rudd v Rudd	(1949)	3668
Re Russell Ltd	(1949) Railway and Canal Commission	3774
Russell v Rudd	[1923] AC 309	1081
Russell v Russell	[1924] AC 687	3914, 3964, 4484
Russoff v Lipovitch	[1925] 1 KB 628	835
Rutherford v Minister of Pensions	(1948) Northern Ireland HC	2785

S & A Services v Dickson	[1940] 2 KB 219	2/1319
Re Saffell	[1945] KB 259	3702
Re Sager	(1874)	1/16
In re Saunders	[1929] Ch 675	4446
Re Scarisbrick	[1950] Ch 226	3756
Scott v Morley	[1887] WN 200	1284
Searle v Wallbank	[1947] AC 341	5611
Seymour v Reed	[1927] AC 554	1049
Sharpe v Minister of Pensions	[1950] 2 All ER 1012n	3720
Re Sheafbrook	[1926] P 61	800
Shell-Mex Ltd v Plymouth Official Receiver	(1930) County Court	703
Shipp v Minister of Pensions	[1946] KB 386	3694, 3703, 3715
Sigley v Hale	[1938] 2 KB 630	1850
Sloane's Application	(1947) Pensions Appeal Tribunal	3725
Re D. S. Smith	(1944) 196 LT 209	26/580
Re P. B. Smith, deceased	(1945) PDA	2/5635
Smith v Mather	[1918] 2 KB 212	3599
Softlaw v Welch	[1899] 2 QB 419	244
Soho Square Syndicate v Pollard & Co.	[1940] 1 Ch 638	1319, 1381
Re a Solicitor	[1944] 1 All ER 523	3921
Re a Solicitor	[1951] 2 All ER 108	5818
Re Somerset	[1894] 1 Ch 231	419

Re Vrint	[1940] 3 All ER 47	1516
Wakeford v Bishop of Lincoln	[1921] 1 AC 813	2/551
Wakeley v Triumph Cycle Co. Ltd	[1921] KBD 214	948, 1124
Wallis v Griffiths		1782
Wallrock v Clare	(1929) HL	1266(1)
Waltho v Waltho	(1944)	3415
Re Ward	30 LJ (NS) 75	355
Re Waring	[1942] Ch 426, [1948] 1 All ER 257	2968
Webster v Southey	(1887) 36 Ch D 9	3576
Weir & Co. v McVicar & Co.	[1925] 2 KB 127	1061
Weston v Smith	(1893) County Court	57
Wigg v Attorney-General of the Irish Free State	[1927] AC 674	910
Re Wigzell	[1921] 2 KB 835	695
Winckley v Baxter	(1931) KBD	1749
Wooding, James, Hawkins v Monmouthshire & South Wales Mutual Indemnity Society Ltd	[1938] 3 All ER 625	1222
Re Woolwich Building Society's Application	[1942] Ch 253	2714
Wright v Bennette & Stephen	[1947] KB 828	3839, 3846, 4099
Young v Minister of Pensions	[1944] 2 All ER 308	2/3694
'The Zamora'	[1916] 2 AC 77	2/1886
Ex p. Ziman	[1915] 2 KB 163	371

BIBLIOGRAPHY

The works listed below are those which are referred to in the text or notes and a few others of particular usefulness. They do not, of course, include all published works material to the history of the Lord Chancellor's Office during the period of the guide. Standard works of reference, such as the **Dictionary of National Biography and Who Was Who** are omitted.

1
BOOKS

Abel-Smith B. & Stevens R.	Lawyers and the Courts (1967)
Allen Sir C. K.	Law and Orders (1945)
Alverstone, Lord	Recollections of Bar and Bench (1914)
Anson Sir W. R.	The Law and Custom of the Constitution (2nd ed. 1896–7)
Arthurs H. W.	Without the Law (1984)
Ashworth H.	The Building Society Story (1980)
Atlay J. B.	The Victorian Chancellors (2 vols., 1906)
Bell E.	These Meddlesome Attorneys (1939)
Bell G. K. A.	Randall Davidson (3rd ed., 1952)
Birkenhead, 1st Lord	Law, Life and Letters (1927) Points of View (2 vols., 1922)
Birkenhead, 2nd Lord	'F.E.' (1960)
Birks M.	Gentlemen of the Law (1960)
Blom-Cooper L. & Drewry G.	Final Appeal (1972)
Bromhead P. A.	The House of Lords and Contemporary Politics, 1911–57 (1960)
Bryce J.	Studies in Contemporary Biography (1903)
Burn W. L.	The Age of Equipoise (1964)
Campbell, Lord	Lives of the Lord Chancellors (8 vols., 1845–69)
Cartwright T. J.	Royal Commissions and Departmental Committees in Britain (1975)
Cheshire G. C.	Private International Law (9th ed., 1974)
Chester D. N. & Willson F. M. G.	The Organisation of British Central Government, 1914–64 (1968)
Childers E. S. E.	The Life and Correspondence of the Rt. Hon. Hugh C. E. Childers, 1827–96 (1901)
Christian E. B. V.	A Short History of Solicitors (1896)
Cleary E. J.	The Building Society Movement (1965)
Cocks R.	Foundations of the Modern Bar (1983)
Cohen E. W.	The Growth of the British Civil Service, 1780–1939 (1941)
Colcridge E. H.	The Life and Correspondence of Lord Coleridge (2 vols., 1904)
Cornish W. R.	Intellectual Property (1981) The Jury (1968)
Dale H. E.	The Higher Civil Service of Great Britain (1941)
David Dudley Field	Centenary Essays, ed. A. Reppy (1949)

Denning, Lord	The Due Process of Law (1980)
Derriman J.	The Pageantry of the Law (1955)
Donaldson F.	Edward VIII (1974)
Edwards J. Ll. J.	The Attorney-General: Politics and the Public Interest (1984)
	The Law Officers of the Crown (1964)
Egerton R.	Legal Aid (1945)
Elmsley K. & Fraser C. M.	The Courts of the County Palatine of Durham from the Earliest Times to 1971 (1984)
Englander D. A.	Landlord and Tenant in Urban Britain, 1838–1918 (1983)
Fay E. S.	The Life of Mr. Justice Swift (1939)
Finlayson G. B. A. M.	The Seventh Earl of Shaftesbury, 1801–85 (1981)
Fitzroy Sir A.	Memoirs (2 vols., 1925)
Fry G. K.	Statesmen in Disguise (1969)
Grey of Falloden, Lord, and others	Viscount Haldane of Cloan (1928)
Haldane, Lord	An Autobiography (1929)
Hare C.	Tragedy at Law (1942)
Harvey C. P.	The Advocate's Devil (1958)
Herbert Sir A. P.	The "Ayes" Have It (1937)
Heuston R. F. V.	Lives of the Lord Chancellors, 1885–1940 (1964)
Hewart, Lord	The New Despotism (1929)
	Not Without Prejudice (1937)
The Holmes-Laski letters, ed. M. D. Howe (2 vols., 1953)	
Holdsworth, Sir W. S.	A History of English Law (18 vols., 1922–66)
Howell P. A.	The Judicial Committee of the Privy Council, 1833–1876 (1979)
Iremonger F. A.	William Temple, Archbishop of Canterbury (1948)
Jackson R.	The Chief (1959)
Jackson R. M.	The Machinery of Justice in England (1940)
Jacob Sir J. I. H.	The Reform of Civil Procedural Law and other Essays in Civil Procedure (1982)
Jennings Sir W. I.	Parliament (2nd ed., 1957)
Jeyes S. H. & How S. D.	The Life of Sir Howard Vincent (1912)
Johnston J.	An Orator of Justice (1932)
Jones K. A.	A History of the Mental Health Services (1972)
Jones Sir T. A.	Without my Wig (1944)
Kahn-Freund O.	The Law of Carriage by Inland Transport (2nd ed., 1949)
Karlen D.	Appellate Courts in the U.S. and England (1963)
Keeton G. W.	Modern Developments in the Law of Trusts (1971)
	The Passing of Parliament (1952)
	Trial by Tribunal (1960)
Kent Sir H. S.	In on the Act (1979)
Kirk H.	Portrait of a Profession (1976)
Koss S. E.	Lord Haldane, Scapegoat for Liberalism (1969)
Laski H. J.	Studies in Law and Politics (1932)
Liddell A. G. C.	Notes from the Life of an Ordinary Mortal (1911)
McGregor O. R.	Divorce in England (1957)

Mackintosh Sir J. P.	The British Cabinet (1962)
Mallet Sir C. E.	A Memoir of Lord Cave (1931)
Manchester A. H.	Modern Legal History (1980)
Mansergh N.	The Irish Free State (1934)
Lord Maugham	At the End of the Day (1954)
Maurice Sir F.	Haldane (2 vols., 1937)
Maxwell-Lyte H. C.	Historical Notes on the Great Seal (1926)
May Sir T. E.	Treatise on the Law, Proceedings and Usage of Parliament (17th ed., 1964)
Mockler A.	Lions under the Throne (1983)
Montmorency J. E. G. de	Lord Gorell, 1848–1913 (1920)
Mullins C.	Fifteen Years' Hard Labour (1948)
	In Quest of Justice (1931)
Muir C.	Justice in a Depressed Area (1936)
Newsam Sir F. A.	The Home Office (1954)
O'Brien R. B.	The Life of Lord Russell of Killowen (1901)
Page Sir L.	The Justice of the Peace (1936)
Parry E. A.	The Law and the Poor (1914)
Paterson A. A.	The Law Lords (1982)
Pellew J.	The Home Office, 1848–1914 (1982)
Pierson C. G.	Canada and the Privy Council (1960)
Pollock Sir G.	Lord Hanworth (1929)

The Pollock-Holmes Letters, ed. M. D. Howe (2 vols., 1942)

The Reform of the Law, ed. Williams G. L. (1951)

Richards P. G.	Patronage in British Government (1963)
Robbins L. C.	Autobiography of an Economist (1971)
Roberts-Wray Sir K.	Commonwealth and Colonial Law (1966)
Robson W. A.	Justice and Administrative Law (1928)
Rosenbaum S.	The Rule Making Authority in the English Supreme Court (1915)
Ross A.	The Penguin Cricketer's Companion (1978)
Rubin G. R. & Sugarman D.	Law and Society in England, 1750–1914 (1984)

Russell on the Law of Arbitration (13th ed., A. Walton, 1979)

Schuster Sir C.	Postscript to Adventure (1950)
Selborne, Lord	Memorials, Personal and Political, ed. Lady S. Palmer (2 vols., 1898)

Select Essays in Anglo-American Legal History (1968)

Shetstreet S.	Judges on Trial (1976)
Simon, Lord	In Retrospect (1952)
Skyrme Sir W. T. C.	The Changing Image of the Magistracy (1979)
Slesser Sir H. H.	Judgment Reserved (1941)
'Solicitor'	English Justice (edition of 1941)
Somner, D.	Haldane of Cloan (1960)
Stephens H.	A Memoir of Lord Hatherley (2 vols., 1873)

Stevens R.	Law and Politics: The House of Lords as a Judicial Body, 1800–1976 (1979)

Studies in the Growth of Nineteenth Century Government, ed. G. Sutherland (1972)

Troup Sir E.	The Home Office (1925)
Tusa J. & A.	The Nuremberg Trial (1983)
Underhill Sir A.	Change and Decay (1938)
Underhill N.	The Lord Chancellor (1978)
West W. T.	The Trial of Lord de Clifford 1935 (1984)
Wheeler-Bennett Sir J. W.	King George VI (1958)
Wilson Fox A.	The Life of Lord Halsbury (1929)
Wiswall F. L.	The Development of English Admiralty Jurisdiction and Practice since 1800 (1976)
Wollaston Sir G. Woods	The Court of Claims (1903)

2
ARTICLES AND LECTURES

Asquith, Lord	The Court of Appeal	[1950] JSPTL 350
Baker P. V.	Reforming the Moneylenders Act	(1967) 83 LQR 196
Ball R. E.	The Chancery Master	(1961) 77 LQR 331
Ball Sir W. V.	The Central Office of the Supreme Court	(1947) 9 CLJ 107
Bicknell B. A.	The Landlord and Tenant (War Damage) Act 1939	(1939–40) 4 Conv. (N.S.) 39
Blackford R.	A Challenge to Chancery	(1981) 78 LSG 590
Bowen, Lord	The Law Courts under the Judicature Acts	(1886) 2 LQR 1
Campbell E. M.	The Decline of the Jurisdiction of the Judicial Committee of the Privy Council	(1959) 33 ALJ 196
Judge Chalmers	The County Courts Consolidation Act	(1889) 5 LQR 1
Chorley R. S. T.	The Hire Purchase Act 1938	(1938–9) 2 MLR 51
	The Unpaid Magistrate and his Future	(1945) 8 MLR
Cohen, Lord	Jurisdiction, Practice and Procedure of the Court of Appeal	(1953) 11 CLJ 3
Cohen J.	The History of Imprisonment for Debt and its Relation to Development of Discharge in Bankruptcy	(1982) 3 JLH 153
Cohn E. J.	The Political Parties and Legal Aid	(1945) 8 MLR 97
Coldstream G. P.	The Lord Chancellor's Office	(1962) Graya 13
Diamond A. S.	The Queen's Bench Master	(1960) 76 LQR 504
Drewry G.	Lord Haldane's Ministry of Justice—Stillborn or Strangled at Birth?	(1983) 61 Public Administration 396
Evans F.	Winding Up	(1900) 15 LQR 86
Finer M.	The War Damage Act 1941	(1941–2) 5 MLR 54
Finer, M. & Harnick M.	The Liabilities (War-Time Adjustment) Act 1941	(1941–2) 5 MLR 120
Foster J.	Law Revision	(1938–9) 2 MLR 14

Gardiner, Lord	The Machinery of Law Reform in England	(1953) 69 LQR 46
	The Trials of a Lord Chancellor	Holdsworth Club, 1968
Goodhart A. L.	Law Reform	Holdsworth Club, 1952
Goddard, Lord	The Court of Criminal Appeal	(1952) 2 JSPTL (N.S.) 1
Gower L. C. B.	Baxter v. Baxter in Perspective	(1948) 11 MLR 176
	Building Societies and Pooling Agreements	(1939–40) 3 MLR 33
	The Cost of Litigation	(1954) 17 MLR 1
	English Legal Training	(1950) 15 MLR 137
	Statute Law Consolidation and Revision	(1951) 14 MLR 320
Griffith J. A. G.	Delegated Legislation	(1949) 12 MLR 297
Hailsham, 1st Lord	The Duties of a Lord Chancellor	Holdsworth Club, 1936
Hailsham, 2nd Lord	The Problems of a Lord Chancellor	Holdsworth Club, 1972
Haldane, Lord	The Work for the Empire of the Privy Council	(1921) 1 CLJ 143
Heuston R. F. V.	Judges and Biographers	(1967)
Hutton N.	The Mechanics of Law Reform	(1961) 24 MLR 18
Jackson R. M.	The Incidence of Jury Trial during the Past Century	(1937–8) 1 MLR 132
Jenks E.	Recent Changes in Family Law	(1928) 44 LQR 314
Jennings W. I.	Emergency Powers (Defence) (No. 2) Act 1939	(1940–1) 4 MLR 132
Jowitt, Lord	Statute Law and Consolidation	Holdsworth Club, 1951
Keely T. C. S.	One Hundred Years of Lunacy Administration	(1944) 8 CLJ 195
Keeton G. W.	The Charity Muddle	(1949) 2 CLP 86
Keith A. B.	The War and the Constitution	(1940–1) 4 MLR 1,82
Kilmuir, Lord	The Office of Lord Chancellor	(1956) 9 Parliamentary Affairs 132
Lloyd D.	The Cost of Litigation	(1954) 7 CLP 55
	Final Report of the Committee on County Court Procedure	(1949) 12 MLR 354
	Leasehold Property (Temporary Provisions) Act, 1951	(1951) 14 MLR 465
Manson E.	The City of London Chamber of Arbitration	(1893) 9 LQR 86
Mitchell J. D. B.	Limitations on the Contractual Liability of Public Authorities	(1951) 14 MLR 478
Napier A. E. A.	The Office of Lord Chancellor	(1950) 1 Nisi Prius 88
Offer O.	The Origins of the Law of Property Acts, 1910–25	(1977) 40 MLR 505
Potter H.	Strict Settlement and Trust for Sale	(1944) 8 Conv. (N.S.) 147
Rankin Sir G.	The Judicial Committee of the Privy Council	(1941) 7 CLJ 2

Rogers R. H. T.	The Compensation (Defence) Act 1939	(1939–40) 4 Conv. (N.S.) 54
Rosenbaum S.	Rule Making in the County Courts	(1915) 31 LQR 304
	Studies in English procedure	(1914–5) 63 Univ. of Pennsylvania LR 151,273,380,505,550
	The Rule Committee and its Work	(1915) 40 Law Magazine and Review 129
	Rule Making in the Courts of the Empire	(1915) 15 Journal of Comparative Legislation (N.S.), 128
Rowntree G. and Carrier N. H.	The Resort to Divorce in England and Wales 1858–1957	(1958) 2 Population Studies 188
Russell-Jones A.	The Administration of the Workmen's Compensation Acts	(1942–3) 6 MLR 157
	Workmen's Compensation: Common Law Remedies and the Beveridge Report	(1944) 7 MLR 13
Samuels A.	The Law Commission: Do We Really Need It?	(1986) 136 NLJ 747
Schuster, Lord	The Office of the Lord Chancellor	(1949) 10 CLJ 175
Shawcross Sir H.	The State and the Law	(1948) 11 MLR 1
Schwelb E.	The Diplomatic Privileges (Extension) Act, 1944	(1945) 8 MLR 50
Snow T. E.	The Waste of Judicial Power	(1891) 7 LQR 256
	The Reform of Legal Administration	(1892) 8 LQR 129
Stevens R.	The Final Appeal: Reform of the House of Lords and Privy Council 1867–76	(1964) 80 LQR 343
Sweet C.	The Report of the Land Transfer Commissioners	(1912) 28 LQR 6
Wade E. C. S.	Administration of Justice (Miscellaneous Provisions) Act 1938	(1938–9) 2 MLR 307
	The Machinery of Law Reform	(1961) 24 MLR 3
	Regency Act 1937	(1937–8) 1 MLR 66
Wade H. W. R.	Land Charge Registration Reviewed	(1956) 14 CLJ 216
Withers A. H.	Twenty Years Experience of the Property Legislation of 1925	(1947) 62 LQR 167

Abbreviations

ALJ	Australian Law Journal
CLJ	Cambridge Law Journal
CLP	Current Legal Problems
Conv.	Conveyancer
JLH	Journal of Legal History
JSPTL	Journal of the Society of Public Teachers of Law
LQR	Law Quarterly Review
LSG	Law Society's Gazette
MLR	Modern Law Review
NLJ	New Law Journal